Masterworks of the Nō Theater

Masterworks of the Nō Theater

Kenneth Yasuda

Indiana University Press ✸ Bloomington & Indianapolis

Frontispiece: Yagi Yasuo, *Shite-kata* of the Kanze school, performing the role of the *shite* in *Eguchi*. (Photo courtesy of Shelley Fenno Quinn.)

Quotations from the speeches of Martin Luther King, Jr., are reprinted and adapted by permission of Joan Daves. Copyright © 1963, Martin Luther King, Jr.; copyright © 1968, Estate of Martin Luther King, Jr.

Manufactured in the United States of America

Library of Congress Cataloging-in-Publication Data

Masterworks of the Nō theater.

  Includes bibliography.
  1. Nō plays—Translations into English. 2. English drama—Translations from Japanese. I. Yasuda, Kenneth
PL782.E5M27 1989   895.6'2'008   87-45833
ISBN 0-253-36805-7

  1 2 3 4 5 93 92 91 90 89

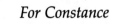

For Constance

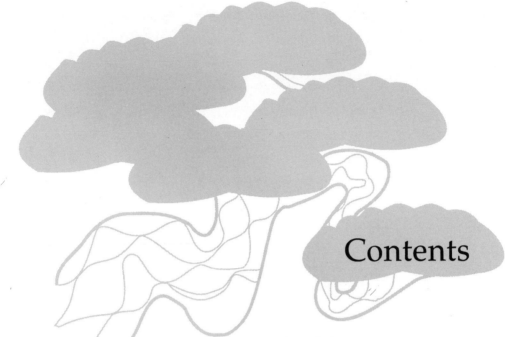

Contents

vii

FOREWORD

The Nō discussed so fully and originally by Kenneth Yasuda took on definitive form in the fourteenth century. During the Edo period (ca. 1603–1868), acting tempo slowed. As a result, the original program of five Nō with comic interludes (*kyōgen*) is today usually reduced to one or two Nō (and a *kyōgen*). But the history of performance is unbroken. It is as if the dramatic forms of Chaucer's time survived not only in texts but also in continuous performance. When we add to Nō and *kyōgen* the later theaters of bunraku (or *jōruri*, using large puppets) and kabuki, we see that classical Japanese theater is unrivaled by any other dramatic tradition for variety, richness, and authenticity of survival. There is only one Nō with laughter, the seldom-performed *Sanshō*, and the height of the art is taken to be those pieces in which the *shite*, or principal role, is the specter of a woman. Comedy is left to the earthier *kyōgen* (although both enjoyed patronage from the warrior aristocracy), and a *kyōgen* figure commonly enters a two-part Nō during the absence of the *shite*.

Besides the text—which is uncommonly narrative and lyric in character for theater—Nō requires a special, fully lit theater, gorgeous robes for the *shite*, largely symbolic stage properties (including the *shite*'s mask and fan), chanting close to singing, movements that are dancelike, a small band of musicians, and a chorus. These details are wholly familiar to anybody who has seen Nō performed, perhaps indeed to nearly every reader of this book. The point of mentioning them is to underscore the great difficulty faced by anyone, even someone as learned as Professor Yasuda, who seeks to describe on paper what transpires in the experience of Nō in the theater. He has found ingenious ways of clarification and his book is of a rare kind: the more a reader knows of the subject, the more the book teaches.

Kenneth Yasuda has long had close association with the Kita School, the most recent of the *shite* schools, emerging in the 1600s. Of course, he is familiar with the somewhat variant texts and acting traditions of the other four schools. In "Of Studies," Bacon writes, "Some books are to be tasted, others to be swallowed, and some few to be chewed and digested." This book is one of those few, and, to continue the metaphor, the order of courses should be followed as the menu gives them on the contents page. Random tasting will give pleasure, but full satisfaction requires following through in order.

Over the years the author has put us in his debt, sometimes before others of us had the sense to appreciate what he gave us. I think in particular of his early anticipation of current studies of Japanese linked poetry (*renga*), which in fact had a considerable impact on Nō. The present book crowns a distinguished career. Like the Japanese gardens he has designed and supervised in the making, in Japan as well as the United States, it will last as living testimony to his artistic insight. As it teaches our understanding to grow, it will—like his garden designs—gradually take on for those who follow him the shape that his learning and imagination have projected, even to future generations.

I take great pleasure in saluting this splendid book about a splendid art by someone who is a valued teacher, colleague, and friend: "Viewing this, we know the past and the future" (*Ataka*).

EARL MINER

x

Foreword

My involvement with Nō began after World War II. While serving as the assistant representative of the Asia Foundation in Tokyo, I was fortunate to have the time and opportunity to meet the great Nō master Kita Roppeita and his successor, Kita Minoru. They asked me to prepare simple English synopses and translations of the Nō texts they performed for foreign guests. During these years, with their aid, the synopses grew into numerous small pamphlets, and I began to see many aspects of the plays that I had not perceived earlier.

This experience taught me how little I knew about Nō and how much the Japanese take for granted. Western students, as I found during my teaching at Indiana University, read and analyze Nō with the fulcrum of their own cultural background. This produces problems and barriers.

To help ease the reader through these difficulties, I have tried to present the depth and precision of Nō in a gradual way. I have written introductions, of varying degrees of complexity, to each play. Those to the first three plays in the volume, *Himuro, Nonomiya,* and *Funabenkei,* are minimal, little changed from the way they were published by the Kōfūsha in 1967. My analyses of the plays in Part II, *Ataka, Hagoromo,* and *Izutsu,* dig more deeply into the underlying structure and the overt techniques of Nō. The eleven plays that follow in Part III are arranged according to the modern classification, and each one is preceded by a short introductory remark.

The last play in the volume was written as an experimental attempt to create a Nō play in English. Its subject is Martin Luther King, Jr., and it was composed when I heard about the designation of 15 January as a national holiday. I hope that more plays of this nature will be written in the future.

All the translated plays were selected from those that I had worked with many years ago for the performances in Tokyo and had subsequently revised in response to suggestions made by the audiences. When I began with the Kitas, I simply prepared synopses and rough translations of the Nō texts. Then I added section numbers, according to the works of Sanari Kentarō,[1] in the left margin at the beginning of each section. These numbers, which are retained here, corresponded with numbers placed at lower stage left and allowed viewers to follow the progression of the plays. Later, I designated the verse forms of the poetic passages, *shidai, issei, machiutai, sageuta, ageuta,*[2] etc. These changes helped give the audiences a definite sense of how Nō is structured.

The next step was to refine the manner in which I rendered the passages in verse; for example, I re-rendered *shidai* passages in measured verse with the original Japanese syllabication of 7–5, 7–5, and 7–4 carried out as closely as possible. I noted the style of singing, such as *tsuyogin, yowagin, au, awazu, hiranori,* or *ōnori,* used for each passage. I also added stage directions so that the reader could recognize the movements of the actors and could follow the three-stage *jo-ha-kyū* progression of the chanting.

I have tried in my translations to do justice to the tone, meaning, and form of the Nō play as they complement one another, creating a whole as the narrative elements are strung together. Special attention is given to those literary techniques and devices employed by the playwrights in the works included here. The use of poems (*tanka*) in other literary works was well known before Zeami. The skillful handling of famous poems in the plays is reproduced in English, as a noted poem or a part of it appears and reappears at calculated places throughout the play—for example, a poem of Tadanori, a poem of an old woman in *Obasute,* or a poem of a dancer in *Higaki.* Each one functions in the play like a theme song in a motion picture; not only does it enrich the passages, but it also unifies the whole play. The same is true of the poetic images that appear again and again in a play, as W. B. Yeats noted in *Certain Noble Plays of Japan.* For instance, in the plays translated here, prominent poetic images are the cherry blossoms in *Tadanori* and *Saigyōzakura,* the water in *Higaki* and *Izutsu,* and the moon in *Obasute* and *Tōru.*

In addition to the literary techniques mentioned above, such time-honored devices as *kakeshi, engo, tōin,* etc., add grace to the texture of the lyric passages in the play. A dramatic instance of the *kakekotoba,* or pivot device, occurs as follows in *Atsumori:*

Atsumori mo	Atsumori, too,
uma hikikaeshi	wheeled his steed and turned ashore
nami no	through the waves
uchimono nuite	that came pounding back and forth
futauchi	he drew his sword
miuchi wa	and twice or thrice
utsu zo to mieshi ga . . .	he seemed to strike the enemy. . . .

In this combat scene, the word "forth" is the pivot, linking two phrases and shifting meanings as it moves from one to the next: "through the waves / that came pounding back and forth / (forth) he drew his sword / and twice or thrice / he seemed to strike the enemy. . . ." Here the sudden dramatic change takes place effectively and effortlessly. In the next example, a whole line, "crossing one another," serves as a pivot device:

itsu made	"How long," they cried,
Ikutagawa	"must we linger on?"
nagaruru mizu ni	as the Ikuta flows down

yūshio no	at the eventide
sachichigaete	crossing one another
munashiku nareba	with their swords, life ebbs away. . . .

This passage is from *Motomezuka*, depicting two young suitors who met their end because of an ill-fated maiden called Unai.

There are other literary devices used by Nō playwrights. Among them, one worthy enough to be noted here is the technique I call "role exchange," which is used to resolve a conflict between two characters effortlessly, as in *Hagoromo*.

While my analyses of the plays refer to the original Japanese, I have carefully compared the original text to the English renderings and at times have retranslated passages so that the analyses can be understood through the translation with the least explanation. Some of the translated passages, however, fared better than others in capturing the beauty of the Japanese lines. I hope that improvement will be made in the future and that more works will also be made available. Although the translations are based on various texts (see "Nō Texts Consulted"), Sanari's *Yōkyoku Taikan* was the source of all Interludes and *Kyōgen* parts throughout the volume.

Finally, it should be mentioned that each Nō play is presented in transliteration according to the romanization system adopted by the Library of Congress, and appears side by side with the English translation. In the hope of avoiding cumbersome footnotes, I have appended a glossary of Japanese Nō terms, which readers can consult whenever they encounter unfamiliar words.

While I sincerely hope that these translations may eventually reach a broader audience, this collection is presented as a handbook for students of Japanese literature, comparative literature, and drama.

Needless to say, this work could not have reached its present state without the rich resources of Japanese scholarship and the direct assistance in many forms given me by institutions, colleagues, associates, and friends. My sincere gratitude to them is duly noted in the acknowledgments.

ACKNOWLEDGMENTS

This book is the outcome of my interest in Nō, and I am deeply indebted to many individuals and institutions here and abroad for their encouragement and support. I would like to thank the Japan Foundation for supporting my research and providing publication assistance. I would also like to offer thanks to the Office of Research and Graduate Development of Indiana University for funding part of the research and awarding a Grant-in-Aid to help prepare the manuscript.

For those individuals in Japan, I thank Kita Roppeita, Kita Minoru, Okano Seiken, Toki Zenmaro, Omote Akira, and both Kamegai Satoru and Hara Katsu for the encouragement they extended to me. Here those who have read all or parts of my work while it was in various stages of preparation have been helpful in numerous matters. I wish to express my sincere gratitude to John McCluskey, Eugene Eoyang, George Elison, and Shelley Fenno Quinn. Thanks are due to Earl Miner for the foreword and to Don Carlton, whose knowledge of religion was of great assistance to me in writing the introduction. Kenneth Inada supplied a great deal of information on Buddhist terminology and on the passages from the various sutras in the Taishō Edition of the Tripitaka. Thanks are also due to Daryl Shadrick for the transliteration of the Nō texts. I wish to express my gratitude to Sharon Sieber, Lena Lo, and Bruce Leeds, who went through the entire manuscript and were generous in providing numerous comments, suggestions, and important changes. I would especially like to thank Sharon Sieber for her most careful preparation of the final manuscript. Above all, I thank Constance Murayama, my wife, for her patience and support.

Special thanks are due to the Kōfūsha for permission to reprint *Himuro, Nonomiya,* and *Funabenkei;* to *Monumenta Nipponica,* for *Ataka;* and to the *Harvard Journal of Asiatic Studies,* for *Hagoromo* and *Izutsu.* I am also grateful to Yagi Yasuo, who appears in the frontispiece for this book.

Finally, I should like to thank John Gallman, the director of Indiana University Press, and also his staff, especially Risë Williamson, with her exceedingly careful editing and thoughtful comments and suggestions, which have been of great assistance.

Masterworks of the Nō Theater

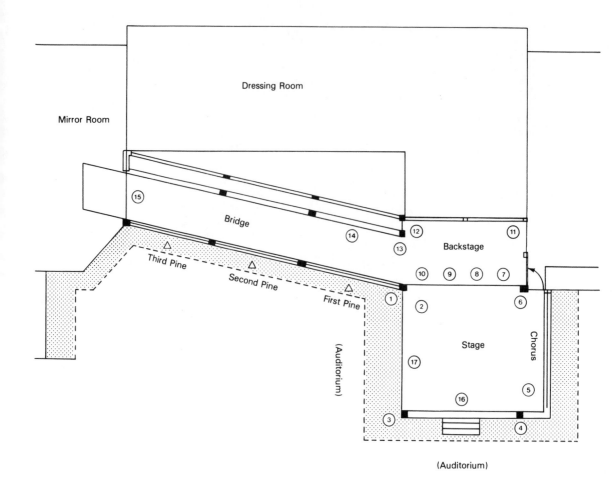

The Nō Stage

1. *Shite* pillar
2. *Shite* seat
3. Eye-fixing pillar
4. *Waki* pillar
5. *Waki* seat
6. Flute player's pillar
7. Flute
8. Small hand-drum
9. Large hand-drum
10. Drum
11. Sliding door
12. Stage attendant's seat
13. *Kyōgen* pillar
14. *Kyōgen* seat
15. Curtain
16. Stage front
17. *Waki* front

Introduction

Nō is the ancient Japanese theater whose multiple dimensions echo and reinforce one central aim, the baring of a soul. That soul may have the form of a human or of a god. It may have the trappings of good or of evil. It may be famous or previously unknown. It may be living or long dead. Whatever, it will be stripped to a core that each person may touch with intimacy.

Anyone viewing Nō is struck by its richness, by the lush interplay of symbolism and evangelism, dialogue and lyrics, music and dance, masks and costumes. But there is a skeletal ruthlessness in their use—like the drum rising in intensity and tempo, all must point steadily to the heart that is being forever opened.

The play in which that soul is caught can include almost any form or technique. The Nō is described as "minimalistic," yet it has absorbed and borrowed hundreds of items from other arts and other dramatic forms and will use most of these techniques and artifacts in any one play. Even the learned eye and ear, however, will be led swiftly past these items by the artistry of the form.

Many conventions of drama are sacrificed in Nō, and these sacrifices intensify the symbolic feeling. The play need not have a plot, and most Nō plays have only a suggestion of a story, with that played out only in memory. The music, if heard apart from the play, may seem like semiregular noise. The dances will be nonacrobatic, usually choreographed for the agility of older men. The dialogue and lyrics will often be hard to hear, difficult to understand, and, when understood, may alternate a single thought among different actors, distorting identity and the origin of the thought. Time will lose its patterns as the actors take minutes to show a few seconds of action, or several seconds will show the passing of a day, or time will simply stop. Props are few and often only suggestive of their function. Only one character is presented in any depth and that character is never developed, only unwrapped.

In the Nō, paradox is piled upon paradox and the multiple surprises create such an aura of mental and emotional echoes that even the most devoted Nō enthusiast can never learn enough to dispel the wonder. Yet, the singlemindedness of Nō so transcends its own features that it can also profoundly affect those who have never seen it before and who know little of Japanese culture and language. This experience can occur despite the extensive weaving of Japan's cultural and religious developments into most structures of Nō.

For the audience, Nō begins with a pine tree. This particular tree is a representation of the Yōgō Pine at Kasuga Shrine in Nara. It is painted on the backdrop and dominates the empty stage of every Nō theater. Within that pine is the unchanging eternalness and strength of the pine symbol, and also a god, the god of the Kasuga Shrine. Sometime before the twelfth century, an old man was seen dancing beneath that tree. He was the god of the shrine. Nō, as we know it, began with a priest standing beneath that tree and allowing the god to descend and inspire his dance. The invocation of that spirit, and that history, continues on the modern stage.

The Nō stage carries its history lessons further. The stage itself resembles a temple or shrine. There are three small steps, never used, at the threshold of the stage, where a priest might rise for a ritual. Sand and gravel are placed to represent the dried-up river- and seabeds where early Nō was performed. The seating area resembles an imperial courtyard, reminiscent of the extended periods of time when Nō was performed almost exclusively for the courts of royalty and the military rulers (shoguns).

Such lessons could continue, but an unobtrusive brocaded curtain is lifted at stage left and the chorus enters. Before the anticipation of the drama fully takes over, someone in the audience may remember that the chorus, now so intimately a part of Nō, was scorned by Zeami, the founder of Nō. Despite his distaste, the chorus was absorbed into Zeami's Sarugaku Nō tradition from a competitor, the Dengaku Nō, which died in the fifteenth century. Nō originally meant "talent" or "performance." As Dengaku faded, Sarugaku Nō became simply Nō.

The eight-to-ten-man chorus (in most cases every performer on the stage, even actors performing female roles, will be male) will emphasize or echo the words of the central character, the *shite* (performer), sometimes speaking for him when he dances. The chorus kneels stage left next to the two-to-four-man orchestra seated in front of the pine at the rear of the stage.

In most plays, the windy sound of the bamboo flute signals the opening of the Nō. Two drums, sometimes three, serve as the "heartbeat" of the drama, setting the rhythmic tone and emphasizing the actors' phrases or breaking them apart as the mood dictates. The flute sets the melodic tone with sparse phrases that are not in melodic concert with the singing of the actors or the beat-chanting of the drummers.

With the call of the flute, the *waki* (bystander) enters the bridge passageway at stage right and moves slowly toward the stage, announcing himself with an opening song. There are only two main characters in Nō, the *shite* and the *waki*. Other characters may appear if the story demands assistants, but their contribution is generally comparable to that of page turners at a recital. The *waki* always appears first. In his opening song, he announces that he is a traveler, often a priest, heading for some famous place. In his "traveling song," he discusses places and events along the way with his attendants or just for the benefit of the audience. His destination, always of historical or religious importance, will have special meaning to a Japanese audience.

Masterworks of the Nō Theater

Now the *shite* enters, but in the guise of an ordinary person. Under questioning, the seemingly ordinary person begins to reveal special knowledge or longing. He eventually hints at or tells of his real identity—that of a particular god, hero, heroine, mad person, or demon whose destiny is unfulfilled. The *waki* stands, literally, between the audience and the *shite* and performs a "priestly" function by asking questions for the audience and serving as a conduit for the words and emotions of the *shite*.

In most Nō plays, a break occurs after the *shite* reveals his/her identity. At such a time, an *ai-kyōgen* (wild-word interlude) is often performed in which the *waki* gathers further details about events associated with the destination. This segment is performed straightforwardly, with clear enunciation, and allows the audience to understand events referred to in the heavily stylized and obscure language of the Nō. Meanwhile, the *shite* is changing costume or mask.

The *waki* is usually a religious person, even if he is not a priest. Religious quotations and discussions are common in the "traveling song" before he meets the *shite*. These thoughts are often given a scholastic touch, which reverberates off the fiery reality of the *shite* and his sufferings.

As the second part begins, the *shite* reappears, this time in the full splendor or tragedy of his past. This is the climactic part of the drama. The full force of the character's emotional-spiritual situation is revealed in song and dance. His final words, which may be supported by prayers or action of the *waki*, point toward greater peace for the character and perhaps greater harmony for the universe.

Nō is normally performed with a series of three plays at one session. A *kyōgen* (wild words) will take place between plays. *Kyōgen* are humorous plays designed to break the tension while providing, at least obliquely, some kind of moral uplift. They often parody Nō subjects and are chosen to enhance the particular mood of the Nō series being performed.

Originally, five plays were presented in a day-long production, one from each of the five categories of plays named for the character type the *shite* plays—gods, warriors, women, mad persons, and devils. The Nō precursors were religious forms that included secular entertainments. As Sarugaku (monkey music) Nō and Dengaku (field music) Nō developed, they integrated the religious and secular elements into one package. From humble beginnings as sideshow acrobatics associated with the chants and rituals of performing Buddhist priests, the drama reached such austere heights that it became necessary to reintroduce a sideshow, the *kyōgen*, between the somber plays.

Religion is so vitally integrated into the structure of Nō that some understanding of basic Japanese beliefs may be necessary to follow the Nō experience more deeply. Of particular importance are the notions of god-manifestation and remembering the dead.

3

The worldly manifestation of gods, especially the descent of a god or a spirit into men and women, is an absolute reality in Japanese religions. It is important to note that each god or spirit is seen as a manifestation of one "aspect" of nature or of a transcendent god. The names of the deities literally depict these aspects. This idea is reflected in the various identities of the *shite*—a greater spirit trapped in ordinary form, revealed to be a personality shared or understood by everyone and pointing to something even larger.

Spirits sometimes seem to wait around every tree in Nō. This is true for even the semidevout Japanese in everyday life. Aspects of divinity are everywhere, as are the souls of the dead who cannot cut their bonds to the earth. People in Japan commonly pray for the dead and feel their presence. Thus, one of the most common Nō themes is remembering a spirit and praying for that spirit's release from suffering. Perhaps the most extreme example of this is in *Genji Kuyō,* where the *shite* is Lady Murasaki, author of the novel *The Tale of Genji.* She is forced to dwell on earth, away from salvation, because she wrote the book without including a prayer service for a dead character in her novel. She asks the *waki* to pray for her.

Japanese religion is a quilt, with most people practicing some parts of two or three religions. The fundament is the indigenous Shintō, "The Way of the Gods." Shintō and Shintō culture provide the basic imagery and aesthetic principles of Nō. Shintō tenets and practices are freely intermingled with Buddhism in Nō, as they are in everyday life. Buddhism provides the primary ideological stances and confrontations, especially its highly developed theories of karma and rebirth. One sect of Buddhism, Zen (Meditation) radicalized the aesthetics of Nō as well as most other Japanese art.

Amidism, a moralistic form of Buddhism teaching that Amida Buddha will give anyone rebirth into his paradise, is the most popular Buddhist school in Japan. It was the religion of the medieval commoner. Most overt Buddhist quotations in Nō are Amidist. Zen, a nonmoralistic form emphasizing discipline, was favored by the shogunate (military rulers) and thus by much of the upper classes. Its current runs deeply through Nō, but less overtly. Shingon, favored by royalty, and Tendai are esoteric sects that are more submerged in Nō but flavor its syncretistic approach and attitudes.

The relative positions of these religions in the Nō texts reflect the groups that supported the art at various times. Patronage has changed hands about every two centuries since Nō's beginnings, alternating between public support, imperial support, and that of the military aristocracy.

Nō appeared, under the Yōgō Pine, in the middle of the fourteenth century as a popular entertainment. Kannami Kiyotsugu developed the style within his Sarugaku Nō tradition, building it with elements from Dengaku and other religious and secular dance and drama forms. The venerated *Okina* is performed as a Nō and predates Kannami by about two centuries, but the bursting forth of the art form started with Kannami. He passed the tradition to his son, Zeami Motokiyo, at the end of the fourteenth century. Both Zeami and Kannami were not only actors but also playwrights, composers, directors, and promoters. Zeami, however, consolidated the Nō and gave it the vast theoretical underpinnings that are largely responsible for its sustained vigor.

Zeami's courtship of the Shogun Yoshimitsu resulted in government patronage and gave him the finances and the time to change the course of theater. Yoshimitsu's contributions may have gone deeper, for he is reported to have instructed Zeami in the Zen principles and disciplines that so profoundly influenced his theoretical work and teaching methods.

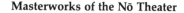

4

Many writers have called Zeami "Japan's Shakespeare," but that may be an understatement of Zeami's contributions. Not only did he formalize most of the techniques currently seen in Nō; he killed off the competition, wrote many plays and scores (the exact number is still in dispute), founded a teaching lineage that has continued, and wrote the critical and theoretical "bibles" of Nō.

Primary among Zeami's aesthetic contributions were the concept of *yūgen,* the introduction of the *jo-ha-kyū* framework as a high dramatic structure, the insistence upon "restraint" as an essential tool of art, the elevation of "borrowing" to a dramatic principle, and the spiritual conception of the "flower" as the supreme end of Nō.

Yūgen is an aesthetic principle that implies "depth," "mystery," "dark beauty," "grace," and "elegance." This quality Zeami pursued relentlessly as the primary vehicle for reaching the souls of the audience and connecting them to the *shite*.

Jo, ha, kyū (introduction, development, and climax) was a musical concept Zeami borrowed from Bugaku court music and raised into a structure for all drama. Every element of Nō is viewed as having that structure. Every play follows it and every production of a series of plays is planned according to it. *Jo* is slow and deliberate, *ha* builds and vacillates, *kyu* can reach a state of controlled frenzy.

Zeami insisted upon "restraint" as an essential tool of Nō, not merely an aesthetic preference. Much of the stylized and symbolic nature of the art is a result. Imitation should always appear as imitation, not as the thing imitated. If one comes too close to reality, attention is focused there rather than on the aesthetic-dramatic-spiritual "flower" evoked by the play. Anger must also have gentleness. The depiction of violence must have quietness in some parts of the body. Greater realism demands more background understanding from the audience, while stylized forms strike more at the core of the human experience, independent of class or culture. The playwright must not make every passage so beautiful that the central points are weakened, and the actor must monitor the enthusiasm of the audience for the same reason.

"Borrowing" became a dramatic principle under Zeami's leadership. He not only borrowed dance forms, terminology, and stage techniques; he took phrases, lines, and whole pages of Japanese and Chinese poetry. He demanded familiar stories and themes and places for the Nō. He emphasized *engo* (related words) that could suggest meanings related to the central themes while carrying a different message at a particular point in the play. He used puns, *kakekotoba* (pivot words), and well-known "pillow words," formulaic adjectives borrowed from Tanka poetry—whose 5-7-5-7-7-syllable verse structure had already been absorbed as the basis of Nō poetry. These elements all combine to form an echo chamber of sound and meaning that promotes timelessness and communality of experience by linking and relinking the mental and sensual experiences of the play, and by continually surprising the audience with new meanings emanating from the very familiar.

Zeami insisted that anything be sacrificed in order to produce the "flower" that is the aim of the drama. This flower is both an aesthetic principle and the "soul" of the actor or the character or the play, and it is, beyond that, a spiritual quest. Every element of the play, every gesture, must be devoted to producing the flower. There is a Zen fable that speaks of a fool who asked his master, "What is the moon?" Since it was nighttime with a full moon, the master pointed at it. The fool then went around telling everyone that the moon was his master's finger. The flower is, ultimately, beyond words and human conceptions—but not beyond human experience and recognition. The beautiful but strange mask is pointing to the flower by pointing to the actor. The actor is pointing to it by pointing to the character. The character points toward the soul. The soul points.

5

Egolessness is the necessary precondition of knowing where and how to point; only after that state is achieved can the special vision descend. This is the reason for much of the rigidity of Nō. This is why a *waki* will never play a *shite* role. This is why the mask is designed so that the *shite* cannot see anything but the eye-fixing pillar. Anything else would interfere with proper concentration. (Oddly, the "blind-man" mask is an exception. The slits that emphasize the blindness allow an unimpeded view of the stage, the only mask so generous.)

The final victory is the "frozen Nō"—representation, dance, mime, business, and rapid movement are all eliminated. The actor, the character, and the play meld together, exposing the flower through sheer spiritual force. This phenomenon is most prominent in *Sekidera Komachi,* where the *shite* sits motionless for one and a half hours. The role is considered the most difficult in Nō because the actor has no motions, no words to help his expression of the character. He must rely solely on his inner strength somehow showing through the mask. It is reputed to require an actor possessed of great spiritual power.

❀

Masterworks of the Nō Theater

PART I

Himuro

Introduction

Himuro belongs to the first of the five groups of Nō plays, the *kaminomono*, or god-plays. Zeami, that great source from which Nō as a theater emerged, characterized this type of drama as "above all . . . an auspicious piece."[1] "First [it] should be taken from an authentic original source, it should be elegant but not too complicated, and should be definite and straightforward of style in singing and dancing. Above all it should be an auspicious piece. . . . For this is the Introduction." Considering the present play *Himuro* against Zeami's criteria allows us to explore what is unique about it. For the play is a challenging one, and its difficulties illuminate some interesting aspects of the world of Nō art.

Let us begin with the need for an auspicious tone, which, Zeami implies, arises from the play's function as the opening piece. In this exhortation we hear overtones of strategy, as a clever actor-manager of an established school strives to maintain his position vis-à-vis other schools in competing for public favor. For we are to imagine a gathering where "the people crowd together and the audience is not yet quieted. . . . The auditorium will not yet be settled down, people will be coming in late and the audience moving about in confusion and not yet in the mood for a performance, so that it is difficult to make any impression on them." So he advises certain emphases on "business" that are apparently distasteful to him even as he puts them forward: ". . . the performance of [an opening piece] on such an occasion cannot really be fully successful." But one does the best one can, for, "After all, when the auditorium is quieted and the people are attentive the performance cannot be unsuccessful. . . . Then the success of that day's performance . . . is surely yours."[2]

Hence the call for the auspicious tone, not only to quiet the audience but to engage them immediately, "in tune with the mood of the moment, all their minds deeply moved and in perfect harmony with the actions of the actor. . . ."[3] For the auspicious will surely please. But if "the opening piece is depressing, it is impossible to overcome during the whole [subsequent] performance."[4] And here again the voice of the manager sounds clearly: the actor must please the audience, for "without success, how can the performance be interesting?"[5]

It seems to be for very much the same considerations that Zeami calls for an "authentic original source," by which he seems to mean in part what is well and generally known. The play, too, "should give an account of the story from the opening speech and immediately. . . ."[6]

When we turn from Zeami's dicta to *Himuro*, the call for a well-known story appears problematic. For, unlike the other *kaminomono*,[7] this play deals with no well-known shrine or established tale.[8] Its source seems to be an account in the *Nihonshoki*[9] that is very general and names no specific shrine or locale. In a sense, then, the author, Miyamasu, seems deliberately to have put himself at a disadvantage with regard to the perilous situation that Zeami described of people "coming in late and the audience moving about in confusion and not yet in the mood for a performance. . . ." This decision can hardly be attributed to any lack of knowledgeability in Miyamasu, for, although his troupe was not as powerful as Zeami's, he was famous during his lifetime (fl. 1427–67) as an expert on god-plays and for his contribution to the dramatic aspects of the Nō—in contrast to Zeami's theater, where *yūgen* was the dominant quality.[10]

One suspects, then, that Miyamasu relinquished the weapon of the well-known story or locale to quiet his audience because he counted on the subject itself to do so—the story of ice, preserved through summer months in remote mountains through some mysterious means. Ice seems to have had something of the exotic and extraordinary for his public. Shinkei, the poet much admired by Bashō, exclaims of it, "There is nothing more sensuous than ice," as he attempts to convey his understanding of *yūgen*.[11] Zeami himself uses the concept of what is cold in discussing *yūgen*: "Snow piled in a silver bowl."[12] This conjecture seems further borne out by *Himuro* itself.

The second difficulty of the play arises from the deeply serious and austere sense of auspiciousness that it conveys as it develops. The opening notes prepare us for the lyric joy of spring, as the *waki* and his companions express their contentedness with the godly order of their world:

> These eight isles are balmy too
> like this glorious spring,
> these eight isles are balmy too
> like this glorious spring
> of our sovereign, and all seems
> truly peaceful.

But the opening verse of the *shite* and his *tsure* already sounds a note of the austerity of a winter landscape, for in the mountains now blooming with cherry flowers, "the scenic winter air / lingers clearly still." "Spring will come everywhere," they chant, but at Mt. Himuro, the "gorge-blown wind / sounds so clear and chilly still." Thus we are introduced to what will become a leitmotif of the play.

Now the *waki* is told the story of how the ice is somehow miraculously preserved through the spring and summer months so that it may be sent as tribute to His Majesty, whose benevolence and virtue are so manifest in the blooming of the land. The *waki*—one is tempted to see him as a prosaic soul who thinks he has

10

explained the butterfly when he has dissected it—remarks that, of course, the deep shadowy gorges would probably keep the ice intact through the summer: "Since even the sun could not cast light into such a deep ravine, the snow and ice do not melt through spring and summer. How logical this is, too."

The *shite* is taken aback. Logic has its place, but it alone cannot explain the ice of Mt. Himuro, for everyone knows,

> in the common way of things,
> ice melts all away;
> how strange then when
> spring passes, and summer deepens. . . .

No, the *shite* says, there is some other explanation. For the *waki*'s explanation makes it seem as if there were no power and grace in His Majesty:

> Without the grace bestowed it
> as a tribute
> how can the snow, I wonder,
> still remain unthawed?

Now a note of growing grandeur begins to swell forth, for the ice is only a small part of the great universal order, which itself is a grace.

> This imperial land lasts long and firm
> as the way lies far and wide,
> ever flourishing.
> Buddhas and the Sun are bright,
> and more than ever they shine
> as the holy Wheel of Dharma
> shall ever turn. . . .

The *waki* is invited to stay to witness the sacred rites of the ice, and as the scene changes mysteriously to a snowscape, "the mountains darken [and]"

> . . . rivers, grass, trees
> lie alike in white
> . . . .
> all the world is changed
> into an emerald altar. . . .

The leitmotif of snow and ice and cold sounds more strongly, adding a growing austerity of feeling as Part I ends.

After the Interlude, we are plunged unequivocally into the winter world, with stormy winds, hailstones falling at a slant, and a chill "wrenching at the heart of things." The god emerges, hardly seeming to personify benevolence or auspiciousness with his demonic mask and unkempt hair.[13] The fierce power and rage of the mask are enhanced by the lines that mark his appearance:

11

> streams and mountains shake and tremble
> as the heavens and the earth
> resound, and there blows an icy wind
> wrenching at the heart of things;

Himuro

crowned with ice from Crimson Lotus Hell,
Great Crimson Lotus Hell, appears
the deity of Himuro
shining clear in all the splendor
of his sacred person!

Sakamoto Setchō, the late Nō critic, remarked that the god reminded him of a "strange monster." "In regard to the *shite* in the second part, what a strange long white flowing wig, I thought. . . . The *shite* with a formidable broad countenance, pushing around the stage, appears as if he is a strange monster, walking on with movements indicative of his great strength, scattering eerie fragments [of ice?], and creating a strange impression. . . . In short, it was extremely interesting. I thought the *shite* achieved what was intended." [14]

The ambiguity of this demon-god's identity is furthered by the fact that he performs no dance. Instead, the *shite-tsure,* an unmistakably heavenly figure, does so. Zeami established that the part of a god is "congruous with a charming style of dance, while the performance of a demon has perhaps no means of passing into dance style." [15]

There seems to be no question that traditionally this strange protagonist is a god. According to Toki Zenmaro, the Nō playwright and poet, it is understood that the *shite* represents the deification of the purity of ice. This is also the opinion of Kita Minoru, perhaps the acknowledged master among Nō actors today. Yet the *shite* must present the purity of this god by wearing the demonic *beshimi akujō* mask and seeming like a "strange monster."

It seems to me that the great interest of the play lies precisely here, in the presentation of this ambiguity. It is as this ambiguous figure assumes life that the awesomely auspicious tone of the play begins to sing. For we are to realize that the heart of what is cold is no different from fire. Thus are we to understand Shinkei's saying that there is nothing more sensuous than ice. Just as it is the great O-fudō, the wrathful god of fire, in his reds and blues, who is contained within (or perhaps Dai-nichi Nyorai, the Buddha of Great Illumination), here it is the dreadful *beshimi akujō* mask, monstrous and formidable with passion, that is to convey the inner purity and stillness of the ice god.

This paradox presents an intricate challenge to any Nō actor. Zeami noted that the actor must always determine the *hon'i,* the essence of the role he is playing. Of the essence of god roles, Zeami said: "Because vaguely expressive of anger, it is not inadmissible in playing the part of some [god] for the style to pass into that of a demon. However, the central features of these are entirely different." [16] While he does not explicitly state the central feature of heavenly roles, he says that "the central feature of a demon is strength and fearfulness." This characterization leads to a difficult problem: ". . . in the miming of a demon there is great difficulty for it is logical that the better the performance is done, the less interesting [the less capable of establishing rapport with the audience] it is. . . . For fearfulness and [rapport] are as different as black and white." The problem for the actor in *Himuro,* then, becomes how to convey the godlike through the fearfulness of the demonlike. How is he to reconcile the duality, to convey the divine oneness of identity, and thus to lead the audience through a reexperiencing of the nature of the godly?

Here the thoughts and experiences of Kita Minoru are illuminating. In 1967 he gave his third public performance of the role, the first being in 1937 and the second in the immediate postwar years. In his opinion, *Himuro* is not a play to be presented frequently. He feels that he did not achieve what was in the play the first time he performed it, when he was thirty-seven years old. As he puts it, he did not know where the Nō of this play was to be found.

> Lately I've begun to be concerned about the flow of my performance [in this play]. Since Mr. Yasufuku [a celebrated hand-drummer] didn't lead me out as he usually does, it was quite difficult to move on. I wondered if because the play is so different from *Takasago* he was purposely holding back and later asked him and found that this was so.[17] I also wanted to perform the first chorus section with greater gentleness on the outside and greater strength inside, but as usual both the outer and inner became strong. Although nobody has remarked on it, the only effect seems to be one of strength. . . . Finally I must admit the only thing I did to my own satisfaction was the *hiraki* gesture before the exit [at the end of Part I].[18]

Approximately ten years later, when he again did the role, he remembers that he was very tired afterwards. He ascribes this in part at least to his own poor physical condition immediately following the war, when his diet had been inadequate for a number of years. He also implies that the fatigue rose because he had not yet "found the Nō." For after his performance some twenty years later, he was not in the least tired.[19]

His performance in 1967, when he was sixty-seven years old, showed a "gratifying depth," according to Toki Zenmaro. It was a reaction that was shared by the members of the audience, who seemed profoundly contented by what they had seen. For what was created was not an otherworldly atmosphere; it was the world of men. Hence there was an air not of the exalted, the uplifted, but rather of serenity, beauty, and strength, which left a sense of satisfaction, as if a reaffirmation had been made of some dimly perceived but deeply acknowledged belief. Even the strangeness of the figure, which was nonhuman, did not seem otherworldly. Nor was it fearful. Its nonhuman character had nothing to threaten the humanity of men. It had a great dignity and strength, and the mask at times conveyed a faintly hidden humor.

These many values of Mr. Kita's interpretation can best be understood, to my mind, by placing the entire play within the Shintō context. In that context—so beautifully externalized at the shrines of Ise—man does not lose his identity as man, but neither is he separated in the sense of being opposed to what is outside him or being threatened by it. There is acknowledgment of force and power in nature; hence the fearsome mask. But that power is not felt as being hostile to man. Yamada Chisaburō has said that it is basic to the Japanese *Weltanschauung* to see "the self as part of the universe."[20] Japanese art of the past was based on this notion. The world was apprehended intuitively. This attitude did not foster empirical science in our history but created art of unique beauty—an art with no conflict between image and perception, an art of complete empathy.

13

HIMURO

By Miyamasu

Persons: WAKI: *A court official*
WAKI-TSURE: *His attendants (two)*
SHITE (PART I): *An old man*
TSURE (PART I): *A man*
NOCHI-JITE (PART II): *The god of Himuro*
NOCHI-TSURE (PART II): *A heavenly being*
KYŌGEN: *Two priests of the Himuro Shrine*

Classification: *Primary, Group I*
Place: *Mt. Himuro in the land of Tamba*
Time: *March*
Kogaki: 1

PART I

[*As the flute player, two hand-drum players, and a stick drummer take their places, the stage attendants bring in a mound made of a framework covered with dark-colored cloth, to which leafy sprays are attached; the whole is mounted on a one-mat dais, approximately three feet by six feet. This prop is placed in front of the musicians at the rear of the stage. With introductory music called* shidai, *the* waki, *an official of the Emperor Kameyama, accompanied by two attending officers, makes his entrance as the brocade curtain separating the mirror-room from the bridge is swept back. The* waki *wears a court minister's cap over a head cover, a heavy silk kimono made of thick fabric, and a white broad divided Nō skirt with a brocade waistband tied in front. Over this he wears a lined hunting robe. The* waki-tsure, *his attending officers, are similarly dressed. They proceed in stately procession over the bridge, and, entering the stage, they face one another to chant the introductory verse, also called the* shidai.]

WAKI AND WAKI-TSURE

[1] (*Shidai: au, tsuyogin*)

Yashima[21] mo onaji	These eight isles are balmy too,
Ōkimi no,	like this glorious spring,
Yashima mo onaji	these eight isles are balmy too,
Ōkimi no	like this glorious spring
mi-kage no haru zo	of our sovereign, and all seems
nodokeki.	truly peaceful.

[*The chorus sings the* jidori, *repeating the above verse, except the third and fourth lines.*]

(Jidori: au, tsuyogin)

Yashima mo onaji	These eight isles are balmy too,
Ōkimi no	like this glorious spring
mi-kage no haru zo	of our Sovereign, and all seems
nodokeki.	truly peaceful.

[*The* waki *and the* waki-tsure *sing the* shidai *together once more, which is called the* sanbengaeshi, *or "third repetition."*]

WAKI AND WAKI-TSURE

(Sanbengaeshi: au, tsuyogin)

Yashima mo onaji	These eight isles are balmy too,
Ōkimi no	like this glorious spring
mi-kage no haru zo	of our sovereign, and all seems
nodokeki.	truly peaceful.

[*After the* sanbengaeshi, *the* waki-tsure *kneel while the* waki, *facing stage front, intones the* nanori, *a prose passage in which he introduces himself to the audience.*]

WAKI

(Nanori: awazu, kotoba)

Somosomo korewa Kameyama no In[22] ni tsukaetatematsuru shinka nari. Ware kono hodo Tango no kuni Kuse no To[23] ni mairi, sude ni gekōdō nareba. Kore yori Wakasa-ji ni kakari. Tsuda[24] no irie, Aoba,[25] Nochise[26] no yamayama o mo ikken shi sore yori Miyako ni kaerabaya to zonji sōrō.

I am a subject serving Our Majesty, the ex-Emperor Kameyama. A while ago I went to Kuse in the land of Tango, and since I am already on my way home, from this point on I take the Wakasa Road; therefore I will view the inlet of Tsuda, then Aoba, Nochise, and other mountains too. From there I plan to go back to the capital.

[*The* waki-tsure *rise as the* waki *finishes the above passage. The* waki *and the* waki-tsure *face one another, and they sing together the following passage, called the* michiyuki.]

WAKI AND WAKI-TSURE

(Michiyuki: au, tsuyogin)

Hana no na no	As the blossom known
shiratama tsubaki[27]	as pearly white camellia
yachiyo[28] hete,	blooms eight thousand years,
shiratama tsubaki	as pearly white camellia
yachiyo hete	blooms eight thousand years,
midori[29] ni kaeru[30]	gloriously the blue returns
sora nare ya	to the sky above
haru no Nochise[31] no	Mt. Nochise, too, this spring,
Yama tsuzuku	ranging on ahead
Aoba no kokage	toward Green Leaf we hasten

15

Himuro

kumoji nɔ sue no	and before too long the end
hodo mo naki	of the cloud-hid way.

[*The* waki *faces stage front, advances a few steps and returns, indicating that the party has now reached Tanba-ji, its destination.*]

Miyako ni chikaki	Near the capital appears
Tanba-ji ya	the road to Tanba,
Himuroyama³² ni mo	so here at Mt. Himuro,
tsukinikeri,	we arrive at last,
Himuroyama ni mo	so here at Mt. Himuro
tsukinikeri.	we arrive at last.

[*After the* michiyuki *the* waki *faces stage front and intones the following prose passage, called the* tsukizerifu.]

WAKI

(Tsukizerifu: awazu, kotoba)

Isogi sōrō hodo ni Tanba no kuni Himuroyama ni tsukite sōrō. Kono tokoro no hito o machi himuro no iware o kuwashiku tazunebaya to zonji sōrō.

As we journeyed on our way in haste, we have already come to Mt. Himuro, in the land of Tanba. We will wait for someone from this place, and ask him about the icehouse hereabouts in detail.

WAKI-TSURE

Mottomo shikarubyō sōrō.

That would be fine, indeed.

[*They all go toward the* waki *seat and sit down. Following the most formal type of entrance music, called* shin no issei, *the brocade curtain is swept back, revealing the* shite, *an old man, preceded by his male companion. The* shite *wears an "old man" mask, called* koshi jō, *and an "old man" wig with a wig band, which is tied around the hair and knotted at the back of the head, its ends falling over the outer robe. He wears a small-checked under kimono woven with a warp of unpolished silk and a woof of polished silk, with the neckline accented by three unattached light yellow collars, arranged as if pleated. He also wears a wide divided Nō skirt and a waistband and carries a fan. The* shite-tsure, *his young companion, wears a plain striped kimono with the neckline outlined in red; a black tunic of unpolished, "inferior silk"; and a broad white divided Nō skirt with a waistband tied in front. He also carries a fan. Both of them carry snow rakes over their shoulders. As the* shite-tsure *stops at the first pine on the bridge, and the* shite *at the third pine, they face each other and chant the following verse, also called* issei.]

SHITE AND TSURE

[2] *(Issei: awazu, tsuyogin)*

Himuromori	Oh, Himuro guard,
haru mo sue naru	here the spring is at its end
yamakage ya,	in the mountain shade
hana no yuki o mo	of the cherry blossom snows
atsumuran	do you rake them too?

[*The* shite *and the* tsure *face stage front, and the* shite *sings the following verse, called the* ni no ku.]

16

(Ni no ku)

Mitani ni tateru   In the shades of pines that stand
matsukage ya   by the deep ravine,

[*The* shite *and the* tsure, *facing each other, sing the rest of the lines.*]

SHITE AND TSURE

fuyu no keshiki o   here the scenic winter air
nokosuran.   lingers clearly still.

[*They take the snow rakes from their shoulders and, carrying them in their hands, enter the stage; the* tsure *goes to stage center, and the* shite *goes by the* shite *seat. Then the* shite, *standing, sings the following* sashi *passage.*]

SHITE

(Sashi: awazu, tsuyogin)

Sore ikke[33]	Now, when once the buds
hirakenureba	open up their blossoms
tenga wa mina	underneath the heavens,
haru naredomo	spring will come everywhere,
matsu wa tokiwa no	so forevermore the pines
iro soete	deepen with their hue,

SHITE AND TSURE [*Facing each other*]

midori ni tsuzuku	and toward Mt. Himuro
Himuroyama no	deepened green continues
tanikaze wa	where the gorge-blown wind
mada oto saete	sounds so clear and chilly still,
kōri ni nokoru	as the water's dripping sounds
mizuoto no	on the ice remain,
ame mo shizuka ni	while the rain is quiet, too,
yuki ochite,	and the snowflakes fall,
geni hōnen[34] o	promising a fruitful year
misuru miyo no	for our mighty sovereign;
mi-tsuki no michi mo	straight and righteous lies the road
sugu narubeshi.	for the royal tribute.

[*The* shite *and the* tsure *sing the following low-pitched* sageuta *passage together.*]

(Sageuta: au, tsuyogin)

Kokudo yutaka ni	How abundant is this land
sakayuku ya,	flourishing evermore
Chitose no yama[35] mo	for Millennia Mountain
chikakariki.	rises close at hand.

17

Himuro

[They change to the high-pitched singing style as they sing the following ageuta *passage.]*

(Ageuta: au, tsuyogin)

Kawaranu ya	Oh, how changeless lies
Himuro no yama no	the mountain of Himuro
fukamidori	with its deepened green,
Himuro no yama no	the mountain of Himuro
fukamidori	with its deepened green,
haru no keshiki wa	where the very air of spring
arinagara	fills the scenic views,
kono tanikage wa	but this shaded deep ravine
kozo no mama	stays like last year's scene
mifuyu³⁶ no yuki o	storing snows three winters old
atsumeoki	as they are gathered
shimo no okina no	by a frosty-haired old man
toshidoshi ni	year in and year out;
Himuro no mitsuki³⁷	here Himuro's gift of ice

[While singing, they change their positions. The shite *goes to the center of the stage, and the* tsure *to stage front on the* waki *side of the stage.]*

mamoru nari,	is well protected,
Himuro no mi-tsuki	here Himuro's gift of ice
mamoru nari.	is well protected.

[The tsure *hands his snow rake to a stage attendant. Noticing the* shite, *the* waki *rises and stands. The following prose dialogue, called the* mondai *(or* mondō), *is intoned between the* waki *and the* shite.]*

WAKI

[3] *(Mondai: awazu, kotoba)*

Ikani kore naru rōjin ni tazunubeki koto no sōrō.	Ho, there, old man. I have something to ask you.

SHITE

Konata no koto nite sōrō ka. Nanigoto nite sōrō zo.	Are you speaking to me? What can I do for you?

WAKI

Sate mo toshidoshi ni sasaguru hi no mono no gugo ogami tatematsuredomo zaisho o miru koto wa ima hajime nari. Satesate ikanaru kamae ni yori, haru natsu made mo yuki kōri no kiezaru iware kuwashiku mōshi sōrae.	Indeed, each year I see the ice graciously presented as a tribute and placed before the table of Our Majesty, but this is the first time I have ever seen the place where it is produced. What sort of building keeps the snow and ice from melting in the spring and summer? Please tell us about it.

[The shite *intones the following prose passage, called the* katari, *as he stands.]*

(*Katari: awazu, kotoba*)

Mukashi[38] mi-kari no kōya ni hitomura no mori no shita io arishi ni, koro wa minazuki nakaba naru ni kanpū gyoi no tamoto ni utsuri, sanagara fuyuno no miyuki no gotoshi. Ayashime goranzureba ichinin no okina yuki kōri o yanai ni tataetari. Kano okina mōsu yō sore senka ni wa shisetsu[39] kōsetsu tote kusuri no yuki ari. Okina mo kaku no gotoshi tote, kōri o gugo ni sonaeshi yori hi no mono no gugo wa hajimarite sōrō.

Long ago in the wide imperial hunting ground, there was a hut under a wooded grove of trees. It was in the middle of the month of June, and the chilly wind flapped the sleeves of the royal robes as though on an imperial journey in winter. Finding this odd, His Majesty looked into the hut and discovered that snow and ice were packed high and full inside the hut. The old man said that some wizards kept medicinal snows called purple snow and crimson snow in their huts. He had some too. So he presented it graciously to him. Since then, the custom of presenting it as a royal gift was started.

[*The* waki *sings the following verse passage in free-rhythm style.*]

WAKI

(*Kakaru: awazu, tsuyogin*)

Iware o kikeba
omoshiro ya,
Satesate himuro no
zaisho zaisho
jōdai yori mo
kuniguni ni
amata kawarite
arishi yo nō.

Hearing you explain this gift
is most delightful!
Of course, of course, these places
called icehouses grew
in country after country,
since the olden days.
Every province builds its own
after their own fashion, right?

SHITE

Mazu wa Nintoku Tennō no gyo-o ni Daiwakoku[40] Tsuge[41] no himuro yori sonae some ni shi hi no mono nari.

First of all, in the reign of His Majesty, Emperor Nintoku, the custom of presenting a tribute of ice was started in the icehouse at Tsuge in the Land of Great Peace.

TSURE

(*Kakaru: awazu, tsuyogin*)

Mata sono nochi wa
yamakage no
yuki mo arare mo
saetsuzuku
tayori no kaze o
Matsugasaki,[42]

Then soon after, once again,
in the mountain shade
where snow and hail continue
frozen by the wind
the other was constructed
underneath Pine Point

19

Himuro

Kitayama[43] kage mo himuro narishi o.　In the shade of North Hill there was another.

SHITE

TSURE

(Kakaru: awazu, tsuyogin)

Mata kono kuni ni
tokoro o utsushite

Then they moved its site once more
to this place across the country

SHITE

mitani mo sayakeku　where the deep ravine is chilly;

TSURE

kokufū kanki mo　and both the gorge-blown wind and cold

SHITE

tayori aritote
ima made mo

are considered suitable;
so unto this day

[*The* shite *and the* tsure, *facing each other, sing the following passage.*]

SHITE AND TSURE

matsudai chōkyū no
hi no gugo no tame
Tanba no kuni
Kuwada no kōri ni
himuro o sadame
mōsu nari.

for the royal tribute of the ice
and the sake of future use,
in the land of Tanba,
in its district of Kuwada
they have fixed the icehouse site
at this place, they say.

[*They look at the* waki *and the* waki *intones the following prose passage.*]

WAKI

Geni geni okina no mōsu gotoku, yama mo tokoro mo kobukaki kage no hikage mo sasanu mitani nareba, haru natsu made mo yuki kōri no kienu mo mata wa kotowari nari.

How true it is, indeed. Just as this old man says, these mountains and this place are deeply shaded with trees. [*Faces the mound.*] Since even the sun could not cast its light into such a steep ravine, the snow and ice do not melt through spring and summer. How logical this is, too. [*Faces the* shite.]

SHITE

Iya tokoro ni yorite kōri no kienu to uketamawareba kimi no ikō mo naki ni nitari.

Well. Depending on the place, the ice does not melt away, you say. That is as if there were no powers and grace in His Majesty.

Masterworks of the Nō Theater

(Kakaru: awazu, tsuyogin)

Tada yo no tsune no	Ordinary ice and snow
yuki kōri wa	all throughout the world,

Shite

Hito-yo no ma ni mo	even during a single night when
toshi koyureba [44]	the year is over,

Waki

haru tatsu kaze ni wa	before the rising winds of spring,
kiyuru mono o	will thaw and melt away.

Shite and Tsure

sareba uta ni mo	So even in the poem

Shite, Tsure, and Waki [*All sing together.*]

Tsurayuki [45] ga	by Tsurayuki,

[*As the chorus sings the following high-pitched* ageuta *passage, the* tsure *goes in front of the musicians and kneels while the* waki *takes his seat.*]

Chorus

(Ageuta: au, tsuyogin)

Sode [46] hichite	"Water that I draw
musubishi mizu no	makes my sleeves so cold and damp
kōreru o.	and freezes tightly,
musubishi mizu no	makes my sleeves so cold and damp
kōreru o.	and freezes tightly,
Haru tatsu kyō no	but today the rising wind
kaze ya tokuran to	of spring will melt and loosen it."
yomitareba	Since the poet sang
yo no ma ni kitaru	of how spring can come even
haru ni dani	in a single night,
kōri wa kiyuru	in the common way of things,
narai nari.	ice melts all away,
mashite ya	how strange then when
haru sugi natsu take	spring passes, and summer deepens
haya minazuki ni	and before too long the month
naru made mo	of June approaches,

21

[*The* shite *walks to the left, around the stage.*]

kienu yuki no	but still the thin ice
usugōri	does not melt away.
gugo no chikara ni	Without the grace bestowed it

Himuro

arade wa	as a tribute,
ikade ka nokoru	how can the snow, I wonder,
yuki naran,	still remain unthawed?
ikade ka nokoru	How can the snow, I wonder,
yuki naran.	still remain unthawed?

WAKI

Nao nao haru natsu made mo kōri no kiezaru iware o kuwashiku mōshi sōrae.

Please tell me more and even more about the reason the ice does not melt through spring and summer.

SHITE

Nengoro ni mōshi agyōzuru nite sōrō.

I will tell you about it in detail.

[*The* shite *stands at the* shite *seat, then goes to stage center and kneels. The chorus sings the following passage, called* kuri.]

CHORUS

[4] (*Kuri: awazu, tsuyogin*)

Sore tenchijin no	In this world of the three orders
sansai[47] ni mo	of Heaven, Earth, and Man,
kimi o motte shu to shi	here Our Majesty reigns all supreme;
sankai banbutsu no	and those who live in seas and mountains
shusshō	throughout their lives,
sunawachi ōji no	welcome spring with grace and virtue
ondoku nari	in our sovereign's kingdom.

[*The* shite *sings the following* sashi *passage.*]

SHITE

(*Sashi: awazu, tsuyogin*)

Kōdo[48] nagaku kataku	This imperial land stands long and firm
teito haruka ni	as the way lies far and wide,
sakan nari.	ever flourishing.

22

CHORUS

Butsu nichi hikari	Buddhas and the sun are bright,
masu masu ni shite	and more than ever they shine
hōrin tsune ni	as the holy Wheel of Dharma
tenzeri.	shall ever turn;

Yōtoku ori o	and the virtue of the sun
tagaezu shite	never mistakes the seasons.

CHORUS

uro sōsetsu no	Rain and dew, frost and snow keep
toki o etari.	their respective seasons.

[*While the chorus sings the following passage, called* kuse, *the* shite *kneels. This combination is called* iguse.]

(Iguse: au, tsuyogin)

Natsu no hi ni[49]	Until the coming
naru made kienu	of a summer's day, thin ice
usugōri	never melts away.
haru tatsu kaze ya	Are the rising winds of spring
yogite fukuran.	blowing now the other way?
Geni tae nare ya	Oh, how wonderful it seems!
banbutsu toki ni	How everything is growing!
arinagara.	Each has its season,
Kimi no megumi no	all blessed, besides, with grace
iro soete	from His Majesty;
Miyako no hoka no	and outside the capital
Kitayama ni	by the northside hills,
tsuku ya hayama no	next to the mountains ranging blue
eda shigemi	with verdant branches,
kono mo kano mo no	from the surface, here and there,
shitamizu ni	of the icebound brooks,
atsumuru yuki no	the piles of snow are gathered
Himuroyama	at Mt. Himuro,
tsuchi[50] mo ki mo	while upon the land and trees
ōkimi no	graciously bestowed
mi-kage ni ikade	is the everlasting grace
morubeki.	of His Majesty.

[*The chorus speaks for the* shite.]

Geni ware nagara	Though I know what is my worth
mi no waza no	and that my work counts
ukiyo[51] no kazu ni	as much as all other tasks
arinagara,	in this fleeting world,
mi-tsuki ni mo	still it is unique:
toriwakite	for this gift of ice
nao ama terasu	outshines by far all others
hi no mono[52] ya;	here beneath the sky,
ta ni mo kotonaru	as it differs from the rest
sasagemono	of the royal gifts
eikan motte	which Our Majesty receives

23

Himuro

hanahadashiki	graciously with pleasure;
gyokutai o	so I'm blessed to go
haisuru mo	before his presence.
mi-tsuki o hakobu	All for this the aged old man
yue to ka ya.	brings forth his tribute.

[*The* shite *sings the following lines, called* ageha.]

SHITE

(*Ageha*)

| Shikareba toshi tatsu | Therefore in this auspicious year |
| hatsuharu no [53] | in this first new spring, |

CHORUS

hatsune no kyō no	on this first day of the Mouse,
tamabōki	now as he holds up
te ni toru kara ni	in his hand the jeweled rake,
yuraku tama no	tasseled cords move lightly,
okina [54] sabitaru	as in days as old as he
yamakage o	in the mountain shade,
kozo no mama nite	where the heaping snows keep on
furitsuzuku	dropping from the boughs

[*Looks up toward stage front above.*]

| yuki no shizuri o | as they did the year before; |
| kakiatsumete | he rakes and gathers them |

[*The* shite *moves the rake about.*]

ko no shitamizu ni	and then sweeps them into pools
kakiirete	underneath the trees;
kōri o kasane	and piling ice upon them,
yuki o tsumite	he heaps more snow on ice.

[*The* shite *looks at the mound.*]

machioreba	Now a while he waits
haru sugite	for the spring to pass,
haya natsuyama ni	and before too long the hills
narinureba	turn to summer green;
itodo himuro no	this appears increasingly
kamae shite	like a real icehouse.
tachisaru koto mo	Never leaving here, he lives
natsukage [55] no	by crystal waters
mizu ni mo sumeru [56]	in the summer shade, this guard
himuromori	of the true icehouse
natsugoromo naredomo	appears to dress in summer robes,
sode sayuru	but how cold and chill
keshiki narikeri.	seems the air about his sleeves.

24

[*The* shite *moves around the stage and then sits*[57] *in stage center; the stage attendant removes his rake. The chorus continues to sing the following passage, called* rongi.]

[5] *(Rongi: awazu, tsuyogin)*

Geni tae nari ya	Oh, how wonderful and strange
hi no mono no,	is this thing called ice!
geni tae nari ya	Oh, how wonderful and strange
hi no mono no	is this thing called ice!
mi-tsuki no michi mo	The road he takes to haul it
sugu ni aru	lies before us straight
Miyako ni iza ya	to Miyako let us all now
kaeran.	return at once.

SHITE

Shibaraku matase	Oh, wait a little longer.
tamōbeshi,	Please remain with us;
totemo sanro no	since you'll take this mountain road
o-tsuide ni	as you journey home
koyoi no	this very night,
hi no mi-tsuki	you may watch and see
sonōru matsuri	the festive rite of offering
goranze yo.	the ice as tribute

CHORUS

Somo ya hitsugi no	Well, now I really wonder
matsuri towa	what it will be like,
ikanaru koto ni	the festive rite to offer
aruyaran.	the ice as tribute.

SHITE

Hito koso shirane	People do not know of it,
kono yama no	but in this mountain,
sanjin bokushin no	all the mountain gods and deities
himuro o shugo shi	of the woods are graciously
tatematsuri	guarding this icehouse;
maiya ni shinji	every night there is a rite
aru nari to	of sacred service.

CHORUS

ii mo aeneba	As he barely speaks these words,
yama kurete	the mountains darken,

25

[*The* shite *rises.*]

kanpū shōsei ni	and midst the forest pines piercing winds
koe tate	raise their voices,
toki-naranu yuki wa	and the flakes of snow untimely
furi ochi	fall and scatter;

Himuro

[*The* shite *looks upward and downward.*]

sanka sōmoku	mountains, rivers, grasses, trees
oshinamete	lie alike in white
kōri o shikite	with the crystal ice laid out,
ruridan ni	all the world is changed
naru to omoeba	into an emerald altar;
himuromori no	and the icehouse guardsman
hakubyō o	seems to make his way
fumu to miete	across the sheet of ice
muro no uchi ni	and deep into the house
irinikeri,	he vanishes away,
himuro no uchi ni	and deep into the icehouse
irinikeri.	he vanishes away.

[*The* shite *moves to his right, and at the* shite *seat he makes a* hiraki *gesture and enters the mound. The* tsure *exits over the bridge to musical accompaniment called* raijo.]

Nakairi (Interlude)

[*Following entrance music called* massha-raijo, *the kyōgen Omo, who is a Shintō priest, appears on the bridge. He comes out to the side of the* shite *seat.*]

OMO

Kayō ni sōrō mono wa Tanba no kuni Kuwada no Kōri Himuro no myōjin ni tsukaemōsu shinshoku no mono nite sōrō. Makoto ni waga chō wa rissan henchi no shōkoku naredomo shinkoku nite, ōi medataku yutaka naru on-koto nite sōrō. Sareba masumasu kimi anzen no hakarigoto o megurashi, kono yama ni himuro o kamae, hi no mono no gugo o sonaemōshi sōrō. Sōjite himuro no shisai to mōsu wa ninnō jūni-dai Keikō Tennō[58] mi-kari no kōya ni hitomura no mori no shita ni iori no arishi ni, koro wa satsuki sue no koto naru ni, kanpū shikiri ni shite gyoi no mi-sode ni utsuri, tada sanagara fuyuno no mi-kari no gotoku nite goza sōrō aida, fushin ni oboshimeshi yoku-yoku eiran aru ni, ie no uchi ni yuki kōri o tsumi kasanete oki sōrō aida, ikanaru koto zo to tazunetamaeba, hitori no okina mōsu yō, sore senka ni wa shisetsu kōsetsu kusuri no yuki ari. Okina mo kore o fukusuru yue ni jumyō chōen sokusai enmei nari tote, sunawa-

I am a Shintō priest serving the deity at the Himuro Shrine in the district of Kuwada in the land of Tanba. Truly, indeed, our country is so remote and small that it resembles scattered millet seeds, but it is a land blessed with kami, so the throne is rich and flourishing. In order to keep our sovereign healthy and sound, every precaution is taken, and on this mountain an icehouse was built so that ice could be presented as a tribute. Generally speaking, the custom originated, they say, in the reign of the twelfth sovereign, the Emperor Keikō. His Majesty went hunting in a wild field, and he saw a hut under a grove of trees. It was in June, but the chilly wind blew strong and shook his sleeves as if he were hunting in a winter field. Finding it strange, he looked into the hut where snow and ice were piled high inside. When he asked what this was, an old man said that in some wizard's hut there were purple and crimson snows, which were

chi kōri o kudaki gugo ni sonaemōshi sōrō. Sore yori hi no mono no gugo to mōsu koto hajimaritari. Sono nochi Nintoku Tennō no gyo-o ni Yamato no kuni Tsuge no himuro yori Yamashiro no kuni Matsugasaki Kitayama ni kamae, sono nochi kono kuni ni kamaemōshi sōrō. Sareba kono kitsurei ni makase ima ni itaru made rokugatsu tsuitachi hi no mono no gugo o sonaemōshi sōrō. Sate mata tadaima Kameyama no In e tsukae on-mōshiaru shinka-dono himuro o goran arubeshi tote. Kono tokoro e go-gekō nite sōrō aida, on-rei no tame idete sōrō. Isoide on-rei mōsō.

used for medicine. "Since I take them, I live long and free from cares," he said. Then he chipped off some ice and presented it to His Majesty. Ever since then, a tribute of ice has been made. Later, in the reign of Emperor Nintoku, an icehouse was built on North Hill, at Matsugasaki in Yamashiro, and was modeled after that of Tsuge in the land of Yamato. Later on, one was also built at this place. Therefore from that lucky occasion until this day, ice is presented on the first of June. Now at present, an officer who serves the ex-Emperor Kameyama is here to see the icehouse. I come out here to give thanks for his coming. I must do that at once.

[*The* kyōgen *goes to the* waki *and bows low, with both hands on the floor.*]

Kore wa Himuro no myōjin ni tsukaemōsu shinshoku no mono nite sōrō. Onrei no tame idete sōrō. Sate tōsha wa shinpen kidoku no on-kami nite sōrō. Tadaima nite mo yuki o koi sōraeba, furimōshi sōrō. Yuki o kōte o-me ni kakemōsōzuru ga, nan to gozaarōzuru zo.

I am a priest serving the Himuro Shrine. I have come here to thank you for your coming. This shrine is full of wonders. Even right now, if I pray for snow, it will snow. Would it please you if I prayed for snow?

WAKI

Sa araba yuki o kōte miserare sōrae.

If you can do that, then pray for snow and show us how it can be done.

OMO

Kashikomatte sōrō. Yareyare ichidan no koto ja. Sareba ima hitori yobidasō. Ikani watari sōrō ka.

Yes, sir. [*Goes to the* shite *pillar.*] Ah, well, this is quite a job. I'd better call my helper. [*Calls toward the curtain.*] Is there someone there?

[*A second* kyōgen, *Ado, a Shintō priest, appears from behind the curtain, dressed like the first* kyōgen.]

ADO

Nanigoto nite sōrō zo.

What is this all about?

27

OMO

Shinka-dono no yuki o kōte mise yo to no on-koto nite sōrō aida, yobidashite sōrō.

The honorable official wants us to show him how to pray for snow. So I called for you.

Himuro

Warera mo sono koto nite arōzuru zo to omoi, migoshirae shite idete sōrō.

I thought that was probably it, so I have prepared myself for it and I have come out here.

OMO

Sareba warera ni mo migoshiraeno shite tamawari sōrae.

That is the case, so I'd better prepare myself too.

ADO

Kokoroe mōshi sōrō.

I see.

[*Relieved, he slips one of his arms out of his tunic sleeve.*]

OMO

Nani to migoshirae wa yoku sōrō ka.

Are you prepared and ready?

ADO

Ichidan to yoku sōrō.

By far the best, sir.

OMO

Sareba yuki o koimōsō.

Then let's pray for snow.

[*Omo goes to the name-saying pillar and Ado near the* waki *seat. They open their fans with both hands and, continuing to use both hands, they fan the air vigorously.*]

OMO AND ADO

Yuki koō, koō, koō.

Snow, snow, I beg of you; I beg of you; I beg of you.

Arare koō, koō, koō.

Hail, hail, I beg of you; I beg of you; I beg of you.

OMO

Sareba koso sora ga kumotte kita wa.

Well, the sky is becoming cloudy.

OMO AND ADO

Yuki koō, koō, koō.

Snow, snow, I beg of you; I beg of you; I beg of you.

OMO

Nani to obitadashiku futta.

Remarkable! It's snowed a lot!

ADO

Sono tōri ja.

Why, it's just as you say!

Masterworks of the Nō Theater

Omo

Yuki marome o itasō. Yuki o atsumete kuresashime.

Let's make a snowball. You gather it, please.

Ado

Kokoroeta.

I will.

Omo

Yuki korobakase.

Let's roll it.

Ado

Yuki marumakase.

Roll it into a ball.

Omo

Koto no hoka okyū natta. Itsumo no tōri[59] naijin ni osamyō. Yuki korobakase.

It's getting unusually big. Let's offer this to the inner shrine as usual. We'll roll it there.

[*They motion, as if they were rolling a snowball toward the mound.*]

Omo and Ado

Yuki maromakase. Kuiri, kuiri, kuiri. Ei ei ō.

Let's roll it! Roll it on, roll it on. Ey, ey-ho!

Omo

Ichidan to medetai. Sareba mata itsumo no gotoku hakusetsu koō.

This is really a lucky sight. Now then, let's go on to the next step and pray for light snow as usual.

Omo and Ado

Yuki koō, koō, koō. Hakusetsu koō, koō, koō.

Snow, snow, let it fall, let it fall. Snow, snow I beg of you; I beg of you; I beg of you. Light snow, light snow, I beg of you; I beg of you; I beg of you. Snow, snow, I beg of you; I beg of you; I beg of you.

[*They sing the following.*]

Waga ya no kaki ya ki ni,
fure ya, tamare,
koō, koō, koō.

On the trees and fences in our yard
let it fall and let it pile;
I beg of you; I beg of you; I beg of you.

[*They stamp their feet and make their exit behind the curtain.*]

Himuro

PART II

[*Following introductory music called* deha, *the* shite-tsure, *a heavenly being, appears as the rich brocade curtain is swept back. She wears a* tsure *mask; a long black wig with a wig band tied around it, knotted at the back of the head with its long ends falling over the outer robe; and a heavenly crown. She is dressed in a silk kimono of a plain white with a satinlike finish, on which a pattern is painted in gold or silver; a broad scarlet divided Nō skirt with a brocade waistband; and a loose cord tied with a central knot below the breast and ending in tassels just above the hem. Similar but smaller cords are attached to the bottom edge of each sleeve. She carries a fan. She moves across the bridge and stands by the first pine. The chorus sings the following verse, during which the* tsure *enters the stage.*]

Chorus

[6] *(Issei: awazu, tsuyogin)*

Gaku ni hikarete	Enticed along by music
Kotoriso[60] no	now the dancers start
mai no sode koso	to dance the Old Bird Measure
yurugu nare.	as they wave their sleeves.

[*The* tsure *performs the Angel Dance* (tennyo no mai). *She then goes in front of the musicians and sits down.*]

Tennyo no mai

[*The* shite, *who has now become the deity of Himuro, stays inside the mound, where he has made a costume change with the stage attendant's help. He wears a* kobeshimi *mask with a flowing red wig and a small round cap called* tōkan, *which rests just above the forehead, secured by cords tied under the chin. He wears a heavy plain silk kimono, and a brocade broad divided Nō skirt with a waistband tied in front. Over this he wears a lined silk hunting robe. He carries a fan. In special performances, he wears a* beshimi akujō *mask with a flowing white wig. He chants the following verse within the mound, representing the icehouse.*]

Shite

(Waka: awazu, tsuyogin)

Kawaranu ya	Unchanged forever,
Himuro no yama no	the mountain of Himuro
fukamidori	deepens into green;

Chorus

yuki o megurasu	swirling all around the snow
mai no sode kana.	how the dancer's sleeves appear!

30

Shite

[7] *(Issei: awazu, tsuyogin)*

Kumori naki	Under cloudless skies
miyo no hikari mo	in his reign its glorious light
ama terasu,	shines in heaven too;
Himuro no mi-tsuki	the tribute from Himuro
sonō nari.	will be offered now.

(*Noriji: ōnori, tsuyogin*)

Sonae yo ya,	Make the offering!
sonae yo ya.	Make the offering!
Samo isagiyoki	Oh, how one pure grain of sand
minasoko no isago	at the bottom of the water

SHITE

(*Awazu, tsuyogin*)

chōjite wa[61] mata	grows to be a mighty stone!
iwao no kage yori	And from behind its deepened shade,

CHORUS

(*Noriji: ōnori, tsuyogin*)

sanka mo shindō shi	streams and mountains shake and tremble
tenchi mo hibiki	as the heavens and the earth
kanpū shikiri ni	resound, there blows an icy wind
kimo o tsuzumete	wrenching at the heart of things,
guren daiguren no	crowned with ice from Crimson Lotus Hell,
kōri[62] o itadaku	Great Crimson Lotus Hell, appears
Himuro no shintai	the deity of Himuro
sae kagayakite zo	shining clear in all the splendor
arawaretaru.	of his sacred person!

[*The stage attendant lets the walls of the icehouse fall, later removing them, to reveal the* shite *seated on a stool, holding white blocks of wood representing ice in each hand.*]

SHITE

(*Noriji: ōnori, tsuyogin*)

Kokufū suihen	These dell winds and water edges
sae kōrite,	are of frozen crystal.

CHORUS

Kokufū suihen	These dell winds and water edges
sae kōrite,	are of frozen crystal.

31

SHITE

tsuki mo kagayaku	Brightly also shines the moon
kōri no omote[63]	on the surface of the ice,
bankyō o utsusu	ten thousand images reflect
kagami[64] no gotoku	as on the Yama mirror.

Shite

Seiran kozue o	The stormy wind blows clear and sweeps
fukiharatte	all across the treetops;

Chorus

kage mo kobukaki	shadowed deep and dark the trees,
tani no to ni	at the gorge's door

Shite

yuki wa shibuki	snows slash upon them,

Chorus

arare wa yogirite	and all aslant the hailstones run;
iwa moru mizu mo	water dripping from the rocks,
sazareishi no	like little grains of sand,
fukai no kōri ni	drop by drop, is firmly welded
tojitsukeraruru o	upon the deep well's crystal ice,
hikihanashi	and tearing, tearing
hikihanashi	all of them apart,

[*The* shite *jumps down from the dais to the stage floor and gestures as if he were tearing the ice from the rocks.*]

ukamiidetaru	setting all of them afloat,
Himuro no kamikaze [65]	appears Himuro's godlike wind.
ara samu ya,	How piercingly cold!
hiyayaka ya.	How terribly chill!

[*The* shite *performs the* hataraki, *a heroic dance with very energetic, forcefully executed steps.*]

Maihataraki

Shite

(Noriji: ōnori, tsuyogin)

Kashikoki miyo no	In his glorious sovereign's reign
mi-tsuki nare ya.	this is our royal gift;

Chorus

Kashikoki miyo no	in his glorious sovereign's reign
mi-tsuki nare ya.	this is our royal gift.

[*The* shite *moves to stage front.*]

Nami o osamuru mo	What keeps the waves serenely calm
kōri	is the ice;

[*The* shite *looks at the ice.*]

Masterworks of the Nō Theater

mizu o shizumuru mo	what makes the water peaceful too,
kōri no	the ice again.
hi ni soe tsuki ni yuki	Day after day, and month after month,
toshi o machitaru	waiting for a year we keep
hi no mono no sonae	this ice to make a tribute;
sonae tamae ya.	present it as a tribute.

[The shite *goes toward the* tsure.]

| Sonae tamae to | Present it as a tribute, |
| uneme no mai no | oh, ye maidens, while you dance, |

[The shite *gives the ice to the* tsure.]

| yuki o megurasu | swirling like the snow, |
| omigoromo no | white sleeves of sacred robes you wear, |

[The shite *steps back to center stage.]*

tamoto ni soete	never let them touch thin ice
usugōri o	lest they should break its gems
kudaku na, kudaku na	into pieces, into pieces;

[The shite *stamps his feet on the floor.]*

tokasu na, tokasu na to	oh, never melt it, never thaw it,
Himuro no kami wa	for the god of Himuro
kōri o shugo shi	graciously protects the ice,
hikage o hedate	keeping it from the bright sun,

[The shite *makes a turn to the left and points the fan toward the* tsure.]

| kansui o sosoki | pouring down the freezing water, |
| seifū o fukashite | allowing the clear chill winds to blow; |

[The tsure *lifts up the ice and exits behind the curtain.]*

| hana no Miyako e | and to flowering Miyako |
| yuki⁶⁶ o wake | through the flaky snows, |

[Near the waki *seat, the* shite *turns toward the curtain.]*

kumo o shinogite	staving off the clouds he comes
Kitayama⁶⁷ no	past North Hill's Suwa
Suwa⁶⁸ ya Miyako mo	where the capital is near,
mietari, mietari	within our sight, within our sight
isoge ya, isoge	let us hurry, hurry on,

[The shite *sees the* tsure *off the* shite *seat.]*

33

hi no mono o	with our gift of ice.
sonōru tokoro mo	From many places it is brought
Otagi⁶⁹ no kōri⁷⁰	like Otagi's country ice,
sasaguru gugo mo	as a tribute to our lord,
hi no moto no kimi ni	our sovereign of the sun, for whom,
mi-tsukimono koso	indeed, this royal tribute
medetakere.	is most auspicious!

[The shite *stamps his feet and exits.]*

Nonomiya

Introduction

There are many Nō plays based on *Genji monogatari* (Tale of Genji), the greatest of the classical Japanese tales, written shortly after the year 1000 by Lady Murasaki. *Nonomiya*, or *The Meadow Shrine*, is one of them. It is often contrasted with another, *Aoi no Ue* (Lady Hollyhock), since in both of these plays by Zeami, the main character is Rokujō no Miyasudokoro, a memorable figure in the gallery of Genji's many loves. If among these women Yūgao is simple devotion incarnate; Fujitsubo, love rued for honor's sake; and the red-nosed princess of Hitachi Palace, love inspired by pity, then Rokujō is perhaps love as prideful passion itself. She is a complex figure, pursued by her conflicting emotions to the fearful shadows of human consciousness from which she herself begs release.

Rokujō is introduced offhandedly. "It was at the time when he was secretly visiting the lady of the Sixth Ward,"[1] Murasaki begins, and then goes on to quite another matter. We learn that Genji at seventeen, already the practiced courtier, was beginning to be uneasy in this affair; the first bloom had passed, and "The lady in the grand mansion was very difficult to get on with. . . ."[2] A whole series of other attachments are described, and next we learn that the lady, widow of the ex-emperor's brother, Prince Senbō, had decided to retire with her daughter to the Ise Shrine, where the latter was to serve as the official priestess. Rokujō allowed it to be known that this move was caused by her resentment at Genji's neglect.[3] Here already was an inkling of the extent and ambivalence of her emotions, for she had deliberately allowed herself to be gossiped about to embarrass Genji—a regrettable example of nose-cutting to spite one's own face. Then followed the famous incident of the tussle between her grooms and those of Genji's wife, Aoi, as their carriages were jostled about in the crowds that had come to see the procession of the Kamo virgin. Rokujō's curtained litter was pushed back among the commoners while Aoi's stood in the front row of spectators, where all the members of the courtly escort of the Kamo virgin paid their respects as they passed. Her humiliation was

34

so extreme that she lost all control and wept, though "It was hideous that her servants should see her in this state."[4] When Genji heard of the incident he was disturbed and called on her to express his regrets. She, however, turned him away, and, in spite of his sympathy, "he was feeling rather tired of coping with injured susceptibilities."[5]

The incident seems to have plunged her deeper into the chaos of her conflicting emotions. She was undecided as to whether she should accompany her daughter and thus renounce any hope of maintaining her relationship with Genji. "Yet what had she to stay for?"[6] To remain meant only to expose herself to the continued exacerbation of "the torment of her desires"[7] and to Genji's growing neglect. She could expect nothing more, for Aoi, his official wife,[8] was about to have his child and therefore Aoi's hold upon him would grow stronger, while her own could only become more attenuated, for she held no recognized position in his life. "She felt herself . . . swirled this way and that by paroxysms that sickened her but were utterly beyond her control."[9] Her condition worsened: "She began to feel that the violent and distracting emotions which continually assailed her had in some subtle way unhinged her mind. . . . "[10] Now terror was added: the fear that she might be responsible for the strange illness of Genji's wife, which was said to be due to possession by some malignant spirit. Tormented by that unspeakable horror, she brooded "constantly upon the nature of her own feelings towards Aoi, but could discover in herself nothing but intense unhappiness. Of hostility . . . she could find no trace at all. Yet she could not be sure whether somewhere in the depths of a soul consumed by anguish some spark of malice had not lurked." She saw that since the "hateful incident of the coaches" she had been "utterly bruised and shattered," and as she relived the humiliation of that day, "it seemed as though she had lost all control over her own thoughts." She dreamed that she was beating Aoi in "an outburst of brutal fury" that appalled her. "How terrible! It seemed then that it was really possible for one's spirit to leave the body and break out into emotions which the waking mind would not countenance." If her hideous crime became known, she would be reviled as a "fiendishly venomous and malignant character." Aghast, she lay "dazed and helpless."

Aoi's condition worsened; her seizures intensified. Incantations and rites of exorcism were redoubled. At last, a spirit spoke and called for Genji, looking at him with "forbearance and tender concern." It spoke "wistfully and tenderly"[11] of her longing for him and revealed itself as being indeed the spirit of Rokujō.[12] The attacks upon Aoi continued while the mortal Rokujō felt "as though she were a stranger to herself," subject to a "strange process of dissolution." Shortly after the birth of her child, Aoi died in a fit of choking.

Genji found the revelation of the possessing spirit ghastly and unbelievable; he was filled with horror. Yet worldling that he was, he soon reduced his dismay to a "painful impression" and finally to a wish: "If only he had chanced never to see or hear the fatal operation of [Rokujō's] spirit!" While he knew that he could never again find the same intimacy he had felt before with this woman, endowed with "every talent and charm," nevertheless he did not wish to be "harsh" or "unfeeling" or to incriminate her in Aoi's death by abruptly breaking off their liaison, for the great world would be all too ready to seize upon it and to speculate. Hoping to comfort her, he wrote, advising her not to "brood overmuch on what has happened." Rokujō rightly divined that Genji suspected her, her own fears were confirmed, and her misery was increased.[13] She felt that she had become "utterly odious" to him. Her only salvation was to forget him, but her attempts to do so only intensified her preoccupation, swerving now to longing and now to resentment. As the time approached for departure to Ise, Genji found himself bemused by his memories of her beauty, intelligence, and breeding, and by his knowledge that his neglect of her had led to this dreadful impasse between them.[14] Such was the state of affairs between them when the meeting took place at the Meadow Shrine, where the Ise virgin was in retreat as part of the purification ritual.

It is with this meeting, as recollected by Rokujō's spirit, that the present play, *Nonomiya*, opens. Structurally, the play is cast in the classic formula of the wandering Buddhist priest who hears the story of an unsettled spirit and prays for its repose, bringing enlightenment to it. The play is regarded as one of Zeami's greatest and is said to embody to a marked degree one type of that beauty which he called *yūgen*, the essence of this theater, particularly of the sort that characterizes the third group of plays among the five classifications—the *kazuramono*, or woman-play. What he wished to convey in this play can be deduced in part by examining what he takes from the *Tale of Genji* and what he omits, and by a comparison with *Aoi no Ue*, the second play with the same heroine.[15]

What he omits is startling. Through the viciousness of her own resentment and jealousy, though beyond her conscious control, Rokujō has caused the deaths of three of Genji's loves—Yūgao, Aoi, and Murasaki. Yet of these most heinous spiritual crimes, there is no mention. In a play ostensibly concerned with the salvation of a tormented soul and its release from earthly karma, such an omission can only alert us to some recondite purpose in the author.

Again, the novel's dramatic description of the storms of indecision and agonizing introspection that torment Rokujō is passed over in the play in four lines:

> but what lies within the depths
> of the human heart?
> So uneasy now and then
> grows the tie between them. . . .

The reader may appropriately ask what the playwright gains by the omission of material that so well presents the deeply human complexity of Rokujō's character.

The meeting between Genji and Rokujō at the Meadow Shrine is presented in detail in the novel, particularly the nuances and changes of Genji's emotions toward her, which surprise even him. He is at first clear in his own mind that their past relationship is over, for he does not write to her at all after the death of his official wife—an event that eliminates the barriers between them—except to acknowledge her condolences. Even when her impending departure moves him to send her letters full of tenderness and solicitude, he does not propose a meeting until a few days before she is to leave. But when he actually sees her, to his own surprise, he "immediately [finds] himself feeling toward her precisely as he had before their estrangement. . . . Now all was over. It was too horrible. He burst into tears." He begs her repeatedly to remain and broaches "what had lain so heavily on his heart." (Murasaki's sureness of touch here is successful and is recognizable even in modern novels, especially in those classified as *jun bungaku*, or "pure literature.") "But no sooner was it openly mentioned . . . than all the pent-up bitterness of so many weeks was suddenly released and vanished utterly away." Rokujō is wildly tempted to remain, for she is as attached to him as ever. And yet, even with his letter the next morning in her hands, "full and affectionate," she cannot

36

deny what she feels is the truth. ". . . his feelings toward her (she was convinced) [were not] of a sort to warrant such a step. Much of what he has said was inspired simply by pity for her." She is overcome by her loss and longing, and sinks "into a state of utter collapse."[16]

This scene—between two lovers whose relationship is so richly textured and iridescent—contains such moving drama that it seems impossible for a playwright to ignore it. Yet this situation too is abandoned by Zeami with the lines:

> and his deep compassionate
> feelings he relates
> through his varicolored words
> dewdrop-bright with love
> all within his heart so moved which seems
> so sadly touching.

With so much dramatic material excluded from the Nō, the wonder is that anything remains that can beguile an audience into that willing suspension of disbelief which all theater establishes. That this play, *Nonomiya*, is a great favorite is surely for its ability to convey a live experience, and the understanding of that experience can begin by emphasizing that it is precisely the dramatic that is excluded.

For such exclusion is in the interest of establishing the special lyricism of *aware*, which, among many other attributes, is a treatment of experience always at one remove. The degree of detachedness can of course vary greatly, and it is the exploitation of those differences in degree that can keep us moving in and out of experience, as in Proust's *Remembrance of Things Past*. The effect of differing layers of detachedness, arising not only from differences in time and context but also from increasing intensity or recall, is the dramatic element of the first part of *Nonomiya*. It is the dramatic substructure for the lyrical appeal to the ear.

The immediate reality is the presence of the priest and of the setting itself. But the *waki*-priest here is an anonymous convention, while the setting of the Meadow Shrine is emphasized for its evocation of the past. Its past, however, is not confined to the heroine's story but includes its connection with the great Shrine of Ise. Thus a serious note is struck immediately, which widens the scope and background of the play. The ineffable simplicity and majesty of Ise, with its great trees, unpainted shrines, and air of gladsome sanctity, is evoked by the *waki*:

> straight and righteous is the way
> taught by Holy Laws.
> To this place I come to seek
> out the old shrine site.
> And my heart grows calm and clear
> in the evening.

The principal actor, or *shite*, establishes the second characteristic of *aware* in this play in the tone of mourning for the past set by the opening verse (*shidai*), the bitterness of longing for love lost in an illusory world, and the hints of her otherworldliness. We move between the present scene, where

> underneath the grove of trees
> where this autumn ends . . .
> Midst the withering tips

Nonomiya

of the grass leaves, wasted sere,
lies the Meadow Shrine . . .

and the past when Genji visited the site, and the even more distant past of Rokujō's marriage and widowhood. Yet the present and the past are all relative, for it is through ghostly eyes that these scenes are conjured up.

With the second description of Genji's trip, this time through the autumn landscape, the sense of *aware* is intensified, as Genji felt it, filled with regret. Zeami has here borrowed heavily from the *Tale*, lifting key nouns and adjectives, as the following comparison will show:

Nonomiya	*Genji monogatari*	English
Tsuraki mono ni wa	Tsuraki mono ni	as heartless
sasugani omoi	omoi	think
hate tamawazu	hate tamainan *mo ito koishiku*	end
harukeki *nonomiya ni*	harukeki no*be wa*	far-off meadow
wakeiri tamoo	wakeiri tamoo *yori*	graciously made
on kokoro		his way
ito mono aware	ito mono aware	touched deeply
nari keriya	nari	is
aki no hana mina	aki no hana mina	all the autumn flowers
otoroe *te*	otoroe *tsutsu*	have faded
	asaji ga hara mo	
mushi no *koe mo*	karegare *naru*	faintly dying
karegare *ni*	mushi no *ne ni*	insects
matsu fuku kaze	matsukaze *sugoku*	pine winds
hibiki made mo	fuki *awasete*	blow
samishiki		

The English rendering of the *Nonomiya* passage follows:

> Even so he cannot bear
> leaving her to think of him
> as unkind, and journeys
> over to the distant Meadow Shrine
> graciously he makes his way;
> in his gentle heart
> there are many moving thoughts
> piercing keenly deep;
> all the autumn flowers are
> withering away
> and the insect voices
> chirping hoarser too;
> even echoes of the wind
> blowing through the pine grove
> whisper sadly. . . .

38

In this passage,[17] it is the anguish of beauty lost—the flowering autumn landscape and Rokujō's love—that emerges strongly. Yet since the sense of personal loss is conveyed mainly through a description of the landscape, heightened in Nō by the vocal quality of the chanting, the refined elegance that underlines the tone of this play is apparent. This is an elegance rising from strength and should not connote fripperies or a narcissistic display of suavity. For Genji, flitter among his dalliances though he is, has the strength of a feeling heart; without it, he could not have submitted himself to this farewell to Rokujō, knowing beforehand how harrowing an experience it would be. The motivation here delineates a whole system of relationships with finely limned devoirs and considerations, a code of personal honor as exacting within its context as that of the Kamakura samurai and requiring as much coolness and nerve.

This is the only section of the play—aside from the poems that are quoted—that follows so closely the actual *Genji* text. Its choice therefore reinforces the interpretation of the play as one designed to present a live experience of the beauty (*yūgen*) arising from a recollection of the past (*aware*) with tones of the serious, mournful, elegant, and sensuous. Too often *aware*, as noted in what is fast becoming a cliché among Western scholars, denotes sentimental nostalgia, as *yūgen* can connote the surface graces,[18] the effeminate or the weak. To limit these two central aesthetic terms in Japanese literature largely to these meanings alone, however, closes the door on a whole range of richly human response. Just as Western critics have at last begun to reexamine Japanese culture in terms other than Victorian ones (*haiku* as epigram; Japanese art as one of wood, paper, and bamboo), it is devoutly to be hoped that a similarly limiting stasis does not overtake these terms—*yūgen* and *aware*.

In this play, *aware* is clearly not the recollection of the past only for the sake of emotional immersion in regret; the austerity and discipline of the Nō theater tradition itself discourages the bathetic (as kabuki does not), while the structuring of this play controls any ungainly efflorescence. Specifically, these reminiscences are directed to salvation; they are confession. This distinction emerges clearly in comparing the use of the carriage scene in the second half of this play with that in *Aoi no Ue*.

The latter play, with its revenge theme, belongs to the Group IV pieces, where a dramatic immediacy is sought. Thus the wraith of the living Rokujō is shown in the actual process of attacking her hated rival, and the imagery of the play, rich in the wheels of the carriage-karma-salvation figure, is charged with emotion as it is being felt (of course within the nonrealistic context of the Nō). Rokujō, appearing first as a woman wraith (wearing the *deigan* mask), is unquestionably human; in the second half, in the *hannya* mask,[19] she has become a hideous demon, with horns, gaping mouth, and protruding eyes. Corresponding to the dramatic impact of the mask, what is presented is understood as happening in the theatrical now.

In *Nonomiya*, the actual event itself is described in greater detail and length than in *Aoi no Ue*, but the essential difference is that since the prevailing tone of the play is one of *yūgen-aware*, the description is not a reliving of Rokujō's humiliation and anger; it only adumbrates these emotions in the vigor of the diction: brawl, clamor, push, deafening noises, jerk, etc. Hence the principal actor wears the same mask throughout the play.[20] In a round-table discussion following a performance, Mr. Kita Minoru, the great interpreter of Nō, said of a previous performance that he had been too strong in the carriage scene:

39

DR. TOKI ZENMARO: When I saw *Nonomiya* some time before, I felt the carriage-brawl scene was overdone. But the other day, in contrast, the

| | overall effect was of a gentleness with a great strength. I was pleased to see the play brought to this level. |
| Kita Minoru: | When I was young, after a performance, Mr. Yamazaki [a critic] said to me, "In a play so typical of the third group, a scene like this in *Nonomiya* was most unusual. Although it usually plays more smoothly and quietly, suddenly there was a commotion. It was very much like a commotion to be found in a fourth-class play and to insert it into this third-group one was a bold move." What he meant was that my performance had some different quality in it, and he meant to be critical.[21] |

The whole passage is controlled by and directed toward the lines that are its raison d'être, the insight into the weary repetition that is mortal life:

> no one can escape
> penalties imposed by sins
> from our former lives.
> As her little ox-drawn cart
> turns and turns again
> round and round returning still,
> how long will return
> these dark delusions?

Such structuring stiffens the potential pathos of Rokujō's feelings of helplessness as she is buffeted about by the crowds in the carriage brawl, an incident that becomes heightened into the emotional equivalent of her unhappy love. Her helplessness then merges into the total human situation before the inexorable workings of the divine laws. Only insight and grace can save her. The *shite* prays: "these dark delusions / save her from them graciously." With these words, as Dr. Toki has said, she enters the state of *hōge*, freed from earthly bonds and enlightened.

These lines also serve as a transition to the quiet of the slow dance, the *jo no mai*; as Mr. Kita remarks, he felt no difficulty in passing from the carriage scene to the tranquility of the following section: "If I went from the carriage scene to the *jo no mai*, it would be difficult. Fortunately there is the passage—'even though she thinks of this / no one can escape'—and to flow into the *jo no mai* is not at all awkward. As I perform, I like this section."[22]

The following climactic passage contains another beautifully effective movement in and out of differing layers of temporal detachment. From the comparative immediacy of her appeal to the priest for salvation—veiled and less immediate for having been made by a ghostly presence—we get a glimpse of her earthly grace that had so charmed Genji:

40

> To the past long gone return
> the sleeves of blossoms;
> to the moon they wave and turn
> with a dancing air!

These lines, coming as they do after the release from anger and longing, gain added dimension, for they can be intensified to show the exquisite ecstasy, resembling almost a frozen frenzy, of the enlightened soul. Dr. Toki has called the quality of this scene *yūkyōteki*: "In the passage beginning 'I recall those ancient days,' there is an element of what seems like frenzied play (*yūkyōteki*). Separated from the actual events of this sort, in an atmosphere of retrospection, she seems to be miming—in a spirit similar to performing within an art of a high level—and she proceeds to dance. In that dance all attachment is gone." [23]

There is no hallelujah of thankful joy here, however. Rokujō's salvation has come after too great suffering, too great anguish. (Genji remembers her expression as full of "rage and misery.") There is release and it is beautiful, but the beauty is somber, not joyous. As we face the immediate scene again, the chorus reminds us of the ephemeral dew that is human life:

> How forlornly shines its light
> on the dew beneath the trees,
> on the dew beneath the trees. . . .

The ghost is now truly a ghost; she accepts the past as illusion.

> comes the one who visits me;
> so he who calls me
> and I, too, are just a world
> of passing dreams at these old ruins. . . .

The deep note of suffering and regret (*aware*) sounds forth again, as we see that where Rokujō waited for Genji, now only the crickets wait:

> where all wait for whom the crickets still
> sound their piercing *rin lin rin,*
> as the winds blow dark and deepen
> at the Meadow Shrine. . . .

But the suffering is enlightened; *aware* is now without pain. Thus the crickets' notes are piercing, light and clear—*rin lin rin*—in the world of illusion where the winds blow—*bō, bō*—with a thickly muted sound. [24]

In this passage Zeami's cryptic remarks about "frozen Nō" assume a transcendent content. Although he is speaking of the actor's art, what he says illuminates the total drama. In the Nō that comes from the spirit, the actor does not particularly attract us with his skills. He gives us nothing to admire, but "in the austerity of his art, he deeply moves us in some mysterious way. This may be called frozen Nō or the mindless Nō." [25] In the state of mindlessness, "the actor conceals even from himself his own intent." [26] At this climax of *Nonomiya*, the audience too is held in a mindless state of experience.

The *shite* is ready to depart. The quick dance, *ha no mai*, begins, miming the going of the soul to its salvation. Rokujō leaves the burning mansion.

41

NONOMIYA

By Zeami

Persons: WAKI: *A traveling Buddhist priest*
SHITE (PART I): *A village woman*
NOCHI-JITE (PART II): *The ghost of Miyasudokoro*
KYŌGEN: *A man of the place*

Classification: *Primary, Group III*
Place: *At Nonomiya in the land of Yamashiro*
Time: *September*
Kogaki: *5*

PART I

Jo no Dan

[*As the musicians, a flautist and two hand-drum players, take their seats in the rear, the stage attendants bring in an entrance gate (torii) of a Shintō shrine flanked by small brushwood fences, placing them at center-front stage. With introductory flute music called* nanoribue, *the* waki *appears. He wears a pointed hood, a plain kimono, a broad-sleeved, unlined tunic-like robe of unpolished silk, and a waistband. Carrying a fan and a rosary, he advances along the bridge to the name-saying seat.*]

WAKI

[1] *(Nanori: awazu, kotoba)*

Kore wa isshō fujū no sō nite sōrō. Ware kono hodo wa Miyako ni sōraite, Rakuyō no jisha nokori naku ogamimegurashite sōrō. Mata aki mo suetsu kata ni nari sōraeba, Sagano no kata yukashiku sōrō hodo ni tada ima Nishiyama e to kokorozashi sōrō. Kore naru mori o hito ni toeba, Nonomiya no kyūseki to ka ya mōshi sōrō hodo ni, tachiyori ikken sebaya to omoi sōrō.

I am a Buddhist priest without any fixed abode. I have come to the capital at this time to pay homage before all the shrines and temples in the eastern district of the city.[27] And since it is almost the end of autumn, the Saga Meadow must be worth seeing now, so I am going to the western mountains. [*After a well-marked pause, representing the journey, he turns toward the Shintō gate to indicate that he has arrived at Saga.*[28]] When I asked about the grove of trees that stands there, some men said that it was the old site of the Meadow Shrine. So I think I would like to stop there and see that place. [*Advances to stage center, looks at the shrine, and sings the following verse.*]

42

(Sashi: awazu, yowagin)

Ware kono kyūseki ni	As I come to see this ancient site,
kite mireba	the Shintō shrine-gate,
kurogi no torii[29]	built of trees unstripped of bark
koshibagaki	with its small brush fence,
mukashi ni kawaranu	has not changed in appearance still,
arisama nari.	since days of long ago.
Kakaru jusetsu ni	In a season such as this
mairiaite	I have come to visit
ogamimōsu zo	so that I can pay homage.
arigataki.	I feel most grateful.

[*Kneeling, he holds his hands together in prayer, singing in the lower range* (sageuta).]

(Sageuta: au, yowagin)

Ise no kamigaki	Ise's sacred fence will make
hedate naku	no distinction here,[30]
nori no oshie no	straight and righteous is the way
michi sugu ni	taught by Holy Laws.
koko ni tazunete	To this place I come to seek
miyadokoro,	out the old shrine site.
kokoro mo sumeru	And my heart grows calm and clear
yūbe kana.	in the evening.

Second Dan

[*As the* shidai *entrance music for the* shite *is played, the* waki *rises and proceeds to the* waki *seat, where he sits in the low, half-kneeling position. The* shite, *in the guise of a village woman, appears as the curtain is swept back. She carries a small branch of sacred* sakaki. *Wearing a* ko-omote *mask, she is gorgeously costumed, with under robes of plain white silk with a satinlike finish, painted with gold patterns; three unattached white collars, one over the other, shaped to follow the neckline; a loosely hanging outer robe of richly patterned brocade, woven in relief upon unpolished silk with threads of gold and polished silk; and a wig with a brocade wig band tied around the hair and knotted at the back of the head, its long ends falling over the outer robe. A fan is inserted into the waistband. She advances along the bridge and stops at the* shite *seat; facing the chorus, she sings the following.*]

SHITE

[2] *(Shidai: au, yowagin)*

Hana ni nare koshi	Accustomed to the flowers[31]
Nonomiya no,	at the Meadow Shrine,
hana ni nare koshi	accustomed to the flowers
Nonomiya no	at the Meadow Shrine
aki yori nochi wa	I stay, but what will happen
ika naran.	when this autumn ends?

43

CHORUS [*Jidori*[32] *in lower tones.*]

(Jidori: au, yowagin)

Hana ni nare koshi	Accustomed to the flowers
Nonomiya no	at the Meadow Shrine
aki yori nochi wa	I stay, but what will happen
ika naran.	when this autumn ends?

SHITE [*Facing stage front, sings the following as recitative* sashi.]

(Sashi: awazu, yowagin)

Ori shimo are	On this occasion now,
mono no sabishiki	lonely and forlorn, the fall
aki kurete,	turns to evening,
nao shiore yuku	still the things lie withering;
sode no tsuyu,	dewdrops on my sleeves[33]
mi o kudakunaru	shatter this life all away
yūmagure	at deepened twilight,
kokoro no iro wa	and the colors in my heart,
onozukara,	glowing of themselves,
chigusa no hana ni	seem to find an outward form
arawarete,	in a thousand flowers;[34]
otorōru mi no	as is the way of the flesh,
narai kana.	all must fade away.

[*Recitative heightens into song in low tones* (sageuta).]

(Sageuta: au, yowagin)

Hito koso shirane	Though nobody knows me here
toshidoshi ni	any longer now,
mukashi no ato ni	still I come year after year
tachikaeri,	to this ancient site

[*The singing heightens further into song in high tones* (ageuta).]

(Ageuta: au, yowagin)

Nonomiya no	at the Meadow Shrine
mori no kogarashi	through the groves of trees the fall
aki fukete,	deepens with chill winds,
mori no kogarashi	through the groves of trees the fall
aki fukete,	deepens with chill winds,
mi ni shimu iro no	piercing me with poignant hues
kiekaeri	that are fading now.
omoeba	Must I go on
inishie o	thinking of the past?
nani to shinobu no	There is nothing left for me

[*Facing stage right, takes two or three steps forward and faces front.*]

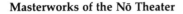

44

kusagoromo,	even though I come
kite shimo aranu	dressed in traveling robes of grass,[35]
kari no yo ni	to this makeshift world,
yukikaeru koso	still returning, back and forth
urami nare,	it is so hateful,
yukikaeru koso	still returning, back and forth
urami nare.	it is so hateful.

Third Dan

WAKI

[*Remains seated and turns toward the* shite.]

[3] (*Mondai: awazu, yowagin*)

| Ware kono mori no | As I stay beneath the shade |
| kage ni ite | of this grove of trees |

inishie o omoi kokoro o sumasu orifushi ni, ito namamekeru nyoshō ichinin kotsuzen to shite kitari tamō wa

thinking about the ancient days, my heart grows serene. Then suddenly there comes a very captivating and bewitching lady;

| ika naru hito nite | What sort of person is she, |
| mashimasu zo. | I truly wonder. |

SHITE

Ika naru mono zo to towasetamō. Sonata o koso toimairasu-bekere. Kore wa inishie Saigū ni tatasetamō hito kari ni utsurimasu Nonomiya nari. Sono nochi wa kono koto taenuredomo mukashi o omō toshidoshi ni

"What sort of a person am I," you ask. It should be I who questions you. This is the Meadow Shrine to which the person who was to become the priestess of the Ise Shrine[36] retreated for a time. Though afterward this custom was abandoned, I think of the past year after year.

SHITE [*Sings the following.*]

(*Kakaru: awazu, yowagin*)

hito koso shirane	No one would recognize me,
miyadokoro o kiyome	though I purify this old shrine site
go-jinji o nashi	with the sacred rituals
samurō tokoro ni	I perform; meanwhile a person
yukue mo shiranu	from a place unknown like you
on-koto naru ga,	makes a rude intrusion here
kitaritamō wa	at this sacred shrine compound.
habakari ari,	It is disrespectful.
tokutoku kaeri-	Quickly, very quickly now
tamae to yo.	leave this place and go.

[*The* shite *takes two steps toward the* waki.]

Nonomiya

(Kakeai: awazu, yowagin)

Iya iya kore wa kurushikaranu mi no yukusue mo sadame naki, yo o sutebito no kazu narubeshi, satesate koko wa furinishi ato o kyō-goto ni mukashi o omoitamō

No, no, on the contrary, there is no reason to be suspicious of me. I am among those who have renounced the world and have no fixed place in this life. Well, you say, here at this old site each year on this very day you think of the past.

iware wa ika naru
koto yaran.

What can really be the reason
for this I wonder.

SHITE

Hikaru Genji kono tokoro ni mōdeta-maishi wa Nagazuki nanuka no hi kyō ni atareri. Sono toki isasaka mochi-tamaikeru sakaki no eda o igaki no uchi ni sashiokitamaeba Miyasudokoro toriaezu,

It was the Shining Prince Genji, who paid a visit to this place on the seventh day of the ninth month, and today falls on that day again. On that occasion he had in his hand just a spray from the sacred tree, which he inserted in the sacred hedge of the shrine compound. Then Miyasudokoro[37] responded in haste:

Kamigaki wa
shirushi no sugi mo
naki mono o
ika ni magaete
oreru sakaki zo

At the sacred hedge
isn't there too a redwood tree
growing as a mark;
how have you mistakenly
come to break the sacred tree?[38]

to yomi tamaishi mo kyō zo kashi.

Thus she composed a verse for him, and today is that day too.

WAKI

Geni omoshiroki
koto no ha no
ima mochitamō
sakaki no eda mo
mukashi ni kawaranu
iro yo nō

How truly interesting
are these words, indeed!
Even now you hold the spray
from the selfsame sacred tree
that remains unchanged in color
as in days long past.

SHITE

46

Mukashi ni kawaranu iro zo to wa, sa-kaki nomi koso tokiwa no

"Unchanged in color as in days long past," you said, the sacred tree is for-ever and ever green, its shade

kage no

on the path

mori no shitamichi	underneath the grove of trees,
aki kurete	where this autumn ends

SHITE

momiji katsu chiri	and the crimson maples scatter,

SHITE AND WAKI [*Together.*]

asaji ga hara mo	while miscanthus meadows fade.

CHORUS [*Sings in high tones.*]

(Ageuta: au, yowagin)

uragare no	Midst the withering tips
kusaba ni aruru	of the grass leaves, wasted sere,

[*The* shite *advances to the shrine gate, offers her spray, and kneels in prayer.*]

Nonomiya no,	lies the Meadow Shrine,
kusaba ni aruru	midst the grass leaves, wasted sere
Nonomiya no,	lies the Meadow Shrine
ato natsukashiki	which remains so dear to me;
koko ni shimo	even at this place

[*The* shite *rises and returns to center stage.*]

sono Nagazuki no	here today that seventh day
nanuka no hi mo	of bygone September
kyo no meguri	makes its round as ever,
kinikeri.	and forlornly
Mono hakanashi ya	stands the little brushwood fence

[*The* shite *advances two steps and looks at the fence.*]

koshiba gaki	ephemerally,
ito karisome no	so these living quarters too
on-sumai	temporary seem.

[*She turns toward the eye-fixing pillar.*]

ima mo hitakiya no	Even now the dimming flicker[39]
kasuka naru	from the sentry fire

[*Turning to the right, she returns to the* shite *seat.*]

47

hikari wa	at the cottage
waga omoi,	stirs my longing thoughts
uchi ni aru iro ya	deep within me,[40] but its color
hoka ni mietsuran.	seems to show itself outwardly.
Ara sabishi	How forlornly sad
miyadokoro,	is the old shrine site!

[*She looks stage front.*]

ara sabishi	How forlornly sad
kono miyadokoro.	is this very old shrine site!

Fourth Dan

WAKI

[4]

Nao nao Miyasudokoro no on-koto ku-washiku on-monogatari sōrae.	More, still more, tell me all you can about Miyasudokoro.

[*The* shite *goes to stage center and kneels.*]

CHORUS

(*Kuri: awazu, yowagin*)

Somosomo kono	First of all this lady
Miyasudokoro to	named Miyasudokoro
mōsu wa	was the consort
Kiritsubo no	of the late great heir
Mikado no on-nototo	and young brother of the Emperor[41]
Senbō to mōshi-	who resides at Kiritsubo.
tatematsurishi ni	Senbō he is called,
tokimeku hana no	thriving like the glorious blooms
iroka made	fragrant in all hues;
imose no kokoro	never shallower grows the love
asakarazarishi ni	shared between their hearts; however,

SHITE

[*The recitative* sashi *is sung alternately with the chorus.*]

(*Sashi: awazu, yowagin*)

Esha jōri no	all those who meet must part.[42]
narai moto yori mo	This has been the way, no matter

CHORUS

odorokubeshi ya	what surprise may lie ahead
yume no yo to	in this world of dreams;
hodonaku okure-	so she's left behind too soon
tamaikeri.	he has passed away.

SHITE

Sateshi mo aranu	But she was hardly fated
mi no tsuyu no	for a life of dew

48

CHORUS

Hikaru Genji no	Shining Genji pays court
warinaku mo	against all reason
shinobi shinobi ni	secretly and secretly
yukikayō	back and forth he goes,

SHITE

kokoro no sue no	but what lies within the depths
nado yaran.	of the human heart?[43]

CHORUS

Mata taedae no	So uneasy now and then
naka narishi ni	grows the tie between them;

[*Since the* shite *remains seated, the following passage is an* iguse.]

CHORUS

(Kuse: au, yowagin)

tsuraki mono ni wa	even so he cannot bear[44]
sasuga ni omoi-	leaving her to think of him
hate-tamawazu	as unkind, and journeys
harukeki Nonomiya ni	over to the distant Meadow Shrine
wakeiri-tamō	graciously he makes his way;
on-kokoro	in his gentle heart
ito mono aware	there are many moving thoughts
narikeri ya.	piercing keenly deep;
Aki no hana mina	all the autumn flowers are
otoroete	withering away
mushi no koe mo	and the insect voices
karegare ni	chirping hoarser too;
matsu fuku kaze no	even echoes of the wind
hibiki made mo	blowing through the pine grove
sabishiki	whisper sadly
michi sugara	all along the path
aki no kanashimi mo	where, too, the autumn sorrow lies
hate nashi.	with no ending.
Katsute kimi koko ni	In this way he comes to call upon her
mōdesase-	at this very place
tamaitsutsu	ever graciously;
nasake o kakete	and his deep compassionate
samazama no	feelings he relates
kotoba no tsuyu mo	through his varicolored words
iroiro no	dewdrop-bright with love
on-kokoro no uchi zo	all within his heart so moved which seems
aware naru.	so sadly touching.

49

Nonomiya

(Ageha)

Sono nochi Katsura no on-parai	Soon after comes the cleansing rite by the Katsura;[45]

CHORUS

Shirayū kakete	let the sacred streamers drift[46]
kawanami no	down the river waves,
mi wa ukigusa no	like the floating weeds[47] she goes
yorube naki	with no place to stay
kokoro no mizu ni	on the water's merciful heart
sasowarete,	that entices her
yukue mo	on the journey
Suzukagawa	"down the Suzuka[48]
yasose no nami ni	by its eighty rapids' waves,
nure nurezu	and if I am splashed,
Ise made tare ka	who'll ask and think about me
omowan no	in distant Ise?"[49]
koto no ha wa	Leaving just these words,
soiyuku koto mo	an unprecedented pair,[50]
tameshi naki mono o	mother and daughter together
oya to ko no	join like bamboo joints
Take[51] no Miyakoji ni	taking up the *Take* road
omomukishi	they journey onward,
kokoro koso	and her heart indeed
urami narikere.	appears regretful.

CHORUS [*Speaking for the* waki.]

(Rongi: au, yowagin)

Geni ya iware o	Listening to the words you say,
kiku kara ni	you are not, it seems,
tadabito naranu	just a commoner
on-keshiki	with the air you have.
sono na o nanori-	Please reveal your name to me
tamae ya.	so graciously.

SHITE

Nanorite mo	Even if I tell
kai naki mi tote	you my name, it is useless.
hazukashi no	How ashamed I feel
morite ya yoso ni	for others to know of this
shiraremashi,	as it may leak out.
yoshi saraba	What must be must be,
so no na mo	name me only
naki mi zo to	as the nameless dead.
towasetamae ya.	Please chant a holy prayer.

50

CHORUS

Naki mi to kikeba	"As the nameless dead," I hear,
fushigi ya na	Oh, how strange it sounds!
sate wa kono yo o	You are then the one who passed
hakanaku mo	vainly from this world

SHITE

sarite hisashiki	long ago and ever since
ato no na no	the name remembered

CHORUS

Miyasudokoro wa	as Miyasudokoro

SHITE

ware nari to	is my own, she says,

CHORUS

yūgure no	as the twilight falls
aki no kaze	with the autumn wind

[*The* shite *rises.*]

mori no ko no ma no	rising through the moonlit rifts
yūzukuyo	in the grove of trees

[*Moving to the* shite *seat, she looks to her right.*]

kage kasuka naru	and beneath the shadowy trees
ko no shita no	pale and dimly dark
kurogi no torii no	between the trees unstripped of bark

[*She looks at the shrine gate.*]

futabashira ni	of the Shintō shrine-gate
tachikakurete	in and out she scurries[52]
usenikeri,	as she disappears,
ato tachikakure	in and out of sight she goes
usenikeri.	as she disappears.

[*The mask is lowered, then raised; she exits.*]

Nakairi (Interlude)

[*The* kyōgen, *a man of the place, wearing a striped heavy silk kimono* (dan noshime), *a long two-piece garment* (naga kamishimo), *a waistband* (koshiobi), *a fan* (ōgi), *and a short sword* (chiisa gatana), *comes out to the name-saying seat,* nanoriza, *and intones the following prose dialogues with the* waki.]

51

Nonomiya

KYŌGEN

Kayō ni sōrō mono wa kono atari ni su-mai suru mono nite sōrō. Kyō wa No-nomiya no go-shinji nite sōrō aida mai-raba ya to zonzuru. Iya kore ni minare-mōsanu o-sō no goza sōrō ga, izuku yori izukata e o-tōri nasare sōraeba kore ni wa yasurōte goza sōrō zo.

I am a person living in this neighbor-hood. Since there is a Shintō service at the Meadow Shrine today, I am thinking of going there. [*Sees the* waki.] Well, I see an unfamiliar Buddhist priest. Since you come from somewhere and are going someplace, I'd guess you are just rest-ing here.

WAKI

Kore wa issho fujū no sō nite sōrō. On-mi wa kono atari no hito nite watari sōrō ka.

I am a wandering Buddhist priest with-out any fixed abode. Are you a resident of this vicinity?

KYŌGEN

Nakanaka kono atari no mono nite sōrō.

Yes, indeed, I am of this neighborhood.

WAKI

Sayō ni sōrawaba mazu chikō on-niri sōrae. Tazunetaki koto no sōrō.

If that's so, first of all please come closer to me. I have something to ask you.

KYŌGEN

Kashikomatte sōrō. Sate o-tazune nasa-retaki to wa ikayō naru go-yō nite sōrō zo.

Of course, holy priest. [*Advances to center stage and sits down.*] What do you wish to ask me?

SHITE

Omoi mo yoranu mōshigoto nite sōrae-domo, kono Nonomiya no iware, Miya-sudokoro no on-koto ni tsuki samazama shisai arubeshi. Go-zonji ni oite wa kat-tate on-kikase sōrae.

Indeed, this is something you may not expect from me, but in regard to this Meadow Shrine, there must be many significant things concerning the story of Miyasudokoro. If you know about it, please tell me.

KYŌGEN

52

Kore wa omoi mo yoranu koto o uketa-mawari sōrō mono kana. Warera mo kono atari ni wa sumaitsukamatsuri sō-raedome, sayō no koto kuwashiku wa zonzezu sōrō, sarinagara hajimete on-me ni kakari o-tazune nasare sōrō koto o, nani to mo zonzenu to mōsu mo ikaga nite sōraeba, ōyoso uketamawari oyobitaru tōri on-monogatari mōsōzuru nite sōrō.

How strange that you should ask me about this. Though we live in this neighborhood, I don't know too much about the details. But since I am asked by a person that I meet for the first time, it would not be nice to say that I know nothing about it at all; so I shall tell you the story the way I've heard it.

Chikagoro nite sōrō.

I would be grateful.

Saru hodo ni kono Nonomiya to mōsu wa, Ise Saigū ni tatasetamō on-kata, kari ni utsurimashimasu go-seishinya nite goza aru to mōsu. Sunawachi kono tokoro nite on-mi o kiyomerare, Katsura no harai to mōsu ni awasetamai, Take no miyako ni sumasetamō. Sono on-kata mo tadabito narazu. Kiritsubo no Mikado no on-nototo Senbō no on-himemiya, Saigū ni o-tachiaran tote, kono Nonomiya ni utsuritamo. Mata Miyasudokoro kono tokoro ni utsuritamō on-koto wa, Senbō ni okureta-maite nochi Hikaru Genji Miyasudokoro o go-chōai nasare on-chigiri asakarazu goza sōraishi go nakagoro susamimairase sōrō aida nyoshō no hakanasa wa Genji no on-kokoro kawa-riyukite wa, Miyako no arite mo sen na-shi tote on-himemiya morotomo ni Ise ni on-gekō arubeshi tote, kono Nono-miya ni utsuritamō o, Genji kikoshi-meshi sasuga ni tsuraki mono ni wa oboshi-meshi hatetamawaneba, Naga-zuki namuka no koro, kono Nonomiya ni mairitamaedomo, go-seishinya no koto nareba, igaki no uchi e wa kanai-mōsazu. Sono toki Genji no on-te ni sakaki no eda o isasaka mochite maira-reshi ga, kawaranu iro o shirushi ni to igaki no uchi e sashiokitamaeba, Miya-sudokoro goranjite,

Well. This Meadow Shrine was a temporary residence for the person who was to become the sacred priestess of the Ise Shrine. Here she purified herself and held a sacred rite, called the Ka-tsura Purification, and she lived at the capital of Take. She was not an ordinary person. The daughter of the crown prince, Senbō, the younger brother of the sovereign at Kiritsubo, was trans-ferred here to be the priestess of the Ise Shrine. After the passing of the Impe-rial Prince Senbō, Miyasudokoro moved here, and Prince Genji, the Shining One, had a deep affection for her. How hopeless it was for Miyasudokoro, be-cause in the middle of their relation-ship, they grew distant, and Genji's heart changed and the relationship became meaningless. Even though she stayed at the capital, all appeared hope-less; so she decided to go down to Ise, and came to this place with her daugh-ter. Prince Genji, on hearing this, was deeply touched and came to this Meadow Shrine around the seventh of September. But since this is a sacred place, he did not go inside the holy hedge. A spray of the sacred tree, which he held in his hand, was inserted in the sacred hedge as a sign of his constancy. Miyasudokoro, seeing this, wrote:

Kamigaki wa
shirushi no sugi mo
naki mono o
ika ni magaite
oreru sakaki zo

At the sacred hedge
isn't there too a redwood tree
growing as a mark;
how have you mistakenly
come to break the sacred tree?

53

to yomi tamaeba, Genji no go-henka ni

To this Prince Genji replied in a song:

Otomego ga
kazashi to omoeba
sakakiba no
ka o natsukashimi
tomete koso ore

Thinking of the spray
as the girl's hair ornament,
longing to keep it,
I break the sacred tree branch
for the fragrance of its leaves.

Nonomiya

Kayō ni go-henja nasare, akegata ni Genji sugosugo to on-kaeri aritaru to mōsu. Soreyori Miyasudokoro wa Ise e go-gekō aritaru to uketamawari-oyobite sōrō. Mazu warera no uketamawari-oyobitaru wa kaku no gotoki nite goza sōrō ga, nan to oboshimeshi o-tazune nasare sōrō zo. Chikagoro fushin ni zonji sōrō.

And at dawn Prince Genji returned home with a heavy heart, I hear. Then, Miyasudokoro went down to Ise. Well, this is what we have heard. Please tell me why you ask about this. Lately I have felt something strange around here.

WAKI

Nengoro ni on-monogatari sōrō mono kana. Tazunemōsu mo yo no gi ni arazu. On-mi izen ni izuku to mo naku, nyoshō ichinin korare sōrō hodo ni, sunawachi kotoba o kawashite sōraeba, Miyasudokoro no on-koto tadaima on-monotatari no gotoku nengoro ni katari Miyasudokoro wa ware nari to ii mo aezu torii no hotori nite sugata o miushinōte sōrō yo.

How kind of you to tell me the story in detail. The reason I asked you is no other than this. A while ago there came a lady from somewhere, and as we spoke with each other, she kindly told me the story of Miyasudokoro in great detail just as you have done. And no sooner had she finished, saying, "I am Miyasudokoro," than I lost sight of her near the Sacred Shrine gate.

KYŌGEN

Kore wa kidoku naru koto o uketamawari sōrō mono kana. Sate wa Miyasudokoro kari ni arawaretamaitaru to zonji sōrō aida, kano on-ato o nengoro ni on-tomurai arekashi to zonji sōrō.

What a strange story you are telling me! I feel she has appeared temporarily, so I think you should sincerely say a holy prayer for her.

WAKI

Shibaraku tōryū mōshi, arigataki o-kyō o dokuju shi, kono on-ato o nengoro ni tomuraimōsōzuru nite sōrō.

I will stay here awhile and chant some holy sutra and say my prayers earnestly for her.

KYŌGEN

Go-tōryū nite sōrawaba, kasanate o-mimai mōsōzuru nite sōrō.

I will call on you if you should stay here awhile.

WAKI

Tanomi sōrōbeshi.

Please do.

KYŌGEN

Kokoroe mōshite sōrō.

Yes sir, good priest.

[*The* kyōgen *goes back to his* ai *seat.*]

PART II

Fifth Dan

[*At the* waki *seat the* waki *sings the high-pitched* ageuta *called* machiutai, *"waiting song."*]

WAKI

[6] (*Machiutai: au, yowagin*)

Katashiku ya	With my sleeves half-spread,
mori no kokage no	in the shade of trees I sit
kokegoromo,	on my moss-hued robe,[53]
mori no kokage no	in the shade of trees I sit
kokegoromo,	on my moss-hued robe,
onaji iro naru	and upon a grassy mat
kusamushiro	of the same green tint,
omoi o nobete	spreading out, I tell those things
yo mo sugara	of the past, night long
kano on-nato o	I will offer holy prayers
tō to ka ya,	to her memory;
kano on-nato o	I will offer holy prayers
tō to ka ya.	to her memory.

[*With the* issei *music, the* shite (*nochi-jite*) *appears. The previously worn brocade outer robe is replaced by a sheer silk, unlined one; under it is an unlined hunting robe of heavy silk with large inwoven patterns, a waistband, and a fully divided red skirt. Other details of the costume are unchanged. Holding a fan, she stands at the* shite *seat.*]

SHITE

[7] (*Issei: awazu, yowagin*)

Nonomiya no	At the Meadow Shrine
aki no chigusa no	with a thousand autumn plants,
hanaguruma,	turns the flower-cart[54]
ware mo mukashi ni	round and round, I, too, return
megurikinikeri.	to the days of long ago.

WAKI

(*Kakeai: awazu, yowagin*)

Fushigi ya na,	Strange! How strange this is!
tsuki no hikari mo	As the moon's bright light now turns
kasuka naru	pale and also dim
kuruma no oto no	sound the creakings of the cart
chikazuku kata o	coming near, and as I look

mireba ajiro no shitasudare omoikake-zaru arisama nari. Ima wa utagō tokoro mo naku

in that direction, how unexpected to see the courtly carriage with the lowered bamboo blinds! Now I know. There is no room for doubt at all.

Miyasudokoro nite	It is Miyasudokoro.
mashimasu ka.	I truly wonder!

Nonomiya

55

samo are	At any rate
ika naru	what kind of cart
kuruma yaran.	could this most likely be?

SHITE

Ika naru kuruma to towasetamaeba, omoi zo izuru sono inishie	As I ask, "What kind of cart?" it brings back once again that day of long and long ago.

Kamo no matsuri no	At the Kamo Festival[55]
kuruma-arasoi	in the carriage brawl, I know
nushi wa sore zo to	not the owner of the cart
shiratsuyu no	on the dew-white path

WAKI

tokoro seki made	which is narrowed everywhere
tatenaraburu	row on row already

SHITE

monomiguruma no	by onlookers' carriages
samazama ni	of all kinds, and one
koto ni tokimeku	for the particularly
Aoi no Ue no	famous Princess Hollyhock[56]

WAKI

on-kuruma tote	"For her carriage, please make way!"
hito o harai	shout the men and scatter
tachisawagitaru	the crowd aside, left and right
sono naka ni	midst the rising din;

SHITE

mi wa oguruma no	"There's no place for us to turn
yaru kata mo	this small cart of ours,"
nashi to kotaete	comes the answer from my men
tateokitaru	while we stand our ground;

WAKI

kuruma no zengo ni	and suddenly in front and back

SHITE [*Looks to the right and then toward the chorus, as she gestures.*]

batto yorite	of our cart the followers

CHORUS [*Song in higher tones.*]

(Ageuta: au, yowagin)

hitobito nagae ni	come and grasp the thill so firmly
toritsukitsutsu	and into the recesses

Masterworks of the Nō Theater

hitodamai no oku ni	of the crowd of viewers she is shoved,
oshiyararete	deeply pushed away.

[*The* shite *steps back three or four steps, expressing resentment.*]

monomiguruma no	In her small sight-seeing cart,
chikara mo naki	all bereft of power,
mi no hodo zo	she is forced to see
omoishiraretaru.	helplessly her true position;
Yoshi ya omoeba	even though she thinks of this,
nani goto mo	no one can escape
mukui no tsumi ni	penalties imposed by sins[57]
yomo moreji.	from our former lives.
Mi wa nao ushi no	As her little ox-drawn cart
oguruma no	turns and turns again
meguri meguri kite	round and round returning still,
itsu made zo	how long will return
mōshū o	these dark delusions?
tasuketamae ya,	Save her from them graciously,

CHORUS [*Speaking for the* shite.]

mōshū o	these dark delusions,
tasuketamae ya.	save her from them graciously.

[*The* shite *extends her hands, folded in prayer, toward the* waki *and, moving forward, sings the following passage.*]

SHITE

[8] (*Ei: au, yowagin*)

Mukashi ni kaeru	To the past long gone return[58]
hana no sode	the sleeves of blossoms;

CHORUS

tsuki ni to kaesu	to the moon they wave and turn
keshiki kana.	with a dancing air!

[*Returning to the* shite *seat, she begins the dance.*]

Jo no mai

SHITE

57

[Waka, *sung at the conclusion of the dance.*]

(*Waka: yowagin*)

Nonomiya no	At the Meadow Shrine
tsuki mo mukashi ya	full of longing thoughts the moon
omōran.	too recalls the past.

Nonomiya

CHORUS

Kage sabishiku mo	How forlornly shines its light
mori no shitatsuyu,	on the dew[59] beneath the trees,
mori no shitatsuyu	on the dew beneath the trees,

SHITE

(Noriji: ōnori, yowagin)

| mi no okidokoro mo | here where I placed this life of mine |
| aware mukashi no[60] | was my dwelling filled with grief |

CHORUS

| niwa no tatazumai | long ago across the garden, |

SHITE [*Moves forward and glances around.*]

| yoso ni zo kawaru[61] | for its changed appearance shows |

CHORUS

| keshiki mo kari naru | too the touching air as makeshift |

SHITE [*Moves toward the gate.*]

| koshibagaki | as the small brush fence,[62] |

CHORUS

| tsuyu uchi-harai | where brushing off the dewdrops |

[*The* shite *brushes the hedge with her fan.*]

towareshi ware mo	comes the one who visits me;
sono hito mo	so he who calls me
tada yume no yo to	and I, too, are just a world
furiyuku ato naru ni	of passing dreams at these old ruins
tare matsumushi no ne wa	where all wait for whom the crickets still

[*Moving in a large circle, the* shite *goes to rear stage.*]

| rinrin to shite | sound their piercing *rin lin rin*,[63] |

[*The* shite *points the fan toward the eye-fixing pillar, as if listening.*]

| kaze bōbōtaru | as the winds blow dark and deepen |

[*The* shite *moves forward to the gate and touches it.*]

| Nonomiya no yo sugara | at the Meadow Shrine throughout the night |
| aware nari. | it seems too touching. |

[*Weeping, the* shite *retreats to rear stage and begins the* ha no mai.]

Masterworks of the Nō Theater

Ha no mai

[At the end of the dance, she stamps and then lowers herself to a half-kneeling position.]

(Kiri: ōnori, yowagin)

Koko wa moto yori	Graciously, indeed, this place

[The shite *holds her hands in prayer.]*

katajikenaku mo	was originally blessed
kamikaze ya Ise no	by the sacred wind of Ise;
uchito no torii ni	in and out there goes the figure

[The shite *rises and moves toward the gate with her fan lifted high, now with the sleeve flipped over her arm.]*

ideiru sugata wa	through the sacred Shintō shrine gate

[She puts one foot through the gate and withdraws it.]

shōji no michi o	on the way of Life and Death.
kami wa ukezu ya	This the deities, she fears,

[She moves toward the eye-fixing pillar.]

omōran to	will not accept at all;

[As the chorus sings, she moves to the shite *seat.]*

mata kuruma ni	so she mounts her carriage
uchinorite	once again and then
kataku no kado o ya	goes through the Burning House's[64] gate,
idenuran,	so she leaves, it seems,
kataku.	the Burning House.[65]

❀

Nonomiya

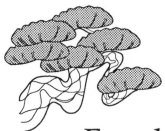

Funabenkei

Introduction

Among many Nō plays constructed in two parts, the *shite*, the principal actor, appears in the first part as an anonymous, humble figure, to be revealed in his true ghostly character in the second part in a dream of the *waki*, or secondary actor, who is often a priest. Typical of these plays, called two-part dream plays (*fukushiki mugen nō*), are *Tōru, Nonomiya,* and *Yuguō Yanagi.* In another group of Nō plays, the two-act dramatic plays (*nidan geki nō*), the principal actor plays the same character in both parts, and that character is depicted as a living person: examples are *Hachi no Ki, Youchi Soga,* and *Genpuku Soga.*

The merits of each form conceal in turn its weaknesses. The dream plays are usually full of a poetic, *yūgen*-like air, dealing as they do with the passions and sorrows of souls who in death still find themselves unreleased from the torments of their earthly existence. But since these are remembered passions narrated by a ghost, the immediate dramatic element is less evident. In the second type of play, where the action is presented as unfolding directly and immediately before the audience, the dramatic reality is strong. However, the poetic, *yūgen*-like quality of the once removed is less paramount. In *Funabenkei,* however, the playwright meets this basic problem: he has attempted to convey vividly both the poetic and the dramatic. This interesting play thus illuminates many of the mysteries of this theater.

The story is part of the well-known cycle of the Genji-Heike clans.[1] As the play opens, Yoshitsune has secretly left the capital to escape the anger of his older brother, Yoritomo, who suspects him of disloyalty. He and his chosen few come to the Bay of Daimotsu to take a boat for Kyūshū, where he hopes to wait for better days in safety. His beautiful mistress, Lady Shizuka, the superb dancer, has followed him, but since the presence of a woman on this rough sea journey is inappropriate, Benkei, the stout warrior-priest and Yoshitsune's devoted follower, advises her to return to Miyako. As she makes her farewells, *sake* is served and she performs a parting dance. In the second half, soon after the party leaves the place, the sea suddenly becomes rough, and the ghost of Tomomori, one of the Heike chiefs, appears to sink Yoshitsune's boat in revenge for the defeat of his clan. Benkei prays mightily, and the vengeful ghost drifts away with the ebbing tide, leaving not a single trace on the snow-white waves.

The construction of this play is unusual in several respects. First, the *shite* in the first part is Shizuka, the beautiful dancer; in the second, the *shite* is Tomomori, the warrior ghost. On the face of it, the abrupt change of emphasis from Shizuka to Tomomori would seem fatal to the unity of the play. Second, the story of the Shizuka episode has no integral connection with the second episode. In the majority of two-part Nō plays, whether they be dream plays or dramatic plays, the first part usually serves as prelude to the second, or climax. Third, the role of the *waki*, or secondary character, Benkei, is given great importance, with more elaboration and particularization than is usual for the *waki*. The *waki* priests of the typical dream-plays are singularly colorless fellows who seem to exist only to ask the *shite* leading questions. Benkei here is a figure in his own hearty, gallant right, such as we have learned to recognize him from the romances and other plays. The danger seems clear that he may run away with the play, overshadowing the *shite* role, or at least distracting our attention from it. Fourth, the same actor is to play the roles of Shizuka and Tomomori. Considering the almost mystical demands that Zeami's criteria for Nō acting make on the actor, as outlined in his *Kadensho* and other writings, this seems a hazardous undertaking. Fifth—although an accepted Nō convention, it seems strange nevertheless—the role of Yoshitsune, the hero supreme among warriors, is assigned to a child actor. It is as if a twelve-year-old boy were cast as Prince Hal: how can romantic credibility be maintained against the strong figure of Benkei-Falstaff?

The author, Kojirō, seems to have deliberately weighted the scales against himself. Nor was he obliged to do so in order to remain faithful to historical sources. For, according to them, Shizuka did not separate from Yoshitsune until after the storm episode.[2] For example, the entry dated November 3, 1158, in the *Heike monogatari* (Tale of the Heike), contains the following:

> On this day, they arrived at the Bay of Daimotsu. On the next day, the fourth, they went down by ship from the Bay of Daimotsu, but since at that time the west wind blew violently, the ship the Hōgan rode was cast by the waves on the shore of Sumiyoshi and from there they went to Yoshino for seclusion. . . . The ten and more ladies who accompanied the Hōgan were all left behind at the Bay of Sumiyoshi. . . . The priest of Sumiyoshi . . . sent all of them back to the capital. . . . The west wind that blew violently and suddenly was, we heard, due to the vengeful spirits of the Heike.[3]

The *Gikeiki* (History of Yoshitsune), giving the same account in detail, says of Benkei: "How terrible it was! If there were no Benkei, it was said, a great disaster might have ensued."[4] Thus Kojirō was not at all obliged by history to deal with the separation of the lovers—as well known an episode as the farewells of Romeo and Juliet. Yet he deliberately rearranges the sequence of events in order to do so and thus seemingly creates for himself a host of problems surrounding the unity of the play.

It must not be supposed that we are dealing with a clumsily melodramatic effort by a playwright who did not know what he was about. For Kojirō wrote several of the most beautiful plays in the Nō repertoire, as severely austere and stripped as any by the master Zeami. His *Yugyō Yanagi* (*The willow tree of Yugyō*) is said to surpass even Zeami's *Saigyōzakura* (*The cherry tree of Saigyō*) in its quality of *yūgen*. Nor are these difficulties of the play raised only by a close reading of it. Kita Minoru, the present head of the Kita school, has said that the great difficulty in staging the play is to prevent it from dividing into two unrelated parts and thus becoming a mere spectacle and vehicle for the *shite* to charm the audience with Shizuka's grace and Tomomori's vengefulness. There is Nō in this play.

As the play opens, we are told immediately that Yoshitsune, the brave hero, finds himself a fugitive, in spite of his former triumphs and glories. His furtive leaving from the capital while "Still in darkness night lies deep" adds to the poignancy of his fall from fortune. Our sympathy is further engaged by the separation scene between Yoshitsune and Shizuka, the sorrowing beauty: "Only choked with tears I weep / in endless sorrow." In a beautiful and typically indirect Japanese sentiment, she delicately reminds him not only of her own love for him but of her faithfulness and dedication, thereby attempting to bind him close even though they must separate.

> Now, indeed,
> more than this parting
> from the one I dearly love,
> how I hold life dear,
> for I hope to meet my lord
> face to face again together
> in the future.

She spares him the burden of a reply, for she is only quoting an old poem; yet she has made her point, and it would be an unfeeling clod who would not remain deeply involved in this relationship in spite of time, separation, or other temptations. As she prays for her lord and encourages him, dancing her farewell, these deeply feminine sentiments and feelings, full of anguish and coquetry, are enriched by the contrast with the manly figure of the Buddhist warrior-priest, the *waki* to this heroine. For as Shizuka is the epitome of feminine love and faithfulness, Benkei is the gallant male counterpart of these qualities.

Then as Yoshitsune's party sets sail, the scene suddenly changes with the downblast of harsh winds from the mountains and the reappearance of the *shite* as the ghost of Tomomori, in his fearsome mask, flowing black hair, and golden horns, armed with a halberd.

> First of all, I am the ninth
> in imperial descent
> of the mighty Emperor Kanmu,
> Tomomori of Taira,
> and I am his phantom.

62

Here we are plunged into a fierce scene as the chorus chants, describing the vengeful ghost moving with heroic steps to the music:

> . . . he regrasps his halberd
> floating on the evening waves aright
> and churns it like the whirlpool-crest
> all around him as he strides

fiercely through the rising tides
and erupts upon us noxious blasts.
So our eyes are blindly shot
like our minds confused, and what
lies before, behind us seems
banished from our sight.

And the *kakeri* dance he performs adds another dimension to this dreadful scene. For the appearance of the ghostly Tomomori is not in a dream but takes place before the very eyes of Yoshitsune and his followers, who find themselves battling their ancient enemy against the background of the raging sea. This fact itself makes the dramatic impact immediate and real. Again Benkei figures largely in this scene, driving the ghost back fearlessly from his lord by his prayers to the divine Myōō. The encounter between Tomomori, the principal role of the second half, and Benkei, as the principal supporting actor, is again mutually enhancing; for if Benkei was the most faithful and courageous of Yoshitsune's followers, Tomomori was one of his most noted foes, known for his wisdom and valor.

The Nō of this play, then, the unifying sense of restraint and heightened beauty, or *yūgen*, emerges in a finely maintained balance of contrasts one after another: between Shizuka and Benkei, between Benkei and Tomomori, between a drama of civil, private life and a warrior's public actions that create history; between the beauty of elegance and gracefulness, and the images of dread and horror, which are vivified by Shizuka's Middle Dance and the warrior's *kakeri* dance respectively. If we assume that the Nō of this play lies in such a concept, then the puzzling aspects of it described previously begin to resolve themselves. First, the shift of principal role from Shizuka to Tomomori must enhance and deepen both characters; we are better able to grasp the essence of Shizuka because we see the essence of Tomomori. Hence the principal actor who undertakes both roles must exercise his power, control, and skill in realizing a unity in tone. Neither role can be done by and for itself: paradoxically, if the actor is too skillful a Shizuka or too skillful a Tomomori, it must be counted a fault. (But perhaps this seems a teasing paradox only to those of us who have not been privileged to enjoy a true repertory theater group but have only been exposed to the crudities of a star system of theatrical presentations. We unfortunately do not see plays; we see performances.)

In this conception of the play, Benkei serves not only as a connecting link in a series of contrasts but also as a bridge for the action from the first episode to the second. In this regard, his passage with the boatman, the *kyōgen* role, is noteworthy in making the transition effortlessly and naturally. Further, the *kyōgen* helps to forward the action since the full presentation of the storm setting depends upon his convincing performance. The *kyōgen* in this play, therefore, rather than merely repeating a summary of the situation, as is so often the function of the role in other Nō plays, is more fully integrated in the dramatic development. As is evident, the role of the *waki* Benkei too demands a fine control of tone and coordination with the *shite* as Shizuka and again with Tomomori. He creates with each role of the *shite* a heightened sense of contrast that gives deeper depths to the poetic quality of the Shizuka episode and the virile rage of Tomomori.

This discussion of the structuring of the play seems to bring this Nō within the confines of the realistic theater; its author, Kojirō (1435–1516), writing a hundred years later than Zeami (1363–1443), brings to the Nō a more dramatic, immediate quality than the *yūgen* of the latter. Yet the assignment of the Yoshitsune role to a *kokata*, or child actor, reminds us how far removed the Nō remains from the realistic drama as we know it. The *kokata* is at times realistically used in child roles, such as the lost son in *Sumidagawa* or the eager Tsuruwaka of *Settai*. At times, as in this play, he is called on to fill adult roles, where that role is not crucial to the central configuration of the Nō. As Dr. Ichikawa Sanki has said, ". . . according to the conventions of the Noh drama, only two leading parts are allowed."[5] Yet, perhaps in part because of the strong class structure of Japanese society during the feudal period, it would seem highly incongruous to designate the roles of such eminent persons as Yoshitsune or the Emperor Kiyomibara (in *Kuzu*) or Yoritomo (in *Daibutsu Kuyō*) as *tsure*, or followers, rather than *kokata*. Perhaps the innocent nature of the *kokata* makes it possible to represent such characters appropriately without crowding the stage or dominating the scene: for the child actor receives a special kind of attention because of the aura of his own youthfulness, as Zeami points out. "First, he has grace (*yūgen*) in all that he does on account of his boyish figure. This is also the period of beautifying of voice, these advantages concealing his demerits and making his merits appear all the more Flowerful. . . . If he is proficient, . . . his performance will be successful whatever he does. With his charming boyish figure, his beautiful voice, and moreover, his skill in performance, how can his performance be unsuccessful?"[6] The assignment of the Yoshitsune role to a *kokata* in *Funabenkei* serves, then, to diminish the dramatic importance of Yoshitsune for the play *qua* play, while preserving the luster that identifies the historical figure in Japanese literature. It therefore allows the central contrasts of the play to emerge, and the question of dramatic credibility previously raised is seen as irrelevant.

However, these considerations do not deal with the *kokata* as he functions within the play. For while the impersonation of adults by a child actor has become a Nō convention, the very acceptance of the convention means, we must assume, that originally it functioned dramatically, serving in the total configuration. The positive advantages of the *kokata* role are especially seen in the second part of this play, where the miming of the slight figure in combat against the towering Tomomori in itself indicates that it is not the crude thrill and suspense of battle that concerns us. It is the innocence and purity of the good, of courage without hate, against the force of vengeance and evil. Thus Benkei, too, great warrior and noted swordsman, opposes the enemy with his rosary and vanquishes him with prayer. All this, relieving us of the anxiety of the real, frees us to experience the heightened beauty of the Nō as a fusion of lyric, dance, and music. For, as Mr. Kita has said, the main problem is always the same—the creation of *bi*, beauty.

The foregoing discussion of this play may appear insufferably schematic and theoretical, as pedantically irrelevant to the actual theater experience as T. S. Eliot's discussion of *Hamlet*. For in spite of Mr. Eliot's close analysis of that play and his conclusion that it is a marred and imperfectly realized conception, as actual experience, whether in the theater or as literature to be read, the play continues to live a life of its own. No doubt *Funabenkei* too will continue as one of the more popular pieces in Nō, even when it is presented as two separate and only loosely connected episodes, as it too often is. For the language of the play is beautiful, the dances are colorful, and the characters and story lines are perennial favorites.

However, I am encouraged to hope that an attempt to grasp the play as a unified whole is not entirely misleading, and that it will lead to a greater understand-

64

ing of the aesthetic configuration of this theater. For the dedicated Nō buff is some-what like the dedicated music lover of the West. If he is expert enough, he hears and experiences the Nō—the chanting, the music, the dancing, the recitations, the rhythmic nuances—even as he reads the text. He has Nō, much as each of us has his *Hamlet*. He therefore demands that the theater experiences give him something of the sense of fulfillment, of completion and realization, of insight that he feels is essential to the play. When this dimension is lacking and he has not experienced the *yūgen* that is the heart of Nō, he remains dissatisfied—as did Sakamoto Setchō, the sensitive Nō critic, when he reviewed the performance of February 2, 1936, of Sakurama Kintarō, an accomplished Nō master: "I went around to the Komaru from Kanze and saw only this number [*Funabenkei*]. Mr. Hōshō Shin, the *waki*, showed unexpectedly his vigor; Mr. Masaki, the *kyōgen*, also showed great re-straint, and the *kokata* was a great success. There was no defect in the *shite*'s per-formance. In view of the elegant charm of the first part, and the heroic sublime in the second, it may be unreasonable to demand of him more than this, but what I want him to show us, I felt, exists still far above this."[7] The venerable Roppeita, now designated an intangible cultural treasure, whose performances are remem-bered with special awe, has said that in Nō, ". . . there is success or failure. There is nothing in between."

On May 13, 1967, Mr. Kita Minoru undertook the *shite* role with Mr. Shigeyoshi Mari as the *waki* Benkei. Mr. Kita, as previously noted, felt that the problem of the play for him was to conceive it as a whole and not to allow it to fall into two disparate parts. In this performance he was most fortunate in his Benkei, whose sensitivity and control matched his own. The experience was enlightening and, together with Mr. Kita's comments, helped me to grasp this play. As Dr. Toki Zenmaro, the noted contemporary poet and Nō playwright, said afterward with great satisfaction, it was a Nō. It was not a *shibai*.[8]

Funabenkei

FUNABENKEI
(Benkei of the Boat)

BY KANZE KOJIRŌ NOBUMITSU

Persons: WAKI: *Musashibo Benkei*
WAKI-TSURE: *Retainers of the Hōgan (three)*
KOKATA: *The Hōgan, Minamoto no Yoshitsune*
SHITE (PART I): *Lady Shizuka*
NOCHI-JITE (PART II): *Ghost of Taira no Tomomori*
KYŌGEN: *Chief Boatman*

Classification: *Primary, Group V*
Place: *At the Bay of Daimotsu*
Time: *November*
Kogaki: *16*

PART I

[*Following introductory music called* shidai, *the* kokata, *Minamoto no Yoshitsune, makes his entrance as the brocade curtain dividing the mirror room from the bridge is swept back. He advances in a stately manner along the bridge, followed by the* waki, *Benkei, and the* waki-tsure, *Yoshitsune's three retainers. The* kokata *wears a tall black cap; a heavy silk kimono, the neckline of which is accented with three unattached red collars arranged as if pleated; a* sobatsugi *robe, indicating that he is in armor; and a white broad divided Nō skirt tied in front with a brocade waistband. He also wears a long sword and a white headband and carries a fan. The* waki *wears a small round cap, a narrow brocade Buddhist stole, a heavy silk kimono, a broad-sleeved robe, a white broad divided Nō skirt with a waistband tied in front, and a short sword. He carries a rosary of diamond-shaped beads. The* waki-tsure, *the three retainers, wear costumes similar to that of the* kokata, *except that their swords are short, their caps are folded over, and their collars are not red. As they enter the stage, they face one another and chant the opening verse, also known as* shidai.]

WAKI AND WAKI-TSURE

[1] (*Shidai: au, tsuyogin*)

Kyō omoitatsu[9]	Today we plan to journey
tabigoromo	dressed in traveling robes,
kyō omoitatsu	today we plan to journey
tabigoromo,	dressed in traveling robes,
kiraku[10] o itsu to	but when will we all return
sadamen.	to Miyako?[11]

[*The chorus sings the* jidori, *repeating the above verse, except the third and fourth lines, in a lower key.*]

Chorus

(Jidori: au, tsuyogin)

Kyō omoitatsu
tabigoromo
kiraku o itsu to
sadamen.

Today we plan to journey
dressed in traveling robes,
but when will we all return
to Miyako?

[*After the* jidori [12] *the* waki, *facing stage front, intones the following prose passage, called* nanori, *introducing himself to the audience.*]

Waki

(Nanori: awazu, kotoba)

Kore wa Saitō [13] no katawara ni sumai suru Musashibō Benkei [14] nite sōrō. Satemo waga kimi Hōgan-dono wa, Yoritomo no on-daikan to shite, ogoru Heike o horoboshitamai, ima wa go-kyōdai no on-naka jichigetsu no gotoku goza arubeki o, yui kai naki mono [15] no zangen ni yori, on-naka tagawase tamō koto kaesugaesu mo kuchioshiki shidai nite sōrō. Shikaredomo waga kimi wa shinkyō no rei o omonjitamai, mazumazu Miyako o on-hiraki atte, on-mi ni ayamari naki yoshi o ōse hirakaren ga tame, konnichi yo o kome, Tsu no Kuni Amagasaki [16] Daimotsu no Ura e to isogi sōrō.

I am Musashibō Benkei, who lives by the West Pagoda. My Lord Hōgan, serving as Yoritomo's chief deputy, has destroyed the clan of the extravagant Heike. The brotherly ties between them should be as close as those of the sun and the moon, but because of false charges spread about by some contemptible person, they have become estranged. This is certainly a serious matter, which we all regret over and over again. In spite of it our lord is fully conscious of the respect due his older brother; so now he plans to leave the capital behind for the time being. Then he will petition his brother for a chance to prove his innocence. So today, while the dark still lingers on, he hastens to Amagasaki on the Bay of Daimotsu in the land of Tsu.

[*The* waki *and* waki-tsure *sing the following verse passage, called* sashi.]

Waki and Waki-tsure

(Sashi: awazu, tsuyogin)

Koro wa Bunji [17] no
hajimetsu kata,
Yoritomo Yoshitsune
fukai no yoshi
sude ni rakkyo shi
chikara naku

When the Bunji Era
had begun we heard
of the disputes Yoritomo
had with Yoshitsune.
This has now been verified,
so, left powerless,

67

Funabenkei

KOKATA

Hōgan Miyako o	Hōgan made his plan to flee
ochikochi[18] no	from the capital,
michi sebaku naranu[19]	long before the roads get narrow
sono saki ni,	near and far away,
saikoku[20] no kata e to	so his heart is set upon the land
kokorozashi	lying in the west.

WAKI AND WAKI-TSURE

mada yobukaku mo	Still in darkness night lies deep;
kumoi no tsuki	how we feel the sorrow
izuru[21] mo oshiki	like the cloud-hid palace moon

[*The* waki *and the* waki-tsure *face one another and sing the rest together.*]

Miyako no nagori,	leaving Miyako behind,
hitotose[22] Heike	so unlike a year ago,
tsuitō no	when we started out
Miyako ide ni wa	to pursue the Heike clan
hikikaete	from the capital,
tada jūyonin[23]	now only ten men or more
sugosugo to	with a heavy heart
samo utokaranu	still they are so intimate
tomo bune no	in this comradeship,

[*The* waki *and* waki-tsure, *still facing one another, sing the following verse passage called* sageuta.]

(*Sageuta: au, tsuyogin*)

nobori kudaru ya[24]	drifting up and floating down
kumo mizu no	like the fleeting clouds
mi wa sadame naki	on the water is the way
narai kana	of uncertain life

[*In a higher tone they sing the following* ageuta *passage, called* michiyuki.]

(*Michiyuki: au, tsuyogin*)

Yo no naka no[25]	In this world of men
hito wa nani to mo	let them whisper as they will,
Iwashimizu,[26]	at the Clear Rock Spring
hito wa nani to mo	let them whisper as they will
Iwashimizu,	at the Clear Rock Spring,
suminigoru oba	whose heart is clear or muddy
kami zo shiruran to	certainly the gods will know.
takaki mi-kage o	To the sacred shrine on high
fushiogami,	down we bow our heads
yukeba hodo naku	as we row before too long
tabigoromo	we find our journey

[*The* waki *faces stage front, steps forward, returns again to his former position, and faces the* kokata, *as if they have arrived at Daimotsu Bay.*]

68

Masterworks of the Nō Theater

ushio[27] mo nami mo   weary on the waves and tides
tomo ni hiku   ebbing all of us
Daimotsu[28] no Ura ni   to the Bay of Daimotsu,
tsukinikeri   we have come at last
Daimotsu no Ura ni   to the Bay of Daimotsu,
tsukinikeri.   we have come at last.

[*When the* ageuta *is finished, the* waki *faces stage front and intones the following prose passage, called* tsukizerifu.]

WAKI

Onnisogi sōrō hodo ni Amagasaki Daimotsu no Ura ni on-tsuki nite sōrō. Kono tokoro ni soregashi zonji no mono no sōrō aida, onnyado no koto o mōshi-tsukyōzuru nite sōrō.

As we traveled so quickly, we have already reached the Bay of Daimotsu at Amagasaki. At this place, I have an acquaintance, so I will ask him for lodgings for us.

[*The* waki *goes out to the* shite *pillar and faces toward the bridge.*]

[2]

Ika ni kono ya no aruji no watari sōrō ka.

Ho, there. Is the master of this house at home?

[*The* kyōgen, *the chief boatman, had entered with the musicians and the chorus before the play began and had taken his place at the* kyōgen *seat. He wears a checked kimono, a two-piece* kyōgen *robe, and a waistband tied in front. He rises, carrying a fan in his hand, and goes to the first pine. The following prose dialogue intoned between the* waki *and the* kyōgen *is called* mondai.]

KYŌGEN

(*Mondai: awazu, kotoba*)

Annai to wa tare nite onniri sōrō zo.

Who is it that is asking for me?

WAKI

Iya Musashi nite sōrō.

Why, I am Musashi.

KYŌGEN

Sate tadaima wa nani no tame ni on-nide sōrō zo.

Well, now, what brings you to this place, sir?

WAKI

San zōrō. Waga kimi o kore made on-tomo mōshite sōrō. Onnyado o mōshi sōrae.

I have escorted my lord to this place. I would like to ask you for some lodgings.

KYŌGEN

Kashikomatte sōrō.

Yes, of course.

69

Funabenkei

WAKI

O-shinobi no koto nite sōrō aida, oku no
ma o yōi serare sōrae. Mata saru shisai
atte saikokugata e on-gekō sōrō aida,
fune o mo yōi atte tamawari sōrae.

Since he is traveling in secret, please
prepare an inner room for him. For certain reasons, he must go down to the
western lands, so please prepare a ship
for us, too.

KYŌGEN

Kokoroe mōshite sōrō. Saraba oku no
ma e on-tōri sōrae. Go-yōjin no koto wa
on-kokoro yasuku oboshimesare sōrae.

I understand. Well, then, please come
into the inner room. As for security,
please put yourself at ease about this
matter.

[*Starting at the* waki *seat, the* kokata, *the* waki, *and the* waki-tsure *stand in a line alongside the
chorus. The* waki *and the* waki-tsure *sit down in front of the chorus while the* kokata *sits on a stool
by the* waki *seat. The* kyōgen *sits down at the* kyōgen *seat. Then the* waki *goes in front of the*
kokata, *speaking as if to himself.* Mondai *between the* waki *and the* kokata.]

WAKI

(Mondai: awazu, kotoba)

Masashiku Shizuka[29] wa on-tomo to
miesasetamai sōrō. Ima no orifushi nani
to yaran, niyawanu yō ni sōraeba soregashi mōshi todomebaya to zonji sōrō.

I am sure that Lady Shizuka is hoping
to accompany him. What does my lord
think of it under these circumstances? I
feel that it is unsuitable. I think I should
advise my lord against this.

[*The* waki *kneels and bows before the* kokata.]

Ika ni mōshiage sōrō. Masashiku Shizuka wa on-tomo to miesasetamaite
sōrō. Ima no orifushi nani to yaran niyawanu yō ni sōraeba kore yori Miyako
e on-kaeshi arekashi to zonji sōrō.

May I speak, my lord? I am sure that
now Lady Shizuka is hoping to come
with us. In circumstances such as these,
it seems inappropriate, my lord; therefore, I feel you must have her return to
the capital from this place.

KOKATA

Tomokaku mo Benkei hakarai sōrae.

However that may be, I leave the matter
up to you, Benkei.

WAKI

Kashikomatte sōrō. Nippon nichi no go-
kigen ni mōshi-agete sōrō. Yagate Shizuka no ya ni tachi koyōzuru nite sōrō.

I understand. I'll put it to her in such a
way that she'll be the happiest person in
all Japan. In a short time I will go over
to her lodgings.

[*The* waki *goes near the bridge and, facing the curtain, he calls out at the first pine.*]

[3]

| Ika kono ya no uchi ni Shizuka no wa-tari sōrō ka. Kimi yori no on-tsukai ni Musashi ga sanjite sōrō. | Is Lady Shizuka staying at this house? Musashi comes here with a message from his lord. |

[*The* shite, *Lady Shizuka, appears from behind the curtain and advances to the third pine. As she does so, she responds. Dialogue* (mondai) *between the* shite *and the* waki.]

SHITE

(*Mondai: awazu, kotoba*)

| Ara omoi yorazu ya. Musashi-dono wa nani no tame no on-tsukai nite sōrō zo. | How unexpected this is, Musashi! What brings you here as a messenger? |

[*The following dialogue is exchanged between the* waki *and the* shite *as the* waki *stands at the first pine, and the* shite, *at the third pine.*]

WAKI

| Waga kimi no go-jō ni wa kore made no on-mairi makoto ni shinbyō ni obo-shimesare sōrō, sarinagara harubaru no hatō o shinogi tomonawaren koto, jinkō shikarubekarazu sōrō aida kore yori Mi-yako e on-kaeri are to no on-koto nite sōrō. | According to my lord's message, his lordship truly appreciates your coming to this place. However, he fears what people might say if your ladyship were to undergo the journey with him across the high waves over the distant seas; thus, he wishes you to return to the capital from this place. |

SHITE [*To the* waki]

| Kore wa omoi no hoka naru ōse kana. Izuku made mo on-tomo to koso omishi ni, | This is a most unexpected thing for him to say. I thought I would follow him wherever he might go. |

[*The* shite *faces stage front again as she sings the following verse.*]

(*Awazu, yowagin*)

tanomite mo	I rely on him,
tanomi sukunaki wa	but how really untrustworthy
hito no kokoro	appears the human heart!

[*The* shite *lowers her face.*]

| ara nani to mo na ya zōrō. | To my sorrow this is truly disappointing. |

71

WAKI

| Geni geni ōse mottomo nite sōrō. Sate on-penji oba nani to mōshi sōrōbeki. | Well, now. What you have said is true enough. Now, what may I tell my lord of your reply? |

SHITE

Warawa on-tomo mōshi kimi no on-daiji ni nari sōrawaba todomari sōrōbeshi.

When I accompany my lord and should it become a grave matter, I would stay behind.

WAKI

Ara kotogotoshi ya. On-daiji made wa arumajiku sōrō. Tada on-tomari aru ga kan'yō nite sōrō.

Well, please don't make too much of this. It is not a grave matter, I'm sure; it's only a question of the need for you to stay here.

SHITE

Yokuyoku mono o anzuru ni kore wa Musashi-dono no on-pakarai to omoi sōrō hodo ni, mizukara mairi jiki ni on-penji o mōshi sōrōbeshi.

The more I consider this, the more I feel that it may be your scheme, Musashi. [*Facing the* waki.] I will go to him myself and give my answer directly.

WAKI

Sore wa tomokaku mo nite sōrō. Saraba yagate on-mairi sōrae.

However that may be, please let me escort you to him.

[*With the* waki *first, followed by the* shite, *they enter the stage. The* waki, *facing the* kokata, *in front of the hand-drum players, puts his hands on the floor.*]

Shizuka no on-mairi nite sōrō.

Lady Shizuka has come, my lord.

[*The* waki, *looking at the* shite, *sits in front of the chorus, while the* shite *goes out toward center stage and kneels. The* kokata, *seated on the stool at the* waki *seat, intones the following prose passage as the* shite *lowers her head and listens to him.*]

KOKATA

[4] (*Mondai: awazu, kotoba*)

Ikani Shizuka. Ware omoi no hoka ochiudo to nariyuku tokoro ni, kore made no kokorozashi makoto ni shin-byō nari, sarinagara harubaru no hatō o shinogi tomonawan koto, jinkō shika-rubekarazu. Mazu kono tabi wa Miyako ni kaeri jisetsu o machi sōrae.

Please listen, Shizuka. I did not anticipate this, but now I have become a fugitive. Truly I appreciate your devotion in coming with me this far. However, I fear what people may say if you should undergo the distant voyage with me over the rough seas. So at this time it is best that you return to the capital and wait for a better time.

SHITE [*Raising her head up slowly.*]

Sate wa kimi no go-jō nite sōrō mono o, yoshi naki Musashi-dono o uramimō-shitsuru koto no hakanasa wa zōrō.

Truly, it was your decision, then, my lord. [*Facing the* waki.] I am ashamed of myself for the suspicions I felt toward Musashi, which have been groundless.

[*The* shite *looks aside toward stage front and lowers her face as she sings the following lines.*]

72

Masterworks of the Nō Theater

(Awazu, yowagin)

kaesugaesu mo	Over and over again
menboku nō	how I feel so shameful
koso sōrae.	that I doubt Musashi.

WAKI

Iya iya kore wa kurushikarazu. Tada jinkō o oboshimesu nari. On-kokoro kawaru to na oboshimeshi so to	No, no, I don't mind it at all. He has only considered what people will say. Never must you think that his heart's concern for you will ever change;
namida o nagashi-mōshikeri.	shedding down his teardrops thus Benkei said.

SHITE

Iya tonikaku ni	Nor at any rate do I
kazu naranu	regret it at all
mi ni wa urami no	as I count for nothing now
nakeredomo,	to his chosen band,
kore wa funaji no	but across the ocean route
kadode naru ni	at my lord's departure,

[*The chorus sings the following* ageuta *passage.*]

CHORUS

(Ageuta: au, yowagin)

nami kaze mo	"why do waves and winds
Shizuka[30] o todome-	leave calmness, Shizuka, too

[*The* shite *faces the* kokata.]

tamō ka to,	here behind?" she asks,

[*She faces stage front.*]

Shizuka o todome-	"leave calmness, Shizuka, too
tamō ka to	here behind?" She fears;
namida o nagashi	so she sheds her tears and speaks
yūshide[31] no	of the hempen cloth
kami kakete	hung before the gods,
kawaraji to	where unchanging love

[*The* shite *lowers her face.*]

73

chigirishi koto mo	they promised, but this too will
sadame na ya.	be her karmic lot.

[*Changing her mood, the* shite *faces the* kokata.]

Geni ya	Now, indeed,
wakare yori[32]	more than this parting
masarite oshiki	from the one I dearly love,
inochi kana,	how I hold life dear,

Funabenkei

[*The* shite *looks at the* kokata *steadily.*]

<table>
<tr><td>kimi ni futatabi</td><td>for I hope to meet my lord</td></tr>
</table>

[*Checking her tears, the* shite *faces stage front.*]

awan to zo omō
yukusue.

face to face again together
in the future.

KOKATA [Mondai *with the* waki.]

[5]

Ika ni Benkei.

Ho, there, Benkei.

WAKI

On-mae ni sōrō.

At your service, my lord.

KOKATA

Shizuka ni shu o susume sōrae.

Let rice wine be served to Shizuka.

WAKI

[Kakeai *in prose and verse exchanged between the* waki *and the* shite.]

Kashikomatte sōrō. Geni geni kore wa
on-kadoide no yukusue chiyo zo to kiku
no sakazuki 33

Yes, certainly, my lord. Truly I agree
that this cup of chrysanthemum wine
[*opens the fan as if to serve her with wine*], worthy of toasting for a thousand years to
come at this departure,

(*Awazu, yowagin*)

Shizuka ni koso wa
susumekere.

calmly, like Shizuka's name,
should be poured for her.

[*The* waki *offers sake to the* shite.]

SHITE

Warawa wa kimi no
onnakare,
yarukata nasa ni
kakikurete
namida ni musebu
bakari nari.

As for me, I must part now
from the one I love,
but with no other person
who could comfort me,
only choked with tears I weep
in endless sorrow.

74

WAKI

Geni on-nageki wa saru koto naredomo,
tabi no funaji no kadode no waka

Indeed, indeed, I sympathize with you
in your grief, but at this departure on an
ocean journey, to a song of farewell,

tada hitosashi to
susumureba

let me urge you to perform
a parting number.

orifushi kore ni eboshi no sōrō. Kore o
meshite hitosashi on-mai sōrae.

Just now here is a tall court hat. Please
put this on and dance a round.

Monogi (Change of Costume)

[*While the* ashirai *music is played, the* shite *goes in front of the flute player's seat and, with the help of the stage attendant, puts on a tall court hat and a courtly over-robe. The* waki *sits down by the* shite. *After the change is completed, the* shite *rises and sings the following* issei.]

SHITE

(*Issei: awazu, yowagin*)

Sono toki Shizuka
tachiagari
toki no chōshi[34] o
toriaezu

At that moment Shizuka,
rising from her seat,
sings a tune in mode to fit
such a time as this.

[*Raising her voice the* shite *chants and looks down to her right, far into the distance.*]

tokō no yūsen[35] wa
kaze shizumatte ide

The ferryboat will leave the crossing,
when these stormy winds are lulled
and still

[*The* shite *faces stage front as the chorus chants the following lines.*]

CHORUS

hatō no takusho wa
hi harete miyu.

out at sea, the place of exile
looms through the clearing skies.

[*In front of the hand-drum players, the* shite, *sighing, faces stage front.*]

SHITE

Tachi mōbeku mo[36]
aranu mi no

In my present state I can
hardly dance a dance;

[*The* shite *makes a* sayū *gesture while the chorus sings the following lines.*]

CHORUS

sode uchifuru mo
hazukashi ya.

even fluttering my sleeves
how ashamed I feel.

[*With the* hayashi *music the* shite *starts to dance the* iroe *dance.*]

Iroe Dance

[*After the* iroe *dance, the* shite *stands in front of the musicians and, facing stage front, she sings the following* sashi *passage.*]

SHITE

(*Sashi: awazu, yowagin*)

Tsutaekiku[37]
Tōshu-kō wa
Kōsen o tomonai

I hear from others
that mighty Tao Chu-kung
has attended Kuo Chien secretly,

Funabenkei

Chorus

Kaikeizan ni	and deep within Mt. K'uai Chi,
komoriite	they're secluded long,
shuzu no chiryaku o	pondering their stratagems
megurashi	in various ways;
tsui ni Go ō o[38]	then the rival King of Wu
horoboshite	was destroyed at last;
Kōsen no honni o	so Kuo Chien's cherished royal wishes
tassu to ka ya.	were fulfilled, we hear.

[*The chorus continues to sing the following passage, called* kuse; *the* shite *dances to the singing of the chorus. This combination is called* maiguse.]

Chorus

(Kuse: au, yowagin)

Shikaru ni	Though once again
Kōsen na	Kuo Chien has conquered
futatabi	his great kingdom
yo o tori	and won the world
Kaikei no haji o	and the deep disgrace at K'uai Chi
susugishi mo	was all rinsed away,
Tōshū kō o	it was the deed that Tao Chu
nasu to ka ya.	carried out, we hear.

[*The* shite *goes out slightly toward stage front.*]

Sareba Etsu no	So among the vassals
shinka nite	at the court of Yueh,
matsurigoto o	he could have had control
mi ni makase	of the state affairs;

[*The* shite *goes out to the eye-fixing pillar, turns in a large arc to her left, and goes to the front of the hand-drum players.*]

kōmei tomi	though all fames and riches,
tattoku	and high honors
kokoro no gotoku	had been graciously bestowed
narubeki o	on him as he wished,
kō nari[39]	when deeds are done
na togete	and fame attained,
mi shirizoku wa	a subject should step down,

[*The* shite *looks toward stage front steadily and, pointing the fan around, looks across to her right.*]

ten no michi to	he thought, as was the way
kokoroete	decreed by Heaven;
shōsen ni	and so in a boat
sao sashite	pole-propelled he went

[*The* shite *makes a* sayū *gesture and opens the fan.*]

Goko[40] no	to enjoy
entō o	distant island views
tanoshimu.	of the Five Lakes.

[*The* shite *makes an* ageōgi *gesture as she sings the following lines, called* ageha.]

SHITE

(Ageha)

Kakaru	This was such
tameshi mo	an instance too;
ariyake[41] no	as the dawn awakes

[*With the* ōzayu *gesture, the* shite *goes out toward stage front as the chorus sings.*]

CHORUS

tsuki no Miyako o	from the moonlit capital
furisutete	to the west you leave
saidai no	far across the waves
hatō ni	on the ocean
omomuki	as you journey.

[*The* shite *looks at the* kokata *steadily.*]

| on-mi no toga no | When you send the very proof |
| naki yoshi o | of your innocence, |

[*Turning to her left, she goes to the* shite *seat.*]

nageki-	pleading truly
tamawaba	for his mercy,
Yoritomo mo	Yoritomo, too

[*The* shite *goes out to the eye-fixing pillar, lifts the fan above, turns around in a large arc, and goes toward the hand-drum players' seats.*]

tsui ni wa nabiku	will join with you together
aoyagi no	finally as close
eda o	as branches
tsuranuru	of the willow
on-chigiri	are joined together.

[*At the front of the hand-drum players, the* shite *makes a* sayū *gesture.*]

| nado ka wa kuchishi | How can such a love be left |
| hatsubeki. | wasted to decay? |

[*After the dance the* shite *sits down at the* shite *pillar as the chorus sings the first line of a verse called* waka. *Then she dances the* jo no mai.]

CHORUS

[6] *(Waka: awazu, yowagin)*

| Tada tanome,[42] | Only trust in me, |

Funabenkei

Jo no mai

[*The* shite *dances the* jo no mai *in five movements to instrumental accompaniment only; she then sings the* waka *verse at the* shite *seat, making an* ageōgi *gesture.*]

SHITE

(Waka: awazu, yowagin)

tada tanome,	only trust in me,
shimeji ga hara no	though how worthless life appears,
sashimogusa	like *mokusa* weeds

[*The* shite *makes a* sayū *gesture as the chorus sings.*]

CHORUS

ware yo no naka ni	in miscanthus moors, so long
aran kagiri wa.	as I live within this world.

[*The* shite *performs the* kakeri *dance. Then the* shite, *facing the* kokata, *sings the following lines.*]

SHITE

(Ōnori, yowagin)

Kaku sonnei no	Since there can be no falsehood
itsuwari naku wa	in this auspicious lyric,

[*Turning to her right, the* shite *goes to the* shite *seat as the chorus sings.*]

CHORUS

kaku sonnei no	since there can be no falsehood
itsuwari naku wa	in this auspicious lyric,

[*Pointing at the* kokata *with her fan, the* shite *goes out toward center stage and kneels.*]

yagate onnyo ni	soon you'll rise across the world
idebune[43] no	with the ship full sail

[*The* shite, *making a* kakaeōgi *gesture, looks at the bridge as the chorus sings the* ageuta.]

(Ageuta: au, yowagin)

funakodomo	oh, all you boatmen,
haya tomozuna o	untie the hawser quickly,
tokutoku[44] to,	hurry, hurry now;
haya tomozuna o	untie the hawser quickly,

[*Toward the* kokata, *the* shite *puts her hands down on the floor.*]

tokutoku to[45]	hurry, hurry now!
susume mōseba	Benkei urges loud.

[*The* shite *faces the* kokata *and the* kokata *rises.*]

Masterworks of the Nō Theater

Hōgan mo	Hōgan, too,
tabi no yadori o	comes out from the traveler's inn
idetamaeba,	graciously before us,

[The shite *clouds her mask and takes off the tall court hat as she sings the following line.]*

SHITE

| Shizuka wa naku naku | but Shizuka, weeping, weeping, |

CHORUS

| eboshi hitatare | lays aside the tall court hat, |
| nugisutete | puts the robe away, |

[Holding back her tears, the shite *goes toward the* shite *seat and holds her steps.]*

namida ni musebu	drowned in sobs and choked with tears
onnakare,	at this leave-taking;
miru me mo aware	those who watch are overwhelmed
narikeri,	by sorrow, too,

[Quietly the shite *goes to the bridge.]*

| miru me mo aware | those who watch are overwhelmed |
| narikeri. | by sorrow, too. |

[The shite *exits behind the curtain, while the* kokata *goes to the* waki *seat and sits on the stool.]*

Nakairi (Interlude)

KYŌGEN *[Coming out to the front of the* shite *pillar.]*

Sate mo sate mo tadaima Shizuka no kimi no nagori o oshimaseraruru tei o mimōshi, warera gotoki no mono made mo rakurui tsukamatsurite sōrō. Mata kimi no go-jō ni wa harubaru no hatō o shinogitomonawan koto jinkō shikarubekarazu to no on-koto, go-mottomo naru on-koto nite sōrō. Hitorigoto o mōsazu to mo saizen Musashi-dono no gozabune no koto o ōsetsukerarete sōrō aida, yōi tsukamatsuri sōrō hodo ni kono yoshi mōsabaya to zonzuru. Ika ni Musashi-dono ni mōshi sōrō. Tadaima Shizuka no kimi ni nagori o oshimaseraruru tei o mishimōshi warera gotoki no mono mo sozoro ni rakurui tsukamatsuri sōrō. Musashi-dono wa nani to oboshimeshi sōrō zo.

Well, now. Well, now. When I saw how sorrowful Lady Shizuka felt at parting from her lord just now, even those like us were moved to tears. And her lord said that people would whisper if she underwent the journey with him over the distant wave-tossed seas. I cannot blame him. Instead of mumbling to myself, I think I should be letting the Reverend Musashi know that the boat he asked me for a little while ago is ready. *[He goes in front of the* waki *and sits down.]* Please, sir, just now I saw how sorrowful Lady Shizuka felt at parting from her lord, and even those like us were deeply moved to tears. What did your reverence think of it?

79

Musashi mo namida o nagashite sōrō. Mata kimi no gojō ni wa harubaru no hatō o shinogitomonawaren koto, jinkō shikarubekarazu to no on-koto kore mo mottomo nite sōrawanu ka.

This Musashi, too, shed tears. Our lord said that people would gossip if she underwent the rough voyage over the distant wave-tossed seas. Do you think that this is right?

KYŌGEN

Geni geni go-mottomo naru on-koto nite sōrō.

Of course, of course, that's right, sir!

WAKI

Mata saizen mōshitsuketaru fune oba yōi serarete sōrō ka.

Have you prepared the boat I ordered a little while ago?

KYŌGEN

San zōrō. Ashi no hayaki fune o yōi tsu-kamatsurite sōrō. Itsu nite mo go-jō shi-dai ni dashimōsōzuru nite sōrō.

Yes, your reverence. A swift-oared one is ready. As soon as your lordship commands, it can be put out to sea at once.

WAKI

Saraba yagate idasōzuru nite sōrō.

Then we will be putting out soon.

KYŌGEN

Kokoroe mōshite sōrō.

I understand, sir.

[*The* kyōgen *returns to the* kyōgen *seat and sits down. The* waki *rises and goes to the* shite *seat. The following dialogue is called* mondai.]

WAKI

[7] (Mondai: awazu, kotoba)

Ara itawashi ya Shizuka no on-shinjū sasshimōshi, warera mo rakurui tsuka-matsurite sōrō. Isogi on-pune o idasō-zuru nite sōrō.

How pitiful it is. We truly understand how Shizuka must feel, and we shed tears, too. But quickly now we must put out to sea.

WAKI-TSURE

Ikani Musashi-dono ni mōshi sōrō. Kimi yori no go-jō ni wa kyō wa nami kaze araku sōrō hodo ni go-tōryū to ōseida-sare sōrō.

Ho, Benkei. I must tell you. According to the order from our lord, it is his wish that we stay here, since the winds are rough today.

Nani to go-tōryō to zōrō ya. Soregashi kitto suiryō mōshite sōrō. Shizuka ni nagori o onnoshimi atte kayō ni ōsei-dasaruru to zonji sōrō. Mazu on-kokoro o shizumete kikoshimesare sōrae. Ima kono on-mi ni on-nari atte, kayō no go-shinjū appare go-un mo sue ni naritaru ka to zonji sōrō. Sono ue hitotose[46] Watanabe Fukushima[47] o onnide arishi toki, motte no hoka no ō-kaze narishi ni, kimi on-pune o idashi tamai, Heike o horoboshitamaishi koto ima motte onaji koto zo kashi.

What? His lordship has decided to stay here, did you say? As far as I can guess I am sure he says so because he feels sorry about leaving Lady Shizuka. Above all, we must keep our hearts calm and understand now that in these circumstances, a decision such as he has made can only mean that his star has set already. A year ago, when he set sail from Watanabe and Fukushima, the wind was extraordinarily terrible, and in spite of it, he put out to sea and destroyed the forces of the Heike. This is the same as then.

Isogi o-fune o
idasubeshi

Quick! We must put out to sea
with no more delay.

Geni geni kore wa
kotowari nari,
izuku mo kataki to
yūnami no[48]

Truly, truly, this will stand
to those who reason why;
foes are everywhere, they say,
like the evening waves

tachisawagitsutsu[49]
funakodomo,

rising raucously aloud
the crew is shouting

eiya eiya to
yūnami ni[50]
tsurete o-fune o
idashikeri.

yo heave ho! And yo heave ho!
all together now
with the evening tide they go
as the boat sets out.

[*During the above exchange, the* kyōgen *hurries into the mirror room behind the curtain and brings out a framework boat that he places in front of the* waki *seat with the bow facing the audience. He steps into it and stands at the stern.*]

Minamina o-fune ni mesare

Please, sir, let us all get aboard the boat.

81

[*The* kokata *gets into the boat and sits on the stool in the bow; the* waki *sits next to him while the rest sit outside, though they are to be looked upon as though they are in the boat also. The* kyōgen *takes up a pole.*]

Sa araba o-fune o idashi mōsō. Ei ei, ei. Ikani Musashi-doni e mōshi sōrō. Kyō wa kimi no on-kadode no funaji ni ichidan no tenki nite medetaku sōrō.

Now let's put out to sea. Yo ho! Yo ho! [*Looks at the* waki.] Your reverence, for his lordship's departure, it is so auspicious a day that the weather is especially fine over the sea.

WAKI

Geni geni ichidan no tenki nite, Musashi mo manzoku mōshite sōrō.

Indeed, it is especially fine, and this Musashi is fully pleased.

KYŌGEN

Mata gozabune no koto nite sōrō aida kyūkyō no funako-domo o sugutte nosete gozaru ga. Musashi-dono ni wa nan to goranji sōrō zo.

Since it was for your lord, I have selected the best among my rowers. What does your reverence think of them?

WAKI

Ichidan to kajite ga sōrōte shukuchaku mōshite sōrō.

They are an unusually good crew of rowers, and I am very much pleased.

KYŌGEN

Tada-ima koso kayō ni saikoku no kata e go-gekō nite sōraedomo, kami wa go-ittai no on-koto nareba ottsuke gojōraku nasareyō wa utagai mo nai. Sono toki wa kono kaijō no kajitori o soregashi hitori ni ōsetsukerarete kudasaruru yō ni o-torinashi atte kudasarekashi to tanomi zonzuru.

Just now your lord is going down to the western land in this way. However, the shogun is his brother, and there is no doubt that soon his lordship will return to the capital. Then will you kindly put in a good word for me with his lordship so that I may be in charge of all the shipping in this sea?

WAKI

Kore wa katagata ni niaitaru nozomi nite sōrō. Kimi yo ni idetamawanu koto wa sōrōmaji. Sono toki wa kono kaijō no kajitori o ba katagata hitori ni mōshitsukyōzuru nite sōrō.

That's a reasonable enough request for you to make. Our lord will unquestionably rise again in the world. And when he does, he will put you in charge of shipping for the western seas.

KYŌGEN

Sore wa chikagoro nite sōrō. Sarinagara o-nushi no go-yō no toki wa iroiro to onyakusoku o mo nasaruredomo oboshimesu mama to naru to wasuresaseraruru mono nite sōrō. Go-shitsunen naki yō ni tanomi zonzuru.

I am very grateful. But when a great one is in need, his men will make all sorts of promises. And once the need is no longer there, they are apt to forget the promises they've made. I hope you will not forget.

82

Iya iya Musashi ni kagitte shitsunen wa arumajiku sōrō.

No, no. This Musashi is the last man in this world to forget.

KYŌGEN

Musashi-dono no sayō ni ōserarureba soregashi ga shishō wa zatto sunda to iu mon ja. Sarinagara mono ni wa nen o ireta ga yoi to mōsu. Kaesugaesu mo tanomi zonzuru. Ei, ei, ei.

So long as your reverence says so, my request is as good as granted, I'm sure. But as the saying goes, it is best to make things double sure, so please, I repeat, please keep it in mind. Yo ho! Yo ho! Yo ho!

[*The* kyōgen *looks above toward the eye-fixing pillar.*]

Ima made wa mie nan da ga Mukoyama no ue ni kumo ga miyuru. Itsu mo ano kumo no deru to kaze ni naritagaru ga. Sareba koso shitataka ni kumo o dashi, kaijō no tei ga arō natta. Minamina sei o dashi sōrae. Ei, ei, ei. Are Kara nami ga uttekuru wa nami yo, nami yo, nami yo. Shikare, shikare, shikare. Shii, shii, shii. Ei, ei. Kayō ni mōsu okashimashii yō ni oboshimesō ga, nami to mō su mono wa yasashii mono de shikareba sono mama yamu koto nite sōrō. Iya arekara nami ga uttekurui wa. Nami yo, nami yo, nami yo. Shikare, shikare, shikare. Arya, arya, arya. Shii, shii, shii.

Up to now, I didn't see any clouds, but now I see them over Mt. Muko. Every time that cloud comes out, it's likely to get windy. Then the wind brings more clouds, and the sea begins to get very rough. All you rowers, do your best! Yo ho! Yo ho! Yo ho! See the waves come surging toward us from yonder. Oh, you waves, waves, waves! Now begone, begone, begone. Yo ho! Yo ho! You may think we're only noisy, as you listen to us. But the waves are simple, and when we scold them, they get quiet. Look, from over there, the waves come beating toward us! [*Looks toward the* waki *seat.*] Oh, you waves, waves, waves! Now begone, begone, begone! Oh, my! Oh my! Oh my! Be still, be still, be still!

PART II

[8]

WAKI

Ara fushigi ya. Kaze ga kawatte sōrō. Ano Mukoyamaoroshi[51] Yuzuriha ga Dake[52] yori fukiorosu arashi ni kono on-pune no rokuji ni tsukubeki yō zo naki. Minamina shinjū ni go-kinen sōrae.

How strange! How strange! See how the wind changes! With those downblasts from Mt. Muko and those from the lofty peak of Yuzuriha, I'm afraid this boat may not be able to reach land. All of you, all of you, pray from the bottom of your hearts!

83

Ikani Musashi-dono ni mōsubeki koto no sōrō.	Ho, Benkei, I have something I want to tell you.

WAKI

Nanigoto nite sōrō zo.	What do you wish to tell me?

WAKI-TSURE

Kono on-pune ni wa ayakashi ga tsukite sōrō.	This boat is possessed by some evil spirit.

WAKI

Shibaraku. Senchū nite wa sayō no koto oba mōsanu koto nite sōrō. Nanigoto mo Musashi to sendō ni on-makase sōrae.	Hold on a minute! On board a ship, don't talk about such things. Please, leave everything to this Musashi and the chief boatman.

KYŌGEN

Aa koko na hito wa saizen fune ni o-na-riyaru toki ara nani yara hitokoto iitaso na kuchimoto de atta to omōta ni shi-tataka na koto o ossharu. Senchū nite sayō na koto wa mōsanu koto nite sōrō.	Ah, these folks here, the minute they came aboard, I could tell from the way their lips were set that they had some-thing they wanted to say. But to say a stupid thing like that! On board a ship you can't say things like that!

WAKI

Iya iya senchū fuannai no koto nite sōrō aida, nanigoto mo Musashi ni menze-rare sōrae.	Now, now. Since they don't know any-thing about ships, please overlook it for Musashi's sake.

KYŌGEN

Musashi-dono no sayō ni ōserarureba mōsu de wa gozaranu ga, amari no koto o ossharu ni yotte no koto nite sōrō. Ei, ei, ei. Saraba koso mata are kara nami ga uttekuru wa. Nami yo, nami yo, nami yo. Shikare, shikare, shikare. Shii, shii, shii. Ei, ei, ei.	If Musashi says so, I won't say any more. But they really go too far. That's why I spoke up! Yo ho! Yo ho! Yo ho! Look, those waves come beating toward us again from yonder. Oh, you waves, waves, waves. Oh, begone, begone, be-gone! Be still, be still, be still. Yo ho! Yo ho! Yo ho!

WAKI [*Looks toward the bridge far into the distance as he sings the following.*]

(*Awazu, tsuyogin*)

Ara fushigi ya	How strange it now appears!
kaijō o mireba	As I look across the ocean,

saikoku nite	I can see the chieftains
horobishi	of the Heike
heike no ichimon	who were vanquished in the Westlands,
onoono ukami	each one rising from the waves

idetaru zo ya. Kakaru jisetsu o ukagaite, urami o nasu mo kotowari nari.

to appear before us. In this way, seizing this opportunity, it stands to reason that they will wreak their vengeance on us.

KOKATA [*Kneeling.*]

(Mondai: awazu)

Ikani Benkei.

Ho there, Benkei.

WAKI

On-mae ni sōrō.

At your service, my lord.

KOKATA

Imasara odorokubekarazu. Tatoi akuryō urami o nasu to mo, nani hodo no koto no arubeki zo.

Now that things have come to this, we need not be afraid. Even if those evil spirits try to wreak their vengeance on us, what harm can they inflict?

[*The* kokata, *facing stage front, sings the following* kuri *passage.*]

(Kuri: awazu, tsuyogin)

Akugyaku butō no	Think of sins and crimes committed
sono tsumori	pile on deadly pile
shinmei butsuda no	all against the gods and Buddhas!
myōkan ni somuki	They defied the will of heavens!
tenmei ni shizumishi	And since destiny has sunk and drowned
Heike no ichirui	the kindred of the Heike

[*All look toward the curtain across the bridge.*]

CHORUS

ichimon no gekkei	and the nobles of that mighty clan,
unka no gotoku	now like a swarm of insects
nami ni	all floating
ukamite	across the waves,
mietaru zo ya.	they appear before us.

85

[*Following the quickened entrance music of the flute, called* hayabue, *the* shite, *the ghost of Taira no Tomomori, appears as the brocade curtain is swept back. He wears the* ayakashi *mask, a flowing black wig with golden horns, and a golden headband. He is dressed in a heavy silk kimono, the neckline of which is accented with three unattached white collars arranged as if pleated; a divided skirt with a brocade waistband tied in front; and a sword. Over this he wears a gold brocade robe, and he carries a halberd on his shoulder. He proceeds along the bridge and at the third pine he looks at the stage; he then goes back behind the curtain, reappears, and speeds across the bridge. As he enters the stage, he stands at the* shite *seat, resting the butt of his halberd on the stage floor.]*

SHITE

Somosomo kore wa
Kanmu Tennō
kyū-dai⁵³ no kōin
Taira no Tomomori⁵⁴
yūrei nari.

First of all, I am the ninth
in imperial descent
of the mighty Emperor Kanmu,
Tomomori of Taira,
and I am his phantom.

Ara mezurashi ya. Ikani Yoshitsune.

Oh, how extraordinary! Hail, O hail, Yoshitsune!

omoi mo yoranu
uranami no

When I least expected you,
over inlet waves,

[The shite *stamps the floor as the chorus sings the following verse passage in* ōnori.]*

CHORUS

(Ōnori, tsuyogin)

koe o shirube ni
idebune no,
koe o shirube ni

guided by your voice I came
as your boat set out,
guided by your voice I came

[The shite *goes out slightly toward stage front.]*

idebune no   as your boat set out

SHITE

Tomomori⁵⁵ ga shizumishi   at the stern where Tomomori sank

[The shite *looks at the* kokata.]

sono arisama ni   at the bottom of the deep,

[The shite *stares at the* kokata, *who in turn puts his hand on his sword.]*

CHORUS

mata Yoshitsune o mo
umi ni shizumen to

let also Yoshitsune sink
in like manner in the ocean;

[Turning to his left and going toward the eye-fixing pillar, the shite *swings his halberd.]*

86

yūnami ni⁵⁶ ukameru
naginata torinaoshi
tomoenami no mon
atari o harai

so saying, he regrasps his halberd
floating on the evening waves aright
and churns it like the whirlpool-crest
all around him as he strides

[The shite *kicks up the waves.]*

ushio o ketate   fiercely through the rising tides

[He stares at the kokata.]

Masterworks of the Nō Theater

akufū o fukikake	and erupts upon us noxious blasts.

[*Turning to his right he goes to the* shite *seat.*]

manako mo kurami	So our eyes are blindly shot
kokoro mo midarete	like our minds confused, and what
zengo o bōzuru	lies before, behind us seems

[*At the* shite *seat, he makes a* hiraki *gesture.*]

bakari nari.	banished from our sight.

[*With* hayashi *music, the* shite *performs a dance.*]

Maihataraki

[*Seated on the stool, the* kokata, *facing stage front, sings the following lines in* ōnori.]

KOKATA

(Ōnori, tsuyogin)

Sono toki Yoshitsune	At this moment Yoshitsune
sukoshi mo sawagazu,	is not the least disturbed at all;

[*The* kokata *rises, draws his sword, and holds it high above his head.*]

CHORUS

sono toki Yoshitsune	at this moment Yoshitsune
sukoshi mo sawagazu	is not the least disturbed at all;
uchimono nukimochi	he draws his sword and holds it high,
utsutsu no hito no	and defies the ghost as though

[*The* shite, *holding the halberd up, approaches the boat and exchanges blows with the* kokata.]

mukō ga gotoku	he were still the living brave.
kotoba o kawashi	Hurling war cries back and forth,
tatakaitamaeba	they engage in mortal combat.

[*The* waki *rubs his holy rosary toward the* shite *as he prays.*]

Benkei oshihedate	Benkei pushes them apart,
uchimonowaza nite	shouting out aloud, "no weapon
kanōmaji to	can be used against him."
juzu sarasara to	Rubbing fast his rosary
oshimonde	in prayer he invokes

[*The* shite, *turning to his left, flees toward the front of the flute player, and then comes out to the eye-fixing pillar.*]

Tōbō Kōzanze[57]	Kōzanze, who's in the East,

[*Holding his halberd high, the* shite *challenges the* kokata, *but he retreats.*]

nanbō Gudariyasha	Gudariyasha in the South,
saihō Daiitoku	in the West, Daiitoku,

[*Again the* shite *tries to face the* kokata *but cannot approach him.*]

Funabenkei

hoppō Kongō	and in the North, Kongō
Yasha Myōō	Yasha Myōō,
Chūō Daishō	then at the very Center Seat

[Through the power of the holy prayer, the shite *is forced to retreat to the front of the hand-drum players.]*

Fudō Myōō no	Great Fudō Myōō
sakku ni kakete	for the ropes to bind the foes!

[Dragging his halberd, the shite *retreats to the bridge.]*

inori inorare	Through this the evil phantoms
akuryō shidai ni	are struck down and they fall away
tōzakareba	slowly in the distance;
Benkei funako ni	then Benkei puts his strength

[The shite *turns his face toward the third pine and looks at the boat. He throws away the halberd and, drawing out his sword, runs into the stage.]*

chikara o awase	together with the boatmen
o-fune o koginoke	to row the boat away from them,
migiwa ni yosureba	and toward the shore they steer it,
nao onryō wa	yet the vengeful spirits come,
shitaikitaru o	still pursuing after us,

[The shite *tries to challenge the* kokata, *but he is chased away by the holy rosary.]*

opparai inorinoke	but now our prayer drives them back out to sea,
mata hiku shio ni	on the ebbing tides again
yurare nagare,	they're rocked and wash away
mata hiku shio ni	by the ebbing tides once more
yurare nagarete,	they are rocked and wash away;

[The shite *retreats to the bridge.]*

ato shiranami[58] to zo	and we know naught of their traces
narinikeru.	but for those white waves.

[At the third pine the shite *stamps the floor and exits across the bridge.]*

Masterworks of the Nō Theater

PART II

Ataka

Introduction

Ataka, written by Kanze Kojirō Nobumitsu (1435–1516), is one of the Nō plays based on the cycle of the epic struggle of the Genji-Heike clans in the second half of the twelfth century.[1] Among the Group IV plays to which it belongs, it is classified as a one-act *genzaimono* (living-person drama). The fourth group as a whole is marked by strong dramatic effects, and the *genzaimono* is particularly dramatic. Chronologically, *Ataka* follows the flight of the Hōgan Yoshitsune and Benkei that began in the play *Funabenkei*.[2] Forced to abandon his plan of escaping the wrath of his brother, the general Yoritomo, by sailing to Kyushu in the south, the star-crossed Yoshitsune now turns northward toward the land of Mutsu, where he hopes to obtain sanctuary from Lord Hidehira, who sheltered him in his youth.[3] Travel by land is perilous, for the military arm of Kamakura, the location of Yoritomo's headquarters, is long and powerful. Attempting to escape detection, Yoshitsune's faithful band disguise themselves as traveling *yamabushi*, the eccentrically individualistic monks who follow the secret rites of the mystic En-no-Gyōja, the seventh-century master of the strange powers in Buddhist chants and esoteric mysteries. It is at this point that the play begins, as the opening speeches of the secondary actors establish.

The journey has been long and hard, past historic mountains and ancient shrines where other men in other times have lived out their destinies. Even the thick, tough hemp of the monks' robes is torn, and, like their desperate hopes for safety, their sleeves are bedraggled and drenched with the dews of the wild places they have passed through and with the tears of their sorrows.[4] The *shite*, or actor of the main role,[5] in this case Benkei, and the *tsure*, the followers of Yoshitsune, chant,

> Though our traveling robes are made
> of the hemp monks use,

> though our traveling robes are made
> of the hemp monks use,
> drenched with dew from bamboo sprays
> will our sleeves turn limp?

They travel through the snow, "on the way to Koshi spring." But as the audience knows only too well, it was not the haven of spring that they found at Koshi; in the author's sources—*Gikeiki* and *Heike monogatari*—so well known as to assume almost the character of folk material, their sad end is related. Our foreknowledge is crucially relevant to an appreciation of this play, for it heightens perception. Whatever is gallant in Benkei, courageous in his followers, noble in Yoshitsune, is compounded and enlarged in a dramatically profitable way against the background of their tragic end.

By means of a travel song that moves from place-name to place-name through a deliberately opaque and massive series of *kakekotoba* (or *kakeshi*, pivot words or puns), *engo* (associated words), *makurakotoba* (pillow words),[6] and alliterations that seem to suggest the weary journey, the band arrives at Ataka, where it finds that an inspection barrier has been set up to intercept and examine all passing mountain monks. Yoritomo, the supreme commander, has ordered this blockade, and the officer in charge, the lord of Togashi, obeys. The fugitives confer among themselves and Yoshitsune's followers are prepared to batter their way through. Benkei does not doubt that they can fight and win, but it is the aftermath that concerns him: "Hold on a moment. As you say, it is easy to crash through this barrier. The matter of serious concern pertains to the future journey." He hatches a plot. Yoshitsune will disguise himself as the baggage carrier, with a mushroom-shaped hat pulled well down over his face, while the real baggage carrier will join the band as one of the monks. As Yoshitsune takes over the porter's belongings, the carrier is sent ahead to spy out the situation.

"What a monstrous plan" of embattlement this is, the carrier exclaims. Seen through his simple eyes and described in his colloquial speech, the danger that confronts the band is established. For only if the danger is serious can the true scope of Benkei's figure be realized. In particular, the heads of three executed mountain monks become a reality and symbol of the extremity of their situation. Of course, the gory sight is not seen directly, but it is perceived vividly, in a typical ploy, in the fright and bumbling braggadocio of the baggage carrier. Benkei teases him briefly as he gathers the group together to proceed on toward the barrier. But then he looks at the *kokata*,[7] or child actor, Yoshitsune, and the depth of his loyalty and the beauty of his devotion flash briefly:

> How true that even one safflower
> planted midst the garden blossoms
> cannot be hidden!

92

In this series of sudden shifts we see the Benkei we know—prudent, adroit, resourceful, a beloved leader, a man at his ease among all men, lords and laborers alike, and above all, a man deeply committed, with the lively sensibilities that make his commitment tenderly human. They approach the barrier and there they are challenged.

The challenge is made by the lord of Togashi, the role assumed by a secondary actor, or *waki*, and he addresses the band in ordinary civil speech. But as Benkei parleys with the barrier guards, establishing his group's identity, the lord of To-gashi suddenly breaks in with the coarsest sort of address to Benkei, as might be used for the lowest ruffian: "Why, this is too much. Your questions do you no good." What has Benkei done to cause this about-face? He has only asked a simple question: "Well, was the Hōgan among the *yamabushi* you beheaded?" Why should this produce such a crude outburst? This is a point to be kept in mind.

Threatened with mass execution, Benkei says that the monks will begin their last religious rites.

SHITE: . . . So let us begin our last rites [*looks at the* waki] and accept death squarely. All of you, comrades, come closer.
TSURE: Yes, we understand.

The *tsure* have much to understand from Benkei's look at them. They understand that they are still to restrain themselves, although they are eager to bring the issue to the test (the stage directions have them hitching up their sleeves at the shoulder, a typical Japanese gesture of preparation for fighting and not for praying). Benkei feels that there is still room to maneuver in spite of the *waki*'s threats, because he has taken a long look at the lord of Togashi;[8] that as long as there is a chance to negotiate a peaceful passage, they must take it for the sake of Yoshitsune's safety; that they must hold themselves in readiness; that this is facing the matter "squarely."

Benkei and the followers begin. He invokes the awesome name of their religious founder, En no Mubasoku, or En-no-Gyōja, master of the mysterious and hidden in Buddha's godhead, which emerges in the fierce grimace of the frightful Fudō Myōō, the god form of the divine and purifying wrath against evil. From head to toe, the *shite* and *tsure* describe the costume of the mountain monk, each item a sacred symbol. "Ah!" they breathe the sacred syllable, and we see the gaping, open mouth of the dread guardian god at the temple gate. "Un," they drone menacingly, and the feared companion god, with his mouth clamped tightly shut, towers above the stage. Together these deities protect Buddha's temples from evil, and they will protect the monks also.

TSURE: "Each body of *Yamabushi*
           a living Buddha!"
SHITE: At this place whoever now
           beheads him can't escape
TSURE: the witness of Amida
           hid deep from human ken,
SHITE: and the dreadful punishment
           of all mighty Yuya Gongen
TSURE: instantly shall fall upon this spot.

Each word of Benkei's last line falls separately, like a long roll of thunder: "Let there be no doubt of this among you!" Pious "last rites" have turned into fierce, urgent threats.

In the face of this band of large, strong, wild-eyed religious fanatics, who have apparently worked themselves up into a threatening frenzy, the barrier commander remains collected and regains his civility. His calmness is not surprising—he is, after all, a warrior. But the politeness demands attention when we remember how a straightforward question startled him into the coarsest diction. And yet here, when he is overtly defied, he is courteous and suave. Added to this mystery is the fact that Benkei, even after the explicit threat of execution, restrains his warriors with a look and launches into a fiery diatribe, obviously maneuvering because he has sensed that there is still some margin for negotiation. Our suspicions are aroused. What is being negotiated between the two men?

At this point the barrier chief is perhaps ironic, and we can only admire the inner control that this stance connotes. He suggests civilly that, since they are monks soliciting contributions to rebuild the great Tōdaiji Temple at Nara, Benkei should read to him from the solicitation scroll so that they may all be enlightened by the pious appeal. Of course, there is no such scroll.

SHITE: What? [*Seeming to pause before standing.*] Do you mean to say that I am to read from the subscription book?
WAKI: Yes, if you please.

With this passage at arms, we begin to see. The two men understand each other. Yet each would preserve his own countenance by appearing not to understand that a deadly game is being played. The game is a final one: there are those three blackened heads. The lord of Togashi suspects. But he is a man to match the man in Benkei, and only at the beginning was he jolted when Benkei asked him, "Well, was the Hōgan among the *yamabushi* you beheaded?" The question could startle only if it were completely out of the character that Benkei had put on up to this point. So it becomes clear that Benkei has acted only too well the part of a pious monk, intent upon his holy affairs, whose reactions should have been shocked horror at the revelation of the murder of three fellow monks and not polite curiosity about the success of the manhunt.

The lord, then, suspects, and he probes. For he has his duty too, as a warrior, to his lord, the general Yoritomo. In this lies his integrity. And his integrity and duty to his leader and to himself lie in his being worthy of his post and showing due decency. It may be objected that this is hardly an appropriate word for a man who has already killed three mountain monks. But we have to remember the fanatically intractable character of *yamabushi* in general. And more to the point, we recall the baggage carrier's song, in which he reports what he was told[9] when he went a-spying: the mountain monks were running away. They were not peaceable men who had established their credentials and were nevertheless relentlessly and brutally cut down. But cut down they were. The lord of Togashi knows his duty. He will certainly do it, but it is the *kyōgen*, his sword-bearer, who prattles about it. This lord is a man of rare parts. So now he commands with civility that the pious message be produced.

Benkei rises to the occasion. The rolling impromptu phrases are powerful and sonorous as he pretends to read. But, as Sakamoto Setchō says, the aura of heroic violence is not enough. "The scroll-reading scene was matchlessly delightful [as done by Roppeita]. Compared to other masters . . . whom I have seen many times, I realized that interest was lacking [in their performances], with only the taste of heroic violence, with little change or thoughtfulness."[10]

What some of these "changes" may be can be deduced from the reading of the play up to this point. For, on the one hand, Benkei must hold back his own men,

94

all too ready to take to force and crash their way through the barrier, as they are perfectly capable of doing. He held them back in their first council; he held them back again, even when the threat of execution was thrown at them, with a look that spoke. And he holds them back now, as violence quivers in the air about them, by the sheer intensity, strength, and agony of his inner resolve that he will effect this passage. On the other hand, he can restrain the forces of Togashi only by his pretended reading.

Other changes that can be rung on the passage of the scroll reading rise from the two levels of intent in Benkei. The surface, literal meaning is a pretended reading of the churchly message of the priest Shunjōbō Chōgen.[11] The second rises from the intense resolve, even to the death ("in this night of life and death / where our dream is long"); his own actual agony as he describes Emperor Shōmu's grief ("his flowing tears / over-brimmed his weeping eyes"); his desperate appeal for help as he reads Shunjōbō Chōgen's appeal ("I, Shunjōbō Chōgen, appeal abroad"); and his own intense prayer to Buddha as he pretends to read Chōgen's words ("Truly trust Lord Buddha / with deep reverence, / thus I proclaim").

Benkei is convincing. The lord commander watches and listens. If he cannot obtain his proof through the ear, he will try the eye. He edges closer to see the scroll. Benkei edges back, holding it away from him as he continues with his pretended reading. Again, the crushing intensity of his inner resolve makes it impossible for the *waki* to demand to see the scroll. There is a barrier of common decorum that precludes a demand to examine such sacred writings. This is the opening that Benkei uses and exploits. For if the *waki* is probing and watching for self-betrayal in Benkei, Benkei too is measuring the margin of doubt in the commander that leaves room for maneuver. He sensed it successfully the first time and widened it so that the barrier commander could only fall back into his former civility. Once more his guard must be so alert that he leaves no space for the fatal lunge that will rip the fiction. And added to the intensity of his search for safety is his anxiety for Yoshitsune, some paces behind the group, alone as the lowly baggage carrier.

In the growing tension, as he ad-libs the bogus message, he traces the grief of the Emperor Shōmu over the death of his wife, a grief so intense that the emperor was inspired to enter religion and construct the Great Buddha of Nara. Scholarly footnotes will primly point out that this is in error, since Shōmu died before his wife. So much the worse for scholarship. The enormity of the error beggars description. For Shōmu had been such a devout believer that he had established monasteries and convents in every province, while accounts of the eye-opening ceremonies of the gigantic Buddha of Nara showed that the rites had been of a brilliance thitherto unknown in the country. His empress, Kōmyō, almost as well known for her piety as she was famed for her beauty, had assembled in her sorrow at his death many of the holy articles used in that ceremony as well as other mementos of her husband in the Shōsōin treasure house. Benkei had served an apprentice priesthood in one of the great temples of Mt. Hiei. He could never have missed hearing an item of knowledge as common as the widowhood of Shōmu's empress. Additionally astonishing is the fact that not only does Benkei make such an error and dwell on it at some length, but it passes without comment from the lord commander and without attack from his officious underling, the *kyōgen*, who have both been eagerly waiting for such a self-betrayal from Benkei.

It hardly seems neccessary to discuss the impossibility of attributing the error to the playwright's ignorance. If Kojirō, some three hundred years after the event, can name correctly the monk in charge of rebuilding the Nara Temple—Shunjōbō Chōgen—the error in regard to the vastly more important figure of Shōmu can only be considered deliberate. The lapse can be accounted for neatly as the dramatist's device to show the frenetic pitch of the controlled tension of violence and irresistible resolve. Benkei's words speak of the saintly Shōmu, who turned to "the Way of Virtue." Benkei's message is quite another matter. His final words ring out like a swinging sword: "Echoes crack the very skies / as loud he reads the scroll."

The dangerous, potent mixture of fanatic religious fears, the aura of violence, and the irresistible thrust of Benkei are fully measured by the reaction of the barrier guards:

WAKI: [*Faces stage front.*]
            All here at the barrier
            are struck numb at heart.
CHORUS: Stunned and fearful, full of dread,
            they allow them to pass.
            [*The* shite *rolls up the scroll and faces the* waki.]
            Stunned and fearful, full of dread,
            they allow them to pass.
WAKI: Quickly, now. You may pass on.
SHITE: Yes, we shall.
KYŌGEN: Come on, come on. Quickly pass along there.

The people of the barrier cannot wait to get rid of this party. The *kyōgen* is off-balance and he bustles about, trying to hide how thoroughly shaken he is by Benkei's reading. But the commander is a man of another stripe. He faces stage front, as the *waki* always faces when he communicates to the audience as their informant on the scene. Impressed he may be, but he is in command of himself, for he can still make the report. Benkei reacts again to the manhood of the commander, as his facing the *waki* and his reply clearly show. And the monks pass through the barrier, up the Nō bridge to the third pine, while behind them the precious baggage carrier slowly rises with his burden.

What is Nō in this play is now clear. It must be insisted upon. For, as with *Funabenkei*, the present play can only too readily be corrupted into sentimental spectacle, like its kabuki adaptation, *Kanjinchō*, in which the barrier commander is torn by his sympathy for Yoshitsune and his duty to his general, and Benkei has only to present a sufficiently convincing spectacle so that the lord can in good conscience let him pass. Setchō makes the point several times that the Nō play must not be allowed to become a *shibai*,[12] or a mere spectacle. Maruoka Akira maintains, "The difficulty in producing this play lies in how to act it so as to bring out positively the Nō in it."[13] In kabuki's fulsome cultivation of the pathetic, the whole thesis of the Nō play is vulgarized and is of a piece with the demand that vice be punished and virtue rewarded—a demand deplored by Aristotle as a sign of the "debility of the audience."[14]

In Benkei's words, "Let there be no doubt of this among you!" The lord of Togashi, *qua* commander of the barrier, is relentless. The testimony of the three blackened heads is irrefutable. At the slightest weakening in Benkei the entire

96

party would be set upon, the issue joined, and a fight to the death begun. Only the inner resolve within Benkei maintains the perilous balance along the sword's edge between two forces of fairly equal strength and warlike determination. For as Benkei has noted, his band is not inferior to the barrier guard. The lord commander and the audience too know this; they see eleven men on the stage opposing only the *waki* and the *kyōgen*. Yet the commander would attack if he were given the slightest excuse.

And he needs the excuse of some self-betrayal in Benkei, for, as has been argued, he is no simple brute. Dramatically, the playwright could not allow this. Only a thoroughly worthy foe can bring out the full conception of Benkei. Only a deadly issue is worthy of two such men. Only equal forces can convey the dramatic intent.

For this is the Nō of the play: the inward duel and fateful testing of two quintessential men, in each of whom power, honor, integrity, and loyalty are equally strong. "Inward" is the key word. The live experience of Nō to be imparted by the actor is expressed, as Abe Nōsei has said, "as centripetally and yet as effectively as possible," while power is "put in, inwardly, inwardly as much as possible."[15] Outwardly what we can see and feel is communicated through a form that resembles sculpture in motion.[16]

If the Nō of the play is found in such a concept, then the exchange of two lines between the lord and Benkei after the scroll reading serves almost as a recognition scene. Surrounded by the tension and terror, the *shite* and *waki* still face each other directly to exchange words, eyeball to eyeball, as it were.

> WAKI: Quickly, now. You may pass on.
> SHITE: Yes, we shall.

This is the climax of the inward duel. In the confrontation there is acknowledgment that each has measured up to the mark. Both sides can now retire with honor.

The last episodes seem to be the outward miming of what has remained deeply inward up to this point. For the first time there is an explicit declaration of the hitherto unspoken suspicion that this is Yoshitsune's group.

> WAKI: [*Without giving ground.*] He looks like Lord Hōgan, so my men say. Therefore, until this is settled, I'll detain him.

Benkei here explicitly holds back the followers twice, just as he had done earlier through his inward determination. The beating that he gives Yoshitsune in order to deceive the guards as to his identity is an action implicit in the disguise of Yoshitsune as a baggage carrier: such a man is always the potential victim of beatings. The stage directions call for the lord to take two or three actual steps toward the *kokata*, just as he has been in pursuit of him throughout the previous two episodes. In the following lines, Benkei's improvisation in this scene reaches a climax, and he at last finds an excuse for direct action, with which he has indirectly threatened the lord in both of his long earlier speeches (the last-rite speech and the scroll reading):

> SHITE: . . . Why do you keep such a sharp eye on the pannier? You must be a thief, indeed!

97

Ataka

In truth, the lord has kept a sharp eye out for the box (the surrogate for Yoshitsune), which he wishes to "steal." The followers now enter the stage proper from the bridge to protect their "box." The stylized struggle during the first long chant of the chorus actualizes the previous inner stuggle, while Benkei holds the followers back. The outcome is the same.

WAKI: [*Returns to* waki *seat; utters the next lines simply.*] This is an error, such as is not often made. You may leave directly.

The *waki*'s delivery is low-key since the line is the conclusion to an acting out of what has already been settled on a more intense, inward level. Clearly, as far as the lord is concerned, the episode is closed. His official duty, to which he gave his best (note the previous stage direction—"without giving ground"), has been completed and he feels that he can retire honorably. Otherwise, he would never have used the word "error."

There is a great deal of movement in this scene, in particular the beating of Yoshitsune, that would readily lend itself to "spectacle" treatment. Undoubtedly, it may frequently be staged in this way. However, if in the interest of the pure Nō intent of the play it is considered only as an outward capitulation of the inward drama, the entire scene can be considered, in the dramatic whole, to function as a device for release and completion. The action is not important in and of itself; consequently, the chorus changes, diminishing action to narration. After the scene is run, the playwright is free to proceed, with some assurance of taking his audience with him, to the last appearance of the *waki* in the final scene, in which the "meaning" of the conflict is given.

But before this can be done, an interval is needed, and this is provided in the concluding sections of Part II. If these sections seem long, their length is perhaps a measure of the intensity of the preceding scenes of struggle, since the tone of the final scene is completely different from that of the first. Hence there is a separation between the two parts through a series of modulations, so that the joyful, congratulatory tone of the conclusion may be arrived at naturally. The suggestion of musical terms here may be taken as an admission of critical inadequacy that resorts to the crutch of analogy; however, when we consider how integrated a part of the whole the music is for Nō and how musical these scenes are, the terms may not be wholly inappropriate.

First comes a recapitulation of the previous scene, with Benkei apologizing to Yoshitsune for the beating, so unnatural in the right order of relations between follower and lord. The first modulation is sounded when Yoshitsune answers that since the present is a result of past causes, Benkei's actions are not so self-evidently a violation of heaven's laws.

KOKATA: We see effect that manifests
in the present, people say,
so we understand the past
and the future. . . .

A second modulation, in the long *kuse* section, which is always the most musical, moves with allusions in a minor key to Yoshitsune's heroic past and the glorious victories that he won through many hardships. A third turns to the injustice of his present position, arising from the immutable natural order of cause and effect.

CHORUS:	Can this be man's fate?
KOKATA:	Oh, how true!
	our deepest wishes
	are seldom granted to us
	so goes the fleeting world,
CHORUS:	and this I know,
	still when I think back,
	my thoughts twang like straight, true bows
	for all the straight, true men
	who must suffer
	agonies. . . . [17]

The last tonal modulation protests against unmerited sufferings, but desperation is muted by the line "and this I know" in the above passage. Hence Yoshitsune's explanations about the wretchedness of the world are an expression not of rage or frustration but of sorrow and suffering. Plainly, at this point we have left the fearful intensity of struggle for a more inward, tragic air, which allows for a transition to a concluding scene.

The final section begins with the *waki* again, for he orders his guard to overtake the party. His reasons are touching.

WAKI:	My rude behavior toward those *yamabushi* a while ago does something less than credit to my name. Therefore, I think I'll follow to offer them some *sake*.

Benkei's stern warning to his followers to be on guard against self-betrayal is to be taken at face value, for the *shite* faces stage front to inform not only the followers but also the audience. But his precaution does not preclude his warmly returning the lord's courtesy in the camaraderie of song and dance: he refers to the "chrysanthemum wine" that they drink together—wine particularly suited for noble and auspicious occasions. Again, the two men understand each other and know the limits of the area of friendship that their chance confrontation allows them. Neither would do the other the discourtesy of overstepping these limits; hence Benkei would not embarrass the lord by forcing him to remember his duty—and remember it he would—because of some casual, untimely lapse by the followers. With complete deliberation, within the context of light conviviality, the lord in turn toasts Benkei, expressing his esteem indirectly through the subtle compliment of asking for the well-known, auspicious song and congratulatory Ennen dance created around it:

> the booming of the waterfall;
> though the sun burns brightly
> still the booming sounds below. . . .

The import of the verse is the happy hope that good fortune may continue as abundantly and eternally as the booming waterfall. In Benkei's acceding to the lord's request, we understand that the compliment is returned, although Benkei, too, maintains the framework of inconsequential gaiety: "I am drunk with *sake*. Now allow me to serve you more."

In the disciplined delicacy and manly refinement of this final delineation of the relationship between the two men lies the "meaning" of the confrontation. In a

99

Ataka

word, it is also the basic configuration of this play: the profoundly moving beauty of a relationship between two honorable warriors, who savor a moment together:

> in this
> mountain shade that serves
> as their makeshift lodging . . .

Following as it does the recitation of Yoshitsune's tragic life, this beauty is also tinged with feelings of sorrow and regret; the play ends on a note of tempered joy that is an austere catharsis. There is no need for this Nō to submit to the "debility of the audience."

The examination of the play has raised several questions that may now be considered. First, it has been maintained that to assume a hidden sympathy for Yoshitsune in the barrier commander would vulgarize the Nō concept of the play. Yet the friendly camaraderie of the concluding section seems to present an insurmountable problem. The difficulty may be solved in a roundabout fashion by pointing out the harm done to the structure of the play by such vulgarization. For in this case the concluding section would add nothing to the play except to provide in a most inept way an occasion for the final dance of the *shite*. This unsatisfying rationale for the final section is difficult to reconcile with the author's acknowledged mastery of the Nō form. Kojirō is no amateur.

The beautifully tight construction of the play is testimony. We have already cited the reasonable explanation for the baggage carrier's knowledge that the executed *yamabushi* were running away; the importance of this detail in establishing the character of the *waki* is clear. The meaningful parallelism between the *shidai-jidori* and the carrier's view of the enemy camp and his song is clear in the text. The enchanting adroitness of the *jidori* in sounding the tonality of the play, both in its tragic echoes and in its moment of gay respite at the conclusion, is masterly. The first *ageuta* of the play starts with the phrase "the second month," which is then repeated twice more; in the *kuse* we are reminded that two of Yoshitsune's most brilliant victories fell in the second month of other years. And after the escape through the barrier, the second month is again mentioned as the time of these "dread dangers." These instances of the evident care with which Kojirō, mindful of his craft, wrote this play must demand from his audience the same careful attention to the clues he provides concerning the controlling *gestalt* of the work.

A more direct answer to the question of the commander's attitude may lie in maintaining that the lord of Togashi is supposed to be so iron-willed that he suppresses entirely his personal inclinations while acting in his official capacity. Hence he will be relentless in the pursuit of his duty, but once he has quit that role he feels free to indulge his private preferences. This may be a possible interpretation and may serve in the absence of a more convincing solution.

Still, however convenient it may be, it seems to miss the mark. For the target is the Nō of the play, and when we aim at this target it becomes clear that the entire question is irrelevant to Nō. When it is raised, we are applying to Nō concepts derived from the more realistic Western theater, in which character study and motivation must be clearly consistent and full, since the total dramatic meaning depends largely upon these elements. So essential do they seem that a theater based on other premises appears unimaginable. However, it is also clear that the realistic and naturalistic emphases in theater—as in the novel—have been exploited to their farthest limits, a realization that may account for the theater in the round or the more singular experiments of the theater of the absurd, the experiential theater, or "happenings." At this time, therefore, when other dramatic strategies are being sought, the premises and techniques of Nō may be both instructive and stimulating, for they are minutely calculated to a most definite and aesthetic end, as amply shown, for example, by Zeami's prose work on the theater arts.

This aesthetic end is the creation of the quality of an experience, with a greater emphasis on quality. Needless to say, the elements of music, dance, and poetry are not mere accessories to the text of the play. All elements are equally important and integrated in Nō as they are in no other form of dramatic presentation current in the West. Whatever the action directly presented on the stage—a fight, a madwoman's search for her child, a vengeful spirit beating her rival—it is never important in and of itself; the play must convey the quality of each action or what an experience of it would be like.

It is from this basic dramatic intent that the nonrealism of Nō rises: the exaggerated delivery, the slow walk, the gorgeous costumes of village women, the use of the mask, the third-person references a character makes to himself,[18] the preponderance of narrative over action, and so on. It also gives rise to some of the delightful paradoxes that Zeami postulates: a second-rate voice is to be preferred to a first-rate one; dance patterns that suggest actual realism are poor, although *monomane* (literally, "imitation of things") is basic to the art; the interlude-*kyōgen* role can be entrusted only to a very accomplished actor, and so on. In this particular play the presentation of the beauty of the testing of manhood is the intent of the dramatist. Hence whatever does not contribute to that intent—for example, the determination of the *waki*'s feelings toward Yoshitsune—is not relevant. Perhaps this point is difficult for a modern audience to accept in this play because the kabuki version is so insistently present, somewhat like an obtrusive jingle. It may be easier to consider the example of a play like *Yuya*.[19] When we read or view this play, the question of whether Yuya is in love with Munemori, whether there is a conflict between her desire to return to her ailing mother and her urge to remain with her lover, indeed the question as to the nature of her emotional relationship with him, does not rise in any important way, although her actual relationship as a *shirabyōshi*[20] subtly enhances the situation. It does not occur to us to ask such questions because we are totally involved in the quality of her sorrow, and released and enlightened by her joy. It may also be noted as a corollary that the spectator is never intended to enjoy his tears when a sorrowful experience is represented in Nō, for enlightenment is beyond tears. Indeed, if the Nō actor elicits nothing more than such a response, he does not know his business. Or else he is not performing Nō, although he may be forgiven if we discover to our surprise that our cheeks are wet when we waken from the Nō world as the *shite* stamps before exiting.[21] Nor does this mean that Nō is an impossibly attenuated art: its close allies, dance, music, and sculpture, are also forms that do not customarily call for a directly simple response.

If it is granted that the nonrealism of Nō is hardly indicative of a primitive theater not yet fully developed, one that is merely a patchwork of borrowed phrases and tired formulas, full of self-contradictions such as poetic peasants and unrealistic diction—common disparagements among critics both Western and Japanese—then the exploitation of well-known subjects in this theater is explainable. It does not indicate a poverty of imagination on the part of the playwright. For again, the play is not the unfolding of a plot. It is intended not to tell a story but to tell what the story is telling—that is, the nature of the experience that the story conveys. The use of well-known materials or characters relieves, in a sense, the playwright of the necessity of developing a story line, or a character, or a system of motivations, freeing him to exploit the material for its other values. Hence tension, suspense, and meaning can come from sources other than curiosity or apprehension as to the outcome of events.

These observations can now be concluded by a remark that may seem to be a peculiarly faint-hearted hedging of bets. For having maintained that this Nō must not be vulgarized or sentimentalized, I must note that the text itself is so elastic as to adapt readily to such deplorable emphases. It does not preclude other types of interpretation beside the one urged here, or readings other than those suggested, provided that these do not violate the careful unity and depth which Kojirō has breathed into this play. While it is generally recognized that the *waki* role in fourth-group plays is fuller than that in other plays, the actual speeches of the *waki* in *Ataka* are extremely short and few. The temptation, then, is for the actor playing the *waki* to add entertaining gestures, in order to compensate for the terseness of the speeches. While this point cannot be expanded here, Zeami's remark that an actor must adapt his style to his particular audience seems pertinent.[22] One may suppose that in the days when Nō troupes performed in both town and country, a less austere style was adopted for a less experienced audience, which preferred to enjoy the spectacle so possible in this delightful play.

Masterworks of the Nō Theater

ATAKA

By Kanze Kojirō Nobumitsu

Persons: WAKI: *Official of Togashi*
KYŌGEN: *Sword-bearer*
KOKATA: *The Hōgan, Minamoto no Yoshitsune*
SHITE: *Musashibō Benkei*
TSURE (TACHISHŪ): *Nine followers of the Hōgan*
KYŌGEN: *Gōriki (Baggage carrier)*

Classification: *Primary, Group IV; Variant, Group II or III*
Place: *Ataka, in the land of Kaga*
Time: *February*
Kogaki: *6*

Jo no Dan[23]

[*Following introductory flute music called* nanoribue,[24] *the* waki, *an official of Togashi, followed by the* kyōgen, *his sword-bearer, appears as the rich brocade curtain dividing the mirror room from the bridge is swept back. The* waki *wears a tall black cap and a white headband, tied at the back of the head and across his forehead. He is dressed in a heavy silk kimono of thick fabric with warp of polished silk threads and woof of unpolished silk, a lined over-robe, and a trailing divided skirt worn over broad divided underskirts. He also wears a short sword and carries a fan. The* kyōgen *wears a silk kimono, a* kyōgen *suit bound with a waistband, into which a short sword and fan are tucked. He carries the long sword of his lord. Both proceed along the bridge to the stage. The* waki *stands near the* shite *pillar, facing stage front, while the* kyōgen *kneels behind him.*]

WAKI

[1] *(Nanori: awazu, kotoba)*

Kayō ni sōrō mono wa Kaga no Kuni Togashi[25] no nanigashi nite sōrō. Sate mo Yoritomo Yoshitsune[26] on-naka fuwa ni narasetamō ni yori Hōgan-dono[27] jūninin no tsukuriyamabushi to natte Oku[28] e on-gekō no yoshi, Yoritomo kikoshimeshioyobare, kuniguni ni shinseki o tatete, yamabushi[29] o kataku eramimōse to no on-koto nite sōrō. Saru aida kono tokoro oba soregashi uketamawatte yamabushi o todomemōshi sōrō. Konnichi

I am an official of Togashi, in the land of Kaga. Since the discord has developed between Yoritomo and Yoshitsune, Yoritomo has heard that the Hōgan, with his retainers in a band of twelve, disguised as *yamabushi*, has started on his way to Oku. Therefore Yoritomo has erected new barriers in each land, giving orders to subject all *yamabushi* to a strict examination. The charge of this barrier has been given over to me, with

103

mo kataku mōshitsukebaya to zonji sōrō.

orders to stop them. Today again I must enforce the order. [*Advances to center stage and faces toward the* kyōgen.]

WAKI

Ikani tareka aru.

Is anyone about?

[*The* kyōgen *comes out in front of the* shite *pillar and kneels down.*]

KYŌGEN

On-mae ni sōrō.

At your service, my lord.

WAKI [*From center stage, looks at the* kyōgen.]

Kyō mo yamabushi no on-tōri araba konata e mōshi sōrae.

If any *yamabushi* pass through this place again today, let it be reported to me.

KYŌGEN

Kashikomatte sōrō.

Yes, my lord.

[*The* waki *goes to the* waki *seat and sits on the stool. The* kyōgen *comes out to the name-saying seat.*]

Minamina uketamawari sōrae. Hōgan-dono jūni-nin no tsukuriyamabusi to nari Oku e on-kudari nite sōrō aida kyō mo mata yamabushitachi no on-tōri a-raba konata e mōshi sōrae. Sono bun kororoe sōrae, kokoroe sōrae.

Now listen to me, all of you. Since the Hōgan, with his retainers in a band of twelve, disguised as *yamabushi*, is said to have started on his way to Oku, should any *yamabushi* pass through this place again today, report it to me. Remember this, remember this well.

[*The* kyōgen *crosses over to the flute pillar and sits down.*]

Ha First Dan

[*With entrance music called* shidai, *the* kokata, *Lord Yoshitsune, followed by the* gōriki, *a baggage carrier; the* shite, *Benkei; and the* tsure, *Yoshitsune's followers, appears as the brocade curtain is swept back. The* kokata *is splendidly dressed, with a headdress called* tokin (*literally, helmet-cloth*), *small and cylindrical in shape, which rests just above the forehead and is tied by a pair of cords under the chin. He wears a heavy silk kimono of thick fabric, the neckline of which is accented with three unattached red collars arranged as if pleated; a wide-sleeved, unlined tunic made of unpolished silk; a brocade stole; a broad white divided Nō skirt with a brocade waistband; and a short sword and fan. He carries a rosary of diamond-shaped beads. The* shite *and* tsure *wear costumes similar to that of the* kokata, *except that their heavy silk kimonos are striped and their collars are light yellow. The* gōriki *wears a small round cap, a heavy silk kimono, a* kyōgen *skirt tied at the knees, and leggings. He carries a box on his back and a staff on his shoulder, with a broad-brimmed mushroom-shaped hat tied to it. They enter the stage and stand in the center in a double row, facing one another as they chant the* shidai[30] *verse.*]

104

[2] *(Shidai: au, tsuyogin)*

Tabi no koromo wa [31]	Though our traveling robes are made
suzukake no,	of the hemp monks use,
tabi no koromo wa	though our traveling robes are made
suzukake no	of the hemp monks use,
tsuyukeki sode ya	drenched with dew from bamboo sprays,
shioruran.	will our sleeves turn limp?

[Instead of the jidori usually sung by the chorus, the gōriki sings the following verse.]

GŌRIKI

(Au, tsuyogin)

Ore ga koromo wa [32]	These outfits of mine are made
suzukake no	of the hemp monks use,
yaburete koto ya	but torn by bamboo branches,
kakinuran.	they do me no good.

[The shite and the tsure sing the following passage together, called sashi,[33] as they face one another.]

SHITE AND TSURE

(Sashi: awazu, tsuyogin)

Kōmon [34] tate yabure	Not at Hung-men but at Miyako
Miyako no hoka no	shields are broken, so we flee,
tabigoromo, [35]	dressed in traveling clothes;
hi mo harubaru [36] no	for endless days we journey
Koshiji [37] no sue	crossing Koshi toward
omoiyaru koso	our destination lying
haruka nare.	distant in our thoughts.

[The shite looks at the tsure standing in array.]

SHITE

Sate on-tomo no	Here we are, among all those
hitobito wa	accompanying our lord;

TSURE

Ise no Saburō [38]	Ise no Saburō,
Suruga no Jirō [39]	Suruga no Jirō,
Kataoka [40] Mashio [41]	Kataoka, Mashio,
Hitachibō [42]	Hitachibō,

[The shite faces front and sings.]

SHITE

Benkei wa	and Benkei,
sendatsu no	disguised, is with us,
sugata to narite	as the chief among the monks.

[*The* shite *and the* tsure *face one another, and the* tsure *sing the following verse.*]

TSURE

Shujū ijō	Both the lord, the vassals,
jūninin	two and ten in all,
imada narawanu	are in holy traveling cloaks
tabisugata	not accustomed yet;
sode no suzukake	brushing dews and frost away
tsuyu shimo o	with our hempen sleeves
kyō wake somete	we set forth this very day,
itsu made no	though until what day
kagiri mo isa ya	it will take no one can know,
shirayuki no[43]	now across the snow
Koshiji no haru ni	on the way to Koshi spring
isogu nari.	here we hasten on.

[*The* shite *and the* tsure, *facing one another, sing together the following passage, called* ageuta.][44]

SHITE AND TSURE

(*Ageuta: au, tsuyogin*)

Toki shimo koro wa	It was then about the time
Kisaragi[45] no,	of the second month,
toki shimo koro wa	it was then about the time
Kisaragi no,	of the second month,
Kisaragi no,	of the second month
tōka no yo	in the dark tenth night,
tsuki no Miyako o	from the moon-bright capital
tachiidete,	we go on our way.
kore ya kono[46]	Here it is, indeed,
yuki mo kaeru mo	where all those who come and go
wakarete wa,	meet and part again
yuku mo kaeru mo	where all those who come and go
wakarete wa	meet and part again,
shiru mo shiranu mo	both friends and utter strangers . . .
ōsaka no	in brief encounters
yama kakusu[47]	on Big Hill now hid,
kasumi zo haru wa	how the trailing mist of spring
urameshiki.	lingers willfully.

[*The* shite *and the* tsure, *still facing one another, continue to sing the following verse passage, called* sageuta.][48]

(Sageuta: au, tsuyogin)

Namiji haruka ni	On the way of waves, far off,
yuku fune no,	out we sail our boat,
namiji haruka ni	on the way of waves, far off,
yuku fune no	out we sail our boat,
Kaizu[49] no Ura ni	toward the Bay of Kaizu
tsukinikeri.	which we now have reached.
Shinonome hayaku	As dawn grows purple early
akeyukeba	we go on our way
asaji irozuku	where the sedge is faintly red,
Arachiyama.[50]	by Mt. Arachi,

[*The* shite *and* tsure *sing the following* ageuta *passage.*]

(Ageuta: au, tsuyogin)

Kei no Umi[51]	past the Kei Bay,
miyai hisashiki	its shrine that stood for ages
kamigaki ya	with the sacred hedge,
matsu no	and ahead
Kinomeyama[52]	pine-groved Tree Bud Pass,

[*The* shite *faces stage front.*]

nao yuku saki ni	then before us comes in view
mietaru wa	Forest Hill beyond
Somayamabito[53] no	woodsmen's Timber Haul,
Itadori[54]	a village-town,

[*The* shite *turns his face slightly to his right.*]

kawase no mizu no	and now the shallow rapids
Asōzu[55] ya	at Ramie Ferry

[*The* shite *goes out toward the eye-fixing pillar.*]

sue wa Mikuni no	flowing down to Tristate Port
Minato[56] naru	where the river ends,

[*The* shite *looks toward the right as if into the distance.*]

ashi no Shinowara[57]	by the reed-hemmed Bamboo Fields
nami yosete	the tide comes surging

[*The* shite *returns to center stage.*]

nabiku	wave on wave,
arashi no[58]	with stormy winds
hageshiki wa	fatal to the flowers

[*Takes the original position at stage front in a row with the followers, facing stage front.*]

hana no Ataka[59] ni	at blossoming Ataka,
tsukinikeri,	we have now arrived,

107

Ataka

hana no Ataka ni   at blossoming Ataka
tsukinikeri.   we have now arrived.

[*The* waki *and the* kyōgen, *who sat at the* waki *seat, move to the railing by the chorus and sit down, while the* shite, *facing stage front, intones the following prose passage, called* tsukizerifu.]

SHITE

(*Tsukizerifu: awazu, kotoba*)

On-nisogi sōrō hodo ni kore wa haya Ataka no Minato ni on-tsuki nite sōrō. Shibaraku kono tokoro ni onnyasumi arōzuru nite sōrō.

Since we traveled in haste, we have already reached the port of Ataka. [*The* shite *faces the* kokata.] Please rest for a while at this place.

Ha Second Dan

[*The* shite *moves far back to the stage attendant's seat. The* kokata *goes to the* waki *seat and sits on the stool supplied by a stage attendant, while the* gōriki *goes back to the* kyōgen *seat and sits down. After they have taken their positions, the* shite *starts to come out toward center stage. Before this, Togashi and the followers had changed their seats to the side of the chorus, making the stage appear unoccupied.*]

KOKATA

[3] (*Mondai: awazu, kotoba*)

Ikani Benkei.   Ho, Benkei.

[*Kneeling, the* shite *puts both hands on the floor and bows. The following prose passages are exchanged between the* shite, kokata, *and* tsure.]

SHITE

On-mae ni sōrō.   At your service, my lord.

KOKATA

Tadaima tabibito no mōshite tōritsuru koto o kiite aru ka.

Just now some travelers passed by, talking to each other. Did you hear what they were saying?

SHITE

Iya nani to mo uketamawarazu sōrō.   No, my lord. I have not heard anything.

108

KOKATA

Ataka no Minato ni shinseki o tatete yamabushi o kataku eramu to koso mōshitsure.

A new barrier has been erected at the port of Ataka, they say, and all *yamabushi* are to be subjected to a strict inspection.

Gongo dōdan no on-koto nite sōrō mono kana. Sate wa on-gekō o zonjite tatetaru seki to zonji sōrō. Kore wa yuyushiki on-daiji nite sōrō. Mazu kono katawara nite shibaraku go-dankō arōzuru nite sōrō. Kore wa ichidaiji no on-koto nite sōrō aida, minamina shinjū no tōri go-iken on-mōshi arōzuru nite sōrō.

What a shocking and monstrous thing this is, I must say. Well, I think that having learned of your lordship's journey this way, they must have set up the barrier. This is, indeed, a grave matter. First of all, let us draw aside and discuss this for a while. [*Looks at the followers.*] Since this is most important, please, all of you, speak truly what is in your heart.

Warera ga shinjū ni wa nani hodo no koto no sōrōbeki. Tada uchiyabutte on-tōri arekashi to zonji sōrō.

In our hearts what fear should there be? We have only to crash through the barrier and pass on.

Shibaraku. Ōse no gotoku kono seki issho uchiyabutte on-tōri arōzuru wa yasuki koto nite sōraedomo onnide sōrawanzuru yuku sue ga on-daiji nite sōrō. Tada nani tomo shite bui no gi ga shikarubekarōzuru to zonji sōrō.

Hold on a moment. As you say, it is easy to crash through this barrier. The matter of serious concern pertains to the future journey. I think it is best to go through here somehow without causing any trouble.

[*Turning toward the* kokata, *he puts both hands on the floor and looks at him for a decision.*]

Tomokaku mo Benkei hakarai sōrae.

In any event, Benkei, I leave the matter up to you.

Kashikomatte sōrō. Soregashi kitto anji idashitaru koto no sōrō. Warera o hajimete minamina nikkui yamabushi nite sōrō ga, nani to mōshite mo on-sugata kakure gozanaku sōrō aida kono mama nite wa ikaga to zonji sōrō. Osore ōki mōshigoto nite sōraedomo on-suzukake o nokerare ano gōriki ga oitaru oi o soto on-kata ni okare, on-kasa o fukafuka to mesare ikani mo kutabiretaru on-tei nite warera yori ato ni hikisagatte on-tōri sōrawaba nakanaka hito wa omoi mo yori mōsumajiki to zonji sōrō.

Yes, my lord. [*Faces stage front.*] Here is a plan that has come to me by chance. [*Looks at the followers.*] To start with, all of us, we can pass as the outlandish *yamabushi*. [*Faces the* kokata.] However, nothing can disguise the noble features of our lord. I fear for your appearance as you are now. [*Puts his hands on the floor.*] With all respect, may I suggest that you remove the hempen cloak, put on your back the pannier the baggage carrier bears, and, pulling his hat well over your eyes, you should drag behind us as if your fatigue were great. Then, I am sure, no one will suspect who you are.

109

Ataka

Geni kore wa mottomo nite sōrō. Saraba suzukake o tori sōrae.

How excellent a plan this is! So you may take my hempen cloak off from me.

SHITE

Kashikomatte sōrō. Ika ni gōriki.

Yes, my lord. [*To the* gōriki.] Baggage carrier.

[*The* gōriki *comes out in front of the* shite.]

GŌRIKI

On-mae ni sōrō.

Here I am, sir.

SHITE

Oi o mochite kitari sōrae.

Bring your pannier over here.

GŌRIKI

Kashikomatte sōrō.

Yes, sir.

[*The* gōriki *goes to the* kyōgen *seat and brings the box. The* shite *puts it on the* kokata. *Then he faces the* gōriki.]

SHITE

Nanji ga oi o on-kata ni okaruru koto wa nanbō myōga mo naki koto nite wa naki ka.

What a lucky fellow you are! Our noble lord will carry your pannier for you on his back.

GŌRIKI

Geni geni myōga mo naki koto nite sōrō.

Indeed! Indeed! This is more than I deserve.

SHITE

Mazu nanji wa saki e yuki seki no yōdai o mite, makoto ni yamabushi o eramu ka mata sayō ni mo naki ka nengoro ni mite kitari sōrae.

First of all, you go ahead of us and observe how things are at the barrier. Find out whether it is true or not that all *yamabushi* are put to a strict examination.

GŌRIKI

Kashikomatte sōrō.

Yes, sir.

[*The* gōriki *goes out to the name-saying pillar.*]

Sate mo sate mo ichidaiji naru koto o ōsetsukerarete sōrō. Isoide seki no yōdai o mite mairō. Mitogamerarete wa narumai. Tokin o totte mairō.

Well, well! What a terrible thing I am ordered to do! I will go quickly and see how things are at the barrier. I must not be suspected. I'll take off my small round cap and go.

[Taking the cap off his head, he slips it into his bosom and goes to the bridge, where he looks stage front, as if far into the distance.]

Sate mo sate mo obitadashii koto kana. Yagura kaitate o age sakamogi o hiki, tori mo kayowanu tei nite sōrō. Mata ano ki no shita ni kuroi mono ga futatsu mitsu miyuru. Are wa nan ja. Yamabushi no koko ja to iu ka. Ara itawashi ya. Isshu tsuranete mairō.

Well, well! What a monstrous plan this is! There's a watchtower set up with a shield-fence all around it, and a barricade bounded with thorny branches pointing outward so that even a bird could not get through. I see two or three dark things under that tree over there. I wonder what they are? *[Points his left hand at his head.]* They are this part of some *yamabushi*, are they? Poor fellows! I'll string some verses together for them before I leave.

Yamabushi wa
kai fuite koso
nigenikere,
tare oikakete
abiraunken.[60]

Those *yamabushi*
blew their trumpet-shells—Oh! Oh!—
while they ran away!
Is there someone after me?
Great Buddha, save me, save me!

Isoide kono yoshi mōsō.

I'll go back quickly and report this.

[The gōriki *comes out in front of the* shite.]*

Ikani mōshiage sōrō. Seki no yōdai o mimōshite sōraeba, yagura kaitate o age sakamogi o hiki, tori mo kayowanu tei nite sōrō. Mata ki no shita ni kuroi mono ga futatsu mitsu gozaaru aida, nani zo to tazune sōraeba,[61] yamabushi no koko ja to mōsu ni yotte itawashū zonji isshu tsuranete sōrō.

May I report to you, sir? As I looked to see how things are at the barrier, I found that they have set up a watchtower, built a shield-fence and barricades bounded with thorny branches sticking outward so that even a bird could not get through. Since there were two or three blackened things under the tree, I asked what they were *[points his hands at his head]*; they said they were this part of some *yamabushi*. I felt sorry for them and strung some verses together for them.

SHITE

Sore wa nani to tsuranete aru zo.

Well, now! What did you string together then?

GŌRIKI

Yamabushi wa
kai fuite koso
nigenikere,
tare oikakete
abiraunken

Those *yamabushi*
blew their trumpet-shells—Oh! Oh!—
while they ran away!
Is there someone after me?
Great Buddha, save me, save me.

abiraunken to tsuranete sōrō.

Great Buddha, save me, save me, this I strung, sir.

111

Ataka

SHITE

Nanji wa kozakashiki mono nite sōrō.	What a clever fellow you are, indeed!
Yagate onnato yori kitari sōrae.	Now come along and follow us.

GŌRIKI

Kashikomatte sōrō.	Yes, sir.

[*The* gōriki *returns to the* kyōgen *seat. The* shite *bows his head toward the* kokata.]

SHITE [Intones the following.]

Saraba on-tachi arōzuru nite sōrō.	Well, we can take up our journey, my lord.

[*All of them rise. The* shite *looks at the* kokata *and the following verse exchange is sung between the* shite, tsure, *and* kokata, *called* kakeai.]

[4] (*Kakeai: awazu, tsuyogin*)

Geni ya kurenai wa [62]	How true that even one safflower
sonoo ni uete mo	planted midst the garden blossoms
kakurenashi.	cannot be hidden!

TSURE

Gōriki ni wa	On a baggage carrier
yomo me o kakeji to	no one will cast suspicious eyes.
on-suzukake o	Let us exchange the cloak
nugikaete	made of hempen cloth
asa no koromo o	for the one of coarser weave
on-mi ni matoi	to disguise our noble lord;

SHITE

ano gōriki ga	then the pannier borne this far
oitaru oi o	by the baggage carrier

KOKATA

Yoshitsune totte	Yoshitsune fastens fast
kata ni kake	across his shoulder;

TSURE

oi no ue ni wa	above it both the rain gear
amagawa katabako	and the little shoulder boxes
toritsukete	are tightly fastened.

KOKATA

ayasugegasa nite	Within the hat of woven sedge
kao o kakushi	I wholly hide my face

112

TSURE

| kongōzue[63] ni sugari | leaning on the diamond staff heavily |

KOKATA [*In* yowagin *style.*]

| ashi itage naru gōriki nite | as if he were sore and lame, he looks the very part |

[*The* kokata *takes two or three forward steps as the chorus sings the following verse passage.*]

CHORUS

(*Awazu, yowagin*)

| yoroyoro to shite ayumi tamō | of a baggage carrier! Tottering on his feet, |

[*All "cloud" their faces.*]

| onnarisama zo itawashiki. | his pitiful appearance is deeply touching. |

SHITE [*Facing the* kokata, *he intones the following.*]

(*Awazu, kotoba*)

| Warera yori ato ni hikisagatte onnide arōzuru nite sōrō. Saraba minamina on-tōri sōrae. | My lord, please stay behind and follow us at some distance. [*To the others.*] Well then, all of you! Comrades, let us go. |

TSURE

| Uketamawari sōrō. | Yes, let us go. |

Ha Third Dan

[*Led by the* shite, *all the followers go up the bridge in a line. The* kokata *follows them, but at the stage attendant's seat he sits down. The* waki, *followed by the* kyōgen, *stands up behind the musicians at stage rear and comes out to sit at the* waki *seat, while the* kyōgen *sits in front of the chorus. Looking at the* shite *and the followers coming back to the stage from the bridge, the* kyōgen *stands up. The* shite, waki, *and* kyōgen *exchange the following prose passages, called* mondai.]

KYŌGEN

[5] (*Mondai: awazu, kotoba*)

| Ika ni mōshi sōrō. Yamabushitachi no ōzei on-tōri sōrō. | Please be informed, my lord. A large band of *yamabushi* is coming. |

WAKI

| Nani to yamabushi no on-tōri aru to mōsu ka. Kokoroete are. | What? You say a large band of *yamabushi* is coming? Very well. |

Ataka

[*The* waki *stands, and as the* shite *and followers are about to enter the stage, he addresses them.*]

Nō nō kyakusōtachi kore wa seki nite sōrō.

Ho, there, holy monks! This is a barrier.

[*The* shite *stops at the* shite *seat, calmly, facing the* waki.]

SHITE

Uketamawari sōrō. Kore wa Nanto Tō-daiji[64] konryū no tame ni kuniguni e kyakusō o tsukawasare sōrō. Hokuri-kudō[65] oba kono kyakusō uketamawatte makari tōri sōrō. Mazu susume ni onniri sōrae.

Yes, so we see. We monks have been sent throughout the land to raise funds for the reconstruction of the great To-daiji Temple at the southern capital. We travel this way as we are responsible for the provinces along the Northland Route. Would you kindly join in making a contribution?

WAKI

Chikagoro shushō ni sōrō. Susume ni wa mairōzuru nite sōrō, sarinagara kore wa yamabushitachi ni kagitte tomemōsu seki nite sōrō.

It is an admirable cause, such as we don't hear about these days. At your invitation, I will contribute. However, this is a barrier set up to stop only you *yamabushi*.

SHITE

Sate sono iware wa zōrō.

Well, what is the reason for this?

WAKI [*In a dignified tone.*]

San zōrō. Yoritomo Yoshitsune on-naka fuwa ni narasetamō ni yori Hōgan-dono wa Oku Hidehira o tanomitamai, jūni-nin no tsukuri-yamabushi to natte on-gekō no yoshi sono kikoe sōrō aida, ku-niguni ni shin-seki o tatete yamabushi o kataku erami-mōse to no on-koto nite sōrō. Saru aida kono tokoro oba sore-gashi uketamawatte yamabushi o tome-mōshi sōrō. Koto ni kore wa ōzei goza sōrō aida, ichinin mo tōshi mōsuma-jiku sōrō.

This is the reason. Since open discord has broken out between Lord Yoritomo and Yoshitsune, the Hōgan looks to Hi-dehira, Lord of Mutsu, for protection. Disguised as *yamabushi*, in a noble com-pany of twelve, he and his followers are traveling this way, so rumor has it. Therefore Yoritomo has ordered that new barriers be erected in every prov-ince to subject all the passing *yamabushi* to a strict examination. Being in charge of this place, I am stopping all of them. Since this reverend group is unusually large, I cannot let a single one of you pass.

SHITE

Isai uketamawari sōrō. Sore wa tsukuri-yamabushi o koso tomeyo to ōseidasare sōraitsurame. Yomo makoto no yama-bushi o tome yo to wa ōserare sōrōmaji.

I understand your reasons very well. I presume the order was to stop false *ya-mabushi*, but surely, you are not ordered to stop real monks.

Masterworks of the Nō Theater

[*The* kyōgen, *the sword-bearer, comes out in front of the* shite.]

KYŌGEN

Yō no ka wa oshatsu zo. Kinō mo san-nin kitte kaketesu.

Don't gibber and grumble so much. Yesterday we beheaded three of them and put their heads on show.

SHITE [*Looks at the* kyōgen *sharply.*]

Sate sono kittaru yamabushi wa Hōgan-dono ka.

Well, was the Hōgan among the *yamabushi* you beheaded?

WAKI

Ara mutsukashi ya. Mondō wa mu-yaku. Ichinin mo tōshi mōsumajii ue wa zōrō.

Why, this is too much. Your questions do you no good. Not a single soul shall pass as long as my order stands.

SHITE

Sate wa warera o mo kore nite chūserare sōrawanzuru na.

What! [*Stares at the* waki.] Does that mean you plan to kill us here, too?

WAKI

Nakanaka no koto.

Yes, that is right.

SHITE [*Facing stage front.*]

Gongo dōdan. Kakaru fushō naru to-koro e kikakatte sōrō mono kana. Kono ue wa chikara oyobanu koto, saraba saigo no tsutome o hajimete jinjō ni chūseraryōzuru nite sōrō. Minamina chikō watari sōrae.

How shocking! How could we have come to such an ill-fated place, I wonder. When things have come to this, we are powerless. So let us begin our last rites [*looks at the* waki] and accept death squarely. All of you, comrades, come closer.

TSURE (FIRST)

Uketamawari sōrō.

Yes, we understand.

[*The* shite *and the* tsure *put their fans to their bosoms. They tuck up their sleeves at the shoulder and enter the stage to the musical accompaniment,* notto.[66] *The* shite *advances to stage front and center as the followers arrange themselves in two wedge-shaped rows behind him; all sit down cross-legged. The* shite *and the* tsure *have the following verse exchange, called* kakeai.]

115

SHITE

(*Kakeai: awazu, tsuyogin*)

Ide ide saigo no
tsutome o hajimen.

Here, comrades, let us now begin
our last and final offices.

Ataka

Sore yamabushi to ippa	Those who are the mountain monks receive
En no Mubasoku[67] no gyōgi o uke	En no Mubasoku's ways through the rites he practiced.

TSURE

Sono mi wa	In their persons
Fudō Myōō[68] no	they symbolize the dread divine
sonnyō o katadori	as the figure of the god of fire;

SHITE

tokin to ippa	and our helmet-caps are crowns
goji[69] no hōkan nari	bejeweled brightly with his five wisdoms,

TSURE

jūni innen[70] no hida o	creased upon the top, the folds we wear reveal
suete itadaki	the twelve karmic sources;

SHITE

kue mandara[71] no	in persimmon-brown the cloak
kaki no suzukake	is the ninefold Mandala.

TSURE

taizō[72] kokushiki no	We wear the jet-black leggings showing
habaki o haki	the all-embracing Womb.

SHITE

sate mata yatsume no	And again the rice-straw sandals
waranzu wa	with the eight eyelets

TSURE

hachiyō no renge[73] o	that tread upon the eight bright-petaled
fumaetari	lotus flower in bloom.

116

SHITE

ideiru iki ni	Breathing out and breathing in
aun no niji o tonae[74]	"Ah-om," twin holy syllables, we chant,

TSURE

sokushin sokubutsu no	"Each body of a *yamabushi*
yamabushi o	a living Buddha!"

Shite

koko nite uchitome
tamawan koto

At this place whoever now
beheads him can't escape

Tsure

myō no shōran
hakarigatō

the witness of Amida
hid deep from human ken,

Shite

Yuya Gongen[75] no
go-batsu o ataran koto

and the dreadful punishment
of almighty Yuya Gongen

Tsure

tachidokoro ni oite

instantly shall fall upon this spot.

Shite

utagai arubekarazu.

Let there be no doubt of this among
you!

Chorus

(Au, tsuyogin)

Onnabira
unken to
juzu sarasara to
oshimomeba

Oh! Earth, Water, Fire,
Wind, and Air! They chant
rubbing hard the rosaries
raucously aloud.

[*The* shite *makes magical signs with his fingers while the followers rub their hands together vigorously, with their rosaries between their palms, making a loud clacking sound.*]

Ha Fourth Dan

Waki [*In a polite tone, the* waki *intones.*]

[6] *(Mondai: awazu, kotoba)*

Chikagoro shushō ni sōrō. Saki ni uketamawari sōraitsuru wa Nanto Tōdaiji no kanjin to ōse sōrō aida sadamete kanjinchō no goza naki koto wa sōrōmaji. Kanjinchō o asobasare sōrae. Kore nite chūmon mōsōzuru nite sōrō.

This is an admirable teaching, such as we don't hear these days. As I heard you say a while ago that you are raising funds for the rebuilding of the great Tōdaiji Temple at the southern capital, doubtless you must have the subscription book with you. It would be kind of you to read aloud the message from it. Here I may be privileged to hear it.

117

Ataka

Nan to kanjinchō o yome to sōrō ya.

What? [*The* shite *seems to pause before standing.*] Do you mean to say that I am to read from the subscription book?

WAKI

Nakanaka no koto.

Yes, if you please.

SHITE

Kokoroe mōshite sōrō.

Very well.

[*The* shite *goes to the stage attendant's seat and receives from him a scroll; he speaks, as if to himself, as he returns to stage front.*]

Moto yori kanjinchō no araba koso, oi no naka yori ōrai no makimono ikkan toriidashi kanjinchō to nazuketsutsu

As if there were ever such a subscription book! Taking a scroll from the pannier and calling it the subscription book,

takaraka ni koso
yomiagekere

boldly in a booming voice
he reads the scroll aloud.

[*The* shite *is now at center front; the* tsure, *at* waki *stage front, line up in double rows. The* shite *holds the scroll with both hands and recites the following passage, called* yomimono.]

SHITE

(Yomimono: tsuyogin)

Sore tsuratsura
omon mireba
Daion kyōshu[76] no
aki no tsuki[77] wa
nehan no
kumo ni kakure
shōji jōya no
nagaki yume
odorokasubeki
hito mo nashi.
Koko ni
nakagoro
Mikado
owashimasu
on-na o ba
Shōmu[78]
Kōtei to
nazuke
tatematsuri
saiai no
fujin[79] ni wakare
renbo
yamigataku

As I deeply meditate,
all lost in thought, I see
that as the Giver of the Laws,
like the moon in autumn,
is hidden deep
behind Nirvana-clouds
in this night of life and death
where our dream is long,
no one comes to startle us
and rouse us from it.
Hereupon,
there came to us
a ruler
in the middle age;
graciously his name
was renowned
as the emperor
Shōmu,
honored by all men,
but when he parted
from his beloved consort,
his longing
never seemed to end,

118

teikyū	his flowing tears
manako ni araku	over-brimmed his weeping eyes
nanda tama o	as they fell like strings
tsuranuku	of threaded pearls.
omoi o	Then reflecting
zento ni	he turned his thoughts
hirukaeshite	to the future truly
Rushanabutsu[80] o	to Rushana Buddha he
konryū su.	dedicated it.
Ka hodo no	That such a place
reijō no	so blessed and sacred
taenan koto o	has been reduced to ruins
kanashimite	saddens me; so I,
Shunjōbō	Shunjōbō
Chōgen[81]	Chōgen,
shokoku o	appeal abroad
kanjin su.	for contribution.
Isshi	He who gives
hansen no	one sheet of paper
hōsai no	or half a penny
tomogara wa	from his humble store
kono yo nite wa	shall know a matchless joy
muhi no	and delight
raku ni hokori	within this world of ours;
tōrai nite wa	and in the world hereafter,
susen renge no	on some thousand lotus flowers
ue ni zasen.	he shall sit forever!
Kimyō kesshu	Truly trust Lord Buddha
uyamatte	with deep reverence,
mōsu to	thus I proclaim.

[*Holding the scroll high at arm's length, he reads in a heroic crescendo.*]

ten mo hibike to	Echoes crack the very skies,
yomiagetari.	as loud he reads the scroll.

[*During the recitation, the* waki, *leaning sideways, tries to look at the scroll twice, and each time the* shite *retreats slightly and continues unconcernedly.*]

WAKI [*Faces stage front and sings.*]

(*Au, tsuyogin*)

Seki no hitobito	People's hearts are thunderstruck
kimo o keshi	at the barrier.

119

CHORUS

osore o nashite	Stunned and fearful, full of dread,
tōshikeri,	they allow them to pass.

[*The* shite *rolls up the scroll and faces the* waki.]

Ataka

| osore o nashite tōshikeri. | Stunned and fearful, full of dread, they allow them to pass. |

Ha Fifth Dan

WAKI

(Mondai: awazu, kotoba)

| Isoide on-tōri sōrae. | Quickly, now. You may pass on. |

SHITE

| Uketamawari sōrō. | Yes, we shall. |

KYŌGEN

| Sa sa isoide on-tōriyare. | Come on, come on. Quickly pass along there. |

[*The* shite *moves from center front to the bridge in a right-hand curve, while the* tsure *rise and follow him in single file. He goes up the bridge to the third pine, while the followers array themselves along the bridge behind him. The* kokata *rises at the stage attendant's seat. The* kyōgen *comes out to center stage and, looking at the* shite *seat toward which the* kokata *starts to proceed, he kneels and intones.*]

KYŌGEN

[7] *(Mondai: awazu, tsuyogin)*

| Ikani mōshiage sōrō. Hōgan-dono no o-tōri nite sōrō. | May I inform you, my lord, there comes the Hōgan. |

WAKI

| Kokoroete aru. | I'll keep that in mind. |

[*The* waki *slips his arm out of the sleeve of the outer robe and, holding his sword under his left arm, prepares himself. Meanwhile, the* kokata *leaves the stage attendant's seat and, leaning on his staff, enters the stage; from the* shite *seat, he comes out toward the front.*]

| Ika ni kore naru gōriki tomare to koso. | Ho, there! Halt, baggage carrier. Halt, I say! |

[*The* waki *stands, puts his hand on the hilt of the sword, and glares at the* kokata. *The* kyōgen *also rises. Surprised, the* kokata *steps back to the* shite *seat, half kneels, and, leaning the staff on his right shoulder, lowers his face. At the bridge, the* tsure *turn their faces all together toward the* kokata, *ready to rush forward.*]

TSURE

| Suwa waga kimi o ayashimuru wa ichigo no fuchin kiwamarinu to | Good gracious! Now suspicion falls upon our master. Here our lives depend on it, here we all sink or swim. |

120

[*They put their hands on the hilts of their swords.*]

mina ichidō ni tachikaeru. All together they return to the barrier!

[*From the third pine, the* shite *moves to the first pine and, at the head of the retainers, stops them.*]

SHITE

Ō shibaraku. Awatete koto o shison- Hold back a moment! Don't botch up
zu na. our plans through your hastiness.

[*The* shite *enters the stage, looking at the* kokata.]

Yā nani tote ano gōriki wa tōranu zo. Well, now! You, baggage carrier, why
don't you step along?

WAKI

Are wa konata yori tomete sōrō. I ordered him to stop.

SHITE [*Standing behind the* kokata.]

Sore wa nani tote on-tome sōrō zo. Then, will you tell me why you stopped
him?

WAKI

Ano gōriki ga chito hito ni nitaru to That baggage carrier looks a little like
mōsu mono no sōrō hodo ni sate tomete someone, so my men say. Therefore I
sōrō yo. stopped him.

SHITE

Nani to hito ga hito ni nitaru to wa, me- What! Some man looks like another
zurashikaranu ōse nite sōrō. Sate tare ni man, you say? This is nothing unusual.
nite sōrō zo. Well, whom does this baggage carrier
look like?

WAKI [*Without giving ground.*]

Hōgan-dono ni nitaru to mōsu mono He looks like Lord Hōgan, so my men
no sōrō hodo ni, rakkyo no aida todo- say. Therefore, until this is settled, I'll
mete sōrō. detain him.

SHITE

Ya, gongo dōdan. Hōgan-dono ni Well, I'm surprised. [*Looks at the* kokata.]
nimōshitaru gōriki-me wa ichigo no To look like Lord Hōgan will be the
omoide na. Haratachi ya hi takaku wa memory of a lifetime for this stupid fel-
Noto no Kuni made sasōzuru to omoi- low! How angry I am. While the sun
tsuru ni wazuka no oi ōte ato ni sagareba was still high, I thought we could
koso hito mo ayashimure. Sōjite kono stretch our legs and get on to Noto. But
hodo, nikushi nikushi to omoitsuru ni, here you drag along behind us, though
idemono misete kuren tote kongōzue you carry such a light pannier. That's

121

Ataka

o ottote sanzan ni chōchakusu. Tōre to koso.

why people suspect you. [*Approaches the* kokata.] Lately, I've become more and more disgusted with you. I must teach you a lesson. Snatching up the diamond staff, I beat him repeatedly, shouting, "Pass on!"

[*The* shite *suits his action to his words and pushes the* kokata *behind him. The* kokata *goes to the stage attendant's seat and sits down. The* waki *takes two or three steps forward toward the* kokata *as if in pursuit. Seeing this, the* shite *approaches the* waki *and looks at him.*]

SHITE

Ya, oi ni me o kaketamō wa tōjin zo na.

Why do you keep such a sharp eye on the pannier? You must be a thief, indeed!

[*The followers move onto the stage, form a double row, and press after the* shite *as he advances; the* shite *holds them back with the diamond staff. During the following passage, there is a lively vying, with the two parties advancing and retreating until the* waki *is pushed back to the* waki *seat. The* tsure *sing the following passage, called* ageuta.]

TSURE

(*Ageuta: au, tsuyogin*)

Katagata wa	Oh, all you guardsmen,
nani yue ni,	what are the reasons,
katagata wa	oh, all you guardsmen,
nani yue ni,	what are the reasons
kahodo iyashiki	that you draw the swords and blades
gōriki ni	against so lowly
tachi katana	and all too humble
nukitamō wa	a baggage carrier,
medaregao no	in this unmanly way
furumai wa	to act the bully?
okubyō no	Have you now become
itari ka to	such utter cowards?
jūichinin no	Speaking thus, the mountain monks,
yamabushi wa	one and ten in all,
uchi katana	start to draw halfway
nukikakete	their swords all ready
isami	and against
kakareru	this heroic
arisama wa	move to face the foe,
ikanaru tenma	all devil-fiends whatever
kijin mo	and demons all,
osoretsubyō zo	horror-struck and filled with awe,
mietaru.	would surrender!

[*The* waki *returns to the* waki *seat and intones the following prose* mondai.]

Masterworks of the Nō Theater

(Mondai: awazu, kotoba)

Chikagoro ayamarite sōrō. Haya haya on-tōri sōrae.

This is an error, such as is not often made. Quickly, quickly, you may pass and go.

Kyōgen

Makoto no yamabushi ja. Isoide o-tōri yare.

You are real *yamabushi*. Now quickly, pass along.

Ha Sixth Dan

[*The* waki *and* kyōgen *retire to the stage attendant's seat. The* tsure *stand in single file from the* waki *seat and pass in front of the chorus, to the hand-drum player's seat, while the* kokata *goes to the* waki *seat and stands. The* shite, *pulling down the outer robe from his shoulder at the stage attendant's seat, comes out to the* shite *seat; facing stage front the* shite *intones.*]

Shite

[8] *(Mondai: awazu, kotoba)*

Saki no sekisho oba haya batsugun ni hodo hedatarite sōrō aida, kono tokoro ni shibaraku onnyasumi arōzuru nite sōrō. Minamina chikō on-mairi sōrae.

Now that we are greatly far away from the barrier we left a while ago [*turns to the* kokata], I think we should rest here for a time. All of you, comrades, please come closer.

[*The* kokata *sits on a stool at the* waki *seat; the retainers sit in front of the musicians, while the* shite *advances to center stage and bows to the* kokata, *putting both his hands on the floor.*]

Shite

Ika ni mōshiage sōrō. Sate mo tadaima wa amari ni nangi ni sōraishi hodo ni, fushigi no hataraki o tsukamatsuri sōrō koto.

Please let me speak, my lord. It was indeed a most difficult moment we came through just now, and I acted in a way I never expected I would.

[*Somewhat heightened in* yowagin *style.*]

kore to mōsu ni
kimi no go-un
tsukisasetamō ni yori

What I mean to say, my lord,
is that fortune's turning
seems stopped for you, to turn no
more to good

ima Benkei ga
tsue ni mo atarase-
tamō to omoeba
iyoiyo asamashū

when I think you were attacked
even by Benkei's diamond staff
as happened a short while ago,
thinking of this more and more, my
lord,

koso sōrae.

I am ashamed and wretched.

123

Ataka

Sate wa ashiku mo kokoroenu to zonzu.	Well now, I am afraid he sees this
Ika ni Benkei, sate mo tadaima no kiten	wrongly. Listen, Benkei, the ready wit
sara ni bonryo yori nasu waza ni arazu.	you showed just now could never have
Tada ten no on-kago to koso omoe.	been an act sprung from an ordinary
	man. Think of it only as a grace from
	heaven. [*Facing stage front.*]

Seki no monodomo	When the barrier guardsmen cast
ware o ayashime,	suspicious eyes upon me,
shōgai kagiri	and this life of mine, I thought,
aritsuru tokoro ni,	had come then to its final hour,
tokaku no zehi oba	decisively, with no questions
mondawazushite	of the right or wrong of it,
tada makoto no	taking me in my guise
genin no gotoku,	of a lowly serving man,
sanzan ni utte	you hit and beat me thoroughly,
ware o tasukuru.	and rescued me from peril.
Kore Benkei ga	Could this not have been perhaps
hakarigoto ni arazu	a plan not made by Benkei
Hachiman[82] no	but a way revealed

[*The* chorus *sings the following* sageuta *passage.*]

CHORUS

(*Sageuta: au, yowagin*)

go-takusen ka to	by the mighty God of War?
omoeba	a miracle!

[*The* kokata *holds back his tears.*]

katajikenaku zo	When I think of this I feel
oboyuru	deep gratitude.

[*The chorus sings the following passage, called* kuri.][83]

CHORUS

(*Kuri: awazu, yowagin*)

Sore yo wa masse[84] ni	Say that this world of ours has now
oyobu to iedomo	entered the later stage of time,
nichi gatsu wa imada	still the sun and the moon on high
chi ni ochitamawazu,	have not yet fallen on this earth.
tatoi ikanaru	Say whatever may be said,
hōben naritomo	for my improvisation,
masashiki shukun o	still, with a staff I struck my lord,
utsu tsue no	our rightful master.
tenbatsu ni	Is it then not true
ataranu koto ya	that the judgment of Heaven
arubeki.	must fall on me?

[*The* kokata *sings the following passage, called* sashi.]

124

Masterworks of the Nō Theater

(*Sashi: awazu, yowagin*)

Geni ya genzai no	We see effect that manifests
ka o mite[85] kako	in the present, people say,
mirai o shiru to	so we understand the past
iu koto	and the future,

CHORUS

ima ni shirarete	as now I do, from sorrows
mi no ue ni	suffered in my flesh
uki toshi tsuki no	from months and years of hardship
Kisaragi[86] ya	coming to this end
shimo no tōka no	of the frosty second month;
kyō no nan o	that we survived somehow
nogaretsuru koso	the dread dangers of this day
fushigi nare.	is a miracle!

KOKATA

Tada sanagara ni	Overwhelmed, the chosen band
jūyonin	of ten men and more

CHORUS

yume no sametaru	are held by the sensation
kokochi shite	of a dreamer roused,
tagai ni omote o	and not yet wakened from his dream,
awasetsutsu	staring numb and blank

[*The* shite *and followers face one another.*]

naku bakari naru	from one face to another,
arisama kana.	they cry and weep aloud,

[*The chorus sings the following passage with Nō dance accompaniment, called* iguse.][87]

CHORUS

(*Iguse: au, yowagin*)

Shikaru ni	even noble
Yoshitsune	Yoshitsune,
kyūba no ie ni	scion of a warrior's house
mumare kite,	of bows and horses,
mei o	who offered
Yoritomo ni	to Yoritomo
tatematsuri,	his life or his corpse,
kabane o[88]	plunging all his foes
Seikai no	deep beneath the waves
nami ni shizume,	down in the western seas;
sannya	in meadows,
kaigan ni	hill, and by the shore,

125

Ataka

okifushiakasu	rising, to lie down once more
monono no	through long nights to dawn,
yoroi no	with no moment
sodemakura	to pillow his head
kata shiku hima mo	on his armor sleeves, half-spread
nami[89] no ue,	by the lapping waves.
aru toki wa	There were other times
fune ni ukami	when his life he trusted
fūha ni	to drifting boats
mi o makase,[90]	tossed by storm-whipped seas.
aru toki wa	There were other times;
sanseki no	on mountain ridges,
batei mo mienu[91]	his horses left no hoofprints,
yuki no uchi ni	laboring through deep snows,
umi	and when
sukoshi aru[92]	the sea lies closer
yūnami no	come the charging sounds
tachikuru oto ya	of the eve-tide toward Suma
Suma[93] Akashi[94] no	across Akashi Strait
tokaku[95]	he destroyed
mitose no[96]	the deadly foe
hodo mo naku	within three short years
teki o horoboshi	and peace rules the world that bows
nabiku yo no	before his brother,
sono chūkin mo	and counts his matchless exploits
itazura ni[97]	as empty trifles
narihatsuru	done with like his life
kono mi no	brought to this end
somo nani to ieru	what is left to say of this?
inga zo ya.	Can this be man's fate?

[*The* kokata *sings the following lines, called* ageha.]

KOKATA

(*Ageha*)

Geni ya	Oh, how true!
omō koto	our deepest wishes
kanawaneba koso	are seldom granted to us;
ukiyo nare to.	so goes the fleeting world,

[*The chorus continues to sing the second half of the* kuse *passage.*]

126

CHORUS

(*Kuse: au, yowagin*)

Shiredomo	and this I know;
sasuga nao	still when I think back,
omoikaeseba	my thoughts twang like straight, true bows

azusayumi no	for all the straight, true men
sugu naru	who must suffer
hito wa [98]	agonies
kurushimite	while the slanderers
zanshin wa [99]	prosper more and more
iyamashi ni	in this fleeting world
yo ni arite [100]	the Way lies distant,
ryōen	vast before us
tōnan no [101]	to the East and South,
kumo o okoshi	where men rise up like clouds,
seihoku no [102]	to the West and North,
yuki shimo ni	tortured by the frost,
semerare umoru	buried in the wretched deep snows
ukimi o	of human life,
kotowari tamō-	where there ought to be someone
beki naru ni,	to judge right from wrong,
tada yo ni wa	in this world of men,
kami mo	is it true
hotoke mo	that no Buddhas
mashimasanu ka ya,	or gods are left to judge us?
urameshi no	Oh, how hateful is
ukiyo ya,	this wretched world!
ara urameshi no	Oh, how truly hateful is
ukiyo ya.	this wretched world!

Kyū Dan

[*Toward the end of the singing, the* waki *and the* kyōgen *rise from stage rear and go to the bridge; by the end of the song, the* waki *stops at the second pine, and the* kyōgen *near the first pine.*]

WAKI [*Intones the following prose* mondai.]

[9] (*Mondai: awazu, kotoba*)

| Ika ni tare ka aru. | Ho, there, is someone about? |

KYŌGEN [*At the first pine.*]

| On-mae ni sōrō. | I am here, sir. |

WAKI

127

Sate mo yamabushitachi ni ryōji o mōshite, amari ni menboku mo naku sōrō hodo ni ottsukimōshi shu o hitotsu mairashōzuru nite aru zo. Nanji wa saki e yukite tomemōshi sōrae.

My rude behavior toward those *yama-bushi* a while ago does something less than credit to my name. Therefore, I think I'll follow to offer them some sake. You go ahead of me and stop them.

Ataka

KYŌGEN

Kashikomatte sōrō. Haya batsugun ni onnide arōzuru mono o. Iya kore ni goza sōrō. Ikani annai mōshi sōrō.

Yes, my lord. [*Facing stage front.*] Probably they are far away by now. Well, well, here they are. [*Facing the stage, the* kyōgen *speaks.*] Please, sir.

[*The* gōriki *comes out to the* shite *seat.*]

GŌRIKI

Tare nite watari sōrō zo.

I wonder who is there.

KYŌGEN

Kore wa saizen no sekimori nite sōrō ga, saizen wa ryōji o mōshite sōrō aida, tokoro no meishu o mochite kore made mairite sōrō. Sendatsu e sono yoshi on-mōshi atte tamawari sōrae.

I am a guard from the barrier you have just passed. A while ago, our lord spoke too rudely to you; therefore, he wished to bring some *sake,* for which this place is famous. Please report this to your leader.

GŌRIKI

Kokoroe mōshi sōrō. Ika ni mōshiage sōrō. Saizen no sekimori amari ni ryōji mōshite sōrō aida, tokoro no shu o mochite mairitaru yoshi mōshi sōrō.

I understand. [*Faces the* shite.] Please let me make a report. Since the officer at the barrier feels that he spoke too rudely to you a while ago, he wants me to tell you that he has brought some *sake* produced in these parts.

SHITE

Gongo dōdan no koto. Yagate on-me ni kakarōzuru nite sōrō.

How unusual this is! I shall see them at once.

GŌRIKI [*Faces the* waki.]

Sono yoshi mōshite sōraeba, koko on-tōri are to no on-koto nite sōrō.

I spoke to our leader, who asks that your lord come this way.

KYŌGEN

Kokoroe mōshite sōrō. Koko on-tōri are to no on-koto nite sōrō.

I understand. [*Faces the* waki.] They ask that you come this way.

128

[*The* kokata, *urged by the* shite, *retires to the stage attendant's seat. The* waki *enters the stage and faces the* shite.]

WAKI

Saki ni wa ryōji o mōshite sōrō aida, shu o motasete kore made mairite sōrō.

Let me apologize for my rudeness a short while ago. I have had my men bring some *sake,* since I am come to see you.

SHITE

(Awazu, kotoba)

Kō on-tōri sōrae.	Please come this way.

[*The* waki *takes the* waki *seat. The* shite *goes to the first pine.*]

Geni geni kore mo kokoroetari. Hito no nasake no sakazuki ni ukete kokoro o toran to ya. Kore ni tsukitemo naonao hito ni	Indeed, I know the real reason for this. With a cup of kindness, he would make us feel afloat and seize our hearts. So regarding this, now more than ever [*the* shite, *facing the* tsure, *sings in* tsuyogin *style*],

kokoro na kure so	do not give your hearts away
kurehatori[103]	for rare goods from Wu,

[*The chorus sings the following passage. The* shite *faces the* tsure.*]

CHORUS

(Au, tsuyogin)

ayashimeraru na[104]	do not let this novelty
menmen to	betray anyone;
Benkei ni	carefully cautioned
isamerarete	thus by Benkei,

[*The* shite *looks into the distance, to the right from stage front.*]

kono	in this
yamakage no	mountain shade that serves
hitoyadori ni	as their makeshift lodging,

[*He moves forward a little.*]

sarari to	arrayed they sit;
matoi shite	by the mountain trail
tokoro mo	this place lies too;

[*The* shite *makes a* hiraki *gesture.*]

yamaji no	so let this *sake*
kiku no sake[105] o	be chrysanthemum wine,
nomō yo.	let us drink it.

SHITE

[10]

Omoshiro ya	What a delight it is
yamamizu ni	on the mountain stream,

[*As the chorus sings the following passage, the* shite *moves out to the eye-fixing pillar, turns to the right, and goes by way of the* waki *seat to the front of the musicians' seat.*]

129

Ataka

omoshiro ya	What a delight this is!
yamamizu ni	On the mountain stream
sakazuki o	*sake* cups are set
ukamete wa	afloating, drifting
ryū ni hikaruru [106]	down the water's rippling flow
kyokusui no	to the crescent bend
te mazu	where the hands
saegiru	arrest them first
sode [107] furete	with the brushing sleeves,

[*The* shite *makes a* hiraki *gesture toward stage front.*]

| iza ya mai o | so come and let us dance |
| maō yo | and dance a round. |

[*The* shite *stamps the floor a few times.*]

| moto yori | Originally |
| Benkei wa | Benkei served |

[*The* shite *faces full toward stage front again.*]

Santō no [108]	the Three Pagodas
yūsō	as a young page
mai ennen no [109]	dancing at the Ennen Dance
toki no waka	to the timely song.

[*He goes out to the eye-fixing pillar.*]

| kore naru | Oh, over here |
| yamamizu no | the mountain water |

[*Holds his fan high, looks down, and stamps firmly once.*]

| ochite iwao ni | falling on the rocks below |
| hibiku koso | echoes back the line: |

(*Waka: awazu, tsuyogin*)

"Naru wa taki no mizu . . ." [110]   "The booming of the waterfall . . ."

[*While the chorus sings this last line, the* shite *goes to the* shite *seat; he then comes out to center stage and offers* sake *with his fan.*]

SHITE [*Intones the following prose line.*]

(*Awazu, kotoba*)

Tabe eite sōrō hodo ni sendatsu o-shaku ni mairōzuru nite sōrō.

I am drunk with *sake*. [*To the* waki.] Now allow me to serve you more.

WAKI

Sarabe tabe sōrōbeshi. Tote mono koto ni sendatsu hitosashi on-mai sōrae,

I thank you for it. But, reverend monk, I would rather have you dance to that song:

[*The* shite *folds his fan, ready for the dance. The chorus starts to sing the first line of a verse called* waka.]

CHORUS

(Waka: awazu, tsuyogin)

> naru wa taki no mizu,   "the booming of the waterfall,"

[*The* shite *performs the heroic dance called* otoko mai *in five movements.*]

Otoko Mai

[*After the* otoko mai, *the* shite *sings the following* waka *line, making an* ageōgi[111] *gesture at the* shite *seat.*]

SHITE

(Waka: awazu, tsuyogin)

> naru wa taki no mizu,   "the booming of the waterfall";

[*The* shite *stamps the floor and continues to dance to the singing of the following passage by the chorus in* ōnori.]

CHORUS

(Noriji: ōnori, tsuyogin)

> hi wa terutomo   though the sun burns brightly
> taezu tōtari,   still the booming sounds below,
> taezu tōtari,   still the booming sounds below.

[*He looks at the* tsure *on his left.*]

> toku toku tate ya   Quickly, quickly let us go.
> tatsukayumi no   Like the bow you hold,

[*Goes out to center stage.*]

> kokoro yurusuna   don't relax your heart-string now;

[*Kneels and bows toward the* waki.]

> sekimori no hitobito[112]   listen, guardsmen of the barrier,
> itoma mōshite   we must say our parting words,
> saraba yo tote   and bid you all farewell.

[*Gestures as if putting a box on his back.*]

> oi o ottori   Lifting up the pannier
> kata ni uchikake   they pack them on their shoulders,
> tora no o o fumi   stepping on the tiger's tail

[*Stamps a few times.*]

> dokuja no kuchi o[113]   they all feel as though they go

[*The* shite *moves to the front of the* waki *seat and then rushes across to the* shite *seat.*]

131

Ataka

nogaretaru kokochi shite	escaping from the serpent's poison jaws
Mutsu no Kuni e zo kudarikeru.	and to the land of Mutsu they go on their way.

[*At the* shite *seat, the* shite *assumes the* hiraki *form, stamps deliberately twice, and exits up the bridge, disappearing behind the curtain.*]

Masterworks of the Nō Theater

Hagoromo

Introduction

The story of *Hagoromo*, one of the greatest pieces of the Nō theater, is simple. A fisherman named Hakuryō finds a beautiful robe of feathers hanging on a pine tree by the seashore one balmy spring morning. He resolves to take it home with him to keep as a "treasure of his house." An angel appears, laying claim to the robe. He refuses to return it to her. She grieves, since without it she must remain on earth. Hakuryō, touched by her sorrow as he sees the "five signs that taint a sacred form" begin their slow corruption of her purity, agrees to return the robe if she will dance for him. Full of joy and gratitude, she prepares to dance as angels dance "about the palace of the moon above," and says she must have her robe to perform. Hakuryō suspects that once she has the robe, she will fly away, but the gentle being replies, "Oh, no indeed! Doubt exists only among you mortals. In heaven there can never be deceitfulness." Hakuryō is ashamed and forthwith hands over the robe. She dances, for mankind's joy, she says, and returns to heaven.[1]

Described thus baldly, *Hagoromo* must seem perhaps simpleminded and childish, "chiefly a framework or excuse for the dances," in Waley's words. He says further of it: "It is thus a Nō of the primitive type, and perhaps belongs, at any rate in its conception, to an earlier period than such unified dramas as *Atsumori* or *Kagekiyo*." He finds some of the text "irrelevant" to the play.[2] The discrepancy between Waley's comments and the actual importance of the play in the Nō repertory is ascribable in part to his lack of experience in the totality of this theater. For *Hagoromo* is structurally and thematically a very solidly constructed Nō. Probably basic to his misjudgment is the fact that Waley never saw an actual performance in Japan. This is not to diminish the sensitive understanding he brings to certain of the plays. In the case of *Hagoromo*, however, having only the text, he is unable to visualize the fullness of the play as performed. Consequently, he finds it thin. Yet within the actual theater of Nō, it is regarded as one of the most graciously serene and pure of the plays, much loved and often performed.[3] The problem, then, is to explore the conception of this play so that the experience conveyed by it can be understood. The experience may be worth the effort, for it must be held as an article of faith that whenever an art form endures among a people, it must be based on some deeply felt and important human perception that speaks to the human condition.

Four aspects of the play, which yield themselves up through descriptive reference to the text and musical terms, will be dealt with here. These will show that *Hagoromo*, far from being a minor play, is marked by a complex of significances. These four related questions are the classification of the play; the implications of the name Hakuryō; the relation of the terms *waki* and *shite* to the characters of a play; and the musical and lyrical structure in which the intent of the play can be found.

As far as its classification goes, *Hagoromo* has had a checkered history. It began life as a fourth-class play[4] and persists on occasion as a fifth-class play today in the Hōshō school.[5] It has generally been presented as a third-group wig-play since the Edo period (1600–1868). This quaintly antiquarian bit of information can be valuable for what it reveals about the changing conceptions of this piece.

The division of a day's program into five parts is along varied lines and for different purposes. The categorization of individual plays into the five groups has now become conventional but seems to have been much more flexible in the days of Zeami (1363–1443), the great playwright and actor, whose prose works are the fountainhead of the tradition. At present, the usual basis for categorization, based on convenience, is the character of the leading part, or *shite*; the first group deals with the gods, the second with warriors, the third with women, the fourth with mad persons, and the fifth with demons. This rough-and-ready means of classification breaks down so easily when subjected to close examination that the existence of some deeper criteria is clear. One outward manifestation of the criteria can be found in the variant, or *kogaki*, versions of a play, when *Yamauba*, for example, with a *tachimawari* dance is a fifth-class demon-play, while with a *chū no mai* dance, it becomes a first-class god-play. Another interesting example is *Taema*, which Sanari classifies without comment as either a fourth- or fifth-class play. Maruoka categorizes it as a fifth-class play and points out two *kogaki* versions that can render it playable as either a first-class or a third-class piece.[6] Since a single play can be so variously labeled, the identity of the main character is clearly not the sole factor in classification.

As we have already observed, Zeami was a practical man, especially in his role as manager and as titular and hereditary head of an established theatrical troupe on which the fortunes of his family depended.[7] Consequently, it can be supposed that the classification of plays based on his precepts arose from urgent reasons. For his concern was to capture, sustain, and bring to a climax the interest of an audience that at times included huge, unruly mobs as well as intimate private groups of the upper classes, rustic provincial viewers as well as the most sophisticated devotees.[8] Hence he gave much thought to the composition of a day's total program, in which five or more plays were presented, according to the sequential principle of *jo-ha-kyū*, or introduction, development, and conclusion, so as to win his audience and triumph over his competitors.[9]

His general remarks, therefore, on characteristics suitable for openings, for middle sections, and for conclusions, when applied to individual plays, give us a good idea of what qualities he found conveyable through them. He speaks of these qualities in many ways: in terms of the story line, the tempo, the mood, the relative importance of dance and music in individual plays, the degree of simplicity or ornateness, the appropriate amount of stage business, or the types and styles of dances. This multiplicity of terms can be a fatal Minoan maze, strewn with the boulders of exceptions and the dead ends of qualifications. One Ariadne-thread through the maze can be, to my mind, the function of the classifications vis-à-vis the audience, as set forth by Zeami. With a generalized description of what a type of play is required to do in a certain place in the total day's program, we can examine the individual and unique way in which a particular drama creates its moment of reality.

This is not haphazard or recondite theorizing. Recall, for example, the situation at the beginning of a day's program as Zeami saw it: "The auditorium will not yet be settled down, people will be coming in late and the audience moving about in confusion and not yet in a mood for the performance, so that it is difficult to make any impression on them." [10] It would be a self-evident blunder to bring on at this point a third-group play such as *Nonomiya* or *Izutsu*,[11] with its intense and delicate creation of a woman's emotions toward her lover. A fourth-class *genzaimono* ("living-person play") will not easily entice such an audience, itself freshly arrived from the familiar daily quality of the mundane world, into the magic circle of heightened experience. A warrior-play is perhaps too exciting or strongly rhythmed; such a mood on stage and in the audience, in each case arising from different sources, would create a non-Nō atmosphere, for it is a trait of this theater not to stun or overpower the audience into receptivity but rather to lure and entice it. The audience, according to Zeami, needs initially to be soothed and calmed, cajoled into receptivity by a play celebrating the auspiciousness of the occasion, of nature, or of the times, with very little plot action other than the actual dance and singing.[12] The principle of *jo-ha-kyū* underlying the classification of the plays is seen, then, as rising from a practical consideration. Zeami, stressing repeatedly the need to win over an audience,[13] cites as a skill belonging only to seasoned actors the ability to sense and mold the mood of the spectators. He implies that tempo of presentation is one factor when he states that the ending piece (*kyū*) has a definite tempo of its own.[14] More important, the actor himself maintains a sense of what is appropriate for an opening number of a developmental section, or an ending climax, and at times must make adjustments to fit special circumstances, as when some eminent personage walks into the performance late:

> While the Nō is in progress and has arrived at the end of the developmental section and is approaching the climactic ending, a nobleman may make his entrance. Here the Nō is already at the climax, but the feeling of this illustrious person is still at the beginning state. If with this *jo* feeling, he then looks at a Nō already in the climax stage, nothing about it will please him. Also, those others who have already been watching will have their spirits somewhat dampened. The mood will be changed to the feelings prevailing at the beginning. The performance on such an occasion will not go well. You may think you should start over, with feelings appropriate to a beginning, but this too will not go well. This is a very delicate situation.[15]

135

Aside from the problem of the late-arriving illustrious guest, so important that his entrance destroys the established mood, there are the difficulties of facing an audience that is somewhat inebriated:

Or again, there are times when you are unexpectedly asked to perform. Wine has already been served and the feelings of those assembled are already heightened. You are suddenly called in to perform and asked to give a Nō. The feeling of the room is already at the climax. [But] the Nō you perform will be the first piece. This is a delicate situation. On an occasion such as this, in your first Nō, you must present it somewhat as if it were the developmental Nō. . . . Taking a less sedate attitude, you should pass quickly over to a feeling proper to Nō of the middle developmental and ending climactic [portion of a total program].[16]

The function of the fourth- and fifth-group plays, as is evident from the last quotation, is to extricate the audience from the deeply inward, poetic style of the wig-play that precedes them and to prepare the way for the faster paced, climactic ending of the fifth group, with its "appeal to the eye."

Interesting in themselves as an indication of the circumstances under which Zeami at times performed Nō, the two quotations given perhaps reveal only "a good sense of timing . . . the stock-in-trade of any adequate public performer [making] conscious efforts . . . to see that the theatrical effects were as telling as possible," as O'Neill has said of other precepts in the writings.[17] Much deeper than such usual professional skills are the methods described by Zeami in *Shūdōsho*, dated 1430. Here Zeami gives interesting details on how such adjustments in timing were to be made, in this instance when a Nō program contained more than five numbers, as was not infrequently ordered by powerful patrons. He is most reluctant in this situation.

Since it is ordered by the honored persons, it is beyond our control. The whole troupe must give this careful consideration. In the place where we come to the middle and ending, we must leave something in reserve. The secret important details of performance should be held back [*te o oshimu*]. The piece should not be played for its maximum effects [*kyoku o hikaeru*]. We must devise a plan, item by item, so that a play need not be shown in its fullest depths. This reveals the expertness of the master. By such planned devices, the *jo-ha-kyū* structure can be adjusted. The study of Nō programming is like this.[18]

Zeami's descriptions of the "secret, important details of performance," found scattered throughout his prose writings, are one of the rewards of reading them. The effect of such adjustments would be to keep the time span of a total program within manageable limits, however unwilling the actors were to alter the usual presentation of a play. With such in-depth familiarity with the plays, Zeami gives the impression that a day's program was almost to be orchestrated. Professor Makoto Ueda has described the idea perceptively when he says,

. . . many variations are possible. The director of a Nō performance may use a fairy play like *The Robe of Feathers* for the Woman Play [Group III]; this will give a lighter tone to the whole sequence. Another director may adopt *Birds of Sorrow* or *Akogi* in place of the Frenzy Play [Group IV]; this will add a graver, more subdued color to the sequence. One of the unique features of the Noh drama is that one may give a different tone and color to the performance by a different five-play combination. . . . In the golden years of the Noh there must have been more than two thousand plays in the repertoire; in those days one had an infinite number of choices in arranging a five-play performance.[19]

The fact that *Hagoromo* has been variously presented as a fourth- and fifth-group play in the past and as a third-group play at present can now begin to yield up its meanings, the central significance of which is that the play can cover a large part of the Nō spectrum. A consideration of those characteristics which seem to make credible the fourth- and fifth-group classifications must begin with the play's inclusion of the *taiko*, the large stick-drum.

While the small hand-drum and the large hand-drum appear in all the plays in all five groups, the use of the *taiko* is distributed as follows:[20]

GROUP I	38 plays	All with *taiko*
GROUP II	16 plays	3 with *taiko*
GROUP III	38 plays	9 with *taiko*; two optional
GROUP IV	89 plays	32 with *taiko*; one optional
GROUP V	51 plays	All with *taiko*

From these figures, it is apparent that the use of the *taiko* is operative in underlining the characteristics that make any play appropriate for a given place in a day's program. Since *Hagoromo* has never been classified as a Group I or Group II play, the figures for these two groups, interesting enough for what they reveal, will not enter into this discussion. What is directly pertinent is to examine the eleven plays in Group III in which the *taiko* appears. They are the following: *Obasute, Seiganji, Kazuragi, Ume, Fuji, Kakitsubata, Mutsura, Kochō, Yoshino Tennin, Hatsuyuki,* and *Hagoromo.* It is clear that none of them is regarded as of the sort that most strongly characterizes the wig-play, in which the ambience created around a beautiful and sorrowing woman is the theme. Six are what Donald Shively has classified as Nō dealing with the "nonsentient,"[21] the spirits of the plum, the wisteria, the iris, the maple tree, a butterfly, and a bird. The beautiful *Obasute* centers on an anonymous old village woman. *Kazuragi* deals with the deity of a mountain. *Yoshino Tennin* and *Hagoromo* deal with celestial beings. Only *Seiganji* treats of a well-known aristocratic woman, the poetess Izumi Shikibu, a character from the same mold as those of the better-known wig-plays. However, in this play Shikibu is already an enlightened goddess of poetry; her earthly sorrows have vanished. Consequently, the treatment is quite different from that of the usual wig-play and closer to the joyous, celebratory tone of most of the other Group III plays with *taiko.*[22] This group of nine plays may be considered an important variation on the central theme of the wig-play, and it may be concluded that the use of the *taiko* in Group III is not generic to that central theme.

The figures given above also make clear that the *taiko* is much at home in plays of Groups IV and V. Why this is so is apparent in Zeami's remarks about plays now in these two categories. In his essay entitled *Nōsakusho*, Zeami deals in detail only with the composition of Group I plays. His writing precepts about the remaining four groups are set forth in connection with a discussion of the different types of roles, based on the art of acting. Since he considered that part of that art was the ability to write actable plays, a good deal can be gathered indirectly from what he says about the roles. For the Group IV plays, he comments on *Hōka-mono*, a subtype dealing with a kind of Buddhist priest who turned scripture teaching into semi-entertainment, singing and dancing to a hip drum.[23] Examples are the plays *Hōka-sō, Kagetsu, Tōgan Koji,* and *Jinen Koji*, according to Nose. For Zeami, the *Hōka-*

137

mono is related to the Group II warrior-play, but it must have an air of *saidō-fū*; the movements are executed without a show of strength. Zeami applies the same qualifications to the plays dealing with madmen and women, which are very similar, he says, to those on the subject of a search for a loved one abducted or lost through misunderstanding—all further types of Group IV. What he seems to be calling for is well-defined projection without an aura of brute violence or force. His mad persons are not uncontrollable psychotics but confused and disoriented sufferers. Zeami follows a discussion of *Hyakuman* with a warning on the need to write skillfully and in detail about a madwoman; the words and gestures should be appropriate. And if the form has beauty, he says, no matter what she does, it will be interesting. Even in the treatment of the hatred of Rokujō for her rival in *Aoi no Ue*, it is not her hatred that enthralls Zeami but rather the contrast between her two persons—the marvelously gifted and beautiful aristocrat possessed by the evil of her hate. "This is a good theme for Nō," Zeami says, and adds that it is even better than the paradox expressed in the old song that goes: "Giving the cherry blossoms the fragrance of the plum flowers, I want them to bloom on the weeping willow."

The quality of *omoshiroi*—interesting, paradoxical, amusing—is a recurrent motif. Zeami calls for interesting dialogue (*omoshiroi monku*), interesting points, and interesting phrases. He finds it appropriate for this group that the costume of the drummer monk is *hanayaka*—flashy. He speaks several times of rhythm, emphasizing what seems to be an *allegro* effect in connection with both *Hōka-mono* and *Hyakuman*. The notation must call for a light and buoyant rhythm; recitative (*sashi*) must be written so that an *issei* type of song can follow.[24] *Issei* is an appreciably vivid, rhythmically varied musical pattern. Thus it can be seen even from these fragmentary remarks how the *taiko* is more apt to be found in Group IV plays. It is found in lively or vivid Nō.[25] Conversely, the presence of the *taiko* in its instrumentation allows us to understand much about what is found in *Hagoromo*, and that understanding is validated by the figures given above.

Kazamaki Kejirō has noted that there is a group of plays in Category IV that can be termed playful or entertaining. He gives as examples of this type *Makiginu*, *Aridōshi, Ikkaku Sennin, Kiku Jidō, Jinen Koji, Tōgan Koji*, and *Hōka-sō*.[26] Examination of these plays makes clear what is meant. *Hōka-sō* will be selected as an example, since Waley's translation is available. The plot of the play is centered on revenge, and thus its treatment is even more surprising. The comedy—one is tempted to call it low comedy—of the servant's first encounter with the revenge-seeking brothers, the parody of Zen flatulence as the symbolism of the fan is explained, the restraining of the overeager brother by a mumbo jumbo of nonsensical pieties—all this is very clear.[27] It strikes a note that is not generally associated with Nō in the West but is not foreign to it.[28] Echoes of this quality can be found in *Hagoromo*.

138

For the general character of the fifth-group plays, Zeami's remarks on the devil-plays are pertinent, since these form an appreciable portion of the plays in this category. He calls for an air of liveliness with overtones of gaiety (*hanayaka*) in the rapid devil dance. In the two-part plays, he counsels that the first part should be as concise and short as possible. The tempo of the singing should be fast and light. Speaking of *Yamauba*, he calls for a very fast tempo in the final portion of the most important musical section.[29] The emphasis on a quickened tempo is intended to create a spirited finale to the day's program. In the plot of the plays themselves, the same upbeat air is preserved, since it would be inept to end a day's program with a minor-keyed Nō. Kazamaki points out that the spirits within the plays can be divided into those who help human beings and those who hinder them, and the latter are finally overcome and the play concludes happily.[30]

When we turn to *Hagoromo* with Zeami's descriptions of the fourth- and fifth-group plays in mind, its origin as a fourth-group play is readily observable. The lively tempo that the *taiko* later induces is marked from the opening verse of the play and by its accompaniment, an *issei* in *tsuyogin* style, musical terms that will be dealt with later. The opening verse is a poem from the eighth-century *Man'yōshū*, the first anthology of Japanese poetry. "Once upon a time," the fairy tale begins, and with that magic formula it creates its own structure of expectations. So does this opening of *Hagoromo*. There is a joyous tone of "early dawn" in the poem, as there is throughout the whole anthology, which marks a spontaneity of vision that was never again to be reached in Japanese poetry. For example, never again could Japanese poets see the fisherfolk of the bay, in and for themselves, as they are seen here; what is interesting in this description lies wholly in the live picture, in its freshness and spontaneity.

> Kazahaya no   Round about the shore
> Mio no ura wa o   of Mio's windswept inlet
> kogu fune no   fishers row their boats,
> urabito sawagu   shouting loudly as they ride
> namiji kana   down the ocean road.[31]

If these lines are compared with a great poem from a later period, the special freshness of the *Man'yō* vision can be seen. The priest Saigyō writes:

> Kokoro naki   Even for the one
> Mi ni mo aware wa   who has given up the world,
> shirarekeri   loneliness is known,
> shigi tatsu sawa no   when the snipe dart from the marsh
> aki no yūgure.   in the deepening autumn eve.[32]

Here the poet makes the scene touchingly interesting. It is because his musing, reflective tone is imbued in the scene that the second poem is memorable. In contrast, the strongly swinging, cadenced rhythm and spontaneity of the opening *Man'yō* verse sets the tone of this play.

Overtones of gaiety and amusement, a characteristic of Group IV plays, and intimations of the upbeat, happy-ending plot, characteristic of Group V, can be found particularly in the first exchanges of verse dialogue between the secondary character and the *shite*. The story line of the play, as simple as it is, contributes to the air of happy innocence that makes gaiety possible, as a comparison of the Nō with earlier versions of the story in the eighth-century *Fudoki* clearly reveals. In one, the angel is trapped into marriage and, after the birth of four children, ferrets out her robe to escape with it back to the heavens, mourned by her husband and presumably abandoning her children. In another, the maiden is eventually disowned by her earthly foster-parents, after she has enriched them.[33] In both these versions, the sense of an underlying and rather mean conflict between the mortals and the heavenly being is clear. However, in the Nō piece, the fisherman wishes

139

to keep the robe not from personal avarice but for the sake of "future generations" and as a "miracle and treasure of the land." He will "show it to the elders." The high-mindedness of these motives, from the point of view of the conception of this Nō, transfers the dramatic construct immediately to a higher plane. On that plane, his pity for the grieving angel and his distress over the signs of corruption gradually overtaking her are motive enough for surrender of the gorgeous robe in exchange for heavenly dances. The triumph of sweet virtue is complete when the angel gently shames the fisherman into a realization of the grossness of his suspicions that she will renege on her part of the bargain. The confrontation between the fisherman and the angel is so attenuated as to be a miming of confrontation. From such reasonable and high-minded adversaries, we expect an agreeable conclusion to their differences.

The allocation of dialogue within the play as preserved by the Hōshō school[34] substantiates this contention and shows the gaiety of tone in the play. In an analysis of the *kakeai* section, Igarashi Chikara concludes that the confrontation is attenuated by the device of allotting to one character speeches that logically belong to the other, or by having a character speak what the chorus would normally be expected to take over. The *kakeai* section is an alternation of dialogue in verse between two characters, in which the speeches become progressively shorter, until at last the chorus takes up the text. The *kakaru* notation, which calls for a heightening from intoned prose to recitative, hints that the passage is too interesting or charming to be left as common speech, as Igarashi maintains, while the progressive shortening "seems to express clearly the artistic inner nature of it." This "artistic inner nature" seems to me to be the growing intensity inherent in such a patterning. When the speeches are allocated illogically, the dramatic effect is the "delight [the characters] discover in the exchange of their roles." There are elements of light, even rueful, mockery as well as empathetic sympathy in such role exchange. It is amusing to see "the struggle that comes from the confusion between friend and foe during the push-and-pull between them."[35] The similarity between the therapeutic use of role exchange in modern psychiatric practice and the dramatic use in this old classical Japanese play is striking.

Other elements in the internal structuring of the play that reveal its relationship to the plays of Groups IV and V are the elimination of the conventional formal entry pattern for the secondary actor (*waki*), and the exit of the *shite* to the strong cadences of the *ōnori* rhythm pattern rather than the *hiranori*, which marks the more deeply reflective plays in Group III;[36] these matters are dealt with later. The element of spectacle, an important factor in fifth-group plays, in the physical beauty of the angel; the emphasis on dance throughout the text, with its verses on the dance of the Rainbow Skirt and the old Azuma dances; the praise songs in the latter part of the play; and the less conventional treatment of the *waki* role are also relevant. While none of these elements in itself is absolutely indicative of category, the presence of all of them in one play is the operative factor.

140

Some of the variant *kogaki* versions of *Hagoromo* indicate how flexibly rhythmed the play can be. According to Miyake Noboru,[37] there are nine variants, although none is labeled in such a way as to indicate a change in categorization, such as *Waki Nō no shiki* (Play as a Group I play) or *Sanbanme no shiki* (Play as a Group III play), *kogaki* subtitles that do appear for variant versions of *Taema*, *Shōjō*, and other plays. Some of the changes called for in *Hagoromo* variants have to do with tempo. *Wagō no mai*, a variant of the Kanze and Umewaka schools, calls for the last section of the *jo no mai*, usually a slow dance, to be performed at the faster *ha no mai* tempo. *Saishiki no den* of these two schools substitutes the short *iroe* movement for the *ha no mai*, which has the effect of speeding the tempo since it shortens the play. In the *banshiki* variant of the Hōshō and Kongō schools, the stately *jo no mai* is performed in the *banshiki* mode more usual for the quick dance, rather than the conventional *ōjikichō*.[38] Sakamoto Setchō points out that no true wig-play has a *banshiki* variant.[39] These three variants eliminate large portions of the text. The question of time is, among other factors, probably the reason for such shortening. The Kita school has a *kogaki* entitled *Kumoi no mai*, a variant presented at the Imperial Palace and shortened variously to fit the time allotted to the Nō in the ceremonial program of the day.[40]

The accepted category of the play at present is the third-group wig-play, since the piece lends itself to a presentation of the inner, transcendent beauty inherent in the divinity of the heavenly being. It has gradually assumed the third-play position, the most important in the total programming since the Edo period, as previously noted. According to the Kanze school, a notation exists from the Kyōhō era (1716–35) that "this Nō may be used as an auspicious wig-play," which indicates its suitability for such special celebrations as the New Year.[41] Thus, even as a third-group play, it occupies a special place. Kita Roppeita, the survivor among the great Meiji masters, showed the transcendent insight popularly ascribed to those actors when he chose *Hagoromo* to perform at the Imperial Court on December 8, 1915, during the celebration attendant on the coronation of the Taishō Emperor. Certainly the joyous tone of the play, as well as its references to the supraearthly origins of the imperial family, its inclusion of a line identical with the first line of the modern national Japanese anthem, and its lyrical celebration of the beauties of the land the emperor was to rule, make it a particularly graceful, congratulatory piece and act of homage for such an occasion. What Stephen Orgel has said of the Jacobean poet is equally true for the older Japanese artist: ". . . the idealization of the virtue embodied in the king and aristocracy was in the highest sense a moral act."[42]

It is possible that the high moral plane implicit in the play is also operative in the choice of it for such an occasion; the ruler is respectfully and indirectly advised, through joyous celebration and praise, as to what is expected of him as ruler of such a land:

. . . ametsuchi wa	. . . here heaven and earth
nani o hedaten	have nothing to divide them,
tamagaki no	for our sovereign hails
uchito no kami no	from the godhead in the shrines
mi-sue nite	by the jeweled fence;
tsuki mo kumoranu	so the moon is cloudless too
hinomoto ya	in this sun-blessed land.

There is here no less majesty, for in a wig-play the qualities of beauty of the sort called *yūgen* are paramount. Consequently, the public "message" of the play is understood to lie in the experience of that beauty. *Hagoromo*'s *yūgen* is obviously a different sort from that found in other great wig-plays like *Izutsu* or *Nonomiya*; after all, this is a totally happy play. Hence it adds an important dimension to the difficult concept of *yūgen* itself; there can be *yūgen* in joy as well as in sadness.[43]

This dimension reaches its climax in the dancing of the central figure of the *shite*, as described by Zeami:

> The style for an angel's dance should be full and ample. With the power of the spirit filling the entire body, dance the dance. Then the dance will begin to turn you about, making visible small things and large things, like flowers and birds swaying and fluttering in the spring breezes. Show the audience a subtle and profound style, smoothly uniting in one form the skin, the flesh, and the bones. I repeat and repeat: this is a big, important dance. The angel's dance should not appear to be of human style. . . . However, there is something feminine in it. Although it is a large (*ōmai*) dance in Nō, with a general understanding of it, it is not particularly difficult to change it into a human dance. . . . it belongs to the final stage of learning.[44]

The structure of the passages in *Hagoromo* following the angel's dance, as will be shown, indicates how "big" and "important" a dance it is within the play. It seems so overpowering that special lyrical and musical strategies are needed to allow for an exit by the *shite* and for a conclusion to the play. The impossible ideal, then, is a mysterious amalgam of strength, magnitude, subtlety, profundity, smoothness, the suprahuman, and the feminine. With this description, the lyrical monumentality of the conception of the play is clear. The question is whether an actor can approximate it.

Sakamoto Setchō in his reviews of masterly performances seems to feel that it is possible. He was fortunate, for he is commenting here on performances by Kita Roppeita, whose mastery is legendary: "There is nothing rare about Roppeita's performing *Hagoromo*, but each time, we are moved and impressed. If I were to describe a performance as passionate and jewel-like, I must also say that there is in it a jewel-like coolness. In the art of this master, so cool and gem-like, there is moreover a sensuousness brought to the very point of overflowing. . . . In the shimmering gaiety and smoothness of his performance, there was something to enthrall the audience completely."[45] On his final exit, Roppeita is said to have given the impression of actual levitation—the "mist exit"—as the angel flies back to the heavens.[46]

While Roppeita's performance, in the memory of many knowledgeable persons, was extraordinary, Setchō's description of it seems to bear out something of Nose's remarks on the lamentable womanizing of the angel's role, for he feels that Zeami's description calls for what is strong, large, dashing, and stately.[47] Setchō's review of another performance describes an air different from what he ascribes to Roppeita, and one perhaps closer to Nose's conception: "From the sonorous skillful tones of the *yobikake*, the performance was most delightful. Although the angel's gestures were quite daring, almost to the point of being violent, this did not in the least mar the refinement of it; the reason he could maintain such a beautiful concept throughout the play comes from a thoroughly practiced and mastered art."[48] One last comment from Setchō will give another characteristic of the particular kind of *yūgen* in this play, arising from Zeami's dictum that the nonhuman nature of the angel must be expressed: ". . . I feel that this Nō called *Hagoromo* should be without anything suggestive of the human element, and that the concluding section should in an ample and uplifted way be colorful and joyous." He understood this,

142

he says, not from anything concerning the angel, but chiefly from the chanting of the chorus.[49] The fact that he saw such an abstruse and essential element in the play through the quality of the chanting of the chorus illustrates the totality of what Malm calls the "*gestalt* of equally contributing arts," which is the hallmark of Nō.[50]

For that *gestalt*, the name of the secondary character, *waki*, is most significant. The *waki* introduces himself as a fisherman whose name is *Hakuryō*, which is too dignified and resonant a name for a common fisherman, for the literal meaning of the name is "white dragon"; it is found in a widely known Chinese story:

> The King of Wu wished to go disporting among the common people. Wu Tzu-hsü remonstrated by saying, "This should not be done. Formerly, a white dragon descended to a clear, cool spring and transformed [itself] into a fish. A fisherman by the name of Yü-ch'ieh shot an arrow and hit the eye of the fish. The white dragon ascended to heaven to lodge a complaint with the Heavenly King. The Heavenly King said, 'at the time of the occurrence, what was the shape you had assumed?' The white dragon replied, 'I went down to a crisp cool spring and transformed [myself] into a fish.' The Heavenly King then said, 'A fish, after all, is what ordinary mortals shoot at. If so, how can Yü-ch'ieh be accounted guilty?'
>
> "Now let me say: A white dragon is the nobility among the domesticated animals that belong to the Heavenly King, whereas, Yü-ch'ieh is but a low-ranking minister of the Sung Kingdom. If the white dragon had not been transformed, Yü-ch'ieh would never have shot at it. Now, [for you] to forsake your position as a king of ten thousand chariots and to go disporting with commoners—I fear that there might follow a calamity just like Yü-ch'ieh's."
>
> The King of Wu thereupon desisted [from carrying out his wish].[51]

The probability that the use of the name is calculated can be argued in several ways, which will also show how it is operative in the structure of the play. First, there is Zeami's dictum on the use of Chinese poems in the text, which by extension I apply to the name from the Chinese story: "Use only the texts of Chinese and Japanese poems which are elegant and the meaning of which is understood at once."[52] Second, immediately following the *waki*'s name announcement, there come four lines from a Chinese poem by Ch'en Wen-hui, included in the well-known collection called *Shijin gyokusetsu*.

Banri no kōzan ni	On ten thousand miles of lovely peaks
kumo tachimachi ni okori	suddenly the clouds come up and hover,
ichirō no meigetsu ni	and above the tower shines the brilliant moon,
ame hajimete hareri	as now the passing shower clears away.

The juxtaposition draws attention to the name and creates an expectation that it may be significant. As Kitto has remarked, in the art of drama, juxtaposition is one way of saying "things of the utmost importance without using a single word."[53] Third, the name occurs in the phrase *Hakuryō gyofuku* in a well-known line of Chinese poetry based on the legend, meaning literally "the white dragon in the disguise of a fish." To have used the full phrase would be irrelevant since the play does not make use of the legend itself. But the derived denotation of the disguised nobleman is retained in this play by naming a fisherman Hakuryō:

Hagoromo

Kore wa Mio no matsubara ni Hakuryō to	By the Bay of Mio and among the groves of
mōsu gyofu nite sōrō.	pine trees, I am Hakuryō, the fisherman, so
	they call me.

Fourth, as will be seen, the original Chinese legend sets up a clear division between the dragon and the fisherman. In this play, they are incorporated into one character. What is celestial and what is earthly are bound together.

The *waki*, then, is not the simple fisherman he claims to be, and he wishes us to know it. But he also wishes us to accept him in his guise and makes this clear in two ways immediately. The first is his misquotation of the Chinese lines, which originally read:

Senri no kōzan ni	On a thousand miles of lovely peaks,
kumo tachimachi ni osamari	suddenly the clouds recede and clear,
ichirō no meigetsu ni	above the tower shines the brilliant moon,
ame hajimete hareri	as now the passing shower clears away.

It is of course more logical to see a brilliant moon in a clear sky, as here, than in a cloudy one, as in the *waki*'s version. But a simple fisherman might be expected to make such an obvious error.[54] Second, the *waki* refers to himself as a "lowly heart"; the spring view is so delightful that even to his "humble eyes" the beauty is enjoyable. Later, he characterizes himself as "heartless and unkind," implying a low, somewhat brutish nature.

The *waki*'s guise as a lowly person is made necessary by the original *Hagoromo* story as given in the *Fudoki*, where, as previously noted, the confrontation is between a heavenly being and greedy earthlings. Since the play is based on a retelling of that well-known story, the general nature of the main characters in it are kept.

But in his dimension as Hakuryō, the *waki* has us understand that what was crude and avaricious in the behavior of the mortals in the older stories is not a part of this play. For the fisherman is a nobleman in disguise. He is Hakuryō, who reverses himself and, far from being "heartless and unkind," realizes the angel's agony.

> WAKI: How shall I express my thought aloud? Now that I realize from your cast and countenance how terrible and deeply agonizing are the depths of your distress, here I would like to say that now truly I will return this robe to you.

He can be shamed into realizing how corrupted he has become in the world of men, when he can not even remember that there is another world in which "there can never be deceitfulness," as the angel reminds him.[55]

144

WAKI

Ara hazukashi ya	Ah, what shame, what shame is mine,
saraba to te	uttering these words,
hagoromo o kaeshi	he returns the robe of feathers . . .

The high-mindedness of the dialogue between the angel and Hakuryō is made probable because of the "true" identity of the fisherman. And in view of the auspicious, happy tone of the play, we can come in a full circle to say that if Hakuryō is disguised as a fisherman, the fisherman is also Hakuryō. That is to say, in this world where "heaven and earth have nothing to divide them," the nature of even the lowly man responds to the celestial and is transformed. Man in his true being is good. It is fitting that he should receive angelic visitations. This play is gay with celestial celebration and rejoicing. The chorus sings:

Omoshiro ya	What delight is this!
ame nara de	Though it's not heaven
koko mo taenari	here how wondrous all is too!

The role reversal of the fisherman into Hakuryō is effected in the *kakeai* passage, previously cited for its overtones of gaiety and as evidence of the attenuation of conflict in the play. Such attenuation leads to resolution, and in the resolution the transformation of the fisherman into nobleman is completed, though not yet revealed. As Igarashi has noted, the tone of the passage is one of delight, while the audience reaction is a puzzled amusement at the seeming illogic of the role exchange between the angel and Hakuryō. She says what he should logically say; he says what she should say.[56] When the role exchange comes to its farthest limits, as the lines become shorter and shorter, the chorus rescues the situation musically, with an *ageuta* swelling forth in the higher ranges of song.[57] This passage restores logic; the characters are sorted back into their proper persons.

The reader is asked to hold in abeyance the questions raised by the reference of each character to himself in the third person in the following *kakeai*; these will be dealt with shortly. The allocation according to the Hōshō text is as follows:

Waki (I)

Kono on-kotoba o	Now barely were these grieving words
kiku yori mo	said and heard alike,
iyoiyo Hakuryō	when more and more Hakuryō
chikara o e	becomes resolute.

| moto yori kono mi wa kokoro naki, ama no hagoromo torikakushi. | Unkind and cruel is the heart of this fisherman. The heavenly robe of feathers he takes down and hides. |

| Kanōmaji tote | It cannot be helped, he says, |
| tachinokeba | and prepares to leave. |

Shite

ima wa sanagara	Now even one from heaven
tennin mo	seems as though she were
hane naki tori no	only like a helpless bird,
gotoku nite	without wings to rise

Waki (II)

| agaran to sureba | to the heavenly realm above, |
| koromo nashi | for she has no robe; |

145

Hagoromo

chi ni mata sumeba   if she dwells upon the earth
gekai nari.   that's the world below.

WAKI (III)

To ya aran   Should she turn this way?
kaku ya aran to   Should she turn some other way?
kanashimedo   Though she deeply grieves,

SHITE

Hakuryō koromo o   Hakuryō does not return
kaesaneba   the robe of feathers.

WAKI (IV)

chikara oyobazu   She who seems so powerless

SHITE

senkata mo   lingers helplessly,

CHORUS

namida no tsuyu no   on the blossoms in her hair
tamakazura   gemlike tears of dew
kazashi no hana mo   and their petals start to droop
shioshio to   sorrowfully too . . .

Igarashi states that in Nō the allocation of dialogue to specific characters is usually based on the nature of the speeches' content. The chorus of course may speak for either the *waki* or *shite*. The *waki* and *shite* may recite lines usually sung by the chorus. In these instances, the character recites chorus lines appropriate to himself. This *Hagoromo* passage is most unusual, since in no other play is Igarashi aware of a misallocation of dialogue among the characters. He bases his analysis on both meaning and grammar. He concludes that the misallocation is deliberate and serves a dramatic function, about which he makes some interpretative suggestions.[58]

He finds that the second, third, and fourth speeches of the *waki* are illogically allocated; they should be said by the angel. Or they could be allocated to the chorus, which would then be expressing the angel's thoughts for her and describing the situation from her point of view—both conventional functions of the chorus. Logically, then, the total passage of eleven lines, beginning with the *shite*'s first speech, is a "moan" of the angel, to use Waley's word. Allocation of part of the angel's moan to the fisherman shows not only his sympathy, as Igarashi points out, but also, to my mind, the progressive process of the fisherman's identification with her situation, as he comes to sense her feelings and to complete her thoughts.

The second *waki* speech shows, Igarashi suggests, the fisherman, still in the stance of being "heartless and unkind," mocking the angel, and yet also beginning

Masterworks of the Nō Theater

to pity her. This interpretation seems strengthened by the third *waki* speech, which shows his deeper involvement, to my mind; he knows now what she is thinking and senses her panic.

The angel's speech at this point, after the end of her moan, belongs logically to the chorus, as Igarashi points out. What is conveyed by having the *shite* recite these lines is to my mind the sympathetic empathy of the angel, in her turn, for Hakuryō's state of mind. She expresses his inner thought for him, as he has previously done for her. She forces him to face up directly to what he knows but has not yet expressed. Even in distress, the angel's ability to empathize is strong. Such is the nature of celestial beings.

With the fourth speech, the fisherman is now completely identified with the angel's situation. "So all grace will pass away," he says. He begins to understand fully the dreadful consequences of her dilemma; the angel's last speech puts the stamp of finality on it. The celestial nature of the angel is beginning to fade away. The chorus, in a rising heightened *ageuta*, sings that the flowers of her jeweled coronet are beginning to droop, and "The five dread signs that taint an angel / appearing here before our eyes / are all too cruel." The signs of corruption in the celestial maiden are themselves symbols of the grossness inherent in his mean earthly nature. The fisherman is struck dumb and overcome by the enormity of his refusal, as we are by the realization of the lowness of an unenlightened self. He has no dialogue for the next thirty-five or so lines. Thus the *waki*'s silence, customary during the musical and lyrical passage initiated by the first *ageuta* of the chorus and shared with the *shite*, is dramatically significant in this play. This fisherman is very much there, though silent, as the chorus and the *shite* describe the angel's longings to return to heaven; she calls to the sea gulls and the plovers, envying them their flight. Their freedom is of course symbolic of the spiritual freedom of the enlightened self possible to man.

When at last the *waki* speaks, he has capitulated completely. "How shall I express my thought aloud?" he begins. "Now that I realize . . . how terrible and deeply agonizing . . . [is] your distress . . . I will return this robe. . . ." When the angel responds, "Oh, how this gladdens me!" and repeats the cry one speech later, her joy is not only for the return of her feathered robe but also for the fisherman's return to goodness and to his Hakuryō self; just as in the beginning, she cried, "How this saddens me!" both for his refusal to return the robe and for the grubby meanness of his earthly nature.

With the Hakuryō in the fisherman now fully revealed, the Nō world of this play comes full circle, back to the innocence of "early dawn" of the opening *Manyōshū* lines of the play, when "heaven and earth have nothing to divide them." Performing moon-dances for mankind's joy, the angel dances the celestial patterns, while the chorus sings of the very beginnings of the world with Izanagi and Izanami. ". . . the two gods first appeared," and "ten directions through all space / for the world they fixed; / for the skies they set no bounds. . . ." A primordial freshness and such joy as attended the first appearance of a lovely world carry the remainder of the play along.

The tone set here in the description of the physical setting is an echo of the opening lines, which follow the *Man'yō* poem. For the physical setting described in the beginning is significantly placed at the very edges of the meeting of land, sea, and skies, an appropriate locale for angelic visitations, all in the freshness of an early spring day. The *waki* and his companions sing:

147

Hagoromo

Geni nodoka naru	How delightful it all seems,
toki shi mo ya	this balmy season!
haru no keshiki	These spring scenes we long for,
matsubara no	where the groves of pines
nami tachitsuzuku	crest and roll, wave after wave,
asagasumi	to the morning haze,
tsuki mo nokori no	paling where the moon still hangs
ama no hara	far on heavenly plains. . . .

The imagery here suggests some indeterminate place. The green of the ocean waves rolls onward, merging with the thick pine groves, which are now become wavelike, fading in the distant haze of the spreading plains of heaven. The fresh buoyancy is of the time when the earth, sea, and sky were still young, and the tired, harsh divisions between them had not yet hardened. The images in the play repeat the motif: floating clouds appear like ocean waves rising up, blossoms fall from the skies, a sweet fragrance is "floating everywhere," heavenly music comes from some indeterminate source, and laurels are flowering in the moon. Almost literally, "heaven and earth have nothing to divide them." This is a place where man and heavenly beings can meet.

One further way in which the dual nature of the *waki* is operative within the concept of the play is that it establishes initially a theater world of second remove from the audience. In effect, we are told that there will be a play within a play; Hakuryō will play the part of a fisherman.[59] This device neatly takes care of the problem of the credibility of the angel; disbelief is thus more willingly suspended. The fisherman is not a fisherman, although we are asked to accept his disguise. So the angel is understood not to be "truly" an angel, and we accept that fiction also. It is within the matrix of such an illusion that the miming of confrontation and the role exchange in the *kakeai* section described by Igarashi can assume their overtones of playful, refined charm. But with the unfolding of the spiritual and physical *yūgen*-beauty of the angel as the play progresses, the initial coordinates of the illusion fade away, and the play within the play emerges as the only reality. Hakuryō is no longer playing the part of the fisherman; the fisherman has become Hakuryō, and the dignity of man matches the stature of the heavenly being. The Nō reality is created by the force of *yūgen*. Some inkling of the dynamics of Nō *yūgen* can be grasped through a consideration of the relation of the actors, the *waki* and *shite*, to the characters in the play.

However, the creative force of *yūgen* does not arise from the person of the angel, as played by the *shite*, for the *shite* is not beautiful in himself. He is of course a male actor, perhaps a "man in his sixties with a cracked bass voice and large, ugly hands," as Keene has said.[60] The costumes, of beautiful materials, not lacking in vivid colors though often monochromatic, give less the impression of grace than of a puzzling bulk and massiveness that seem designed not to enhance the human form but to overwhelm it. The mask worn is so small as to leave "a disillusioning sallow or reddish fringe of jowls" visible around its edges.[61] The net effect is of a shapeless mass, somewhat pyramidal, topped by a stark white, impressionless blob, approximating the human face.

Other instances of the mystifyingly cavalier rejection of realistic representation in the staging of Nō have been recounted many times and are perhaps one source of the fascination of this art. The same lack of realism extends to the text itself: the

148

element of narration (*katari*) rather than dialogue, the references by a character to himself in the third person rather than the first, the illogical allocation of dialogue, the use of the first person by the chorus as it utters dialogue for the character or the unspoken thoughts of the character. For example, in the final section of *Yuya*, the chorus chants the heroine's thoughts in the first person, a passage that in Western drama would be an aside spoken by her.[62]

From the standpoint of realistic Western drama, these are antidramatic arrangements of the text, which would generally weaken and perhaps even destroy the imaginative involvement of the audience in the dramatic whole. This is not a consideration in Nō. For example, in this play, the angel has made her first appearance to a most celestial *yobikake*, which wafts like a faint stir of air made vocal, coming from everywhere and nowhere, like the "sweet fragrance . . . floating everywhere" that the fisherman has remarked on. But then, she immediately enters into an argument with the fisherman.

SHITE *(Yobikake)*

Nō. Sono koromo wa konata no nite sōrō. Nani shi ni mesare sōrō zo.	Oh! [*Drawn out.*] Please, that cloak you have taken down from the pine tree is mine. Why do you take it and carry it away with you?

WAKI

Kore wa hiroitaru koromo nite sōrō hodo ni torite kaeri sōrō yo.	This is a cloak I found by myself alone. Therefore I have taken it down, to be my own, and now I will carry it home.

She remonstrates, in a speech. He is adamant. She is saddened and mourns. This exchange can be translated in the first person. The fisherman's next speech, which begins the *kakeai* previously given, is all in the third person.[63] ". . . Hakuryō becomes resolute," he says; "this fisherman is heartless, unkind. He . . . hides the robe. . . ." In the further exchanges between the *shite* and the *waki*, the speeches remain in the third person, with the angel referring to herself as "one from heaven" (*tennin*), and the fisherman, in the Kanze text, continuing to refer to himself as Hakuryō.[64]

Characters frequently refer to themselves in the third person throughout all the plays. The use of the third person in the dialogue has been dealt with in several ways by Japanese critics. Yokomichi and Omote, for example, maintain that first-person dialogue makes for greater intensity; they find that third person references show the "nondramatic tendencies" of many Nō plays. The implication is that, in the evolution of Nō, such plays are closer to the older narrative form than to a later and more developed dramatic form. However, as they point out, "the interesting fact is that these third-person passages are more numerous in the *genzai* Nō [living-person plays], and in the pure dream Nō they are very rare. Such an explanation as '. . . thus the spirit said,' or '. . . thus the spirit wept' is hardly ever found in the pure dream Nō. . . . Judging from this, it would seem the *genzai* Nō are more narrative-like and the dream Nō are more drama-like."[65] Conventionally, it is said that the living-person plays are comparatively realistic, since the action is presented in the theatrical present, dealing with human emotions as actual, unfolding occurrences. It is a canon of Nō criticism that the living-person plays excel in dra-

Hagoromo

matic construction because of their realism.[66] Consequently, one would expect that *genzaimono* would use the more immediate *I* form of dialogue, rather than the narrative third person. It becomes clear, then, that a different set of conventions than that dictated by logic is exploited in Nō.

That the drama is presentation rather than narration is clear, but that direct presentation of events as they happen makes for the dramatic in Nō is debatable. The difficulty arises from two concepts of what is real and what makes for intensity. It is more real, in the sense of realistic, for a character to refer to himself as "I" rather than as "this fisherman," but such realism does not necessarily create what is real, in the sense of experiential, in the Nō. Nor is it the source of dramatic intensity in Nō. For in Nō, the actor is not meant to be mistaken for the character. The *shite* is not the angel, in the sense that Hamlet exists in the person of the actor on stage. The *waki* is not the fisherman, in the sense that a Horatio is equated with the actor.

The angel becomes "intense" and "real" in the total experience we have while listening to the *shite* and *waki,* the chorus and the orchestra, and while watching the dances and other action. That is to say, it is our experience of the totality of the *gestalt* that creates the reality of the angel. The astonishing intensity and absolute stillness that usually prevail in the theater during a successful performance perhaps find their source in the audience involvement in the *gestalt* process. The sense of timelessness that is also a generally acknowledged characteristic of Nō comes from its power to create a total experiential configuration. Donald Richie characterizes the experience as "that extraordinary bond between the mind of the actor and the minds of his audience."[67] The actor is not the angel, but is the *shite,* a part of the structure of the total play. Hence, as Keene has said, "The roles in a Nō play are known not by the names of the characters, as in a Western drama, but by the category of the role,"[68] such as *shite, waki, tsure* (companion), and so on. In the Japanese text of this play, as in all others, the speeches are allotted to the *shite* and not to the *tennin,* to the *waki* and not to Hakuryō.

The remarks of performers, at times rather cryptic because experiential, can be understood, I believe, on the assumption that an intensely single creation, a *gestalt,* is the aim of all the performers—what both Malm and Richie call the "chamber-music" aspect of Nō.[69] At the same time, these remarks will throw some light on how the aim is attained. We recall that Kita Minoru, the present actor-head of the Kita school, said of one performance that when the drum player "didn't lead me out as he usually does, it was quite difficult to move on" to make a first entrance.[70] Keene reports that unless the musicians and the chorus know which mask is to be used by the *shite,* they cannot perform;[71] they must presumably know the level at which the play is to be performed. The chorus leader complains of the "suffering" he feels when the two drummers are not in harmony with each other in the striking of rhythmic patterns and the patterns of tempo; the words the chorus must utter will not come "to ride the beat, no matter how we struggle. Really, as the chorus leader, I feel as if I must weep" when this happens.[72] Malm's analysis of the relationship between the two drums and of the various patterns that they beat makes the singer's quandary clear.[73] For his part, the drummer complains that when a singer gave a poor performance, he could not get his own hand to strike the drum.[74] What the actor Hōshō Shin says brings out clearly the singleness of the effort in which the *shite* and *waki* are engaged:

Masterworks of the Nō Theater

In the *kakeai* and *mondō* sections, I feel strongly the delicacy in contrast [between the roles of *waki* and *shite*]. The art of receiving and giving back the *utai* (song) is very difficult. Depending on your partner, there is nothing more troublesome than this . . . nothing more taxing. Generally speaking, the *shite* begins softly and gently. The *waki* receives this in a smooth and responding style. On returning it to the *shite*, he must give it back openheartedly. The *shite* receives it and does what he will. On the other hand, if the *waki* elevates his own dignity and, for example, becomes calm (*shizuka*), the partner finds it a very awkward matter. The same principle applies to the gestures.[75]

The celebrated bareness of the Nō stage itself is a capsule statement of the nature of the experience unique to this theater. For it is not the material devices but the inward experiences that will fill the emptiness. Displaying nothing, the stage can become anything—a seashore, a mountain valley, a room. In addition to this, it has a special relation to the bulky massiveness of the costuming; the bareness concentrates attention on the figure, while the figure's mass seems sculpture-like in the empty space and uses it, as a statue needs the space around it.

The reference by a character to himself in the third person is of course not unknown in English drama. When it occurs in the masques of Ben Jonson, for example,[76] one of its effects, to my mind, is to maintain a heightened heroic tone consonant with the pageantry and spectacle of a court celebration. The latter elements are not lacking in *Hagoromo* and result in the gay auspiciousness of the piece. Where pageantry and spectacle are dominant, the third-person reference serves to emphasize the visual, as in the masques. The actor turns the character into a visual object. When with the third-person reference to the character he is playing, the Nō actor detaches it from his own person, it is to free the character from such diminishment, to assume a larger life than his physical person can give it within the conventions of Nō. Thus the *shite* remains always the *shite*; the *waki*, the *waki*. In Nō, where the visual is minimal, the detachment sustains the inward experience that begins out of necessity because of the bareness of the stage and continues because of the other elements of antirealism, so to speak, such as the extremely slow tempo of movement, the exaggerated delivery, the nonrealistic costuming, the use of masks, the expressionless face of the unmasked *waki*, and so on. Where the text is comparatively closer to actuality, as in the living-person plays, more speeches in which the characters refer to themselves in the third person are perhaps needed to maintain the inward existence of the play and to ensure that the actor is not mistaken for the character; whereas in the dream Nō, already inward since an ancient story is unfolding in a dream of the *waki*, the device is less needed. Consequently, as Yokomichi and Omote tell us, the device is hardly ever found in the texts of the pure dream Nō and indeed occurs more frequently in the living-person plays.

I have pointed out that *Hagoromo* is one of the great successes of the Nō theater. It owes much of its felicity to the adroitness with which, through a most simple story line, it conveys a stunningly ample theatrical experience of purity, warm with joy and beauty. A large part of its success is due to the solidly conceived lyrical and musical structure of the play, which differs in some respects from the norm. Our examination of its structure will be preceded by some general statements of the norm as found in the body of the plays. In some instances, I shall give figures to

151

indicate that norm. Awareness of the frequency of formal musical and lyrical patterns and the circumstances of their use within the entire repertory may yield greater knowledgeability in the analysis of individual plays. The figures also give some insight into the structuring of the *jo-ha-kyū* principle as applied to the five groups of plays. Although the number of plays in the current repertory is said to range from 200 to 240, I have accepted Sanari's figure of 235 as a working number.[77] I wish to indicate only certain tendencies within the repertory and feel that the figures will do so adequately, no matter which total or what system of classification is followed.

In a large majority of the pieces, the lyrical and musical elements of the play begin with the entrance of the *waki*. While the musical accompaniment and first speech of the *waki* can take several forms, in approximately 118 plays the musical accompaniment to the entry walk is a *shidai,* and the first verse uttered is a *shidai.*[78] The strong introductory value accruing to the *shidai* can be seen particularly in the fact that of the some 40 Group I plays, approximately 88 percent begin with some form of *shidai*. It is the introductory element in the first play on a program, a play that itself is considered as the introductory piece. Of the 16 plays in Group II, 9, or 56 percent, begin with *shidai*. In Group III, 45 percent are *waki-shidai* openings; in Group IV, 38 percent, and in Group V, 47 percent. This decreasing trend in *shidai* openings between the first two groups of plays and the last three groups perhaps indicates that, as the program progresses, the need for strong, formal introductory openings diminishes, as the *jo-ha-kyū* principle of development, applied to a complete program of five plays, is fulfilled.

The term *shidai* is adapted from the name given to a Buddhist chanting style, in which the leader of the group chants the first two lines, called a *ku,* consisting of seven and five syllables respectively. The group repeats the two lines; the next *ku* is then recited by the leader. In Nō, the *shidai* verse always has six lines, with lines three and four being repetitions of the first two lines, and lines five and six being different. The sixth line is shortened to four syllables. All six lines are chanted by the *waki* or the *waki* group. The last four lines are repeated by the chorus, this repetition being called a *jidori.* In Group I plays, the *waki* may then repeat the *shidai,* and the whole pattern is then known as *sanbengaeshi.* This series reinforces the introductory function. The effect of the pattern of repetition is a gain in formality and importance, and, like the final couplet in Shakespearian sonnets, it provides a conclusiveness, a rounding off. There is freedom to approach a new subject. Thus a recurring opening pattern that is frequently found is *shidai* and *jidori,* followed by a *nanori,* or intoned prose speech in which the *waki* identifies himself, a traveling song (*michiyuki*), and an intoned prose statement that the destination has been reached (*tsukizerifu*).

Aside from its introductory function in bringing on the *waki,* the *shidai* verse also serves as a prelude to the whole play. The affective theme of the entire play must be suggested in it. Consequently, it may be sung by the *shite,* who conventionally makes the second entry, in which case the *waki* has usually entered to other patterns. It is not a dominant pattern for a *shite* entry. It occurs in thirty-two pieces from the five groups of plays.[79] As a theme poem, the *shidai* is often "enigmatic,"[80] to use Waley's appropriate word, with fateful overtones suggesting some as yet unrevealed significance. Its dramaturgical function becomes clear only as the play unfolds. The opening *shidai* of the plays *Tomoe, Sotoba Komachi,* and *Ama* are good examples of this type of *shidai*.[81] One consequence of the enigmatic tone of this type of opening *shidai* is that the same poem can be found as the *shidai* for more than one play. For example, the *shidai* of *Ataka* is also found in *Settai* and *Kurozuka*.[82]

For both *shite* and *waki*, the art of singing the *shidai* must encompass the two functions of entry and theme, and Miyake Kōichi warns that the singer must be clear that it is quite different from an ordinary *ageuta* (song in a higher range of tones) in its tonal feeling.[83] The song begins in the high range (*jo*), moves primarily between that and the middle range (*chū*), and ends on the low range (*ge*). It is simple and without rich ornamentation.[84] Kobayashi says that terms such as *iri* and other notes for vocal colorings are never indicated for it. The rhythm of the *shidai* is always the *hiranori*, the basic and most common of the three Nō rhythmic patterns; no variation is allowed.[85]

The *jidori* is sung in a lower range of tones.[86] Rhythmically, it is also different from the *shidai*, being in a free, or noncongruent, rhythmic pattern, which will be discussed in connection with the *issei*. Consequently, through these musical variations, variety is added to the pattern of verse repetition. In the most formal of entries, the *sanbengaeshi*, however, the *jidori* follows the rhythmic pattern of the *shidai*, thus gaining even greater formality by eschewing variety.[87] An example follows from *Takasago*, a play from Group I:

WAKI AND WAKI-TSURE: *(Shidai)*	Let us now start on our way, dressed in traveling clothes, let us now start on our way, dressed in traveling clothes, long the days before us, too, lie far and fair.
CHORUS: *(Jidori)*	Let us now start on our way, dressed in traveling clothes, long the days before us, too, lie far and fair.
WAKI AND WAKI-TSURE: *(Sanbengaeshi)*	Let us now start on our way, dressed in traveling clothes, let us now start on our way, dressed in traveling clothes, long the days before us, too, lie far and fair.

Sanari as well as Yokomichi and Omote suggests that the last two lines of this *shidai* imply an unbounded, limitless future, as is consonant with the auspicious cast of the play.[88] Prosodically, the four-syllable last line, in place of the expected five syllables, strengthens the expansive thrust. Thus the *shidai* establishes the affective tone of the play.

153

The *shidai*, although it is a *yaku-utai*, a song usually sung by a specific role, in this case the *waki*, may also appear in the body of the play, sung by the chorus, in which case it is referred to as a *ji-shidai* (chorus *shidai*). Frequently, after an exchange of dialogue that has become progressively shorter, the chorus takes up the thread of the text. Usually it does so with a song in the high range (*ageuta*), which is a comparatively longer passage of verse, resolving or commenting on the matter

Hagoromo

of the dialogue. When resolution is wanted without length, the six-line *shidai* by the chorus may be used. The conclusive rounding off provided by the verse form, as previously mentioned, is evident in these contexts. The *ji-shidai* in *Kinuta* is an example. Miyake Kōichi has said that in such cases the *ji-shidai* serves to "bring out the feeling [at this point] briefly and symbolically."[89] Another instance of the *ji-shidai* is found in the *kuri-sashi-kuse* pattern, which will be discussed later.

As the *shidai* is the role song of the *waki*, so the *issei* is said to be the role song of the *shite*, who usually enters after the *waki*'s introductory passages are completed. The term *issei* can apply to both the verse form and the musical accompaniment to the *shite*'s entry. As a verse form, it consists of five lines of alternating five and seven syllables, thus beginning and ending with five syllables. At times, it can be followed by four further lines, alternating between seven and five syllables; this addition is called a *ni no ku*. An example, again from *Takasago*, follows:

SHITE AND TSURE: *(Issei)*	At Takasago
	through the pine the spring wind fades
	into evening,
	and the bell upon the peak
	too is echoing.
TSURE: *(Ni no ku)*	The ocean waves are hidden
	by the shoreward mists
SHITE AND TSURE:	yet the voices of the sea
	tell of ebb and flow.

Rhythmically, the first line of five syllables serves as an introduction to the usual pattern of Nō verse, which proceeds in sets of two-line units (*ku*) of seven and five syllables. The shortened first line, then, is vivid prosodically, in contrast to the regularity of the conventional *ku* of seven and five syllables.[90] It will be noted that there is no repetition of the lines, as there is in the *shidai* verse. This lack has the effect of leading onward; there is no sense of closure. The verses following the *issei*, the *ni no ku* or a *sashi*, usually amplify the nature of the *shite* or the feelings and emotional tone of the character, according to Miyake Kōichi. He also points out that the content of the verse is often a visual description of the view of the surrounding natural scene.[91] This follows logically, since the *waki* has previously traveled, in a *michiyuki* passage, to the place where the *shite* is to be found, and the *waki* announces his arrival at this definite place in a *tsukizerifu*. The *shite*'s description of the natural scene may be imbued with the emotional state of the character. For example, in *Motomezuka*,[92] though the scene is one of early spring with maidens gathering spring herbs, the *issei*, with its line on chillness, suggests that this is not gay celebration of the coming on of spring:

SHITE AND TSURE: *(Issei)*	In Ikuta Field,
	where the maidens pick young greens
	in the morning breeze,
	still the chillness comes and stirs
	waves and turns their sleeves.
SHITE: *(Unmarked verse)*	Though the buds begin to swell,
	with the soft spring snow
SHITE AND TSURE:	underneath the grove of trees
	still the grass lies cold.

Musically, the *issei* is more vivid than the *shidai*. Miyake Kōichi notes that it begins and ends in the high range, which is predominant through it; it contains tones from the higher range (*kuri*). Various ornamentations such as *kuri*, *iri*, and *iri ma-washi* are allowed.[93] Rhythmically it is free, like the *jidori* previously referred to; the notation is made that it does "not match the beat" (*hyōshi ni awazu*). That is to say, it does not follow any of the three basic patterns for fitting a *ku* of twelve syllables to the basic musical unit of eight beats.[94] Minagawa has said of such free-rhythm sections:

> The rhythm of Noh is quite fascinating. Free rhythm sections . . . , such as *sashi*, *issei* and *kuri*, are sung with considerable freedom, in much the same manner as western recitative, in which likewise some important words and melodic patterns are given special treatment. In Noh, these sections are rather simple, but nevertheless interesting rhythmically. The voices proceed in their own rhythm, conforming to the notation, but freely . . .—and the drums proceed independently in theirs (the *kotsuzumi* and *ōtsuzumi* drums, however, always share the same rhythm), these instruments creating the effect of background music, just as does the flute. When the end of a section in free rhythm is approached, the rhythmic divergences are gradually and smoothly supplanted by rhythmic agreement, and all the participants produce a cadence at the same time.[95]

There is, therefore, in the *issei* a freedom to the rhythmic structure that is in contrast to the *shidai*. The vivid musicality of the *issei* is perhaps also shown in the fact that *issei* music itself can be an entry pattern; an appreciable number of entries are made to the music alone, while the following verse is not in the *issei* pattern. The music may also be omitted, and an *issei* verse sung. The frequent separation between music and lyric in the *issei* is not true for the *shidai*. In only one instance is there such a separation in the latter pattern when it is used as a *waki* entry; this occurs in the play *Hakurakuten*. I have therefore considered as *issei* entries those with music alone, verse alone, or with music and verse together.[96]

The identification of the *issei* with the *shite*'s first entrance is fully evident only in the first group of plays; in 88 percent of them, the *shite*'s entrance has *issei* elements, and in twenty-nine of them, the most formal pattern is used, the *shin no issei*,[97] which is found only in Group I plays, with the one exception of *Matsukaze*. As with the large percentage of *waki-shidai* openings in this group of plays, the large percentage of the *shite-issei* entrances seems consonant with the introductory role of the first group plays in the total programming. And, as might be expected, the following four groups of plays have nothing like so large a correspondence. In the second group, the figure is 31 percent; for the third group, 8 percent; the fourth group, 27 percent; and the fifth group, 44 percent. There are several generally plausible reasons for these figures. Perhaps the simplest is that there are many more formal elements of verse and music that are usable for the *shite*'s first entrance than for the *waki*'s, since the focus of the play is on the *shite* role. More variety is possible since the *shite* is being introduced into an established situation, the main outlines of which have already been drawn. Hence the playwright's concern to introduce and identify the *shite* can be subordinated to the desire to establish nuances of character and mood in ways other than that provided by the *issei*. For example, it was noted that only 8 percent of the wig-plays have *shite-issei* entries. Approximately 17 percent have *shite-shidai* entries. Miyake Kōichi has commented

Hagoromo

that "when a role that normally enters on *issei* enters on *shidai*, it is to reinforce a more tranquil (*seijaku*) tone about the *shite*. . . . The total feeling around a *shidai* is a much more tranquil effect."[98] Again, in this connection, the occurrence, with only one exception, of *shidai* music and verse form together supports his characterization of it, as is clear when the more frequent separation of *issei* music from its verse form is remembered.

In the overall pattern of *jo-ha-kyū* that governs the tempo of a program of five plays, it is significant not only that the Group I plays introduce the *shite* most frequently (88 percent) with the *issei*, but also that only four other kinds of entry are used, and each type is used by only one play: *yobikake* (*Urokogata*), *shidai* (*Fujisan*), *sashi* (*Kinsatsu*), and *shin no raijo* music (*Tsurukame*). This lack of variety is in contrast to the Group IV plays, in which at least nine different patterns of *shite* entry are used, and to the Group V plays, in which at least ten are found. As with the decreasing trend in *waki-shidai* openings, the increase in entry patterns for the *shite* in the fourth- and fifth-group plays is apparently evidence of a growing lack of concern for formal introductory elements as the five-play program moves away from its development (*ha*) and approaches, in the fourth group, and reaches, in the fifth group, its end (*kyū*).

However, the *issei* is apparently needed for a strongly marked introduction of the *shite* role in one particular place in the second-, third-, and fourth-group plays. That is in the second part of the two-part plays, after the *nakairi* (*shite* exit), which can be an intermission or can at times be merely a *monogi* (an addition to or change of apparel or of appearance), which is effected on stage. In the Group II plays, there are twelve two-part pieces; in nine of these, the *shite* reappears in the second half to some *issei* element, music or verse. In the third-group wig-plays, twenty-seven are in two parts; of these, the *shite* in the second part (*nochi-jite*) enters to some *issei* pattern in eighteen. In Group IV plays, forty-seven are in two parts; of these the *nochi-jite* comes on to *issei* in twenty-three. The percentages are 75 percent, 66 percent, and 49 percent, respectively, as compared to percentage figures for the first entry of the *shite* to *issei* in all the plays in each group, which, as previously noted, are 31 percent, 8 percent, and 27 percent, respectively. These differences in percentages seem significant and large enough to justify a more closely detailed study of the musical and lyrical structures of the individual plays than is possible here. In connection with the present study of *Hagoromo*, these figures are cited to show not only the function of the *issei* in connection with the *shite* role, but also the musical and lyrical details that must be considered in an understanding of the individual Nō, as a drama in which singing, instrumental music, poetry, and dancing play so large a part that a reading of the text is immeasurably deepened by awareness of them.

One general conclusion may be drawn. Since plays from the second, third, and fourth groups constitute the developmental section of a five-play program, it may be supposed that a certain balance is desirable between the first and second halves of these plays. Such balance may be gained when the entrance of the *nochi-jite* is structured with the definitely identifying and vivid *issei* entry pattern. The *issei* and *issei* verse, dealing as they often do with the inner emotional state of the *shite*, as previously noted, carry with them an intimation of matters to be developed, since the form is one that leads onward, without the *shidai*'s sense of closure. The second half of the play can be weighted further, as Nogami has pointed out, by the

156

placement of a very important pattern—the *kuri, sashi, kuse* section—after the intermission in Groups II and III.[99] Zeami himself recommends that the *kuse* section follow the *nakairi* in the warrior-plays.[100] My own count shows that, in the Group II plays, the *kuse* section comes after the *nakairi* in 83 percent of the two-part pieces; in Group III, in 68 percent. In Group IV, thirteen of the two-part plays have no *kuse*. The remaining thirty-four are fairly evenly divided: fifteen plays (44 percent) have the *kuse* section before the intermission, and in nineteen plays (56 percent) it appears after it. The importance of the pattern among the formal structural units of the plays is shown by the fact that, out of the total repertory, only sixty-eight plays do not contain it.[101]

Examination of the *nochi-jite* entries in Groups I and V tends to support the conclusion that the *nochi-jite-issei* entry in the three middle groups of plays is related to the *jo-ha-kyū* principle as applied to the five-play program. For none of the thirty-nine two-part plays in Group I have a *nochi-jite* entry. Further, in this group, the *kuse* sections all come before the intermission.[102] Both factors deemphasize the final half of the plays. In Group V, among the forty-one two-part plays, only two *nochi-jite* enter to an *issei*: in *Yamauba* and *Eboshiori*. Five other plays in this group have an *issei* element after the *nakairi*, carried by other roles; they are *Kurama tengu*, *Zegai*, *Chōryō*, *Tsuchigumo*, and *Rashōmon*. Expressed as a percentage, this is 5 percent for the *nochi-jite* entry and 16 percent for all second-half *issei* openings, which is markedly less than percentages for Groups II, III, and IV. As in the Group I plays, the elements in the second half of the Group V plays are in general less strong. Nogami's prototype shows a musical entry, a short dance, and the ending verse by the chorus.[103] My count shows only 5 percent of the two-part plays in Group V with the *kuse* section after the intermission. Again, both factors deemphasize the concluding half of the plays. For Group I plays, the shortening of the final part of the play is probably in the interests of an emphasis on introductory elements; in Group V, in the interests of an allegro ending.

Deemphasis of the second half of the plays in both groups is correlated with the frequency of another formal structural element. The majority of the *nochi-jite* entries in Groups I and V are marked by character-identifying, as contrasted to role-identifying, musical passages. The percentages are 95 percent for Group I and 73 percent for Group V. Role songs are structural. The character-identifying music seems to me limited and local, so to speak, somewhat like a musical theme that serves as a signature for a character in Western opera. Among such signature passages are the *ōbeshi* for genii and goblins; *hayabue* for devils, serpent deities, and other gods; *ranjo*, which announces the lion's dance; *sagariha* for nonhuman *shite* such as gods, the spirit of an animal, or an angel; and the *deha*, which is somewhat less specific than the others and can cover human beings as well as male and female gods, ghosts, a saint, etc.[104] There are no verse forms identified with any of these musical entries. This lack suggests their limited use. The relative paucity of the *nochi-jite* entries to such signature music in the second, third, and fourth groups of plays also tends to support such a contention; they are present in 25 percent, 22 percent, and 34 percent of the plays, respectively. They may be profitably compared to the *nochi-jite-issei* entries previously given for these three groups: 75 percent, 66 percent, and 49 percent.

Just as the limiting nature of the signature music makes it suitable as an introduction for a shortened second half, that nature apparently unfits it for the beginning of plays, when a development must be undertaken. Only four first *waki* entries from among all the plays are made to character pieces: three to *shin no raijo*, denoting a Chinese emperor (*Kōtei, Seiōbo,* and *Tōbōsaku*), and one to *hayatsuzumi,* denoting a warrior (*Tsuchigumo*). This paucity also seems consonant with the functional and structural nature of the *waki* role, which is almost always more important than his individual identity, as is plainly evident from a reading of the texts. Among the first-half *shite* entries to signature music, there is one in Group I (in *Tsurukame,* to *shin no raijo*), none in Groups II and III, one in Group IV (in *Kanayōkyū,* to *shin no raijo*). Group V has two of these entries out of forty-three plays; one *sagariha* (*Shōjō*) and one *hayabue* (*Matsuyama Kagami*). In the case of the first-half *shite,* the *mae-jite,* the few such entries probably stem not from a lack of interest in the identity of the *shite* but rather from the structural thrust of the plays, which is often aimed toward the discovery or establishment of that identity.

Just as the *shidai,* the role song for the *waki,* is found in thirty-two plays as a *shite* entry pattern, as previously noted, so the *issei,* normally the role song for the *shite,* sometimes occurs as a *waki* entry pattern. Such instances are apparently rare; I have identified among the five groups of plays only nineteen occurrences.[105] Of these nineteen, ten are in fourth-group plays, seven are in fifth-group plays, and two are in wig-plays. The *waki-issei* entries can be separated into three categories, based on their placement within the individual pieces.

In five plays, there appears to be in a musical sense a conventional patterning, with the *issei* serving as usual as the second strong entry unit of the musical structure. The *shite* in three plays and the *tsure* in one have entered first to a well-developed *shidai* pattern, after which the *waki-issei* entry occurs; these plays are *Shichikiochi, Sekihara Yoichi, Momijigari,* and *Zenji Soga.*[106] In *Kanayōkyū,* the *shite* enters first to introductory signature music, after which the *waki* enters to *issei.* The reversal of the conventional order of entry and the consequent reversal of the role assignment of formal musical patterns will probably provide important clues as to the dramatic intent and experiential significance of these plays.

In ten plays, the *waki* entry to *issei* seems to function as an introductory element for the second half of the play, which is not an unusual function for the *issei,* as previously shown, though it is usually the *nochi-jite* who enters to it. In four plays, the *nochi-waki* enters to *issei* music only: *Chōryō, Rashōmon, Orochi,* and *Hachi no ki.* In *Daibutsu kuyō* and *Zegai,* the *mae-jite* has entered to a well-developed *shidai* pattern, there is no *mae-waki,* and the second half of each play begins with *issei* music and *issei* verse to which the *nochi-waki, waki-tsure, kokata,* or others enter. The seventh play in this group, the well-known *Shunkan,* is particularly interesting. This play has no *shite* exit in it—that is to say, it is a one-act play. However, the *waki* exits early in the piece, to reappear later on, where the role is designated as *nochi-waki,* and the entry is to *issei* music and *issei* verse.[107] There is a clear conclusion to one part of the play, and a second beginning, but the break is not marked by the *shite* exit as is usually done. The *nochi-waki-issei* entry, therefore, serves to mark the beginning of the second development of the play. In *Nishikido,* a *monogi* marks the division of the play into two parts, with a *nochi-waki* entry to *issei* music and *issei* verse following it. In *Tsuchigumo,* a two-part Group V play, the first half is conventionally structured with an opening *shidai* and *jidori,* here sung by the *tsure,* and a *shite-issei* entry. However, only after the *shite* has exited does the *waki* make a brief appearance, marked by entry and exit to *hayatsuzumi,* a drum pattern denoting a warrior. After the usual prose recounting of the story by the *ai-kyōgen*, who also enters to *hayatsuzumi*, the *nochi-waki* appears to *issei* music and *issei* verse. The *nochi-jite*'s true nature as a giant spider is revealed when the covering of the prop on stage, representing a cave, is dropped.

The unusual musical pattern of the last play in this group, *Ohara gokō*, is similar to that of *Aoi no Ue* in several respects. In both plays, what precedes the *issei* entry is introductory in nature and somewhat short. In *Ohara gokō*, the section of the play that precedes the *shite* exit is abnormally short, especially for a Group III play; it contains no strong introductory musical elements, beginning with a prose *nanori* with no music by the *waki-tsure*, an unveiling of the *shite* in a hut, with no introductory music, followed by a recitative, a song in the low range of tones (*sageuta*), and short verses before the *shite* exit. The strength of the following musical pattern, to which the *waki* and others enter, thus seems appropriate: *issei* music, *issei* verse, *shidai*, *jidori*, and a one line prose *tsukizerifu*. The same pattern can be seen in *Aoi no Ue*. A short prose *nanori* with no music by the *waki-tsure* and a short verse by a *tsure* are given first, after which they exit. The *shite* then enters to *issei* music and sings an *issei* verse and a *ni no ku* on the bridge. A musical pattern called *ayumi ashirai* is played for the entry to the stage proper. After an *uchikiri* ending, the *shite* sings a *shidai*, *jidori*, *sashi*, *sageuta*, and *ageuta*. *Matsukaze* also incorporates such a pattern in the texts of the Kongō, Komparu, and Kita schools,[108] after a somewhat unmusical introduction and prose conversation. While the dramaturgical function of such a cluster of formal patterns is different for the three plays, it seems probable that the short and relatively unmusical introductions in them are a relevant factor. This factor probably does not apply to *Taema*, in which a well-structured *waki* entry precedes an elaborated *shite* entry of the same type as discussed here. The problem posed by the unusual patterning of this play can perhaps be profitably approached by a consideration of the five variant versions, some previously mentioned, which make it playable as a piece for Groups I, III, IV, or V, since these may yield clues as to the structural function of its parts. As will be seen, a variant version of *Hagoromo* has proven illuminating for this study.

It seems clear that musical, lyrical, and plot structuring should be considered as an integrated whole, within which the total concept for an individual play can be found. Such an assumption needs of course to be tested for each play and may be helpful in avoiding what Roy E. Teele characterizes as a weakness of certain Western Nō studies: "the cheapening of tone, the misconception of motive and emotion."[109] The fact, then, that only four plays open with *mae-waki-issei* entries indicates that such openings probably serve a special purpose. Two are fifth-group plays, both in two parts: *Ōyama* and *Kuzu*. *Hagoromo* and *Sagi*,[110] an extremely short, one-act fourth-group play, are the other two. All four plays have strongly lyric passages before the *shite* enters. The proportion of prose to verse is comparatively small. In *Kuzu*, the *shite* and *tsure* enter to *ashirai* music, which is short, quiet, and graceful. It is not identified with a specific character. In the remaining three, there is no music indicated. Three of the *shite* begin to speak in prose, while in *Sagi*, the *shite*, which is a heron, does not speak after the entrance until *tsure*, *waki*, and chorus have uttered lines and chanted passages. All these details seem to suggest an adjustment in the *shite*'s entrances because of the vivid musicality of the *waki*'s entrance, beginning as it does with *issei* and continuing with preponderantly verse passages. The omission of the *shidai* and the comparatively unstructured *shite*

159

Hagoromo

entry suggest that the plays begin musically *in medias res*. In light of the *jo-ha-kyū* principle, the supposition seems strengthened by the classifications of the four plays: two in the fourth group (*Hagoromo* was originally played as a fourth-group play, it will be remembered), and two in the fifth group. Consequently, truncation of the introductory elements of these four plays is consistent with the larger rhythmic structure of a day's program of five plays.

These theoretical constructions offered to accommodate the *waki-issei* entrance within the general rhythmic patterning of Nō have been necessary and preliminary to my central discussion of certain musical and lyrical structures of *Hagoromo*, as these support the intent of the play. Some of the observations to be offered are implicit in the foregoing presentation. *Hagoromo* as the only play presented as a third-group piece that opens with a *waki* entrance to *issei* thus betrays its fourth-group origins, with the elimination of the formal *shidai* entry. But such an omission is not dissonant with the total *gestalt* of *Hagoromo* as a wig-play, for the rare *issei* opening contributes to the creation of the special kind of *yūgen* to be found in it. For if it is to be actable as a wig-play, it must have a certain quality of *yūgen*.

Of the forty wig-pieces in the present repertory, twenty-six of them have women as the *shite*. Two plays have heavenly beings in the role with female masks. One has a goddess. In nine plays dealing with trees, flowers, a butterfly, and a bird, the *shite* representing the nonhuman role wears a female mask. In the two remaining plays, in which the spirits of a willow tree and a cherry tree are the *shite* roles, the actor is represented as an old man. The preponderance of the feminine in the *shite* role in the wig-plays is consonant with the *yūgen* aim of this group. Zeami states in his *Nikyoku santai ezu* (1421) that "The dance of women belongs especially to the superior style and appears to be an exquisite sort of *yūgen*. Considering even the sight of youthful dancing and singing, or the three basic forms, still the highest form is found in the woman's dance." In *Shikadō* (1420), he isolates two aspects of *yūgen*: "What is courtly and graceful in the air of *yūgen* arises from the dynamic aspects of the womanly form."[111] Only one of the wig-plays, *Ohara gokō*, has no dance, while thirty have the elegant and courtly *jo no mai*, or prelude dance. The identification of the *jo no mai* with the wig-play can be shown by a summary of its appearances in all the plays: the second and fifth groups have none; the first group, four; the fourth group, four.[112]

In passing, it should be noted that the two early descriptions of *yūgen* by Zeami given above, from among the many comments he makes on it, arise basically from a concept of *yūgen* as a type of *monomane* (imitation of things). As P. G. O'Neill has shown, the school of Nō of Zeami's father, Kannami (1333–84), emphasized the art of *monomane*, in contrast to the school of Inuō, another master performer, whose forte was *yūgen*. It is with this difference between the two schools in mind that Kannami's famous lifelong refusal to dance the angel dance, which was a speciality of Inuō's school, becomes significant. The concept of *monomane*, which originates at least—though with transformational, modifying refinements under Zeami— from realistic tendencies, is perhaps particularly difficult to apply to heavenly beings. Kannami did allow Zeami to perform the angel dance, however; in this connection, we remember the close ties and mutual admiration that existed between both Kannami and Zeami and Inuō. O'Neill goes so far as to say, "It was from him [Inuō] that Zeami derived his understanding of *yūgen*. . . . " Citing the *Kakyō* of 1424, one of the last essays of Zeami's middle period, O'Neill goes on to say that Zeami "made it clear that his conception of *yūgen* was typified by the appearance

160

and bearing of the nobility. . . . It was in mimicry that the beauty of *yūgen* found its clearest expression."[113] These conclusions are undoubtedly valid for Zeami's thinking before his later period. What must be added to this account is that, in Zeami's later prose work, he consistently shows a deepening insight into his earlier concepts, as Konishi has shown. He points out that Zeami "in his early period . . . valued *yūgen*. But he did not think every Nō should be colored by *yūgen*. In contrast to [Inuō's] school, which chiefly stressed *yūgen*, [Kannami's school] valued many varieties of *monomane*." Zeami's treatment of *yūgen* as a category of *monomane* can be seen particularly in the third section of the sixth entry in *Kadensho*, entitled "Kashū ni iu," which Konishi dates before 1408.[114] Later, Zeami seems to have moved from specifics toward a concept of *yūgen* as an aesthetic statement of the nature of beauty. Konishi points out that Zeami "in his middle years says almost no word about *monomane*. The reason is probably that his interest was concentrated on the idea of *yūgen*."[115]

It is to the end of the middle period (1424) that Zeami's famous statements on frozen Nō (*hietaru* Nō) and "no-action" Nō belong.[116] These are concepts of a sublime level. In *Kyūi* (1428) of his last period, a theoretical and highly abstract statement of the various levels of *yūgen* appears, where a certain level of beauty is described metaphorically as "snow in a silver bowl." In 1430, Zeami repeats the ice metaphor in *Sarugaku dangi*, commenting on the appearance of a rival, Zōami.[117] While this difficult area of *yūgen* remains to be further clarified, it is clear that the *yūgen* concept became a great deal larger and deeper than mimicry of courtly manners. It is probable that the growing depth of theoretical insight was based on what Zeami discovered in his art as he matured. From these deeper meanings of *yūgen*, *Hagoromo* exercises its absorbing dramatic hold.

In the third-group plays, then, *yūgen* in the narrow sense that arises from *monomane* is based on what is feminine, with an overlay, however thin, of the sensuous, what in Japanese is called *iro* or *en*. Whatever has *iro* will have *tsuya* (luster or sheen). Without *tsuya*, a performance is dead, as Kita Roppeita once told me. This is easily seen when the *shite* role is that of a young woman. The great interest in the performance of those plays in which the *shite* is an older or old woman lies in part in the intimations of an enduring sexuality, as a beautiful life force, which is associated readily with the feminine. The play *Bashō* is not an unusual example of the *shite* as an elderly woman, who is in this play the spirit of the banana tree. Of this piece a commentator says that, "Aside from illustrating the doctrine of the universal Buddha nature, its chief interest lies in the graceful dance by an elderly woman clad in a 'robe of ice' and a 'skirt of frost' designed to awaken chaste emotions in the hearts of the audience."[118] Along these same lines, Komachi, that most passionately erotic, intense, and beautiful poetess, is presented in the guise of an ancient poor woman in three plays: *Sotoba Komachi*,[119] *Ōmu Komachi*, and *Sekidera Komachi*. In the remaining two of the five plays about her, she is beyond the first bloom of youth; these plays are *Kayoi Komachi* and *Sōshiarai Komachi*.[120] While the dramatic focus is different in *Ōmu Komachi*, *Sekidera Komachi*, and *Sōsharai Komachi*, these being wig-plays, from that in the remaining two, both fourth-group plays, the significance of the old- or mature-woman guise for Komachi may arise from what is characteristically Nō.[121]

161

So forceful is her personality that it can successfully be presented indirectly. The very intensity of it makes for interest when it is seen in an outward form so at variance with the inner self. The tone of such an intent will be seen to be consonant with certain general aesthetic aims underlying the Japanese sensitivity, as expressed in such concepts as *sabi* and *hie*.[122] With varying differences in quality, the same principle would account for the old-man guise of the *shite* in the wig-plays *Yugyō Yanagi* and *Saigyōzakura*. The willow tree, particularly in the very early spring, with its slender branches swaying in a flush of green, generally represents a refined but pronounced sensuousness. However, in *Yugyō Yanagi* the time is autumn and the spirit of the old willow wears a *shiwajō*, a wrinkled old man's mask. In terms of Nō sensibility, it is altogether characteristic to present the spirit of the old cherry tree in spring not as a beautiful young girl.[123] (The *shite* mask in *Saigyōzakura* is also a *shiwajō*.) The whole symbol of the flowering cherry embraces a more massive and intellectually responsible content than such a simple metaphor might suggest.

Although *yūgen* as an aesthetic notion became larger in scope than the *monomane* manifestations of it described by Zeami in his early works and found in the wig-plays, because of the great success of these plays, the concept itself is burdened by at least one aspect of its formulation in the wig-plays. As previously noted, *yūgen* is thought to have as a necessary element a certain somber quality. The attribution is understandable in view of the great wig-plays whose heroines have troubled memories. Even so pure and sweetly loving a *shite* as the one in *Izutsu* has a certain pall over her. It is perhaps a measure of the affective thrust of these plays, in which the *yūgen* of a beautiful and sorrowing woman is raised beyond the pathetic and beyond easy tears, that the element of a "universal sadness," as one critic has put it, is considered essential. In truth, the sense of *lacrimae rerum* is essential to these plays; but it is optional for the concept of *yūgen*, for such a definition cannot account for those third-class plays in which there is no such element, such as *Kakitsubata, Fuji, Ume, Mutsura,* or *Seiganji*.[124] All of these plays, in addition to *Hagoromo*, deal with nonhuman *shite*. Their inclusion of the *taiko* also marks them as a variation on the central theme of the wig-play, as previously noted. In this context, however, these seem to me not decisive considerations. For these plays have come to be considered as belonging to Group III; they are presented as wig-plays. What is conveyed by them cannot be ignored in arriving at an understanding of the term *yūgen*, both as it applies narrowly to the wig-play and as it functions as a larger aesthetic concept.

The kind of wig-play *yūgen* to be found in *Hagoromo*, then, arises from the celestial beauty of the angel; the identity is precisely the point. This is an angelic and heavenly being; the being is also totally good and therefore totally joyous. An *issei* opening for a play with such a *shite* is seen to be most appropriate. The rhythmically textured pattern, the usual, comparatively high, range of the song (here muted by the *tsuyogin* style),[125] and the various ornamentations allowable in the vocal style, which make for musical richness, can convey the active sense of joy in a way for which the *shidai*, with its lower range, regular rhythm, and lack of ornamentation is not easily adaptable. Miyake Kōichi, it will be remembered, characterizes the *shidai* as tranquil. Further the *tsuyogin* (literally "strong") mode, is characterized by Minagawa as suitable for "descriptive and bright sections," with accent, dynamic stress, and tone color as important elements. It can be heroic and vigorous. *Yowagin*, the alternative mode (literally "weak"), is suitable for "gentle" characters in sections that are lyrical, elegant, and emotional.[126] Thus, unusual as it is for a play to open with a *waki-issei* entry, it can be seen that, in *Hagoromo*, the breach of musical form not only enhances but clarifies the intent of the play. The lyrics of

162

the song also are well suited to the nature of the *issei,* as was previously touched upon. The simple candor, typical of the *Man'yō* quality, which delights straightforwardly in the rush of boats putting out to sea as the fishermen shout to each other, is bright and lively.

> Round about the shore
> of Mio's windswept inlet,
> fishers row their boats,
> shouting loudly as they ride
> down the ocean road.

The *waki*'s name-saying speech that follows is a *sashi,* which Minagawa characterizes as a recitative, with a simple melodic movement.[127] A musical pattern of *issei, sashi, sageuta,* and *ageuta* is normal for a *shite* entry.[128] When very formal, it becomes *shin no issei* (with the additional verse *ni no ku*), *sashi, sageuta,* and *ageuta. Takasago* is the classic formal example. *Hagoromo* contains the less formal pattern but in a fully developed sequence. What is unusual about it here is the use of the *sashi* to deliver the name-saying passage,[129] which is in prose form with *sōrō* endings, as is usual. Such prose generally is not sung but intoned. Hence the effect of a *sashi* here is to enhance the name of the *waki,* Hakuryō, as a dynamic element in the play; again this is unusual, but necessary here, as the previous discussion has shown. Once more, we find the musical element supporting the dramatic structure of the play. Unusual patterns, both lyrical and musical, must be examined for what they may reveal about a play.

It is only at the end of the *ageuta* that another prose passage of the *waki* entry appears, which, though intoned, is less elevated than the prior passages. As previously noted, it may be considered that, musically, the usual *waki* entrance, beginning with a *shidai,* has been eliminated, and the play begins *in medias res* with the customary *shite* passage (here allotted to the *waki*), which is usually considered the beginning of the three-part developmental section of the individual play. One effect of such beginnings is a certain spontaneity, to which effect later reference will be made.

Miyake Kōichi has pointed out that the usual content of an *issei* section is a description of the site of the play that has already been arrived at, or of the feelings and general tone of the *shite.* The travel song is a separate section. Here, however, an *issei* section is used to move the *waki* along as well as to prepare the atmosphere and situation of the *shite.*

> As for the *waki*'s entry, the *shidai* is the standard form; however, there are occasionally some plays with the *issei* entry. For instance, the entry of the *waki* in *Hagoromo* and *Momijigari* takes the *issei-sashi* form like that of the *shite* entry. Though such entry is made in the *shite*-entry format, since its content is nevertheless about travel or something similar to it [in *Hagoromo* the *waki* is coming home from fishing[130]], this *issei* and other passages that follow must be sung with movement (*dōteki*) as its lyrical feeling is different from that of the *shite* entry.[131]

163

Specifically, the *issei* section here is used in three ways: to set the affective tone of the play, as the "enigmatic" *shidai* generally does; to move the *waki* to the meeting place (usually accomplished with a *michiyuki*), and to foreshadow the nature of the *shite* (usually a function of the *shite-issei*). Perhaps it is for these reasons also that

Miyake uses the word *dōteki*. It seems reasonable to suppose that the several unusual functions of this entry musically and lyrically are in this case a musical reflection of the dual nature of the *waki* himself, in his guise as Hakuryō and as a common fisherman.

The principle of perspective holds together the following verses. The Chinese verse immediately following the *nanori*, in addition to underscoring the significance of the name Hakuryō, opens up the "distant" view, so that the next line, "How delightful it all seems," is given ample scope. As Hakuryō looks about him from the inlet to the incurving shoreline leading to Mio Point, he first sees the ocean waves, which merge through drifts of rising morning haze with "wave on wave" of green pines into a distant perspective, adorned by a paling moon, where they seem to be growing "far on heavenly plains." The recitative is then succeeded by a low-pitched song followed by a high-pitched song, which continues the theme of a merging perspective, this time from the sky to the sea, to the immediate scene about him: clouds in the sky merge with and are mistaken for the ocean waves, on which the fishermen are at work. This marks the end of the first section of the play, with a repetition of two verse lines in a closure pattern. A word may now be said about the divisions in a play.

The plays are divided into *dan,* or sections, to indicate the beginning, developmental, and concluding parts of the plays. Conventionally, the first *dan* is the introduction; the second, third, and fourth *dan* constitute the development; and the fifth *dan,* the conclusion. There can be great diversity among Japanese critics in the placement of the divisions. I have followed the divisions made by Tanaka in view of his experience as a performer and acknowledged master of the *kotsuzumi,* since they seem to me, particularly in this play, a manifestation of musical development.[132]

With the discovery of the robe, the second *dan* begins. Here an appeal to the senses is one unifying thread. First, as Hakuryō approaches, "a sweet fragrance is floating everywhere." He realizes that this is no ordinary robe he has found, for its fragrance is exquisite. The *shite* enters to claim the robe with a *yobikake* from behind the curtain. Such *yobikake* entries appear in all groups of plays. The distribution is as follows: Group I, one; Group II, two; Group III, seventeen; Group IV, four; and Group V, five. As for role distribution, the call may be allotted to the *shite,* the *shite-tsure,* or a *kokata.* It is sounded from behind the curtain and must give the impression of coming from a considerable distance. Miyake Kōichi notes that, as a shortened form of *shite* entry, it is most effective.[133] This quality of the *yobikake* is here reinforced by the spontaneity accruing to the *waki-issei* entry previously noted. In the wig-plays, all *yobikake* entries are followed by prose exchanges between the *shite* and *waki*, called *mondō* or *mondai*, which are usually in the form of questions and answers. In *Hagoromo*, the prose exchanges become elevated into a verse exchange, a *kakeai* sung in recitative in a free-rhythm style, in which the amusing role exchange of the protagonists delicately and touchingly takes place. The *shite* here introduces the bird imagery, which is more fully developed later in this section. The verse exchange becomes progressively shorter, until one line is said by the *shite* followed by one line by the *waki*. The growing intensity inherent in such a pattern is taken up by the chorus song in the high range, which continues indirectly the appeal to Hakuryō, through his sight; the gradual disintegration and corruption of the angelic form is described, more horrid because the form is celestial, just as the celestial self in man is corrupted by his refusal to surrender to enlightenment.

164

The next five-line *shite* song is in performance usually a delight; it conveys sadness but such sadness as a heavenly being might feel. Sorrow is expressed in such a way as to allow us to enjoy the beauty of the song, yet it engages our genuine concern.

Ama no hara	As I look far out
furisake mireba	across the plains of heaven
kasumi tatsu	the mists are rising,
kumoji madoite	and the could-land path is lost,
yukue shirazu mo	so I do not know the way . . .

Significantly, this poem is taken, with one minor change, from the ancient source of the play, the *Fudoki*. Its use here is an example of the skillful and dramatic way in which poems are incorporated into the text, arousing echoes and thus gaining amplitude.

The chorus takes up the angel's moan in a low-range song, which quickly changes to one in a higher range that makes an appeal to the ear, with references to the kalavinkas' faint voices and the call of geese returning homeward. All this is heard and not seen. Next the gulls and plover are seen and the spring breeze is felt. As the images subtly move from far to less far, not only spatially but experientially, beginning with the sound of faint songs, then proceeding to the stronger call of the unseen geese, and then to the sight of the plover and gulls, what unifies them is their enviable freedom, in sharp contrast to the state of the angel herself, "like a helpless bird / without wings to rise." Just so the godly self in man is unable to rise. The section ends again with two lines repeated in a closure pattern, as the *shite* makes a weeping gesture.

In the third *dan* the theme of joy that began in the first resumes and continues through this and the following sections, gradually intensifying and becoming purer. The section repeats the opening forms of the second *dan*. Hakuryō's change of heart and the angel's cry of joy begin the prose *mondō* section, which again becomes elevated into a verse exchange. The exchanges become progressively shorter, and end again with one verse line by the *waki* and one by the *shite*. Perhaps because it is a repetition of pattern, the *kakeai* section becomes shorter than in the previous *dan*; this shortening begins to quicken the pace of the play.[134] As before, the chorus resolves the increase in intensity. However, in place of the usual high-range song, the resolution takes place here in one of the most interesting formal units in the play, a chorus *shidai* and *jidori*. Its use here is related to the development and elevation of the theme of joy.

To recapitulate, the *issei* opening and *Man'yō* poem set the happy tone, full of joy, which is thematically treated and progressively elevated. First we note the spontaneous joy the fisherman expresses as he admires the spring scene. His joy is unselfish as he finds the robe, and he determines to "make it a treasure of my house." When he knows what a rare treasure he has found, his joy becomes more high minded and civic; he will keep it not from personal greed but for the joy of "future generations" and as a "miracle and treasure of the land." His rejoicing is made poignant by the angel's sorrow, mourning both the loss of her robe and the cruelty in corrupted man. In the third section, joy is elevated as the angel rejoices for the return of her robe and the revelation of man's innate goodness. This thematic elevation of joy is paralleled by the gradual revelation of the identity of the fisherman as truly a Hakuryō, as previously pointed out. Both themes meet in

165

Hagoromo

the angel's cry of gladness. She repeats it in the next speech. It is with just such joy as this that she will perform her dances, for the origin and the heart of dance is pure joy. This is what the chorus conveys to us in the *shidai*, when it sings:

Azumaasobi no	amid Azuma measures,
Surugamai	this Suruga dance,
Azumaasobi no	amid Azuma measures,
Surugamai	this Suruga dance
kono toki ya hajime	was first indeed performed at such
naruran.	a time as this.

With its reference to such ancient times, the content arouses echoes of the first *issei* verse from the old *Man'yō* age. This *shidai* is of the type that Miyake Kōichi says serves to "bring out the feeling briefly and symbolically." It takes the place of the normal *ageuta*, that is the pattern seen in section two, in the chorus verse describing the corruption of the angel's form. Its closure pattern parallels the repetitions that marked the end of the first and second *dan*, but it is stronger, especially with the *jidori*. The strength of the closure apparently balances the *shite* song from the *Fudoki*, and the *sageuta* and *ageuta* by the chorus ending the second *dan*—in all twenty-eight lines of verse. Consequently, it operates as a second quickening of the tempo of the play, leading directly into the fourth *dan*.

Besides further elevating and expanding the theme of joy, the *shidai* and *jidori* combination serves as a pivot verse between the two sections.[135] Like a verse in *renga*, with which it is now believed Zeami was familiar,[136] it is to be read as a concluding verse to the third *dan* and as the introductory verse to the *kuri-sashi-kuse* pattern that follows in the fourth *dan*. Its function as a concluding verse is self-evident, but its role as an introductory one needs examination. The appropriate passages follow.

WAKI

ama no hagoromo	The heavenly robe of feathers
kaze ni kwashi	waves harmoniously;

SHITE

ame ni uruō	with the winds and rain-bedewed
hana no sode	are its blossomed sleeves,

WAKI

ikkyoku o kanade	as she plays a piece of music

CHORUS

(Shidai)

Azumaasobi no	amid Azuma measures,
Surugamai	this Suruga dance,
Azumaasobi no	amid Azuma measures
Surugamai	this Suruga dance
kono toki ya hajime	was first indeed performed at such
naruran	a time as this.

(Jidori)

Azumaasobi no	Amid Azuma measures,
Surugamai	this Suruga dance
kono toki ya hajime	was first indeed performed at such
naruran	a time as this.

(Kuri)

sore hisakata no	Oh say, why do the heavens
ame to ippa	spread eternally?
ni-jin shusse no	When the two gods first appeared
inishie	long, long ago,
jippō sekai o	ten directions through all space
sadameshi ni	for the world they fixed. . . .

The first sequence flows simply and effortlessly enough. We can see that the angel dances the Suruga dance; the chorus repeats the two lines, emphasizing the image created. With the final two lines, we see that more than emphasis is intended, and what was object becomes now subject. The *jidori* establishes the second pattern firmly, freeing it from what preceded. Since it is sung in a lower range than the *shidai* and in a different rhythmic pattern, it creates musically a swift contrast, vivifying the definite sense of closure. At the same time, by the reference to such olden days as when the ancient Suruga dances were first created from the pure joy at the heart of dance, the *shidai* leads to even older times, when the joy of the gods was the source of all creation. The creation is then described. Thus the theme of joy is further elevated and amplified.

Aside from functioning thematically as a pivot verse connected to its preceding and succeeding lines through content, structurally the *shidai* may also be considered as the first unit of the large musical pattern that follows it: *jidori, kuri, sashi,* and *kuse.*[137] This pattern is said to be derived from an older form of dance and song, *kusemai,* which Zeami's father incorporated into Nō. In its fullest form, the concluding lines of the *kuse* repeat the lines of the introductory *shidai;* the repetition, however, is not noted as *shidai. Hyakuman, Kakitsubata, Utaura, Tōgan Koji,* and *Yamauba* contain examples. Thus the importance of this *shidai* thematically and structurally is evident, and Miyake's sound characterization of such *shidai* as functioning "briefly and symbolically" seems a brilliant understatement for this particular case. In many cases, the use of a chorus *shidai* as a substitute for the *ageuta* following a *kakeai* and the use of it as an introductory element to the *kuri-sashi-kuse* pattern are not combined as they are here.

The *kuri,* which opens the fourth *dan,* begins the most brilliantly musical pattern in Nō.[138] The *kuri* is in the higher range, beginning on *jō,* coming to *chū,* and, through a cadential sequence called *honyuri,*[139] reaching the low *ge.* Generally the pitch is set higher than the *jō* notation suggests.[140] It contains the types of ornamentation known as *kuri, iri,* and *mawashi;* its melody is, according to Miyake, magnificent. The description makes it seem most appropriate for a song celebrating the creation of the world. It is in the free-rhythm group of songs, like the *issei* that it resembles. As for role distribution, it is generally sung by the chorus, although there may be some exceptions; in *Kakitsubata,* the *shite* sings the first part and the chorus the second, and in *Yorimasa,* the *shite* sings it. As the introduction to the *kuse* section of the play, in which the mood changes radically from what precedes, it is sung in an ample manner (*ōkiku*), gaily, splendidly, and flowingly. The mood shift is emphasized by the contrast between the low pitch of the preceding *jidori*

167

Hagoromo

and the high pitch of the *kuri*. The general terms describing the musical attack are to be adapted to the particular play. For *Takasago*, Miyake suggests the phrase *tō tō taru* (swiftly rushing); for *Hagoromo*, the characterization is *seiro ryūrei* (clear, flowing, elegant). It has no particular verse pattern and deviates freely from the usual seven and five syllable unit.

An old metaphor for the entire section compares the *kuri* to a waterfall, the *sashi* to flowing water, and the *kuse* to a brimming pool.[141] The metaphor is usefully suggestive.

Again throughout the structure, we note the use of a proportioned perspective, from the far and immense, through a middle ground, to the near, which is here still large. From the vaulting ". . . infinite / they have named the skies" in the *kuri*, we come in the recitative *sashi* to the moon palace, made "with the axe of jewels / so as to last eternally" and tended by the band of celestial maidens. Miyake tells us that the mode changes abruptly with the *sashi*, which is sung deliberately and with restraint (*jikkuri*), and in a lower pitch.[142] It is begun generally by the *shite* and at times by the *shite-tsure* or *waki*. It is continued by the chorus. There may be several alternations between *shite* and chorus. Miyake differentiates between the *sashi* found in the *shite* entry pattern and the *sashi* found in the *kuse* pattern, pointing out that the first is a development of the *issei*, dealing with the subjective feelings of the *shite*, while the *sashi* in this pattern generally contains objective description without deep elaboration, since it is an introduction to the *kuse* rather than a development of a prior element.

From the middle ground of the *sashi*, the chorus takes up the final unit, the *kuse*, bringing us from the moon palace to the glories of the earthly spring scene without diminishment, for the vistas here are large and gracious, trailing their own clouds of glory from the first days of creation. "Fuji's timeless snows / . . . At this spring dawn / so matchless by the waves," the chorus sings. The perspective is proportioned, and even what is near is still large, as the theme of joy is further elevated in a glowing song of praise.

Musically, the *kuse* stresses what is melodious and delicate. "This is the place where melody is enjoyed," Miyake says.[143] Unlike the free rhythm of the two preceding units, it is in regular Nō rhythm, *hiranori*. It is a long passage, usually sung by the chorus, with an insertion of a very short passage by the *shite*, known as *ageha*. The *kuse* is divided into three parts, corresponding to the beginning, development, and conclusion. The first two parts come before the *ageha*, and the last follows it. There are variations on this module; some sections may be omitted, the *ageha* may be missing, and, in the most elaborate form, there may be two *ageha*, as in *Kakitsubata*, *Hyakuman*, and *Yamauba*, in which the *jo ha kyū* divisions are differently placed.

In *kuse* with one *ageha*, as in *Hagoromo*, the end of the *jo* section may be marked by the concluding *uchikiri* drum pattern. In the verse, it is marked by a strong pause. In *Hagoromo*, the pause follows the lines: ". . . with the pine-breeze too / how calm and balmy / glow the inlet scenic views!" The middle section concludes before the *ageha* by the *shite*.

The opening and middle sections are comparable to song in the low range. They begin in the middle range and end on the low *ge*. The usual ornamentations are allowable (*kuri*, *iri*, *irimawashi*, *uki-furi*, etc.). In the first section, since it follows the deliberate tempo of the preceding *sashi*, there is a gradual *accelerando*, with some *ritardando* before its end. The verse content at this point fosters such a slowing:

nodoka naru / ura no arisama. The second section has perhaps a return to regular tempo—marked in the verse by the phrase "and what is more"—with slight *ritardando* before the *ageha.* The second section is sung *legato (surasura).*

The *ageha* that begins the third and concluding section of the *kuse* is sung in the higher *jō* range.[144] The singing of it is adjusted to the type of *shite* in the play. In *Hagoromo,* the *ageha* continues the praise song begun in the previous unit. The higher range therefore seems to enhance it. The chorus section that follows, though not usually marked *kuse,* is understood to be a continuation of it. It is similar to song in the high pitch, since it centers on the *jō-on.* However, there are more ornamentations, called *kuri-on,* and the melody is animated and gorgeous (*nigiyaka, hade*). Zeami called the *kuse* the "ear-opening" section. Here the whole universe is filled with joyful sounds, with "voices singing / to many panpipes, / bamboo flutes and harps and zithers, / spreading, swelling high above / the lonely cloudlets. . . ." The *kuse* ends, bringing the developmental section of the play to a close, in the low range, as do all *ageuta.*

The *shite* verse that marks the beginning of the fifth and final *dan* of the play brings the theme of joy to its logical and pure climax in the prayer of the *shite,* in praise of the Daiseishi Bosatsu incarnate in the moon. In contrast to the low-range ending of the *kuse,* it begins in the high range and ends in the high range, reaching also into the higher range (*kuri*). An *issei*-type of song, it is in free rhythm, in contrast to the regular rhythm preceding it.[145] The angel folds her hands in reverence and half-kneels,[146] acknowledging the bodhisattva, before she begins the angel's dance. This is the *jo no mai* previously dwelt upon, which constitutes the section that Zeami characterized as the "eye-opening" section. The significance of its placement here, after the prayer and gesture of reverential joy, is strengthened by the preceding *shidai,* sung by the chorus, in which joy as the source of dance was celebrated. Here, joy as the source of prayer becomes a fitting climax to the whole play, which is a celebration of a godly and glorious world. The angel reminds us that the true essence of prayer is joy, in praise of the divine. For man, such a realization is profoundly joyful. Dealing as it does with such a theme, the great esteem accorded this play is understandable. *Yūgen* arising from such a concept is seen in a most powerful and sublime aspect.

The section that follows the angel's dance is marked *waka,* signifying the major verse form of five lines, consisting of two parts in the following pattern of syllabication: 5, 7, 5 and 7, 7, which Zeami considered two *ku.* In the plays, such sections may contain well-known lines from *waka* or complete traditional Japanese poems. In *Matsukaze,*[147] for example, the complete poem is given; the first line is recited by the chorus, and the last four lines by the *shite.* The allocation of lines may be variously made. In the Kanze school, the *waka* is regarded as an *issei*-type of song. In some plays the other schools mark it in the *ōnori* rhythm.[148]

The *waka* section of *Hagoromo* is unusual in that the first three lines of seventeen syllables are represented by only four syllables: *aruiwa.* Yokomichi and Omote give an interesting explanation for irregularities in versification, which seems pertinent here. They suggest that the verbal hiatus is left to accommodate changes in movement on stage, where a basic tempo is maintained even if left unplayed. They go on to say that the lines following such a hiatus will be found to be quite full—that is, to contain the usual twelve syllables, accommodated to the basic eight-beat rhythmic unit. They suggest that the fullness of such lines is intended to restrain the movement within the rhythm section.[149] Minagawa, it will be remembered,

169

Hagoromo

stated that "When the end of a section in free rhythm is approached, the rhythmic divergences are gradually and smoothly supplanted by rhythmic agreement, and all the participants produce a cadence at the same time." It may be that an interval for rhythmic accommodation is needed here, particularly after the "big" angel dance, and that the hiatus created by the extremely truncated first half of the *waka* provides this interval. It will be noted that five of the six succeeding lines are of seven syllables, while one has eight syllables—that is to say, they leave very little in the way of interval.[150] What follows the four syllables—*aruiwa*—is marked *ōnori* by Tanaka, one of the three basic patterns for fitting syllables to the eight-beat unit. In it, each syllable falls on a downbeat, with the result that the "music that is cast in it is sung with each accent very clear," as Minagawa says. It has a "calm and majestic effect,"[151] which suggests that the lingering effects of the larger-than-life angel dance cannot end with the dance itself but carry over to these following lines, effectively smothering the usual *waka* section. This factor may underlie the extreme compression of seventeen syllables into four. These are the lines following the end of the angel's prelude dance.

SHITE (*Waka*)

(*Ōnori*)

Aruiwa	At times she seems
amatsu mi-sora no	dressed in robes as deeply blue
midori no koromo	as the glorious skies of heaven,

CHORUS

mata wa haru tatsu	or again in robes as soft
kasumi no koromo	as the mists that rise in spring;

SHITE

iroka mo tae nari	how superb in hue and fragrance
otome no mosuso.	is the maiden's trailing gown!

The parallelism between the first pair of seven-syllable lines, which are the second half of the *waka*, and the next pair of seven-syllable lines is effectively brought to a conclusion in the third pair of lines. In a subtle closure, the eight syllables in the penultimate line function as a signal that the succession of seven-syllable lines is ended.

The next line, "left, right and left," is shortened to four syllables, paralleling the shortened *waka aruiwa*. By breaking the preceding pattern of long lines, it marks the attenuation of the powerful majesty of the angel dance and prepares for the lighter rhythms that will enable the *shite* to exit. These next lines, using the name of Nō dance movements, graphically, onomatopoetically, and rhythmically introduce the *ha no mai*, the quick dance. The onomatopoetic alliteration is particularly important here.

170

Sayū sa	Left, right and left,
sayū sassatsu no	left and right it swirls and swishes
hana o kazashi no	with the blossoms up she holds
ama no hasode	the heavenly feathered sleeves

<pre>
nabiku mo kaesu mo   that flutter, stream and turn and wave
mai no sode   in a dance of sleeves.
</pre>

Sayū sa is the name of a Nō dance movement involving the hands and feet, mentioned by Zeami in *Shichijū igo kuden*.[152] There he asks his successor to pay special attention to this movement and to its reversed form. The modern form, called *sayū*, belongs to this dance pattern or is perhaps derived from it, according to Nose.[153] Masuda describes the modern movement as follows: as the dancer raises toward the left his left hand rather high and the right hand lower in the same direction, he takes a specific number of steps forward on a diagonal line; he then raises his right hand high toward the right and lowers the left hand in the same direction, taking a number of steps forward on the opposite diagonal. He thus moves forward in a zigzag fashion. The number of steps taken depends upon the size of the dance movements—large, medium, or small.[154]

Prosodically speaking,[155] the first line divides syllabically into three and one (technically a second epitrite), suggesting the lyric movement of the dancer's hands, together with his half-turning body as he moves forward on the diagonal. The repetition in the initial three syllables of the second line (a cretic foot) flows into the five-syllable, onomatopoetically rich phrase in Japanese, imitating the silken sounds of the trailing gown in the wind; I have tried to capture the rhythmic movement with the combination of iambic and amphibrachic feet, and the onomatopoeia with a repetition of *s*, as in the Japanese. In contrast to this ending, the third line repeats the cretic foot of the second, here given rhythmic variety by the diambic ending, introducing a new movement. The diambic, functioning as a pivot phrase in Japanese as in the translation, then flows naturally into the fourth line. Here are two contrasting three-syllable feet—amphibrach and cretic—which modulate the contrasting rhythm and suggest the dance rhythms. The fifth line repeats the amphibrach of the fourth, punctuated by the vigorous half spondee that vividly accents the dance movement. The flowing four-syllable foot (a choriamb) creates a smooth liquid rhythm that is reinforced by the contrast in the last line. The whole passage, with its emphasis on rhythmic and onomatopoetic elements, serves as a prelude to the *ha no mai*. This passage, composed in such a way that movements flow naturally from it, is a good example of Zeami's dictate in *Kadensho* that ". . . the norm is for the action to develop from the singing; and to sing in conformity with the actions is an inversion of the normal order." Zeami warns that the actor who regulates his singing by the business (*waza*) is a novice.[156]

The *shite* can now dance the short *ha no mai*. The immensity of the angel's dance, so intensely described by Zeami, can be glimpsed by the careful preparations needed to conclude it and to free the play to move on to its close.

The description given here of the function of the shortened *waka* and of the intervening lines before the final chorus is supported by the *kogaki* version of *Hagoromo* called *wagō no mai*, in the repertory of the Kanze and Umewaka schools. According to Miyake Noboru's description of the variant form, the last section of the angel's dance approaches the character of the *ha no mai*: "That is to say, the *jo no mai* and the *ha no mai* are harmonized with each other. The forms and the costuming are changed." The angel dance then is on a smaller scale. Thus the *waka* section is eliminated. A slight musical *tsuzumi* pattern (*uchiage*) is played in its place, and the text goes immediately to the final chorus song.[157]

The final lines of *Hagoromo* deserve special attention, since there is no repetition

171

of lines in a closure pattern as is usual. Of the forty Group III plays, nineteen end with the last two lines repeated; fifteen end with the repetition, and a further single line added. Only six plays, including *Hagoromo*, end with no repetition.[158] This detail seems particularly appropriate for *Hagoromo*. With no definite sense of closure, the angel does indeed mingle "with the mists of heaven," gradually fading away.

Kita Roppeita has created an ending that is now recognized as a *kogaki* for his school, named the *kasumidome*, or mist exit. In it the chorus pauses at the end of the penultimate line, while the instruments continue to play. In the pause, Roppeita straightens his knees, which are always slightly bent during the performance, giving the effect of actual levitation, and exits quickly as the curtain falls behind him, while the chorus delivers the last line very softly. The *waki* gives the final stamp that indicates the end of the play. The *waki* and the *waki-tsure* then make their exit in silence.[159] It is generally agreed that it is a most beautiful and effective variant.

The concluding verse, here marked *kiri*, is chanted by the chorus. It should be, in Sakamoto Setchō's words, "in an ample and uplifted way, colorful and joyous." It is in the "calm and majestic" *ōnori* rhythm pattern. The angel returns to the heavens, leaving the spellbound audience listening to the chorus sing:

Fuji no takane	to Fuji's lofty peak
kasuka ni narite	she flies and faintly distant
amatsu mi-sora no	in the heavenly sky she grows,
kasumi ni magirete	and intermingling with the mists
usenikeri.	vanishes away.

Masterworks of the Nō Theater

HAGOROMO

Author Unknown

Persons: WAKI: *Hakuryō, a fisherman*
WAKI-TSURE: *His companion (one or more)*
SHITE: *An angel*

Classification: *Primary, Group III; Variant, Group IV or V*
Place: *At the Bay of Mio in the land of Suruga*
Time: *Spring (March)*
Kogaki: *9*

Jo no Dan

[*A stage attendant places a pine tree at stage center front and hangs a loose, unlined silk robe on its branches, representing the robe of feathers. The time is spring, within the pine groves of Mio Bay. With* issei *music, the* waki, *accompanied by his attendant, appears on the bridge. Both carry fishing poles. The* waki *wears a striped kimono of silk, a waistband, and a broad, unlined tunic of unpolished silk. He also wears a white broad divided skirt, with a hunting robe of heavy silk with inwoven large patterns. The* waki-tsure *wears a similar costume, except for the kimono, which is plain. They proceed to center stage, where they stand facing each other. They sing the following* issei *verse.*]

WAKI AND WAKI-TSURE

[1]   *(Issei: awazu, tsuyogin)*

Kazahaya no	Round about the shore
Mio no urawa o	of Mio's windswept inlet [160]
kogu fune no	fishers row their boats,
urabito sawagu	shouting loudly as they ride
namiji kana	down the ocean road. [161]

[*After the opening verse, the* waki *turns stage front and, facing the audience, he sings the "name-saying" passage in* sashi.]

WAKI

(Nanori: awazu, tsuyogin)

Kore wa Mio no matsubara ni Hakuryō to mōsu gyofu nite sōrō.	By the Bay of Mio, and among the groves of pine trees, I am Hakuryō, the fisherman, so they call me.

WAKI AND WAKI-TSURE [*Facing each other again.*]

Banri no kōzan ni	On ten thousand miles of lovely peaks
kumo tachimachi ni okori	suddenly the clouds come up and hover,
ichirō no meigetsu ni	and above the tower shines the brilliant moon,
ame hajimete hareri.	as now the passing shower clears away.[162]
Geni nodoka naru	How delightful it all seems,
toki shi mo ya	this balmy season!
haru no keshiki	These spring scenes we long for,
matsubara no	where the groves of pines
nami tachitsuzuku	crest and roll, wave after wave,
asagasumi	to the morning haze,
tsuki mo nokori no	paling where the moon still hangs[163]
ama no hara	far on heavenly plains
oyobi naki mi no	high above these humble eyes
nagame ni mo	that behold the view;
kokoro sora naru	even to our lowly hearts
keshiki kana.	all seems delightful.

(*Sageuta: au, tsuyogin*)

Wasureme ya	No one can forget
yamaji o wakete	how he takes the mountain path
Kiyomigata	down toward the shore
haruka ni Mio no	of the Clear View Bay[164] far out
matsubara ni	over Mio's pines.[165]
tachitsure iza ya	Come, let us go together
kayowan	and hurry there,
tachitsure iza ya	come, let us go together
kayowan	and hurry there.

(*Ageuta: au, tsuyogin*)

174

Kaze mukō	Mistaking cloudlets
kumo no ukinami	drifting on before the wind
tatsu to mite	for the rising waves,
kumo no ukinami	drifting on before the wind
tatsu to mite	like the rising waves,
tsuri sede hito ya	are you now returning home,
kaeruran.	pulling in your lines?[166]
Mate shibashi	Oh, wait a moment,
haru naraba	now that spring has come,
fuku mo nodokeki	even with the blowing breeze
asakaze no	at dawn it's balmy
matsu wa tokiwa no	through the pines forever green
koe zo kashi	we hear its voice while
nami wa oto naki	the ocean waves grow soundless

Masterworks of the Nō Theater

asa nagi ni   in the morning lull,
tsuribito ōki   and fishers are as many[167]
obune kana   as their little boats.

[*The* waki *and the* waki-tsure *exchange positions.*]

tsuribito ōki   And fishers are as many
obune kana.   as their little boats.

[*While chanting the above line the* waki-tsure *moves toward the chorus and sits in front of it, while the* waki *goes to the stage-attendant's seat in the rear, puts down his fishing pole, takes a folding fan in his hand, and advances to the name-saying seat. He intones the following prose passage.*]

Second Dan

WAKI

[2] *(Kotoba: awazu)*

Ware Mio no matsubara ni agari, ura no keshiki o nagamuru tokoro ni kokū ni hana furi ongaku kikoe reikō yomo ni kunzu. Kore tadagoto to omowanu tokoro ni, kore naru matsu ni utsukushiki koromo kakareri. Yorite mireba iroka tae ni shite tsune no koromo ni arazu. Ikasama torite kaeri, furuki hito ni mo mise, ie no takara to nasabaya to zonji sōrō.

Upon the seashore of Mio's grove of pines I land, and as I look about me and marvel at the inlet view, from out of the sky blossoms fall and heavenly music is heard. A sweet fragrance is floating everywhere. As I come to realize that this is quite unusual, upon the branch of a pine tree I see there a robe of beautiful cloth hanging. [*Looks at the robe.*] As I come nearer, I find its hue and fragrance most exquisite. It is not a common cloak. [*Advances to the pine tree.*] Well, I will bring it down and take it home. [*Holds the robe in both hands.*] Then I'll show it to the elders too, and as the richest treasure in my humble house I will keep it ever.

[*As the* waki *starts toward the* waki *seat, indicating that he is going home, the* shite *calls out from behind the curtain as she enters* (yobikake). *She wears the refined* zō *mask, used to represent young women of a divine nature; a long-haired wig gathered with a strip of white paper at the back of the head and allowed to fall loosely down the back; and a brocade wig-band tied around the head and knotted at the back, with its long ends falling over the outer robe. Her head is adorned with a heavenly crown, a coronet surmounted with a crest of some kind and hung with pendants. She is gorgeously costumed, wearing under robes painted with gold patterns, made of plain white silk with a satinlike finish; at the neckline are three white collars, one over the other, indicating her noble character. An embroidered kimono is wrapped around her body from the waist down, with both sleeves hanging loosely behind her, in the* koshimaki *style. She holds a fan and proceeds slowly down the bridge.*]

175

SHITE

(Yobikake: awazu, yowagin)

Nō. Sono koromo wa konata no nite sōrō. Nani shi ni mesare sōrō zo.

Oh! [*Drawn out.*] Please, that cloak you have taken down from the pine tree is mine. Why do you take it and carry it away with you?

WAKI [*Stands at the* waki *seat and faces the* shite.]

Kore wa hiroitaru koromo nite sōrō hodo ni torite kaeri sōrō yo.

This is a cloak I found by myself alone. Therefore I have taken it down, to be my own, and now I will carry it home.

SHITE [*Advances toward the end of the bridge.*]

Sore wa tennin no hagoromo tote, tayasuku ningen ni atōbeki mono ni arazu. Moto no gotoku ni okitamae.

That robe is the robe of feathers meant for heavenly beings, and not intended to be given indiscreetly to a mortal being. Please, put it back there in the place where you found it.

WAKI

Somo kono koromo no on-nushi to wa sate wa tennin nite mashimasu ka ya. Samo araba masse no kidoku ni todomeoki, kuni no takara to nasubeki nari. Koromo o kaesu koto arumaji.

Well, then! Are you saying that the real owner of this robe is indeed a being from heaven? Did you say that to me? Then now, all the more, for future generations,[168] as a miracle and a treasure of the land it should be held and kept. There can be no good reason to give you back the robe.

SHITE

Kanashi ya na. Hagoromo nakute wa higyō no michi mo tae, tenjō ni kaeran koto mo kanōmaji. Sari tote wa kaeshitabitamae.

How this saddens me! Without my feathered robe, I can no longer fly, for the way is closed. For me to reach my home above in the heavens is impossible. Do not deny me. Return it, oh please, return it.

[*The* waki *responds in* sashi. *The* kakaru *notation indicates a change from intoned prose to heightened verse.*]

176

WAKI [*Facing stage front.*][169]

(Kakaru: awazu, yowagin)

Kono on-kotoba o
kiku yori mo
iyoiyo Hakuryō
chikara o e.

Now barely were these grieving words
said and heard alike,
when more and more Hakuryō
becomes resolute.

Masterworks of the Nō Theater

[*Returns to prose.*]

Moto yori kono mi wa kokoro naki, ama no hagoromo torikakushi,

Unkind and cruel is the heart of this fisherman. The heavenly robe of feathers he takes down and hides.

[*Returns to* sashi.]

kanōmaji tote tachinokeba

It cannot be helped, he says, and prepares to leave.

[*The* waki *advances two steps forward.*]

SHITE

Ima wa sanagara
tennin mo
hane naki tori no
gotoku nite
agaran to sureba
koromo nashi

Now even one from heaven
seems as though she were
only like a helpless bird,
without wings to rise
to the heavenly realm above,
for she has no robe;

WAKI

chi ni mata sumeba
gekai nari.

if she dwells upon the earth
that's the world below.

SHITE

To ya aran
kaku ya aran to
kanashimedo

Should she turn this way?
Should she turn some other way?
Though she deeply grieves,

WAKI

Hakuryō koromo o
kaesaneba

Hakuryō does not return
the robe of feathers.

[*The* shite *enters the stage and stands at the* shite *seat, while the* waki *chants the above lines.*]

SHITE

chikara oyobazu   She who seems so powerless

WAKI

senkata mo   lingers helplessly,

[*The chorus takes up the text in an* ageuta, *describing the gradual corruption in the angel's appearance and her agitation.*]

CHORUS

(*Ageuta: au, yowagin*)

namida no tsuyu no
tamakazura

on the blossoms of her hair
gemlike drops of dew

177

Hagoromo

kazashi no hana mo	and their petals start to droop,
shioshio to	sorrowfully too,[170]
tennin no gosui mo	the five dread signs that taint an
	angel[171]
me no mae ni miete	appearing here before our eyes
asamashi ya.	are all too cruel.

[*While chanting the following lines, the* shite *darkens the mask by tilting it slightly downward. The* shite *then turns toward the right and looks up.*]

SHITE

(*Awazu, yowagin*)

Ama no hara	As I look far out
furisake mireba	across the plains of heaven
kasumi tatsu	the mists are rising,
kumoji madoite	and the cloud-land path is lost,
yukue shirazu mo.	so I do not know the way[172]

CHORUS

(*Sageuta: au, yowagin*)

Suminareshi	back to the heavens
sora ni itsu shika	where I used to dwell before,
yuku kumo no	when, how soon, can I
urayamashiki	go like those returning clouds
keshiki kana.	I see with envy?

(*Ageuta: au, yowagin*)

Karyōbinga no	The kalavinka voices[173]
narenareshi	I'm used to hearing,
karyōbinga no	the kalavinka voices
narenareshi	I'm used to hearing

[*The* shite *moves forward.*]

koe ima sara ni	sound more faintly than before
wazuka naru	at this moment now
karigane no	when I hear the call
kaeriyuku	of geese returning
amaji o kikeba	by the path across the sky,
natsukashi ya.	how I envy them!

178 [*The* shite *looks ahead and above.*]

| Chidori kamome no | The plovers and the seagulls |
| okitsunami | on waves at offing, |

[*The* shite *turns to the left.*]

| yuku ka kaeru ka | moving in and out at will, |
| harukaze no | even those spring winds |

sora ni fuku made	blowing high across the blue,
natsukashi ya	how I envy them,
sora ni fuku made	blowing high across the blue,
natsukashi ya.	how I envy them!

[*Returning to the* shite *seat, the* shite *looks upward at the sky and moves slightly backward. The* shite *makes the* shioru *gesture,*[174] *raising one hand slightly toward the mask and tilting it downward, to indicate weeping. Now the* waki *at the* waki *seat and the* shite *at the* shite *seat begin the following prose* mondō *or* mondai[175] *passage.*]

Third Dan

WAKI

[3] *(Mondai: awazu, yowagin)*

Ikani mōshi sōrō. On-sugata o mitate-matsureba amari ni onnitawashiku sōrō hodo ni koromo o kaeshimōsōzuru ni-te sōrō.

How shall I express my thought aloud? Now that I realize from your cast and countenance how terrible and deeply agonizing are the depths of your distress, here I would like to say that now I truly will return this robe to you.

SHITE

Ara ureshi ya. Saraba konata e tamawari sōrae.

Oh, how this gladdens me! Please, oh please, then, give me back my precious robe.

[*The* shite *moves two steps toward the* waki.]

WAKI

Shibaraku.

Wait a moment.

[*The* waki *moves two steps backward.*]

Uketamawarioyobitaru tennin no bu-gaku tadaima koko nite sōshitamawaba koromo o kaeshimōsubeshi.

Long, long ago I've heard the story men tell of the dances of the angels. So now, at once, here in this place if you will perform and dance, then and only then will I return your garment.

SHITE

Ureshi ya sate wa tenjō ni kaeran koto o etari. Kono yorokobi ni totemo saraba, ningen no gyo-yū no katami no mai, gekkyū o megurasu bukyoku ari. Ta-daima koko nite sōshitsutsu yo no uki hito ni tsutōbeshi. Sarinagara koromo

This gladdens me! Indeed, then, back to heaven above I will be able to go once again. Yielding to the thankfulness within me, I will dance, a dance I leave you as a keepsake for your sweet mer-riment, which we dance about the Pal-

179

nakute wa kanōmaji. Saritote wa mazu kaeshitamae.

ace of the Moon above. So now, at once, here in this place I will perform it. Among you sorrowful men, let it be handed down. Though I wish to dance, without my heavenly robe I cannot do so. Therefore now, before all else, please return it to me.

WAKI

Iya kono koromo o kaeshinaba, bukyo-ku o nasade sono mama ni ten ni ya agaritamōbeki.

Oh, no, indeed! If I return the robe to you now, without dancing any dance, once you have the robe, straight to the skies far above you might fly away.

SHITE

[*Delivers the following with dignity and an air of purity.*][176]

I ya utagai wa ningen ni ari. Ten ni i-tsuwari naki mono o.

Oh, no, indeed! Doubt exists only among you mortals. In heaven there can never be deceitfulness.[177]

[*The* waki *is touched. He responds.*]

WAKI

(Kakaru:[178] awazu, yowagin)

Ara hazukashi ya
saraba to te
hagoromo o kaeshi
atōreba

Ah, what shame, what shame is mine,
uttering these words,
he returns the robe of feathers;
when he gives it back,

[*The* waki *gives the robe to the* shite *and returns to the* waki *seat. The* shite *retires to the stage attendant's seat. While* ashirai[179] *music is played, the stage attendant helps the* shite *put on the robe, a procedure called* monogi. *After the* monogi, *the* shite *advances to the* shite *seat.*]

SHITE

(Kakeai: awazu, yowagin)

Otome wa koromo o
chakushitsutsu
geishō-ui no
kyoku o nashi

the maiden puts the garment on.
"The Robe of Feathers
and the Rainbow Skirt"[180] she swings
and steps the measure.

WAKI

ama no hagoromo
kaze ni kashi

The heavenly robe of feathers
waves harmoniously

SHITE

ame ni uruō
hana no sode

with the winds and rain-bedewed
are its blossomed sleeves

180

WAKI

ikkyoku o kanade   as she plays a piece of music

SHITE

mō to ka ya   while she dances now

[*The chorus takes up the text with a* shidai.]

CHORUS

(*Shidai: au, yowagin*)

Azumaasobi no	amid Azuma measures,[181]
Surugamai	this Suruga dance;
Azumaasobi no	amid Azuma measures,
Surugamai	this Suruga dance
kono toki ya hajime	was first indeed performed at such
naruran.	a time as this.

(*Jidori*)[182]

Azumaasobi no	Amid Azuma measures,
Surugamai	this Suruga dance
kono toki ya hajime	was first indeed performed at such
naruran.	a time as this.

Fourth Dan

[*The* shite *moves in front of the musicians, making certain graceful movements*[183] *that follow a conventional pattern. The chorus begins the most musical section of the play with the following* kuri.]

CHORUS

[4] (*Kuri: awazu, yowagin*)

Sore hisakata no	O say, why do the heavens
ame to ippa	spread eternally?
ni-jin shusse no	When the two gods first appeared[184]
inishie	long, long ago,
jippō sekai o	ten directions through all space[185]
sadameshi ni	for the world they fixed,
sora wa kagiri mo	for the skies they set no bounds
nakereba tote	stretching endlessly on
hisakata no	ever without end;
sora to wa	the infinite
nazuketari.	they have named the skies.

181

[*The* shite *begins the* sashi *section, alternating with the chorus.*]

Hagoromo

(*Sashi: awazu, yowagin*)

Shikaru ni	Fair is the sight
gekkyūden no	of the bright Moon Palace,
arisama	for it was made
gyokufu no shuri	with the axe of jewels
tokoshinae ni shite	so to last eternally.

CHORUS

byakue kokue no	Dressed in either white or black,[186]
tennin no	the heavenly maidens
kazu o san-go ni	are divided in two groups
wakatte	of three fives;
ichigetsu yaya no	and each month, night after night,
amaotome	a heavenly maiden
hōji o sadame	is assigned her turn to go
yaku o nasu.	to fulfill her task.

SHITE

Ware mo kazu aru	I, too, am of that number,
amaotome	a heavenly maiden

CHORUS

tsuki no katsura no	from the moon-bright laurel fruit[187]
mi o wakete	who comes incarnate
kari ni Azuma no	to the eastern land awhile
Surugamai	this Suruga dance
yo ni tsutaetaru	she will dance for you to keep
kyoku to ka ya.	for the world of men.

[*While the chorus sings the* kuse, *the* shite *moves gracefully in time to it. Consequently, it is classed as a* maiguse, *or dance* kuse.]

CHORUS

(*Maiguse: au, yowagin*)

Harugasumi	All across the sky
tanabikinikeri	the mists of spring are trailing,
hisakata no	far in the distance.
tsuki no katsura no	Are the laurels of the moon
hana ya saku.	in full bloom above?[188]
Geni hanakazura	Now the blossoms in her hair
iromeku wa	glow deep with colors,[189]
haru no shirushi ka ya.	can it be the first sign of spring?
Omoshiro ya	What delight is this!
ame narade	Though it's not heaven
koko mo tae nari.	here how wondrous all is too!
Amatsukaze	Oh, winds of heaven,

Masterworks of the Nō Theater

kumo no kayoiji	swiftly blow and block the way
fukitoji yo	homeward through the clouds,
otome no sugata	that the vision of this maid
shibashi todomarite	may linger on a little while [190]
kono matsubara no	here across the grove of pines
haru no iro o	from Mio's point we see
Miogasaki	hues of spring, the sights
tsuki Kiyomigata	over Clear View Bay, the moon,
Fuji no yuki	Fuji's timeless snows.
izure ya haru no	Which one surpasses others?
akebono	At this spring dawn
taguinami mo	so matchless by the waves,
matsukaze mo	with the pine-breeze too
nodoka naru	how calm and balmy
ura no arisama.	glow the inlet scenic views! [191]
Sono ue ametsuchi wa	And what is more, here heaven and earth
nani o hedaten	have nothing to divide them,
tamagaki no	for our sovereign hails
uchito no kami no	from the godhead in the shrines [192]
mi-sue nite	by the jeweled fence;
tsuki mo kumoranu	so the moon is cloudless too
hinomoto ya.	in this sun-blessed land. [193]

[*The* shite *continues as she chants the following verse, called* ageha, *literally "lifted wing" or "high ridge," since it contains notes in the high range.*]

SHITE

(*Ageha*)

Kimi ga yo wa	Oh, thy reign shall stand,
ama no hagoromo	more than crags that wear away
mare ni kite	though brushed but rarely

CHORUS

nazutomo tsukinu	by an angel's feathered robe,
iwao zo to	oh, rock eternal! [194]
kiku mo taenari	How superb it is to hear
Azumauta	this Azuma song
koe soete	with voices singing
kazukazu no	to many panpipes,
shō chaku kin ku go	bamboo flutes and harps and zithers, [195]
koun no hoka ni	spreading, swelling high above
michimichite	the lonely cloudlets, [196]
rakujitsu no	as the crimson red
kurenai wa	of the setting sun
someiro no	dyes bright the mountain
yama o utsushite	mirroring Mt. Sumeru, [197]
midori wa nami ni	while deep green upon the waves
Ukishima ga	Floating Island Field [198]

183

Hagoromo

harō arashi ni	is swept by winds that scatter
hana furite	the cherry blossoms;
geni yuki o megurasu	indeed their snows that swirl and flutter
hakuun no sode zo	from the white clouds of her sleeves
tae naru.	are exquisite![199]

Fifth Dan

[*As the* shite *finishes the movements of the* kuse, *she half-kneels at the* shite *seat. The* shite *chants the following verse, in the style of* issei-*like singing, holding both her hands in prayer.*]

SHITE

[5] *(Ei: awazu, yowagin)*[200]

Namu kimyō	All praise and glory
Gattenshi	to thee, Moon-Monarch,
honji Daiseishi	O, thou almighty Seishi![201]

CHORUS

Azumaasobi no	Amid Azuma measures
mai no kyoku.	this dance she dances.

[*The* shite *rises from the* shite *seat and dances the prelude dance.*]

Jo no mai

[*After the dance, she continues to move gracefully, in unison with the following* waka *verse.*]

SHITE

(Noriji: ōnori, yowagin)

Aruiwa	At times she seems
amatsu mi-sora no	dressed in robes as deeply blue
midori no koromo	as the glorious skies of heaven,

CHORUS

mata wa haru tatsu	or again in robes as soft
kasumi no koromo	as the mists that rise in spring;

184

SHITE

iroka mo tae nari	how superb in hue and fragrance
otome no mosuso.	is the maiden's trailing gown!

CHORUS

Sayū sa	Left, right and left,
sayū sassatsu no	left and right it swirls and swishes

hana o kazashi no	with the blossoms up she holds
ama no hasode	the heavenly feathered sleeves
nabiku mo kaesu mo	that flutter, stream and turn and wave
mai no sode	in a dance of sleeves.

[*The* shite *dances the quick dance.*]

Ha no mai

[*At the end of this brief dance, the* shite *is at the* shite *seat. The* shite *stamps and continues her graceful movements, as the chorus chants the final verse passage.*][202]

Chorus

(*Kiri: ōnori, yowagin*)

Azumaasobi no	Amid Azuma measures
kazukazu ni	with many numbers,
Azumaasobi no	amid Azuma measures
kazukazu ni	with many numbers,
sono na mo tsuki no	as each is named, a maiden
miyabito wa	of the moon appears,
san-go yachū no	shining in the skies again
sora ni mata	on this three-fives night
mangan shinnyo no	in a form so full and perfect[203]
kage to nari	with the light of truth,
go-gan enman	for the Vows are all fulfilled,[204]
kokudo jōju	the kingdom realized;
shippō jūman no	and letting all the seven treasures[205]
takara o furashi	fall and scatter like the rain
kokudo ni kore o	everywhere throughout the land,
hodokoshitamō	they are graciously bestowed;
saru hodo ni	then, before too long,
toki utsutte	the hour flies swiftly.
ama no hagoromo	The heavenly robe of feathers
urakaze ni tanabiki	trails upon the blowing inlet breeze,
tanabiku	and as it trails

[*While the chorus sings, the dancing* shite *begins to move toward the bridge, gradually ascends it, and finally, with the last words of the chorus, delivered very softly, disappears beyond the curtain.*]

Mio no matsubara	over Mio's grove of pines,
Ukishima ga kumo no	past cloud-skirted Floating Island,
Ashitakayama ya	above Mt. Ashitaka
Fuji no takane	to Fuji's lofty peak
kasuka ni narite	she flies and faintly distant
amatsu mi-sora no	in the heavenly sky she grows,
kasumi ni magirete	and intermingling with the mists
usenikeri.	vanishes away.

185

[*The* waki *stamps, indicating the end of the play.*[206] *The* waki *and the* waki-tsure *make their exit.*]

Hagoromo

Izutsu

Introduction

> A playwright must understand the heart of the
> music; he must make the words turn from one
> to another beautifully.
>
> —ZEAMI[1]

Izutsu, a wig-play written by Zeami, is based loosely on the twenty-third episode
of the classic *Tales of Ise* (ca. 950). According to popular tradition, Ariwara no Narihira (825–80), the famous poet, and the daughter of Ki no Aritsune (815–77)[2]
were childhood playmates. As they grow older, their camaraderie gives way to a
newfound love, and after a courtship forwarded by an exchange of poems, they
are married. Sometime thereafter, Narihira begins an affair with another woman,
but the sweet longing of his wife, expressed in a well-known poem, draws him
back to her. "His heart swelled with love for her, and his visits to [the lady in]
Kawachi ceased."[3]

In the Nō play, this plot kernel is embedded in the conventional framework of
the two-part ghost play. A traveling Buddhist priest visits a ruined site connected
with the two lovers, meets there a mysterious woman who tells him the story, and
finally learns the identity of his visitor, who is the ghost of Narihira's wife. She
thereupon disappears. After being given a straightforward résumé of the story by
a "person of the place" in less elevated language, the priest sings a "waiting song"
as he prepares to spend the night. The spirit then reappears in his dream in her
proper guise as Narihira's wife. She performs an abstract and expressive dance,
demonstrates once again the purity and sweetness of her tender love, and then
departs as the priest awakens from his dream.

In the oblique fashion of this theater, a most important character in this play
never appears and yet is constantly present. This is Narihira himself, "one of
the greatest of all the Court poets" of the Heian period (794–1185), as Brower

186

and Miner say, going on to characterize him further as "quick-minded yet reflective, overwhelmingly attractive yet humanely considerate, many-sided yet profound. . . ."[4] Helen Craig McCullough concludes that "like Prince Genji, Narihira seems to personify the supreme Heian ideals of elegance and sensitivity."[5] Add then to this commonly accepted portrait of the man the fact that his poetry is one of the major glories of the Japanese poetic tradition, and we are already prepared for the refined and graceful tone of a subtle, high court culture. Zeami hardly needs to establish a groundwork of expectation—only to exploit it in the lyrics, the singing, the music and dance of Nō.

I have urged elsewhere[6] that one method that can make a Nō play accessible to a reader is to pay much greater attention to the formal lyrical and musical elements in a play than has been the usual case in discussions of individual plays. (The use of these elements within a single play must of course be evaluated in terms of their use throughout the repertoire.) What I mean by a play's being accessible is that it enables a reader to get some grasp of the living theater experience that emerges from the text. Such attention to Nō structure is perhaps not so needful for the more overtly dramatic or theatrical plays, since vivid battle descriptions, or a strong, sequential plot line, or the use of melodramatic masks and costuming can convey some of the thrust of a play. But the Group III plays generally eschew such explicit devices. This may be why these wig-plays have been comparatively less appreciated in the West, as can be inferred from Roy E. Teele's comment that the success of "Pound's and Waley's books has been emphasis on the fourth- and fifth-class plays, the most dramatic [i.e., theatrical] of the five groups."[7] Thus, particularly in the "true" wig-plays (*jun-sanbanme* like *Izutsu*, in which a diaphanous, luminous *glissando*, ringing the changes of a tender lost love, is the intent), some attention to the Nō structure can be profitable, as I hope to show.

For in *Izutsu*, it is the conventional Nō format of the two-part ghost-play itself, rather than a plot line, that provides a sequential linear thread. Hence this play may seem stultifyingly formulaic, unless we are aware of its affective content, conveyed not only through the lyrics and music but through its use of Nō conventions.

So it is clear that what is horizontally sequential in *Izutsu* is less consequential for the play than is the clarity of the rendering of the pure and tender longing of Narihira's wife. What is more important in this play than the "dramatic horizontal . . . line" is the "series of verticals, moments of chorded experience," as Marvin Rosenberg has said in another connection in his well-known essay. *Izutsu* is meant to form a whole as a "texture, rather than a line."[8] What this texture is in Nō can be revealed in part by attention to the total structure, to what Waley calls the "architecture" of the plays: "It is above all in 'architecture,' in the relation of parts to the whole that these [plays] are supreme."[9]

This examination will deal with the significance of the large configuration of the *waki*'s entry pattern taken together with the *shite*'s entry pattern in the wig-plays; the arrangements of the text, especially in its use of repeated motifs and of some of Narihira's greatest poems; and the use of musical elements to support the experiential intent. 187

Prior to the performance, the members of the chorus enter silently and modestly through the hurry-door[10] and seat themselves stage left. The musicians—the two hand-drum players and the flutist—move slowly down the bridge from the mirror room and take their places in the rear. A highly stylized prop representing the well curb is placed at center front. There is silence. The harshly vivid tones of the Nō flute, piercing, breathy, and blurred of pitch,[11] begin the set pattern for the *nanori* entry by the secondary actor (*waki*). He emerges and at the right rear pillar opens the play with an intoned prose announcement of his identity as a wandering Buddhist priest and the statement that he is at the site of the Ariwara Temple, now no longer standing. Advancing to center stage, his voice heightens slightly from prose to recitative (*sashi*) as he identifies the site with Narihira and his wife. He quotes, in a throwaway fashion, the first three lines of the wife's poem from the *Tales of Ise*, with which she won back Narihira's heart:

> Kaze fukeba   "When the wind rises,
> okitsu shiranami   the white waves from the offing
> Tatsutayama . . .   Mount Tatsuta's Pass . . ."

"So goes her famous poem," he says, "and surely at this very place / she must have written it." It will be seen that the first two lines of the poem (the *joshi*, or introduction) are very loosely connected to the third line through a pun on "mount," which approximates the Japanese pivot word (*kakekotoba* or *kakeshi*, translated elsewhere in this book as "pun").[12] The effect is so conventional as to be very flat in the poem, but as will be seen, the Nō text exploits that very flatness for some deeply intensified effects.

The rhythm of the singing changes from the free rhythm of recitative to the usual Nō rhythm (*hiranori*) of song,[13] here in the low tones, as the *waki* recalls how lost in the past is the famous story and clasps his hands in prayer to the memory of the storied pair. This entry pattern concludes with the closure of repetition of two lines of verse, and the *waki* proceeds to the *waki* seat, where he sits in the usual low, half-kneeling position. This ends the first of the five *dan*, or units into which the plays are divided.[14]

Kazamaki has pointed out how low-keyed this entry is: "The traveling priest is already here and knows that this is the ancient site [of the story of Narihira and his wife]. This is an easygoing entrance."[15] In contrast to the fully developed pattern for a *waki* entry, with formalistic alternations of song, prose, song, and prose (*shidai* and *jidori, nanori, michiyuki, tsukizerifu*),[16] the grouping of formal elements here fosters the impression of subdued quiet: prose, recitative, and song in the low tones (*sageuta*). In particular, the omission of the "traveling song" often sung by an itinerant priest—always a variety of song in the high tones (*ageuta*) and therefore more vivid musically[17]—must be taken as calculated, for the sake of immediately setting the tone of this play as quiet (*shizuka*) and restrained (*tsutsushimu*), to give Sakamoto Setchō's characterization of the play.[18] In performance, that omission is marked by a well-defined pause,[19] following the name-saying, after which the *waki* begins an entirely different attack.

Aside from giving the necessary "information," the *waki* here strikes the theme of the importance of the past. The wordplay that occurs here on *nari* (to be) and Narihira, the poet's name, is repeated several times throughout the play, as is that on *tsune* (forever) and Aritsune, the given name of the wife's father. The thrust of these pivot words is lost in translation, but in Japanese they give added dimension to the theme of the past: what was here is here no longer; what was to be forever has passed away.

The second *dan*, or beginning of the developmental section, opens as the main actor or *shite* enters to the musical *shidai*, normally a *waki* pattern. I have stated elsewhere that of the 235 plays in the repertoire, the *shite* enters to the *shidai* in only 32.[20] Thus it is not a common *shite* entry pattern. Miyake notes that "when a role that normally enters on *issei* [i.e., the *shite*] enters to *shidai*, it is to reinforce a more tranquil (*seijaku*) tone about the *shite*. . . . The total feeling around a *shidai* is a much more tranquil effect."[21] So the subdued tone already noted in the *waki*'s entry in *Izutsu* is further reinforced here with the uncommon *shite-shidai* entry, with its deliberate patterns of repetition.

The verse content is one of great purity, gentleness, and calm. The *shite* sings:

Akatsuki-goto no	With each dawn I come to draw
aka no mizu	the holy water,
akatsuki-goto no	with each dawn I come to draw
aka no mizu	the holy water,
tsuki mo kokoro ya	and the moon, too, makes my heart
sumasuran.	peaceful, calm, and clear.

The chorus sings in lower tones, repeating the last four lines:

Akatsuki-goto no	With each dawn I come to draw
aka no mizu	the holy water,
tsuki mo kokoro ya	and the moon, too, makes my heart
sumasuran.	peaceful, calm, and clear.

This gently tender *shidai* fulfills very well its *shidai* function of sounding the affective theme of the entire play. These qualities are gracefully created by the homonymic alliteration of the syllables *aka* (*akatsuki*, or "dawn," and *aka no mizu*, or "holy water") as well as by the broad and open sound of *a* in the syllables, and by the explicit statement of the last line, terminating with the alliterative flow of the repeated syllable *su* (*sumasuran*), which is turned back to the preceding pair of lines by the word *mo* (too) and the alternate homonym of *tsuki* in line five. The attempt in the translation to approximate the texture of the Japanese verse through alliter-ation (dawn and draw; with and water; moon, makes, and my; clear and calm) and vowel sounds (dawn, water, calm; peaceful and clear) is self-evident. The particle *ya* also functions to open out the feeling and dimension, adding a spreading amplitude.[22] Gentleness rises too from the action itself of drawing holy water to use as a religious offering.

Yeats's perceptive observation on the unity of imagery in the Nō plays is well known—what he calls the "playing upon a single metaphor as deliberate as the echoing rhythm of line in Chinese and Japanese paintings." He cites the "woven grass [that] returns again and again in metaphor and incident" in *Nishikigi*.[23] Just such an example of imagistic unity can be found in *Izutsu* in the recurring water theme. The first instance appears in the half-quoted Tatsutayama poem in the *waki*'s first recitative, where white waves are mentioned. Here in the *shidai*, holy water is drawn. After several further unobtrusive mentions of water, the image is fully and intricately developed in the *sashi* section of the important *kuri-sashi-kuse* pattern and in the *kuse* passage itself. Finally, at the climactic moment of the play, the *shite* looks into the well to see the image of her lover on the water. In a play entitled the *Well Curb*, where the theme of purity of feeling figures importantly, the purifying and cleansing function implied in the water images seems appropriate.

I have dealt elsewhere with the *shidai* as the dominant entry pattern for the

189

waki.[24] The "name-saying" to which the *waki* enters here is the second most common *waki* entry throughout the current repertoire of 235 plays. Its distribution among the five groups of plays is as follows: Group I, 3 percent (1 play); Group II, 37 percent (6 plays); Group III, 45 percent (18 plays); Group IV, 41 percent (39 plays); Group V, 30 percent (13 plays). Taking the 118 *waki-shidai* entries and the 77 *waki-nanori* entries together, they constitute 83 percent of the *waki* entries in the entire repertoire. The *waki-nanori* entries vary greatly in their patterning, from very slight (*Futari Shizuka*, for example) to elaborate (*Ume*). One important factor in evaluating their dramaturgical and expressive function seems to be their relationship with the *shite* entry. I will consider here only the *waki-shidai* (17 plays) and *waki-nanori* (18 plays) entries in the 40 plays of Group III, to which *Izutsu* belongs.

It will be remembered that the third group of plays is the climax or most experientially intense of the day's program of five plays, which in the early days of Nō proceeded sequentially with introduction (the god-plays of Group I), development (Groups II, III, and IV), and conclusion (the lively Group V, which includes those plays with demons).[25] Thus, before the wig-play, the restless audience has already been settled down and cajoled into receptivity by a god-play, celebrating the auspiciousness of the occasion, of nature, or of the times, with very little plot action other than the actual dance and singing. The Group II warrior-play marks the beginning of a deepening intensity. Thus, with the Group III wig-play, the playwright is not concerned with introductory or preliminary measures, designed to capture the audience. These have already been taken care of. He is free to enter more quickly into the deeper experiential levels, the series of "verticals, moments of chorded experience." We can note this in the relative paucity of the formal structural introductory elements, considered singly. Only seventeen (43 percent) of the forty wig-plays begin with the conventional *waki-shidai* openings, and in only three (8 percent) is the *shite* first brought on to the vivid *issei*, the conventional *shite* role-song (*yaku-utai*). These figures become more meaningful when compared with those for the introductory Group I plays, where 88 percent begin with *waki-shidai* openings and 88 percent have *shite-issei* entries. These larger percentages are consonant with the introductory function of the god-plays in the day's program.[26]

Further significance is found in examining the relationship between the seventeen conventionally formal *waki-shidai* entries in the Group III plays and the *shite* entries in them. For no wig-play begins with the stately tempo of the introductory god-plays, with a structured *waki-shidai* entry followed by a formal *shite-issei* entry. Thirteen have *shite-yobikake* entries,[27] in which the *shite* comes on, having called out to the *waki* from behind the curtain, as if from a considerable distance. All *yobikake* entries throughout the repertoire are followed by a prose exchange (*mondō* or *mondai*) between the *shite* and *waki*. In short, while very effective,[28] the *yobikake* is not a musical entry and leads directly to the matter of the play. Significantly, 58 percent of all *shite-yobikake* entries throughout the repertoire are found in the wig-plays.[29]
The *shite* entries in the remaining four plays of this group are also relatively unstructured as far as formal musical elements are concerned.[30] Thus these wig-plays are free to come quickly to the heart of their matter.

This conclusion is strengthened by the fact that the total absence of relationship between *waki-shidai* entries and *shite-issei* entries is not true of the other four categories of the plays. The number of such relationships for each category follows: Group I, thirty-three *shite-issei* entries can be found in the thirty-five plays with *waki-shidai* entries; Group II, four *shite-issei* entries among the nine *waki-shidai* en-

190

tries; Group IV, eleven among thirty-six; Group V, twelve among twenty. If the criterion becomes simply the massiveness of musical patterns (in contrast to the slimness of the *shidai-yobikake* pattern of the wig-plays), and the *shite-shidai* entries are added to the frequency of the *shite-issei* entries in the above figures, they increase as follows: Group I, thirty-four; Group II, six; Group IV, thirteen; Group V, unchanged.

When the *shite* entries in the eighteen plays in Group III with *waki-nanori* entries are examined, it is found that nine are formally musical and nine are marked with slight musical elements. The breakdown is as follows: three to *issei*, six to *shidai*, three to *yobikake*, four to *ashirai* music and recitative, one to *ashirai* music and prose dialogue, and one to no music and prose dialogue.[31] What is of interest is that this *nanori-waki* group contains all the *shite-issei* entries and all but one of the *shite-shidai* entries in the forty plays of Group III. (In the one exception in the latter group, *Minobu*, the *waki* entry is quite unstructured: there is no entry music and the *waki* begins with recitative.) The comparatively less assertive nature of the *nanori* entry in Group III plays is shown since it is used to accommodate, so to speak, these more importantly structured types of *shite* entry.

Such patternings might be considered the reverse of the *waki-shidai, shite-yobikake* configuration previously considered. In the latter, the setting of tonality through musical means is accomplished by the *waki*'s entry to *shidai*, thus allowing for the brevity of the *shite*'s *yobikake* entry, followed immediately by prose dialogue. In the former, the musically truncated *waki* entry to *nanori* immediately establishes the informational coordinates of the play, while the *shite*'s entry to *shidai* or *issei* sets the musical tonality.

The above characterization of one function of the *nanori* entry seems to be supported by the fact that in all categories, it occurs in 50 percent (fifteen) of the pieces with the uncommon *shite-shidai* entries (although there are thirty-two of the latter, two plays do not have a *waki*).[32] The rate of relationship between the two patterns seems large enough to be significant. Further, the distribution pattern is illuminating: of the fifteen, six are found in Group III, as noted, and eight in Group IV. In Group III plays, the relationship between such *waki* and *shite* entries seems to be in the interest of a more rapid development of the *yūgen* intensity that particularly characterizes this group. For the Group IV plays, it may function as part of the foreshadowing of the quickened tempo of the concluding group of plays. As one group of Japanese scholars has said, the fourth-class plays "should be produced with such rapidity as to suggest the coming of the [last] play."[33]

To summarize: the relationship between the two types of *waki* entries, *shidai* and *nanori*, which together account for 87 percent of the wig-plays, and the *shite* entries in the same plays in Group III indicates a general lack of concern for formal or massive musical patterning. The lack serves to diminish the thrust of the horizontal line of the Nō structure. It is in the interest of developing with some rapidity a "vertical" intensity. The position of the wig-plays as the third piece in a program of five plays allows for such rapid development.

In *Izutsu*, the recitative that the *shite* sings following the *shidai* entry illustrates how quickly and directly this wig-play can sound the tone of *yūgen-sabi*, an elusive and mysterious beauty arising from the deep seclusion of the neglected temple grounds in autumn. Zenchiku (1405–68), Zeami's son-in-law and himself a Nō playwright, cites this passage as an outstanding example of *yūgen*.[34] The first lines, giving an effect of sinking ever deeper into the heart of the mystery of this kind of beauty, contain a dazzling ellipsis between lines three and four. The sensation of penetrating deeper is intensified further by succeeding images of increasing distance. To show the ellipsis, an English equivalent of the first seven lines is given.

Sa naki dani	Already
mono no samishiki	a loneliness of things
aki no yo no	of an autumn night
	[how much more lonely when]
hitome mare naru	people too are rarely seen
furu-tera no	in the old temple
niwa no matsukaze	garden where the pine wind
fukesugite	blows and passes on

A more liberal translation follows:

	Even at the best,
	loneliness lies deep in things
	in the autumn night,
	deepened here where so few come
	to old temple grounds
	where the wind blows through the pines
	farther into night
tsuki mo katamuku	there the moon, too, westers low
nokiba no kusa	aslant the sagging eaves
wasurete sugishi	where the bracken cling forlorn
inishie o	for days forgotten,
shinobu gao nite	filling me with yearning thoughts. . . .

The movement of the passage from the first commonplace observation to an intensified instance flows further into a mysterious distance, with the autumn wind blowing deeper into the garden and the growing lateness of the hour into night (*fuke*), while the moon sinks lower too—all images of increasing distance—compounded next by a past that has been forgotten, until at the last there is nothing:

itsu made ka	how long, I wonder,
matsu koto nakute	with nothing here to wait for
nagaraen	shall I linger on?

Zeami has brought us and the *shite* to the farthest limit. But he has brought us there tenderly, as shown by the gentleness of the *shidai*, with "yearning thoughts." Thus, the *shite*'s acknowledgment of her attachment to this world in the last four lines of the recitative is most touching. For it is tenderness that ties her to the past.

Geni nanigoto mo	How true that whatever comes
omoide no	leaves its memories
hito ni wa nokoru	in the minds of those who love
yo no naka kana	within this changing world.

Attachment, in Buddhistic terms, is usually a source of torment and suffering, but not for this gentle, loving *shite*. Thus she can pray for her own salvation. As many commentators have pointed out, the usual request by the ghostly presence to the *waki* priest for redemptive prayers is lacking in this play.[35]

The recitative is now heightened slightly to song in the low tones and heightened further to song in the high tones as she prays in affirmation of her faith that the benevolence of Buddha will truly lead man to the Western Paradise from the unreal world of actuality. The theme of the supremacy of the nonactual over the actual, begun in the *waki*'s entry as he honors the past, is continued here as the world of salvation becomes the real world and the actual world only one of dreams from which man must be spiritually awakened.

sadame naki yo no	in this fleeting world of men
yume-gokoro	that our hearts dream of,
nani no oto ni ka	what will be the sound that calls
sametemashi	to awaken us,
nani no oto ni ka	what will be the sound that calls
sametemashi	to awaken us?

The felicity of these closing lines of the second *dan* in maintaining the unity of the play is fully realized in the concluding choral song of the play, where it is the sound of the wind-tossed plantain leaves[36] that awakens the *waki* from an actual state of dreaming, and the world of this Nō releases us into experiential enlightenment with yet another turn:

matsukaze ya	as the pine-wind tears
bashō-ba no	at the plantain leaves,
yume mo yaburete	broken, too, the dream he dreams
samenikeri	and he awakens,
yume wa yabure	for the dream is broken
akenikeri	and the day has dawned.

In the concluding lines of the second *dan*, the imagistic concreteness of the calling pine-winds, as the *shite* tilts the mask in a listening gesture, becomes the more abstract "sound that calls" man to religious enlightenment. In the last verses of the play, image and abstraction have become totally one. The same syllepsis-like technique, which moves the focus easily from one level to the other, can be seen in the second *dan* in the immediately preceding lines. The concept of the Buddha's guiding light leading the way to enlightenment becomes the imagistic moon, the Buddhist symbol of wisdom, in the western sky where paradise is located.

After the extended song of the *shite*'s entry, the third *dan* begins. The prose dialogue that follows between the *shite* and *waki* contributes to the texture of the play through contrast with the preceding long musical passage. The prose then heightens to a verse exchange in recitative, called *kakeai*, in which the speeches become progressively shorter until one line is sung by the *waki* and one line by the *shite*. The intensity inherent in such patterning is then resolved by the chorus with a song in the high range, which concludes the *dan* with a repeated two-line unit. This sequence (*mondō, kakeai, ageuta*) is conventional. The first *dan*, or *waki* entry, might be considered a *waki* solo, the second *dan* a *shite* solo, and in the third *dan*, we now have the first extended song by the chorus. It is possible that this clear-cut allocation of a *dan* to each of the principal voices may figure in Zeami's passing comment that *Izutsu* is a straightforward (*sugu naru*) piece.[37]

193

In this first choral song, the verbal play on names, first noted in the *waki*'s entry, is repeated with Ariwara. The description of the abandoned grounds again makes reference to the past, but now with added overtones of longing and regret. The temptation that the intensifying musical patterning offers for a well-defined attack by the chorus in this first song is thus compounded by the lyrics. However, as Setchō notes, the quiet tone should still be maintained "prudently" here: "In a piece as quiet as this, there is no way, indeed, but to perform it prudently. . . . In the first chorus song, [at the line] 'Grasses / growing, growing wild,' of course the *shite* [in his movements] as well as the chorus was very cautious."[38]

His comment on the performance qualities appropriate for the following line is one example of the "vertical" moments necessary for successful presentation.

> I did not think that the [*shite*'s] movement of looking at the desolate scene of the ancient mound at the line "Dew drops deeply, deeply still" and the use of the eyes gazing off toward the *waki*-seat were very effective. . . . I do not mean that the eyes were not used. I mean that a force that would make me believe the eyes were alive was lacking. Of course, the style of this piece does not require that the eyes shine. And I admit that the mask used is not a strong mask. Nevertheless, at this point I thought there could be in the eyes of the mask a power alive with the charming appeal of gazing sadly.[39]

Setchō's comments here might be comparable to those of a dance critic who finds one performance of a traditional ballet fully satisfying and another mechanical, although the same forms are executed. For in Nō, too, the prescribed movements and gestures, known as *kata*, are traditional and inserted at set moments in the plays. It will also be remembered that for the most part, the actions of the actors on stage are slow and controlled, with many moments of silence and no action. Earle Ernst notes that the slowness, "like that of a figure in slow-motion film reveals more . . . than can be observed in actuality."[40] Thus, the slight tilting of the mask, after a long-held stance, can be deeply expressive.[41] The signifying power of the traditional *kata* is of course enhanced by a style of singing in which a musicianly expressiveness rather than melody per se or a richly endowed voice is the focus of appreciation. How minutely the texts are studied can be seen in some comments by Kita Minoru on singing; for example, his suggestions for the singing of the nine syllables of "Grasses / growing, growing wild / and dense" (*kusa / bōbō to / shite*) deal with six syllables separately, giving directions on breath control, volume, enunciation, attack, rhythm, emphasis, and pitch for each syllable.[42] Thus, the "cracked bass voice" of a man in his sixties miming a beautiful young girl, to return to Donald Keene's example, is not disturbing to the Nō audience, for whom musicianly expressiveness is the supreme value.[43]

The fourth *dan* is devoted to the most brilliantly musical Nō pattern, the three-part *kuri-sashi-kuse*.[44] In content, the plot kernel of the play is given. No sequential time line is followed in the narration. The short *kuri* deals with Narihira's young manhood. The *sashi* tells of their marriage. The concluding *kuse* backtracks, to tell the story of their childhood days and courtship. The disregard for a chronological line may be a variation on the theme of the importance of the nonactual over the actual. It is a construction that emphasizes the "vertical" moment at the expense of the horizontal, sequential line. Zeami speaks of the value of such dramatic shifting of the material: "To write in this way does not follow the order of events. In order to create *jo ha kyū* [introduction, development, and conclusion] in an actual

Masterworks of the Nō Theater

performance, the composition goes back and forth, back and forth in time."[45] In *Izutsu*, what is secondary is given first, and the more crucial is then treated. For the feeling tone of childhood innocence and joy, and the sweet purity of the first days of love are at the heart of the play. Significantly, the *kuse* is the most delicately melodious section of the three-part pattern.[46]

In the *kuri*, a carefree Narihira is shown,

hana no haru	viewing flowery springs,
tsuki no aki tote	and praising moon-bright autumns
sumitamaishi ni	as he whiled his days away.

In the following recitative, the Tatsutayama poem, three lines of which were sung at the beginning of the play, is given at last in its entirety. The water metaphor is developed in an intricate way, with six references to be noted later. The recitative concludes with four lines in praise of poetry, but these four lines contain as pivot words the nouns "foam" (*utakata*) and "froth" (*awa*), which echo delicately the "white waves from the offing" of the Tatsutayama poem. With such echoes, then, we understand how this simple poem could win back the husband's heart, since it expresses, as only poetry can, "the whole of sorrow."

In the three-part choral *kuse*, the first section deals with the days of childhood, as the two children play "happily / chatting together" by the well that stands before their houses. They look at themselves reflected in the water, an important fore-shadowing of the climactic moment of the play in the fifth *dan*. The very short second section describes Narihira's unfolding love. The concluding section on their courtship begins with the high-pitched *ageha*[47] sung by the *shite*, in which the first three lines of what Masuda calls the theme poem of the play are given.[48] It is found in the twenty-third episode of the *Tales*.

SHITE

(Ageha)

Tsutsu izutsu	"By the round well-curb,
izutsu ni kakeshi	our heights we used to measure,
maro ga take	now that little boy

CHORUS

(Kuse)

oinikerashi na	has outgrown the marks you made
imo	since last
mizaru ma ni to	he came to meet with you."

The placement of the first three lines of this theme poem in the vivid *ageha* passage is another instance of the use of musical structure to support the lyric.

Much use is made of this first, shyly indirect love poem. The first two lines are repeated with variations in the concluding lines of this *dan*. The first four lines are repeated in the last *dan* of the play, where a most important "vertical" moment is created around them. Two references are made to the *shite* as the "well-side woman," while the strongly cadenced and alliterative first line, *tsutsu izutsu*, occurs almost like a snatch of a song, together with two similarly treated lines from another poem (*mayumi tsukiyumi*), in the beginning of the fifth *dan*. There the happy fact that the syllables *tsutsu* in the word meaning "well" (*tsutsui*) can also mean "nineteen" is deftly exploited by Zeami, who is then blessed with a nineteen-year-old well-side woman neatly packaged in an alliterative and homonymic phrase that gently echoes the theme poem. The hapless translator must heavy-footedly separate the two thoughts into ". . . from the time I was nineteen / since those well-curb years . . ." and the like.

In contrast to the *kuse,* with its irregular verse pattern and its low-pitched *ge* ending, is the following *rongi,* with its regular pattern of seven and five syllables, beginning in the high tones and set like the *kuse* to *hiranori* rhythm.[49] Another factor that serves to contrast it with the choral *kuse* is the alternation of the song between the chorus and the solo *shite.* Its placement here is conventional. As for content, the chorus, speaking for the *waki,* questions her about her identity, which she is conventionally reluctant to reveal.[50] As she shyly resists answering, there is again an echo from the Tatsutayama poem, hinting of her true guise. In the next speech, glowing with love like Mount Tatsuta "in the red and golden hues / of its maple stands," the *shite* reveals herself as the "well-side maiden."

Zeami considered it most important that in the *rongi* a delicate "fragrance" (*nioi*), leading here to the important revelation of identity, be incorporated. Otherwise, the *shite*'s acknowledgment of identity would not "enter the listener's ear."[51] Here the shyness suggested by the shifting pivot words (dealt with in the translation of the play), the fragmentary echo from the Tatsutayama poem, and the fuller sounding of that echo in the second explicit reference make this *rongi* a good example of Zeami's concept of fragrance—a linking effect that enhances the flow from one line to the next. What rises from tonality is *nioi.*

In the final choral song, the theme poem is again echoed as the chorus sings of her faithfulness since her "nineteenth year" and of the *shite*'s disappearance, with the homonymic first line from the theme poem, behind the well curb as she exits. The fourth *dan* ends with a repetitive closure.

I have said that the water metaphor is intricately developed in the *sashi* section of the *kuri-sashi-kuse* pattern. The development moves in six references from simple to complex. In the process, the previously noted flat conventionality of the wordplay in the third line of the Tatsutayama poem is deftly exploited. For only as it is simple can it be enhanced and amplified into a song in praise of poetry. The first two references, which are self-explanatory, are in italics:

imose no kokoro	the feelings shared between them
*asaka*razarishi ni	were not *shallow,* but soon after
mata *Kawa*chi no kuni	in the land of *River* Deltas. . . .

The first two syllables of the proper noun Kawachi (here given somewhat freely as "River Deltas"; see n. 160) denote "river." The third reference is in the Tatsutayama poem:

Kaze fukeba	"When the wind rises
okitsu shira*nami*	the white *waves* from the offing
Tatsutayama	Mount Tatsuta's Pass,
yowa ni ya kimi ga	in the deepest midnight dark,
hitori yukuran to	do you cross there all alone?"

The fourth reference is in the line immediately following; in English it is a pivot line, applying equally to Narihira and to her "heart," as is suggested in the Japanese:

obotsuka-*nami* no	as unsure as the lapping *waves*
yoru no michi	nearing the night road,
yukue o omō	her heart that follows after
kokoro togete	where her lover wanders. . . .

The syllable *na* in *nami* (waves) serves as a pivot between *obotsukanai* ("unsure") and *nami*. The word *yoru* operates in both its meanings of "nearing" and "night" (the last from the reference to "night" [*yowa*] in the poem). Taken as "nearing," it amplifies the noun "waves," making them active and thus prolonging the echoes of the poem.

The fifth and sixth references are found in the four concluding lines of the recitative, which, as previously noted, explain how the simple Tatsutayama poem won back the husband's affection:

geni nasake shiru	*froth*-like, the whole of sorrow
*uta*kata no	songs alone can sing,
*awa*re o nobeshi mo	sweet with pity, they are their own
kotowari nari.	good reason for being.

Uta (song) pivots between *shiru* (to know) and *utakata* (foam). The second meaning vivifies the sense of "froth" (*awa*) in the next noun, *aware*, here translated "sweet with pity." The conventional feeling tones around the images of foam and froth are those of regret for the ephemerality of beauty, impressions firmly fixed in the historically important concept of *aware*.[52] These delicate echoes can be sounded just because of the unassertive conventionality of the Tatsutayama poem itself.

The references to water images in the *kuse*, which also number six, are straightforward and are pointed out in the text of the play.

After the prose repetition of the story by "a man of the place" during the Interlude, the fifth and final *dan* begins with the "waiting song" of the priest. The *machiutai* is always a song in the higher tones,[53] sung *legato* and with grace. If a god is awaited, there is an air of reverence and brightness; if a spirit, a sense of prayer. While the song is being sung, the instruments enter, and after the song is ended they proceed without a break to play the entry music for the *shite*.[54] The priest in *Izutsu* waits for dreams of the past, he says, as he prepares to sleep. Thus he has no further lines in the play, unlike the *waki* in some dream plays who has dialogue with the *shite* after the reentry.

The *nochi-jite* (the principal role in the second half), now in her true guise as Narihira's wife, enters wearing a keepsake robe of Narihira and his courtly hat, to the vivid music of *issei*.[55] Kazamaki notes how appealing, with overtones of sensuousness, is the appearance of the *nochi-jite* as a woman dressed in man's clothing; it suggests something of the *shirabyōshi*, the professional female dancers and singers prominent during the Kamakura period (1185–1333).[56] The *nochi-jite* first sings in recitative yet another poem from the *Tales of Ise*, found in episode 17, and names herself "a woman waiting for someone," a familiar image of lovelornness. Then comes the first line from the well-side theme poem, *tsutsu izutsu*, followed by a

197

second strongly cadenced line, *mayumi tsukiyumi,* from yet another poem from the *Tales* (episode 24), the first depending on homonymic word play and the second on an associative word (*tsuki*) for junction to the text. As previously noted, the two lines are so strongly cadenced and alliterative that they seem to be snatches of songs. They heighten the effectiveness of the entrance, which moves immediately to a "vertical" moment, as the *nochi-jite* gazes at the sleeve of Narihira's robe. Setchō has described it: "At the line 'these robes of Narihira,' the gesture of bring-ing the left sleeve to the breast was full of heart-felt charm (*jō mi*)." [57]

According to the notation of Yokomichi and Omote,[58] the song that follows is an *issei,* with its heightened melody in free rhythm. It is considered as part of the reentry pattern of the *nochi-jite.*[59] One effect of the three-part pattern of *issei* music, recitative (*sashi*), and *issei* song in muting the musical thrust of *issei* is the enhance-ment of a quiet tone. It indicates much about the delicate tonality of the wig-plays that Sanari shows only two with *issei* music and *issei* verse as the reentry: *Genji kuyō* and *Fuji.*[60]

In *Izutsu* the lyric has the prescribed form of the *issei* verse: five lines with a syl-labication pattern of 5, 7, 5, 7, 5. However, in the second half of other plays in the whole repertory, the verse form is extremely irregular, as the following examples show. The two repetitive seven-syllable lines first sung by the *nochi-jite* in *Yamanba* are marked as *issei.*[61] A Chinese verse in *Hōkazō* that divides into lines of 8, 6, 9, 5 is marked *issei.*[62] The two lines of 7 and 5 syllables sung by the *nochi-jite* in *Miidera* after a recitative are in *issei.*[63] That such passages are sung as *issei* is made clear from the markings in the *utai-bon,* the song books issued by the five schools of Nō, giving the text as the school presents it, along with song markings for the lines. However, not all such passages are labeled. The *issei* notation for the reentry verse following the recitative, in the three-part pattern seen in *Izutsu,* is made by Sanari for only eight plays throughout the repertoire, although in performance the num-ber may be greater.[64] There seem to be several reasons for such omissions and the prosodical irregularity of the verse in the second half of the plays, as compared to the entry *issei* in the first half.

First, it will be remembered that in the first half of the dream plays, the *shite* is usually in another form—perhaps an old man or an anonymous village woman. In the second half, since the *nochi-jite* is in his true guise, the introductory function of the *issei* verse in the first half, where the *shite-issei* established the feelings and emotional tone of the character,[65] is no longer necessary. Hence the term becomes in the second half of the plays almost exclusively a musical and not a prosodical one, as the extreme variations in the verse form indicate. What the truncated verse form does not convey is not necessary since it has already been established. The *issei* music, with the two hand-drums and the flute, is enough.

198

Second, according to Miyake, all dances are introduced with *issei*-like lines.[66] In plays such as *Izutsu* or *Miidera,* where the dance follows closely on the second entry, the notated *issei* verse seems to be almost pivotal in its function, serving to lead from entry to the dance. Since Miyake writes for the singer, he may mean that an *issei*-like tone (*kanji*) gradually pervades the delivery of the verse preceding the dance, even though it may be marked as *kuse* (as in *Uneme*),[67] be a verse exchange (*Takasago*),[68] or be only the first line of a poem, which is then given in its entirety after the dance in the *waka* section that conventionally follows it (*Matsukaze* or *Tō-boku*).[69] As the music and song introducing the dance, the open-ended character of the *issei*[70] seems apparent in the fact that almost all such lines center on five syl-lables and seldom have the common repetitive closure pattern before the dance.[71]

Third, with regard to the omission of markings, which is so apparent in Sanari, Miyake suggests of a passage in *Yorimasa* that such omissions may be in the interest of interpretative freedom, not only for the actor but for the five Nō schools, each of which has its own tradition of performance practices. He remarks that an example of *issei* "which is often not marked" in the song books can be found in this play. The line "ara enbu koishi ya" is sung as recitative, but the next unmarked line, "Ise musha wa," must be in *issei*, as the notations show; vocal colorings like *kuru* indicated here never appear in recitative but are characteristic of *issei*.[72] Miyake seems to indicate here how much leeway a Nō performer has in spite of the supposed rigidity of convention in this theater. Helen Julia Bryant says that "melody need not necessarily be performed exactly according to the notation. . . . As with everything in Nō careful attention is paid to formal detail, while at the same time great skill is required to handle the freedom in general interpretation."[73]

With this general description of the opening patterns of the second half in *Izutsu*, they may be considered in light of such openings in all the wig-plays. In general, the fifth *dan* of a play, as the concluding section, is relatively rapid. It can be expected that it will open with effects calculated to move on to the kind of conclusion consonant with the play. In Group III plays in two parts, these openings have some uniformity. In over half, it is with the *waki-machiutai* and *shite-issei* entry, considered together as a large configuration, that an appropriately heightened effect through musical forms is achieved. Zeami implies that such effects can keep the play from becoming "sluggish" (*nunari to shite*).[74]

Of the twenty-seven plays in two parts in Group III, the fifth *dan* opens with a "waiting song" in nineteen.[75] In these, the *nochi-jite* enters to *issei* music in fifteen.[76] The four remaining *nochi-jite* enter to *deha* music.[77] The *issei*-like function of the *deha* can be found in its old designation: *taiko no issei*.[78] The addition of the stick drum to the ensemble adds to the theatrical element, as becomes clear when the dramatic gestures available to the *taiko* player come to mind.[79]

Of the remaining eight two-part wig-plays without a *waki-machiutai*, one (*Hatsuyuki*) has no *waki*. In four, the *nochi-jite* enters to some form of *issei*;[80] in one, to *deha* (*Yoshino tennin*); and in one to *shidai* (*Sōshiarai Komachi*). The most musically restrained reentry, to *ashirai* music, is found in *Ohara gokō*, a play abounding in unusual patterns.[81]

Beginning with the *issei* song in *Izutsu*, throughout the remainder of the play, the expressiveness of the rhythmic changes used to underline the text is illuminating. Unfortunately, a meaningful comparison of the pattern of rhythmic changes here with that in other plays is not possible since detailed rhythmic notations are given only by Yokomichi and Omote, whose work covers only selected pieces from the repertoire. However, even the cursory sampling made possible by them indicates that rhythmic patternings assume various sequences. *Eguchi* seems to resemble closely the pattern in *Izutsu* after the dance.[82]

As well as serving in an attenuated way as part of the musical patterning of the *nochi-jite* reentry, the *issei* song here is introductory to the dance, as Miyake states, including as it does the phrase *utsuri mai* (dancing as he danced), which can indicate that the dancer is either imitating someone or is possessed by a spirit as she dances. While both nuances are said to be present in this dance,[83] the latter meaning seems to be clarified by the *waka* that follows: she is possessed by the reality of the past and relives it so intensely that she later believes for one moment that she sees her lover again.

Elsewhere I have touched on the relationship between the dance in the wig-

199

plays and the concept of *yūgen*.[84] Here the dance is the *jo no mai*, found in thirty of the wig-plays. It is a large, important dance, marked by elegance and refinement, in five movements (which can be shortened to three),[85] accompanied by the flute and two hand-drums. Masuda tells us that in *Izutsu*, "throughout the whole dance a mood of longing is created."[86]

The section that follows is marked *waka*, a homonym applying equally to music and verse. In its fullest form as verse (*waka*), it consists of two parts: 5, 7, 5 and 7, 7. Zeami treated these units as two standard *ku*, although both parts have more than the standard twelve syllables. Here in *Izutsu*, the three-line upper hemistich is sung by the *nochi-jite*, the lower two lines, by the chorus. The parts can be variously allocated.

In other plays, the verse in the musical *waka* section deviates freely from the norm, although not to the same extent as the *issei*-like verse preceding the dance. For example, only the upper hemistich appears in *Fuji* and *Hotoke-no-hara*. In *Senjū*, only two lines of seven and six syllables are given. Four syllables (*aruiwa*) replace the seventeen-syllable upper hemistich in *Hagoromo*, followed by the usual fourteen syllables of the lower hemistich. The full form of thirty-one syllables is found in the majority of the wig-plays where the *waka* is notated: examples are *Ume*, *Sumizome sakura*, *Sumiyoshi mōde*, and *Tōboku*. An interesting and frequent pattern is found in the latter play. One five-syllable line precedes the dance (presumably sung as *issei*, following Miyake) and is repeated as the first line of the complete *waka* that follows the dance. The same repetition is found in *Fuji* and *Hajitomi*, although the verse is reduced to the upper hemistich alone.[87] One effect of such an arrangement of the verse is to incorporate the dance into the play as an integral element. It may also signal the tone to be found in it. In *Funabenkei*, for example, the *issei* line preceding the dance and repeated in the following *waka* expresses the *shite*'s desire to encourage and console her lover:

CHORUS

(Issei)

Tada tanome   "Only trust in me,"

[*The* shite *dances the* jo no mai.]

SHITE

(Waka)

Tada tanome	"Only trust in me,
shimeji ga hara no	though how worthless life appears,
sashimogusa	like *mokusa* weeds

CHORUS

ware yo no naka ni	in miscanthus moors, so long
aran kagiri wa	as I live within this world."[88]

Often the last seven-syllable line of the verse is repeated, like a closure pattern, showing that the dance section is ended. In *Tōboku*,[89] the last line is given three times, illustrating the conclusive function of the *waka* section.[90]

For just as the open-ended *issei* music and verse leads to the dance, the *waka*

200

section serves to "receive" it, in Miyake's words. During the dance, there is a gradual *accelerando*. Thus the *waka* is sung in a lively but nevertheless *legato* manner.[91] As a formal musical structure, the *waka* is apparently not quite so protean as the preceding *issei*-like section. Sanari notates the verse following the dance as *waka* far more often than he does the verse preceding it as *issei*.

The open-ended nature of *issei* and the conclusive nature of *waka* is evident in the very verse forms themselves. For in the 5, 7, 5 and 7, 5 syllabication pattern of the full *issei* verse, the first five-syllable line is introductory rhythmically, while the following pair of 7, 5 lines, identical to the *ku* or usual pattern of Nō verse,[92] suggests an ongoing continuation as in the longer verse sections.[93] The frequent use of pivot words and lines as well as associative words throughout the verse, together with the *katari* (narrative) element,[94] makes such passages a seamless whole, at one with the musical line. This is one result of Zeami's demand that "a playwright must understand the heart of the music; he must make the words turn from one to another beautifully." Particularly in the "true" wig-plays, the most important in the day's program of five plays, where import is content, the texture, communicated by musical elements in great part, becomes more accessible as attention is paid to structure.

In contrast to the *issei*, the *waka* verse form, with its rhythmically repetitive final lines of 7 and 7 syllables, can adapt itself to closure, signifying that the dance section is ended. The playwright is of course not confined to such simple closure techniques as repetition—whether of rhythm or verse lines—as is shown in the verses following the angel's dance in *Hagoromo*.[95]

As for content, the *waka* sections may contain lines from well-known *tanka* poems; the complete poem, as in *Funabenkei* given above; or verse that forwards the action. As music, the first lines are considered a type of *issei* song and sung in free rhythm. However, in some plays, schools other than the Kanze mark the section following the dance in the *ōnori* rhythm: for example, *Hagoromo* or *Momijigari*.[96] In this rhythm, in its simplest form, each syllable falls on a downbeat. The result, as Minagawa says, is that the music "that is cast in it is sung with each accent very clear." It has a "calm and majestic effect."[97]

In *Izutsu*, the *waka* section does not contain a well-known poem, perhaps because of the famous poem that comes afterward. The first three lines are in free rhythm. The next three lines are in *ōnori*, with the repetitive third line reinforcing the deliberate rhythmic pattern and concluding the dance section, as well as providing a skillful transition to the famous poem that follows. The *nochi-jite* establishes explicitly the reality of the past, as she makes a large, formal movement with the fan, the *ageōgi*.[98]

NOCHI-JITE

201

(Waka: awazu)

Koko ni kite	To this place I come
mukashi zo kaesu	turning time back to the past
Ariwara no	at Ariwara . . .

We are now present in the past, a change of scene that facilitates the transition to the imagery of the moon that follows, underlined by the rhythmic change to *ōnori* and the pivot function of the line "at Ariwara."

CHORUS

(Ōnori)

terai ni sumeru	in the temple-well how clear
tsuki zo sayakeki	the moon is in its splendor,
tsuki zo sayakeki	the moon is in its splendor . . .

This is an emphatic introduction to the next passage, which includes two lines from one of Narihira's most famous and characteristic poems on the sorrows of love. The *nochi-jite* sings in free rhythm:

tsuki ya aranu	"Is this the moon no more?
haru ya mukashi to	Is the spring no more a spring . . . ?"
nagameshi mo	Gazing longingly,
itsu no koro zo ya	when was it he sang so well. . . .

The free rhythm not only provides contrast to the preceding *ōnori* pattern but is particularly suited to the subtle shades and nuances of this difficult poem on love's sorrows. Again, the imagistic moon reflected in the well becomes the moon of Narihira's lament, just as in the second *dan* the imagistic content of the "winds calling / through those pines . . ." became the "sound that calls" to spiritual enlightenment. The seeming incongruity of having the *nochi-jite* in the guise of Narihira's wife sing these famous lines from a poem written by Narihira for another woman apparently does not discommode the audience during performance, for reasons that will be discussed.[99]

A variant (*kogaki*) of the play inserts an *iroe* movement after the last line given above. The *nochi-jite* stamps lightly after the line, and as the two drums and the flute play, the company makes a large circle around the periphery of the stage, to return once again to stage rear.[100] Possibly an interest in further deepening this moment created by the famous poem prompted this variant.

With the strongly cadenced line *tsutsu izutsu* from the theme poem that follows, the rhythm again changes to *ōnori,* and the line's repetition by the chorus serves to make the rhythm even more marked.

NOCHI-JITE

(Ōnori)

tsutsu izutsu	by the round well-curb

202

CHORUS

(Ōnori)

tsutsu izutsu	"By the round well-curb
izutsu ni kakeshi	our heights we used to measure,

NOCHI-JITE

(Ōnori)

maro ga take	now that little boy

Masterworks of the Nō Theater

CHORUS

(*Ōnori*)

>   oinikerashi na   has outgrown the marks you made . . ."

With the following variation on the fourth line of the poem comes one of the most deeply important moments of the play:

NOCHI-JITE

(*Ōnori*)

>   oinikeru zo ya   has outgrown his childhood days!

Masuda says that in the slow and deliberate singing of this line, fostered by the two emphatic particles (*zo* and *ya*), the actor must show us the "passage of time of one entire life, shortened and contained within one moment."[101] The moment is marked by the performance of the *hiraki* movement—an important formal stance—which holds the "vertical" intensity in a timeless stasis.

The *ōnori* rhythm continues as the chorus sings of the *nochi-jite*'s resemblance to her lover, dressed as she is in his robes and court hat. At the line "now she seems no more a woman," the actor softly flips back one sleeve over the arm, ready to approach the well. The chorus continues deliberately:

CHORUS

(*Ōnori*)

>   otoko narikeri   but that very man himself,
>   Narihira no   Lord Narihira . . .

The *nochi-jite* parts the pampas grass by the well and gazes into it.

>   omokage   reflected there . . .

There is a well-marked pause.[102] Then the *nochi-jite* sings, the rhythm changes to *hiranori*, and the climactic moment of the play is reached.

NOCHI-JITE

(*Hiranori*)

>   mireba natsukashi ya   I see! Oh, how dear he is!

It is from her love and joy that she imagines the reflection of Narihira, just as she gazed at his image in their childhood days (described in the *kuse* passage), when they shared a pure and innocent affection. She is filled with tenderness and deep joy. "If this crucial moment is achieved," says Setchō, "the peak of this Nō has been attained."[103] Masuda remarks that the moment seems like "neither a few seconds nor an eternity . . . as the *shite* sings with deep feeling, 'Oh, how dear he is!'"[104] Kita notes that the delivery is quiet and the feeling tone serious and keen. The rhythmic change from the emphatic *ōnori* to the more flexible *hiranori* underlines the full expressiveness of the moment, and the play continues to the end in *hiranori*, as do all the *jun sanbanme* wig-plays.[105]

203

Izutsu

From the well curb at center-front stage, the *nochi-jite* retreats slowly to right stage rear as the chorus sings for her:

CHORUS

(Hiranori)

ware nagara	though it is myself,
natsukashi ya	oh, how dear he is!
bōfu	A lover
hakurei no	in a phantom shape,
sugata wa	a fleeting form. . . .

As the *nochi-jite* realizes that the vision of her lover was her own image dressed in his robes and court cap, reflected in the water, the heightened quality of the climactic moment returns slowly to reality. So the second singing of the line "Oh, how dear he is!" is perhaps modulated with overtones of yearning, as the *nochi-jite* mourns the passing of her love. At right stage rear, she half kneels and lightly flips one sleeve over her arm. She gradually hides the mask behind her open fan, as if shrinking into herself while she sorrows tenderly. Describing the action, Setchō says of one performance at this moment, "The sitting form was totally perfect."[106]

The chorus continues to describe the passing of love.

CHORUS

(Hiranori)

shibomeru hana no	a lovely flower withered,
iro nōte	with its colors gone,
nioi	the fragrance
nokorite	lingers faintly. . . .

These four lines are from the famous preface by Ki no Tsurayuki (884–946) to the *Kokinshū* (ca. 905), the first imperial anthology of Japanese verse.[107] Quoted extensively over the centuries, they were and are widely known, an essential item in everyone's literary baggage. It seems particularly audacious to quote them here, for they are Tsurayuki's disparaging remarks on Narihira's poetry and contain much that is valid.[108] They are operative in this Nō context in a varied and complex way.

On the simplest level, Narihira is mourned—the flower is "withered / with its colors gone," as he is described in Tsurayuki's words. But he is so described after the *nochi-jite* has created and projected whole his image through the power of her sweet love. Kitto has said that in the art of drama, juxtaposition is one way of conveying "things of the utmost importance without using a single word."[109]

204

Hence the juxtaposition of the two images of Narihira has us understand that the poetry, too, has beauty, as does the *nochi-jite*'s image of the poet. That beauty lies precisely in those qualities which Tsurayuki found displeasing. Thus these famous *Kokinshū* lines become here lines of praise.

The quotation conjures up Tsurayuki also. The reminder of what his famous preface has meant as a manifesto for the worth of Japanese poetry against the prevailing vogue for writing Chinese poetry, and for the unique beauty of the Japanese poetic sensibility helps us, from the vantage point of historical remove, to appreciate more justly both poets. It brings, too, intimations of the varied, ample, and splendid thing which is the Japanese poetic tradition, not only for its quality and quantity but for its livingness and its ability to communicate feeling over the centuries. The sense of a timeless past, so important to this play, is here imbued with great dignity and with an awareness of the reality that is beyond change, beyond the actual, thus reconciling us to loss, through the *yūgen* beauty of the sorrowing *shite*'s kneeling form. All these meanings seem to operate here, no doubt centrifugally, with the largest implications on the very fringes of consciousness. They serve to give gravity and substance—what in Japanese is called *omomi*—to the configuration conveyed by this play. The groundwork for such extended meanings was laid in the choral celebration of poetry in the conclusion of the *sashi* in the *kuri-sashi-kuse* in the fourth *dan*: poetry, which sings "the whole of sorrow," is its own "good reason for being."

Such extended meanings may also account for the inclusion of the three poems not found in episode 23 of the *Tales*, the most important of which is the poem on the moon beginning *Tsuki ya aranu*. Narrowly considered in their own contexts in the *Tales*, they seem to go against the grain of the play, as even a casual reading of the classic makes clear.[110] Since the popularity of the *Tales* from the Heian period is well established, it cannot be supposed that Zeami or his aristocratic audience did not know the prose context of the poems and that therefore their inappropriateness for the Nō in the light of the *Tales* escaped them. Then, too, the fact that the Nō play has survived as an acknowledged masterwork for some five hundred years indicates that this inappropriateness does not weaken the play. Why this incongruity is overlooked, to my mind, is that the poems function in the Nō play without reference to their context in the *Tales* (unlike the three from episode 23, which help to "tell the story"). They are a vertical element. They function as part of the thrust of the play itself as an experience—not through poetry, but in poetry.

A successful poem is an experience; it is not about an experience. Thus with the one great poem in this play, *Tsuki ya aranu*, introduced with such careful strategy, it no longer matters for the play that the poem was written by Narihira for another woman. Its significance as a poem keening a lost love is what matters. All six poems are an example of the Nō use of *honkadori*, or allusive variation,[111] the concept that borrowings from older works are successful only if what is borrowed assumes new meanings or freshness or another kind of importance, as was shown with the simple Tatsutayama poem.

I have discussed elsewhere the relation between a particular role and the term *shite*. The person of the *shite* is never meant to be identified with the character. For, masked or not, a sixty-year-old man can never in his person be taken for a beautiful young girl. Yet conventional Nō wisdom holds that it is just the old actor who can best play such parts. The fact that the Nō play is not the unfolding of a plot but is the conveying of an experience inherent in the plot has also been dealt with.[112]

Both of these ideas seem to me to clarify further the central thrust of Nō as shown in this play. For the theater experience in Nō does not depend primarily on an illusion of reality, either from the actor or from the happenings described; rather it centers on the apprehension of beauty within the audience—comparable to the experience, not through poetry, but in poetry. Stephen Orgel has said of Inigo Jones's hugely elaborate settings for the Elizabethan masques that they "were making the most far-reaching statements about the nature of the theatrical illusion; for a realistic scene implies that seeing—not hearing or understanding—is believ-

205

ing."[113] In an analogous way, the exposed, uncurtained Nō stage makes its unique statement about the nature of its theater experience. A metaphor for Nō might be its empty stage. For in Nō, believing comes from experiential understanding.

Masuda notes that, as part of the construct of the play itself, the *Kokinshū* phrase is used as a fragrant expression of the fading away of a dream from classical literature, just as the dream of the *waki* is beginning to fade and the ghostly *shite* will soon leave.[114] She stamps softly three lines later, perhaps signaling her tender acceptance of her loss: Setchō says of one performance at this point that the stamp was lightly sounded and "deep with tonal interest." He praises the quality of the choral singing of the concluding lines, to which the *nochi-jite* exits, by saying that it was "courageously committed" to a low-keyed quietness.[115] He seems to mean that as important as are exits and conclusions, the chorus is disciplined enough to maintain the tone without resorting to a heightened singing in order to bring the play to an end with some éclat.

The foreshadowing of the last six lines of the play in the *shite's* first *ageuta* in the second *dan* has been noted. The abstract sound that will call man to enlightenment by waking him from his dream, which is worldly attachment, becomes here the imagistic sound of the pine-wind and the rustling plantain leaves, which wakens the *waki* from his dream and leaves us with the experiential enlightenment of the Nō, as the chorus concludes:

CHORUS

matsukaze ya	as the pine-wind tears
bashō-ba no	at the plantain leaves,
yume mo yaburete	broken, too, the dream he dreams
samenikeri	and he awakens,
yume wa yabure	for the dream is broken
akenikeri	and the day has dawned.

The open *a* sounds of these concluding lines function as they do in the *shite's shidai*, while the *ya* particle of the first line opens wide the perspective as it did there—here from the intensity of memory to the actual temple grounds. The change from *mo* (too) in line three to *wa* (topic marker indicating the subject) in line five, and the rhythmic surprise created by dropping the suffix *te* from the verb, in a variant repetition at the end of the fifth line, as the statement moves from the dream of the *waki* to the dream of the Nō, are admirable. The quiet appropriateness of these subtle changes in the repetitive closure can be seen if one substitutes for the last two lines a simple repetition of the preceding two. The somewhat forbidding portentousness then achieved is less desirable for this delicate play.

206

Literally, the Japanese lines on the plantain leaves read: "The dream of the plantain leaves is also broken." The *also* likens this dream to the *waki's*. The reference is to a well-known Chinese tale in which a woodcutter has the good luck to kill a deer, which he caches for fear of losing it, covering it with plantain leaves. Overcome with the joy of his windfall, he forgets where he hid it, tries to remember, and finally concludes ruefully that the event was only a dream.[116] The Chinese story provokes a sympathetic smile, where the comparable tale of the self-serving rationalization of Aesop's fox and his grapes does not. The difference lies in the joy of the woodcutter and the mean greed of the fox. The allusion in the Nō text is a passing one, but nevertheless telling. Like the dream of the plantain leaves, the *waki*'s dream too has had a patina of joy, while recounting the "whole of sorrow / sweet with pity" of a tender love, now lost.

The *shite* in this jewel-like play leaves us as she came to us. We have not progressed with her through some change. What has happened? Very little. What has been conveyed? Much. In this lies the vertical character of this theater, in which the "moments of chorded experience" so possible in Nō are satisfyingly sounded, their echoes trailing like the tolling bell at Ariwara Temple.

Izutsu

IZUTSU

By Zeami

Persons: WAKI: *A traveling priest*
SHITE (PART I): *A village woman*
NOCHI-JITE (PART II): *The ghost of Aritsune's daughter*
KYŌGEN: *A man of the place*

Classification: *Primary, Group III*
Place: *At Ariwara Temple*
Time: *September*
Kogaki: *5*

PART I

First Dan

[*After the chorus and musicians have entered and taken their places, the stage attendants bring in a well curb with a spray of pampas grass attached to one corner and place it at center-front stage. With entrance music on the flute (nanoribue), the* waki, *an itinerant Buddhist priest, appears as the rich brocade curtain dividing the mirror room from the bridge is swept back. He wears a pointed hood, a plain kimono woven with a warp of unpolished silk and a woof of polished silk, a broad-sleeved, unlined tunic made of unpolished "shrunk" silk, and a waistband. He carries a fan and a rosary. Walking slowly along the bridge,*[117] *he stops at the name-saying place (*nanoriza*).*]

WAKI

[1] (*Nanori: awazu, kotoba*)

Kore wa shokoku ikken no sō nite sōrō. Ware kono hodo wa Nanto shichidō ni mairite sōrō. Mata kore yori Hatsuse ni mairabaya to zonji sōrō. Kore naru tera o hito ni tazunete sōraeba Ariwara-dera to ka ya mōshi sōrō hodo ni tachi-yori ikken sebaya to omoi sōrō.

I am a Buddhist priest traveling from province to province. Recently I paid homage to the seven temples in the southern capital.[118] Now I intend to go on to Hatsuse.[119] [*During a well-marked pause, he looks toward the well curb.*] When I asked people about that nearby temple, they said that was Ariwara Temple.[120] So I thought I would stop along the way to see the place.

[*The* waki *advances toward center stage; facing stage front, he sings the following verse as recitative.*]

208

(*Sashi:*[121] *au, yowagin*)

Satewa kono	So this is the place
Ariwara-dera wa	where Ariwara Temple
inishie Narihira	stood long ago, when Narihira
Ki no Aritsune no	and Aritsune's daughter
sokujo	lived together
fūfu sumitamaishi	ever graciously as man and wife,
Iso no Kami narubeshi.	and this must be Iso no Kami.[122]
Kaze fukeba	"When the wind rises,
okitsu shiranami	the white waves from the offing
Tatsutayama	Mount Tatsuta's Pass . . ."[123]
to eijiken mo	so goes her famous poem
kono tokoro nite no	and surely at this very place
koto narubeshi.	she must have written it.

[*The following is sung in the lower range of tones.*]

(*Sageuta:*[124] *au, yowagin*)

Mukashigatari no	As I come to see the site
ato toeba	of the storied past,

[*The* waki *sits in the half-kneeling, erect position.*[125]]

sono Narihira no	I find Lord Narihira,
tomo to seshi	who had befriended
Ki no Aritsune no	Aritsune of the Ki,
tsune[126] naki yo	in this world no more.
imose o kakete	To his memory and hers

[*With his rosary, he holds his hands in prayer.*]

tomurawan	let me raise my prayer;
imose o kakete	to his memory and hers
tomurawan.	let me raise my prayer.

Second Dan

[*As introductory* shidai *music is begun, the* waki *rises and proceeds to the* waki *seat, where he sits in the low, half-kneeling position.*[127] *The* shite, *a village woman, now appears as the brocade curtain is swept back. She wears the mask of a beautiful young girl*[128] *with a wig and a wig band that is tied around the hair and knotted at the back of the head, its long ends falling over the outer robe. She wears a rich under-robe of plain white silk with a satinlike finish and three unattached white collars, one over the other, shaped to follow the neckline of the robe.*[129] *Over this, she wears hanging loosely from her shoulders a gorgeous outer-robe of richly patterned brocade, which is woven in relief upon unpolished silk with threads of gold and flossed silk. She carries a small wooden pail, a spray of leaves, and a rosary. Moving slowly down the bridge, she stops at the* shite *seat. She looks toward stage left, as she sings the* shidai.]

209

Izutsu

(Shidai: au, yowagin)

Akatsuki-goto no	With each dawn I come to draw
aka [130] no mizu	the holy water,
akatsuki-goto no	with each dawn I come to draw
aka no mizu	the holy water,
tsuki mo kokoro ya	and the moon, too, makes my heart
sumasuran.	peaceful, calm, and clear.

CHORUS

(Jidori: au, yowagin)

Akatsuki-goto no	With each dawn I come to draw
aka no mizu	the holy water,
tsuki mo kokoro ya	and the moon, too, makes my heart
sumasuran.	peaceful, calm, and clear.

[*Facing stage front, the* shite *sings the following as recitative.*]

SHITE

(Sashi: awazu, yowagin)

Sa naki dani	Even at the best,
mono no samishiki [131]	loneliness lies deep in things
aki no yo no	in the autumn night,
hitome mare naru	deepened here where so few come
furu-tera no	to old temple grounds
niwa no matsukaze	where the wind blows through the pines
fukesugite [132]	farther into night
tsuki mo katamuku [133]	there the moon, too, westers low
nokiba no kusa [134]	aslant the sagging eaves
wasurete sugishi [135]	where the bracken cling forlorn
inishie o	for days forgotten,
shinobu [136] gao nite	filling me with yearning thoughts,
itsu made ka	how long, I wonder,
matsu koto nakute	with nothing here to wait for
nagaraen.	shall I linger on?
Geni nani goto mo	How true that whatever comes
omoide [137] no	leaves its memories
hito ni wa nokoru	in the minds of those who love
yo no naka kana	within this changing world,

[*Still facing stage front, the* shite *changes her singing from the free rhythm of recitative to the regular* hiranori *rhythm of song in the low range.*]

(Sageuta: au, yowagin)

tada itsu to naku	where continually I pray
hitosuji ni [138]	for redeeming grace

Masterworks of the Nō Theater

tanomu hotoke no	with a single-minded faith,
mi-te no ito	with that cord you hold,
michibikitamae [139]	oh, Holy Buddha, guide us
nori no koe,	as we call your name; [140]

[*The singing now heightens to song in the high pitch.*]

(*Ageuta:* [141] *au, yowagin*)

mayoi o mo	even for the lost,
terasasetamō	you have vowed to lead the way
on-chikai	with your hallowed light,
terasasetamō	you have vowed to lead the way
on-chikai	with your hallowed light [142]
geni mo to miete	truly pointing toward the place
ariyake no	where the moon at dawn
yukue wa nishi no	departs beyond the mountains
yama naredo	to the holy west, [143]
nagame wa yomo no	while everywhere around us
aki [144] no sora	vacant autumn skies

[*The* shite *turns slightly, facing toward the right and appearing to listen closely.*]

matsu no	seem wearied [145]
koe nomi	with winds calling
kikoyuredomo	through those pines, we hear

[*The* shite, *quietly raising the mask, faces stage front.*]

arashi wa	but cannot know
izuku [146] to mo	from where the storms rise

[*As the* shite *sings the following lines, she takes one or two steps forward and assumes the erect half-kneeling position, on one knee. She holds up the spray of leaves, as if making an offering, and places it on the stage. Holding the rosary, she joins her hands in prayer.*]

sadame naki yo no	in this fleeting world of men
yume-gokoro	that our hearts dream of,
nani no oto ni ka [147]	what will be the sound that calls
sametemashi [148]	to awaken us,
nani no oto ni ka	what will be the sound that calls
sametemashi.	to awaken us?

[*With the chanting of the last line, the* shite *rises and returns to the* shite *seat. She faces stage front. The following exchange in prose, called* mondai, *takes place between the* waki, *seated at the* waki *seat, and the* shite, *standing at the* shite *seat.*] [149]

Third Dan

WAKI

[3] (*Mondai: awazu, kotoba*)

Ware kono tera ni yasurai kokoro o su-masu orifushi ito namamekeru nyoshō	As I rest at this temple, praying and meditating, there comes a very charm-

Izutsu

niwa no itai o musubiage hanamizu to shi kore naru tsuka ni ekō no keshiki mietamō wa ika naru hito nite mashimasu zo.

ing woman. At the wooden well over there, she scoops up water for the flowers which she places before that mound as if it were an offering. I wonder who you are.

SHITE

Kore wa kono atari ni sumu mono nari. Kono tera no hongan Ariwara no Narihira wa yo ni na o tomeshi hito nari. Sareba sono ato no shirushi mo kore naru tsuka no kage yaran. Warawa mo kuwashiku wa shirazu sōraedomo hana mizu o tamuke onnato tomuraimairase sōrō.

I am one who lives near this place. This temple was built to honor Narihira's wishes, who made a name for himself in this world. Therefore the stone that marks his remains may lie behind the mound over there. [*The* shite *lowers the mask.*] Although I do not know much about the matter, I offer up some flowers and water and recite prayers.

WAKI

Geni geni Narihira no on-koto wa yo ni na o tomeshi hito nari, sarinagara ima wa haruka ni tōki yo no mukashi gatari no ato naru o shikamo nyoshō no on-mi to shite kayō ni tomuraitamō koto sono Ariwara no Narihira ni

How very true! Narihira was one who left his mark on this world. However, this ruined site is told about in stories from a time remote and far. So I am surprised to find someone praying here for Ariwara no Narihira, especially a woman.[150]

[*The* waki *changes from intoned prose and sings the following.*]

| ikasama yue aru | Are you related in some way? |
| on-mi yaran. | What are your ties with him? |

SHITE

[*The following is intoned prose.*]

Yue aru mi ka to towasetamō. Sono Narihira wa sono toki dani mo mukashi otoko[151] to iwareshi mi no mashite ya ima wa tōki yo ni yue mo yukari mo arubekarazu.

You ask about my ties with him, and if we are related. But even in his own time Narihira was called a man of ancient days. Now he belongs to a remote past, indeed. So how can I be related to him?

[*The following verse exchange, called* kakeai, *is sung in free rhythm between the two.*]

212

WAKI

Mottomo ōse wa	What you say cannot be doubted;
saru koto naredomo	but still and all, the fact remains
koko wa mukashi no	that this is the very place
kyūseki nite	of those ancient times.

SHITE

Nushi koso tōku	Though the lord's remains are gone
Narihira[152] no	and long passed away,

WAKI

ato wa nokorite	Narihira still remains
sasuga ni imada	even to this present day,

SHITE

kikoe wa kuchinu	still undying is his fame
yogatari o	in the world of tales

WAKI

katareba ima mo	as men retell those stories

[*The* shite *takes one or two steps toward the* waki.]

SHITE

mukashi otoko no	of the Man of Ancient Days

[*The* shite *faces stage front. The singing now heightens to song in the high pitch, in regular* hiranori *rhythm.*]

CHORUS

(*Ageuta: au, yowagin*)

na bakari wa	stays his name alone
Ariwara-dera[153] no	at Ariwara Temple
ato furite	with its old remains,
Ariwara-dera no	at Ariwara Temple
ato furite	with its old remains,
matsu mo oitaru[154]	where the aging pines still stand
tsuka no kusa.	by the grass-grown mound.

[*The* shite *advances slightly to stage front.*]

Kore koso sore yo	This must be the very place,
naki ato no	though nothing lingers

[*The* shite *advances toward the well curb and gazes at the pampas cluster.*]

hitomura-	but the single[155]
zusuki no	pampas cluster
ho[156] ni izuru wa	forming silvery ears,
itsu no nagori	when was it planted there
naruran.	to his memory?

[*She looks about at the grass.*]

Kusa[157]	Grasses
bōbō to	growing, growing wild

213

Izutsu

shite	
tsuyu shinshin to	and dense
furuzuka[158] no	dew drops deeply, deeply still
	lies the aging mound,

[*The* shite *lowers the mask as if lost in the past.*]

makoto naru kana	and how real it truly seems,
inishie no	like those distant days,
ato natsukashiki	how dear these scenes around me
keshiki kana	of the old remains,

[*The* shite *turns in a large circle to return to the* shite *seat; while the chorus concludes its song, the* shite *faces front toward the* waki *and stamps once.*]

ato natsukashiki	how dear these scenes around me
keshiki kana.	of the old remains.

[*While the chorus sings, the* kyōgen *appears inconspicuously through the half-raised curtain and sits at the* kyōgen *seat.*]

Fourth Dan

WAKI

[4]

Nao nao Narihira no on-koto kuwashiku on-monogatari sōrae.	Will you not tell me all you can and all you know of these old tales concerning Narihira?

[*The* shite *advances to center stage and assumes a low half-kneeling position, on one knee. The following long passage, consisting of a* kuri, sashi, *and* kuse, *is the most elaborately developed and heightened musical section of the play. The* kuri, *which begins on a quite high pitch, is in free rhythm.*]

CHORUS

(*Kuri: awazu, yowagin*)

Mukashi Ariwara no chūjō	Long ago, the Middle Captain Ariwara
toshi hete koko ni	passed many a year at this
Iso[159] no Kami	Iso no Kami,
furinishi sato mo	even in this old village,
hana no haru	viewing flowery springs,
tsuki mo aki tote	and praising moon-bright autumns
sumitamaishi ni	as he whiled his days away.

[*The following recitative alternates between the* shite *and the chorus. The water image is developed here. It is sung deliberately and with restraint.*]

SHITE

(*Sashi: awazu, yowagin*)

Sono koro wa	It was then he pledged
Ki no Aritsune ga	his true love to the daughter
musume to chigiri	of Ki no Aritsune;

Masterworks of the Nō Theater

imose no kokoro	the feelings shared between them
asakarazarishi ni	were not shallow, but soon after,

CHORUS

mata Kawachi no kuni	in the land of River Deltas
Takayasu no sato ni	at the town of Takayasu,
shiru hito arite	there was someone else he knew,
futamichi ni	whom he went to see
shinobite kayoi-	in secret, walking often
tamaishi ni,	on this double path;

SHITE

kaze fukeba	When the wind rises
okitsu shiranami	the white waves from the offing
Tatsutayama	Mount Tatsuta's Pass,

CHORUS

yowa ni ya kimi ga	in the deepest midnight dark,
hitori yukuran to	do you cross there all alone?[160]
obotsuka-nami no	as unsure as the lapping waves
yoru no michi	nearing the night road,
yukue o omō	her heart that follows after
kokoro togete	where her lover wanders
yoso no chigiri wa	moves him deeply, and he meets
karegare nari.	the other one no more.

SHITE

Geni nasake shiru	Froth-like, the whole of sorrow
utakata no	songs alone can sing,

CHORUS

aware o nobeshi mo	sweet with pity, they are their own
kotowari nari.	good reason for being.

[*The final* kuse *passage, sung by the chorus with an* ageha *by the* shite, *is the most delicately melodious section. It has its own pattern of introduction, development, and conclusion (jo ha kyū), with* ritardandos, accelerandos, *and* rubatos *in tempo. As the* shite *remains half-kneeling throughout the song, this type of* kuse *is known as an* iguse, *in contrast to the "dance* kuse" *(mai-guse). In* iguse, *the emphasis is on the song.*][161]

215

CHORUS

(Kuse: au, yowagin)

Mukashi	Long ago
kono kuni ni	in this land of ours,
sumu hito no	there were some persons
arikeru ga	whose houses were placed

Izutsu

yado o narabete	near each other, side by side,
kado no mae	and before their gates,
izutsu ni yorite	leaning over the well curb,
unaiko no	their long-haired children
tomodachi	played happily,
kataraite	chatting together,
tagai ni kage o [162]	peering at their images
mizu-kagami [163]	mirrored in the well,
omote o narabe	cheek by cheek, their sleeves across
sode o kake	each other's shoulders,
kokoro no mizu mo	hearts flowing fresh as water
sokoi naku	from the unfathomed well
utsuru [164] tsukihi mo	while uncounted moons and suns
kasanarite	were reflected there;
otonashiku	and so time passed by,
hajigawashiku	and they grew more gentle,
tagai ni ima wa	bashful, and somehow undone
narinikeri.	before each other.

[The introduction of the kuse *ends here, marked by* ritardando *and in the low range of tones. The beginning of the developmental section returns to normal tempo, with slight* ritardando *before the* shite's ageha *passage, and is sung* legato.]

Sono nochi	And later on
kano	sometime
mameotoko	from this faithful youth,
kotoba no tsuyu [165] no	there came a gemlike letter,
tamazusa no	filled with dew-fresh words,
kokoro no hana mo	colored with the fragrant flowers
iro soite	blooming in his heart.

[The following shite *passage, which begins the concluding section of the* kuse, *is sung in the high range* (jō-on). *The choral continuation also centers on the high range with many musical ornamentations and an animated melody.]*

SHITE

(Ageha)

Tsutsu izutsu	"By the round well-curb
izutsu ni kakeshi	our heights we used to measure,
maro ga take	now that little boy

CHORUS

oinikerashi na	has outgrown the marks you made
imo	since last
mizaru ma ni to	he came to meet with you." [166]
yomite okuri	Thus he composed these lines
keru hodo ni	and sent them to her.
sono toki	Then she in turn
onna mo	replied in verse:

kurabekoshi	"Since last we measured,
furiwake-gami mo	long my parted hair, too, grows
kata suginu	below my shoulders,
kimi narazu shite	for whom else if not for you
tare ka	should I bind
agubeki to	and comb it up?" [167]
tagai ni yomishi	So they sang for one another,
yue nare ya	surely this is why
tsutsu izutsu no	she is known so widely
onna to mo	as the "well-side maid"
kikoeshi wa	in the world of men,
Aritsune ga	where this dear old name
musume no furuki	is given to the daughter
na narubeshi.	of Aritsune.

[The kuse, *with its irregular lines, ends in the low tones. The verse form of the following* rongi *is very regular; the seven- and five-syllable pattern is sung in the basic* hiranori *rhythm and begins in the high range of tones. The chorus speaks for the* waki.*]*

CHORUS

[5] *(Rongi: au, yowagin)*

Geni ya furinishi	This is indeed a story
monogatari	from those days long past.
kikeba taenaru	As I listen, it appears
arisama no	so very charming,
ayashi ya nanori	so mysterious you seem!
owashimase.	Tell me who you are.

SHITE

Makoto wa ware wa	If the truth must now be known,
koi-goromo [168]	dressed in robes I love,
Ki [169] no Aritsune ga	that Aritsune's daughter
musume to mo	might have worn and come,
isa [170]	unknown,
shiranami no [171]	where the snow-white waves
Tatsutayama	Mount Tatsuta high,

[The shite *looks at the* waki.*]*

| yowa ni magirete | and now I've come back under |
| kitaritari. | favor of midnight. |

CHORUS

Fushigi ya satewa	Oh, how strange and wonderful!
Tatsutayama	Like Mount Tatsuta [172]
iro [173] ni zo izuru	in the red and golden hues
momijiba no	of its maple stands

217

Izutsu

SHITE

| Ki[174] no Aritsune ga | Lord Aritsune's daughter, |
| musume to mo | blushing with my love, |

CHORUS

| mata wa izutsu no | or as the world has named her, |
| onna to mo | the "well-side woman," |

SHITE

| hazukashi nagara | though ashamed, I will confess |
| ware nari to | that I am that one, |

CHORUS

| iu[175] ya | and barely |
| shimenawa no | had she said these lines |

[*The* shite *rises quietly and begins to move toward the* shite *seat.*]

nagaki yo o	truthful as the ties
chigirishi toshi wa	binding her for long to vows
tsutsu izutsu[176]	since her nineteenth year,
izutsu no kage ni	when behind the round well-curb

[*At the* shite *seat, the* shite *bends forward slightly from the hips and then straightens up to exit slowly over the bridge, while the chorus concludes.*]

kakurekeri	away she vanished,
izutsu no kage ni	and behind the round well-curb
kakurekeri	away she vanished.

Nakairi (Interlude)

[*The* kyōgen, *a villager of Ichinomoto, stands and advances onto the stage. He wears a striped kimono, a sleeveless robe over a trailing divided skirt, which is tied with a waistband in front, and a small sword. He carries a fan. As he reaches the name-saying place, he intones the following prose.*]

KYŌGEN

[6]

218

Kayō ni sōrō mono wa Washū Ichino-moto ni sumaisuru mono nite sōrō. Soregashi shukugan no shisai atte Ari-wara-dera e sankei tsukamatsuri sōrō. Konnichi mo mairabaya to zonzuru. Iya kore ni minaremōsanu go-sō no goza sōrō ga, izuku yori izukata e o-tōri na-sare sōraeba kore ni wa yasurōte goza sōrō zo.

I am a villager of Ichinomoto in Washū.[177] I have been coming to the Ari-wara Temple for some time to ask that my prayer be granted. I think I will pay homage there today too. [*He sees the* waki.] There's a Buddhist priest I haven't seen here before. They all come from some-where and wander off again somewhere else. He must just be resting there.

Kore wa issho fujū no sō nite sōrō. On-mi wa kono atari no hito nite watari sōrō ka.

I am a Buddhist priest who has no fixed abode. Are you a native of this place?

KYŌGEN

Nakanaka kono atari no mono nite sōrō.

Yes, I live nearby.

WAKI

Sayō nite sōrawaba mazu chikō onniri sōrae. Tazunetaki koto no sōrō.

If that is so, please come closer. I have something to ask.

KYŌGEN

Kashikomatte sōrō. Sate o-tazune na-saretaki to wa ikayō naru go-yō nite sōrō zo.

Yes, reverend sir. [*Advances to center stage and kneels.*] What would you like to know?

WAKI

Omoi mo yoranu mōshigoto nite sōrae-domo, inishie Narihira, Ki no Aritsune no musume fūfu no on-koto ni tsuki samazama no shisai arubeshi. Go-zonji ni oite wa katatte o-kikase sōrae.

Though it may be strange for me to ask about this, there must be various stories from the olden times concerning that couple, Narihira, and the daughter of Ki no Aritsune. If you know any of them, please tell me.

KYŌGEN

Kore wa omoi mo yoranu koto o ōse sōrō mono kana. Ware mo kono atari ni jūkyo tsukamatsuri sōraedomo sayō no koto kuwashiku wa zonzezu sōrō. Sari-nagara, hajimete o-me ni kakari o-tazune nasare sōrō mono o nan to mo zonzenu to mōsu mo ikaga nite sōraeba oyoso uketamawarioyobitaru tōri on-monogatari mōsōzuru nite sōrō.

This is most surprising—what you've just asked me! Though I live in this dis-trict, I don't really know much about these things. But if I tell you nothing, it might seem unobliging, especially since this is the first time we've met. So I'll tell you the story the way I've heard it.

WAKI

Chikagoro nite sōrō.

I would be most grateful.

219

KYŌGEN

Saru hodo ni Ariwara no Narihira to mōshitaru on-kata wa Aho Shinnō no sue no mi-ko nite gozaaritaru to mōsu. Sunawachi kono tokoro ni sumawase-

Well, to begin. The great person who is called Narihira of Ariwara was, I hear, the youngest son of Prince Aho, and he used to live in this place. In those days

Izutsu

tamō ga. Sono koro Ki no Aritsune to mōsu on-kata no go-sokujo no gozaari-shi ga, Narihira tsune ni tomonaitamai, kore naru izutsu ni tachiyori kage o u-tsushite on-asobi arishi ga, otonashiku naritamaite wa tagai ni hajigawashiku omoshite deaitamō koto mo naku sōrō ni, aru toki Narihira no kata yori uta o yomite sokujo no kata e okuraru. Sono on-uta wa

> Tsutsu izutsu
> izutsu ni kakeshi
> maro ga take
> oinikerashi na
> imo
> mizaru ma ni

Kayō ni asobashikereba, sokujo no go-henka ni

> Kurabekoshi
> furiwake-gami mo
> kata suginu
> kimi narazu shite
> tare ka
> agubeki to.

Kayō ni go-henka atte, hodo naku fūfu no katarai nashitamai, on-chigiri asa-karazu aritaru to mōsu. Mata sono koro Narihira wa Takayasu no sato ni to aru onna to chigiritamaite Takayasu e kayoi-tamō ni sokujo wa uramitamō kokoro mo naku, Takayasu e kayoitamō ori-fushi wa kigen yoku shite idetatasetamō aida, Narihira fushin ni oboshimeshi, moshi futagokoro ya aru to oboshime-shi, Kawachi e kayoitamō fuzei nite niwa naru hitomura no susuki no kage ni tachiyori uchi no tei o go-ran aru ni, sokujo wa itsu yori mo utsukushiku idetachi, kō o taki, hana o sonae, en ni idete Takayasu no hō o go-ranji, isshu no uta ni

> Kaze fukeba
> okitsu shiranami

the daughter of Aritsune of Ki lived here too. Narihira was always with her. They used to stop by that well curb over there, and, looking at their reflections on the water, they played together. But when they grew older and became self-conscious, they began to feel shy before each other and they did not meet. One day Narihira wrote a poem and sent it to her. It said:

> "By the round well-curb
> our heights we used to measure,
> now that little boy
> has outgrown the marks you made
> since last
> he came to meet you."

This is the way his poem went. So she replied in a verse:

> "Since last we measured,
> long my parted hair, too, grows
> below my shoulders,
> for whom else if not for you
> should I bind
> and comb it up?"

This is the way she answered, and soon afterward they became man and wife. It was no shallow love that bound these two together, I hear. Then about this time, Narihira began to know a certain person in the village of Takayasu, and he went there, back and forth. But his wife was not jealous. Each time he went to Takayasu, she sent him off pleasantly. Then Narihira suspected that she might not be faithful. So he pretended he was going to Kawachi and hid behind the bushy pampas grass in his garden. As he looked inside the house, she ap-peared more beautiful than usual: she burned incense before the altar, offered up some flowers, and then came out on the porch. Looking towards Takayasu, she recited a poem:

> "When the wind rises
> the white waves from the offing

220

Tatsutayama
yowa ni ya kimi ga
hitori yukuran

Mount Tatsuta's Pass,
in the deepest midnight dark,
do you cross there all alone?"

to yomitamai, ika ni mo ajikinaki tei nite oku e onniri sōrō o Narihira gorōjite, sate wa futagokoro naki mono o to, Kawachi-gayoi o todomaritamaitaru to mōsu ga. Mata sono nochi sokujo mo Narihira mo munashiku naritamō ni yori, sono ato ni tera o tate Ariwara-dera to nazukemōshi sōrō. Mazu warera no uketamawari-oyobitaru wa kaku no gotoku nite goza sōrō ga. Nan to obo-shimeshi o-tazunenasare sōrō zo. Chi-kagoro fushin ni zonji sōrō.

How touchingly weary she must have looked as she went inside. When Nari-hira saw this, he knew how faithful she was and he stopped going to Kawachi, I hear. And later on, when they passed away, men built this temple for their re-mains and named it the Ariwara Temple. This is the story I have heard. Why did you ask me about it? Lately, it has been rather strange around here.

Nengoro ni on-monogatari sōrō mono kana. Tazunemōsu mo yo no gi ni a-razu. On-mi izen ni izuku to mo naku nyoshō hitori kitarare, kore naru itai o musubi, hana o kiyome, kō o taki, are naru tsuka ni ekō nashimōsare sōrō hodo ni, ika naru koto zo to tazune sō-raeba, Narihira, Ki no Aritsune ga so-kujo no on-koto tadaima on-monogatari no gotoku nengoro ni katari, nan to ya-ran mi no ue no yō ni mōsare, izutsu no atari nite sugata o miushinōte sōrō yo.

How detailed a story you have told me! I had no particular reason to ask you about it. But a while ago, I saw a woman come from somewhere. She drew water from that wooden well, prepared some flowers, burned incense, and offered prayers before the mound over there. When I talked to her, she told me about Narihira and the daughter of Aritsune exactly as you did. And it sounded as if the story were her own. Then I lost sight of her around this well curb.

Sate wa go-sokujo no go-bōshin arawa-retamaitaru to zonji sōrō aida, shibaraku go-tōryū atte Narihira fūfu no on-ato o-tomurai arekashi to zonji sōrō.

Well! That must have been the spirit of the daughter, I'm sure. You should stay here awhile, I think, and pray for both their souls.

Warera mo sayō ni zonji sōrō aida, shi-baraku tōryū mōshi, arigataki o-kyō o dokushō-shi, kano on-ato o nengoro ni tomurai mōsōzuru nite sōrō.

Yes, indeed, I agree with you. I will stay here for a while and chant the holy su-tras and recite prayers for them.

221

Go-tōryū nite sōrawaba, kasanete go-yō ōse sōrae.

If you have something for me to do dur-ing your stay here, please call me again.

Izutsu

Tanomi sōrōbeshi.   Yes, I shall. Thank you.

Kokoroe mōshite sōrō.   Please call on me. [*Retires to the* kyōgen *seat.*]

PART II

Fifth Dan

[*As the* kyōgen *retires, the* waki *sings the following "waiting song"* (machiutai), *a song in the high range of tones in the set* hiranori *rhythm. While he is singing, the instruments enter and proceed without a break after the song is ended to play the entry music for the* nochi-jite. *In accordance with the practice in Japanese texts, the role will be designated as* shite *in what follows.*]

[7] (*Machiutai: au, yowagin*)

Fukeyuku ya	It is growing late,
Ariwara-dera no	over Ariwara Temple
yoru no tsuki	hangs the moon tonight,
Ariwara-dera no	over Ariwara Temple
yoru no tsuki	hangs the moon tonight,
mukashi o kaesu[178]	inside out I turn my robe
koromode ni[179]	turning back in time
yume[180] machisoete	to the past I wait for dreams,
karimakura	pillowing my head
koke no mushiro ni	on the spreading mat of moss,
fushinikeri	let me lie and sleep,
koke no mushiro ni	on the spreading mat of moss,
fushinikeri.	let me lie and sleep.

[*As* issei *entry music is played, the brocade curtain is swept back and the* nochi-jite *appears in her true guise as the daughter of Ki no Aritsune. She is gorgeously costumed, wearing under robes painted with gold patterns, made of plain white silk with a satinlike finish, and the three white collars at the neckline as before. An outer robe, woven in relief upon unpolished silk with thread of gold and flossed silk, painted and embroidered magnificently, is wrapped around her body from the waist down, with both sleeves hanging loosely behind her, in the* koshimaki *style. Over all, a loose, unlined purple robe hangs. The mask and wig are the same as in the first half. Holding a fan, she proceeds slowly along the bridge to the* shite *seat, where she stops and faces stage front. She sings the following as recitative.*]

222

[8] (*Sashi: awazu, yowagin*)

Ada nari to	"Fruitless and too frail—
na ni koso tatere	such is the reputation
sakurabana	of cherry blossoms,

tóshi ni mare naru	though for one who seldom comes
hito mo machikeri.	throughout the year, they waited." [181]

[*The* shite *faces the* waki.]

Kayō ni yomishi mo	The maiden who first sang that song,
ware nareba	that one too was I,
hito matsu onna to mo	a woman waiting for someone—
iwareshi nari	so that name too was mine,

[*The* shite *faces stage front once again.*]

ware tsutsu izutsu no [182]	and from the time I was nineteen,
mukashi yori	since those well-curb years,
mayumi tsukiyumi	many moons have come and gone,
toshi o hete [183]	drawn like crescent bows,
ima wa naki yo ni	in this world where nothing stays
Narihira no [184]	except this keepsake,

[*The* shite *gazes at her left sleeve and brings it up slowly to her breast.*]

katami no nōshi	these robes of Narihira
mi ni furete	which I have put on,

[*Facing stage front, the* shite *softly sings the following* issei *in free rhythm, beginning and ending in the high range of tones and inserting various ornaments. Notes from an even higher range may be sung.*]

SHITE

[9] (*Issei: awazu, yowagin*)

hazukashi ya	stirring me shyly
mukashi otoko ni	like that Man of Ancient Days,
utsuri mai [185]	dancing as he danced,

[*The next two choral lines conclude the* issei.]

CHORUS

yuki o megurasu	with these flower-sleeves I wave,
hana no sode	scattering cherry snows.

[*While the chorus sings the above, the* shite *turns at the* shite *pillar and stands with her back to the audience (*kutsurogu*), a stance that prepares the way for the dance. Introductory music for the prelude dance (jo no mai) is played by the two hand-drums. The* shite *then performs the dance, during which the flute takes the lead, accompanied by the drums. The dance usually consists of five sections (*dan*).*]

223

Jo no mai

[*After the dance, the* shite *stands near the* shite *pillar and sings the following* waka *verse in free rhythm, during which the formal movement known as* ageōgi *is made. The opened fan is held at the level of the mask and then extended forward, horizontal to the floor, as the feet move backward—left, right, and left. The extended fan is raised upward and lowered to the right in a large movement.*] [186]

SHITE

(Waka: awazu, yowagin)

Koko ni kite	To this place I come
mukashi zo kaesu	turning time back to the past
Ariwara no	at Ariwara

[The rhythm changes to the well-defined ōnori, with each syllable falling on a downbeat.]

CHORUS

(Ōnori: au, yowagin)

terai ni sumeru[187]	in the temple-well how clear
tsuki zo sayakeki	the moon is in its splendor,
tsuki zo sayakeki	the moon is in its splendor,

SHITE *[Sings in free rhythm]*

tsuki ya aranu   "Is this the moon no more?

[As the shite *begins, she advances front slightly and then moves in a circle back to a position in front of the musicians, while singing the following.]*

haru ya mukashi to	Is the spring no more a spring . . . ?"[188]
nagameshi mo	Gazing longingly,
itsu no koro zo ya	when was it he sang so well

[The rhythm changes again to the regularity of the ōnori*. The* shite *is now facing stage front.]*

SHITE

(Ōnori: au, yowagin)

tsutsu izutsu   by the round well-curb—[189]

[The shite *moves forward slightly, toward the well curb.]*

CHORUS

tsutsu izutsu	"By the round well-curb
izutsu ni kakeshi	our heights we used to measure,

SHITE

maro ga take   now that little boy

224

CHORUS

oinikerashi na[190]   has outgrown the marks you
made . . ."

[The shite *makes the* hiraki *movement, facing stage front. She extends the arms away from the body and downward at the sides as she steps back on the left foot, then right and left, and stops. At the conclusion, with the arms held outward and downward at the sides, an important, formal stance is created.[191] The following line is sung with slow deliberation.]*

(Ōnori: au, yowagin)

oinikeru zo ya   has outgrown his childhood days!

[The shite *moves forward to the eye-fixing pillar (*metsukebashira*), right stage front.]*

CHORUS

sanagara mi-mieshi	just as when he came to meet you,
mukashi otoko no	dressed in courtly cap and robes
kamuri naoshi wa	of the Man of Ancient Days,

[Moving in a large circle to the left, the shite *goes past the chorus and to stage rear, in front of the musicians. She then advances stage front up to the well curb, where she gently flips back a sleeve over one arm. She mimes the action of parting the pampas grass and looks into the well, as the chorus has all the while been singing the following.]*

onna to mo miezu	now she seems no more a woman
otoko narikeri	but that very man himself,

*[The next two lines are sung slowly and deliberately (*jikkuri*).]*

Narihira no	Lord Narihira,
omokage	reflected there

[There is a well-defined pause. The ōnori *rhythm changes to and continues as* hiranori. *The* shite *looks at the reflection in the well and sings softly with deep feeling.]*

SHITE

mireba natsukashi ya   I see! Oh, how dear he is!

[The shite *takes a few steps backward.]*

CHORUS

ware nagara	though it is myself,
natsukashi ya	oh, how dear he is!

[Turning to the right, the shite *moves back even further to a position in front of the stick-drum player's seat.]*

bōfu[192]	A lover
hakurei no	in a phantom shape,
sugata wa	a fleeting form,

[The shite *slowly sinks into the half-kneeling position and lightly flips one sleeve over her arm. Gradually she covers the mask behind her open fan, as if shrinking into herself as she mourns tenderly.]*

225

shibomeru hana no	a lovely flower withered,
iro nōte	with its colors gone,

[The shite *rises slowly and lightly.]*

nioi[193]	the fragrance
nokorite	lingers faintly

Izutsu

Ariwara no[194]   as the temple bell
tera no kane mo   here at Ariwara

[*The* shite *tilts the mask slightly, as if listening to the bell. She stamps delicately.*]

honobono to[195]   trailing softly too
akureba   tolls of dawning

[*Looks up slightly, as if at the eastern sky.*]

furu-tera no   at this old temple

[*Holding the closed fan straight out in front, the* shite *moves forward to left stage front, to the* waki *seat, and returns to stage rear, to the* shite *seat, in a diagonal line across the stage, as the next lines are sung.*[196]]

matsukaze ya   as the pine-wind tears
bashōba no   at the plantain leaves,
yume[197] mo yaburete   broken, too, the dream he dreams
samenikeri   and he awakens,

[*Facing stage front, the* shite *makes the* hiraki *movement.*]

yume wa yabure   for the dream is broken
akenikeri   and the day has dawned.

[*As the chorus sings the last lines, the* shite *turns toward the* waki *seat. She stamps again, and exits slowly over the bridge.*]

226

PART III

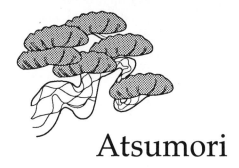

Atsumori

Introduction

Atsumori is a warrior, or *shura*, piece, which belongs to Group II of Nō plays. It occupies a place between the god-play and the wig-piece in the Nō program of five plays. Compared with the former, there are some structural changes in the *shura* piece, but it demonstrates the formal elements of the god-play more than those of the wig-piece. Also, the *shura* piece lacks the poetic richness of the *yūgen* quality that dominates the wig-piece. Zeami is aware of this, as he states in the "Shura" section of his essay entitled "Kadensho": "This [*shura* piece] is also one type. Though we perform it well, interesting points are rare."[1] The reason for this problem is that "the *shura* madness is apt to assume a demon's action. It should not be performed often." Consequently, he advises the playwright as follows: "If the Nō is well done by combining the beauties of nature with the theme of those who are famous among the Genpei, it is also interesting."

True to this insight, Zeami chose the excellent theme of the story of the young warrior-aristocrat Taira no Atsumori, told in the ninth chapter of the *Tale of the Heike* and in the thirty-eighth chapter of the *Rise and Fall of the Genpei*. In this story, Kumagae no Jirō Naozane beheaded Atsumori, who carried the famous bamboo flute, Little Branch, in the brocade bag at his hip and played it the night before he was slain. This sense of courtly elegance in the midst of the battleground made the gallant Genji warriors from the Eastern Land shed tears.[2] Atsumori was then only seventeen, with his teeth dyed black, as was customary for the aristocratic class of the time.

In this play, the candidate whom Zeami selects for the *waki* is not the usual Buddhist priest who travels from province to province. Zeami introduces him to the audience in the *nanori* passage as follows: "I am Kumagae Jirō Naozane, a native of the province of Musashi. I have renounced this world and become a Buddhist priest, calling myself Rensei. Since Atsumori was slain by my hand, the sorrow I felt led me to a form such as this."

The karmic relation between the *waki* and the *shite* sets the touching tone of the play as it opens. In addition, Zeami uses the sound of the bamboo flute so subtly that it serves as a prelude to the coming of the *shite*. The flute and music appear then throughout the play to unify this warrior-piece.

The grass cutters (*tsure*) are ushered in by the following powerful line from a poem by Kakinomoto no Hitomaro, one of the great *Man'yōshū* poets: "There upon the hill / stands the man who cuts the grass," a line that had also impressed Yeats with its image. Among the three grass cutters, Zeami cast the *shite* as a young man without a mask, which is exceptional, as Gondō Yoshikazu observes.[3] This innovation is, indeed, refreshing and appropriately satisfying, and it unfolds the character of the *shite* effortlessly. The dialogue between the *waki* and the *shite* also subtly foreshadows the elegant, artistic side of Atsumori, who never directly reveals his identity, as the chorus sings in his behalf:

> though I have not said
> my name should be apparent
> day and night you say
> the Buddhist holy prayers
> before the altar
> for that one whose name is mine.

After the Interlude, Part II opens with the usual "waiting song" (*machiutai*), and the *nochi-jite* appears with the *issei* music as a young noble warrior, elegantly costumed with a mask called *juroku*. When he stands at the *shite* seat, as Sakamoto Setchō observed of the *nochi-jite* as played by Kanze Sakon (1895–1939), "He appears, though warrior-like, somehow sorrowful, and with a loneliness akin to a phantom in a dream, which shows very deep charm."[4] Then "a confession"[5] serves as a turning point to unfold the "original source" of the story, and there ensue the *kuri-sashi-kuse* passages, where the *nochi-jite* tells of the fall of the Heike and of the life at the First Ravine (*Ichi no Tani*). This section is followed by the gay scene of music and singing that Atsumori enjoyed with his father, Lord Tsunemori, which culminates in the *chū no mai,* instead of in the quick *kakeri* dance that appears in seven plays of Group II, while the other seven are classified as *quasi-kakeri* pieces.[6] "In this piece the *chū no mai* is perhaps used for the first time," says Gondō Yoshikazu.[7] Nogami also states the following in regard to the *chū no mai*:

> The *chū no mai* is extraordinary for a *shura* piece; the *shura* piece is expressed as though it were a wig-piece. . . . In *Atsumori* the play is divided into two parts and structured after the typical *shura* piece, but following the *kuse* in the second part, the *chū no mai* danced by the *nochi-jite* is exceptional. Atsumori is a young noble warrior, and is the same age as Tomoakira and Tomonaga.[8] The pitiable fact that the lovely youth is beheaded by the mighty valor of the Eastern Land made the playwright, I believe, construct the play with the *yūgen*-centered *chū no mai*.[9]

230

Here I feel the *chū no mai* is most appropriate, but not for the reasons that Nogami gives. For Zeami it is illogical to use the standard *kakeri* dance, because it generally expresses the warrior's agony in the Ashura World,[10] and here, Atsumori's unsettled spirit has found peace for the most part. This state is due to the devoted prayers offered "every day and every night" by Rensei, and it is for this reason that Zeami's use of the *chū no mai* is significant. This is why a description of Atsumori's endless sufferings in the Ashura World is absent here, revealing the playwright's deep insight into the play. Consequently, for Zeami, the heart of this play is to reveal the soul of the artistic side of Atsumori, who loves music and his treasured bamboo flute, which he could not bear to leave behind in the enemy's hands. It is not only most appropriate, then, but also natural that the *chū no mai* follows the gay scene of music.

The *kakeai* between the *shite* and the chorus leads to the combat scene on the shore. Then, in a blind moment of attachment, Atsumori tries to settle old scores, as the concluding passage shows. The chorus sings for the *shite* in *tsuyogin* style:

> and at last,
> slain and vanquished,
> on the Wheel of Fate
> that ever turns,
> he returns to meet with you.
> "My enemy is here," he shouts
> as he's about to strike him . . .

but here his warring spirit is calmed by the grace of the holy prayers. The chorus continues:

> "Evil I'll repay with good"
> for the prayers
> you have said for me,
> calling on Amida's name. . . .

At the end of the play, as he makes the *tome* stamp, he asks Rensei for the last prayer for his final rest and eternal peace:

> oh, say the holy prayers
> for my memory.

The figure of this young noble, Atsumori, in the concluding section is most memorable; the expression of the Nō mask lingers vividly even after he has made an exit.

231

Atsumori

ATSUMORI

By Zeami

Persons: WAKI: *Priest Rensei*
SHITE (PART I): *Ghost of Atsumori (appears as a grass cutter)*
TSURE: *The fellow grass cutters (three)*
NOCHI-JITE (PART II): *Ghost of Taira no Atsumori (appears as himself)*
KYŌGEN: *A man of the place*

Classification: *Primary, Group II*
Place: *Ichi no Tani in the land of Settsu*
Time: *August*
Kogaki: *4*

PART I

[*Following introductory music called* shidai, *the* waki, *Priest Rensei, wearing a pointed hood (kaku-bōshi), a less-formal heavy silk kimono (noshime), a broad-sleeved robe (mizugoromo), a waistband (koshiobi), a fan (ōgi), and a rosary (juzu), comes out to the name-saying pillar and, facing the musicians' seats, sings the following* shidai *verse.*]

WAKI

[1] *(Shidai: au, yowagin)*

Yume no yo nareba	As the world is but a dream,
odorokite,	so surprised by this
yume no yo nareba	that the world is but a dream,
odorokite	so surprised by this;
sutsuru ya utsutsu	then renouncing of this world
naruran.	is truly real?

[*The chorus sings the* jidori, *repeating the above verse, except the third and fourth lines, in a lower key.*]

232

CHORUS

(Jidori: au, yowagin)

Yume no yo nareba	As the world is but a dream,
odorokite	so surprised by this;
sutsuru ya utsutsu	then renouncing of this world
naruran.	is truly real?

[*After the* jidori, *the* waki *intones the following prose passage, called* nanori, *introducing himself to the audience in free-rhythm recitative style.*]

Masterworks of the Nō Theater

(Nanori: awazu, kotoba)

Kore wa Musashi no Kuni no jūnin Kumagae no Jirō Naozane[11] shukke shi,
Rensei to mōsu hōshi nite sōrō. Sate mo
Atsumori[12] o te ni kake mōshishi koto
amari ni onnitawashiku sōrō hodo ni
kayō no sugata to narite sōrō. Mata kore
yori Ichi no Tani[13] ni kudari Atsumori
no go-bodai o tomurai mōsabaya to
omoi sōrō.

I am Kumagae Jirō Naozane, a native of
the Province of Musashi. I have renounced this world and become a Buddhist priest, calling myself Rensei. Since
Atsumori was slain by my hand, the
sorrow I felt has led me to a form such
as this. From here I think I will go west-
ward to the First Ravine and there I will
perform a holy Buddhist service for Atsumori's memory.

[*After the* nanori, *the* waki, *still facing stage front, sings the following verse* ageuta *passage, called* michiyuki, *"travel song."*]

(Michiyuki: au, yowagin)

Kokonoe no	From the ninefold clouds
kumoi[14] o idete	girding round the capital,
yuku tsuki no,	now the moon departs,
kumoi o idete	from the cloud-girt capital
yuku tsuki no	like the moon we part
minami ni meguru	rolling on the southward round
oguruma[15] no	as the little wheel
Yodo[16] Yamazaki[17] o	turns at Pool and Mountain Point
uchisugite	we pass and journey
Koya no Ike[18] mizu	across Koya's lake water
Ikutagawa[19]	and the Ikuta;

[*The* waki *faces to his right, goes forward two or three steps, and then returns to his former position, indicating that he has traveled; he finishes the rest of the lines.*]

nami koko moto ya[20]	then here where the waves rise up
Suma no Ura[21]	at the Suma Bay
Ichi no Tani nimo	where the First Ravine lies deep
tsukinikeri	I have also come,
Ichi no Tani nimo	where the First Ravine lies deep
tsukinikeri	I have also come.

[*After the* michiyuki, *the* waki *faces stage front and intones in free-rhythm style the following prose passage, called* tsukizerifu.]

233

(Tsukizerifu: awazu, kotoba)

Isogi sōrō hodo ni Tsu no Kuni Ichi no
Tani ni tsukite sōrō. Makoto ni mukashi
no arisama ima no yō ni omoi iderarete
sōrō. Mata ano Ueno[22] ni atatte fue no
ne no kikoe sōrō. Kono hito o aimachi

I have traveled so fast that here I am already at the First Ravine in the Province
of Tsu. Truly I still recall that scene of
long ago as though it were today. [*Facing
to his right.*] Besides, over in the direction

Atsumori

kono atari no kotodomo kuwashiku tazunebaya to omoi sōrō.

of High Meadow I can hear the music of
a flute. I will wait for that person. [*Facing
stage front again.*] Among other things, I
would like to ask him about the stories
of this place. [*The* waki *goes to the* waki *seat
and sits down.*]

[*Following the* shidai *music, the* shite, *the grass cutter, enters the stage wearing a Nō mask, a collar
in pale blue (*eri asagi*), a striped, less-formal silk kimono (*dan noshime*), an "inferior silk" broad-
sleeved robe (*shike mizugoromo*), a waistband (*koshiobi*), and a fan (*ōgi*). He is followed by his
fellow grass cutters, similarly dressed; all holding sprays of flowers and facing one another, they sing
the following* shidai *verse together.*]

SHITE AND TSURE

[2] (*Shidai: au, yowagin*)

Kusakaribue no	For the flute grass cutters play,
koe soete	the breeze comes blowing,
kusakaribue no	for the flute grass cutters play,
koe soete	the breeze comes blowing,
fuku koso nokaze	to accompany its voice
narikere.	across the field.

[*The chorus sings the* jidori, *repeating the above verse, except the third and fourth lines, in a lower
key.*]

CHORUS

(*Jidori: au, yowagin*)

Kusakaribue no	For the flute grass cutters play,
koe soete	the breeze comes blowing,
fuku koso nokaze	to accompany its voice
narikere.	across the field.

[*After the* jidori, *the* shite *faces stage front and sings the following verse, called* sashi.]

SHITE

(*Sashi: awazu, yowagin*)

Kano oka ni[23]	There upon the hill
kusakaru onoko	stands the man who cuts the grass,
no o wakete	and across the field
kaerusa ni naru	he will be returning home
yūmagure.	as the twilight falls.

SHITE AND TSURE [*Facing one another.*]

Ieji mo sazona	His way home may lead him, too,
suma no umi	near the Suma Sea;
sukoshi ga hodo no	short may be the path he takes
kayoiji ni	on his daily rounds
yama ni iri	deep into the hills

Masterworks of the Nō Theater

ura ni izuru	down toward the inlet,
uki mi no waza koso	still the work of man's sad life
monoukere.	is too wearisome.

[*The* shite *and the* tsure *sing the following low-pitched song, called* sageuta, *in strict-rhythm* yowagin *style.*]

SHITE AND TSURE

(*Sageuta: au, yowagin*)

Towaba koso	Should one ask of you
hitori wabu tomo	if I live alone and sad,
kotaemashi.[24]	let you then reply:

[*They continue to sing the following high-pitched song, called* ageuta.]

(*Ageuta: au, yowagin*)

Suma no Ura	by the Suma Bay
moshio tare tomo[25]	dipping seaweed brine I live;
shirarenaba,	if someone knows me,
moshio tare tomo	dipping seaweed brine I live,
shirarenaba	if someone knows me,
ware ni mo tomo no	then there ought to be a friend
arubeki ni	that I too might find,
amari ni nareba[26]	but this fisher's life I lead
wabibito no	as a wretched man,
shitashiki dani mo[27]	those who are so dear to me
utoku shite	keep their distance now.

[*The* shite *goes to the* shite *seat, and the* tsure *to the front of the chorus. All stand and sing.*]

sumeba to bakari	Hoping only to survive,
omou ni zo	I resign myself
uki ni makasete	as I yield the rest to fate
sugosu nari,	living out my days,
uki ni makasete	as I yield the rest to fate
sugosu nari.	living out my days.

[*At about the time the singing comes to an end, the* waki *rises. Then, during the following prose dialogue, called* mondai, *the* waki *stands at the* waki *seat and the* shite *at the* shite *seat, and they respond to each other.*]

WAKI

[3] (*Mondai: awazu, kotoba*)

| Ika ni kore naru kusakaritachi ni tazune mōsubeki koto no sōrō. | Ho, there. Grass cutters. I have something that I must ask you. |

SHITE

| Konata no koto nite sōrō ka. Nanigoto nite sōrō zo. | Are you speaking to me? What can I do for you? |

Atsumori

Tadaima no fue wa katagata no naka ni fukitamaite sōrō ka.	About the flute I have just heard, is it played among you?

SHITE

San zōrō. Warera ga naka ni fukite sōrō.	Yes. The flute is played among us.

WAKI

Ara yasashi ya. Sono mi ni mo ōzenu waza. Kaesugaesu mo yasashū koso sōrae.	How elegant! The performance is unbecoming for folks like you, but it is very, very elegant indeed, I should say.

SHITE

Sono mi ni mo ōzenu waza to uketamawaredomo sore masaru o mo[28] urayamazare. Otoru o mo iyashimu na to koso miete sōrae. Sono ue shōka bokuteki[29] tote,	Though I hear you say the performance is unbecoming for folks like us, there is a saying: "Do not envy those who excel you. Do not despise those who fall short of you." Besides, in the case of the "woodsman's song" and the "herdsman's flute,"

[*The* shite *and the* tsure *face one another and sing the following verse passage.*]

SHITE AND TSURE

(*Awazu, yowagin*)

kusakari no fue	for the flutes grass cutters play,
kikori no uta wa	and the songs the woodsmen sing
kajin no ei ni mo	are recorded in the verses
tsukuriokarete	written by the poets too;
yo ni kikoetaru	how well known throughout the land
fuetake no	and superb they are

[*Facing toward the* waki *they make a* tsumeashi *gesture.*]

fushin na[30] nasasetamai so to yo.	made of bamboo out of joint you ought not find us so.

[*They remain standing in the same positions. There follows the* kakeai, *in free-rhythm* yowagin *style.*]

WAKI

(*Kakeai: awazu, yowagin*)

Geni geni kore wa	Yes, indeed, what you have said
kotowari nari.	appears reasonable;
Sate sate shōka	what you've said of woodsmen's songs
bokuteki to wa	and of flutes for shepherds;

kusakari no fue   they're grass cutters' bamboo flutes,

WAKI

kikori no uta no   and woodcutters' songs for all

SHITE

ukiyo o wataru   help them through the fleeting world
hito fushi o   with the melody,

WAKI

utō mo   as they sing them,

SHITE

mō mo   dance the rounds,

WAKI

fuku mo   blow the tunes,

SHITE

asobu mo   and play as well

[*The* shite *makes a* tsumeashi *gesture toward the* waki. *During the following* ageuta *passage sung by the chorus, the* kyōgen *comes out quietly through the half-lifted curtain, goes to the* kyōgen *seat, and sits down. As the chorus starts to sing, the* shite *makes a* hiraki *gesture toward stage front.*]

CHORUS

(*Ageuta: au, yowagin*)

mi no waza no   as they work, which seems
sukeru kokoro ni   pleasing to their hearts, they find
yoritake[31] no,   drifted bamboo-joints,

[*The* waki *sits down at the* waki *seat.*]

sukeru kokoro ni   pleasing to their hearts they make
yoritake no   drifted bamboo-joints
Saeda[32] Semiore[33] into various types of flutes
samazama ni   such as Little Branch,

[*The* shite *goes out slightly toward stage front and makes a* hiraki *gesture.*]   237

fue no na wa   Broken Cicada,
ōkeredomo   as the names are many
kusakari no   for those famous flutes.
fuku fue naraba   So the name we gave, "Green Leaf,"
kore mo na wa   should be considered
Aoba no Fue to   suitable for the flute
oboshimese.   grass cutters play.

Atsumori

[*As the chorus sings the following passage, the* shite *goes out to the eye-fixing pillar and, turning around to his left, goes to the* shite *seat, while the* tsure *make an exit across the bridge.*]

Sumiyoshi no	Were we at the shore
migiwa naraba	of Sumiyoshi,
Komabue³⁴ ni ya	the flute of Koguryō
arubeki.	should suit us well.
Kore wa Suma no	Since at Suma inlet
shioki no	the name "Burnt End" left

[*The* shite, *at the* shite *seat, faces toward the* waki.]

ama no Takisashi³⁵ to	from fishermen's salt-making woods
oboshimese,	should be considered,
ama no Takisashi to	from fishermen's salt-making woods
oboshimese.	should be considered.

[*The following dialogue, called* kakeai, *is exchanged between the* shite *and the* waki.]

WAKI

[4] *(Kakeai: awazu, yowagin)*

Fushigi ya na. Yo no kusakaritachi wa mina mina kaeritamō ni on-mi ichinin todomaritamō koto nani no yue nite aruyaran.

How strange! The other grass cutters have all gone home, but you are still here by yourself. I wonder why.

SHITE

Nani no yue to ka yūnami no³⁶ koe o chikara ni kitaritari, jūnen³⁷ sazuke owa-shimase.

Why do you ask? Guided by the voices calling across the evening waves I have come. Please repeat for me the Holy Name ten times.

WAKI

Yasuki koto jūnen oba sazukemōsube-shi. Sore ni tsuketemo okoto wa ta so.

I shall be glad to repeat the Holy Name ten times. Though I shall do so, I still must ask you who you are.

SHITE

Makoto wa ware wa	To relate to you the truth,
Atsumori no	I am really one
yukari no mono nite	who was once in close connection
sōrō nari.	with Lord Atsumori.

WAKI

Yukari to kikeba	I hear you are connected;
natsukashi ya to	you are so dear, he says,

[*With the rosary, the* waki *folds his hand in prayer.*]

tanagokoro o	and clasping tight his hands
awasete	together, prays:
namuamidabu	holy Amida Buddha!

[*The* shite, *too, folds his hands in prayer as he kneels on one knee; both chant the following lines from the sutra.*]

SHITE AND WAKI

Nyakuga jōbutsu[38]	Should I gain enlightenment,
jippō sekai	through this ten-sphered world, let all
nenbutsu shujō	those who call my name be saved
sesshu fusha.	from abandonment.

[*As the chorus starts to sing for the* shite, *the* shite *looks at the* waki *and lowers his hands from the prayer position.*]

CHORUS

(*Au, yowagin*)

Sutesasetamō na yo	"Oh, do not abandon me," I ask,
hitokoe[39] dani mo	though one call alone would be
tarinubeki ni	good enough to save us,
mainichi	truly daily,
maiya no	ever nightly
o-tomurai	you have said a prayer

[*Lowering his face, the* shite *rises and starts to go toward the* shite *seat.*]

Ara arigata ya	and I am so grateful too,
waga na oba	though I have not said
mōsazu tote mo	my name should be apparent
ake kure ni	day and night you say

[*Returning to his former position, the* shite *gazes at the* waki *and moves slightly forward.*]

mukaite ekō	the Buddhist holy prayers
shitamaeru	before the altar
sono na wa ware to	for that one whose name is mine.

[*Turning to his right, the* shite *goes to the* shite *seat.*]

ii sutete	With these words he left;
sugata mo miezu	there his figure, too, is lost
usenikeri,	and is seen no more,

[*At the* shite *seat, the* shite *makes* hiraki *toward stage front as if he were vanishing.*]

239

sugata mo miezu	there his figure, too, is lost
usenikeri.	and is seen no more.

[*The* shite *makes an exit quietly behind the curtain.*]

Atsumori

Nakairi (Interlude)

[*The* kyōgen, *wearing a striped, less-formal heavy silk kimono* (dan noshime), *the* kyōgen *two-piece* (kyōgen kamishimo), *and a waistband* (koshiobi), *and carrying a fan* (ōgi) *in his hand, comes out to the name-saying pillar and intones the following prose passage.*]

KYŌGEN

(*Mondai: awazu, kotoba*)

Kayō ni sōrō mono wa Suma no Ura ni sumai suru mono nite sōrō. Kyō wa makariide fune no kayoi o nagame, kokoro o nagusamebaya to zonzuru. Iya kore ni minare mōsanu o-sō no goza sōrō ga, izukata yori o-ide nasare sōrō zo.

I am a person living by the Bay of Suma. Today I will go out to watch the boats sailing by and amuse myself. [*Noticing the waki.*] Well, I see an unfamiliar Buddhist priest here. Where did you come from?

WAKI

Kore wa miyakogata yori idetaru sō nite sōrō. On-mi wa kono atari no hito nite watari sōrō ka.

I come from the capital and I am a Buddhist priest. Do you live around this vicinity?

KYŌGEN

Nakanaka kono atari no mono nite sōrō.

Yes, I come from this neighborhood.

WAKI

Sayō nite sōrawaba mazu chikō onniri sōrae. Tazunetaki koto no sōrō.

If that's so, please come closer. I have something I would like to ask you.

KYŌGEN

Kashikomatte sōrō. Sate on-tazune nasaretaki to wa ikayō naru go-yō nite sōrō zo.

Yes, holy priest. [*Goes to the center of the stage and sits down.*] Well, you would like to ask me something. What sort of business do you have in mind?

WAKI

Omoi mo yoranu mōshigoto nite sōraedomo kono tokoro wa Genpei ryōke no kassen no chimata to uketamawari oyobite sōrōchū ni mo, Heike no kindachi Atsumori no hatetamaitaru yōtei gozonji ni oite wa katatte on-kikase sōrae.

Indeed, this is something you may not expect from me, but I hear that, among other things, this place was the very battlefield where the two houses of the Taira and of the Minamoto had fought. Please tell me the story if you know about the death of Atsumori, a noble of the Heike clan.

KYŌGEN

Kore wa omoi mo yoranu koto o uketamawari sōrō mono kana. Warera mo kono atari ni wa sumai tsukamatsuri

How strange that you should ask me about such things. Though we live in this neighborhood, I don't know too

240

Masterworks of the Nō Theater

sōraedomo sayō no koto kuwashiku wa zonzezu sōrō, sarinagara hajimete o-me ni kakari o-tazune nasare sōrō mono o, nan tomo zonzenu to mōsu mo ika nite sōraeba ōyoso uketamawarioyobitaru tōri on-monogatari mōsōzuru nite sōrō.

much about the details. But since I am asked by a person that I meet for the first time, it would not be quite right to say that I know nothing at all; so I shall tell the story roughly the way I've heard it.

WAKI

Chikagoro nite sōrō.

I would be most grateful.

KYŌGEN

Saru hodo ni Heike wa Juei ninen aki no koro Kiso Yoshinaka ni Miyako o otosare, kono tokoro e utsuritamō ga, Genji wa Heike o horobosan to rokuman'yoki o futate ni wake sayū nō uchiyaburi go-ichimon wa chirijiri ni ochitamō. Naka ni mo Shuri no Tayū Tsunemori no on-ko Mukan no Tayū Atsumori wa gozabune ni noran tote nagisa no kata e onnide arishi ni Koeda to mōsu go-hizō no fue o honjin ni wasuretamō ga, ato nite teki ni toraren koto o kuchioshiku oboshimeshi, mata honjin ni o-kaeri arite fue o tori nagisa e onnide arishi ni gozabune o hajime hyōsen domo kotogotoku oki e idemōshi sōrō aida, uma wa tsuyoshi oyogasen tote uma o umi e uchiiretamō tokoro ni Musashi no Kuni no Jūnin Kumagae Jirō Naozane ōgi o hiraki manekikereba Atsumori yagate totte kaeshi, namiuchigiwa nite muzu to kumi ryōba ga aida ni dō to ochiru. Kumagae wa daigō no mono nareba sono mama totte osae kubi o kakan to shite uchikabuto o mireba, jūgoroku bakari to miete keshō shite kane kuro-guro to tsuketamō aida, appare yoki musha kana. Tasukebaya to ushiro o mireba, Dohi Kajiwara [40] jikki bakari tsuzukitari. Kumagae mōsu yō wa tasukemōshitaku sōraedomo goran no gotoku mikata ōzei tsuzukitari. Kumagae ga te ni kake onnato nengoro ni tomuraimōsan tote on-kubi kakiotoshi on-shigai o mitatematsureba koshi no nishiki no fukuro ni fue no goza sōrō aida, sunawachi taishō no kenzan ni ire-

Well. It was about autumn of the second year of the Juei era that the Heike were defeated at the capital by Kiso Yoshinaka and the Heike moved to this place. The Genji, however, determined to destroy them. Dividing their gallant warriors six hundred thousand strong into two forces, the Genji crushed the Heike right and left, and as the Heike fell, they scattered and dispersed. Among them the son of Lord Tsunemori, the vice-minister of the Service Bureau, was Atsumori, who held no office. He went out to the shore to board the royal ship, but as he forgot his treasured bamboo flute called Little Branch in the main camp, he was vexed at the thought that later it might fall into the enemy's hands. So he went back to the main camp and recovered it. When he came out to the shore again, the royal ship and those of the soldiers were all out at sea. His steed was strong. He tried to make him swim but as he spurred him, Kumagae Jirō Naozane, who came from the Province of Musashi, opened his fan and beckoned him back with it. Soon Atsumori returned ashore. They grasped each other and down they fell between the horses by the shore. Huge heroic man that Kumagae was, he held Atsumori accordingly and pressed him down, but, looking under the helmet as he was about to behead him, he saw that Atsumori seemed fifteen or sixteen years old, with his face powdered and his teeth dyed deep black. He seemed

241

Atsumori

shi ni makoto ni kakaru orifushi fue o mochitamō koto wa, kindachi no naka nite mo yasashiki on-kata nari tote, minamina yoroi no sode o nurashitaru to mōsu. Sono nochi on-na o tazunuru ni Tsunemori no on-ko Mukan no Tayū Atsumori nite goza aritaru to mōsu. Makoto ya hito no mōsu wa Kumagae wa shukke shite Atsumori no go-bodai o tomurō to mōsu ga, sayō no mono naraba sono toki tasukemōsōzuru ni, tasukenu mono naraba kore wa itsuwari nite sōrōbeshi. Sono Kumagae ga kono tokoro e kitarekashi. Uchikoroshite Atsumori no kyōyō ni itashitaku to no mōshigoto nite sōrō. Mazu warera no uketamawarioyobitaru wa kaku no gotoku nite goza sōrō ga, nanto oboshimeshi otazune nasare sōrō zo. Chikagoro fushin ni zonji sōrō.

splendid and gallant. Kumagae wanted to spare him, but as he glanced back there came galloping Dohi and Kajiwara, followed by some ten other braves. "I would like to spare you," he said, "but many on my side are coming, as you see. By my hand you must fall. I shall pray most earnestly for you." So saying, Kumagae beheaded him. As he looked at the corpse, there was a bamboo flute in a brocade bag worn by his hip. Thereupon it was presented to the general for inspection. Certainly in a situation such as this, anyone who still carried his bamboo flute, even among the nobles, was most elegant, they said, and all wet their armor's sleeves with tears. Later when they investigated who he was, it was Atsumori who held no office, the son of Lord Tsunemori. According to what people say, Kumagae renounced this world to pray for Atsumori's memory; however, if he were such a man, he should have saved Atsumori at that time. Since he did not, he must be a hypocrite. Let that Kumagae come to this place, and he would be struck down to be offered as a prayer for Atsumori's memory. So they say. Well, this is what we've heard. Please tell me why you ask me about this. Lately I have felt something strange around here.

WAKI

Nengoro ni on-monogatari sōrō mono kana. Ima wa nani o ka tsutsumimōsubeki. Kore wa Kumagae no Jirō Naozane shukke shi Rensei to mōsu hōshi nite sōrō. Atsumori no go-bodai o tomuraimōsan tame kore made mairite sōrō yo.

How kind of you to tell me all about the story. Now why should I conceal anything about myself from you? I am Kumagae Jirō Naozane who renounced this world and is now called Rensei. I have come to this place in order to perform a holy service for Atsumori's memory.

KYŌGEN

Sate wa sono toki no Kumagae-dono nite sōrō ka. Sayō no koto to mo zonzezu yaji naru monogatari mōshite sōrō.

Well. So you're the Kumagae of that time. Without meaning to, I'm afraid I've told Atsumori's story. Please forgive

242

Gomen sōrae. Sate zen ni tsuyoki wa aku nimo tsuyoshi to mōsu ga katagata no koto ni sōrōbeshi. Yaya Atsumori no onnato on-tomurai arekashi to zonji sōrō.

me. Well, as the saying goes, "He who is strong for good deeds is strong for bad ones." That is the warrior. I hope you say some holy Buddha's prayers for Atsumori.

WAKI

Iya iya kurushikarazu sōrō. Kono to-koro e kitari sōrō mo Atsumori no on-nato tomuraimōsan tame nite sōrō aida, shibaraku tōryū mōshi yaya arigataki on-kyō o dokuju shi kano on-nato o nengoro ni tomuraimōsōzuru nite sōrō.

No, no. I am not offended. I do not mind all this. The reason I came to this place is that I wanted most earnestly to say some holy prayers for Atsumori's memory. I will stay here for a while and with the recitation of sutra, I would like to hold a holy service.

KYŌGEN

Sayō nite sōrawaba o-yado o mōsōzuru nite sōrō.

If that is so, may I offer you lodgings.

WAKI

Tanomi sōrōbeshi.

That is kind of you. Thank you.

KYŌGEN

Kokoroe mōshite sōrō.

Not at all, good priest.

PART II

[*After the Interlude, at the* waki *seat, the* waki *sings the following* ageuta *verse, called* machiutai, *"waiting song."*]

WAKI

[5] (*Machiutai: au, yowagin*)

Kore ni tsuketemo	For this connection let me
tomurai no,	say a holy prayer,
kore ni tsuketemo	for this connection let me
tomurai no	say a holy prayer
hōji o nashite	and the Buddhist service too
yomosugara	let me hold nightlong
nenbutsu mōshi	calling out Amida's name
Atsumori no	for Atsumori
bodai o nao mo	that his soul may find true rest
tomurawan,	as I pray still more,
bodai o nao mo	that his soul may find true rest
tomurawan.	as I pray still more.

243

Atsumori

[*Following the* issei *music, the* nochi-jite, Taira no Atsumori, *wearing the Atsumori mask; a flowing black wig (kuro tare); a tall black cap (nashiuchi eboshi); a "long silk," loose, unlined, broad-sleeved outer robe (chōken); a white headband (shiro hachimaki); a collar in white and red (eri shiro aka); a "thick board" heavy silk kimono (atsuita); a white broad divided skirt (shiro ōguchi); a waistband (koshiobi); a fan (ōgi); and a long sword (tachi), enters the stage and stands at the* shite *seat, where, facing stage front, he sings the following verse.*]

SHITE

[6] (*Au, yowagin*)

Awajigata[41]	On Awaji-bar
kayō chidori no	I hear the plovers' voices
koe kikeba	passing back and forth.
nezame mo Suma no[42]	Wakeful, too, from sleep nightlong
sekimori wa ta so.	who is he like Suma's guard?

[*During the following exchange between the* waki *and the* shite, *called the* kakeai, *the* shite *stands at the* shite *seat, while the* waki *sits at the* waki *seat. The* shite, *facing the* waki, *finishes the rest of the verse.*]

(*Kakeai: awazu, yowagin*)

Ika ni Rensei	Listen now, Rensei,
Atsumori koso	here is Atsumori
mairite sōrae.	who has come before you now.

WAKI

Fushigi ya na	Oh, how strange this seems!
fushō o narashi	As I tap the gong I hold
hōji o nashite	a holy Buddhist service
madoromu hima mo	when I have no time to spare
naki tokoro ni	for a moment's dozing,
Atsumori no	Atsumori came,
kitaritamō zo ya.	or it so appeared and surely
Sate wa yume nite	this, I thought, was but a dream.
aruyaran.	Am I dreaming still?

SHITE

Nani shi ni yume nite arubeki zo. Utsu-tsu no inga o harasan tame ni kore made araware kitaritari.	Why must it be a dream? It is to atone for the sins of my life that I come here before you in a visible form.

244

WAKI

Utate na ya.	What a foolish thing to say!
Ichinen Midabutsu[43]	With one clear call of Mida's name
sokumetsu muryō no	at once the guilt of all your sins,
zaisho o harasan	countless though they be, is cleansed away;
shōmō no	ceaselessly I hold
hōji o taesezu	in the Holy Name the service,

tomurō kuriki ni	and with grace so given by it
nani no inga wa	what karma can still remain
arisoumi[44] no	crag-bound like the ocean

fukaki[45] tsumi o mo	fathomless my sins may be
toiukame	should I still be saved?

WAKI

mi wa jōbutsu no	Yes, by prayer I hope it serves
tokudatsu no en.	for my own salvation too,

SHITE

Kore mata tashō no	as this is Dharma's power
kuriki nareba	on our next existence

WAKI

higoro wa kataki	so the long-time enemy

SHITE

ima wa mata	of the past shall now

WAKI

makoto ni nori no	once again become a friend

SHITE

tomo narikeri.	by Amida's mercy.

[*The* shite *makes a* tsumeashi *gesture toward the* waki.]

CHORUS

(*Au, yowagin*)

Kore ka ya	In the saying

[*The* shite *makes a* hiraki *gesture toward stage front.*]

akunin no tomo o	that "one should leave his friend
furisutete	if he's evil;

[*With his left hand the* shite *points to the* waki *and, while moving forward and flipping his left sleeve, looks at the* waki.]

zennin no	if the foes are good,
kataki o	bid them welcome,"
maneke to wa,	you're indeed the proof
on-mi no koto ka	of the very words just said!
arigata ya.	How truly grateful!
Arigatashi,	I am so grateful,

Atsumori

[*Changing his mood, the* shite *goes around to his left toward the* shite *seat.*]

arigatashi.	I am so grateful.
Totemo sange no	Now I wish I could relate
monogatari	all of my story
yosugara iza ya	to you in this confession
mōsan,	throughout the night,
yosugara iza ya	to you in this confession
mōsan.	throughout the night.

[*At the* shite *seat, the* shite *faces toward the* waki. *Then, from in front of the musicians, the* shite *goes out toward center stage and sits on the stool provided by the stage attendant as the chorus sings the following passage, called* kuri.]

[7] (*Kuri: awazu, yowagin*)

Sore haru no hana[46] no	All the flowers in the springtime
jutō ni noboru wa	rising toward the treetops higher
jōgu bodai no	lift us and inspire us all
ki o susume	to true salvation,
aki no tsuki no	and the moon at autumn
suitei ni shizumu wa	shines across the water on its bed
geke shujō no	to reveal its form to save
katachi o misu.	all the lowly beings,

[*While all sit, the* shite *sings the following* sashi *passage in free-rhythm* yowagin *style.*]

SHITE

(*Sashi: awazu, yowagin*)

Shikaru ni ichimon	yet in spite of this the Heike
kado o narabe	lined their mansions' gateways,
ruiyō eda o	flourished like a mighty tree
tsuraneshi yosooi	intertwines its leafy branches.

CHORUS

makoto ni kinka	As the morning glory blooms
ichijitsu[47] no	only for a day
ei ni onaji,	with its glowing splendor,
yoki o susumuru	so the law that glorified
oshie ni wa	good and teaches men
ō koto kataki[48]	did not realize its goal
ishi no hi no	for a moment brief
hikari no ma zo to	like flintstone's spark
omowazarishi	for we were all thoughtless,
mi no narawashi koso	hampered by accustomed habits
hakanakere.	in this fleeting world.

SHITE

Kami ni atte wa	From on high, the mighty look
shimo o nayamashi	on the low whom they oppress,

246

tonde wa ogori o   As they prosper, rich and haughty
shirazaru nari.   they grow and know no end.

[*The* shite *rises from the stool and dances, periodically making appropriate gestures, during the following* kuse *passages sung by the chorus in strict-rhythm* yowagin *style.*]

(*Kuse: au, yowagin*)

Shikaru ni Heike   On the other hand, indeed,
yo o totte   here the Heike
nijūyonen   ruled this world for twenty
makoto ni   years and longer,
hitomukashi[49] no   but a generation
suguru wa yume no   passes only like a span
uchinare ya.   of a dream we dream.

[*The* shite *advances slightly forward toward stage front.*]

Juei no   In Juei
aki no ha no   as the autumn leaves
yomo no arashi ni   are all tossed before the storm,

[*Pointing the fan around, the* shite *looks to his right.*]

sasoware   raging fiercely
chirijiri ni naru   scattering and scattering
ichiyō no   like a single leaf
fune ni uki   floating in a boat

[*The* shite *makes a* sayū *gesture, indicating a stop.*]

nami ni fushite   upon the waves we slept
yume ni dani mo   dreaming, never turning
kaerazu.   even homeward,

[*The* shite *goes out toward the eye-fixing pillar.*]

Rōchō no[50]   like the caged birds
kumo o koi,   longing for the clouds
kigan tsura o   and returning columned geese
midaru naru,   left astray behind

[*Looking at the sky, the* shite *turns in a large arc to his left.*]

sora sadamenaki   in the skies unsettled still
tabigoromo   dressed in traveling robes
hi mo[51] kasanarite   days that piled on days we found
toshitsuki no   months turned into years,
tachikaeru   ending to return
haru no koro   with the spring again

247

[*From the front of the chorus the* shite *goes forward toward center stage.*]

kono Ichi no Tani ni   in the First Ravine we sheltered
komorite   in seclusion

Atsumori

[*The* shite *makes a* sayū *gesture, indicating a stop.*]

shibashi wa koko ni   for a little while and lived
Suma[52] no Ura.   by the Suma Bay.

[*The* shite *opens the fan, makes an* ageōgi *gesture, and sings the following verse, called* ageha.]

SHITE

(Ageha)

Ushiro no   Roaring downward
yamakaze   from behind us
fukiochite   comes the mountain blast,

[*With an* ōzayū *gesture, the* shite *goes out toward stage front as the chorus sings the rest of the* kuse *passage.*]

CHORUS

(Kuse: au, yowagin)

no mo saekaeru   till the fields turned frosty too
umigiwa ni   by the ocean shore
fune no   where our boats
yoru to naku[53]   were afloat at hand,
hiru to naki   day and night throughout
chidori no koe mo   came the plovers' crying too

[*At stage front the* shite *flips up his left sleeve, and, using it for a pillow, he sits down.*]

waga sode mo   dampened with sea spray,
nami ni shioruru   like the beach we slept upon,
isomakura,   are our sleeves with tears.
ama no   In the huts

[*The* shite *rises and goes out toward the eye-fixing pillar; then, turning to his left, he goes to the* shite *seat.*]

tomaya ni   of the fishers,
tomone shite   close with them we slept
Sumabito[54] ni nomi and were used to Suma folks,

[*Raising the fan up, the* shite *goes out toward stage front from the chorus front, holds the fan out horizontally, and folds it.*]

sonarematsu no   wind-embraced like shore-pines
tatsuru ya   twisting upward
yūkemuri   rose the evening smoke,
shiba to yū[55] mono fed by what they called brushwood
orishikite   which we broke and lay,
omoi o Suma no   thinking of this Suma-life

[*Pointing upward with his fan, he looks above to his right.*]

Masterworks of the Nō Theater

yamazato no	at the village-town
kakaru tokoro ni	in a mountain such as this
sumai shite	we endured our days,

[*Going around in a large arc to his left, the* shite *proceeds toward chorus front.*]

Sumabito ni	and became at last
narihatsuru	like those Suma folks;

[*In front of the chorus the* shite *makes a* sayū *gesture and finishes the dancelike movement, as the chorus concludes the* kuse *passage.*]

ichimon no hate zo	thus our clan has faced its ending
kanashiki.	lamentably.

[*During the following passage exchanged between the* shite *and the* waki, *called* kakeai, *the* shite *stands in front of the hand-drum players, and the* waki, *at the* waki *seat. The prose passage is intoned by the* shite.]

SHITE

[8] *(Kakeai: awazu, tsuyogin)*

Sate mo Kisaragi muika no yo ni mo narishikaba, oya nite sōrō Tsunemori warera o atsume imayō o utai maiasobi-shi ni.	Then it was around the sixth day of the second month. My father, Tsunemori, called us all together. And we sang modern ballads as we danced and played.

WAKI

Sate wa sono yo no	That was how it happened then
onnasobi narikeri.	in the night you held your feast,
Jō no uchi ni	safe within your stronghold;
sa mo omoshiroki	notes of joyous lyric songs
fue no ne no	of the flute were heard
yosete no jin made	even at the camped position
kikoeshi wa	of your enemy.

SHITE

Sore koso sashimo Atsumori ga saigo made mochishi fuetake no	Yes, indeed, that was until the final moment Atsumori kept the bamboo flute,

WAKI

ne mo hitofushi o	playing such a melody,
utaiasobu	singing, too, enjoying

249

SHITE

imayō[56] rōei	modern ballads, chanting verses

WAKI

koegoe ni	line by line aloud

Atsumori

[*Turning to his right, the* shite *goes toward the* shite *seat and starts dancing as the chorus sings the following* issei *verse.*]

CHORUS

(*Issei: awazu, tsuyogin*)

| hyōshi o soroe | keeping time in unison |
| koe o age | we raised our voices. |

[*The* shite *dances to the* hayashi *music. This dance should be performed invigoratingly in four or five movements.*]

Chū no mai

[*After the dance, the* shite *makes an* ageōgi *gesture and sings the following lines.*]

SHITE

[9] (*Awazu, tsuyogin*)

| saru hodo ni | Sometime afterward, |
| mi-fune o hajimete | first the royal barge was launched |

[*The* shite *stamps the floor as the chorus sings the following passage.*]

CHORUS

(*Noriji: ōnori, tsuyogin*)

| ichimon minamina | and as all the mighty clansmen |

[*Pointing outward with his fan and turning to his right, the* shite *goes out toward stage front from the* shite *seat.*]

fune ni ukameba	had put out their boats to sea,
noriokureji to	shouting loud, "We will not be
migiwa ni uchiyoreba	left behind," and Atsumori rushed
gozabune mo hyōsen mo	to the shore, but all the soldiers' boats

[*At stage front, the* shite *makes a* kumo no ōgi *gesture and looks into the distance.*]

| haruka ni nobitamō. | and royal barge had fled far out to sea. |

[*The* shite *sings the following in free-rhythm* tsuyogin *style as he retreats to the* shite *seat.*]

SHITE

250

(*Awazu, tsuyogin*)

| Senkata nami ni[57] | Left so helplessly behind |
| koma o hikae | against the surging waves |

[*The* shite *makes a* yūken *gesture with his fan, indicating his feeling.*]

| akirehatetaru | Atsumori held his steed, |
| arisama nari. | overwhelmed completely |

[*The* shite *goes out toward* waki *front; the chorus sings the following verse.*]

(Chūnori, tsuyogin)

Kakarikeru	in a circumstance
tokoro ni	like this. Meanwhile,

[The shite *looks back toward the curtain and goes forward to the* shite *seat, as if to welcome his foe, as the chorus sings the following lines.]*

ushiro yori	from behind there came
Kumagae no	brave Kumagae
Jirō Naozane	Jirō Naozane,
nogasaji to	bent on his capture,
oikaketari.	chasing after him.

[Turning to his left as if to pull on the reins, the shite *goes to the* shite *seat.]*

Atsumori mo	Atsumori, too
uma hikikaeshi	wheeled his steed and turned ashore
nami no	through the waves

[Drawing his sword, the shite *goes out toward stage front and strikes his foe.]*

uchimono⁵⁸ nuite	that came pounding back and forth
futauchi	he drew his sword
miuchi wa	and twice or thrice
utsu zo to mieshi ga	he seemed to strike the enemy,

[While the waki *and the* shite *are locked in combat, the* shite, *turning back to his left, kneels on one knee.]*

uma no ue nite	and on their steeds they grappled,
hikkunde	one another, then
namiuchigiwa ni	falling by the surf-rushed shore
ochikasanatte	dropped atop each other hard,
tsui ni	and at last,
utarete	slain and vanquished,
useshi mi no	on the Wheel of Fate

[Looking over at the waki, *the* shite *rises.]*

inga wa	that ever turns
meguriaitari⁵⁹	he returns to meet with you.

[Lifting up the sword, the shite *goes in front of the* waki.]*

kataki wa kore zo to	"My enemy is here," he shouts
utan to suru ni	as he's about to strike him:

251

[Retreats to position in front of the hand-drum players.]

ada oba on nite	"Evil I'll repay with good,"
hōji⁶⁰ no	for the prayers

[Kneeling, the shite *turns around and faces stage front.]*

nenbutsu shi	you have said for me
tomurawarureba	calling on Amida's name,

Atsumori

[*Looking at the* waki.]

tsui ni wa tomo ni	so at last we surely too
mumarubeki	shall be born again
onaji hachisu no	on the same sweet lotus seat.

[*As the* shite *rises, he goes out toward the eye-fixing pillar, and, turning to his right, he goes to the* shite *seat.*]

Rensei hōshi[61]	Rensei, truly named
kataki nite wa	you are no mortal foe
nakarikeri	anymore, oh, priest,

[*Throwing down his sword, the* shite *clasps his hands in prayer.*]

ato tomuraite	who says the holy prayers
tabitamae,	for my memory,

[*Turning toward* waki *front, the* shite *makes a* tome *stamp.*]

ato tomuraite	oh, say the holy prayers
tabitamae.	for my memory.

252

Masterworks of the Nō Theater

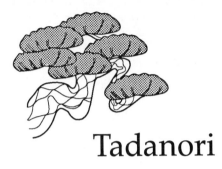

Tadanori

Introduction

One of the most attractive figures among the Genpei warriors for Nō playwrights is, indeed, Tadanori, as Zeami selected him for this *shura* piece, which belongs to Group II of Nō plays. There are, among other factors, two good reasons for Zeami to do so: namely, Tadanori was a noted poet and equally renowned for his valor as a great general of the Heike clan. The fact that the Heike were defeated in war adds to the story an acute sense of sadness, tinged with an air of mutability. Moreover, the famous ninth chapter of *The Tale of the Heike*[1] is highly praised for its literary excellence, which Zeami used as if providing the very proof for his conviction, which he stated in his essay entitled "On Nō Composition": "The image of the warrior. If, for instance, your source is about a famous captain of the Genji or the Heike, take special care to write as it is told in the *Tale of the Heike*."[2] As a playwright, he seems to have had great confidence in this piece, for he dictated in the "Sarugakudangi": "*Michimori, Tadanori, Yoshitsune,* these three numbers are good Nō for the *shura* style." This opinion is reiterated by Zenchiku (1405–72) in his "Kabuzuinōki": "*Satsuma no Kami Tadanori* has the Deeply Hidden Style and the *Yūgen* Style." He also considered it as the representative piece among the Group II plays.

Since Tadanori excelled in the arts of both poetry and arms, Zeami emphasizes his ties to poetry in this play rather than the agonies he suffered in the Ashura World. Among the attachments that continue to bind him to the temporal world, the strongest is the fate of his poem "On the Flowers at my Native Place":

> Though the capital
> at ripple-lapping Shiga
> lies in ruined waste,
> the mountain cherry blossoms
> are the same as long ago.

Although Lord Shunzei included this poem in the *Senzaishū*, an imperial anthology of Japanese poetry, he attributed it to an anonymous author rather than to Tadanori. Zeami uses the cherry blossoms that echo this song as the most important flower image throughout the play; in addition to this, the poem on the cherry flowers entitled "At the Inn" appears and reappears as the theme song in this piece. The poems bind and unify the play against the world Zeami sets so remarkably.

It is spring at Suma, a setting chosen not only for its cherry trees in full bloom but also for its numerous associations with the *Tale of Genji*, which enrich the tone and poetic nuances of the play. As the *shidai* verse opens the play with the very word "flowers"—"As the flowers are fleeting too, / I renounce this world . . ."—it suggests that the *waki* is a Buddhist priest, which is confirmed as he introduces himself: "I am the one who once served in the house of Shunzei. After Toshinari passed away, I became as you see me now. . . ." This *waki*'s relation to Lord Shunzei not only provides far more than the function of the usual *waki*, who says the prayers for the *shite*, but also gives a special reason for the *shite* to show up.

The *shite* appears as an old woodcutter, who brings home from each trip to the mountain a bundle of firewood with a spray of flowers, which he offers to a nameless grave marked only by a single young cherry tree. Here the *shite* encounters the *waki*. A dialogue ensues between them, as the chorus finishes singing the following lines on behalf of the *shite*:

> as the young sweet cherry tree
> over Suma
> and the sea are separated
> almost not at all,
> back and forth
> blows the inlet wind;
> the mountain cherry flowers
> fall before it too.

While "the mountain cherry flowers" echoes Tadanori's anthologized song mentioned above, the dialogue continues and the *waki* asks for lodging for a night. Then the following passage is intoned by the *shite*: "Caught by the nightfall, should I lodge beneath the shade of the sheltering trees, then throughout this night my host would be the cherry flowers." Though this passage is printed as prose, it was originally a poem by Tadanori, and it serves as the theme song throughout the play. The *waki* repeats it and says, "He who wrote this poem was / the Lord of Satsuma," to which the *shite* adds, "Tadanori is his name. . . . This is the tree his kinsmen planted to mark his resting place." And at the end of the first part of the play, the *shite* vanishes, leaving the audience with the following words:

> beneath the twilight flowers
> let sleep come to you,
> wait for what I will disclose
> in the dream you dream,
> and return to the capital
> with this news. . . .

In Part II, after the usual "waiting song" following the *issei* music, the *shite* makes his appearance dressed in full costume with a long sword. Through the elaborate verse structures, with the *shite*'s *sashi* and *kuri* and the *waki*'s *sageuta* and *ageuta*, the poet-warrior is depicted in a detailed close-up. This segment is followed by the heroic combat scene, presented with an onrushing subtlety through various angles one after another, now from Tadanori's side, then from his foe's, like modern camera shots, culminating in the *waki*'s discovery of the paper strip with the poem written on the theme of "At the Inn." The chorus sings:

> "Caught by the nightfall,
> should I lodge beneath the shade
> of the sheltering trees. . . ."

The *shite*, holding a paper strip in his hand, dances the *kakeri*. Then, holding out the paper strip, the *shite* looks at it and finishes singing the last two lines of the above verse.

There is no *sashi* or *kuse* passage, which usually precedes the *kakeri* dance in the *shura* pieces. The reason for this omission is that Zeami emphasized the role of the poet in *Tadanori*. This is the main chord that runs throughout the play to create an air of *yūgen* in the heroic mode. And, just as in music the resolution is achieved with the same note that began the symphony, so this piece is resolved with the same flower image that started the play, as we observe how the chorus concludes the *kiri* passage:

> offer prayers when you pray
> for my last remains
> and beneath the trees you lodge,
> as you journey on,
> then indeed your host will be
> the cherry flowers.

255

Tadanori

TADANORI

By Zeami

Persons: WAKI: *A traveling Buddhist priest*
WAKI-TSURE: *Companion priests (two)*
SHITE (PART I): *An old man*
NOCHI-JITE (PART II): *Ghost of Tadanori*
KYŌGEN: *A local person of Suma Bay*

Classification: *Primary, Group II*
Place: *At the Bay of Suma*
Time: *Spring (March)*
Kogaki: 2

PART I

Jo no Dan

[*Following the* shidai *music, the* waki, *accompanied by two followers, enters the stage. They are similarly costumed, wearing a pointed hood* (kakubōshi), *a plain, less-formal heavy silk kimono* (muji noshime), *a broad-sleeved robe* (mizugoromo), *a waistband* (koshiobi), *and a rosary* (juzu). *They face one another and sing the following* shidai *verse.*]

WAKI AND WAKI-TSURE

[1] (*Shidai: au, yowagin*)

Hana o mo ushi to	As the flowers are fleeting too,
sutsuru mi no,	I renounce this world,
hana o mo ushi to	as the flowers are fleeting too,
sutsuru mi no	I renounce this world,
tsuki ni mo kumo wa	so the clouds across the moon
itowaji.	I do not mind.

CHORUS [*Sings the* jidori *in a lower tone.*]

(*Jidori: au, yowagin*)

Hana o mo ushi to	As the flowers are fleeting too,
sutsuru mi no	I renounce this world,
tsuki ni mo kumo wa	so the clouds across the moon
itowaji.	I do not mind.

256

[*Facing stage front, the* waki *intones the* nanori *in prose.*]

(*Nanori: awazu, kotoba*)

Kore wa Shunzei[3] no mi-uchi ni arishi mono nite sōrō. Sate mo Toshinari naku naritamaite nochi kayō no sugata to narite sōrō. Mata saikoku o mizu sōrō hodo ni kono tabi omoitachi saikoku angya to kokorozashi sōrō.

I am the one who once served in the house of Shunzei. After Toshinari passed away, I became as you see me now. Besides, as I have not yet seen the Western Land, I thought that this time I would like to make a holy pilgrimage there.

WAKI

(*Sashi: awazu, yowagin*)

Seinan no rikyū[4] ni omomuki
To the palace of the southwest side I go and then

Miyako o hedatsuru Yamazaki[5] ya
past Mountain Point that separates Miyako from here

Sekido[6] no Shuku wa na nomi shite
where the inn at Barrier Gate now remains in name

tomari mo hatenu tabi no narai,
with no place to rest I go the way of travel now

ukimi wa itsu mo majiwari no
in our life of misery mixed and stained with dust

chiri no ukiyo no Akutagawa[7]
of the fleeting world along the Rubbish River

Ina[8] no ozasa o wakesugite
through this Ina's bamboo field, I journey onward,

WAKI AND WAKI-TSURE

[*The* waki *turns to the* waki-tsure, *and, facing one another, they sing.*]

(*Sageuta: au, yowagin*)

Tsuki mo yado karu Koya no Ike[9]
then by Cottage Pool the moon is a lodger, too,

minasoko kiyoku suminashite[10]
dwelling clearly in the depth of the water still.

(*Ageuta: au, yowagin*)

Ashi no hawake no[11] kaze no oto,
Rustling through the reedy leaves come the sounds of winds,

ashi no hawake no kaze no oto
rustling through the reedy leaves come the sounds of winds,

kikajito suruni
though I try to hear them not,

uki koto no
still the fleeting things

sutsuru mi made mo
I've renounced appear to me

257

Tadanori

Arimayama[12]	like Mt. Arima
kakurekanetaru	I can scarcely hide myself
yo no naka no	in this fleeting world
uki ni kokoro wa	fraught with weary woes my heart
adayume no	finds an empty dream
samuru makura ni[13]	on the pillow, where I wake
kane[14] tōki	to the distant bell
Naniwa wa ato ni	left behind in Naniwa;
Naruogata[15]	over Echo Bay
okinami tōki	on the offing-waves how far
obune kana,	are the little boats,
okinami tōki	on the offing-waves how far
obune kana.	are the little boats!

Waki

[Intones the tsukizerifu *in prose, facing stage front.]*

(Tsukizerifu: awazu, kotoba)

| Isogi sōrō hodo ni kore wa haya Suma no Ura ni tsukite sōrō. Shibaraku kono tokoro ni yasurai, hana no sama o nagamyōzuru nite sōrō. | As we traveled in haste, we have already arrived at the Bay of Suma. Resting for a little while at this place, let us view the cherry trees in bloom. |

[The waki *and* waki-tsure *go to the* waki *seat, take their respective positions, and sit down.]*

Ha no Ichi Dan

[Following the issei *music, the* shite, *wearing the* asakura jō *mask, an old-man wig (jō gami), a collar in pale blue (eri asagi), a plain, less-formal heavy silk kimono (muji noshime), a brown "inferior silk" broad-sleeved robe (cha shike mizugoromo), a waistband (koshiobi), and a fan (ōgi), and holding the leaves in his left hand and a cane in his right hand, enters and stands at the* shite *seat.]*

Shite

[2] *(Sashi: awazu, mixed)*

Geni yo o wataru	This has been the way men take
narai tote	all throughout the world,
kaku uki waza ni mo	though most harsh their toil, they never
korizuma[16] no	quit the Suma Bay;
kumanu toki dani	when there is no brine to draw,
shioki o hakobeba,	there is wood to haul for salt-fires,
hosedomo hima wa	with no time to dry the clothes
naregoromo[17] no	old, work-worn, by going

[Faces to the right.]

| Ura[18] yama kakete | to the sea and hills behind |
| Suma[19] no Umi. | the Bay of Suma. |

258

Masterworks of the Nō Theater

Ama no yobikoe[20]	As the fisher's calling voice
hima naki ni	sounds continuously,

[*The* shite *faces stage front once more.*]

shiba naku chidori	once in a while a plover
ne zo tōki.	cries in the distance.

(Sashi: awazu, mixed)

Somosomo	This is the place
kono Suma no Ura to	men have called the Bay of Suma;
mōsu wa	and the reason
samishiki yue ni	why it has received that name
sono na o uru.	is for its solitude.
Wakurawa ni[21]	Should there be by chance
tō hito araba	someone who asks after me,
Suma no Ura ni	then you should reply
moshio taretsutsu	that here I live at Suma
wabu to kotae yo.	drenched with seaweed brine and tears.
Geni ya isari no	Truly from the little boats
amaobune	fishing out at sea,
moshio no kemuri	from the smoke of seaweed fires,
matsu no kaze	from the pine-swept winds,
izure ka	there is nothing
samishikarazu to	we can choose which is, we say,
yū koto naki.	not forlorn and lonely.

[*Facing to his right, he delivers the next lines in prose.*]

Mata kono Suma no yamakage ni hitoki no sakura no sōrō. Kore wa aru hito no naki ato no shirushi no ki nari.	There is, too, one cherry tree growing on the mountainside at Suma. It stands for the memory of someone who passed away long ago.

Kotosara toki shimo	Especially now it's the time
haru no hana	for the flowers of spring,
tamuke no tame ni	in remembrance of the dead;
gyakuen nagara	though I am but a stranger,

[*Sings the* sageuta *in a lower tone.*]

259

(Sageuta: au, tsuyogin)

ashibiki no	every time I come
yama yori kaeru	homeward down the mountain slope,
origoto ni	in the gathered wood
takigi ni hana o	I insert a flowering spray
orisoete	of the tree I break
tamuke o nashite	for an offering to him

Tadanori

kaeruran,	on my way back home,
tamuke o nashite	for an offering to him
kaeruran.	on my way back home.

Ha no Ni Dan

[Giving the feeling that he is offering the branch, the shite *puts the branch down, holds his hands together in prayer, and rises. The* waki *rises too.]*

WAKI

[3] *(Mondai: awazu, yowagin)*

| Ika ni kore naru rōjin okoto wa kono ya-magatsu nite mashimasu ka. | Ho there, old man, are you one of the folks who live among these mountains? |

SHITE

| San zōrō. Kono ura no ama nite sōrō. | Yes, I am a fisherman of this bay. |

WAKI

(Kakaru)

Ama naraba	As a fisherman
ura ni koso	you should live indeed
sumubeki ni	close along the shore;
yama aru kata ni	if you frequent back and forth
kayowan oba	where the mountain rises,
yamabito to koso	then you should describe yourself
yūbekere.	as a mountain man.

SHITE

| Somo amabito no kumu shio oba ya-kade sono mama oki sōrōbeki ka. | That may be so, but should the salt-water that the fisherman draws be left unboiled, for lack of wood? |

WAKI

Geni geni kore wa	Yes, indeed, indeed, that is
kotowari nari.	right and stands to reason;
Moshio taku naru	you must keep the salt-fire smoke
yūkemuri.	rising at the eve.

SHITE

| Taema o ososhi to | Without waiting for a break |
| shioki toru. | salt-firewood I get. |

WAKI

| Michi koso kaware[22] | Different may be the roads, |
| satobanare[23] no | distant lies the village, |

260

SHITE

| hito oto mare ni | with few human sounds I live |
| Suma no Ura | by the Suma Bay. |

WAKI

| chikaki ushiro no | Behind the mountain village |
| yamazato ni | lying close at hand, |

SHITE

(Ageuta: au, yowagin)

| shiba to iu mono no [24] | there is something that the native |
| sōraeba | people call brushwood, |

CHORUS

shiba to iu mono no	there is something that the native
sōraeba	people call brushwood,
shioki no tame ni	so I go there back and forth
kayoikuru	for salt-making wood

SHITE

amari [25] ni	as a fisher
orokanaru	all so foolish, too,
o-sō no	oh, holy priest,
go-jō kana ya na.	are the words you said to me.

CHORUS

[*The* shite *looks toward the* waki *seat in the distance.*]

Geni ya	Lives are lived
Suma no Ura	so differently
yo no tokoro ni ya	at this Suma Bay indeed
kawaruran.	than they seem elsewhere

[*The* shite *goes to the eye-fixing pillar.*]

Sore hana ni	the cherry blossoms
tsuraki wa	feel heartbroken
mine no arashi ya	from the storms across the peaks,
yamaoroshi no	and so the mountain blasts,

261

[*The* shite *looks around.*]

oto o koso	hateful and severe,
itoishi ni	are the sounds they loathe,
Suma no wakaki [26] no	as the young sweet cherry tree
sakura wa	over Suma
umi sukoshi dani mo	and the sea are separated
hedateneba [27]	almost not at all,

Tadanori

[*The* shite *turns to his right and returns to the* shite *seat.*]

kayō	back and forth
urakaze ni	blows the inlet wind;
yama no sakura mo	the mountain cherry flowers
chiru mono o.	fall before it too.

Ha no San Dan

[*The* shite *gazes at the cherry flowers. Meanwhile, the* ai (kyōgen) *enters through the half-raised curtain inconspicuously, and silently takes the* kyōgen *seat.*]

WAKI

[4] (*Mondai: awazu*)

| Ikani jō-dono. Haya hi no kurete sō-raeba, ichiya no yado o on-kashi sōrae. | Ho there, old man. As the sun has set already, I would like to ask you to give me lodgings for a night. |

SHITE

| Utate ya na. Kono hana no kage hodo no o-yado no sōrōbeki ka. | How unobservant you are! Are there better lodgings than this shade beneath the flowers? |

WAKI

| Geni geni kore wa hana no yado nare-domo sarinagara tare o aruji to sada-mubeki. | How true, how true! This is a flowery shelter; however, I wonder who the host will be. |

SHITE

| Yukikurete ko no shita kage o yado to seba hana ya koyoi no aruji naramashi[28] to | Caught by the nightfall, should I lodge beneath the shade of these sheltering trees, then throughout this night my host would be the cherry flowers. |

(*Tsuyogin*)

| nagameshi hito wa | Here how pitifully lies |
| kono koke no shita | one who once composed the verse, |

[*Looking at the place where the offering was made a little while ago.*]

262

itawashi ya	deep beneath the moss.
warera ga yō naru	Even folks as poor and lowly
ama dani mo	as we fishermen
tsune wa tachiyori	always stop a little while
tomuraimōsu ni	and recite some Buddhist prayers.
o-sōtachi wa	But holy priests like you,
nado gyakuen nagara	though it's true you are but strangers here,

tomuraitamawanu	why do you forget your prayers?
oroka ni mashimasu	Would you like to be considered
hitobito kana.	as a foolish person?

[*The* shite *takes a step or two toward the* waki.]

WAKI

Yukikurete ko no shita kage o yado to seba hana ya koyoi no aruji naramashi to	Caught by the nightfall, should I lodge beneath the shade of the sheltering trees, then throughout the night my host would be the cherry flowers.

(*Yowagin*)

nagameshi hito wa	He who wrote this poem was
Satsuma no Kami	the Lord of Satsuma.

SHITE

Tadanori to mōshishi hito wa kono Ichi no Tani no kassen ni utarenu. Yukari no hito no ueokitaru shirushi no ki nite sōrō nari.	Tadanori is his name, and in the battle of the First Ravine he was slain. This is the tree his kinsmen planted to mark his resting place.

WAKI

(*Yowagin*)

Ko wa somo fushigi no	Well, this is a strange connection
chigu no en,	by affinity
sashimo sabakari	I meet you who're related
Toshinari no	to Toshinari

SHITE

waka no tomo tote	closely with such intimacy
asakaranu	as a friend of verse.

WAKI

(*Yowagin*)

yado wa koyoi no	"At the Inn," this evening

SHITE

(*Yowagin*)

aruji no hito.	you are the master host

CHORUS

(*Rongi: au, yowagin*)

Na mo Tadanori no[29]	whose name is Tadanori,
koe kikite	which means "only Laws,"

Tadanori

[*The* shite *goes out to center stage and sits, while the* waki, *facing stage front, folds his hands in prayer and sits down.*]

| hana no utena ni | so upon the flowered seat |
| zashitamae. | graciously you sit. |

SHITE

[5] (*Rongi: au, yowagin*)

Arigata ya.	O, how blessed I am!
Ima yori wa	From this moment on,
kaku tomurai no	listening to the voice that chants
koe kikite	Buddhist holy prayers,
bukka o en zo	Mida's grace I would receive
ureshiki.	and am joyful.

[*The* waki *faces toward the* shite.]

CHORUS

Fushigi ya ima no	Strange, how strange! That aged old man
rōjin no	I have met just now,
tamuke no koe o	listens to the prayer I say
mi ni ukete	as though it's for him:
yorokobu keshiki	from his looks, he seems to feel
mietaru wa	joy and happiness.
nani no yue nite	Surely, now, for all of this
aruyaran.	there are some reasons.

SHITE

| O-sō ni towaremōsan tote kore made ki-tareri to | Gentle priest, I wished to ask for prayers on my behalf, so I have come to this place; I say, |

CHORUS

| yūbe[30] no hana no | beneath the twilight flowers |
| kage ni nete | let sleep come to you, |

[*The* shite *rises.*]

264

yume no tsuge o mo	wait for what I will disclose
machitamae,	in the dream you dream,
Miyako e kotozute	and return to the capital
mōsan tote	with this news. So saying,
hana no kage ni	beneath the flowering shade
yadoriki[31] no	like a mistletoe
yuku kata shirazu	sheltered where we do not know
narinikeri,	he has disappeared,
yuku kata shirazu	sheltered where we do not know
narinikeri.	he has disappeared.

[*As the chorus sings the line "like a mistletoe," the* shite *goes to the* shite *pillar and makes a* hiraki *gesture; as the chorus finishes this passage, the* shite *quietly makes his exit.*]

Nakairi (Interlude)

[*The* kyōgen, *wearing a striped, less-formal heavy silk kimono* (dan noshime), *the* kyōgen *two-piece* (kyōgen kamishimo), *a waistband* (koshiobi), *and a fan* (ōgi), *comes out to the name-saying seat* (nanoriza).]

KYŌGEN

(Mondai: katari)

Kayō ni sōrō mono wa Suma no Ura ni sumai-suru mono nite sōrō. Kyō wa makariide wakagi no sakura o nagame-baya to zonji sōrō. Iya kore ni minare-mōsanu o-sō no onnide nasare sōrō ga, izukata yori onnide nasare sōrō zo.

I am one who lives by the Bay of Suma. Today I will go out and look at the young cherry tree in bloom. [*Noticing a Buddhist priest.*] There is a Buddhist priest I have not seen before. I wonder where you came from.

WAKI

Kore wa Miyakogata yori idetaru sō nite sōrō. On-mi wa kono atari no hito nite watari sōrō ka.

I am a Buddhist priest from the capital. Are you a native of this vicinity?

KYŌGEN

Nakanaka kono atari no mono nite sōrō.

Yes, I live in this neighborhood.

WAKI

Sayō nite sōrawaba mazu chikō onniri sōrae. Tazunetaki koto no sōrō.

If that is so, please come closer. I have something to ask you.

KYŌGEN

Kashikomatte sōrō.

Yes, holy priest.

[*The* kyōgen *advances to center stage and kneels down.*]

Sate o-tazune nasaretaki to wa ikayō naru go-yō nite sōrō zo.

What would you like to know? You said you have something to ask me.

WAKI

Omoi mo yoranu mōshigoto nite sōrae-domo, wakagi no sakura no iware mata Tadanori no hatetamaitaru yōtai go-zonji ni oite wa katatte on-kikase sōrae.

Though it may be strange for me to ask about the young cherry tree and how Tadanori met his death, if you know anything about them, please tell me.

KYŌGEN

Kore wa omoi mo yoranu koto o o-ta-zune nasare sōrō mono kana. Warera mo kono atari ni sumaitsukamatsuri

This is most surprising—what you have just asked me. Though we live in this neighborhood, we don't know much

Tadanori

sōraedomo sayō no koto kuwashiku wa zonzezu sōrō. Sarinagara, hajimete o-me ni kakari o-tazune nasare sōrō koto o sukoshi mo zonzenu to mōsu mo ikaga nite sōraeba oyoso uketamawari-oyobitaru tōri on-monogatari mōsōzuru nite sōrō.

about these things in detail. But if we don't say anything, it might be awkward, especially since this is the first time we've met. So I'll tell you the story the way I've heard it.

WAKI

Chikagoro nite sōrō.

I am grateful.

KYŌGEN

Saru hodo ni Heike no kindachi ni Satsuma no Kami Tadanori to mōshitaru on-kata wa, Heike no go-ichimon no naka nite mo bunbu nidō ni sugure, yoki taishō nite goza aritaru to mōsu. Shikaru ni Tadanori kono tokoro e on-gekō no toki, Gojō no San'i Shunzei no Kyō ni on-mōshi sōrō wa ware moto yori waka no michi moppara ni tsukamatsuri sōrō aida, kajin no kazu ni hairitaki yoshi on-mōshi sōraedomo Shunzei-kyō notamō yō wa Heike wa chokkan no on-koto nareba kanōmajiki yoshi ōse sōraedomo Tadanori zehi ni mo to on-nageki ari. Yamazaki yori totte kaeshi, mata Shunzei no kata e on-mairi ari, yomiokitamō uta kazu ōku mairaserare, kono naka ni shikarubeki uta mo sōrawaba onnire kudasare sōrae tote, sono mama on-gekō aritaru to mōsu. Sono go Goshirakawa no In no gyo-o ni Senzaishū o eramareshi ni, Tadanori no uta o isshu onnire sōraedomo yomibito shirazu to kakaretari. Mata go-saigo no yōtai wa, Heike wa kono tokoro ni tazei nite komoritamō o, Genji wa Heike o horobosan to rokumanyoki ofutate ni wakachi Noriyori Yoshitsune oshiyose-tamai, sayū nō uchiyaburi, kindachi amata uchijini ari, sanzan ni ochitamō. Tadanori wa nishi no te no taishō nite sōrō ga, haya go-honjin yori yabureshi-kaba zōhyō ni uchimagire shizushizu to ochi tamō tokoro o, Okabe no Rokuyata Tadazumi yoki teki to me o kake shichi-

Well, among the noblemen of the Heike clan, the Lord of Satsuma was called Tadanori. He was excellent in both the arts of letters and arms, and a great general, I hear. When he came down to this place, he said to Lord Shunzei of the Third Rank, of Gojō, that he devoted himself, of course, to the way of poetry and he wished to be considered among the poets. Then Lord Shunzei said that since the Heike was under imperial displeasure, his wish could not be granted. Whether right or wrong, Tadanori took it hard to heart. From Yamazaki he went back to the residence of Lord Shunzei once more, taking with him many songs he had composed, and pleaded with him, saying that if among these songs there were some good ones, please select them; and he left, I hear. Then in the reign of His Majesty, the Emperor Goshirakawa, the *Senzaishū* was compiled and one of the songs by Tadanori was included in it, but it is stated that the song was by an unknown author. As for his last hour of life, the Heike clan held this place with a great number of their men; and the Genji planned to destroy them. They divided their forces, more than sixty thousand strong, into two, and Noriyori and Yoshitsune surged their forces upon the Heike and easily broke their lines. Many noblemen died, and others fled and scattered. Tadanori was the general of

266

hachiki nite okkakeru. Tadanori yagate Rokuyata to kumitamō ni, moto yori ki-koyuru tairiki nareba Rokuyata o totte osaetamō tokoro o Tadazumi ga rōtō Tadanori o uchimōshite sōrō aida, ita-washiki koto tote mina-mina namida o nagashitaru to mōsu. Mata kono wakagi no sakura to mōsu wa Tadanori no ue-saseraretaru to mo mōsu. Mata Hikaru Genji no uesaseraretaru to mo mōshi sōrō. Warera no uketamawaritaru wa kaku no gotoku nite goza sōrō ga, nan to oboshimeshi o-tazune nasare sōrō zo. Chikagoro fushin ni zonji sōrō.

the western front, but since his head-quarters was already captured by the Genji, he mingled quietly with his com-mon soldiers; then Okabe no Rokuyata Tadazumi recognized him as his worthy foe, and he pursued Tadanori with sev-eral riders. Soon after, Tadanori wres-tled with Rokuyata. Herculean as he was known, he took hold of Rokuyata, but the followers of Tadazumi struck him down. How pitiful it was; all shed their tears, I hear. As for this young cherry tree, I hear that Tadanori had it planted here; or it might be that Prince Genji, the Shining One, had it planted at this place. This is the story I've heard. Why did you ask me about it? Lately I've felt something strange.

WAKI

Nengoro ni on-monogatari sōrō mono kana. Tazunemōsu mo yo no gi ni ara-zu. Kore wa Shunzei no Kyō no miuchi ni arishi mono nite sōrō ga, Shunzei naku narasetamaite nochi, kayō no su-gata to makarinarite sōrō. On-mi izen ni rōjin hitori kitarare sōrō hodo ni, suna-wachi kotoba o kawashite sōraeba, oiki no sakura no iware tadaima on-mono-gatari no gotoku nengoro ni katari Ta-danori no koto o mi no ue no yō ni mōsare, Miyako e kotozute-sen to ii mo aezu, hana no kage nite sugata o miu-shinaite sōrō yo.

How detailed a story you have told me. The reason I asked you is not too spe-cial. I am the one who once served the House of Shunzei, and after he had passed away, I became as you see me now. Before I saw you, there came an old man here alone and as we ex-changed words, he told me the story about the aged cherry tree in detail, as you have done just now. He also told me the story about Tadanori as if it were about himself; and no sooner did he leave a message for me to take back to the capital than I lost sight of him be-hind the shade of the cherry flowers.

KYŌGEN

Kore wa kidoku naru koto o uketama-wari sōrō mono kana. Sate wa Tadanori no go-bōshin araware o-kotoba o ka-washitamō to zonji sōrō aida, shibaraku go-tōryū atte Tadanori no onnato on-to-murai arekashi to zonji sōrō.

This is most surprising—what you have just said. Well, that must have been the ghost of Tadanori and I think you must have talked to him. You should, I think, stay here for a little while and pray for his soul.

267

WAKI

Shibaraku tōryū mōshi arigataki o-kyō o dokuju-shi kano onnato o nengoro ni tomuraimōsōzuru nite sōrō.

Yes, I will stay here for a little while and chant the holy Buddhist sutra and recite reverently some prayers for him.

Tadanori

KYŌGEN

Go-yō no koto mo sōrawaba kasanete ōse sōrae.

If you should have something for us to do, please call me again.

WAKI

Tanomi sōrō beshi.

Yes, I shall, and thank you.

KYŌGEN

Kokoroe mōshite sōrō.

Oh, not at all, holy priest.

[*The* kyōgen *retires to the* kyōgen *seat*.]

PART II

Kyū no Ichi Dan

WAKI

[6] *(Awazu, kotoba)*

Mazu mazu Miyako ni kaeritsutsu,

First, oh, first of all, I must return to the capital;

(Awazu, yowagin)

Teika[32] ni kono koto mōsan to

and at once, report this story to Lord Teika.

WAKI AND WAKI-TSURE

(Machiutai: au, yowagin)

Yūzuki[33] hayaku kagerō[34] no,	As the evening moon sets low quickly pale and dim,
Yūzuki hayaku kagerō no	as the evening moon sets low quickly pale and dim,
ono[35] ga tomo yobu	the flocking plovers calling
murachidori no	their mates are seen no more,
ato mienu	nor any traces
isoyama no	of the beach-side hills
yoru no hana ni	where among the flowers
tabine shite	here I rest at night,
urakaze made mo	fearful even of the noise
kokoro shite	of the inlet winds.
haru ni kikebaya	Only in the spring do they
oto sugoki	sound harsh; I wonder
Suma no sekiya no	where at Suma Barrier
tabine kana,	sleep the travelers,
Suma no sekiya no	where at Suma Barrier
tabine kana	sleep the travelers.

268

[*Following the* issei *music, the* nochi-jite *appears. He wears a* chūjō *mask, a long black wig (*kuro tare*), a tall black hat (*nashiuchi eboshi*), a white headband (*shiro hachimaki*), a collar in pale blue (*eri asagi*), a "thick board" heavy silk kimono with* karaori-*like figures woven in relief (*atsuita karaori*), an unlined gold brocade robe (*hitoe happi*), a hued broad divided skirt (*iro ōguchi*), a waistband (*koshiobi*), a fan (*ōgi*), and a long sword (*tachi*), and at his side an arrow with a poem card tied at its end. He enters the stage and stands at the* shite *seat.*]

SHITE

[7] *(Sashi: awazu, mixed)*

Hazukashi ya	How ashamed I feel
naki ato ni	here where I was slain
sugata o kaesu	in a form as once I was
yume no uchi,	I return in dream
samuru kokoro wa	where, awakened, now my heart
inishie ni	yearns for days long past,
mayō amayo no[36]	like a fisherman astray
monogatari	through the rainy night,
mōsan tame ni	to relate this narrative;
konpaku ni	so myself disguised

[*The* shite *faces toward the* waki.]

utsurikawarite	in a phantom form I came
kitaritari.	before your presence.

[*The* shite *faces stage front again and continues to sing the following* kudoki.]

(Kudoki: awazu, yowagin)

Sanaki dani	Even at the best
mōshū ōki	there are many deep delusions
shaba naru ni	in this fleeting world.
nani nakanaka no	For the *Senzaishū*
Senzaishū[37] no	indiscreetly chosen were
uta no shina ni wa	verses and among them all
iritaredomo	one was mine; however,
chokkan no mi no[38]	His Majesty's displeasure
kanashisa wa	cast on me is sad
yomibito shirazu[39]	because "the author is unknown"
to kakareshi koto	was written, and this fact
mōshū no naka no	was, among all things, the foremost
daiichi nari.	of my deep delusions.
Saredomo sore o	Now this great anthology
senjitamaishi	was compiled so graciously
Toshinari sae	by Lord Toshinari,
munashiku nari-	but even he left this world
tamaeba	all behind him;
on-mi wa	oh, holy priest,

269

[*The* shite *faces the* waki.]

Tadanori

mi-uchi ni arishi	you who once served in that house,
hito nareba	carry this and tell
ima no Teika	noble Lord Teika,
kimi ni mōshi	who succeeds his father:
shikarubeku wa	"Can it be corrected?
sakusha o tsukete	Let the author graciously
tabi tamae to	be named of that poor verse."
yumemonogatari	Thus I tell you in the dream
mōsu ni	all my story.

[*The* shite *goes to stage center a little, and, pointing his fan, he looks across the* waki *stage front.*]

(*Au*)

Suma no Urakaze mo	Oh, wind from Suma's inlet,
kokoro se yo.	be very careful.

CHORUS

[*While the chorus sings, the* shite *moves forward to stage center and sits down.*]

[8] (*Kuri: awazu, tsuyogin*)

Geni ya waka no	Born to a family
ie ni umare[40]	where the verse is honored,
sono michi o tashinami	he pursued its way assiduously
Shikishima[41] no kage ni	and found himself beneath the shade
yotsushi koto	of the Spangled Isles;
jinrin ni oite	in the realm of human duty,
moppara nari.	nothing is more splendid.

WAKI

(*Sashi: awazu, mixed*)

Naka ni mo	Among all men,
kono Tadanori wa	Tadanori was endowed
bunbu nidō o	with the art of poetry
uketamaite	and arms so graciously
sejō ni	and considered
manako takashi.	by the world most highly.

CHORUS

Somosomo	Now in the reign
Goshirakawa[42] no	of Goshirakawa,
In no gyo-o ni	by the sovereign's order,
Senzaishū o	this *Senzaishū*
erawaru.	was collected;
Gojō no Sanmi[43]	noble Lord Shunzei
Shunzei no Kyō	of the Third Rank of Gojō
uketamawatte	was so honored as the one
kore o senzu.	to select the poems.

Toshi wa Juei⁴⁴ no	In the era of Juei,
aki no koro	in the fall it was

[*The* shite *rises.*]

Miyako o ideshi	when we left in haste and fled
toki nareba	from the capital.

[*The* shite *makes a* hiraki *gesture toward stage front and stamps the floor.*]

(*Ageuta: au, yowagin*)

Samo isogawashi-	Though these harrowing events
karishi mi no,	kept me occupied,
samo isogawashi-	though these harrowing events

[*The* shite *starts to go to the* shite *seat.*]

karishi mi no,	kept me occupied,
kokoro no hana⁴⁵ ka	may the flowering heart let me
rangiku no⁴⁶	leave the Fox among
Kitsunegawa⁴⁷ yori	chrysanthemums and orchids;

[*The* shite *stamps the floor.*]

hikikaeshi	to the residence
Toshinari no	of Toshinari

[*Faces stage front, goes forward slightly, and makes a* hiraki *gesture.*]

ie ni yuki	I returned to plead
uta no nozomi o	earnestly with him again
nagekishi ni	for my poem's sake.
nozomi tarinureba	When its wish was really granted,
mata kyūsen ni	with the arrows and the bow
tazusawarite	once again I hurried

[*Goes out to the eye-fixing pillar and makes a large arc to the left and goes to the front of the musicians.*]

Saikai no	to the Western Sea.
nami no ue⁴⁸	Drifting on the waves
shibashi to tanomu	for a while we set our hopes
Suma no Ura	on the Suma Beach

[*In front of the musicians, the* shite *stamps the floor a few times.*]

Genji no	but for the doomed
sumidokoro⁴⁹	house of Heike,
Heike no tame wa	where once Genji had lived,

[*The* shite *makes a* sayū *gesture.*]

yoshinashi to	it promised nothing,
shirazarikeru zo	though we did not know that then,
hakanaki.	to our sorrow.

Tadanori

Kyū no Ni Dan

CHORUS

[9] *(Kuri: awazu, tsuyogin)*

Saru hodo ni	Sometime afterward
Ichi no Tani no	here at the First Ravine
kassen	we battled hard.

[*The* shite *goes to the bridge.*]

ima wa kō yo to	Now how clear it all became
mieshi hodo ni	that the end was drawing
minamina fune ni	very near, so everyone
torinotte	got aboard the ships
kaishō ni ukamu.	and went straightway out to sea.

[*At the first pine the* shite *looks across the sea.*]

SHITE

(Katari: awazu, kotoba)

Ware mo fune ni noran tote[50]   I too thought to board my ship,

[*The* shite *enters the stage.*]

migiwa no kata ni uchiideshi ni   and as I galloped toward the beach

[*Goes to the* waki *seat.*]

ushiro o mireba Musashi no kuni   and looked behind me, there came a

[*Faces the curtain.*]

no jūnin ni Okabe no Rokuyata Tada-zumi[51] to nanotte rokushichiki nite ok-kaketari. Kore koso nozomu tokoro yo to omoi   doughty warrior, shouting his name aloud, "Tadazumi Rokuyata of the Okabe from the land of Musashi." In a band of six or seven, he pursued after me. He seemed, I thought, to

[*Looks at the* waki *stage front and goes forward a little.*]

koma no tazuna o hikkaeseba Rokuyata yagate muzu to kumi ryōba ga ai ni dō to ochi   be the worthy foe I sought; so I wheeled my horse by the reins. Soon Rokuyata seized me hard and we tumbled down between our horses.

272

[*Sitting on the floor, the* shite *makes a gesture as if they grapple and tumble down.*]

kano Rokuyata o totte osae,   Then grasping Rokuyata, I pressed him to the

[*With his left hand the* shite *presses him down.*]

sude ni katana ni te o kakeshi ni   ground, sword in hand, at the ready, when

Masterworks of the Nō Theater

CHORUS

(Uta: au, tsuyogin)

Rokuyata ga	Rokuyata's man
rōdō	came suddenly,
onnushiro yori	circling round, to stand behind
tachimawari	Lord Tadanori,
ue ni mashimasu	who bestrode Rokuyata;
Tadanori no	down he swung the sword
migi no kaina o	with a single mighty blow
uchioroseba	and cut off his right arm.

[*The* shite *lowers his right hand.*]

hidari no	With his left arm
on-te nite	Lord Tadanori,
Rokuyata o totte	grasping Rokuyata so hard,
nagenoke	hurled him aside;
ima wa kanawaji to	knowing then he could no longer
oboshimeshite	fight against the foe,

[*The* shite *makes a gesture with his left hand as if he hurls his foe and sits down cross-legged.*]

Soko	"Stand back!
nokitamae	stand aside from me,
hitobito yo.	all of you, stand back!

[*Looks around to his left and right.*]

Nishi ogaman to	Towards the Western Paradise
notamaite	let me turn," he cried.

[*With his one hand, the* shite *prays.*]

Kōmyō	"How brightly shines
henjō[52]	the holy light
jippō sekai	everywhere upon this world,
nenbutsu shujō	blessing all who call his name:
sesshu fusha to	none be left abandoned,"
notamaishi	graciously chants he

(Yowagin)

on-koe no	who seems more touching
shita yori mo	than the final note

[*The* shite *straightens his hand from the prayer position.*]

273

itawashi ya	underneath his voice!
aenaku mo	For at that instant,
Rokuyata tachi o	Rokuyata draws his sword
nukimochi	swiftly, grasps it
tsui ni on-kubi o	firmly and at last beheads him
uchiotosu.	with a downward blow.

[*The* shite *lowers his mask as if he is beheaded.*]

Tadanori

(*Yowagin*)

Rokuyata	Rokuyata
kokoro ni	ponders on it
omō yō	deeply in his heart:

[*Straightens his mask.*]

(*Yowagin*)

itawashi ya	This is pitiful!
kano hito no	As I see his corpse

[*The* shite *rises and goes to the* shite *seat.*]

on-shigai o	lying now before me,
mitatematsureba	judging from the look of him,

[*Looks at the place where he sat before.*]

sono toshi mo	he's not far advanced
madashiki	in years as yet
Nagazukigoro no	this September marks the month
usugumori	of the fleecy clouds,

[*Looks at the skies.*]

furimi furazumi[53]	off and on the rains come down
sadame naki	from the changeful skies
shigure zo kayō	in passing drizzle, dyeing
muramomiji no	maples dapple-colored

[*Goes to the place where he sat before.*]

nishiki no	in rich brocades
hitatare wa	like his courtly robe,
tada yo no tsune ni	which is extraordinary
yomo araji.	for the common world.

[*The* shite *sits and looks down.*]

Ikasama kore wa	So, indeed, among the great
kindachi no	offerings from the braves
on-naka ni koso	of nobility is he:
arurame to	and a while I wish

274

[*Rises and goes to the* shite *seat.*]

on-na yukashiki	I could find out what would be
tokoro ni	his noble name;
ebira o mireba	on a quiver, strange I should
fushigi ya na	say, I see a long

[*Taking out an arrow.*]

tanjakuo	strip of paper
tsukeraretari.	is securely fastened.

[*Looks at a paper strip for writing verse.*]

Mireba ryoshuku no	As I see it, "At the Inn"
dai o sue [54]	is the given theme:

(*Ue no uta: awazu, yowagin*)

"Yukikurete	"Caught by the nightfall,
ko no shita kage o	should I lodge beneath the shade
yado to seba,	of these sheltering trees,

[*Holding a paper strip in his hand, he dances.*]

Kakeri

[*Still holding the paper strip in his hand, the* shite *looks at it.*]

SHITE

hana ya koyoi no	then throughout this night my host
aruji naramashi.	would be the cherry flowers,

(*Uta: au, yowagin*)

Tadanori" to	by Tadanori,
kakaretari.	so the verse is signed

CHORUS

Sate wa utagai	as clearly unmistakable
arashi [55] no oto ni	as the storm's resounding roar,
kikoeshi	proclaiming high
Satsuma no	the far-famed name
kami nite masu zo	of the Lord of Satsuma,
itawashiki.	all deeply touching!

[*In a sitting position, the* shite *lowers the mask.*]

CHORUS

[10] (*Kiri: au, yowagin*)

On-mi	Holy priest,
kono hana no	when you stopped to rest
kage ni tachiyori-	for a while beneath the flowers
tamaishi o	of the cherry tree,
kaku monogatari	where in this way I wanted
mōsan tote	to narrate my story,
hi o kurashi-	I hastened nightfall
todomeshi nari.	and made you stay behind;
Ima wa	so by now

275

Tadanori

utagai	on no account
yomo araji.	does a doubt remain.
Hana wa ne ni[56]	"To the roots all flowers
kaeru nari,	must return when they fall."
Waga ato toite	Offer prayers when you pray
tabitamae.	for my last remains,
Kokage o tabi no	and beneath the trees you lodge,
yado to seba	as you journey on,
hana koso aruji	then indeed your host will be
narikere.	the cherry flowers.

[*At the* shite *seat, the* shite *makes a* tome chōshi *gesture.*]

Masterworks of the Nō Theater

Matsukaze

Introduction

Matsukaze, which belongs to the Group III Nō plays, is perhaps one of the most popular pieces. As an old saying goes, "Three things that the Japanese cannot miss even for a day are *Matsukaze*, *Yuga*, and cooked rice." The play has enjoyed this reputation throughout its five-hundred-year history. It is indeed the love piece (*renbo kyoku*) par excellence; Zeami considered and graded it as the "Deeply Hidden Flower" (grade 8), a judgment that Zenchiku, Zeami's son-in-law and the excellent Nō theorist and playwright, reiterated in his *Kabu Zuinōki*.[1]

This play illustrates, among other things, three important points. First, the present text is the result of three talented Nō masters' hands. In *Nōsakusho*,[2] Zeami cited *Matsukaze Murasame* as one of the models for new plays and called it *Shiokumi*. He further cited *Matsukaze* as his late father's piece in *Go-on*,[3] where he also stated that *Shiokumi* was possibly the work of Kiami, the noted Dengaku Nō master. As Zeami indicated, the part his father revised begins with the *sashi* passage in the present text that comes after the *ni no ku* of the *issei* verse. What Zeami added or changed is, in Zeami's words, the "later part" (*nochi no dan*).[4] The passage begins with the following lines: "How true that hidden grief / however deep within" (*Geni ya omoi / uchi ni areba*), which come before the *kudoki* passage in the present text. This may be the reason that *Matsukaze Murasame* was mentioned in *Sarugaki Dangi*[5] as Zeami's work.

Second, contrary to the practice of many noted Nō plays, the protagonist (the *shite*) and her sister (the *tsure*) in this play are based on "no authentic source," a point that Zeami considered very important. In fact they are fictitious! Thanks to this play, however, they appear truer and larger than life. In this regard, Zeami clearly stated in *Nōsakusho*: "Also, for what is called made-up Nō, which has no authentic source but is newly conceived and formed in connection with a noted place or historical site, there are times when the play can give rise to moving visual effects. This task demands the skill of the consummate master."[6] True to these words, Zeami selected Suma as the place of action for this play, as Lady Murasaki did for her hero, Prince Genji, in the *Tale of Genji* some four hundred years before Zeami. As she says: "His residence is near the house where the Middle Counselor Lord Yukihira lived, drenched with seaweed brine and tears." So Zeami chose Lord Yukihira as his hero, but he never appears in the play; his famous poems are in evidence, however, and, like a theme song, play an important part in this piece. In addition to the poems, Zeami used different passages from the *Tale of Genji* twelve times.[7] As they are strewn throughout the play, these allusions not only deepen the lyric tone but also enrich the texture. Here the moon over the Bay of Suma, the sound of the ocean waves, the salty smell of the sea spray, the pine winds, and the plovers' cries—all serve as the eternal background for the *shite*'s longing thoughts that never cease or change.

Among the best-known parts of the play, as Zenchiku pointed out in his *Go-on Sankyokushū*, is the *sashi*, which begins with the following lines:

> our hearts are sadly wearied
> by the autumn wind
> though the sea is lying
> at a little distance. . . .

The passage continues through the *sageuta* to the end of the *ageuta*, with the concluding lines sung by the chorus: "wasting all away to naught / like our sleeves decayed." This segment is an example of a *yūgen* passage totaling sixty-two lines![8]

Another famous section, known as "the brine-dipping scene," is most memorable; it runs in part as follows:

CHORUS

Ureshi ya kore mo tsuki ari.	How delightful, too, in this the moon appears!

SHITE

Tsuki wa hitotsu	The shining moon is one,
kage wa futatsu	I see it's mirrored, too,
mitsu	full, three,
shio no	on the tide
yoru no kuruma ni	for tonight they load the moon
tsuki o nosete	upon the cart they draw,
ushi tomo	never thinking
omowanu	of the hardship
shioji	on the road
kana ya.	by the sea.

278

These passages are some of the most popular Nō scenes, accompanied as they are by the superb movements and gestures and stunning visual forms of the *shite* and the *tsure* in their splendid costumes. Here, unity is created as the theme of the moon unfolds. The scene takes place by the moonlit shore, where the *shite* and *tsure* "load the moon upon the cart they draw," a lyrical description of the reflected image of the moon in the wooden pails of sea water they carry home. The single moon above is reflected nightly below on the surface of the water, as in their two pails, and as on the sea itself, becoming two (too), three, and four (for) moons. As in the original Nō text, expressed in charmingly playful puns, the forward movement of the lyric is propelled onward by the numerical progression, binding all the elements mentioned into a poetic whole.

Sakamoto Setchō, the great Nō critic, commented on the superb performance of this play by Umewaka Manzaburō, the modern Nō master, as follows:

> . . . taking the cart-rope, the *shite* looks high above as she sings:
>
> "the shining moon is one"
>
> and in the following line, she sings as she looks upon the sea:
>
> "I see it's mirrored, too . . ."
>
> She continues singing:
>
> "full three
> on the tide
> for tonight they load the moon
> upon the cart they draw . . ."
>
> Then she turns around, looking at the moon in a posture which, I should say, is magnificently superb, but her position is near the front of the stick drum (*taiko*), and too close to the *tsure* on her right. This is regrettable. . . .[9]

The last comment is significant because Setchō is pointing out that the relation between the postures and the players' respective positions is extremely important in Nō, not only in this play but in other pieces as well, as the play unfolds and their relative positions shift aesthetically in the well-realized performance. The reason for this emphasis is perhaps that the *shite*'s posture demands its own space, or sphere of influence, which I call her "soul-field," surrounding her as a magnetic field surrounds a magnet.

Third, this play is an excellent example of what Zeami referred to as a play without an Interlude (*nakairi*). As he observed in the *Seshi Kokujū Igo Sarugaku Dangi*:

> In general, a play written in two parts, in which the *shite* leaves the stage and then returns, is relatively easy to compose. A Nō that is played straight through must be written so that there is sufficient variation for the audience. The point is a vital one. If such variation is not provided, the play will languish and seem ineffective. In the case of *Matsukaze*, for example, the play appears to have such a break, even though it follows straight through. When the line "I no longer feel the pain" is finished, the movement and the music come to a brief pause. Such effects must be carefully studied.[10]

Zeami also stated: "Though *Matsukaze Murasame* is too wordy (*koto ōki*), it is fine."[11] Here he refers, it seems, to the following points: (1) In the *waki* entry section (*Jo no Dan*), the *kyōgen* usually does not appear, but in this play, through the dialogues between the *waki* and the *kyōgen*, we are informed about the old site that was the dwelling place of the two sisters. (2) The *waki-shite* dialogue generally takes place after the *shite* entry section (*Ha no Ichi Dan*); however, in this work the next section (*Ha no Ni Dan*) can be considered as an extension of the *shite* entry section because it consists of a dialogue between the *shite* and the *tsure*. It also stands as if it were an extra section by itself. This is the famous "brine-dipping scene," whose passages are graced with the names of famous places associated with salt making. (3) Normally the content of the *shite-waki* dialogue is not very important but serves as an introduction to the section that follows it. In *Matsukaze*, however, this section (*Ha no San Dan*) is not only a prologue for the *kuse* passage to follow; here the dialogue also creates an air of *yūgen*. It is neither simple nor straightforward. In spite of the involved structure, the dialogues are very moving and memorable, as they are effectively realized as integral parts of the whole.

In the *kuse* passage the *shite*'s feeling intensifies, as if she were possessed by madness when she put on the hunting robe and the tall black courtly cap. This agitation culminates in the *chū no mai* followed by the quick *ha no mai*. After the quick dance, the *shite* asks the *waki* to say holy prayers for her memory, and with her last words she withdraws, as the chorus sings the following passage in *ōnori-*rhythm *yowagin* style:

> like the sounds
> of the waves receding
> clear across
> the beach of Suma
> downward roar the mountain blasts
> blowing from behind,
> from the barrier road now, too,
> cocks crow one by one;
> his dream now fades to nothing,
> night now turns to dawn,
> sounds he took for Autumn Shower, too,
> by this morning's light,
> are only those of the pine wind
> that remain behind,
> are only those of the pine wind
> that remain behind.

It is appropriate to conclude here that this is one of the most natural and artless, yet subtle wordplays that the Nō playwright employs in his characteristic way. As the *shite* withdraws and the *waki* wakes, and while night ends and dawn begins, the proper names of the two sisters reassume the natural function of the normal nouns. Only as we hear the wind passing through the pines do we come to realize by the *shite*'s stamps on the floor that the play has come to a close.

280

MATSUKAZE

ADAPTED BY ZEAMI FROM KANNAMI'S WORK

Persons: WAKI: *A wandering Buddhist priest*
KYŌGEN: *A man of the place*
SHITE: *A fisher maiden (ghost of Matsukaze)*
TSURE: *A fisher maiden (ghost of Murasame)*

Classification: *Primary, Group III; Variant, Group IV*
Place: *At the Bay of Suma in the land of Settsu*
Time: *September*
Kogaki: *9*

Jo no Dan

[*First, the stage attendant brings out a prop symbolizing a pine and places it at stage front. Following the* nanoribue, *the* waki *makes an appearance quietly and stands at the name-saying seat (*nanoriza*). He wears a pointed hood (*kakubōshi*), a plain, less-formal silk kimono (*muji noshime*), a broad-sleeved robe (*mizugoromo*), a waistband (*koshiobi*), a fan (*ōgi*), and a rosary (*juzu*). Facing stage front, he intones the following prose passage, called* nanori.]

WAKI

[1] *(Nanori: awazu, yowagin)*

Kore wa shokoku ikken no sō nite sōrō.
Ware imada saikoku o mizu sōrō hodo
ni kono tabi omoitachi Saikoku angya to
kokorozashite sōrō.

I am a Buddhist priest, traveling from
province to province. I have not yet
seen the Western Land, so I have decided to make a pilgrimage there at
this time.

[*Still facing stage front, the* waki *intones the following passage, called* tsukizerifu.]

(Tsukizerifu: awazu, kotoba)

Ara ureshi ya, isogi sōrō hodo ni kore
wa haya Tsu[12] no Kuni Suma no Ura to
ka ya mōshi sōrō. Mata kore naru isobe
o mireba yō arigenaru matsu no sōrō.
Ikasama iware no naki koto wa sōrōmaji. Kono atari no hito ni tazunebaya
to omoi sōrō.

How glad I am! I have traveled so
fast that I am already here at this place
called the Bay of Suma in the province
of Tsu. [*Noticing the pine.*] As I look about
this shore, over here, I see a curious-
looking pine tree. Surely there must be
some reason for this. Perhaps I can ask
someone in the vicinity about it.

281

Matsukaze

[*The* waki *goes to the* shite *seat and calls out to the* kyōgen. *The following dialogue between the* waki *and the* kyōgen *is called* mondai *or* mondō.]

WAKI

(*Mondai: awazu, kotoba*)

Suma no zaisho no hito no watari sōrō ka.

Is there anyone about who is from the village of Suma?

[*The* kyōgen, *wearing the long* kyōgen *two-piece* (chō jōge), *a striped, less-formal silk kimono* (dan noshime), *a waistband* (koshiobi), *a fan* (ōgi), *and a short sword* (chiisa gatana), *rises from the* kyōgen *seat and stands near the first pine* (ichi no matsu).]

KYŌGEN

Tokoro no mono to o-tazune wa ikayō naru go-yō nite sōrō zo.

Did you ask for someone from this place? What do you wish me to do?

WAKI

Kore wa shokoku ikken no sō nite sōrō. Kore naru isobe ni hito-ki no matsu no sōrō ni, fuda o uchi tanjaku o kakerarete sōrō. Iware no sōrō ka, oshiete tamaware sōrae.

I am a Buddhist priest, traveling from province to province. Here on this shore there is a single pine tree with a wooden tablet fixed to it and a strip of poem paper hanging from it. Is there some story behind this? I should like to hear it.

KYŌGEN

San zōrō. Are wa Matsukaze Murasame[13] to mōshitaru futari no ama no kyūseki nite sōrō. O-sō mo tomurōte on-tōri arekashi to zonji sōrō.

Why, yes. That is the old historical spot of the two fisher maidens who were called Pine Wind and Autumn Shower. Perhaps you might say holy prayers for them when you pass by there.

WAKI

Nengoro ni on-oshie shūchaku mōshite sōrō. Sa araba are e tachikoe gyakuen nagara tomurōte tōrōzuru nite sōrō.

Thank you for telling me courteously. Well then, I will go that way, and though I am not related to them, I will offer some prayers before I continue my pilgrimage.

282

KYŌGEN

Go-yō no koto sōrawaba kasanete ōse sōrae.

If you have something further for me to do, please call me again.

WAKI

Tanomi sōrōbeshi.

Yes, thank you. I will.

Masterworks of the Nō Theater

Kokoroe mōshite sōrō.

Please do, holy priest.

[*The* kyōgen *returns to his seat. The* waki *comes out to stage center and, facing the prop, he sings the following passage.*]

WAKI

(Awazu, yowagin)

Sate wa kono matsu wa	So then, is this the pine that marks
inishie Matsukaze	the last remains of those who're called
Murasame tote	Pine Wind and Autumn Shower,
ni-nin no ama no	two sister fisher maidens
kyūseki ka ya.	in days of long ago?

[*The* waki *kneels and folds both hands in prayer.*]

Itawashi ya.	This is pitiful.
Sono mi wa dochū ni[14]	Though their bodies have been buried
uzumorenuredomo	deeply underneath the earth,
na wa nokoru yo no	as a sign to keep their names
shirushi tote	for the future world
kawaranu iro no	still there grows a single pine
matsu hito-ki	in unchanging hue.
midori no aki o	This evergreen left standing
nokosu koto no	through the autumn season
awaresa yo.	seems deeply touching.

[*The* waki *intones the following prose passage.*]

Kayō ni kyō-nenbutsu shite tomurai sōraeba geni aki no hi no narai tote hodo nō kurete sōrō. Ano yamamoto[15] no sato made wa hodo tōku sōrō hodo ni kore naru ama no shioya ni tachiyori ichiya o akasabaya to omoi sōrō.

While I have been reciting the sutra and repeating the Holy Name, night has come quickly, as it always does with autumn days. Since it seems quite far to the village at the foot of the mountain, I will stop at that salt maker's hut, where I hope to pass the night.

[*The* waki *goes to the* waki *seat and sits down.*]

Ha First Dan

[*With the* hayashi *music, the stage attendant brings out a small prop representing a cart and places it by the eye-fixing pillar* (metsukebashira). *Following the* issei *music, the* tsure, *carrying the pails, followed by the* shite, *makes an entry. The* shite *wears a* wakaonna *(young woman's) mask, a wig* (kazura), *a wig band* (kazuraobi), *a collar in white* (eri shiro), *an under kimono with painted gold or silver patterns* (surihaku), *an embroidered silk kimono with painted gold or silver patterns on a red ground, in* koshimaki *style* (akaji nuihaku koshimaki), *a white broad-sleeved robe* (shiro mizugoromo koshimaki), *a waistband* (koshiobi), *and a fan* (ōgi). *The* tsure *wears a* tsuremen *mask, a wig* (kazura), *a wig band* (kazuraobi), *a white silk kimono with painted gold or silver patterns* (surihaku), *an embroidered silk kimono with painted gold or silver patterns on a red ground, in* koshimaki *style* (akaji nuihaku koshimaki), *a collar in red* (eri aka), *a white broad-sleeved robe*

283

Matsukaze

(shiro mizugoromo), *a waistband* (koshiobi), *and a fan* (ōgi). *They stop along the bridge, the* tsure *at the first pine* (ichi no matsu), *and the* shite *at the third pine* (san no matsu), *and, facing each other, they sing the following* shin no issei.]

SHITE AND TSURE

[2] *(Shin no issei: awazu, yowagin)*

Shiokumiguruma	With the cart for drawing brine
wazukanaru,[16]	barely turning round
ukiyo[17] ni meguru[18]	through this fleeting world how sad
hakanasa yo.	is the turn we take.

[*The* tsure, *facing stage front, sings the following lines, called* ni no ku.]

TSURE

(Ni no ku)

Nami koko moto ya[19]	To this place the waves come up
Suma no Ura.	at Suma's inlet,

[*They face each other again and sing quietly.*]

SHITE AND TSURE

tsuki sae nurasu	even here the moon itself
tamoto kana.	dampens, too, these sleeves.

[*With the* ashirai *music, they come out to the stage, the* tsure *at stage center, and the* shite *at the* shite *seat. Then the* shite, *facing stage front, sings the following* sashi *passage.*]

SHITE

(Sashi: awazu, yowagin)

Kokorozukushi no[20]	Our hearts are sadly wearied
akikaze ni	by the autumn wind,
umi wa sukoshi	though the sea is lying
tōkeredomo	at a little distance,
kano Yukihira[21] no	as the Middle Counselor
Chūnagon	Yukihira sang

[*The* shite *and the* tsure *face each other and sing together.*]

SHITE AND TSURE

284

seki fukikoyuru[22] to	so graciously, "the bay breeze blows
nagametamō	over the barrier . . ."
urawa no nami no	where the waves across the bay
yoru yoru[23] wa	come night after night,
geni oto chikaki	surging as they sound so close
ama no ie	to the fisher's hut
satobanare naru[24]	that lies far from the village
kayoiji no	on the path we take,

tsuki yori hoka wa [25]	for no other than the moon
tomo mo nashi.	friendless we would be.

[*The* shite *faces stage front.*]

SHITE

Geni ya ukiyo no	Though we labor in the way
waza nagara	of this fleeting world,
koto ni tsutanaki	we're especially unskilled
ama obune no	with a small fishing boat,

[*The* shite *and the* tsure *sing together the rest of the lines.*]

SHITE AND TSURE

watarikanetaru	barely able to make sail
yume no yo ni	through a dreamlike world,
sumu to ya iwan	so we cannot say we live;
utakata no	but like foam that fades
shiokumiguruma	from the brine we draw the cart
yorube naki	to no place at all,
mi wa amabito no	for we, the fisher maidens,
sode tomo ni	never dry our sleeves,
omoi o hosanu	with our longing thoughts that stir
kokoro kana.	deep within our hearts.

[*They face stage front as the chorus sings the* sageuta *passage.*]

CHORUS

(*Sageuta: au, yowagin*)

Kaku bakari [26]	In this way so harsh
hegataku miyuru	it appears we have to live
yo no naka ni	through this fleeting world,
urayamashiku mo	while how enviably the moon
sumu [27] tsuki no	shines so clear and bright
dejio [28] o iza ya	as it rises with the tide,
kumō yo,	let's draw the brine,

[*They move forward slightly.*]

dejio o iza ya	as it rises with the tide,
kumō yo.	let's draw the brine.

[*The chorus sings the following* ageuta *in a higher pitch. The* shite, *noticing the pool of water, lowers her face.*]

285

(*Ageuta: au, yowagin*)

Kage hazukashiki	Reproached by this reflection
waga sugata,	of our shameful sight,
kage hazukashiki	reproached by our reflection,

Matsukaze

waga sugata	this too shameful sight,
shinobi-	stealthily
guruma o	we hide the cart
hiku[29] shio no	as the tide withdraws

[*The* shite *looks at the pool of water again, as if lost in thought.*]

ato ni nokoreru	leaving standing water-ruts,
tamari mizu	but do they stay clear
itsu made sumi wa	for how long must we subsist
hatsubeki,	until we perish

[*The* shite *changes her mood.*]

| nonaka no kusa no | as if we were but dewdrops, |
| tsuyu naraba | scattered through grass fields? |

[*The* shite *looks about the shore, to the right.*]

hikage ni kie mo	Then we would fade and vanish
usubeki ni	in the shining sun,
kore wa isobe ni	we are but weeds discarded
yorimo kaku	by the fishermen

[*The* shite *advances two steps.*]

ama no sutekusa	from the washed-up plants they rake
itazura ni	on the ocean shore
kuchimasariyuku[30]	wasting all away to naught

[*The* shite *sadly takes two steps backward toward the* shite *seat.*]

tamoto kana,	like our sleeves decayed,
kuchimasariyuku	wasting all away to naught
tamoto kana.	like our sleeves decayed.

Ha Second Dan

[*The* shite, *changing her mood, faces stage front and sings the following* sashi *passage.*]

SHITE

[3] (*Sashi: awazu, yowagin*)

Omoshiro ya	Oh, how delightful!
narete mo Suma no	though I am familiar
yūmagure	with Suma's twilight
ama no yobikoe[31]	where the fisher's calling voice
kasuka nite	sounds so faint and dim

[*The* shite *and the* tsure, *facing each other, sing together the following passage.*]

SHITE AND TSURE

| oki no chiisaki | in the offing very small |
| isaribune no | appear the fishing boats, |

kage kasuka naru	growing misty is the face
tsuki no kao	of the paling moon
kari no sugata ya	intercepted by the geese,
tomochidori[32]	the plovers crying,
nowaki shiokaze	wintry blasts and salty winds,
izure mo geni	how truly all these things
kakaru tokoro no[33]	in surroundings such as these
aki narikeri.[34]	grace the days of autumn,
Ara kokorosugo no	but our hearts feel desolate
yo sugara ya na.	all the long night through.

[*The* shite *lowers the mask. Regaining her composure, she faces stage front to begin the* kakeai *passage.*]

SHITE

(*Kakeai: awazu, yowagin*)

Iza iza shio o	Come, let us go now and draw
kuman tote	the ocean water

[*The* shite *and the* tsure *face each other, and the* shite *continues to sing.*]

migiwa ni michihi no	along the shore where still the tide
shiogoromo no	is moving back and forth,

TSURE

sode o musunde	we tie our sleeves together
kata ni kake	across our shoulders,

SHITE

shio kumu tame to wa	ready to draw the ocean brine,
omoedomo	as we ought to do,

TSURE

yoshi sore tote mo	but even then how heavy

SHITE

onnaguruma	appears a woman's cart

[*The chorus takes up in song and sings the following* ageuta *passage.*]

CHORUS

(*Ageuta: au, yowagin*)

yosete wa kaeru	moving back and forth, the waves
kataonami[35]	half-hide the beaches,

[*The* shite *and the* tsure *face stage front and the* tsure *retreats to the front of the hand-drum players and then stands beside the* shite.]

Matsukaze

yosete wa kaeru	moving back and forth, the waves
kataonami	half-hide the beaches,
ashibe no	along the reeds

[*The* shite *looks to her right as she follows the cranes with her eyes.*]

tazu koso wa	where the cranes take flight,
tachisawage	crying as they rise,
yomo no arashi[36] mo	answered by the gales that whir

[*The* shite *faces stage front again.*]

oto soete	from all directions.
yosamu nani to	How can we pass this night
sugosan.	so cold and chill?

[*She lowers her mask.*]

Fukeyuku	As the night grows deep
tsuki koso	the moon indeed
sayaka nare,	shines so bright and clear;

[*The* shite *looks up to the right at the moon.*]

kumu wa	what we scoop
kage nare ya.	is wholly moonlight!

[*The* shite *looks at the reflection of the moon in the pail on the cart.*]

Yaku shiokemuri	Oh, be careful of the smoke
kokoro seyo	from brine you boil.
sanomi nado	Even though we are
amabito no	lowly fisherfolk,
uki aki nomi o	much more than autumn's sadness
sugosan.	we linger through.

[*The* shite *retreats two steps and "clouds" (*shioru*) the mask. As the chorus sings the following lines, the* shite *approaches the cart and kneels.*]

(*Sageuta: au, yowagin*)

Matsushima[37] ya	At the Isles of Pines,
Ojima[38] no ama no	do Small Island's fisherfolk
tsuki ni dani	under this full moon

[*With the fan, the* shite *mimes dipping saltwater into the pail.*]

kage o kumu koso	take pleasure too in scooping
kokoro are,	its bright reflection,
kage o kumu koso	take pleasure too in scooping
kokoro are.	its bright reflection?

[*As the chorus sings the following* rongi *passage, the* shite *returns to the* shite *seat.*]

Masterworks of the Nō Theater

[4] *(Rongi: au, yowagin)*

Hakobu wa tōki[39] Michinoku's Salt Kiln lies
Michinoku no in distant Chika,
sono na ya Chika[40] no where the ocean brine is hauled,
Shiogama. though near it means.

SHITE [*Facing stage front.*]

Shizu ga shioki[41] o The humble folk drag driftwood
hakobishi wa for the brine they boil,
Akogi ga Ura[42] ni as the tide ebbs from the Bay
hiku shio. of Akogi.

CHORUS

Sono Ise no Umi no Adjacent to the Ise Sea,
Futami no Ura[43] Twice-Seen Bay is famous.
futatabi yo ni mo So I wish I might twice see
idebaya. this world of ours!

[*The* shite *looks far off into the distance to the right as she sings.*]

SHITE

Matsu no Muradachi[44] When the clustered pines become
kasumu hi ni hazy on the day,
shioji ya tōku distant grows the deep beyond
Narumigata[45] this Narumi Bay.

CHORUS

Sore wa There the Bay
Narumigata[46] of Narumi lies;
koko wa Naruo no here this place is Naruo
matsukage ni shaded by the pines

[*The* shite *faces stage front again.*]

tsuki koso saware which cut off the moon from view
Ashi no Ya.[47] like Reed Cottage.

SHITE

Nada[48] no In Nada
shio kumu we draw the brine
ukimi zo to but can tell no one
hito ni ya tare mo of our boxwood combs, for life
tsuge[49] no kushi is harsh and weary

289

[*During the next chorus song, the* tsure *approaches the cart and puts her wooden buckets in it, while the* shite, *standing, looks at them.*]

Matsukaze

Chorus

sashikuru[50] shio o	with the surging waves we dip,
kumiwakete	and dividing them
mireba tsuki koso	in the buckets we can see
oke ni are.	the moon is shining.

[*The* shite *goes to the front of the cart and looks into the pail.*]

Shite

Kore ni mo tsuki no	The moon has also entered
iritaru ya.	this wooden bucket.

[*The* shite *looks into the other pail, as the* tsure *picks up the hauling rope of the cart and hands it to her. The* tsure *retires to the* shite *seat and stands by it.*]

Chorus

Ureshi ya kore mo	How delightful, too, in this
tsuki ari.	the moon appears!

[*The* shite *looks upward at the sky.*]

Shite

Tsuki wa hitotsu[51]	The shining moon is one,

[*The* shite *looks at the two pails in the cart.*]

kage wa futatsu	I see it's mirrored, too,
mitsu	full, three,
shio no	on the tide

[*The* shite *pulls the rope and retires toward the musicians, indicating that they are homebound.*]

yoru no kuruma ni	for tonight they load the moon
tsuki o nosete	upon the cart they draw,
ushi to mo	never thinking
omowanu	of the hardship

[*The* shite *stamps the floor.*]

shioji	on the road
kana ya.	by the sea.

290

Ha Third Dan

[*As the stage attendant takes the cart away, the* shite *goes close to the front of the* ōtsuzumi *(large hand-drum) player; facing stage front, the* shite *sits on the stool, and the* tsure *sits behind on the* shite*'s right, as if they were resting inside the hut. The prose exchange* (mondai) *now begins. The* waki *rises from the* waki *seat.*]

[5] *(Mondai: awazu, yowagin)*

Shioya no aruji no kaerite sōrō. Yado o karabaya to omoi sōrō. Ikani kore naru shioya no uchi e annai mōshi sōrō.

The owner of this salt hut has returned. I will ask for a night's lodging. [*Turns to the* shite.] I beg your pardon. May I come in?

[*The* tsure *rises and moves slightly forward a step or two toward the* waki.]

TSURE

Tare nite watari sōrō zo.

Is someone there? Who is it?

WAKI [*Toward the* tsure.]

Kore wa shokoku ikken no sō nite sōrō. Ichiya no yado o on-kashi sōrae.

I am a Buddhist priest, visiting from province to province. I should like to ask for a room for the night.

TSURE

Shibaraku on-machi sōrae. Aruji ni sono yoshi mōshi sōrōbeshi. Ikani mōshi sōrō. Tabibito no on-niri sōrō ga ichiya no o-yado to ōse sōrō.

Please wait a moment. I must speak to the owner. [*Facing the* shite, *she kneels.*] Excuse me. There is a traveler here who asks to have a room for the night.

SHITE

Amari ni migurushiki shioya nite sōrō hodo ni o-yado wa kanōmajiki to mōshi sōrae.

Since this salt hut is so wretched, please tell him I cannot have him stay for the night.

[*The* tsure *rises and faces the* waki.]

TSURE

Aruji ni sono yoshi mōshite sōraeba shioya no uchi migurushiku sōrō hodo ni o-yado wa kanōmajiki yoshi ōse sōrō.

I have spoken with the owner, but she feels that this salt hut is too poor a place to offer you lodgings.

WAKI

Iya iya migurushiki wa kurushikarazu sōrō. Shukke no koto nite sōraeba hira ni ichiya o akasasete tamawari sōrae to kasanete on-mōshisōrae.

No, not at all. However poor this is, it does not matter for a Buddhist priest like myself who has renounced the world. Please ask once again if I may stay for just this one night.

291

TSURE

Iya kanai sōrōmaji.

No, that cannot be done.

Matsukaze

SHITE [*Speaking to the* tsure.]

Shibaraku.

Wait a moment.

Tsuki no yokage⁵² mo
mitatematsureba
yo o sutebito.
Yoshi yoshi kakaru
ama no ie
matsu no kibashira ni
take no kaki⁵³
yosamusa koso to
omoedomo
ashibi ni atarite
o-tomari are to
mōshi sōrae.

By the moonlight I can see
that the traveler is one
who has renounced the world.
Well, now. As he can well tell,
this fisher's cottage,
constructed with some pine-tree posts
and a bamboo fence,
will be somewhat cold for him
through this night, I fear,
but he is welcome to the warmth
this rush-fire gives. Please tell him
he may stay just this one night.

[*The* tsure *rises and faces the* waki.]

Konata e on-niri sōrae.

Please, come this way and enter.

WAKI

Ara ureshi ya. Saraba kō mairōzuru nite
sōrō.

I am delighted. I will go in with you.

[*The* waki *takes two or three steps forward and kneels, while the* tsure *resumes her former position and sits down. The* shite *speaks to the* waki.]

SHITE

[6] (*Mondai: awazu, yowagin*)

Hajime yori o-yado mairasetaku wa
sōraitsuredomo amari ni migurushiku
sōrō hodo ni sate ina to mōshite sōrō.

From the very first, I wished to offer you
lodgings, but this hut is so miserable I
did not feel I could do so.

WAKI

On-kokorozashi arigatō sōrō. Shukke
to mōshi tabi to ii tomari hatsubeki mi
naraneba izuku o yado to sadamubeki.
Sono ue kono Suma no Ura ni kokoro
aran hito wa waza to mo wabite koso
sumubekere.

I appreciate your kindness. Since I am a
priest and am on a pilgrimage, there is
no place where I remain for long; so I
am not particular about my lodgings.
Furthermore, those who have a liking
for places like this Bay of Suma purposely choose to live in solitude.

"Wakurawa ni⁵⁴
tou hito araba
Suma no Ura ni

"Should there be by chance
someone who asks after me,
living here at Suma,

moshio taretsutsu wabu to kotae yo" to
Yukihira mo eiji tamaishi to nari. Mata
ano isobe ni hitoki no matsu no sōrō

drenched with seaweed brine and tears,
thus you should reply." So Lord Yukihira sang, I hear. [*Facing the prop.*] And

o hito ni tazunete sōraeba, Matsukaze Murasame ninin no ama no kyūseki to ka ya mōshi sōrō hodo ni gyakuen nagara tomuraite koso tōri sōraitsure. Ara fushigi ya. Matsukaze Murasame no koto o mōshite sōraeba ninin tomo ni go-shūshō sōrō. Kore wa nani to mōshitaru koto nite sōrō zo.

when I asked about that single pine tree on the shore, I was told that it was an old site known for the fisher maidens named Pine Wind and Autumn Shower. Though I am not related to them, I said prayers for them as I passed that way. [Shite *and* tsure *weep.*] How strange this is! At the mention of Pine Wind and Autumn Shower, both of you seem sadly grieved. I wonder what's the reason for this.

SHITE AND TSURE [*Raising their faces.*]

Geni ya omoi	How true that hidden grief
uchi ni areba[55]	however deep within
iro hoka ni	will reveal itself
araware samurau zo ya.	outwardly in our own expression still.
Wakurawa ni	"Should there be by chance
tou hito araba no	someone who asks after me."
on-monogatari	So the story of these lines
amari ni natsukashū	sounds too fondly dear to both of us,
sōraite	more than hearts can bear,
nao shūshin no	and so again the teardrops
enbu no namida	out of our deep attachment
futatabi sode o	to the fleeting world we knew

[*The* shite *and the* tsure *weep.*]

nurashi samurō.	wet these sleeves of ours once more.

WAKI

(Mondai: awazu, yowagin)

Nao shūshin no enbu no namida to wa ima wa kono yo ni naki hito no kotoba nari. Mata wakurawa no uta mo natsukashii nado to uketamawari sōrō. Katagata fushin ni sōraeba ninin tomo ni na o on-nanori sōrae.

"Our deep attachment to the fleeting world we knew . . ."; these are words of those who have gone from this world. You say, too, that you are filled with longing by the song that begins, "Should there be by chance . . ." I grow more and more uncertain about both of you. Please tell me your names.

293

SHITE AND TSURE

(Kudokiguri: awazu, yowagin)

Hatsukashi ya	How shame-sick we are!
mōsan to sureba	Though we have often wished to speak,

Matsukaze

wakurawa ni	none has happened by
kototou hito mo	who has even asked of us
naki ato[56] no	at Suma, long dead
yo ni shiojimite	is our world, where drenched by tides
korizuma no[57]	and learning nothing,
urameshikarikeru	our hearts that long still for this world
kokoro kana.	appear so hateful.

[They continue to sing the following passage, called kudoki.]

(Kudoki: awazu, yowagin)

Kono ue wa	Since it's come to this,
nani o ka sanomi	why should we be so careful
tsutsumubeki.	to conceal our names?
Kore wa sugitsuru	Here some little while ago
yūgure ni	fell the evening dusk
ano matsukage no	beneath the shaded mosses
koke no shita	by that single pine,
naki ato toware	the holy prayer is offered
mairasetsuru	for the last remains
Matsukaze Murasame	of the fisher maidens who were
ninin no onna no	named Pine Wind and Autumn Shower,
yūrei kore made	so as far as this place, the ghosts
kitaritari.	of these two have come
Sate mo Yukihira	here, where Lord Yukihira
mi-tose ga hodo	had lived about three years,
on-tsurezure no	whiling away idle hours
mi-fune asobi	and enjoying boating
tsuki ni kokoro wa	with the moon to clear his heart
Suma no Ura	at Suma's inlet;
yojio o hakobu	and from the fisher maidens
amaotome ni	drawing the brine at night
otodoieraware	out he drew these two fair sisters
mairasetsutsu	bestowing names on them,
ori ni furetaru	and thought they were most fitting
na nare ya tote	to suggest the season
Matsukaze Murasame to	he chose "Pine Wind" and "Autumn Shower"
mesareshi yori	to be his favorites,
tsuki ni mo naruru[58]	who became so intimate
Suma no ama no	with this moon at Suma.

294

SHITE

Shioyakigoromo	Clothes we wore to boil the brine
iro kaete	were exchanged for silks,

katori no kinu no   many colored, and perfumed
soradaki nari.   faint with incense fragrance.

SHITE [*Mood changes.*]

Kakute mi-tose mo   In this way these three years too
sugiyukeba   swiftly came and went
Yukihira Miyako ni   Lord Yukihira graciously
nobori tamai   back to the capital,

TSURE

iku hodo nakute   where very shortly after
yo o hayō   from this world of men
sari tamainu to   he has passed away too soon
kikishi yori   we have heard of this.

SHITE

Ara koishi ya   Oh, how I long for him!
saru nite mo   Even though it's so,
mata itsu no yo no   upon the day the message
otozure o   we awaited comes

[*The* shite *holds back her tears, while the chorus continues singing.*]

CHORUS

(*Uta: au, yowagin*)

Matsukaze[59] mo   once again Pine Wind,
Murasame mo   Autumn Shower, too,
sode nomi nurete   dampen these long sleeves with tears;
yoshi na ya na   nothing good could come
mi ni mo oyobanu   from a love so far beyond
koi o sae   their place as Suma
Suma no amari ni   fisher maidens, all too deep
tsumi fukashi   are the sins they sinned.

[*The* shite *faces the* waki *and folds her hands in prayer.*]

ato tomuraite   Oh, let holy prayers be said
tabi tamae.   for their memories.

[*As the chorus sings the following* ageuta *passage, the* shite *turns and faces stage front.*]

[7] (*Ageuta: au, yowagin*)

Koigusa no   Like the dew-thick weeds,
tsuyu mo omoi mo   our love grows rank with longing,
midaretsutsu,   frenzied and disturbed,

295

Matsukaze

[The waki *returns to the* waki *seat and sits down; the* tsure *moves in front of the flautist.]*

tsuyu mo omoi mo	our love grows rank with longing,
midaretsutsu,	frenzied and disturbed
kokoro kyōki ni	both of our hearts as crumpled
naregoromo[60] no	as old clothes we purify
mi no hi no	upon the Day
harai ya	of the Serpent,
yūshide no	but the gods refuse
kami no tasuke mo	the hempen strips we offer;
nami[61] no ue	on the waves afloat
aware[62] ni kieshi	we are left to fade like foam;
uki mi nari.	fleeting is our lot.

Ha Fourth Dan

[The shite *lowers the mask to indicate deep feeling. As the chorus begins the following* kuse *section, she faces stage front.]*

CHORUS

(Kuse: au, yowagin)

Aware	As I call
inishie o	to my mind the days
omoi izureba	that were long and long ago,
natsukashi ya.	they appear so dear.

[The stage attendant hands the shite *a robe and a court hat, representing Yukihira's keepsakes.]*

Yukihira no	Lord Yukihira,
Chūnagon	the Middle Counselor,
mi-tose wa koko ni	sojourned here for those three years
Suma[63] no Ura	at Suma's inlet,
Miyako e nobori-	but before he journeyed back
tamaishi ga	to the capital,
kono hodo no	as fond reminders
katami tote	of the time he spent
on-tateeboshi	both the tall black courtly cap
kariginu o	and the hunting robe
nokoshioki-	he left behind him
tamaedomo	graciously for us;
kore o	so each time
miru tabi ni	we gaze upon them

[The shite *raises the keepsakes and gazes at them.]*

iyamashi no	more and even more
omoigusa[64]	rise our longing thoughts
hazue ni musubu	forming like the leaf-tip dew,
tsuyu no ma mo	for whose brief moment

[The shite *gazes at the robe and moves her eyes down along the flowing long sleeves of the hunting cloak.]*

Masterworks of the Nō Theater

wasurareba koso	we cannot forget which is
ajiki na ya.	wearisome indeed.

[*Again the* shite *raises the keepsakes to gaze at them.*]

Katami koso[65]	"This very keepsake
ima wa ada nare	has become my enemy,
kore naku wa	if it were not here,
wasururu hima mo	there might be some free moment
arinan to	that I could forget."
yomishi mo	So the poet sang,
kotowari ya.	and how true it is!

[*The* shite *lowers the keepsakes as if she were downhearted and holds back her tears.*]

Nao omoi koso wa	Forevermore my anguished love
fukakere.	grows and deepens.

[*The* shite, *struggling to hold back her tears, sings the following lines, called* ageha.]

SHITE

(*Ageha*)

Yoi yoi[66] ni	Just before I sleep,
nugite waga nuru	taking off his hunting robe
karigoromo	each night I hang it . . .

CHORUS

kakete[67] zo tanomu	on my hope that we may live
onaji yo ni	in the self-same world;

[*Holding the keepsakes in her hand, the* shite *stands and moves slightly toward the eye-fixing pillar.*]

sumu kai	this life of mine
araba koso	is scarce worth living;
wasuregatami mo	even these keepsakes of his
yoshinashi to	are scarce worth keeping.

[*The* shite *tries to put the keepsakes away.*]

sutete mo	I cannot cast
okarezu	them all away;

[*She holds them closely with both hands.*]

toreba omokage ni	when I hold them up his figure
tachimasari	rises more and more.

297

[*Making a right-hand turn, the* shite *goes toward the* shite *seat.*]

okifushi wakade	So awake, asleep alike,
makura yori[68]	from the head and foot
ato yori koi no	of my bed love comes to seize
semekureba	and to torture me

[*She looks backward toward the bridge, as if at someone in pursuit.*]

Matsukaze

senkata	and without help
namida[69] ni	I lie face down

[*She faces stage front and sinks down as if collapsing.*]

fushi shizumu koto zo	in tears I turn away and sink
kanashiki.	deep in sadness.

Kyū First Dan

[*The* shite *retreats to the* shite *seat; she weeps as she holds the keepsakes close to her face. While* ashirai *music is played in a short interlude known as* monogi, *costume changes are made with the assistance of the stage attendant. The* shite *puts on the hunting cloak and court hat. Still seated and struggling to control her tears, she sings.*]

SHITE

[8] *(Sageuta: awazu, yowagin)*

Mitsusegawa[70]	In the gloomy shoals
taenu namida no	along the Three-Ford Rapids
uki se ni mo	of the endless tears,
midaruru koi no	there are dark whirlpools of love
fuchi wa arikeri.	that swirl our hearts in madness.

[*The* shite *seems to slip suddenly into madness.*]

(Kakeai: awazu, yowagin)

Ara ureshi ya	Oh, how happy I am!
are ni Yukihira no	Over there Lord Yukihira
o-tachi aru ga	is standing graciously!

[*The* shite, *gazing at the tree, stands up.*]

Matsukaze to	"Oh, Pine Wind," it seems
mesare samurau zo ya	as if he summons me before him
ide mairō	so let me go to him.

[*The* shite *rises and goes to the pine, while the* tsure *follows and takes her sleeve, trying to stop her.*]

TSURE

Asamashi ya	Ah, how miserable!
sono on-kokoro	With such longing in your heart,
yue ni koso	it is no wonder
shūshin no tsumi ni mo	that you are sinking ever deeper
shizumi tamae	in sin-filled attachments

298

[*The* shite *moves backward toward the drum players; the* tsure *retreats toward* waki *stage front* (wakishōmen).]

shaba nite no	to deep delusions
mōshū o nao	in this fleeting world you left,
wasure tamawanu zo ya.	but even now you don't forget them!

[*Speaks the following to the* shite.]

Masterworks of the Nō Theater

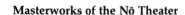

Are wa matsu nite	That is but a pine tree there,
koso sōrae.	oh, nothing more than that!
Yukihira wa	Lord Yukihira
onniri mo	has not graciously
samurawanu mono o.	come out and shown himself before
	you.

SHITE

Utate no hito ni iigoto ya. Ano matsu	How coldly and unfeelingly you speak.
koso wa Yukihira yo.	That pine is surely Yukihira!

[*Heightening into song, the* shite *continues the following passage.*]

Tatoi shibashi wa	"Though we two may be parted
wakaruru to mo	for some little while,
matsu to shi kikaba[71]	should I ever hear you pine
kaerikon to	I will return at once,"
tsuranetamaishi	graciously he strung these lines.
koto no ha wa ika ni.	Is there no meaning in these words?

TSURE

Geni nō wasurete	Truthfully, I had forgotten
samurau zo ya.	those lines he left for us.
Tatoi shibashi wa	"Though we two may be parted
wakaruru to mo	for some little while . . ."
mataba kon to no	if we wait, he will return
koto no ha o	as his poem says,

SHITE

konata wa wasurezu	which I have not yet forgotten,
Matsukaze[72] no	this Pine Wind rises
tachikaerikon[73]	pining for the tidings still
onotozure	that he may return.

TSURE

Tsuini mo kikaba	If we do not hear of him
Murasame no	then Autumn Shower
sode shibashi koso	dampens, too, her sleeves with tears
nururu to mo	for a little while,

SHITE

matsu[74] ni kawarade	as that pine, unchanged, I wait
kaerikoba	for my lord till he

TSURE

ara tanomoshi no	comes back here so full of hope

299

Matsukaze

SHITE

onnuta ya.   is the song he sang!

[*Holding back her tears, the* shite *moves toward the first pine on the bridge. The* tsure *returns to her position in front of the chorus and sits down. The chorus sings the following* waka.]

CHORUS

(*Waka: awazu, yowagin*)

Tachi wakare[75]   "Though I part and go,

[*With the* iroe *dance movement, consisting of a few small, graceful steps, the* shite *returns from the first pine to the stage proper, at the* shite *seat. There is a change of mood, as she begins to dance the Middle Dance, called* chū no mai, *which is generally performed in four movements.*]

Chū no mai

[*After the dance, the* shite, *making* ageōgi *and* sayū *gestures, sings the rest of the* waka *passage.*]

SHITE

(*Waka: awazu, yowagin*)

Inaba no yama no	should I ever hear one pine
mine ni ōru	grow and long for me
matsu[76] to shi kikaba	over Mt. Inaba's peak
ima kaerikon.	presently I will return."

[*The* shite *looks toward the bridge, as if gazing off into the distance, and she sings the following passage in* ōnori yowagin *style.*]

(*Noriji: ōnori, yowagin*)

Sore wa Inaba no	That is the distant mountain pine
tōyamamatsu	of Inaba he passed.

[*The* shite, *pointing her fan at the pine, comes out to center stage, while the chorus takes over the singing.*]

CHORUS

kore wa natsukashi	These pine trees are dear to us
kimi koko ni	for our lord has lived
Suma no Urawa no	here, the Suma inlet pines

[*With the pointing fan, the* shite *draws an arc as if around the bay.*]

matsu no Yukihira   for Yukihira we wait.

[*She turns to her right and goes toward the front of the drummers.*]

tachikaerikoba	Should he graciously return
ware mo kokage ni	then I would draw near the shade

[*She moves to stage front and leans close toward the pines.*]

Masterworks of the Nō Theater

iza tachiyorite	of those wind-embracing pines
sonarematsu no	waiting for him fondly
natsukashi ya.	as I truly do.

[*The weeping* shite *retreats again toward the front of the drummer's seat. Restraining her tears, she raises the mask and begins the* ha no mai *around the pine tree as if she were mad.*]

Ha no mai

[*The* shite *then pauses stage center while the chorus begins the sonorous final verses in the large* ōnori *rhythm pattern, with each syllable receiving a full beat.*]

Kyū Second Dan

Chorus

(Noriji: ōnori, yowagin)

| Matsu ni fukikuru | Through the pines the winds arise |
| kaze mo kyōjite | great with gusts and frenzied, too, |

[*Pointing around with her fan, the* shite *looks about the sea.*]

| Suma no takanami | while at Suma high waves surge |
| hageshiki yo sugara | so fiercely in the night throughout |

[*She goes stage right to the* shite *seat.*]

| mōshū no yume ni | all driven by delusions still |

[*Facing the* waki, *the* shite *comes out to center stage.*]

| miyuru nari. | they appear in dreams, |

[*She kneels, lowers the mask, and folds her hands in prayer.*]

| Waga ato toite | asking for their memories, |
| tabi tamae | holy prayers, they plead, |

[*Raising her head, the* shite *rises.*]

| itoma mōshite | and with parting words withdraw |

(Uta: au, yowagin)

kaeru [77]	like the sounds
nami no oto no	of the waves receding
Suma [78] no	clear across
Ura kakete	the beach of Suma

[*She comes out to the eye-fixing pillar and, with a* kakaeōgi *gesture, gazes off.*]

fuku ya ushiro no [79]	downward roar the mountain blasts
yamaoroshi	blowing from behind,
sekiji [80] no tori mo	from the barrier road now, too,
koegoe ni	cocks crow one by one;

[*She goes in front of the* waki *seat and, making a* kumo no ōgi *gesture, looks up at the eastern sky.*]

Matsukaze

yume mo ato naku   his dream now fades to nothing,
yo mo akete   night now turns to dawn,
Murasame to kikishi mo   sounds he took for Autumn Shower,
                          too,

[*The* shite *returns to the* shite *seat.*]

kesa mireba   by this morning's light,

[*At the* shite *seat, she makes* hiraki *clearly toward stage front.*]

matsukaze bakari ya   are only those of the pine wind
nokoruran,   that remain behind,
matsukaze bakari ya   are only those of the pine wind
nokoruran.   that remain behind.

[*At the* shite *seat, she stamps the floor and makes her exit across the bridge.*]

302

Higaki

Introduction

Higaki, Sekidera Komachi, and *Obasute* are known as "the three old-woman pieces," as Maruoka Akira has described them,[1] and are considered the most difficult plays in the Nō repertoire. *Higaki* is also known by the old title *Higaki no Onna* (The woman of the cypress hedge), a work mentioned in *Nōsakusho*[2] by Zeami as one of the models for the new plays dealing with women. Here it is interesting to note Masuda Shōzō's observation, which runs as follows: "The old-woman play lies where that of the old-man piece and that of the woman's cross each other. This is the secret innermost recess of the Nō, the abysmal chasm of different nature at the end of the woman's journey that can hardly be reached by an old man's state of mind. . . ."[3]

Higaki is just such a Nō play by Zeami, who regarded the old woman as the supreme subject for Nō. In assigning her the most significant position, he also added to Nō a dimension of profound and singular depth, which no other theme could possibly attain. This form therefore demands the consummate skill of the seasoned Nō actor in order to express in full the elevated world of the aged woman, who is at her long journey's end. For this reason *Higaki* is reverently reserved, even today, for a few acknowledged Nō masters; thus any of the rare occasions when it is given will truly be a special event for the audience.

The critic Sakamoto Setchō, for instance, responded excitedly to the 1912 memorial performance for the late Kanze Nō master Kōsetsu (1842–1911), given by the great Umewaka Manzaburō (1868–1940):

> The much-awaited *Higaki* has come at long last. . . . The Nō curtain, which becomes the object of attention and steady gaze, is swept up suddenly. The *shite*, standing in semi-darkness behind the curtain, is even then very slow to make an appearance. As she barely comes out, and the Nō curtain drops behind her, she appears thereafter as if she moves hardly at all. . . . at the first pine she starts to sing the following *shidai* verse in *yowagin* style:

"From this moon-bright White River
I draw the water,
from this moon-bright White River
I draw the water
up, too, the moon that dampens
these long sleeves with tears!"[4]

Here at the very start of this play, the water is introduced "enigmatically," to use Waley's word.[5] It flows throughout the entire play and serves as a unifying image, symbolizing a deep sense of the mutability of life. Against this symbolic water image as the background for life itself, Zeami does not depict the *shite's* beauty, pride, fame, and glory through the dramatic unfolding of her full character as a beautiful dancer. Instead, when the *shite* meets the *waki,* she answers his question of who she is by quoting the following verse:

With these passing years
my raven hair's also turned
this White River made
me stoop and draw its water
till I grew so old and bent.

"It is my poem," she says, and continues: "Once long ago, at Dazaifu in Chikuzen a dancing girl lived in a cottage with a fence made of a cypress hedge. Afterwards, as she grew old, she came to live in the vicinity of this White River." Then, during her dialogue with the *waki,* she subtly hints that when Lord Okinori requested water from her, she composed this poem in reply. And as she asks the *waki* to say holy prayers for her, she fades into the evening dusk.

After the Interlude, through the deep silver mist of the White River, the Hut of the Cypress Hedge comes into view, and the *shite,* dressed in white, appears. She reveals the following:

Once long, long ago I reveled in my fame as a dancer praised by all throughout the world. So deep were the sins I sinned, even now my suffering multiplies by the Three-Ford Rapids, where I shoulder the red-hot iron pails. Holding the bucket of fire I draw this water up,

then the water turns boiling hot,
burning all my scalded body
without cease, ever without rest . . .

Here the White River is replaced by the Three-Ford Rapids, which flow through the netherworld, where the water image still follows her. But now she says, " . . . for the little while I met with you, I was reprieved. And though there yet remains the well bucket, I see the flaming fire no more." Zeami omits a detailed, hellish scene of the dreadful agonies she suffers, as his father did in *Motomezuka.* This understatement, I feel, evokes all the more sharply her tribulations. He continues in his restrained lyrical style the lines that the chorus sings:

on the water mirror
old and feeble
is her form reflected,

304

sunken deeply,
and her hair that once appeared
flowing raven-black
looks like weeds and rubbish now . . .

and she admits:

when I think again
of the world that once was mine,
how I yearn for it. . . .

So, recollecting the time when she was asked to dance for Lord Okinori, she starts to dance the *jo no mai* as she sings the following lines:

I begin the dance
of the Maid of the Cypress Hedge
and her fateful end.

Slow and very graceful is the *jo no mai* as she remembers it, but now, without any gorgeous attire, and with only her white hempen cloth that is too narrow to wrap all the way around herself, her heart is coldly grieved. But her pride is enormously satisfied by the dance, which remains in her still. This dance expresses symbolically the state of her heart as she lingers in the shadow of the once-noted and beautiful dancer known as the "Maid of the Cypress Hedge."

Here Zeami has created a Nō form through which he expresses the old woman's sentiment, crystallized in utter simplicity, from her viewpoint as she approaches the end of her long journey. From this vista, she looks back at herself and her entire life and sees the bygone days of her beauty, pride, fame, glory, and also the sins she has sinned. Moreover, she gazes upon them simultaneously, as though she sees them from some distant point long after she has passed away from the world, where death lasts too long, while the life for which she still yearns was too short. These double perspectives, indeed, help Zeami to transcend time, for only in this way can the true insight into the role that the aged woman plays become immediate, as the "real flower" Zeami cherished.

Sakamoto Setchō summed up Umewaka's performance in the following manner: "This one Nō number required two hours and twenty-three minutes. The audience inhaled as if they were brought back to life, and dazed, perhaps, they forgot to applaud. I'm ashamed to say this is the first time I have seen an 'old woman piece' . . . it is needless to state that there is no flaw in the performance."[6] Indeed, two hours and twenty-three minutes sounds extraordinary! The reason for the protraction can perhaps be seen by analogy in the following modern, although prosaic, example. In a video replay of the Rose Bowl x times slower than the actual speed of the performance, we can see in the perfect thirty-yard pass to the end zone, among other things, exactly what has happened to the football and the players, whereas we would miss it under normal conditions at the stadium. Similarly, under extraordinary conditions filled with the air of *yūgen*, what happens to the soul of the *shite* can be vividly revealed to the audience in the Nō auditorium.

In connection with this aspect of the art, it is appropriate to mention the training of the Nō performers. It consists in the mastering of plays in a strictly prescribed sequence, graded according to the play's *kurai*, or "aesthetic magnitude."

305

A play of fast tempo is said to have "light *kurai*," and a slow one to have "heavy *kurai*." *Higaki* is the heaviest and most difficult of the pieces. This quality is, indeed, the very reason why a play such as this demands not only a lengthy performance time but also, as I stated in the beginning, the highly trained skill of a well-seasoned Nō master. The same may be said of *Obasute*.

Masterworks of the Nō Theater

HIGAKI

By Zeami

Persons: WAKI: *A Buddhist priest*
SHITE (PART I): *Ghost of the woman of the Cypress Hedge*
  (appears as an old woman of Higaki)
NOCHI-JITE (PART II): *Ghost of the woman of the Cypress*
  Hedge (appears as herself)
KYŌGEN

Classification: *Primary, Group III; Variant, Group IV*
Place: *At Iwado in the land of Higo*
Time: *Indefinite (no fixed season)*
Kogaki: *6*

PART I

[The stage attendant brings out a prop symbolizing a cottage and places it in front of the musicians. Following the introductory flute music, called nanoribue, *the* waki *quietly makes an entrance. He wears a pointed hood (kakubōshi), a small-checked kimono (kogōshi), a broad-sleeved robe (mizu-goromo), a white broad divided skirt (shiro ōguchi), a waistband (koshiobi), a fan (ōgi), and a rosary (juzu), and stands at the center of the stage. Facing stage front the* waki *intones the following prose (kotoba) passage called* nanori, *introducing himself and informing the audience of his purpose.]*

WAKI

[1] *(Nanori: awazu, kotoba)*

Kore wa Higo no Kuni Iwado[7] to mōsu yama ni kyojū no sō nite sōrō. Sate mo kono Iwado no Kanzeon[8] wa reigen shu-shō no on-koto nareba, shibaraku sanrō shi, tokoro no chikei o miru ni,

I am a Buddhist priest living by the mountain called Rock Door in the Land of Higo. The Goddess of Mercy enshrined here [*faces toward the eye-fixing pillar*] at this Rock Door Mountain is holy and miraculous. So for a time I am in retreat at this temple to pray and to practice my devotion. As I see the lay of the land around this place,

307

[The waki *faces stage front and sings the following verse passage in* yowagin *style.]*

(Awazu, yowagin)

nansei wa kan-un	to the southwest spreads a sea of clouds,
manman to shite	a vast expanse that retains

Higaki

banko kokoro no	in its heart a feeling
uchi nari.	most primeval,
Hito mare ni shite	where visitors are rare,
nagusami ōku	and many comforts fill me
chikei atte	deep with matchless landscapes,
kyōri o saru,	distant from the village.
makoto ni sumubeki	This, I thought, is truly sacred
reichi to omoite	to live in such a place as this,
mi-tose ga aida wa	so here I've stayed for three long years
kyojū tsukamatte	ever since I chose this very place
sōrō	for my dwelling.

Koko ni mata momo ni mo oyoburan to oboshiki rōjo mainichi aka no mizu o kumite kitari sōrō. Kyō mo kitarite sōrawaba ikanaru mono zo to na o tazunebaya to omoi sōrō.

Now, there is a very old woman who, it seems, must be almost a hundred years old. She comes every day with holy water she has drawn. Should she come this way again today, I think I will ask her who she is.

[After this, the waki *goes to the* waki *seat and sits down. Following the introductory music called* shidai, *the* shite *makes her entrance very quietly. She has a cane in her right hand and a redwood pail in her left hand. She wears an* uba *(old-woman) mask, a wig band (kazuraobi), a collar in white (eri shiro), an under kimono with painted gold or silver patterns (surihaku), a "Cathay fabric" broad outer kimono without red in "tucked up" style (ironashi karaori tsuboori), and a rosary (juzu). On the way across the bridge she pauses a moment, proceeds to the third pine, and rests a little; at the first pine, with her back turned toward the audience, she sings the following verse, called* shidai.]*

SHITE

[2] (*Shidai: au, yowagin*)

Kage Shirakawa⁹ no	From this moon-bright White River
mizu kumeba,	I draw the water,
kage Shirakawa no	from this moon-bright White River
mizu kumeba	I draw the water
tsuki mo tamoto ya	up, too, the moon that dampens
nurasuran.	these long sleeves with tears!

[The chorus sings the jidori, *a repetition of the above verse, except the third and fourth lines, in a lower key.]*

CHORUS

308

(*Jidori: au, yowagin*)

Kage Shirakawa no	From this moon-bright White River
mizu kumeba	I draw the water
tsuki mo tamoto ya	up, too, the moon that dampens
nurasuran.	these long sleeves with tears!

[After the jidori *the* shite, *facing stage front, sings the following* sashi *passage.]*

(Sashi: awazu, yowagin)

Sore rōchō wa [10]	As a bird inside a cage
kumo o koi	longs for clouds above,
kigan wa	and homeward geese
tomo o shinobu,	mourn for their companions,
ningen no mata	even for all mankind too,
kore onaji.	it is all the same.
Hinka ni [11] wa	For the humble home
shinchi sukunaku	few are those who are close friends,
iyashiki ni wa	and old acquaintances
kojin utoshi,	withdraw from lowly folks.
rōsui otoroe	Weakened by old age, enfeebled,
katachi mo naku	and with no figure, now
romei kiwamatte	this transient life is at its end
sōyō ni nitari.	like the frosted leaves all withered,

[*The* shite *sings the following low-pitched* sageuta.]

(Sageuta: au, yowagin)

Nagaruru mizu no	or water bubbles floating
aware [12] yo no	through this wretched world,
sono kotowari o	by drawing up its reason
kumite [13] shiru.	we understand it.

[*The* shite *changes now to a high-pitched* ageuta.]

(Ageuta: au, yowagin)

Koko wa tokoro mo	Here this very area too
Shirakawa no	is called White River,
koko wa tokoro mo	here this very area too
Shirakawa no	is called White River,
mizu sae fukaki [14]	with its waters fathomless
sono tsumi o	like our transgressions,
ukami ya suru to	they will cleanse away all sins,
sutebito ni	so I hope to see

[*As the* shite *starts to sing the following lines, she enters the stage from the bridge and, facing the* waki, *advances to stage center.*]

chigū o hakobu	one who has renounced this world,
ashibiki [15] no	down the long steep slope
yamashita iori ni	to the hut below the hill
tsukinikeri,	I have come at last,
yamashita iori ni	to the hut below the hill
tsukinikeri.	I have come at last.

[*Going toward the* waki, *the* shite *intones the following prose passage, called* mondai.]

309

Higaki

[3] *(Mondai: awazu, yowagin)*

Itsu mo no gotoku kyō mo mata on-mizu agete mairite sōrō

Here again I come today alone, as I always do, and offer holy water.

[*The* shite *sits in the center of the stage and puts down the pail.*]

WAKI [*At the* waki *seat.*]

Mainichi rōjo no ayumi kaesugaesumo itawashū koso sōrae.

Each day this old woman appears on foot, repeatedly renewing my compassion for her sorrow.

SHITE

Semete wa kayō no
koto nite koso
sukoshi no tsumi o mo
nogarubekere.

At the very least, I carry
water in this manner,
so in some degree the burden
of my sins is lightened.

[*The* shite *folds both hands in prayer.*]

Nakaran ato o
tomuraitamai
sōrae.

For the one who passed away,
graciously, oh, holy priest,
hold a service.

[*The* shite *makes a* shiori *gesture.*]

Akenaba mata mairi sōrōbeshi. Onni-toma mōshi sōrawan.

When day dawns again, I will return to this place. Now excuse me, I must go.

[*As the* shite, *facing stage front, leans on her cane and starts to rise, the* waki *speaks.*]

WAKI

Shibaraku. On-mi no na o-nanoritamae.

Wait a moment. Please, tell me your name.

SHITE [*Rising, looks at the* waki.]

Nani to na o nanore to zōrō ya.

What? Did you say you wish to know my name?

WAKI

Nakanaka no koto.

Yes, that is what I asked.

[*The* shite *sits down again. Putting down the cane and facing stage front, she first intones the prose line.*]

SHITE

Kore wa omoi mo yaranu ōse kana. Kano Gosenshū[16] no uta ni

This is something I did not expect you to say. In the anthology of poems called *Gosenshū*, there is this verse:

"Toshi fureba[17]	"With these passing years,
waga kurokami mo	my raven hair's also turned
Shirakawa no	this White River made

mitsuwagumu[18] made oinikeru kana" to	me stoop and draw its water till I grew
yomishi mo warawa ga uta nari. Mu-	so old and bent." Thus it reads. It is my
kashi Chikuzen no Dazaifu[19] ni iori ni	poem. Once long ago, at Dazaifu in Chi-
higaki shitsuraite sumishi shirabyōshi[20]	kuzen, a dancing girl lived in a cottage
nochi ni wa otoroete kono Shirakawa no	with a fence made of a cypress hedge.
hotori ni sumishi nari.	Afterwards, as she grew old, she came
	to live in the vicinity of this White River.

WAKI

Geni saru koto o	Yes, of course, I have been told
kikishi nari.	such a tale as this;
Sono Shirakawa no	and there by that White River
iori no atari o	where once stood the thatched cottage,
Fujiwara no Okinori[21]	Lord Fujiwara Okinori
tōrishi toki	passed by on his journey.

SHITE

mizu ya aru to kowase	"May I have some water at this place?"
tamaishi hodo ni	he requested graciously.
sono mizu kumite	"I will draw fresh water up,
mairasuru tote	for my lord and bear it back,

WAKI

mizu wa kumu to wa	I stoop and draw the water,"

SHITE

yomishi nari.	thus I wrote a verse.

[*During the following* ageuta *passage sung by the chorus, the* kyōgen *enters quietly through the half-lifted Nō curtain and silently takes his* kyōgen *seat.*]

CHORUS

(Ageuta: au, yowagin)

Somo mizu wa kumu to	Stooping down to draw the water
mōsu wa,	just as I've said,
somo mizu wa kumu to	stooping down to draw the water
mōsu wa	just as I've said,
tada Shirakawa no	it was not only water
mizu ni wa nashi.	drawn from this White River
Oite	but also

[*The* shite *faces the* waki.]

311

Higaki

kagameru	this bent figure,
sugata o ba	grown so old and stooped,
mitsuwagumu to	bent from stooping downward,
mōsu nari.	so I should have sung.
Sono shirushi o mo	When you witness graciously
mitamawaba	now its very proof,

[*Facing stage front, the* shite, *holding the cane in her hand, rises.*]

| kano Shirakawa no | here about the neighborhood |
| hotori nite | of this White River, |

[*The* shite *faces the* waki.]

waga ato toite	for my memory, she says,
tabitamae to	please recite some prayers,
yūmagure²² shite	and mixing with the twilight

[*The* shite *goes backward several steps toward the front of the stick-drum player, and, throwing the cane away, she lowers her mask and vanishes into the prop, as the chorus finishes the rest of the lines.*]

usenikeri,	she vanishes away,
yūmagure shite	and mixing with the twilight
usenikeri.	she vanishes away.

Nakairi (Interlude)

[*The* kyōgen, *wearing a striped, less-formal heavy silk kimono* (dan noshime), *the long* kyōgen *two-piece* (naga kamishimo), *a waistband* (koshiobi), *a fan* (ōgi), *and a short sword* (chiisa gatana), *rises from his* kyōgen *seat, goes near the* shite *pillar, and intones the following prose.*]

KYŌGEN

[4] *(Mondai: katari)*

Kayō ni sōrō mono wa kono atari ni sumai suru mono nite sōrō. Makoto ni Iwado no Kanzeon wa reigen arata ni goza sōrō aida, tsune ni ayumi o hakobu koto nite sōrō. Mata kono Iwado ni tōtoki o-sō no on-iri sōrō aida, butsuzen ni mairu tabigoto ni tachiyori sōrō. Kyō mo mairabaya to zonzuru. Kono aida wa okotari mōshi sōrō.

I am a person living in this neighborhood. Truly the Goddess of Mercy at Rock Door is miraculous. So I always come here on foot; besides, a virtuous Buddhist priest is staying at Rock Door. Each time I come before the Buddhist altar, I call on him. Today, I think, I will go there too. [*Goes out toward center stage; facing the* waki, *he sits down.*] I failed to come here the other day.

WAKI

Nani tote okotararete sōrō zo.

Why did you fail to do so?

KYŌGEN

Mottomo mainichi mairitaku sōraedomo kanawanu yō no koto nite okotari mōshi sōrō.

I had wanted to come, in fact, every day, but I had some unavoidable business to do; so I failed to come here.

Geni geni mottomo nite sōrō. Sate katagata ni tazunetaki koto no sōrō. Omoi
mo yoranu mōshigoto nite sōraedomo,
Furu Shirakawa no hotori ni sumishi Higaki no Onna no koto ni wa samazama
shisai arubeshi. Go-zonji ni oite wa katatte on-kikase sōrae.

That is, indeed, reasonable enough.
Well, I have something to ask you. Indeed, this is something you may not expect from me. Regarding the Woman of
the Cypress Hedge, who lived near that
Old White River, there must be many
stories. Please tell me if you know about
them.

Kore wa omoi mo yoranu koto o uketamawari sōrō mono kana. Warera mo
kono atari ni sumai tsukamatsuri sōraedomo, sayō no koto kuwashiku zonzezu sōrō ga, ōyoso uketamawarioyobitaru tōri on-monogatari mōsōzuru
nite sōrō.

How strange that you should ask me
about such things. Though we live in
this neighborhood, I don't know too
much about the details. However, I
shall tell the story the way I've heard it.

Chikagoro nite sōrō.

I would be most grateful.

Saru hodo ni Chikuzen no Kuni Dazaifu
ni shirabyōshi no goza sōrō o, Higaki no
Onna to mōsu shisai wa kano mono higaki o konomite iori ni higaki o shitsurai
sumitaru ni yori Higaki no Onna to mōshi sōrō. Sono nochi toshi yorite Shirakawa no hotori ni sumai tsukamatsuri
sōrō ga koko nite mo iori ni higaki o
shitsurai sumitaru to mōsu. Mata sono
koro Fujiwara no Okinori to mōshitaru
on-kata kono atari o tōritamaishi toki
kano higaki no shitsuraitaru iori nite
mizu o koitamaeba, rōjo idete mizu o
musubite mairase sōrō. Sono toki rōjo
no uta ni

Well, there was a dancing girl at Dazaifu
in the province of Chikuzen. The reason
she was called the Woman of the Cypress Hedge is that she liked cypress
trees, and she lived in her hut fenced all
around with a cypress hedge. Later on,
when she got old, she came to live near
this White River. Here too she fenced
her hut all around with a cypress hedge,
I hear. About this time, when Fujiwara
no Okinori passed this neighborhood,
he begged for water at the hut with the
cypress hedge. The old woman came
out, and, drawing some water, she presented it to him. The old woman's verse
at that time was as follows:

313

Toshi fureba
waga kurogami mo
Shirakawa no
mitsuwagumu made
oinikeru kana

With these passing years,
my raven hair's also turned
this White River made
me stoop and draw its water
till I grew so old and bent.

to, kayō ni yomi tamaitaru to mōsu. Sōjite saizen mōsu gotoku kuwashiki koto

Thus she composed the verse, I hear.
Generally speaking, as I said before, I

Higaki

wa zonzezu sōraedomo, mazu warera no uketamawari oyobitaru wa kaku no gotoku nite goza sōrō ga, nani to oboshimeshi on-tazune nasare sōrō zo. Chikagoro fushin ni zonji sōrō.

don't know too much about the details. Well, this is what I have heard. Please tell me why you ask me about this. Lately, I have felt something strange around here.

WAKI

Nengoro ni on-monogatari sōrō mono kana. Tazunemōsu mo yo no gi ni arazu. Kono hodo izuku to mo naku rōjo hitori mainichi aka no mizu o mochite mairare sōrō. Sunawachi kyō mo mairare sōrō hodo ni ikanaru hito zo to tazunete sōraeba Higaki no Onna no koto o mi no ue no yō ni mōsare. Gosenshū no uta nado o eiji Shirakawa no hotori nite ato toite tabe to ii mo aezu sono mama sugata o miushinōte sōrō yo.

How kind of you to tell me all about the story in detail. The reason why I asked is not special. Some time ago an old woman came to this place from somewhere every day for water, and today she came here too; so when I asked her who she was, she spoke about the Woman of the Cypress Hedge as if it were she. Among other things, she recited a verse from the *Gosenshū*. Then near this White River, no sooner than she said, "pray for my memory," I lost sight of her.

KYŌGEN

Kore wa kidoku naru koto o uketamawari sōrō mono kana. Sate wa Higaki no yūrei arawareide, on-kotoba o kawasaretaru to zonji sōrō ga, kano mono wa shirabyōshi nareba iyoiyo tsumi mo fukaku arubeki to zonji sōrō aida, arigataki o-kyō o mo on-dokuju arite, kano onna no ato o on-tomurai arekashi to zonji sōrō.

It's the strangest story I've ever heard! Well, the ghost of the Cypress Woman must have appeared and exchanged words with you. As she has been a dancing girl, her sins were very deep, I think; so you should recite the holy Buddhist sutra and hold a service for her memory.

WAKI

Chikagoro fushigi naru koto nite sōrō hodo ni, Shirakawa no atari e tachikoe rōjo no ato o nengoro ni tomurai mōsōzuru nite sōrō.

Since this is a very strange thing of late, I will go over to the neighborhood of that White River and hold a service for the memory of the old woman.

314

KYŌGEN

Warera mo on-ato yori mairi mōshi sōrōbeshi.

I will come later too and follow you, holy priest.

WAKI

Katagata mo ato yori on-ide sōrae.

Please come later then.

Kokoroe mōshite sōrō.　　　　　　　Yes, good priest.

[*The* kyōgen *returns to his* kyōgen *seat. Later, through the half-lifted Nō curtain, he makes his exit after the* nochi-jite *enters the stage.*]

WAKI

[5]　(*Awazu, kotoba*)

Sate wa inishie no Higaki no Onna kari ni araware ware ni kotoba o kawashikeru zo ya. Hitotsu wa masse no kidoku zo to omoinagara mo tazune yukeba.

Surely now, that must have been the Woman of the Cypress Hedge from the olden days who appeared before me for a time and exchanged those words with me. Wondering if this might be a rare, miraculous event, to be told to future generations, I go searching out my way.

[*The* waki *sings the following* ageuta, *called* machiutai, *"waiting song."*]

WAKI

(*Machiutai: au, yowagin*)

Fushigi ya hayaku　　How strange this is! How swiftly
hi mo kurete,　　　　day turns into night!

[*The* waki *rises and shows by his gesture that he is walking on his way.*]

fushigi ya hayaku　　How strange this is! How swiftly
hi mo kurete　　　　day turns into night,
kawagiri fukaku　　　as the heavy river mists
tachikomoru　　　　arise and cover
kage ni iori no　　　deep across the gloom a light
tomoshibi no　　　　flickers from a hut,

[*The* waki *goes out slightly toward the prop and sits down.*]

honoka ni miyuru　　and it dimly gleams,
fushigisa yo,　　　　so mysteriously,
honoka ni miyuru　　and it dimly gleams,
fushigisa yo.　　　　so mysteriously.

[*The lonely-sounding* hayashi *music begins, suggesting the entrance of the* nochi-jite. *She sits inside the prop. She takes off the "Cathay fabric," a brocade outer kimono (*karaori*). She wears a "long silk," loose unlined broad-sleeved robe (*shiro chōken*) and a light blue broad divided skirt (*asagi ōguchi*). Without showing herself, still inside the prop, she sings as if whispering.*]

315

SHITE

[6]　(*Awazu, yowagin*)

Ara arigata no　　How truly grateful I feel
tomurai ya na,　　for the holy prayers!

Higaki

ara arigata no	How truly grateful I feel
tomurai ya na.	for the holy prayers!

[*The* shite *sings the following* sashi *passage in free-rhythm* yowagin *style.*]

SHITE

(*Sashi: awazu, yowagin*)

Kaze ryokuya ni	Across the verdant fields
osamatte	quiet grows the wind;
enjō naoshi.	straight the willow branches droop,
Kumo gantō ni	while above the craggy crest
sadamatte	the clouds rest calmly
gekkei matoka nari.	and the moon shines in its perfect sphere.

[*The* shite *continues to sing the high-pitched* kuri *passage.*]

(*Kuri: awazu, yowagin*)

Ashita ni[23]	As morning comes
kōgan atte,	rosy hued our faces glow
seiro ni	and worldly ways
tanoshimu to	are all our pleasure,
iedomo,	so men would say,

CHORUS

yūbe ni wa	but as evening falls
hakkotsu to natte	turning into whitened skeletons
kōgen ni kuchinu.	all decay across the prairie.

SHITE

Ui no arisama	Vicissitudes of seeming!

CHORUS

mujō no makoto	Eternal truth of changes!

SHITE

tare ka shōji no	Who cannot but ponder on
kotowari o	the very reason
ronzezaru.	all that lives must die?

316

(*Au, yowagin*)

CHORUS

Itsu o kagiru	What sets the limit
narai zo ya.	for man's span of life?
Rōshō to ippa	Neither our age nor youth, they say,

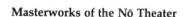

funbetsu nashi.	matters for this question.
Kawaru o motte	When the changeful moment comes,
go to seri.	then is the time.
Tare ka hitsumetsu o	Should not each man be well prepared
go sezaran,	for his final hour?
tare ka wa kore o	Should not each man be ready
go sezaran.	for his final hour?

[*The following passages between the* waki *and the* shite *are called* kakeai.]

WAKI

[7] (*Kakeai: awazu, yowagin*)

Fushigi ya na	Strange! How strange it is!
koe o kikeba	I listen to the voice
aritsuru hito nari.	of the one I've just encountered.
Onajiku wa	So, if possible,
sugata o arawashi	reveal the figure of yourself
tamōbeshi,	graciously to me
onnato toite	that I may say a prayer
mairasen.	for your soul's repose.

[*Still inside the prop, the* shite *sings.*]

SHITE

Saraba sugata o	In a form as once I was,
arawashite	now I should reveal
o-sō no mi-nori o	myself and have the prayer
ukubeki nari.	you recite, oh, priest,
Hito ni wa arawashi	but do not relate this matter
tamaiso to yo.	to the other people.

WAKI

Nakanaka ni	Yes, of course, indeed.
hito ni arawasu	This is not a matter fit
koto arumaji.	to relate to others.
Haya haya sugata o	Come now, come. This is the moment
mietamae.	to reveal yourself.

[*As the* shite *starts to sing the following passage, the cover of the prop is quietly taken away, revealing the aged woman sitting on a stool.*]

SHITE

317

Namidagumori no	So beclouded now with tears
kaobase wa	is her countenance
sore to mo mienu	that one cannot clearly tell
otoroe o	who this old one is,
tare Shirakawa[24] no	bending to scoop the water
mitsuwagumu	of this White River,

Higaki

oi no sugata zo   bent so low, she feels ashamed
hazukashiki.   of her age-old form.

[*The* shite, *sitting on the stool inside the prop, lowers her face.*]

WAKI

Ara itawashi no   Oh, how deeply pitiful,

[*The* shite, *facing the* waki, *folds her hands in prayer.*]

onnarisama ya na.   indeed, is your own appearance!
Ima mo shūshin no   Even now you scoop the water
mizu o kumi   of attachment still
rinne no sugata   as I can see the figure
mietamō zo ya,   of the turning Wheel of Fate.

[*Unfolding her hands in prayer.*]

haya haya   Quickly, quickly
ukami tamae.   may you rise above it.

[*Facing stage front, the* shite *intones the following prose passage.*]

SHITE

Ware inishie wa bujo no homare yo ni   Once, long, long ago I reveled in my
sugure, sono tsumi fukaki yue ni yori   fame as a dancer praised by all through-
ima mo kurushimi o Mitsusegawa²⁵ ni   out the world. So deep were the sins I
nettetsu no oke o ninai myōka no tsu-   sinned, even now my suffering multi-
rube o sagete kono mizu o kumu.   plies by the Three-Ford Rapids, where I
                                         shoulder the red-hot iron pail. Holding
                                         the bucket of fire I draw this water up,

Sono mizu yu to natte   then the water turns boiling hot,
waga mi o yaku koto   burning all my scalded body
hima mo nakeredomo   without cease, ever without rest,

[*The* shite *turns her face toward the* waki.]

kono hodo wa o-sō no chigū ni hikarete   but for the little while I met with you, I
tsurube wa aredomo myōka wa nashi.   was reprieved. And though there yet re-
                                          mains the well bucket, I see the flaming
                                          fire no more.

WAKI

Saraba inga no   If it's so, by drawing up
mizu o kumi   karma-water then
sono shūshin o   deep delusions in your heart
furisutete,   you must cast away
tokutoku ukami   quickly quickly may you rise
tamōbeshi.   from your lot, I pray.

[*The* shite *looks at the water at stage front.*]

Ideide saraba o-sō no tame, kono kake-
mizu o kumi-hosaba

So, here and now, oh, priest, if I should
draw water by the well rope for you until it runs dry,

tsumi mo ya asaku
narubeki to

shallow then the sinful depth
of my life becomes,

WAKI

omoi mo fukaki[26]
sayo-goromo no
tamoto no tsuyu no[27]
tamadasuki

though my longing thoughts are deep
as this night I brace
a cord across my shoulder
for my sleeves bedewed,

SHITE

kage Shirakawa no[28]
tsuki no yo ni

this White River glistens bright
in the moonlit night;

WAKI

soko sumu mizu o   let me draw some water clear

SHITE

iza kuman.   to the riverbed.

[*The* shite *comes out from the prop onto the stage. The* waki *returns to the* waki *seat and sits down as the chorus sings the following* shidai *verse.*]

CHORUS

(*Shidai: au, yowagin*)

Tsurube no mizu ni
kage ochite
tamoto o tsuki ya
noboruran.

On the water in the pail
reflected brightly,
Oh, the moon appears to climb
up along my sleeve.

[*The chorus sings the high-pitched* kuri *passage in free-rhythm* yowagin *style.*]

[8] (*Kuri: awazu, yowagin*)

Sore zansei no
kanae ni wa
hokkei no
mizu o kumi
goya no ro ni wa
nanrei no
shiba o taku.

By the lingering stars at dawn
I draw some water
from the Northern Gorge
for the three-legged pot;
and at the midnight hearth
I burn the brushwood
from the Southern Peak.

319

[*The* shite *sings the* sashi *passage.*]

Higaki

(Sashi: awazu, yowagin)

Sore kōri wa[29]	Men say that ice is made
mizu yori idete	from water, but colder still
mizu yori mo samuku	than water is its icy chill;

CHORUS

aoki koto	as the blue dye comes
ai yori idete	from indigo, but deeper
ai yori fukashi.	than indigo are its blues.
Moto no uki mi no	So my past of wretched sins
mukui naraba	has justly come to this,
ima no kurushimi	and my present agony
sari mo sede,	leaves me not; instead,

SHITE

iya masarinuru	the color of my yearnings
omoi no iro	deepens more than ever

[*The* shite *holds back her tears.*]

CHORUS

kurenai no[30] namida ni	as now my teardrops in crimson hue
mi o kogasu.	set my flesh aflame.

[*The* shite *puts the fan away by inserting it into her bosom; then she goes out toward stage front and makes the appropriate dancelike movement, as the chorus sings the* kuse *passage.*]

CHORUS

(Kuse: au, yowagin)

Tsurube no	The well rope brings
kakenawa	the bucket up
kurikaeshi uki	time and time again it brings
inishie mo	back my wretched past:

[*The* shite *stops the* maiguse *movement, making a gesture as though pulling the long well-rope as she looks into the well.*]

kōka no	crimson blossoms
haru no ashita	in the bright spring morning,
kōyō no aki no	red and golden leaves at autumn
yūgure mo	in the evening
ichijitsu no yume to	already became a dream too,
haya narinu.	lasting but a day!

[*The* shite *goes out to the eye-fixing pillar and, making a big turn to her left, goes to the front of the musicians.*]

Kōgan no	Fair and rosy cheeked,
yosooi	bright in costumes,
bujo no homare mo	as a dancer highly praised
ito semete	at the least is she;
samo utsukushiki	so superbly beautiful,
kōgan no	fair and rosy cheeked
hisui no kazura [31]	with the long kingfisher's wig,
hana shiore	but as flowers wilt

[From the front of the musicians, the shite *goes out slightly toward stage front.]*

katsura no mayu mo	so her crescent eyebrows too
shimo furite	whiten with the frost;

[Bending her body, the shite *looks at her reflection in the water.]*

mizu ni utsuru	on the water mirror
omokage	old and feeble
rōsui kage	is her form reflected,
shizunde	sunken deeply,
midori ni mieshi	and her hair that once appeared

[Lifting up her fan, the shite *points it toward her head.]*

kurogami wa	flowing raven-black
dosui no mokuzu	looks like the weeds and rubbish

[The shite *raises her face up.]*

chiri akuta	in the muddy pool.
kawarikeru	Altered, indeed, are

[The shite *retreats to center stage, holding back her tears.]*

mi no arisama zo	all her old appearances
kanashiki.	sorrowfully.
Geni ya	Ah, indeed,

[The shite, *making a turn to her right, goes to the front of the musicians; then she goes out to stage center, makes a* sayū *gesture, and opens her fan as the chorus sings the rest.]*

arishi yo o	when I think again
omoi izureba	of the world that once was mine,
natsukashi ya,	how I yearn for it
sono Shirakawa no	over these White River waves
nami kakeshi	brightly ripple-blessed,

[The shite *makes an* ageōgi *gesture as she sings the following couplet.]*

SHITE

Fujiwara no	Lord Okinori
Okinori no	of Wisteria Field

[Making an ōzayū *gesture, the* shite *goes out toward stage front as the chorus starts to sing.]*

❁

321

Higaki

sono inishie no	summons forth the dancing girl
shirabyōshi	in the days long past,
ima hitofushi to	saying graciously, "Dance now
arishikaba	to an ancient tune,"
mukashi no	but her sleeves that bloomed

[*At stage front, the* shite *turns her left sleeve and gazes at it.*]

hana no sode	brightly long ago
imasara iro mo	are faded like the color
asagoromo	of this hempen robe,

[*The* shite *steps back to center stage.*]

mijikaki sode o	with her sleeves so short she can
kaeshienu	hardly turn them 'round.

[*The* shite *goes out to the eye-fixing pillar, lifts up the fan, and, making a turn to her left, goes to the front of the musicians.*]

kokoro zo tsuraki	So her heart is grieved, for as
Michinoku no	Kefu's narrow goods
Kefu [32] no hoso nuno	from the distant Eastern Land
mune awazu	meet not at the breast,
nani to ka	try as she may,
shirabyōshi	what remains with her

[*Making a* sayū *gesture in front of the musicians, the* shite *lowers her face.*]

sono omokage no	of the vestige of the girl
arubeki.	as once she danced?

[*Regaining her poise, the* shite *raises her face, as the chorus continues to sing the following passage.*]

CHORUS

[9] (*Iguse: au, yowagin*)

Yoshi yoshi	Do not mind it.
sore tote mo	What does it matter?
mukashi tenareshi	As you danced in days long past

[*The* shite *makes a* sayū *gesture.*]

mai nareba	with such artless ease,
mawademo ima wa	can you bear to leave this now
kanōmaji to	within yourself undanced?

[*The* shite *makes a* hiraki *gesture as she sings.*]

SHITE

Okinori	Okinori
shikiri ni	ever urged me,
notamaeba	ever ardently.

[*The* shite *looks at her left sleeve.*]

Masterworks of the Nō Theater

CHORUS

asamashinagara	Hampered by my misery
asa no sode	in these hempen sleeves,
tsuyu uchiharai	brushing drops of dew away,

[*The* shite *stamps the floor.*]

maiidasu	I begin the dance

[*The* shite *sits down at the* shite *pillar.*]

SHITE

(*Ei: awazu, yowagin*)

Higaki no Onna no	of the Maid of the Cypress Hedge

CHORUS

mi no hate o.	and her fateful end.

[*First, the* shite *takes the formal steps and movements in unison with the introductory hand-drum music. Then, following the* hayashi *music, she dances the* jo no mai, *which is now often performed in three movements.*]

Jo no mai

[*After the* jo no mai, *making an* ageōgi *gesture at the* shite *seat, the* shite *sings the following verse, called* waka.]

SHITE

(*Waka: yowagin*)

Mizu musubu	To draw the water
tsurube no nawa no	up I raise the bucket rope
tsurube no nawa no	up I raise the bucket rope
kurikaeshi	time and time again,

[*The* shite *makes a* sayū *and other gestures, while the chorus sings the following passage in* ōnori *style.*]

CHORUS

(*Ōnori*)

mukashi ni kaere	turning back to days long gone
Shirakawa no nami,	over these White River waves,
Shirakawa no nami,	over these White River waves,
Shirakawa no	on this White River

323

SHITE

[10] (*Awazu, yowagin*)

mizu no aware[33] o	I know full well the sorrow
shiru yue ni	of foam on water;

Higaki

[*The* shite *makes a* tsumeashi *gesture toward the* waki.]

kore made araware so at this place I now appear

[*The* shite *sings the last line in strict-rhythm* yowagin *style.*]

(*Au, yowagin*)

idetaru nari. as I come for water.

[*The chorus sings the following concluding passage in strict-rhythm* yowagin *style.*]

CHORUS

(*Uta: au, yowagin*)

Hakobu	To bring it
ashitazu[34] no	here the cries of cranes

[*Holding the fan horizontally like a plate with both hands, the* shite *goes out to center stage and, kneeling, gazes at the* waki.]

ne[35] o koso tayure	drift away like duckweed roots
ukikusa no	cut off from water
mizu wa hakobite	some I draw and bring here now
mairasuru	as I come to you.

[*The* shite *rises and, stepping back a little, holds both hands in prayer and pleads; then, facing to her right, she stamps the floor.*]

tsumi o ukamete	With your prayers I ask
tabi tamae,	save me from my sins,
tsumi o ukamete	with your prayers I ask
tabi tamae.	save me from my sins.

Masterworks of the Nō Theater

Obasute

Introduction

Obasute is a wig-play belonging to Group III of Nō plays. As are *Higaki* and *Sekidera Komachi*, it is one of "the three old-woman plays," so named because the *shite* in each one of them is an aged woman. In the entire Nō repertoire, this piece is considered as the loftiest and most profound play, reserved for the well-seasoned Nō masters. Consequently it is performed very rarely, as evidenced by Setchō's remark in his *Collected Nō Reviews*: "Since Umewaka Manzaburō [1868–1947] performed *Obasute* in 1914, this is the first time Kanze Sakon (1895–1939) presented this 'secret' piece, which was performed on the second day of the Nō program for the Kanze memorial service in 1927. So I expected it would be a great pleasure for me."[1]

The original source (*honsetsu*) is important in Nō composition, according to Zeami.[2] The oldest text providing a source for this play is poem #878 in the *Kokinshū*, compiled in 905 by Ki no Tsurayuki (868?–945?), with a headnote as follows:

> Theme unknown, author unknown
>
> For this heart of mine
> there's hardly any comfort
> at Sarashina
> on Obasute Mountain
> gazing at the glowing moon.

According to the tenth-century poem-tale collection called *Yamato monogatari*,[3] this anonymous poem is by a man who is urged again and again by his young wife to desert his aged, loving aunt deep in the mountains. The story in *Konjaku monogatari*[4] is similarly treated, with minor differences, but there the poem is also by a man. In contrast to these versions, an abandoned old aunt composed the poem as she gazed at the moon throughout the night from the top of the mountain, according to *Toshiyori Kudenshū*,[5] or *Mumyōshō*, by Minamoto no Toshiyori (1055–1129), the noted poet-critic. "The playwright consults the latter," according to Sanari,[6] while Gondō Yoshikazu mentions the former two tales as the sources for this play.[7] At any rate, this piece creates a unique, in-depth dimension, so characteristic of this theater.

Following the *shidai* music, the *waki*, accompanied by his companions, appears and sings the following verse, also called *shidai*:

> With the harvest moon how near
> has this autumn come!
> with the harvest moon how near
> has this autumn come!
> On Obasute Mountain
> let's pay our call.

The moon appears in many Nō plays—for example, in *Tōru* and *Matsukaze*—but no moon has ever graced a piece with the splendor of the moonlight in this play. Furthermore, it returns and reappears throughout the play as a binding image that unifies the work into a glorious whole.

Unlike the usual traveling Buddhist priest, the *waki* and his companions are city folk who come "deliberately" to see the famous Sarashina moon. As the *waki* intones the "arrival passage" (*tsukizerifu*) with a feeling of satisfaction tinged with a sense of great expectation, the *shite* appears as a village woman, calling out (*yobikake*) to the *waki*. She responds to the *waki*'s questions as she stands at the second pine, and she also tells him where the deserted crone, who sang the poem from the *Kokinshū* cited above, is buried deep in the earth, adding, "yet her heart-attachment seems / lingering behind." She then enters the stage after the *ageuta*, which the chorus sings in her behalf: "More than ever now. . . ." Here again the *Kokinshū* verse appears—"as the evening falls"—and echoes deeply, like a theme song, "from the lonely mountain peak / desolate in view." Thus the chorus concludes this section of the play.

When the *shite* learns from the *waki* that he is from the distant capital, she promises him and his companions that she will come out with the rising moon to sing and dance for their pleasure throughout this long night, illuminated in all the splendor of the moonlight. The chorus sings for the *shite*:

> all deserted too
> in this mountain depth
> still alone I live
> purely shines the harvest moon
> on its round above
> in each autumn as it clears
> dark attachments still
> I have come before you here
> in this eve, she says. . . .

Suddenly she disappears, hinting that it is she herself who is the deserted crone in disguise.

During the Interlude, the *kyōgen*, a local person, tells the legend of the deserted crone in detail. This scene is unique in that unlike the usual Interlude, which generally repeats what has taken place in the first part of the play, it provides a distant backdrop against which the story will unfold, with a deeper dimension, as the play develops in the second part.

Part II of the play opens as the *waki* and his companions sing the "waiting song," praising the splendid rising moon. Following the *issei* music, the *nochi-jite*, robed in silver white, appears and enters the stage as if she were the spirit of the moonlight itself. She celebrates the moon, and, during the ensuing dialogue, she reveals her identity. She also says to the *waki* how wonderful, like a dream, this moon-blessed fellowship is, and starts dancing to the lyrics in the *kuri*, *sashi*, and finally in the *kuse* passages, where she tells the story related to the moon, in praise of both Daiseishi and Lord Amida. This *kuse* is accompanied by the dance, to which Setchō responded in the following words: "The way the *shite* carried her feet, and the fan she opened and closed, were full of deep significance. Among the *kata* the most beautiful, I thought, was the fan she lifted up as if to cover her head when the chorus sang the following line in the *kuse* passage: 'full the moon at times.'"[8] This "ear-opening" section culminates in the *jo no mai* dance.

It is worthy to note here that among the three old-woman pieces, this is the only play in which the *jo no mai* dance is accentuated by the stick drum (*taiko*). This feature suggests that the *shite* is likened almost to the spirit of the radiant moonlight. The reason for this is that there is no hatred left in her, nor does she come to ask that some holy prayers be said in her memory. Lured by ". . . the harvest moon / on its round above / in each autumn . . . ," she makes her appearance for the Dance of Butterflies. Indeed, the *jo no mai* symbolizes her votive state of mind, full of hope and in high spirits, which the *taiko* brings out. Yet after the dance she sings the lines called *waka*, and here once again the *Kokinshū* poem returns as the theme song, for she is still earthbound: "for this heart of mine. . . ." And there soon follows the heightened exchange (*kakeri*) in lyric lines between the *shite* and the chorus:

SHITE:	fluttering in play
	with the dancing sleeves,
CHORUS:	turning, turning back once more
SHITE:	to the autumn of the past
CHORUS:	I return as I recall
	the deep delusion in my heart
	where I have no place to turn
	tonight before the autumn wind. . . .

The chorus continues in her behalf: "with light already / whitening at dawn. . . ." Now the travelers are gone, "leaving here behind, so alone / this ancient woman / all abandoned / as in those days of long ago." She becomes larger than her individual life, like Obasute Mountain itself, as the play comes to a close.

This closing, contrary to the usual ending of the wig-plays, where the *shite* vanishes across the bridge while the *waki* remains on the stage, is indeed most daring and "suitable for this masterpiece entitled *Obasute*," says Gondō.[9] "Truly," Sanari comments, this is "'frozen Nō,' a play which lies perhaps closest to the highest reach of Zeami's *yūgen*."[10]

Obasute

OBASUTE

By Zeami

Persons: WAKI: *Man from the capital*
WAKI-TSURE: *Companions (two)*
SHITE (PART I): *Ghost of the old woman (appears as a village woman)*
NOCHI-JITE (PART II): *Ghost of the old woman (appears as herself)*
KYŌGEN: *One of the mountain folk*

Classification: *Primary, Group III*
Place: *Mt. Obasute in the land of Shinano*
Time: *The fifteenth night of September*
Kogaki: 2

PART I

[*Following the* shidai *music, the* waki, *accompanied by two companions, enters the stage. The* waki *wears a striped, less-formal heavy silk kimono* (dan noshime), *an unlined hempen two-piece over robe* (suō kamishimo), *a waistband* (koshiobi), *a fan* (ōgi), *a short sword* (chiisa gatana), *and a hat* (kasa). *The* waki-tsure *are similarly dressed, except the* kitsuke *is a plain one* (muji noshime). *They face one another and sing the* shidai *verse.*]

WAKI AND WAKI-TSURE

[1] (*Shidai: au, yowagin*)

Tsuki no na chikaki	With the harvest moon[11] how near
aki nare ya,	has this autumn come!
tsuki no na chikaki	With the harvest moon how near
aki nare ya,	has this autumn come!
Obasuteyama[12] o	On Obasute Mountain
tazunen.	let's pay our call.

[*The chorus sings the* jidori, *repeating the above verse, except the third and fourth lines, in a lower key.*]

328

CHORUS

(*Jidori: au, yowagin*)

Tsuki no na chikaki	With the harvest moon how near
aki nare ya,	has this autumn come!
Obasuteyama o	On Obasute Mountain
tazunen.	let's pay our call.

[*Following the* jidori, *the* waki *takes off his bamboo hat, and, facing stage front, he intones the following prose passage, called* nanori, *introducing himself to the audience.*]

WAKI

(Nanori: awazu, yowagin)

Kayō ni sōrō mono wa Miyakogata ni sumaitsukamatsuru mono nite sōrō. Ware imada Sarashina no tsuki[13] o mizu sōrō hodo ni, kono aki omoitachi Obasuteyama e to isogi sōrō.

I am one who lives at the capital. Since I have not yet seen the moon at Sarashina, I have decided to do so this autumn. So I will hurry toward the Mountain of the Abandoned Crone, Obasute Mountain.

[*The* waki *puts on the bamboo hat again and he and the* waki-tsure *face one another. Then they sing the following passage, called* michiyuki, *"travel song."*]

WAKI AND WAKI-TSURE

(Michiyuki: au, yowagin)

Kono hodo no	Now for some few days,
shibashi tabii no	sheltering as travelers must
karimakura,	on makeshift pillows,
shibashi tabii no	sheltering as travelers must
karimakura,	on makeshift pillows,
mata tachiizuru	once again we rise and go;
nakayado no	at the halfway inn
akashi kurashite	we pass the night and journey
yuku hodo ni	on our way ahead
koko zo na ni ou	to the place so widely known

[*The* waki *faces stage front, steps forward, and returns to his former position, indicating that they have traveled and arrived at their destination; again facing one another, they finish the rest of the lines.*]

Sarashina ya,	in Sarashina,
Obasuteyama ni	here Obasute Mountain,
tsukinikeri,	now we reach at last,
Obasuteyama ni	here Obasute Mountain,
tsukinikeri.	now we reach at last.

[*After the* michiyuki, *the* waki *takes off the bamboo hat and faces stage front.*]

WAKI

(Tsukizerifu: kotoba)

Isogi sōrō hodo ni, kore wa haya Obasuteyama ni tsukite sōrō.

As we have traveled so fast, here we are already at Obasute Mountain.

WAKI-TSURE

Mottomo nite sōrō.

Yes, indeed. You are right.

329

Obasute

[*The* waki-tsure *go toward the* waki *seat and sit down next to it, while the* waki *goes out to the center of the stage.*]

WAKI

(*Awazu, kotoba*)

Sate mo ware Obasuteyama ni kite mireba, mine tairaka ni shite banri no sora mo hedate naku senri ni kuma naki tsuki no yo sa koso to omoiyararete sōrō. Ikasama kono tokoro ni yasurai koyoi no tsuki o nagameba ya to omoi sōrō.

Now that I am here at Obasute Mountain and I look about me, I can see that the mountain crest is level. The sky spreads for ten thousand miles, without any barriers, and across a thousand boundless miles in the moonlit night. All is just as I thought it would be. Well, let us rest at this place and tonight, I think, we will be able to view the moon.

[*As the* waki *is on the way toward the* waki *seat, the* shite, *wearing a* fukai *mask, a wig* (kazura), *a wig band* (kazuraobi), *a collar in white* (eri shiro), *an under kimono with painted gold or silver patterns* (surihaku), *a "Cathay fabric" brocade outer kimono without red* (ironashi karaori), *and a fan* (ōgi), *comes out from behind the* Nō *curtain and calls out to the* waki. *This is known as* yobikake.]

SHITE

[2] (*Yobikake: awazu, yowagin*)

Nō nō are naru tabibito wa nanigoto o ōse sōrō zo.

Ho, there. [*Drawn out.*] You travelers! What did you say to me?

WAKI [*Rising from his seat.*]

San zōrō. Kore wa Miyako no mono nite sōrō ga, hajimete kono tokoro ni kitarite sōrō. Sate sate on-mi wa izuku ni sumu hito zo.

Why, yes. We are from Miyako, and this is the first time we have come to this place. Well, now, tell me, where do you live?

SHITE

Kore wa kono Sarashina no sato ni sumu mono nite sōrō. Kyō wa na ni ou aki no nakaba,[14] kururu o isogu tsuki no na no koto ni terisou ama no hara kumanaki yomo no keshiki kana. Ikani koyoi no tsuki no omoshirokaranzuran.

I am a person living in the village of Sarashina. This night is well known as the midpoint of autumn. The famous full moon brings on the nightfall quickly. It will make the vast night skies especially bright, reaching everywhere. How truly wonderful the moon will be tonight!

WAKI

Sate wa Sarashina no hito nite mashimasu ka ya. Sate sate inishie Obasute no zaisho wa izuku no hodo nite sōrō zo.

So, then, you are a person of Sarashina. Well, now, can you tell us about the village where the old woman was abandoned long, long ago?

Masterworks of the Nō Theater

[*During the* waki*'s inquiry above, the* shite *enters the stage and stands at the* shite *seat.*]

SHITE

Obasuteyama no naki ato to towase-tamō wa kokoroenu.

How unfeeling you are to ask about the remains of the woman who was abandoned on Obasute Mountain.

Waga kokoro[15]
nagusamekanetsu
Sarashina ya

"For this heart of mine
there's hardly any comfort
at Sarashina

Obasuteyama ni teru tsuki o mite to ei-zeshi hito no ato naraba kore ni koda-kaki katsura no ki[16] no kage koso mu-kashi no obasute no sono naki ato nite sōrae to yo.

on Obasute Mountain, gazing at the glowing moon." If you wish to know about the remains of the one who wrote that verse, she is over here, in the shade of this slightly high laurel tree. It was truly here, in the old days, that she was abandoned.

WAKI

Sate-wa kono ki no
kage ni shite
sute okarenishi
hito no ato no

Then beneath the shade
of this very tree,
here alone her last remains
have been long abandoned,

SHITE

sono mama dochū ni mumoregusa[17]
kari naru[18] yo tote ima wa haya

she was buried deep in the earth just covered with grass, cut off from this fleeting makeshift world already, they say,

WAKI

mukashigatari ni
narishi hito no
nao shūshin ya
nokoriken,

she became a character
in the ancient story,
yet her heart-attachment seems
lingering behind,

SHITE

naki ato made mo
nani to yaran

desolately, even long
after she had perished,

WAKI

mono susamashiki
kono hara no

why does this plain, I wonder,
lie forlornly wild,

SHITE

kaze mo mi ni shimu   where the winds, too, chill me through

Obasute

331

aki no kokoro.   with the heart of autumn?

[*The chorus comes in and sings the following passage, called* ageuta, *"high-pitched song."*]

CHORUS

(*Ageuta: au, yowagin*)

Ima tote mo	More than ever now,
nagusame kanetsu	there's hardly any comfort
Sarashina ya,	in Sarashina,
nagusame kanetsu	there's hardly any comfort
Sarashina ya	in Sarashina
Obasuteyama no	on Obasute Mountain,
yūgure ni	as the evening falls
matsu mo katsura mo	both the pines and laurel trees,
majiru ki no	scattered through the woods,
midori mo nokorite[19]	leave too their deepened green to mix
aki no ha no	with the autumn leaves
haya irozuku ka	flushed already with their hues
Hitoeyama[20]	over One-Fold Hill
usugiri mo	one thin band of mist
tachiwatari	trails and hovers too
kaze susamashiku	dolefully the whirring wind
kumo tsukite	sweeps the clouds away
samishiki yama no	from the lonely mountain peak
keshiki kana,	desolate in view,
samishiki yama no	from the lonely peak
keshiki kana.	desolate in view.

SHITE

[3] (*Mondai: awazu, yowagin*)

Tabibito wa izuku yori kitaritamō zo.   O traveler, where did you come from?

WAKI

Sareba izen mo mōsu gotoku Miyako no mono nite sōrō ga Sarashina no tsuki o uketamawarioyobi, hajimete kono to-koro ni kitarite sōrō yo.

Well. As I have said before, I am from the capital. I have heard about the moon of Sarashina, so I come to this place for the first time.

SHITE

Sate wa Miyako no hito nite mashimasu kaya. Sa araba warawa mo tsuki to tomo ni araware idete tabibito no yayū o nagusamemōsubeshi.

Then you really are from the capital! If that is so I will come out here, too, with the moon, to sing and dance for your pleasure through this night.

Somo ya yayū o nagusamen to wa, on-mi wa ika naru hito yaran.

What can you mean by saying that you will dance for our pleasure tonight? Please tell me who you are.

SHITE

Makoto wa ware wa Sarashina no mono.

To tell the truth, I am from Sarashina.

WAKI

Sate ima wa mata
izukata ni

So presently where is it
that you make your home?

SHITE

Sumika to iwanna

"Where I make my home?" you ask me.

kono yama no

Here in this mountain,

WAKI

na ni shi oitaru

well renowned throughout the world

SHITE

Obasute no

as Obasute.

[*The chorus comes in and sings the* ageuta *passage.*]

CHORUS

(*Ageuta: au, yowagin*)

Sore to iwan mo
hazukashi ya.

Even to relate it so
how ashamed I feel

[*The* shite *lowers her mask.*]

Sore to iwan mo
hazukashi ya.
Sono inishie mo
suterarete
tada hitori
kono yama ni

even to relate it so
how ashamed I feel
as in days of long ago
all deserted too
in this mountain depth
still alone I live

[*The* shite *goes forward slightly.*]

333

sumu tsuki no[21] na no
aki goto ni
shūshin no yami o
harasan to
koyoi araware

purely shines the harvest moon
on its round above
in each autumn as it clears
dark attachments still
I have come before you here

idetari to	in this eve, she says,
yūkage²² no	as the twilight dusk
ko no moto ni	falls beneath the trees
kakikesu yō ni	suddenly as if effaced
usenikeri,	away she vanishes
kakikesu yō ni	suddenly as if effaced
usenikeri.	away she vanishes.

[*The* shite *turns to her right and, making a* hiraki *gesture, exits quietly.*]

Nakairi (Interlude)

[*The* kyōgen, *one of the mountain folk, wearing a striped, less-formal heavy silk kimono* (dan no-shime), *the long* kyōgen *two-piece* (naga kamishimo), *a waistband* (koshiobi), *a fan* (ōgi), *and a short sword* (chiisa gatana), *comes out to the name-saying pillar* (nanoriza) *and intones the following dialogue with the* waki *in prose.*]

KYŌGEN

(Mondai: awazu, kotoba)

Kayō ni sōrō mono wa kono yama no fumoto ni sumai suru mono nite sōrō. Kon'ya wa meigetsu naraba yama e no-bori, tsuki o nagameba ya to zonji sōrō. Iya kore ni minarenu o-kata no goza sōrō ga, izuku yori izukata e o-tōri sōraeba tsuki ni nagame irite onniri sōrō ka.

I make my home at the foot of this mountain. Tonight the harvest moon is full, so I think I will climb the mountain and look at it. Well, here is a man I have never seen before. [*Looks at the* waki.] As you came from someplace, so you must be going somewhere, but in the meantime, you are here for the moon-viewing, aren't you?

WAKI

Kore wa Miyakogata no mono nite sōrō. Sate on-mi wa kono atari no hito nite watari sōrō ka.

I am from the capital. Well now, are you from this vicinity?

KYŌGEN

Nakanaka kono atari no mono nite sōrō.

Yes. I am from this neighborhood.

WAKI

334

Sayō ni sōrawaba mazu chikō onniri sōrae. Tazunetaki koto no sōrō.

If that's so, please come closer. I have something to ask you.

KYŌGEN

Kashikomatte sōrō. Sate o-tazune nasa-retaki to wa ikayō naru go-yō nite sōrō zo.

Yes, sir. [*Goes out to stage center and sits down.*] Now then, what is it you want to ask me?

Omoi mo yoranu mōshigoto nite sōrae-domo, kono Sarashina no tsuki o shō-gan no koto, mata Obasuteyama no shi-sai go-zonji ni oite wa katatte on-kikase sōrae.

What I ask you may surprise you. But please tell me about the moon-viewing here at Sarashina, and about the stories of Obasute Mountain. I would like to hear whatever you know about these things.

Kore wa omoi mo yoranu koto o uketa-mawari sōrō mono kana. Warera mo kono atari ni sumaitsukamatsuri sōrae-domo sayō no koto kuwashiku wa zon-zezu sōrō. Sarinagara hajimete on-me ni kakari o-tazune nasare sōrō koto o nan to mo zonzenu to mōsu mo ikaga nite sōraeba, ōyoso uketamawari-oyobitaru tōri on-monogatari-mōsōzuru nite sōrō.

How strange that you should ask me about such things. Though we live in these parts, I don't know much about the details of such things. But since I am asked by a person that I meet for the first time, it would not be right to say I know nothing at all about your ques-tion, so I will tell the story the way I have heard it.

Chikagoro nite sōrō.

I would be most grateful.

Saru hodo ni Obasuteyama to mōsu shi-sai wa, inishie kono zaisho ni Wada no Hikonaga to mōsu mono no goza sō-raishi ga, osanaki toki ni ryōshin ni okure, oba no yōiku nite hito to nari sōrō ga, tsuma o kataraite yori kono oba o nikumi, sore ni iroiro zangen shikare-domo Hikonaga sara ni gaten sezu sōrō. Shikaredomo amari ni tsuyoku iware, sūnen no on o wasure, ima no shūen ni hikare aru toki oba ni mōsu yō, kono yama no atari ni tōtoki mi-hotoke no zashite onniri sōrō. Iza ya tomo shite haisen tote, kono yama ni tsurekitari, to aru tokoro ni sute oki, yama o mireba tsuki wa harete kuma naku sōrō aida, mukae ni yukan to zonji sōraedomo, onna no kokoro sagashiku sōrō aida, omoinagara yukisuguru hodo ni oba wa munashiku nari shūshin ishi to nari-mōshite sōrō. Sono nochi Hikonaga tazunekitari kore o mite osoroshiku

Well, the reason it is called Obasute Mountain is that long ago in these parts, there was a man named Hironaga of Wada. He lost his parents when he was very young, and his aunt nursed him and brought him up. But then he grew up and got a wife who hated his aunt and slandered her in many ways. Hi-ronaga turned a deaf ear to her slander-ings. However, as his wife's remarks be-came more vicious, he forgot the debt of gratitude he owed his aunt for her years of care, and, driven by his karma, one day he told his aunt, "There is a holy Buddha enshrined near this mountain. I'll go with you and we'll pay him hom-age together." So he led her to this mountain, and at a certain place, he abandoned her. When he looked back toward the mountain, he saw that the moon was clear and he wanted to go to bring his aunt back, but his wife became

335

omoi shukke tsukamatsuru to mōsu. Sore yori kono yama o Obasuteyama to mōshi sōrō. Sunawachi fumoto no zaisho o mo Obasute no zaisho to mo moshi sōrō. Sono mukashi wa Sarashinayama to mōshitaru geni sōrō. Mazu warera no uketamawaritaru wa kaku no gotoku nite sōrō ga nani to oboshimeshi o-tazune nasare sōrō zo. Chikagoro fushin ni zonji sōrō.

very angry. So a few days went by while he thought about his aunt. In the meantime, she died. Then the attachment in her heart for the world turned her into a stone. Later on, Hironaga came back searching for his aunt, and when he found her, he was deeply shocked. So he renounced this world to become a priest, we hear. Since then this mountain has been known as the mountain where the old aunt was abandoned. Even the village at the foot of this mountain is called Obasute, Abandoned Aunt. Before this it was called something like Sarashina Mountain. Well, this is what I've heard about it. Please tell me why you ask. Lately I have felt something strange around this place.

Nengoro ni on-monogatari sōrō mono kana. Tazunemōsu mo yo no gi ni arazu. Saizen mo mōshishi gotoku kore wa Miyakogata no mono nite sōrō ga, kono Sarashina no koto o uketamawarioyobi, tsuki o min tote waza to kitarite sōrō. Saizen tsuki matsu koro ni izuku tomo naku rōjo hitori kitarare, Obasuteyama no koka nado o yomare, tsuki no yayū o nagusamen to mōsare sōrō hodo ni ika naru hito zo to tazunete sōraeba, inishie wa Sarashina no mono, ima wa kono Obasuteyama ni sumu mono naru ga shūshin no yami o harasan tame, koyoi arawareidetari to ii mo aezu kore naru ueki no kage nite sugata o ushinōte sōrō yo.

Thank you for telling me all this in detail. I had no special reason for asking about it. As I told you before, I am from the capital. When I heard about this Sarashina, I decided I must see its moon and came here deliberately for that purpose. And then, just a little while ago as I waited for the moonrise, an old woman suddenly appeared from nowhere. She recited an ancient poem about this Obasute Mountain. Then she said that she would dance and sing for our moon-viewing party, to entertain us. When I asked her who she was, she said she used to live in Sarashina, but now she lived on Obasute Mountain, and as she said she came here to clear away the darkness of her worldly attachment, no sooner had she spoken than she vanished away behind the shade of the trees planted over here.

336

Kore wa kidoku naru koto o ōse sōrō mono kana. Sate wa utagō tokoro mo naki oba no shūshin arawareide o-kotoba o kawasaretaru to zonji sōrō. Sayō

I've never heard a stranger story! No doubt about it, the aunt's attachment must have brought her back to talk to you here. If that's the case, you should

ni sōrawaba, shibaraku kono tokoro ni goza sōrōte arigataki o-kyō o mo on-do-kuju nasare kano oba no ato o nengoro ni o-tomurai arite, kasanete kidoku o goran arekashi to zonji sōrō.

stay here for a while to pray for her memory by reciting the holy Buddhist sutras. Somehow I feel as though you will see that strange thing again.

Waki

Warera mo sayō ni zonji sōrō aida, tsuki o mo nagame kokoro o sumashi kasanete kidoku o miuzuru nite sōrō.

I agree with you. I would gaze at the moon, too, and refresh my heart. For somehow I feel too that I will see that strange thing again.

Kyōgen

Mata go-yō no koto sōrawaba kasanete ōse sōrae.

If you have something else for me to do, please call me again.

Waki

Tanomi sōrōbeshi.

That is kind of you.

Kyōgen

Kokoroe mōshite sōrō.

Not at all.

[*The* kyōgen *goes to the* ai *seat. Then the* waki *and the* waki-tsure *sing together the following verse, called* machiutai, *"waiting song."*]

Waki and Waki-tsure

[4] *(Machiutai: au, yowagin)*

Yūkage suguru	Gone is the hour of twilight
tsukikage no,	now the moon's begun,
yūkage suguru	gone is the hour of twilight
tsukikage no	now the moon's begun
haya idesomete	arising here already.
omoshiro ya	How delightful now!
banri no sora mo	Skies extend ten thousand miles,
kumanakute	clear and limitless,
izuku no aki mo	everywhere the autumn glows
hedate naki	without boundaries
kokoro mo sumite	and this heart of mine, too, is
yo mo sugara	peacefully serene

337

(Au: yowagin)

sangoya-chū[23] no	all throughout this fifteenth night
shingetsu no iro	of the newly rising moon,
jisenri no hoka no	with my dear old comrades' thoughts
kojin no kokoro.	now two thousand miles away.

Obasute

PART II

[Following the issei *music, the* nochi-jite, *wearing an* uba *(old-woman) wig, a wig band (*kazu-raobi*), an under kimono with painted gold or silver patterns (*surihaku*), a white "long silk," loose unlined broad-sleeved outer robe (*shiroji chōken*), a waistband (*koshiobi*), and a fan (*ōgi*), enters the stage, stands by the* shite *seat, and sings the following passage.]*

SHITE

[5] *(Awazu, yowagin)*

Ara omoshiro no	How delightful all appears
orikara ya na,	at this very moment!
ara omoshiro no	how delightful all appears
orikara ya.	at this moment now!

(Sashi: awazu, yowagin)

Akeba mata[24]	When it dawns again
aki no nakaba mo	here this midpoint of the fall
suginubeshi	will be over too;
koyoi no tsuki no	only for the moon tonight
oshiki nomi ka wa,	such regret there is, I feel.
sanaki dani	Even at its best,
aki machikanete	we await too long this fall
taguinaki[25]	unsurpassed the name
na o mochizuki no[26]	this bright full moon possesses,
mishi dani mo	but when I saw it
oboenu hodo ni	I cannot now remember
kuma no naki	clearly boundless skies
Obasuteyama no	spread across Obasute
aki no tsuki	with this autumn moon
amari ni taenu	moving me to ecstasy
kokoro to ya,	that no heart can bear;
mukashi to dani mo	so I think this is unlike
omowanu zo ya.	those I saw before.

WAKI

(Kakaru: awazu, yowagin)

Fushigi ya na	Strange, how strange this seems!
haya fukesuguru	though it is already late
tsuki no yo ni	in this moonlit night,
hakue no nyonin[27]	here a woman, robed in white,
arawaretamō wa	appears before me graciously.
yume ka utsutsu ka	Am I dreaming? Is it real?
obotsu kana.	I can hardly tell.

SHITE

Yume to wa nado ya	Do you speak of dreams, I ask?
yūgure[28] ni	From the twilight shade

arawareideshi	I appear before you now,
oi no sugata	in an ancient figure
hazukashinagara	shrinking with the shame I feel,
kitaritari.	I return once more.

Waki

(Kakaru: awazu, yowagin)

Nani o ka tsutsumi-	What are you concealing still
tamōran.	graciously from me?
Moto yori tokoro mo	From old days this mountain's name
Obasute no	is Obasute

Shite

| yama wa rōjō ga | Mountain which the crone has made |
| sumidokoro no | for her dwelling place. |

Waki

| mukashi ni kaeru | To that past she now returns |
| aki no yo no | in this autumn night, |

Shite

| tsuki no tomobito | oh, companions of the moon, |
| madoi shite | let us gather round, |

Waki

| kusa o shiki | spread the grasses out |

Shite

| hana ni oki fusu²⁹ | with the flowers, wake and lie |
| sode no tsuyu no | upon our sleeves bedewed; |

Shite and Waki

samo iroiro no	with those who play for pleasure,
yayū no hito ni	many, many ways at night
itsu naresomete	we become familiar
utsutsu na ya.	in no time like dreams.

[*The chorus comes in, and, describing the* shite's *state of mind, they sing the following* ageuta *passage.*]

Chorus

(Ageuta: au, yowagin)

Sakari fuketaru	Past the peak how faded seems
jorōka no,³⁰	the lady-flower,
sakari fuketaru	past the peak how faded seems

Obasute

jorōka no	the lady-flower,
kusagoromo	clad in grassy robe,
shiotarete,	sere and withered now,

[*The* shite *goes out toward stage front.*]

mukashi dani	even in the past
suterareshi hodo no	utterly she was abandoned,
mi o shirade	but she did not know;
mata Obasute no	on Obasute Mountain
yama ni idete	she appears again

[*The* shite *looks beyond.*]

omote o Sarashina no[31]	to expose her sunken face before
tsuki ni miyuru mo	this moon at Sarashina,
hazukashi ya.	shrinking in her shame.

[*The* shite *lowers her mask.*]

Yoshi ya nanigoto mo	In this world of dreams, no matter
yume no yo no	what may come to pass,
nakanaka iwaji	what's the best is not to speak,
omowaji ya	nor to think of it,

[*The* shite *stands at the* shite *seat.*]

omoigusa[32]	as the "longing grass"
hana ni mede	loves the flowers in bloom,
tsuki ni somite	steep ourselves in moonlight;
asoban.	let's make merry.

[*The* shite *looks up above, and, as the chorus starts to sing the* kuri *passage, she goes to the front of the musicians.*]

CHORUS

[6] (*Kuri: awazu, yowagin*)

Geni ya kyō ni[33]	"Truly carried forward
hikarete kitari,	by delight I came," one sang;
kyō tsukite	"when it's at an end,
kaerishi mo	homeward I return."
ima no ori ka to	So I know that such a time
shiraretaru,	is tonight beneath
koyoi no sora no	this celestial scenery
keshiki kana.	all across the sky.

[*The* shite *sings the following* sashi *passage.*]

SHITE

(*Sashi: awazu, yowagin*)

Shikaru ni tsuki no	Though it may be that the moon
nadokoro,	is so famous
izuku wa aredo	in many other places,
Sarashina ya	at Sarashina

Masterworks of the Nō Theater

Obasuteyama no	on Obasute Mountain
kumori naki	without any cloud,
ichirin miteru[34]	in its full and perfect sphere
seikō no kage,	brimming with a crystal light,
dandan to shite	round and round the moon
kaikyō o hanaru.	climbs and leaves the seaside
	mountain.

SHITE

Shikareba shobutsu no	On the other hand, of the Buddhas'
on-chikai	many holy vows,

CHORUS

izure shōretsu	which can hardly be excelled
nakeredomo	one by another,
chōse no higan[35]	yet compared to Mida's Vow
amaneki kage	all illuminating
Mida kōmyō ni	through the world with glorious light,
shiku wa nashi.	none can surpass it.

[*The* shite *dances, accompanying the following* kuse *passage that the chorus sings, called* maiguse.]

CHORUS

(*Maiguse: au, yowagin*)

Saru hodo ni	So in the meantime,
sankō[36] nishi ni	as the sun, the moon and stars
yuku koto wa	turn toward the west,
shujō o shite	guiding the multitudes
Saihō ni	to persuade them all
susume iren ga	to the holy paradise
tame to ka ya	lying in the west,
tsuki[37] wa kano	where the moon is placed
Nyorai no migi no	on the right of Lord Mida
shōji to shite	as the mighty figure,
uen o koto ni	for he guides those with some tie
michibiki	to Amida,
omoki tsumi o	and those with heavy sins,
karonzuru	he can lighten them
tenjō no	since he is bestowed
chikara o	with the power
uru yue ni	of all heaven's might;
Daiseishi[38] to wa	for this reason he is called
gō su to ka.	"Power All Supreme!"
Tengan no	On his heavenly crown
aida ni	all the glitter
hana no hikari	of its gleaming blossoms
kakayaki	shines so brightly

341

Obasute

tama no utena no	from the calyx made of gems
kazukazu ni	numbered countlessly,
tahō no	illumining
jōdo o	paradises
arawasu.	of other realms.
Gyokuju rō no	Here within the towers
kaze no oto	decked with jewelry
shichiku no shirame	music heard among the winds
toridori ni	mixing with the airs
kokoro hikaruru	from the strings and flutes, enthralls
kata mo ari.	joyously our hearts.
Hachi iroiro ni	These the lotus blossoms blow
saki majiru	in white and crimson
takara no ike no	mingled in the Treasure Pond,
hotori ni	while around it
tatsu ya namiki no	stand the rows of waving trees
hana chirite	scattering their flowers
funpō shirikiri ni	ceaselessly, perfuming keenly
midaretari.	in diffusing air.

[*The* shite *sings the following lines, called* ageha.]

SHITE

(*Ageha*)

| Karyōbinga[39] no | The Kalavinka voices |
| tagui naki | singing matchlessly |

[*The chorus takes over and continues to sing the rest of the* kuse *passage.*]

CHORUS

(*Maiguse: au, yowagin*)

koe o taguete	are imitated jointly
morotomo ni	all in one by both
kujaku ōmu no	the peacocks and the parrots
onajiku	similarly
saezuru tori no	sing the birds in unison
onozukara	of their own accord
hikari mo kage mo	as the light shines everywhere
oshinamete	brightly all alike,
itaranu kuma mo	so no cranny is too small
nakereba	for his blessing;
muhenkō[40] to wa	he is therefore justly called
nazuketari.	"Light All Infinite!"
Shikaredomo	Covered by the shroud
ungetsu no	of clouds however
aru toki wa	full the moon at times
kage michi,	shines splendidly,
mata aru toki wa	yet again at other times

342

kage kakuru	its light is hidden.
ui tenpen no,	This tells the eternal truth
yo no naka no	that throughout the world
sadame no naki o	of vicissitudes of life
shimesu nari.	nothing stays the same.

[*The* shite *finishes the dance, which accompanies the above* kuse *passage sung by the chorus. The* shite *sings the following lines.*]

SHITE

[7] *(Issei: awazu, yowagin)*

| Mukashi koishiki | Yearning for the past this night |
| yayū no sode | in play I wave my sleeves. |

[*The* shite *makes some foot movements to the hand drum that plays for the* jo no mai *dance, and then, with the music, she begins dancing very quietly. Generally this dance is performed in three movements.*]

Jo no mai

[*After the dance, the* shite *continues to dance to the song called* waka, *as she sings it.*]

SHITE

(Waka: yowagin)

| Waga kokoro | For this heart of mine |

[*At the* shite *seat the* shite *makes an* ageōgi *gesture.*]

| nagusamekanetsu | there's hardly any comfort |
| Sarashina ya | at Sarashina |

CHORUS

Obasuteyama ni	on Obasute Mountain,
teru tsuki o mite,	gazing at the glowing moon,
teru tsuki o mite,	gazing at the glowing moon,

SHITE

(Awazu, yowagin)

tsuki ni nare	intimate with her
hana ni tawamururu	we become and play with flowers
akikusa no	of autumn grasses
tsuyu no ma[41] ni,	while the dews remain,

343

CHORUS

(Noriji: ōnori, yowagin)

| tsuyu no ma ni | while the dews remain |
| nakanaka nani shini | what I come to do, I wonder, |

Obasute

arawarete	as I now appear
Kochō no asobi[42]	for the Dance of Butterflies,

SHITE

tawamururu	fluttering in play
mai no sode	with the dancing sleeves,

CHORUS

kaese ya kaese[43]	turning, turning back once more

SHITE

mukashi no akio	to the autumn of the past

CHORUS

omoiidetaru	I return as I recall
mōshū no kokoro	the deep delusion in my heart
yaru kata mo naki	where I have no place to turn
koyoi no akikaze	tonight before the autumn wind
mi ni shimijimi to	I feel a shudder deeply
koishiki wa mukashi	with tender yearnings for the past,
shinobashiki wa	with remembrances
enbu no	of this dream-world,
aki yo tomo yo to	of autumn and of comrades
omoioreba	I think awhile, I muse

(Uta: au, yowagin)

yo mo sude ni	as the night grows pale
shirashira to	with light already
haya asama ni mo	whitening at dawn that brings
narinureba,	once again the world
ware mo miezu	where I'm seen no longer,
tabibito mo	gone the traveler, too,
kaeru ato ni	leaving here behind,

[*The* waki *rises and enters behind the curtain.*]

SHITE

hitori	so alone
suterarete	this ancient woman
rōjo ga	all abandoned

CHORUS

[*The* shite *looks at the* waki *and makes a* shiori *gesture.*]

mukashi koso arame	as once she was in days long past,
ima no mata	also once again

344

Obasuteyama to zo	now this Obasute Mountain
narinikeru,	she indeed becomes,
Obasuteyama to	this Obasute Mountain
narinikeri.	she has now become.

[*The* shite *makes a* hiraki *gesture at the* shite *seat and concludes without stamping the floor.*]

Obasute

Saigyōzakura

Introduction

Saigyōzakura belongs to Group III of Nō plays. In *Sarugaku Dangi*,[1] Zeami says that he wrote this piece because he felt that no one else would compose such a Nō play as this. He further states that the *nochi* (the *shite* who appears in the second part of the play) is quiet (*soto ari*), with an air of the old style. It seems to me that Zeami wished to leave this piece for future playwrights as a model of a Nō play in which an aged person (*rōtai*) serves as the *shite*. In this sense, the play is significant.

The *waki* that Zeami selected for this play is the famous poet-priest Saigyō (1118–90). The play is set during Saigyō's later years, when he lived at his retreat on the western side of the capital. The time is spring, when the age-old cherry tree in his yard comes into full bloom. The air is filled with spring merrymaking and the uplifted spirits of the sight-seeing crowd. One of them says, "Yesterday I saw the cherry flowers at Jinushigongen Shrine on the Eastern Hill. Then today I heard that the cherry blossoms at Saigyō's cottage on the Western Hill are in their glory. So with a group of sight-seeing friends, I am hurrying toward his cottage." They sing together on their way:

> . . . and as the number
> of days quickly pass . . .
> with the vernal sky
> stay awhile in fellowship
> beneath the blossoms;
> those who know and do not know
> one another meet
> here, and every heart becomes
> like the flowers in bloom.

They are all unaware of the fact that Saigyō has canceled the viewing of the cherry flowers at his cottage this year and has made a public announcement to that effect.

This decision not only adds an element of sadness to the hearts of the sight-seeing crowd but also stirs all the more their desire to see Saigyō's famous cherry flowers. At the same time, it reveals the aging *waki*'s feeling, which becomes clear as the play unfolds. A great poet and late bloomer as he is, he wants to have a heart-to-heart communion with his age-old cherry tree in full bloom this year. He is quite determined to do so, but, moved by the fellow blossom-viewers' "tender sentiments" that brought them to his place "over such a great distance," he opens the gate door of the brushwood fence for them.

The chorus sings on his behalf:

> Even at this distant place
> in the heart of Saga
> when spring comes
> he's called by all
> here where the mountain
> will, too, become a saga
> of the fleeting world
> he renounced
> and left behind him.
> There can be no other world
> for a mortal man;
> in the end what other place
> can be called his home. . . .

So the *waki* finds the company of the flower lovers somewhat difficult and gives vent to his thought in song:

> Seeking out the flowers,
> the people come together
> gathered in a crowd;
> to my great regret the flowers
> of the cherry are to be blamed.

The chorus continues to sing that, as the dusk deepens, regrettably the cherry blossoms also darken,

> . . . but at moonrise hour
> underneath the trees
> we forget the homeward path
> all together now,
> let's lie down and spend the night
> underneath the blossoms
> viewing them with night together
> till the daybreak.

347

During the night the *shite* comes out as a white-haired old man. Sakamoto Setchō describes the *shite*, as performed by Matsumoto Take (1877–1935), as follows: "This *shite*, wearing a black folded-over cap (*kurokazaori*), a hunting robe in brown, and a light-blue broad divided Nō skirt, appears elegantly quiet. The mask may be called 'mai jō.' It is, indeed, refined and graceful. The singing style is in a low key; however, its strength is enough. . . ."[2] The term "elegantly quiet," chosen by Setchō for the *shite*'s appearance, is what Zeami meant when he spoke about

Saigyōzakura

the *nochi-jite*, and the "mai jō" mask seems to symbolize the heart of the role the *shite* plays, which hints at Zeami's intent in this Nō. It is, I feel, also true that Matsumoto's insight into this play made him choose such a mask to illustrate Zeami's intent. The author's objective becomes clear through the ensuing dialogue, as the *shite* challenges the *waki* about the meaning of the poem he composed. The confrontation, which has a sulky air to it, serves as a dramatically subtle way for Zeami to reveal the deep relation between the *shite* and the *waki*, and their true identity. Here Masuda Shōzō's statement is insightful: "The *shite* in *Saigyōzakura* is the spirit of the cherry blossom, as well as Saigyō's other self, the poet-priest, which can be considered as the reflection-image of the heart of his poetry."[3] Indeed, this view is significant because the *waki* is not only the great old poet-priest Zeami selected for this play, but he is also a great lover of the cherry blossoms. Saigyō even wished he would die when they were in full bloom, and he was so blessed at seventy-three. Consequently, it is natural for Zeami to use the cherry tree, but why such an ancient cherry tree? He could have chosen some trees from Saigyō's other famous poems, which are undoubtedly much greater than the one used in this play; for example, he might have used the willow tree, as his nephew, Kanze Kojirō (1435–1566), did in a two-part dream play,[4] which Zeami perfected. But this would not be "in the old style." Thus, he constructs this play without an Interlude and uses the spirit of an old cherry tree in bloom as the *shite*. There must be a significant reason for Zeami to do so, especially since he is a great Nō playwright and an equally great actor. The answer may lie in the fact that "an age-old cherry tree in bloom" is a metaphor Zeami employed, not only once but twice, to describe the old person as one of the three basic forms (*santai*)[5] in Nō for the *shite*, which he seems to want to illuminate in this play.

After the *shite* reveals who he is, he says in prose: "How grateful I am. Drawn here to meet Your Holiness by chance, all are blessed by this dew of grace, falling everywhere." The *shite* then praises the many surrounding places famous for the cherry trees. He dances the slow, quiet *jo no mai*, expressing the joy that he and the *waki* share, against the background of the blooming cherry trees, which they view in the moon-bright night and which enrich the texture and the atmosphere of the play. While the *shite* dances the *jo no mai*, the stick drum (*taiko*) comes in and accentuates the dance, as it brings out the *yang* nature and the dignity of the ancient cherry tree in bloom. Here, indeed, Zeami's metaphor for the aged *shite* is more than a figure of speech. It becomes truly real as a theater experience through the performance of this play.

348

SAIGYŌZAKURA

By Zeami

Persons: WAKI: *Priest Saigyō*
KYŌGEN: *A servant*
WAKI-TSURE: *A cherry viewer (and three or four companions)*
SHITE: *An old man (the spirit of the old cherry tree)*

Classification: *Primary, Groups III, IV*
Place: *Saigyō's cottage at Nishiyama, Kyoto*
Time: *Spring (March)*
Kogaki: 7

[*The stage attendants bring out a prop representing a hill, covered with a black cloth with a spray of cherry blossoms on it, and place it in front of the chorus. The* waki, *accompanied by the* kyōgen nōriki, *enters the stage. The* waki *wears a pointed hood (kakubōshi), a plain, less-formal heavy silk kimono (muji noshime), a black broad-sleeved robe (kuro mizugoromo), a white broad divided skirt (shiro ōguchi), a waistband (koshiobi), a fan (ōgi), and a rosary (juzu); and the* kyōgen, *a kyōgen head cloth (kyōgen zukin), a striped, less-formal heavy silk kimono (dan noshime), a broad-sleeved robe (mizugoromo), leggings (kyahan), and a fan (ōgi). The* waki *takes his stool at the* waki *seat.*]

WAKI

[1] *(Mondai: awazu, kotoba)*

Ika ni tare ka aru.	Is anyone about?

[*The* kyōgen, *at stage center, bows his head toward the* waki.]

KYŌGEN

On-mae ni sōrō.	Yes, sir, I am here.

WAKI

Zonzuru shisai no aru aida, tōnen wa anjitsu ni oite hanami kinzei to aifure sōrae.	For certain reasons, this year the viewing of the cherry flowers will be prohibited at my cottage. So make an announcement to that effect to the public.

349

KYŌGEN

Kokoroe mōshite sōrō.	Yes, sir. I understand.

[*The* kyōgen *goes to the name-saying seat.*]

Kayō ni sōrō mono wa Saigyō[6] no anjitsu ni tsukaemōsu nōriki[7] nite sōrō. Sate mo anjitsu no hana haru goto ni migoto nite sōrō aida, Miyako[8] yori kisen gunshū tsukamatsuri sōrō ga, tōnen wa nan to oboshimeshi sōrō yaran hanami kinzei to ōseidasare sōrō aida, minamina sono bun kokoroe sōrae. Kokoroe sōrae.

I am an attendant, serving at the cottage of my master, Saigyō. Well, now, the cherry blossoms are so wonderful every spring at this cottage that crowds of people, both high and low, come from the capital. But this year I don't know what my master has in mind. He has canceled the viewing of the cherry blossoms. So let everyone take note of this. Please take note of this.

[*After this announcement the* kyōgen *goes to the front of the flute player and sits down. Following the* shidai *music, the* waki-tsure *and three to four sightseers, each wearing a plain, less-formal heavy silk kimono (*muji noshime*), an unlined hempen two-piece over robe (*suō kamishimo*), a waistband (*koshiobi*), a fan (*ōgi*), and a small sword (*chiisa gatana*), enter the stage and, facing one another, sing the following verse, called* shidai.]

WAKI-TSURE AND COMPANIONS

(Shidai: au, tsuyogin)

Koro machietaru	The long-awaited time's come
sakuragari,	for cherry viewing,
koro machietaru	the long-awaited time's come
sakuragari	for cherry viewing
yamaji no haru ni	by the mountain path to spring
isogan	let us hurry.

[*The chorus sings the above* shidai *verse, except the third and fourth lines, in a lower key, which is called* jidori. *While the chorus sings the* jidori, *the* waki-tsure *faces stage front.*]

CHORUS

(Jidori: au, tsuyogin)

Koro machietaru	The long awaited time's come
sakuragari,	for cherry viewing
yamaji no haru ni	by the mountain path to spring
isogan.	let us hurry.

[*After the* jidori, *the* waki-tsure *intones the following prose passage, called* nanori.]

WAKI-TSURE

350

(Nanori: awazu, kotoba)

Kayō ni sōrō mono wa Shimogyō[9] hen ni sumaitsukamatsuru mono nite sōrō. Sate mo ware haru ni nari sōraeba koko kashiko no hana o nagame, sanagara sannya ni hi o okuri sōrō. Kinō wa Higashiyama[10] Jishu[11] no sakura o ikken tsukamatsurite sōrō. Kyō wa mata Nishiyama Saigyō no anjitsu[12] no hana,

I live in the lower southern section of the capital. When each spring comes, I go about here and there to view the cherry blossoms. Up in the mountains and down in the fields I would go as I spent all my days. Yesterday, I saw the cherry blossoms at the Jishu Shrine on the Eastern Hill. Then, today, I heard

sakari naru yoshi uketamawarioyobi
sōrō hodo ni hanami no hitobito o
tomonai tadaima Nishiyama Saigyō no
anjitsu e to isogi sōrō.

that the cherry blossoms at Saigyō's
cottage on the Western Hill are in full
bloom. So with a group of sight-seeing
friends, right now I am hurrying toward the cottage of Saigyō on the Western Hill.

[The waki-tsure *and his companions face one another again, and they sing the following* ageuta
passage, called michiyuki, *"travel song."]*

WAKI-TSURE AND COMPANIONS

(Michiyuki: au, tsuyogin)

Momochidori[13]	Countless are the birds
saezuru haru wa	with their chirping songs in spring
monogoto ni	everything's renewed,
saezuru haru wa	with their chirping songs in spring
monogoto ni	everything's renewed
aratamariyuku	once more, and as the number
hi kazu hete	of days quickly pass
koro mo yayoi no	it is now the month of March
sora nare ya,	with the vernal sky;
yayo[14] todomarite	stay awhile in fellowship
hana no tomo	beneath the blossoms;
shiru mo shiranu mo[15]	those who know and do not know
morotomo ni	one another meet
tare mo hana naru	here, and every heart becomes
kokoro kana,	like the flowers in bloom;
tare mo hana naru	and here every heart becomes
kokoro kana.	like the flowers in bloom.

[The waki-tsure *faces stage front, takes a few steps forward, and returns again to his original position,
indicating that they have traveled and reached the Western Hill. After they have finished the travel
song, the* waki-tsure *faces stage front and intones the following prose passage, called* tsukizerifu,
"arrival speech."]

WAKI-TSURE

(Tsukizerifu: awazu, kotoba)

Isogi sōrō hodo ni kore wa haya Saigyō
no anjitsu ni tsukite sōrō. Shibaraku
minamina on-machi sōrae. Soregashi
annai o mōsōzuru nite sōrō.

Since we hurried along the way, we
have already reached Saigyō's cottage.
Please, all of you, wait for a while. I will
act as your guide.

351

THE FIRST COMPANION

Shikarubyō sōrō.   Yes, that will be fine.

[The waki-tsure *and his companions go to the bridge, and, at the first pine, the* waki-tsure *faces
stage front.]*

Saigyōzakura

WAKI-TSURE

(Mondai: awazu, kotoba)

Ika ni annai mōshi sōrae.

May I please speak to someone?

[*The* kyōgen *goes out near the* shite *pillar.*]

KYŌGEN

Annai to wa tare nite watari sōrō zo.

Are you speaking to me? I wonder who you are.

WAKI-TSURE

San zōrō. Kore wa Miyakogata no mono nite sōrō ga, kono on-anjitsu no hana sakari naru yoshi uketamawari oyobi harubaru kore made mairite sōrō. Soto on-mise sōrae.

Yes. We are from the capital. I heard that the cherry blossoms at this cottage are in full bloom, so we have traveled a long way to this place. Please, let us see them for a few minutes.

KYŌGEN

Sono koto nite sōrō. Tōnen wa nan to oboshimeshi sōrō yaran, hanami kinzei to ōsei dasarete sōraedomo Miyako yori harubaru onnide nite sōraeba, go-kigen o motte mōshi agyōzuru nite sōrō. Shibaraku kore ni on-machi sōrae.

As for that, sir, I don't know what my master is thinking, but he has ordered me to announce that this year there will be no viewing of the cherry blossoms. However, since you've come such a long way to this place, I'll wait for the right moment and ask him for you. So please wait for a while.

WAKI-TSURE

Kokoroe mōshi sōrō.

I thank you kindly.

[*The* waki-tsure *and his companions sit down. The* kyōgen *goes back to the* kyōgen *seat, and then the* waki *sings the following* sashi *passage, seated on a stool at the* waki *seat.*]

WAKI

[2] *(Sashi: awazu, yowagin)*

Sore haru no hana wa	O say, the flowers in the spring
jōgu honrai no [16]	seeking upward for salvation,
kozue ni araware,	show themselves across the treetops
aki no tsuki	and the autumn moon
geke meian no	on the water down below
mizu ni yadoru.	brightens up our darkness.
Tare ka shiru	Who'd know the hottest
yuku mizu ni	summer's heat is not
sanpuku no [17]	in the running stream
natsu mo naku	through the cool ravine?
kantei no	Through its pines the wind

352

matsu no kaze,	we await.
kantei no	Through its pines the wind
matsu no kaze,	we await one call
issei no aki o	by the fall that makes us feel
moyoosu koto	so invigorated.
sō-moku kokudo	Grasses, trees, the land itself,
onozukara	of their own accord,
kenbutsu-monpō no	keep a tie with us to praise and hear
kechien tari.	Mida and his teachings.

| Sarinagara yotsu no toki nimo sugure-taru wa kajitsu no ori narubeshi. | Even among the four seasons, however, the excellent time is when the flowers and the fruits come out. |

| Ara omoshiro ya sōrō. | How delightful all appears here before us. |

[*The* kyōgen *rises and speaks.*]

KYŌGEN

(*Mondai: awazu, kotoba*)

| Iya ichidan no gokigen nite sōrō. Saraba isoide mōshi agebaya to zonzuru. Ikani mōshiage sōrō. Miyako yori wakaki hitobito anjitsu no hana mitaki yoshi mōshite mairarete sōrō. | He seems to be in a very good mood. So I think I had better hurry and speak to him. [*The* kyōgen *goes to the front of the* waki.] Excuse me, sir. Some young people have come from the capital, saying that they wish to see the cherry flowers at the cottage. |

WAKI

| Nan-to Miyako yori to mōshite kono an-jitsu no hana o nagamen tame ni kore made mina-mina kitari tamō to mōsu ka. | What? From the capital, they say? All of them came from the capital to see the cherry blossoms at this cottage, did you say? |

KYŌGEN

| San zōrō. Anjitsu no hanami kinzei no yoshi mōshite sōraedomo harubaru mairi sōrō aida, misete kureyo to no koto nite sōrō. Soto on-mise arekashi to zonji sōrō. | Yes, sir. Though I told them that the viewing of the cherry blossoms at the cottage was prohibited, they still asked to see the flowers since they had come to this place from such a distance. Please let them have a glance at the flowers. |

353

WAKI

| Oyoso Rakuyō no hanazakari. Izuku mo to iinagara, Saigyō ga anjitsu no hana, hana mo hitoki ware mo hitori[18] to miru | Generally speaking, the capital appears in full bloom, as it seems everywhere else, so they tell me, while at my cottage |

mono o, hana yue arika o shiraren koto ikaga naredomo kore made harubaru kitaritaru kokorozashi o, misede wa ikade kaesubeki. Ano shibagaki no to o hiraki uchi e ire sōrae.

there is but one tree in bloom and only this one person to enjoy it. Though it does not please me that this retreat of mine has become known for its flowers, still I can hardly send these people home without a glimpse of the blossoms, since they have come here from so far away. You may open the gate door of the brushwood fence and let them in.

KYŌGEN

Kashikomatte sōrō.

Yes, sir.

[*The* kyōgen *faces the* waki-tsure.]

(*Mondai: awazu, kotoba*)

Ika ni saizen no hito no watari sōrō ka.

Ho, there. Are the people who came a while ago still out there?

WAKI-TSURE

Nanigoto nite sōrō zo.

Yes. What is it?

[*The* waki-tsure *and all of his companions rise.*]

KYŌGEN

Go-kigen o motte mōshiage sōraeba, soto on-mise arōzuru to no on-koto nite sōrō aida, koko on-tōri sōrae.

My master was in a good mood, so I asked him for you. He said that he would let you have a glance at the cherry flowers. Please come this way.

WAKI-TSURE

Kokoroe mōshite sōrō.

Yes, I understand.

KYŌGEN

Mazu shibagaki no to o akeyo. Sara sara sara.

First of all, let me open the gate door in the brushwood fence.

[*With his fan, the* kyōgen *makes a gesture as if opening the gate door and exits through the* kirido. *The* waki-tsure *and his companions go forward toward the eye-fixing pillar. They sing the following verse.*]

354

WAKI-TSURE AND COMPANIONS

(*Kakeai: awazu, yowagin*)

Sakurabana[19]	As the cherry blossoms
sakinikerashi na	are now, we think, all blooming,
ashibiki no	for out from the gap
yama no kai yori	between the steep-sloped mountains

mieshi mama	they appear in full,
kono ko no moto ni	so beneath this tree we go
tachiyoreba.	near its base and stand.

[*They line up in single file at the* waki *stage front and sit down.*]

WAKI

Ware wa mata	I, too, have feelings
kokoro kotonaru	different from other folks
hana no moto ni	underneath the blossoms
hika rakuyō o	thinking of their scattering
kanjitsutsu	and of falling leaves
hitori kokoro o	as I make this heart of mine
sumasu tokoro ni.	serenely clear, all alone.

WAKI-TSURE

Kisen kunju no	High and low the crowds of men
iroiro ni	come in every sort
kokoro no hana mo	like the flowers in their hearts
sakan nite.	blooming at their best,

WAKI

| mukashi no[20] haru ni | the scenes are turning now |
| kaeru arisama | to the spring that once was mine, |

WAKI-TSURE

| kakuredokoro no | though this mountain may well be |
| yama to iedomo | a good place for one's retreat, |

WAKI

| sanagara hana no | here it's like the capital |

WAKI-TSURE

| Miyako nareba | of the cherry blossoms. |

[*The chorus takes up the above exchanges, called* kakeai, *and sings the following* ageuta.]

CHORUS

(*Ageuta: au, yowagin*)

355

sutebito mo	Though a hermit priest,
hana ni wa nani to	where remains for him to hide
kakurega no,	when the cherry blooms,
hana ni wa nani to	where remains for him to hide
kakurega no	when the cherry blooms?
tokoro wa Saga[21] no	Even at this distant place
oku naredomo	in the heart of Saga,

Saigyōzakura

haru ni	when spring comes
towarete	he's called by all
yama made mo	here where the mountain
ukiyo²² no saga²³ ni	will, too, become a saga
naru mono o,	of the fleeting world
geni ya	he renounced
sutete dani	and left behind him.
kono yo no hoka wa	There can be no other world
naki mono o	for a mortal man;
izuku ka tsui no	in the end what other place
sumika naru,	can he call his home,
izuku ka tsui no	in the end where is the place
sumika naru.	that will be his home?

[*The companions and the* waki *face one another.*]

WAKI

[3] (*Mondai: awazu, kotoba*)

| Ikani menmen kore made harubaru kitaritamō kokorozashi kaesugaesu mo yasashū koso sōrae, sarinagara sutete sumu yo no tomo tote wa hana hitori naru ko no moto ni mi ni wa matarenu hana no tomo, sukoshi kokoro no hoka nareba, | Well, now, all you gentlemen, I marvel again and again over the tender sentiments that brought you here over such a great distance. But for a person like myself who has renounced the world and whose only friend is this one tree in bloom, I do not await flower-loving friends. As I am slightly vexed, I say, |

(*Yowagin*)

hana min to²⁴	seeking out the flowers,
muretsutsu hito no	the people come together
kuru nomi zo,	gathered in a crowd;
atara sakura no	to my great regret the flowers
toga ni wa arikeru.	of the cherry are to be blamed.

CHORUS

(*Au, yowagin*)

Atara sakura no	To my great regret the flowers
kage kurete	darken as the dusk
tsuki ni naru yo no	deepens, but at moonrise hour,
ko no moto ni	underneath the trees,

356

[*The* waki *rises and goes slightly forward.*]

ieji wasurete²⁵	we forget our homeward path,
morotomo ni	all together now,
koyoi wa hana no	let's lie down and spend the night
shitabushi shite	underneath the blossoms,
yo to tomo ni nagame	viewing them with night together
akasan.	till the daybreak.

Masterworks of the Nō Theater

[*As the chorus starts to sing* shitabushi shite *(underneath the blossoms), the* waki *returns to the* waki *seat and sits down, and the* waki-tsure *and his companions go to the front of the chorus and sit down. The stage attendant lets the covered cloth fall from the prop, revealing the* shite, *the spirit of the cherry tree. He wears a* shiwajō *mask, a long white wig (*shiro tare*), a folded-over cap (*kazaori eboshi*), a gold satin damask headband (*kindan hachimaki*), a collar in pale blue (*eri asagi*), a small-checked kimono (*kogōshi*), a waistband (*koshiobi*), and a fan (*ōgi*). As the chorus concludes the last line above, the* shite, *sitting on the stool inside the prop, sings the following* sashi *passage.*]

SHITE

[4] *(Sashi: awazu, tsuyogin)*

Mumoregi no	As fossil logs are
hito shirenu mi to²⁶	buried deep, I stay unknown
shizumedomo,	to the world of man,
kokoro no hana wa	but the blossoms in my heart
nokorikeru zo ya.	are alive with feeling still.
Hana min to	Seeking out the flowers,

[*The* shite *changes the singing style to* yowagin.]

(Yowagin)

muretsutsu hito no	the people come together
kuru nomi zo,	gathered in a crowd;
atara sakura no	to my great regret the flowers
toga ni wa arikeru.	of the cherry are to be blamed.

[*During the following dialogues between the* shite *and the* waki, *the* waki *is at the* waki *seat, while the* shite *sits on the stool inside the prop. The* waki *faces the* shite.]

WAKI

(Kakeai: awazu, yowagin)

Fushigi ya na,	Strange! How strange this is!
kuchitaru hana no	From within this hollow tree
utsuogi yori	of the withered blossoms,
hakuhatsu no rōjin	now an ancient man appears
arawarete	with his snow-white hair,

Saigyō ga uta o eizuru arisama samo fu-shigi naru jintai nari.	my poem is recited in a strangely hu-man manner.

SHITE

357

Kore wa muchū no okina naru ga ima no eika no kokoro o nao mo tazunen tame ni kitarikeri.	Though I am an ancient man in a dream, I have come to learn the mean-ing of the song I heard just now.

WAKI

Somo ya muchū no	By your words, "an ancient man
okina to wa	in a dream," you say,
yume ni kitareru	so across the dream he comes;
hito narubeshi.	you must be that person.

Saigyōzakura

Sore ni tsukite mo tadaima no eika no kokoro o tazunen to wa uta ni fushin no aru yaran.

And even if this is so, since you come to ask about the meaning of the verse I just composed, is there something in the verse so questionable?

SHITE

Iya shōnin no onnuta ni nani ka fushin no arubeki naredomo

No, no there could hardly be anything questionable in a poem by one such as you, but

muretsutsu hito no
kuru nomi zo
atara sakura no
toga ni wa arikeru;

the people come together
gathered in a crowd;
to my great regret the flowers
of the cherry are to be blamed.

sate sakura no toga wa nani yaran.

Now, I wonder what you meant by the blame of the cherry tree?

WAKI

Iya kore wa tada ukiyo o itou yamazumi naru ni kisen kunju no itowashiki kokoro o sukoshi eizuru nari.

Well, I merely composed the lines on the tiresome sentiment of the crowd, both high and low, who come to my mountain retreat where I live to escape the follies of the fleeting world.

SHITE

Osore nagara kono gyoi koso sukoshi fushin ni sōrae to yo. Ukiyo to miru mo yama to miru mo tada sono hito no kokoro ni ari. Hijō mushin no sōmoku no hana ni ukiyo no toga wa araji.

I beg your pardon, but may I say your feeling itself is a little questionable. Whether you see the vanity of the fleeting world or you see the mountains, it comes only from your heart. The flowers of trees and grasses, which have no feeling or desires, can hardly be blamed for the fleeting world.

WAKI

Geni geni kore wa kotowari nari. Sate sate kayō ni kotowari o nasu on-mi wa ikasama kaboku no seika.

How true, how true, it stands to reason. Well, now, considering the way you reason, can it be that you are perhaps the spirit of this flowering tree?

SHITE

Makoto wa hana no sei naru ga kono mi mo tomo ni oiki no sakura no.

The truth is that I am a spirit of the flowers, grown old with this age-old cherry tree.

358

WAKI

Hana mono iwanu[27]	Though the flowers of the trees
sōmoku naredomo	and grasses do not speak at all,

SHITE

toga naki iware o	still they wish to prove how blameless
yūhana[28] no	are the blooming blossoms

WAKI

kage kuchibiru o	like the tulips speaking out

SHITE

ugokasu nari.	as they move their petals.

[*The* shite *looks at the* waki. *The chorus sings the following passage. As the chorus starts to sing, the* shite *lowers his mask.*]

CHORUS

(Uta: au, yowagin)

Hazukashi ya	How ashamed I feel
rōboku no	for the age-old tree
hana mo sukunaku	with its blossoms so few too

[*The* shite *arises, comes out of the prop, and goes to center stage.*]

eda kuchite	withered are the boughs
atara sakura no	to my great regret the flowers
toga no	who are blamed
naki yoshi o	have no fault, so I,
mōshihiraku[29]	the spirit of the flowers,
hana no	shall open
sei nite	my plea for them,

[*The* shite *faces the* waki.]

sōrō nari.	for they are all blameless.

[*While the chorus continues to sing the following lines, the* shite, *changing his mood and turning to his right, goes to the* shite *seat and, again facing the* waki, *comes out to center stage, while the* waki *rises, too, and comes out slightly forward.*]

CHORUS

359

ōyoso	As a rule,
kokoro naki	even with no sentient heart,
sōmoku mo	trees and grasses too
kajitsu no ori wa	don't forget at all the time
wasureme ya	for their flowers and fruits;

Saigyōzakura

sōmoku	trees and grasses
kokudo mina	and the land itself

[They face each other, put their knees to the floor, and fold their hands in prayer.]

jōbutsu no mi-nori	enter Nirvana by Dharma's
narubeshi.	true salvation.

SHITE *[Folding his hands in prayer.]*

[5] *(Awazu, kotoba)*

Arigata ya, shōnin no on-chigū ni hika-rete megumi no tsuyu amaneku,	How grateful I am. Drawn here to meet Your Holiness by chance, all are blessed by this dew of grace, falling everywhere.
hana kanzen ni[30] ende	By the bridge railing, the flowers are smiling,
koe imada kikazu,	still their sweet voices go unheard;
tori rinka ni naite	in the forest, the birds are crying,
nanda tsukigatashi.	still their tears of joy are endless.

[The shite *goes to the front of the musicians and stands facing stage front. The* waki *returns to the* waki *seat and sits down. The chorus then sings the following passage, called* kuri.*]*

CHORUS

(Kuri: awazu, yowagin)

Sore ashita ni[31]	Stepping out at morning
rakka o funde	through the scattered cherry flowers,
aitomonatte izu,	with a group of bosom friends we go;
yūbe ni wa	and at evening,
hichō ni shitagatte	following a flock of flying birds,
ichiji ni kaeru.	to our homes we all return.

[The shite *sings the following* sashi *passage.]*

SHITE

(Sashi: awazu, tsuyogin)

Kokonoe ni	Though these cherries bloom
sakedomo hana no	in the ninefold Palace ground,
yaezakura	they are called "Eightfold";

360

CHORUS

ikuyo no haru o	but how many reigns of spring
kasanuran.[32]	did the blooms unfold?

SHITE

Shikaru ni hana no	While so many places are
nadakaki wa	famous for their flowers,

Masterworks of the Nō Theater

mazu hatsuhana no	first of all, the early buds
isogu naru	rushing out in bloom
Konoe-dono no	are the weeping cherries
itozakura.[33]	of Lord Konoe.

[*The chorus sings the following* kuse *passage; the* shite *dances to it, which is called* maiguse, *or the* kuse *with a dance.*]

(*Kuse: au, tsuyogin*)

Miwataseba[34]	As I look far out,
yanagi sakura o	the willow trees are mingled
kokimazete	with the cherry trees
Miyako wa haru no	and the capital that wears
nishiki	spring's brocade
sanran tari.	glistens bright in splendor.

[*The* shite *goes out slightly forward toward stage front.*]

Chimoto[35] no	Here one thousand
sakura o	blooming cherries
ueoki	are transplanted,
sono iro o	and then their beauty,
tokoro no	bright in color,
na ni misuru	gives the street its name,

[*The* shite *stamps the floor and makes a* hiraki *gesture.*]

senbon no	Thousand Cherry Lane,
hanazakari,	blooming at its best,
unro ya yuki ni	as it passes through the clouds,
nokoruran.	leaving here its snow.

[*The* shite *goes to the eye-fixing pillar, and, making a small turn to his left, he goes to the front of the musicians.*]

Bishamondō no[36]	At the Hall of Bishamon
hanazakari,	glorious are the blooms,
Shiōden[37] no	and the Great Four Heavens
eiga no	in their splendor
kore ni wa ikade	cannot surpass in beauty
masarubeki.	this magnificent sight!
Ue naru	There the others

[*Pointing with his fan high above, the* shite *goes out to center stage, looks down to his left below, and opens his fan.*]

361

Kurodani[38]	are Black Ravine,
Shimogawara[39]	Lower River Beach;
mukashi Henjō[40]	here once Bishop Henjō
Sōjō no	left this fleeting

[*The* shite *makes an* ageōgi *gesture with his fan.*]

Saigyōzakura

(Ageha)

ukiyo o	world behind him
itoishi	and retreated
Kachōzan,[41]	to Flower Crown Mountain,

[*With an ōzayū gesture, the* shite *goes out toward stage front.*]

CHORUS

Washi no Mi-yama[42] no	like Eagle Mountain blooming
hana no iro	bright in hue we see,
karenishi	and then the Grove
Tsuru no	of the Crane,
Hayashi[43] made	withered we recall,
omoishirarete	makes us realize that all
aware nari.	is deeply touching.

[*Making a turn to his right, the* shite *goes to the* shite *seat.*]

Seisuiji[44] no	There at Clear Stream Temple
Jishu no hana	Kannon's cherry flowers
matsu fuku kaze no[45]	blow among the pines the winds
Otohayama[46]	from Mt. Otoha;

[*Pointing the fan toward stage front and making a beckoning gesture with it, the* shite *goes out to stage front.*]

koko wa mata	and here, moreover,
Arashiyama[47]	Mt. Tempest rises
Tonase[48] ni otsuru	on the Tonase there fall
takitsu-	and cascade

[*Going to the eye-fixing pillar, the* shite *holds the fan up over his forehead.*]

nami made mo	every wave on wave,
hana wa	the blossoms
Ōigawa[49]	down the Ōi,
iseki ni yuki ya	where the flash boards dam them white

[*Making a small turn to his left, the* shite *goes out to the front of the musicians, and, making a sayū gesture, he completes the dance that accompanies the* kuse.]

kakaruran.	like the fallen snow.

[*The* shite *sings in free-rhythm* tsuyogin *style.*]

362

SHITE

[6] *(Awazu, tsuyogin)*

Suwa ya kazu sou	Listen, there the hour hand-drum
toki no tsuzumi	adds number to its beat,

goya no kane no ne   while the bell that tells the dawn

[*The* shite *goes out slightly forward and makes a* hiraki *gesture.*]

hibiki zo sou.   echoes with its tolling.

SHITE

Ara nagorioshi no yayū ya na, oshimu-beshi, oshimubeshi, egataki wa toki, aigataki wa tomo narubeshi.

Ah, parting is such sweet sorrow after this night's sport! How I regret it! How I regret it! How hard it is to recover time [*facing the* waki]; how hard to meet with friends in fellowship like this.

Shunshō ikkoku [50]	In the night of spring one moment
atai senkin	is worth a thousand in gold;
hana ni seikyō	clear fragrance is for flowers;
tsuki ni kage	for the moon, its light.

[*The* shite *sings the following first short line of the verse called* waka. *Then the* shite *takes the* kutsurogi *position by the* shite *seat.*]

SHITE

(*Waka: awazu, tsuyogin*)

haru no yo no   On this night of spring

[*With the introductory (jo) hand-drum music, the* shite *takes some preliminary steps, and after this, following the* hayashi *music, he performs a quiet dance called* jo no mai, *which is traditionally performed in five movements, but now usually has three movements.*]

Jo no mai

[*After the above dance the* shite *makes an* ageōgi *gesture at the* shite *seat, and continues his dancing as he sings the* waka *passage.*]

SHITE

(*Waka: awazu, tsuyogin*)

hana no kage yori	behind the cherry blossoms
akesomete	dawn begins to break

[*The chorus comes in and sings the following passage in* ōnori.]

CHORUS

363

kane o mo matanu [51]	without waiting for the bell
wakare koso are,	only farewell now remains,
wakare koso are,	only farewell now remains,
wakare koso are.	only farewell now remains.

[*With his fan, the* shite *beckons to the* waki *and comes out to center stage. The* shite *sings in* ōnori *and* tsuyogin *style.*]

Saigyōzakura

(Noriji: ōnori, tsuyogin)

Mate shibashi mate shibashi	Wait for a moment, wait for a moment,
yo wa mada fukaki zo,	deep upon us night still lingers;

[*The* shite *looks up at the flower on the prop as the chorus sings.*]

CHORUS

shiramu wa hana no	dawning light is but the glow
kage narikeri.	of the flowers' whiteness

[*Making a turn to his right, the* shite *goes to the front of the stick drummer.*]

Yoso wa mada Ogura[52] no	and elsewhere about Mt. Ogura
yamakage ni nokoru	lies dark night-cherry blooms remain
yozakura[53] no	all for those who lie

[*The* shite *flips up his left sleeve and uses it as a pillow as he kneels down.*]

hana no makura no	and pillow on the flowers

[*The* shite *lets the sleeves fall and lifts up his face.*]

SHITE

(Uta: au, tsuyogin)

yume wa	of their dreams
samenikeri,	that are broken now,

[*The* shite *rises and stamps the floor a few times.*]

CHORUS

yume wa	as their dreams
samenikeri.	are now all broken
Arashi mo yuki mo	by the storm and cherry snows
chirishiku ya,	scatter, spread around,
hana o	while stepping
funde wa[54]	through the petals
onajiku oshimu	we regret all equally

[*Making a turn to his right, the* shite *goes to the* shite *seat.*]

364

shōnen no	for the young sweet year
haru no yo wa	of the spring at night
akenikeri ya,	giving way to dawning

[*At the* shite *seat, the* shite *makes a* hiraki *gesture toward stage front and makes the final stamps on the floor.*]

okina sabite	as the aged man's visage
ato mo nashi,	leaves no trace behind,
okina sabite	as the aged man's visage
ato mo nashi.	leaves no trace behind.

Motomezuka

Introduction

Motomezuka belongs to Group IV of Nō plays. In *Go-on*, Zeami lists it as his father's work.[1] It is constructed as a two-part dream play, which deals with the tragic story of the maiden called Unai. Poets in the *Man'yōshū* wrote several poems about her,[2] but this play is based chiefly on episode 147 of the poem-tale collection called *Yamato monogatari*.[3] Kannami (1333–84), however, treats the ending of his play quite differently from the tale. He completely rejects the bloody duel fought by Unai's two young suitors, which continues even after they have died. He creates instead the hell scenes in Part II of the play, in which this lovely, innocent maiden suffers punishment for her offense.

The play begins as the *waki*, a traveling Buddhist priest from the western provinces, appears with two accompanying priests. There are the usual passages called *shidai, nanori, michiyuki,* and *tsukizerifu*. After the *waki* has reached the famous village of Ikuta, he says: "This is the place I have heard so much about before. As I look at that little field, there many folks come out to gather young greens. I will wait for them and ask them about the famous places around here, too."

It is early spring, the season for gathering the first spring shoots, even in this cold mountain area, distant from the capital. The *shite* and her young companions sing:

> Picking fresh young greens
> at Ikuta's Little Field
> in the morning breeze,
> still the coldness comes and stirs,
> waves and turns our sleeves.

365

The wind is crisp and life is harsh in these parts, but there is hope and joy in the air, as the Feast of Seven Herbs of Health symbolizes spring for these simple country folk. But they feel somewhat envious of the spring that comes a little earlier for the city people, for they cannot yet pick the young greens on the cold mountain. They sing:

but young greens at Miyako
will be picked afield,
for the time to gather them
must have come by now!
So even thinking of it,
envy fills us all.

During the dialogue, their responses to the *waki*'s questions sound mischievous, adding a teasing and playful touch to the poetic tone of the passages. The sections that follow in *sageuta*, *ageuta*, and *rongi*, as well as the exchanges between the *shite* and the chorus, express exquisitely the pastoral scene, where the young girls continue to look for the fresh young greens. Famous old poetic lines connected with the subject, and the names of noted places, so characteristic of Nō style as well as being melodiously satisfying, are strewn through the passages like flowers.

As the river wind begins to blow cold, the pickers return home, except for the oldest one. Sakamoto Setchō describes how the younger pickers make their exit: "How silently, or how stealthy in posture, I should say, they went out onto the bridge. This brought out the truth in my heart. The *shite* watched them leave . . . the way she did so is deep in feeling. As she stood there seeing them off, anyone, it seems, could assume such a posture, but it is wondrous that we feel its deep poignancy."[4] The older picker who remains behind offers to guide the priest to Unai's grave. During the ensuing dialogue, which occurs in the middle of the story, we are fully introduced to the tragic legend of Unai, from the point when the two arrowheads of her suitors struck, at the same time, the wing of the same bird. Here the prose narration in the third person changes to verse in the first person, as if she were telling her own story. The atmosphere thereafter begins to assume a tragic tone. Unai cast herself into Ikuta's water, and then the two young men, who arrived together, lovingly searched for her mound. The chorus sings:

"How long," they cried,
"must we linger on?"
As the Ikuta flows down
at the eventide,
crossing one another
with their swords, life ebbed away.
And all for this,
too, the guilt is mine;
save me from the sin I've sinned
with your prayer, she pleads,
and vanishes away
deep into the mound . . .

366

After the waiting song (*machiutai*), and following the *deha* music, the *shite* starts to sing from within the mound, and the exchange between the *shite* and the chorus ensues. Toward the end of the *ageuta*, when the chorus sings for the *shite*,

in the Burning House I live.
O, look upon it,
this Burning House, my dwelling,
O, look upon it,

the black cloth that covers the mound falls, revealing the *shite* sitting on a stool. She folds her hands in prayer and tells the *waki* how she suffers agonies for the death of the water bird and her suitors. Their ghosts attack her fiercely. She describes further her suffering, as she is tortured by fire and water. The chorus continues to sing:

> the demon jailer
> lashes at her with his scourge
> pursuing her quickly;
> stumbling out, she wanders, lost
> among the hells
> eight in number
> with all the means
> of many painful agonies.
> In your holy presence,
> let me repent,
> let me tell you
> of the scenes I've witnessed . . .

The direct descriptions in the hell scenes that follow are most brutal in both tone and length and are unique in the Nō repertory. After the *shite* rises and comes out of the mound, the chorus sings the following passage in strict-rhythm *chūnori* style:

> plunging, hurtling,
> down she falls
> headlong for a period
> of three months and three long years
> with the sufferings that now
> end all bitter agonies . . .

Setchō describes Roppeita's superb *kata* at this point as follows: ". . . holding up the fan high and then slowly bringing it down in reverse, she jerks it low suddenly, as she falls on her knee. Because of this action, I feel, there are few who are able to suppress a groan."[5]

Why must she suffer so much for having committed so small an offense? Her heart is innocent and free from evil thoughts. It is beyond our logical comprehension, yet when we see this play, I recall, it is so powerful and sublime, as Gondō Yoshikazu observed, that it not only makes us transcend such irrationality but also makes the hell that exists only as an abstract idea become immediately real.[6] In contrast to the first part, this scene moves us deeply, leaving us with an endless world of darkness, as the chorus concludes the play:

> . . . the figure
> of the phantom
> vanishes away,
> the shadow of the phantom
> vanishes away.

367

Indeed, *Motomezuka* is considered to be one of the best works of Kannami. Kanze Kasetsu (1884–1959), the great modern Nō master, reinstated this play into the regular Kanze Nō repertory in 1952.

MOTOMEZUKA

By Kannami

Persons: WAKI: *A Buddhist priest*
WAKI-TSURE: *Accompanying priests (two)*
SHITE (PART I): *Ghost of Unai Otome (appears as a village girl)*
NOCHI-JITE (PART II): *Ghost of Unai Otome (appears as herself)*
TSURE: *Village girls (two or three)*
KYŌGEN: *A man of the place*

Classification: *Primary, Group IV; Variant, Group III*
Place: *Ikuta in the land of Settsu*
Time: *Early spring*
Kogaki: *None*

PART I

[*After the musicians take their seats at the rear of the stage, the stage attendant brings in a framework covered with dark-colored cloth, indicating a tomb mound. Following the introductory* shidai *music, the* waki *and the* waki-tsure *enter the stage. The* waki *wears a pointed hood (kakubōshi), a plain, less-formal silk kimono (muji noshime), a broad-sleeved robe (mizugoromo), a waistband (ko-shiobi), a fan (ōgi), and a rosary (juzu); the* waki-tsure *are similarly costumed. Facing one another, they sing the following* shidai *verse.*]

WAKI AND WAKI-TSURE

[1] (*Shidai: au, yowagin*)

Hina[7] no nagaji no tabigoromo,	Over distant country roads, dressed in traveling clothes,
hina no nagaji no tabigoromo,	over distant country roads, dressed in traveling clothes
Miyako[8] ni iza ya isogan.	on the way to Miyako let us hasten.

[*The chorus sings the* jidori, *repeating the above verse, except the third and fourth lines, in a lower key.*]

CHORUS

(*Jidori: au, yowagin*)

Hina no nagaji no tabigoromo,	Over distant country roads, dressed in traveling clothes

| Miyako ni iza ya | on the way to Miyako |
| isogan. | let us hasten. |

[*After the* jidori, *the* waki, *facing stage front, intones the following prose passage, called* nanori, *introducing himself to the audience.*]

WAKI

(Nanori: awazu, kotoba)

Kore wa Saikokugata yori idetaru sō nite	I am a Buddhist priest who comes from
sōrō. Ware imada Miyako o mizu sōrō	the western provinces. As I have not yet
hodo ni, tadaima Miyako ni nobori sōrō.	seen Miyako, I will go up there now.

[*Once the* waki *has introduced himself to the audience and stated his purpose, he and the* waki-tsure, *facing one another again, sing in unison the following verse passage, called* michiyuki, *a traveling song.*]

WAKI AND WAKI-TSURE

(Michiyuki: au, yowagin)

Tabigoromo[9]	Dressed in traveling clothes
yae[10] no shioji no	eightfold there rolls the ocean
urazutai,	by whose road we go,
yae no shioji no	eightfold there rolls the ocean
urazutai,	by whose road we go:
fune nite mo yuku	here by boat we cross the sea;
tabi no michi	there, too, the mountains
umi yama kakete	as we journey on our way
harubaru to	far and far away,
akashi kurashite	spending many days and nights
yuku hodo ni	on we go, and now

[*The* waki *faces stage front, goes forward a step or two, and returns to his former position, indicating that they have all traveled and have now come to their destination. Again, facing one another, they finish the rest of the lines.*]

na ni nomi kikishi	only known by name to us
Tsu[11] no kuni no	in the land of Tsu,
Ikuta[12] no sato ni	the village of Ikuta
tsukinikeri,	we have reached at last,
Ikuta no sato ni	the village of Ikuta
tsukinikeri.	we have reached at last.

[*Facing stage front, the* waki *intones the following prose passage, called* tsukizerifu, *the arrival speech.*]

WAKI

(Tsukizerifu: awazu, kotoba)

Kore wa kikioyobitaru tokoro nite sōrō.	This is the place I have heard so much
Ano Ono o mireba wakana[13] tsumu hito	about. As I look at that little field, there
no amata kitari sōrō. Kano hitobito o	many folks come out to gather young

Motomezuka

machite tokoro no meisho o mo tazunebaya to omoi sōrō.

greens. I will wait for them and ask
them about the famous places around
here, too.

WAKI-TSURE

Mottomo nite sōrō.

Yes, certainly.

[The waki *goes to the* waki *seat and sits down beside his attendant. Following the entrance music
called* shidai, *the* shite, *preceded by the* tsure, *appears. The* shite *wears a* zō *mask, a wig (*kazura*),
a wig band (*kazuraobi*), an under kimono with painted gold or silver patterns (*surihaku*), a white
broad-sleeved robe (*shiro mizugoromo*), an embroidered under kimono with painted gold or silver
patterns in* koshimaki *style (*nuihaku koshimaki*), a waistband (*koshiobi*), and a fan (*ōgi*). The*
tsure *are similarly costumed, except for the mask and the fan. On the bridge they line up and sing the*
issei *verse.]*

SHITE AND TSURE

[2] *(Issei: awazu, yowagin)*

Wakana tsumu	Picking fresh young greens
Ikuta no Ono no	at Ikuta's Little Field
asakaze ni	in the morning breeze,
nao sae kaeru [14]	still the coldness comes and stirs,
tamoto kana.	waves and turns our sleeves.

TSURE

(Ni no ku)

Ko no me mo haru no [15]	Though the tree buds start to swell
awayuki ni	with the soft spring snow,

SHITE AND TSURE

mori no shita kusa	underneath the grove of trees
nao samushi.	still the grass lies cold.

[The shite, *facing stage front, sings the following* sashi *passage.]*

SHITE

(Sashi: awazu, yowagin)

Miyama ni wa	In the deep mountains
matsu no yuki dani	fallen snows have not yet thawed
kienaku ni [16]	even from the pines,

370

SHITE AND TSURE *[Facing one another again.]*

Miyako wa nobe no	but young greens at Miyako
wakana tsumu	will be picked afield,
koro ni mo ima wa	for the time to gather them
narinuran,	must have come by now!
omoiyaru koso	So even thinking of it,
yukashikere.	envy fills us all.

Masterworks of the Nō Theater

Koko wa mata	This too is the place
moto yori tokoro mo	located very far away
amazakaru[17]	from the capital.

SHITE AND TSURE

hinabito nareba	Since we all are backwoods folk,
onozukara	naturally life
uki mo inochi mo	is so harsh and miserable,
Ikuta[18] no umi no	but as long as we survive
mi[19] no kagiri nite	near Ikuta's weary waves
uki waza no	endless is our toil
haru toshi mo naki	as this year when spring is late
Ono ni idete.	to Little Field we go.

SHITE AND TSURE

[*All sing the* sageuta, *a low-pitched song, facing one another.*]

(*Sageuta: au, yowagin*)

wakana tsumu	Picking fresh young greens,
iku satobito no	how many from the village
ato naran,	leave those tracks behind?
yukima amata ni	Now more patches bare of snow
no wa narinu.	show across the field.

[*Changing the key, they sing the high-pitched song,* ageuta.]

(*Ageuta: au, yowagin*)

Michi nashi tote mo[20]	Even though there is no path,
fumiwakete	on we make our way,
michi nashi tote mo	even though there is no path,
fumiwakete,	on we make our way
nozawa no wakana	by the marshland to gather
kyō tsuman,	fresh young greens today
yukima o	but should we wait
matsu[21] naraba	for the snow to melt
wakana mo moshi ya	here and there, in spots, young greens
oi mo sen.	would perhaps grow old.

[*They enter the stage.*]

Arashi fuku	With the blasts that blow
mori no kokage	across the shaded woods
Ono no yuki mo	Little Field lies in snow
nao saete,	growing cold and clear
haru toshi mo	with no spring this year
nanakusa[22] no	for the seven herbs[23]
Ikuta[24] no wakana	let us gather fresh young greens
tsumō yo.	at Ikuta,

371

Motomezuka

[The tsure *go to stage front from the* waki *seat and stand in line with the eye-fixing pillar, and the* shite *stands in front of the musicians. Just before they finish singing, the* waki *rises from his sitting position.]*

Ikuta no wakana tsumō yo.	let us gather fresh young greens at Ikuta.

[The following dialogues, some in prose and some in verse, are exchanged between the waki *and the* shite *or* tsure.]*

WAKI *[At the* waki *seat.]*

[3] *(Mondai: awazu, yowagin)*

Ikani kore naru hito ni tazunemōsubeki koto no sōrō. Ikuta to wa kono atari o mōshi sōrō ka.	Ho there, a moment, please. I have something I would like to ask you. Is this vicinity called Ikuta?

TSURE *[Standing near the eye-fixing pillar.]*

Ikuta to shiroshi-meshitaru ue wa on-tazune made mo sōrōmaji.	Since you know Ikuta's name, there is hardly any need for you to ask some person about this place at all.

SHITE *[Standing in front of the musicians.]*

Tokorodokoro no arisama ni mo nado ka wa goranji shirazaran.	Glancing over here and there at what you see around, you surely should have known at once if this were the place.
Mazu wa Ikuta no na ni shi ou kore ni kazu aru hayashi oba Ikuta no Mori[25] to wa shiroshimesazu ya.	First of all, one of the well-known sights of Ikuta is a thickly wooded grove, which you should have recognized as Ikuta Forest. Don't you think so?

TSURE

Mata ima watari tamaeru wa na ni nagaretaru[26] Ikutagawa[27]	And so graciously just now you've crossed on your way, the river of Ikuta flowing far in fame.

SHITE

372

mizu no midori mo haru asaki yukima no wakana tsumu nobe ni	Its waters reflect the light green of early spring, and in the fields with patches bare of snow, the tender shoots are picked.

TSURE

sukunaki kusa no hara naraba	Since the grass grows little yet across the meadow

| Ono to wa nado ya | how could you fail to wonder |
| shiroshimesarenu zo. | if this were the same Little Field? |

[*The* shite *and the* tsure *face one another and sing.*]

SHITE AND TSURE

Miyoshino[28] Shiga[29] no	Both Yoshino and Shiga
yamazakura,	with mountain cherries,
Tatsuta[30] Hatsuse[31] no	Tatsuta and Hatsuse
momiji oba	with crimson maples
kajin no ie[32] ni wa	are known among the houses
shirunareba	of lyric poets,
tokoro ni sumeru	so you might think those who live
mono nareba tote	in this famous place
Ikuta no Mori to mo	know about Ikuta's forest
hayashi to mo	or its stands of trees;

[*The* shite *goes a step or two closer toward the* waki.]

| shiranu koto o na | you should not ask us about |
| notamaiso yo. | things we don't know at all. |

[*The* waki *looks toward stage front, above and into the distance.*]

WAKI

(Kakeai: awazu, yowagin)

Geni mokuzen no	Indeed, what lies before me
tokorodokoro	stretching here and there,
mori o hajimete	starting from that grove of trees
umi kawa no	to the sea and streams,
kasumi watareru	with the trailing mists that veil
Ono no keshiki	the view of Little Field?

| Geni mo Ikuta no na ni shi oeru. Sate Motomezuka[33] to wa izuku zo ya. | Indeed, all these deserve the fame of Ikuta's name. But where, then, is the Motomezuka? |

SHITE

| Motomezuka to wa na ni wa kikedomo, makoto wa izuku no hodo yaran. Warawa mo sara ni shiranu nari. | I have heard of something called the Motomezuka, but in fact I do not know where it is. I know nothing more about it. |

373

TSURE

Nō nō tabibito	Come now, come now, oh, travelers,
yoshinaki koto o na	why are you pestering us still
notamaiso.	with trifles like these?
Warawa mo wakana o	For we are picking these young greens
tsumu itoma.	with no time to spare.

Motomezuka

SHITE

On-mi mo isogi no	You are also in a hurry
tabi naru ni	as you journey still.
nani shi ni yasurai-	Why do you want to linger here
tamōran.	since you have rested?

SHITE AND TSURE [*Facing one another.*]

Sareba furuki	So in the ancient verse
uta ni mo	it has been said:

[*As the chorus starts to sing the following* sageuta, *all face stage front again.*]

CHORUS

(*Sageuta: au, yowagin*)

Tabibito no[34]	Fresh young greens of spring
michi samatage ni	will keep all travelers
tsumu mono wa	from journeying on
Ikuta no Ono no	through Ikuta's Little Field,
wakana nari.	where young girls pick them.

[*The* shite *faces the* waki.]

Yoshinaya, nani o	What nonsense! Just what is it
toitamō.	that you want to know?

[*The* shite *faces stage front again, as the chorus starts to sing the following* ageuta *passage in high-pitched singing style. At the same time, the* kyōgen *comes out inconspicuously through the half-raised Nō curtain and silently takes the* ai *seat.*]

(*Ageuta: au, yowagin*)

Kasugano no[35]	In Kasuga Fields,
tobihi no nomori	guardsmen of the signal fires,
idete miyo,	step outside and look,

[*The* tsure *go to the front of the chorus and sit down, and the* waki *takes the* waki *seat.*]

tobihi no nomori	guardsmen of the signal fires,
idete miyo	step outside and look,
wakana tsuman mo	we can pick the fresh young greens
hodo araji.	here before too long.

[*The* shite *moves slightly forward toward stage front.*]

Sono gotoku	So, likewise it seems
tabibito mo	that you travelers
isogasetamō	who are hastening on your way
Miyako o	to Miyako

[*Facing the* waki.]

ima ikuka arite	have just a few more days from now
goranzen.	before you arrive.

374

Masterworks of the Nō Theater

[*Changing her mood and turning to her left in an arc, the* shite *goes to the* shite *seat.*]

Kimi ga tame[36]	For your sake I go
haru no no ni idete	out to the meadow in the spring,
wakana tsumu	picking fresh young greens;
koromode samushi	although my sleeves grow chilly
kie nokoru	with the snows that cling
yuki nagara	to the greens half-thawed,
tsumō yo	let us pick them;

[*At the* shite *seat, making a* hiraki *gesture toward stage front, the* shite *turns to the* waki.]

awayuki nagara	together with the light snow
tsumō yo.	let us pick them.

[*The* shite *goes out slightly toward stage front, as the chorus sings the following* sageuta *passage.*]

[4] (*Sageuta: au, yowagin*)

Sawabe naru	Though along the edge
hikori wa usuku	of the marsh the lumpy ice
nokoredomo	still remains so thin

[*Pointing her fan downward, the* shite *looks closely about her and turns her gaze to her right.*]

mizu no fukazeri	in the water, rooted deep,
kakiwakete	watercresses grow;
aomidori	parting them to choose
iro nagara iza ya	the fresh young greens deep blue in hue
tsumō yo,	let us pick them,

[*The* shite *faces the* tsure.]

iro nagara iza ya	the fresh young greens deep blue in hue
tsumō yo.	let us pick them.

[*At the* shite *seat, the* shite *faces stage front. The chorus and the* shite *exchange the following lines, called* rongi.]

CHORUS

(*Rongi: au, yowagin*)

Mada hatsu haru no	Still among the fresh young greens
wakana ni wa	of the first spring day,
sanomi ni tane wa	are there any good enough
ika naran.	for a kind of stock?

375

SHITE

Haru tachite[37]   Though the spring has come

[*The* shite *looks into the distance.*]

Motomezuka

Ashita no Hara[38] no	here I see the fallen snow
yuki mireba	over Morning Field,
mada furu[39] toshi no	so I feel the good old year
kokochi shite,	lingers with us still,
kotoshi oi wa	but how very few appear
sukunashi,	this year's new sprouts.

[*To the* tsure.]

furuha no wakana	Fresh young greens among the old,
tsumō yo.	let us pick them.

CHORUS

Furuha naredomo	Even though they are old leaves,
sasuga mata	as they still remain

[*The* shite *goes out slightly forward.*]

toshi wakakusa no	with the new greens of this year,
tane nare ya.	they're a kind of stock;
Kokoro seyo	gather them with care
haru no nobe.	from the fields of spring.

[*The* shite *stands as if in a recollective mood.*]

SHITE

Haru no no ni,[40]	To the fields of spring,
haru no no ni,	to the fields of spring,
sumire tsumi ni to	for the violet in bloom
koshi hito no	came a man and picked
wakamurasaki no	a green they call "young purple"
na ya tsumishi[41]	in its place instead.

[*The* shite *goes out to the eye-fixing pillar, and, turning to her left in an arc, she goes to the front of the musicians, while the chorus sings the following lines.*]

CHORUS

Geni ya yukari no	So its name and hue retain
na o tomete	an affinity,
imose no hashi[42] mo	like the bridge that lovers crossed
naka taeshi	in twos lies broken

SHITE

Sano no kukutachi[43]	over Sano young and fair
wakatachite	stand the rapeweed stalks

CHORUS

midori no iro mo	glowing all in deepened green
na ni zo somu	justly famous, too,

Chōan[44] no nazuna[45]   like Chang-an's royal shepherd's purse,

CHORUS

karanazuna[46]   pungent shepherd's purse;

SHITE

shiromigusa[47] mo   also white-root cresses
ariyake[48] no   in the moonlit dawn

CHORUS

yuki ni magirete   are mistaken for the snow;

[*The* shite *looks at the light snow on her right.*]

tsumikanuru made   at Little Field how chilly
haru samuki   it is to pick them
Ono no   in the spring

[*The* shite *points her fan at the treetops as she looks across them.*]

asakaze   with morning gusts
mata mori no shizue   across the branches of the pines
matsu tarete   bending down with snow.
izure o   So when spring comes

[*Opening her fan, the* shite *turns to her right.*]

haru to wa   we cannot know
shiranami[49] no   as the white-capped waves

[*From the musicians' seats the* shite *looks toward stage front far into the distance, and, beckoning with her fan, she comes forward and looks at her left sleeve.*]

kawakaze made mo   break before the river wind,
saekaeri   clear and piercing cold,
fukaruru   and blown by it
tamoto mo   our sleeves are still
nao samushi   bleakly chilly too;

[*At this point the* tsure *make their exits through the low door located upstage left, called* kirido.]

tsuminokoshite   so leaving some unpicked,
kaeran,   are they going home?

[*The* shite *goes to the* shite *seat.*]

377

wakana tsuminokoshite   Leaving those unpicked young greens
                              behind,
kaeran.   are they going?

[*As the* waki *stands at the* waki *seat, he speaks to the* shite *in prose. The dialogue between them is known as* mondai, *"questions and answers."*]

Motomezuka

[5] *(Mondai: awazu, yowagin)*

Ika ni mōsubeki koto no sōrō. Wakana tsumu nyoshō wa mina mina kaeri tamō ni nani tote on-mi ichi-nin nokori tamō zo.

Hello, there. The maidens who were picking those young greens have all returned home, so why do you remain behind by yourself?

SHITE

Saki ni on-tazune sōrō Motomezuka o oshiemōshi sōrawan.

I would like to show you the Motomezuka that you were asking us about a while ago.

WAKI

Sore koso nozomi nite sōrō. Onnoshie sōrae.

Indeed, that is what I wanted. Please, show it to me.

SHITE

Konata e onniri sōrae.

Please, come this way.

[*The* shite *takes two or three steps forward toward the mound.*]

Kore koso Motomezuka nite sōrae.

This is, indeed, the Motomezuka.

WAKI

Sate Motomezuka to wa nani to mōshitaru iware nite sōrō zo. Kuwashiku onmonogatari sōrae.

Well then. There must be some reasons why the Motomezuka is here. Please tell me its story in detail.

[*The* waki *goes out toward the mound and faces it.*]

SHITE

(Mondai: katari, kotoba)

Sareba katatte kikase mōshi sōrōbeshi.

Now, I will tell you and let you hear the story.

[*Seated in front of the mound and facing stage front, the* shite *tells the story, which is called* katari, *"narration." The* waki, *at the* waki *seat, listens to her.*]

(Katari: awazu, kotoba)

378

Mukashi kono tokoro ni Unai Otome[50] no arishi ni, mata sono koro Sasada otoko, Chinu no Masurao to mōshishi mono kano Unai ni kokoro o kake, onaji hi no onaji toki ni warinaki omoi no tamazusa o okuru. Kano onna omou yō, hitori ni nabikaba hitori no urami fukakarubeshi to sō nō nabiku koto mo na-

Long ago there lived in this village Unai the Maid. At about that time two young men, Sasada and Chinu the Brave, threw their hearts upon Unai. On the same day and at the same hour, each sent her a love letter filled with declarations of unbearable longing. Then she thought that if she yielded to one, the

karishi ga ano Ikutagawa no mizutori o sae futari no yasaki morotomo ni hitotsu no tsubasa ni atarishikaba.

other's bitter feeling would deepen. So she could not easily give herself to either. But even when they shot at a mandarin duck on the River Ikuta, their two arrowheads struck at the same time the wing of the same bird.

[*The* shite *cannot bear the thought; she lowers her mask and speaks in the first person.*]

Sono toki warawa	At that time I thought of it
omou yō,	deeply by myself:
muzan na ya	how truly cruel!
sashi mo chigiri wa	Deeper were their vows of love
fukamidori	than the deep green hue
mizutori made mo	of that pair of waterfowl.
ware yue ni	Just because of me,
sakoso inochi wa	though they held this life so dear,
oshidori no	now they've passed away;
tsugai sarinishi	gone forever this pair too
awaresa yo.	sad and pitiful!

[*The* shite *continues singing, in free-rhythm* yowagin *style.*]

(*Awazu, yowagin*)

Sumi wabitsu[51]	Weary of this life
waga mi suteten	in the land of Tsu I will
Tsu no Kuni no	cast myself to drown
Ikuta no Kawa wa	in the River Ikuta,
na nomi narikeri to.	"Field of Life," in name only.

[*The chorus takes over and sings the* ageuta *passage.*]

CHORUS

(*Ageuta: au, yowagin*)

Kore o saigo no	With these words she leaves behind
kotoba nite	her final poem;
kono kawanami ni	underneath the river waves
shizumishi o	now she deeply sinks.

[*The* shite *points at the mound with her fan.*]

toriagete

	Then her corpse was raised
kono tsuka no	and they buried her
dochū ni kome	deeply underneath the earth
osameshi ni	in this very mound;
futari no	but soon after
otoko wa	there came these two
kono tsuka ni motome	young gallants, together to this place
kitaritsutsu	searching for her mound:

[*Sadly, the* shite *turns toward the* waki.]

379

Motomezuka

itsu made	"How long," they cried,
Ikutagawa[52]	"must we linger on?"
nagaruru mizu ni	As the Ikuta flows down
yūshio no	at the eventide,[53]
sashichigaete[54]	crossing one another[55]
munashiku nareba	with their swords, life ebbed away.
sore sae	And for all this,

[*The* shite *takes a step or two toward the* waki.]

waga toga ni	too, the guilt is mine;
naru mi o tasuke-	save me from the sin I've sinned
tamae tote	with your prayer, she pleads,

[*Turning to her left, the* shite *goes near the mound.*]

tsuka no uchi ni	and vanishes away
irinikeru,	deep into the mound,
tsuka no uchi ni zo	and vanishes all away
irinikeru	deep into the mound.

Nakairi (Interlude)

[*The* kyōgen, *a man of the place, wearing a striped, less-formal silk kimono* (dan noshime), *the long* kyōgen *two-piece* (naga kamishimo), *a waistband* (koshiobi), *a fan* (ōgi), *and a small sword* (chiisa gatana), *comes out to the name-saying seat* (nanoriza), *stands, and exchanges the following dialogue with the* waki *in prose.*]

Kyōgen

(Mondai: katari, kotoba)

Kayō ni sōrō mono wa Ikuta no sato ni sumai suru mono nite sōrō. Kyō wa Ikuta no atari e mairi kokoro o nagusamebaya to zonzuru. Iya kore ni minaremōsanu o-sō no goza sōrō ga, izuku yori izukata e otōrinasare sōraeba kore ni wa yasurōte goza sōrō zo.	I am a person living in the village of Ikuta. Today I will go out to the neighborhood of Ikuta to amuse myself. Well, I see an unfamiliar Buddhist priest here. [*Looks at the* waki.] As you come from someplace and are going somewhere, I presume you are just resting here.

Waki

Kore wa Saikokugata yori idetaru sō nite sōrō. On-mi wa kono atari no hito nite watari sōrō ka.	I am a Buddhist priest who comes from the western provinces. Do you live around this vicinity?

380

Kyōgen

Nakanaka kono atari no mono nite sōrō.	Yes, holy priest. I am from this neighborhood.

Waki

Sayō nite sōrawaba mazu chikō on-niri sōrae. Tazunetaki koto no sōrō.	If that's so, please come closer. I have something to ask you.

Masterworks of the Nō Theater

Kashikomatte sōrō. Sate o-tazune na-saretaki to wa ikayō naru go-yō nite sōrō zo.

Yes, holy priest. [*Goes out to stage center and sits down.*] Well, then. What is it you want to ask me?

WAKI

Omoi mo yoranu mōshigoto nite sōrae-domo kono Motomezuka ni tsuki sama-zama shisai arubeshi. Go-zonji ni oite wa katatte o-kikase sōrae.

Indeed, this is something you may not expect from me, but there must be vari-ous reasons why the Motomezuka is here. Please tell me the stories if you know about them.

KYŌGEN

Kore wa omoi mo yoranu koto o uketa-mawari sōrō mono kana. Warera mo kono atari ni wa sumaitsukamatsuri sō-raedomo sayō no koto kuwashiku wa zonzezu sōrō, sarinagara hajimete o-me ni kakari o-tazune nasare sōrō koto o, nan to mo zonzenu to mōsu mo ika nite sōraeba, oyoso uketamawari-oyobitaru tōri on-monogatari mōsōzuru nite sōrō.

How strange that you should ask me about such things. Though we live in this neighborhood, I don't know too much about the details. But since I am asked by a person that I meet for the first time, it would not be right to say that I know nothing; therefore, I shall tell the story the way I have heard it.

WAKI

Chikagoro nite sōrō.

I would be most grateful.

KYŌGEN

Saru hodo ni Motomezuka no shisai to mōsu wa inishie kono tokoro ni Unai Otome to mōsu onna no goza sōraishi ga, mata Izumi no Kuni Nobuta to mōsu tokoro ni Chinu no Masurao to mōsu mono goza sōrō ga, Unai Otome o koi shitai mōsu. Mata kono tokoro ni mo Sasada to mōsu mono goza aritaru ga, kore mo otome o koi shitaitaru ga, fu-shigi naru koto no sōrō. Aru toki otome no kata e onaji hi no onaji toki ni, ryōnin no fumi tōri sōrō ga, otome wa fumi o miru ni buntai mo onaji koto nite sōrō aida, izure e henji itasubeki yō mo naku, futaoya e kono yoshi mōshide-reba, oya-domo mōsu yō wa, ryōnin tomo ni Ikutagawa e tomonai mizudori o isase yumi no masaretaru kata o muko ni torubeshi to mōshikereba, ryōnin tomo ōi ni yorokobi, yumiya tazusae

Well, the reason for the Motomezuka is that here Unai the Maid lived long ago, and at the place called Nobuta in Izumi Province, there lived a man named Chinu the Brave, who loved and longed for her. Here there was also a man called Sasada, who also loved and longed for her. It is a strange thing that on a certain day letters came to her from both of them at the same time, and at the same hour. When she looked at the letters, both were the same. She was at a loss as to how to reply. As she told her parents about the letters, they said that she should accompany the two men to the Ikuta River, then ask them to shoot a water bird, and choose the one who excelled with the bow as her groom. When she told them about it, the two men were overjoyed. With their bows

381

Motomezuka

Ikutagawa e mairi, yatsubo o on-sashi are to mōsu. Saraba ichiwa no tori o ryōnin nite asobase to mōsu ni ryōnin nite ryō no hagai o imōshi sōrō aida, otome no oya mo akirehate ori sōrō ga, otome wa mazu ryōnin no mono o kaeshi, kayō no koto mo zense no yakusoku nari. Kono ue wa inochi atte mo sen nashi tote isshu no uta ni,

> sumi wabinu
> waga mi suteken
> Tsu no Kuni no
> Ikuta no kawa wa
> na nomi narikeri

to eiji, Ikutagawa e mi o nage munashiku narimōshi sōrō aida, sono mama tsuka ni tsukikomimōsu ni, ryōnin no otoko kono yoshi o kiki, tsuka no mae ni kitari sashichigae munashiku narimōshi sōrō aida, kore mo sayū no tsuka ni tsuki komi motomete shishitaru tsuka nareba to te, Motomezuka to wa mōshi sōrō. Mazu warera no uketamawari-oyobitaru wa kaku no gotoku nite goza sōrō ga nani to oboshimeshi o-tazune nasare sōrō zo. Chikagoro fushin ni zonji sōrō.

and arrows they went to the Ikuta River. "Notch the bows," she said. "Now shoot a bird, both of you." Both the arrows hit the wing of the same bird. The parents were astonished for a while. Unai made both men return home. "Such a thing as this must be my fate from a former life. Now even though I live on, life has no meaning," she said, and wrote a verse.

"Weary of this life
in the land of Tsu I will
cast myself to drown
in the River Ikuta,
'Field of Life,' in name only."

Then she threw herself into the Ikuta and died. In the mound she's buried as she was. Both men heard of this and came here to the mound. Then they stabbed each other and died. They were also buried, on the right and left of her mound. Since they searched for the mound and died here, it is called the Motomezuka. Well, this is what I have heard. Please tell me why you ask about this. Lately I have felt something strange around here.

WAKI

Nengoro ni on-monogatari sōrō mono kana. Tazunemōsu mo yo no gi ni arazu. On-mi izen ni nyoshō amatu korare sōrō hodo ni, sunawachi kotoba o kawashite sōraeba tokoro no meisho nado o oshie, kono tokoro e dōdō sōraite, Motomezuka no koto o nengoro ni katari, nan to yaran mi no ue no yō ni mōsare, tsuka no hotori nite sugata o miushinōte sōrō yo.

How kind of you to tell me all about the story. The reason I asked is not special. A while ago many young maidens were here, and I exchanged words with one of them. She told me about some famous sites of this place and she accompanied me along the way, telling me kindly about the story of the Motomezuka. She told the story as if it were about herself, and near the mound I lost sight of her.

KYŌGEN

Kore wa kidoku naru koto o uketamawari sōrō mono kana. Sate wa otome no yūrei arawareide, o-kotoba o kawashitaru to zonji sōrō aida, kano ato nengoro ni o-tomurai arekashi to zonji sōrō.

This is as strange a story as I've ever heard! Well, the ghost of the maiden must have appeared; I think you have exchanged words with her. I hope you pray for her memory very kindly.

WAKI

Chikagoro fushigi naru koto nite sōrō hodo ni shibaraku tōryū mōshi arigataki o-kyō o dokuju shi, kano ato o nengoro ni tomuraimōsōzuru nite sōrō.

Since things have been very strange of late, I will stay here for a while, and with the recitation of holy sutras, I would like to hold a sacred service.

KYŌGEN

Go-yō no koto mo sōrawaba kasanete ōse sōrae.

If you have something for me to do, please ask me again.

WAKI

Tanomi sōrōbeshi.

That is kind of you. Thank you.

KYŌGEN

Kokoroe mōshite sōrō.

Not at all, good priest.

[*The* kyōgen *goes to the* ai *seat.*]

PART II

[*The* waki *and the* waki-tsure *sing the following verse, called* machiutai, *"waiting song."*]

WAKI AND WAKI-TSURE

[6] *(Machiutai: au, yowagin)*

Hitoyo fusu	Sleeping through the night,
oshika no tsuno no[56]	short as a buck's new antler
tsuka no kusa,	is the mound's young grass,
oshika no tsuno no	short as a buck's new antler
tsuka no kusa[57]	is the mound's young grass,
kage yori mieshi	the specter-soul is briefly
bōkon o	seen behind its shade,
tomurō nori no	for whose sake I pray aloud
koe tatete	so that she may rest.

[*The* waki *holds his hands together in prayer, facing toward the mound, and sings the following passage from the Buddhist sutra.*]

WAKI

Namu yūrei[58]	Peace to the restless ghost!
Jōtō shōgaku	May you truly win salvation.
shutsuri shōji	You'll be freed completely
tonshō bodai.	from the chains of life and death.

[*Following the* deha *music, the* nochi-jite, *the* shite *in Part II, appears. She has made a costume change within the mound. She wears a* yaseonna *mask, a wig (*kazura*), a wig band (*kazuraobi*), an under kimono with painted gold or silver patterns (*surihaku*), an unpatterned polished white silk robe in* tsuboori *style (*shironeri tsuboori*), a red broad divided skirt (*iro ōguchi*), a waistband (*ko-*]

Motomezuka

shiobi), and a fan (ōgi). Without revealing her form, she sings from inside the mound the following sashi passage.]

SHITE

[7] (Sashi: awazu, tsuyogin)

Ou kōya	Desolate, wide plain!
hito mare[59] nari.	How few men come this way!
Waga kofun narade	There is really nothing other
mata nani mono zo.	than my ancient burial mound;

[Changes her singing style to free-rhythm yowagin.]

(Yowagin)

Kabane o arasou	fighting over scattered corpses
mōjū wa	those ferocious beasts
satte mata nokoru.	retreat and once again return;
Tsuka o mamoru	flying spirits guarding
hibaku wa	this earthen mound
shōfū ni tobi	whirl in the rushing pine winds,
denkō chōro	quick as the lightning flashes,
nao motte	brief as the dewdrop
manako ni ari.	before our very eyes.

[The shite sings in tsuyogin style.]

(Issei: awazu, tsuyogin)

Kofunnōku wa	Many of these ancient mounds
shōnen no hito[60]	are for those who died in youth,

[The shite again changes the singing style to yowagin.]

(Yowagin)

Ikuta no na ni mo	so their lives belie the name
ninu inochi.	of the Field of Life.

[The chorus comes in. The shite looks at the waki.]

CHORUS

Satte hisashiki	It was long ago I fled
kokyō no hito no	from my native place, but here

SHITE

mi-nori no koe wa	I am grateful for the voice
arigata ya.	of the people's prayers.

CHORUS

Ara enbu[61]	How I really long
koishi ya.	for the Jambu!

Masterworks of the Nō Theater

(Ageuta: au, tsuyogin)

Sareba hito	Even though a man
ichinichi ichiya o	should live but for a single night
furu ni dani,	and a single day,
ichinichi ichiya o	should live but for a single night
furu ni dani	and a single day,
hachi oku	eight hundred million
shi sen no	and four thousand
omoi ari.	passions still arise.
Iwan ya	How many more
warera wa	must come to me,
sarinishi ato mo	longing even since my death
hisakata[62] no	for those distant days
Ama no	in the reign
Mikado no	of the heavenly
mi-yo yori	mighty sovereign?
ima wa nochi no	And now, long afterwards,
Horikawa[63] no	in the blessed rule
gyo-o ni awaba	of Gohorikawa,
ware mo	through his grace,

[Changes the singing style to yowagin.]

(Yowagin)

futatabi yo ni	would that I could return
kaerekashi.	to the world once more!
Itsu made	How long, how long
kusa no kage	underneath the moss,
koke no shita ni wa	in the shadows of the grass,
uzumoren.	must I lie buried?
Saraba uzumore mo	Buried here to rot completely,
hatezu shite	but I cannot rest
kurushimi wa	for these agonies
mi o yaku	scorch my body

[As the black cloth that covers the mound falls, the shite appears, sitting on a stool.]

kataku[64] no sumika	in the Burning House I live.
goran-ze yo,	Oh, look upon it,
kataku no sumika	this burning house, my dwelling,
goran-ze yo.	Oh, look upon it.

385

WAKI

[8] (Kakeai: au, yowagin)

Ara itawashi no onnarisama ya na. Ichi-   How pitiful and wretched is this painful

Motomezuka

| nen hirugaeseba muryō no tsumi o mo nogarubeshi. | sight. If for a single moment, you would abandon your attachment, you would be forgiven even countless sins. |

[*The* waki *folds his hands in prayer.*]

Shuju shoakushu	All evil of each and every kind,
jigoku ki chikushō	all worlds of demons, beasts, and hells,
shōrō byōshi ku	all agonies of birth, death, age, and illness—
izen shitsu ryōmetsu.	all shall come to an end.

| Haya haya ukami tamae. | Soon, soon may enlightenment and salvation be yours. |

SHITE

Arigata ya.	How grateful I am!
Kono kurushimi no	Amid these ever ceaseless
hima naki ni	agonies and pain,
mi-nori no koe no	to my ears there comes a voice
mimi ni furete	chanting holy prayers.
daishōnetsu[65] no	Even in the smoke that fills
kemuri no uchi ni	up this Hell of Scorching Heat
harema no sukoshi	I can glimpse a clearing space
miyuru zo ya.	through a little rift!

[*The* shite *folds her hands in prayer.*]

| Arigata ya. | How grateful I am. |

[*The* shite *leaves the mound and comes out to the stage. She gazes to her right.*]

(*Awazu*)

| Osoroshi ya. Okoto wa ta so. Nani Sasada Otoko no bōshin to ya. Mata konata naru wa Chinu no Masurao, sō no te o totte, kitare kitare to semuredomo | Oh, hideous horror! What are you? Is this the ghost of young Sasada? And over here, is this Chinu the Brave? Each takes me by the hand, left and right, urging me to come this way and that; |

(*Tsuyogin*)

| Sankai[66] kataku no | in this Burning House I live |
| sumika oba | in the Threefold World |

386

| nani to chikara ni izubeki zo. Mata osoroshi ya hibaku tobisari me no mae ni, kitaru o mireba oshidori no tetchō[67] to natte kurogane no | what shall I depend on to give me the power to escape? Oh, more hideous! Now those ghosts fly off and what I see approaching me is the mandarin duck. She turns to iron with the steel |

[*The* shite *sings the following passage in* yowagin.]

(Yowagin)

hashi ashi tsurugi no	beak and claws as though they're sharpened
gotoku naru ga	like the keenest daggers;
kōbe o tsutsuki	pecking at my head she eats
zui o kuu.	all the marrow up.

[*The* shite *shrinks back.*]

Ko wa somo warawa ga	Shall this be my fate forever
naseru toga ka ya.	for the evil that I've done?

[*Restrains her tears.*]

Urameshi ya.	Oh, how reproachful!

[*Facing the* waki, *the* shite *pleads.*]

(Kakeai: awazu, yowagin)

Nō on-sō kono kurushimi oba nani to ka tasuketamōbeki.	Holy priest, I beg of you. Find some way to free me from the torment of these pains.

WAKI

[9]

Geni kurushimi no	"Now there comes the final hour
toki kitaru to	of agony and anguish."
ii mo aeneba	Thus no sooner than she speaks,
tsuka no ue ni	above the earthen mound
kaen hito-mura	flies a cloud of flaming fire
tobiōite	covering it over;

SHITE

hikari wa hibaku no	light becomes a hellish demon
oni to natte	to torment my spirit:

WAKI [*Speaking for the* shite.]

shimoto o furiage	up he flings the scourge above him
ottatsureba	and pursues her swiftly.

SHITE

yukan to sureba	When I try to flee, the sea
mae wa umi	is there before me,

WAKI

ushiro wa kaen	the blazing flame, behind her,

387

Motomezuka

hidari mo   on both my left

migi mo   and her right,

suika no seme ni   fire and water torture me,
tsumerarete   hopelessly entrapped,

[*The* shite *looks at the pillar of the mound.*]

senkata nakute   not a way is left for her.
kataku no   As she clutches
hashira ni   at the pillar

[*The chorus comes in and sings the following passage in* chūnori. *The* shite *rises and clings to the pillar.*]

(*Chūnoriji: au, yowagin*)

sugaritsuki   of the Burning House,
toritsukeba   as she holds it tightly,
hashira wa sunawachi   thereupon the pillar changes

[*The* shite *jerks her hands off from the pillar as if it is in flame.*]

kaen to natte   into a rising column
hi no hashira o   of blazing fire and flame
idaku zo to yo.   while embraced in her arms;
Ara atsu ya.   "How white hot," she cries,
Taegata ya.   "I cannot bear it."
Godai wa okibi no   All her body is transfigured

[*The* shite *holds back her flowing tears with both hands.*]

kuro kemuri to   now into jet-black smoke
naritaru zo ya.   from the blazing charcoal.

[*The* shite *raises her face.*]

388

Shikōjite   As I struggle on,
okiagareba   barely rising to my feet,

Shikōjite   as I struggle on,
okiagareba   barely rising to my feet,

gokusotsu wa	the demon jailer
shimoto o atete	lashes at her with his scourge
ottatsureba	pursuing her quickly;

[*The* shite *rises and comes out from the mound.*]

tadayoiidete	stumbling out, she wanders lost
hachi dai-	among the hells
jigoku[68] no	eight in number
kazukazu	with all the means
kurushimi o tsukushi	of many painful agonies.
on-mae nite	In your holy presence,
sange no	let me repent,

[*The* shite *faces the* waki.]

arisama mise-	let me tell you
mōsan, mazu	of the scenes I've witnessed:
Tōkatsu Kokushō	first, the Hell of Never-Healing Gashes,

[*The* shite *looks around.*]

Shugō Kyōkan	then of Iron Ropes, Sword Mountains,
Daikyōkan	Hot Steam, Ferocious Fires,
Ennetsu Gokunetsu	White Heat, and Ruthless Scorching Heat;
Muken no soko ni	lastly, to the Endless Pit

[*Pointing with her fan, the* shite *lets her body sink as she kneels, as if she is falling into the abyss.*]

sokushō	plunging, hurtling,
zuke to	down she falls
otsuru aida wa	headlong for a period
mitose mitsuki no	of three months and three long years
kurushimi hatete	with the sufferings that now
sukoshi kugen no	end all bitter agonies

[*The* shite *rises and walks around a little.*]

hima ka to omoeba	for a while, she thinks a little

[*Suddenly going out toward stage front, the* shite *looks to her left and right, far into the distance.*]

oni mo sari	as the demon fades
kaen mo kiete	and the fires die away.
kurayami to	When the darkness palls,
narinureba	shrouding all around,

❀

[*Turning to her left and then to her right two or three times, the* shite *walks with heavy steps, indicating her wandering.*]

ima wa kataku ni	once again I now come back
kaeran to	to the Burning House,
aritsuru sumika wa	where I've lived so long, but where
izuku zo to	is my dwelling place?
kurasa wa kurashi	Through the blackness of the dark

Motomezuka

anata o tazune	over here and over there
konata o	she looks around,
Motomezuka	as she seeks and asks,
izuku yaran to	"Where's the Motomezuka?"
motome motome	Searching, searching for it
tadori yukeba	on her way, she struggles
motome-	and at last

[*Discovering the mound at stage front, the* shite *lifts her fan over her head and looks on.*]

etari ya	she discovers
Motomezuka[69] no	the Motomezuka
kusa no kageno no	in the deep grass-shaded field
tsuyu kiete,	with the dew that fades,

[*Quietly the* shite *approaches the mound and enters it.*]

kusa no kageno no	in the deep grass-shaded field,
tsuyu kiegie to	like a fading drop of dew
mōja no	there the figure
katachi[70] wa	of the phantom

[*Gesturing as if to cover her head with the open fan.*]

usenikeri,	vanishes away,
mōja no kage wa	the shadow of the phantom
usenikeri,	vanishes away,
mōja no kage wa	the shadow of the phantom
usenikeri.	vanishes away.

Masterworks of the Nō Theater

Kuzu

Introduction

Kuzu belongs to Group V of Nō plays. The background for this play is the famous political uprising concerning the succession to the throne after the death of the Emperor Tenchi in 671. In Japanese history this event is known as the Jinshin Rebellion of 676. The literary sources of the play are the first and fourteenth chapters of the *Genpei Seisuiki* and the fifteenth chapter of the *Uji Shūi monogatari*. Unlike other Nō plays, *Kuzu* is based on varied and novel materials, and the skill and creativeness with which they are organized into a dramatic whole is worthy of our attention.

The play opens with the formal verse structures consisting of *issei, ni no ku, sashi, sageuta,* and *ageuta.* The lyric air is dignified in diction, and its tone is tinged with regret, as the *issei* verse sung by the *waki* and the *waki-tsure* shows:

> One dark night in spring,
> unexpectedly we leave
> the cloud-girt palace;
> over Miyako the moon
> fills us with regret.

Yet the singing continues and concludes in a high-pitched *ageuta,* with a note of hope:

> Though the skies remain so cloudy
> for a while with cherry-mists,
> bright the spring moon shines
> above the cloud-girt palace,
> where he shall return
> in his jeweled palanquin,
> let us set our trust
> on his jeweled palanquin,
> let us set our trust.

The *kokata*, Emperor Tenmu (also known as the emperor Kiyomibara), and his faithful followers escape from the imperial enemy and reach the district of Kuzu, deep in the heart of the Yoshino Mountains.

Following the *ashirai* music, the *shite* (an old fisherman) and the *tsure* (his aged wife) appear. They are the Kuzu people, kind and simple, who have shown their undivided devotion and respect to the imperial throne, as recorded in the *Kojiki* from ancient times. In contrast to the preceding section, the atmosphere changes to a more primeval scene, reflected in the honest tone of their dialogue:

SHITE: Old woman, look, look! . . . Just right above our cottage the purple clouds
          appear. Do you see them?
TSURE: Yes! yes! I see. . . . There, that's no ordinary sight. . . .
SHITE: No ordinary sight, indeed, I think.

Since the ancient times
above the place
where an emperor is dwelling,
such purple clouds,
arise and trail, they say.

They hurry back to their hut and soon learn from the officials about the plight of the emperor. They are asked to present a meal to His Highness, as he has had no food for two or three days. The old man offers his humble cottage. The aged wife describes her own feeling in song as she prepares the greens.

Overcome by far too much
royal honor, now the heart
of this ancient woman beats
with a quickened pulse,
and the watercress she picked
here she washes clean;
old she is but young in heart
as the young green leaves
she arranges neatly
for the royal dish.

The old man, too, among the colored maple leaves, builds a fire and broils the trout he has caught in the Kuzu River.

After the meal the famous trout scene unfolds, as the old man receives from the emperor what is untouched of the fish. As he frees it into the rock-riven waters, he witnesses the very same fish come to life again of its own accord—a great auspicious sign, foretelling that the emperor will return to the capital.

392

Then, following the quickening drum-beats, indicating that the pursuing soldiers are near, the *shite* reassures the emperor and his officials by telling them, "Leave everything to this old man." With his aged wife, the *shite* hauls the boat from the bridge onto the stage, turns it over, and hides the *kokata* under it. The atmosphere changes and the dialogues between the *shite* and the soldiers are filled with drama. Gradually, the old man overwhelms them and finally makes them turn back, which is indeed exhilarating. Sakamoto Setchō comments on Hōshō Jūei's performance of *Kuzu* in the following words: "The feeling . . . in front of the boat . . . is splendid. In the *mondō*, the way the *shite* keeps perfect composure from the beginning is excellent. The timing of his intimidating bluff is magnificent, and this section is wonderfully filled with humor."[1]

After the soldiers have gone the *kokata* thanks the *shite*, and, as the hours slip by, the chorus sings on behalf of the old couple:

> So for now what can we do
> to console the heart
> of His Highness . . .

But soon, at the *shite* seat, the *shite* feels as if he were listening to the tune:

> with the koto notes
> pine winds from the summit come
> mingling back and forth
> descend the heavenly maidens,
> fluttering their sleeves
> in the dance called *gosechi* . . .

As the chorus finishes singing, the *shite* slowly exits over the bridge, followed by the *tsure*, both disappearing behind the curtain. Then, in their place, the angel appears and performs the *gaku* dance.

The great deities of the mountains attend the performance, and, magnificently, the sacred presence of Zaō manifests itself. He flies throughout the void, promising the emperor's safety and bestowing his blessing on the land, and the play thus concludes on a happy note, as do many of the plays in Group V. This auspicious note is significant, as it portrays an affectionate air expressing a warm, spontaneous feeling of mutual love and respect between the people and their ruler, long before he is deified as a living god. "The aged couple are, in fact, manifestations of the deity, Zaō Gongen, and the angels. Reasoning such as this [the concept of the two-part Nō play] comes rather after the form of Nō became standardized," states Gondō Yoshikazu. "It is, I think, natural that some other actors appear as Zaō Gongen and the angel, when the old couple do not make an exit."[2] According to this view, the play can then assume, structurally speaking, the old style, as Zeami speaks of it in connection with *Saigyōzakura*, where, true to the spirit of ancient Japan, the witty, bright, and exhilarating tone combines with an awe-inspiring note to harmonize into a complete whole.

Kuzu

KUZU

Author Unknown

Persons: KOKATA: *Emperor Tenmu*
WAKI: *Attending official*
WAKI-TSURE: *Palanquin bearers (two)*
TOMO: *Followers (two)*
SHITE (PART I): *An old man*
TSURE (PART I): *An old woman*
KYŌGEN: *Pursuing soldiers (two: Omo and Ado)*
TSURE (PART II): *An angel*
NOCHI-JITE (PART II): *Zaō Gongen*

Classification: *Primary, Group V; Variant, Group I or IV*
Place: *Mt. Yoshino in the land of Yamato*
Time: *March*
Kogaki: *3*

PART I

[*Following the* issei *music, the* kokata *appears, wearing a headdress (*uikanmuri*), a collar in red (*eri aka*), an embroidered under kimono with painted gold or silver patterns (*nuihaku*), an unlined hunting robe (*hitoe kariginu*), a "strung-through" embroidered divided skirt (*sashinuki*), a broad divided underskirt (*komi ōguchi*), a waistband (*koshiobi*), and a fan (*ōgi*). He is assisted by two* waki-tsure, *the palanquin bearers, holding the prop over the* kokata. *They wear a "thick board" heavy silk kimono (*atsuita*), a white broad divided skirt (*shiro ōguchi*), a waistband (*koshiobi*), and a fan (*ōgi*), and are followed by two* tomo, *the attendants, each wearing a less-formal heavy silk kimono (*noshime*), an unlined overrobe in two pieces (*suō kamishimo*), a waistband (*koshiobi*), a fan (*ōgi*), and a short sword (*chiisa gatana*). They are followed by the* waki, *an attending official, wearing a "thick board" heavy silk kimono (*atsuita*), a gold brocade robe (*happi*), a white broad divided skirt (*shiro ōguchi*), a waistband (*koshiobi*), a fan (*ōgi*), and a long sword (*tachi*). They enter the stage and line up in a row. Then the* waki *and the* waki-tsure *sing the following* issei *verse.*]

WAKI AND WAKI-TSURE

[1] *(Issei: awazu, tsuyogin)*

Omowazu mo	One dark night in spring,
kumoi o izuru	unexpectedly we leave
haru no yo no	the cloud-girt palace;
tsuki[3] no Miyako[4] no	over Miyako the moon
nagori kana.	fills us with regret.

WAKI

Michimichi taraba	If our way is Heaven's Way
Kuraiyama[5]	to Mt. Royal Crown

WAKI AND WAKI-TSURE

noborazarame ya	may our lord ascend again.
tada tanome	Let us trust the gods

[*The* waki *sings the following passage, called* sashi.]

WAKI

(Sashi: awazu, tsuyogin)

kamikaze[6] ya	of the sacred winds
Isuzu[7] no furuki[8]	blowing from the Three-Fives Bell
sue o ukuru	flows the ancient line
Mimosusogawa[9] no	into the Gown Rinse River
on-nagare	as it reaches down
yagoto naki	to the illustrious
on-kata[10] nite	and the most exalted one
owashimasu.	of the rightful line.

WAKI AND WAKI-TSURE

Kono kimi to mōsu ni	Let it be known of this gracious one:
onnyuzuri to shite	His Highness should have been enthroned
Amatsu-hitsugi o	as the imperial heir,
ukubeki tokoro ni	descendant of the Heavenly Sun.
on-hakubu[11]	But by his uncle,
nanigashi no muraji ni	a certain prince of royal lineage,
osowaretamai	he was assaulted,
Miyako no sakai mo	so from the capital he flees
tōinaka no	to the distant country;
narenu sannya no	through unfamiliar mountains,
kusaki no tsuyu	meadows, trees, and grasses
wakeyuku michi no	thickly dewed, he parts his way,
hate made mo	till it ends in snow,
mi-yuki[12] to omoeba	hopeful that we'll think about it
tanomoshi ya.	as a royal tour.

[*The* waki *and the* waki-tsure *sing the following low-pitched song, called* sageuta.]

395

(Sageuta: au, tsuyogin)

Mi o Akiyama[13] ya	Wearied by this fleeting world,
yo no naka no	past Autumn Mountain,
Uda[14] no mi-kariba	Uda's hunting ground we see
yoso ni mite	in the distance now.

[*Changing their mood, they sing the following high-pitched song passage, called* ageuta.]

Kuzu

(Ageuta: au, tsuyogin)

Ojika[15] fusu naru	Here where the stag finds shelter
Kasugayama,[16]	on Mount Kasuga,
ojika fusu naru	here where the stag finds shelter
Kasugayama	on Mount Kasuga,
mikasa[17] zo masaru	we see the water rising
harusame no	with the rain of spring;
oto wa izuku zo	from where do we hear the sound
Yoshinogawa[18]	of the Yoshino?
yoshi ya shibashi koso	Though the skies remain so cloudy

[*The* waki *goes out toward stage front a few steps and returns to his former position, indicating that they have made the royal journey.*]

hanagumori nare	for a while with cherry-mists,
haru no yo no	bright the spring moon shines
tsuki wa kumoi ni	above the cloud-girt palace,
kaerubeshi	where he shall return
tanomi o kake yo[19]	in his jeweled palanquin,
tama no koshi,	let us set our trust
tanomi o kake yo	on his jeweled palanquin,
tama no koshi.	let us set our trust.

[*After the above song, the* waki *faces stage front and intones the following prose passage, called* tsukizerifu, *"arrival statement."*]

WAKI

(Tsukizerifu: kotoba)

Onnisogi sōrō hodo ni izuku tomo shi-ranu sanchū ni on-tsuki nite sōrō. Mazu kono tokoro ni go-za o nasaryōzuru nite sōrō.

Since we have traveled so fast, we find ourselves in the heart of the deep mountain, and we hardly know where we are. [*Facing the* kokata.] First of all, let us rest in this place.

[*The* kokata *goes to the* waki *seat and sits on a stool provided by the stage attendant; the rest sit down next to the* kokata *in front of the chorus. The stage attendants place a boat by the end of the bridge, indicating that the River Yoshino flows through there. Following* ashirai *music, the* tsure, *carrying a fishing rod, appears. She is followed by the* shite, *carrying a bamboo pole. The* tsure *wears an* uba *mask, an "old-woman" wig (*kazura*), a wig band (*kazuraobi*), a collar in dry-leaf hue (*eri kuchiba iro*), an under kimono with painted gold or silver patterns (*surihaku*), a "Cathay fabric" brocade outer kimono without red (*ironashi karaori*), and a "shrunk silk" broad-sleeved robe (*yore mizugoromo*). The* shite *wears a mask called* asakura jō, *an "old-man" wig (*jō kazura*), a collar in light blue (*eri asagi*), a plain, less-formal heavy silk kimono (*muji noshime*), an "inferior silk" broad-sleeved robe (*shike mizugoromo*), a waistband (*koshiobi*), a hempen-cord skirt (*koshimino*), and a fan (*ōgi*). They walk along the bridge to its end, where the* tsure *gets into the boat and sits in the middle with the fishing pole over her shoulder, while the* shite *gets into the boat at the rear and takes up a pole. He looks toward the stage as if at his cottage, ready to pole the boat back home.*]

396

[2] *(Mondai: awazu, yowagin)*

Muba ya mitamae.   Old woman, look! Look!

SHITE

Nanigoto nite sōrō zo.   What is the matter?

SHITE

Ano ōji ga fuseya no ue ni shiun no ta-   Just right above our cottage the purple
nabiitaru o ogamai tamōta ka.   clouds appear. Do you see them?

TSURE

[*Looks at the stage.*]

Geni geni atari ni shiun tanabiki tada-   Yes! Yes! I see the purple clouds are
naranu sora no keshiki ya na.   trailing about it. There, that's no ordi-
    nary sight across the sky.

SHITE

Ō ṭadanaranu keshiki zōrō yo.   No ordinary sight, indeed, I think. [*Looks
    stage front.*]

(Kakaru: awazu, yowagin)

Mukashi yori   Since the ancient times,
Tenshi no   above the place
gozadokoro ni koso   where an emperor is dwelling,
shiun wa   such purple clouds
tatsu to mōse.   arise and trail, they say.

Moshi mo fushigi ni jō ga sumika ni   What if by some miracle to our cottage

TSURE

(Kakaru: awazu, yowagin)

sayō no kinin ya   such a noble personage should
owasuran to   pay a gracious visit,

SHITE

fune sashiyosete   I would pole my boat ashore
waga ya ni kaeri   and hurry to my cottage.

397

[*The* waki *puts his hands on the pole and makes a gesture as if he were rowing the boat with it.*]

TSURE

mireba fushigi ya sareba koso   As I look into the cottage, strange, how
    strange, indeed! [*Looks at the* kokata.]

Kuzu

SHITE

tama no kōmuri naoshi no sode

He wears a jeweled headdress. Though the sleeves of his formal robe [*looks at the kokata*]

TSURE

tsuyu shimo[20] ni shiore-tamaedomo

are bedraggled and wet with frost and dew,

SHITE

sasuga magirenu
onnyosooi.

unmistakably, indeed,
they are royal garments.

[*The chorus comes in and sings the following passage.*]

CHORUS

Samo yagoto naki
on-kata to wa
utagai mo naku
shiraito[21] no
tsurizao o
sashiokite

How extraordinary!
This is a mighty person!
Beyond all doubt they know it,
so they put aside
now the bamboo fishing pole
with the snow-white line.

[*Both leave their respective poles in the boat and come out upon the stage, the* shite *to the center and the* tsure *to the front of the* waki (waki shōmen), *where she sits down, facing the* waki, *and sings the following verse.*]

(*Ageuta: awazu, yowagin*)

somo ya ika naru
on-koto zo.
Kahodo iyashiki
shiba no to no
shibashi ga hodo no
o-mashi ni mo
narikeru koto yo
ikani sen
ara katajikena no
on-koto ya,
ara katajikena no
on-koto ya.

Whatever is the meaning
of this encounter
in a humble hut like this
with a brushwood door,
that even for a short while
such a one should come
is too unprecedented!
What is to be done?
We are far too undeserving
of such an honor,
we are far too undeserving
of such an honor.

398

SHITE

[3] (*Mondai: awazu, kotoba*)

Kore wa somo nani to mōshitaru on-koto nite sōrō zo.

What is this all about, I wonder?

Waki

Kore wa yoshi aru on-kata nite goza sōrō ga, majikaki hito ni osowaretamai kore made on-shinobi nite sōrō. Nanigoto mo jō o tanomi oboshimesaruru to no on-koto nite sōrō.

This is a person of noble birth. Pursued by a close relative, he has escaped to this place. In all things, His Highness puts his trust in you.

Shite

Sate wa yoshi aru on-kata nite goza sōrō ka. Saiwai kore wa kono jō ga io nite sōrō hodo ni on-kokoro-yasuku onnyasumi arōzuru nite sōrō.

So then, he is a person of noble birth! Fortunately, this humble cottage is mine; if it pleases His Highness, may he stay here and rest at ease.

Waki

(Mondai: awazu, kotoba)

Ikani jō. Menboku mo naki mōshigoto nite sōraedomo, kono kimi nisannichi ga hodo gugo o chikazuketamawazu sōrō. Nani nite mo gugo ni sonae sōrae.

Ho, there, old man. It is so difficult to ask you, but His Highness has had no food for two or three days; therefore, whatever the fare, would you kindly offer him a meal?

Shite

Sono yoshi muba ni mōsozuru nite sōrō. Ikani muba kiite aru ka. Kono nisanni-chi ga hodo gugo o chikazuketamawazu sōrō to no on-koto nari. Nani nite mo gugo ni tatematsuri sōrae.

I will speak to my old wife. [*Facing the tsure.*] Listen closely, old woman. For two or three days, His Highness has had no food. We are therefore called upon to serve him and offer him a meal as best we can.

Tsure

Orifushi kore ni tsumitaru nezeri no sōrō.

At this moment there is some water-cress I picked.

Shite

Sore koso Nippon-ichi no koto. Ware-ra mo kore ni kuzuio no sōrō. Kore o gugo ni sonaemōsōzuru nite sōrō.

That will be the best thing in all Japan! I have some Kuzu fish, which I too would like to offer to him for his dish.

Tsure [*Describes her own feelings.*]

399

(Kakaru: awazu, yowagin)

Muba wa amari no
katajikenasa ni

Overcome by far too much
royal honor, now the heart

Kuzu

[*The* tsure *turns to stage front.*]

mune uchisawagi	of this ancient woman beats
tsumiokeru	with a quickened pulse,
nezeri araite	and the watercress she picked
oi ga mi no[22]	here she washes clean;
kokoro wakana[23] o	old she is but young in heart
soroetsutsu	as the young green leaves
gugo ni sonae	she arranges neatly
tatematsuru.	for the royal dish.

[*The* tsure *faces the* waki.]

Sore yori shite zo	And for this very reason,
Miyoshino no	ever since, it was
Natsumi no Kawa to	called the River Yoshino,
mosu nari.	the Greens-Picked River.

SHITE

Ōji mo iro koki momiji o rinkan ni taki[24]	Now the old man, too, builds a fire
Kuzugawa nite tsuritaru ayu o yaki	among the deeply colored maple leaves and broils the trout he angled from the Kuzu River,

(*Kakaru: awazu, yowagin*)

onajiku gugo ni	and presents it just as she,
sonaekeri.	as a royal dish.

[*The* shite *opens his fan, indicating that the trout is on a plate, rises, and goes to the* waki. *He mimes the presentation of the fish and returns to his former position.*]

CHORUS

(*Uta: au, yowagin*)

Yoshino no kuzu to	For this reason, ever since,
iu koto mo	mountain trouts are known
kono toki yori no	as Kuzu of Yoshino,
koto to ka ya.	so the story goes,
Junsai no atsumono[25]	though hot soups garnished with water shield
rogyo tote mo	or bass in vinegar

[*The* waki *rises, holding his fan with both hands, goes in front of the* kokata, *and offers it to him. The* kokata *looks at him, indicating that he is tasting it. While the chorus continues to sing the following passage, the* waki, *holding the open fan, returns to his former position.*]

kore ni wa ikade	are so famous, how can they
masarubeki.	surpass this menu?

[*The* waki *looks at the* shite *while the chorus speaks for him.*]

Masterworks of the Nō Theater

Majikaku maire
oibito yo
majikaku maire
oibito.

May the ancient man approach
closer to this place,
may the ancient man approach
closer to me.

WAKI

[4] *(Mondai: awazu, kotoba)*

Ikani jō. Gugo no on-nokori o jō ni tamaware to no on-koto nite sōrō.

Ho, there, old man. His Highness is
pleased to tell you that what is untouched
of the trout from the royal dish will be
given to you. [*Shows his fan to the* shite.]

[*The* shite *opens his fan and holds it with both hands as if to receive the trout; then he bows his head
toward the* kokata.]

SHITE

Ara arigata ya zōrō. Saraba uchikaeshite
tamawarōzuru nite sōrō.

How blessed am I! I will turn it over
once and receive it gratefully.

[*The* shite *returns to his former position.*]

WAKI

Somo uchikaeshite tamawarōzuru to wa
nani to mōshitaru koto nite aru zo.

Why do you turn the fish over on its
other side as you receive it?

SHITE

Uchikaeshite tamawarōzuru to mōsu
koso kuzuio no shirushi nite sōrō.

When you receive a Kuzu fish you must
turn it over once, according to the special custom.

[*Faces the* tsure.]

(Mondai: awazu, tsuyogin)

Ika ni muba gugo no nokori o jō ni tamaware to no on-koto nite sōrō ga, kono
io wa imada ikiiki to miete sōrae.

Old woman, this is what was left from
the royal dish and was given to me. But
look at it, this fish seems very much
alive!

TSURE

Geni kono io wa imada ikiiki to miete
sōrō.

Indeed, this fish appears still very much
alive.

SHITE

Iza kono Yoshinogawa ni hanaite miyō.

Let me free this fish into the water of the
Yoshino.

401

Kuzu

TSURE

Suji naki koto na notamai so. Hanaita-
reba tote ikikaerubeki ka wa.

Don't say such senseless things! Even if
you let it go free, it will not come back
to life again.

SHITE

Iya iya mukashi mo saru tameshi ari.[26]
Jingū Kōgō Shiraki o shitagae tamaishi
urakata ni Tamashimagawa[27] no ayu o
tsurasetamō. Sono gotoku kono kimi mo
futatabi Miyako ni kankō naraba

No, no, in the past there was such an
incident. When the Empress Jingū sub-
jugated Silla, she foretold the fortune of
her army by having a trout caught in the
Jewel Island River. Therefore, if [*faces the
kokata*] His Highness is to return to the
capital again,

[*The* shite *looks at his fan and sings the following two lines.*]

(*Kakaru: awazu, tsuyogin*)

kono io mo nadoka
ikizaran to

there is no reason why this fish
shouldn't come to life once more.

CHORUS

(*Ageuta: au, tsuyogin*)

Iwa kiru mizu ni
hanaseba,

Into rock-riven waters
he lets it go,

[*The* shite *goes to stage front.*]

iwa kiru mizu ni[28]
hanaseba,

into rock-riven waters,
he lets it go:

[*Turning over the open fan, the* shite *gestures as if letting the trout go free into the water.*]

sashimo hayase no
takigawa ni
are Miyoshino[29] ya
kichizui o
arawasu io no
onozukara
ikikaeru
kono urakata
tanomoshiku
oboshimesare yo.

even where the rapids rush,
cascading swiftly
down the River Yoshino,
see how it dashes
as a most auspicious sign,
for the fish revives
of its own accord,
and this fortune-telling
should be graciously
received as most promising!

402

[*The* shite *goes toward the chorus seat and, facing the* waki, *he sits down. Quickening drumbeats indicate that the pursuing soldiers are approaching. The* waki *rises and faces the* shite.]

WAKI

[5] (*Mondai: awazu, kotoba*)

Ikani jō. Oite ga kakarite sōrō.

Listen, old man. The pursuers are coming after us.

Konata e on-makase sōrae.	Leave everything to this old man.

[*Faces the* tsure.]

Ikani muba. Ano fune kaite kō.	Listen, old woman. Let's carry that boat over here.

TSURE

Kokoroe mōshi sōrō.	Yes. I understand.

[*The* shite *and the* tsure *go to the bridge to fetch the boat and place it in front of the chorus. As the* kokata *draws near the boat, they tilt it, thus indicating that the* kokata *is hidden under it. The* shite *sits down with his back toward the boat; the* tsure *sits down beside him. The* waki *and his companions sit down by the stage attendants' seat. The* kyōgen, *two pursuing men called Omo and Ado, appear as the curtain is swept back. They wear striped kimonos, sleeveless* kyōgen *robes and divided skirts (*kyōgen kamishimo*), leggings, and short swords. They carry fans. Omo, carrying a spear, and Ado, a bow and arrow, hurry across the bridge, shouting as they enter the stage.*]

KYŌGEN: OMO AND ADO

Yarumai zo, yarumai zo, yarumai zo.	Don't let them get away! Don't let them get away! Don't let them get away!

OMO

Namu-sampō.[30] Miushinōta.	Holy Buddha! We've lost sight of them.

ADO

Sono tōri ja.	Exactly.

OMO

Yama-yama ga fukai ni yotte miushi-nōta. Mazu kochira e watarashime.	All these mountains are too deep: that's why we've lost sight of them. Well, now, come over here.

ADO

Kokoroeta.	Yes, sir.

OMO [Noticing the shite.]

Kore ni rōjin ga iraruru. Tazunete miyō. Ikani rōjin. Kiyomibara[31] no Tennō no yukue o shiranu ka.	There's an old man. Let me ask him. Ho, there, old man. Do you know where the Emperor of Kiyomibara went to?

403

SHITE

(*Mondai: awazu, kotoba*)

Nani kiyomibarae.[32] Kiyomibarae naraba kono kawashimo e yuke.	What? Kiyomibarae, did you say? That means to purify yourself. If you want to do that, go further downstream.

Kuzu

Omo

Kore wa ika na koto. Oi horete musa to shita koto o iu.

He's got it all wrong. He's so old; he talks somewhat dotingly.

Ado

Tadashi mimi ga tōi ka. Takō iute misashime.

Well, now. Maybe he's hard of hearing. Try talking louder.

Omo

Kokoroeta. Ikani rōjin. Kiyomibara no Tennō no yukue o shiranu ka.

I see. [*Raising his voice.*] Ho, there, old man. Do you know where the Emperor of Kiyomibara went to?

Shite

Sate wa Kiyomibara to wa hito no na yo na. Ara kikinarezu no hito no na ya. Sono ue kono yama wa Tosotsu no Naiin[33] ni mo tatoe mata Godaisan Shōryōsen[34] tote Morokoshi made mo tōku tsuzukeru Yoshinoyama. Kakurega ōki tokoro naru o, izuku made tazunetamōbeki. Sumiyaka ni kaeritamae.

Oh, I see. Kiyomibara is somebody's name. That's an unfamiliar name for any man. In addition, these mountains are usually thought of as the Paradise of Miroku. Sometimes they're called Godaisan or Shōryōsen. So for all I know, these mountains of Yoshino may stretch as far as the kingdom of T'ang! There are a lot of hiding places. How far will you go looking for him? You should turn back at once.

Omo

Makoto ni rōjin no iu tōri ja. Iza modorō. Kochira e oriyare, oriyare. Iya kore ni fune ga utsumukete aru. Tazunete miyō. Ika ni rōjin. Ano fune wa nani tote utsumukete aru zo. Fune no naka ga gatten ga yukanu. Sagashite miyō.

What the old man says is true enough. Well, let's go back. Come on over here. Over here. [*Noticing the boat as he is about to turn back.*] Look, there's a boat, turned over. I'll ask the old man about it. [*Facing the* shite.] Ho, there, old man. Why is that boat turned over? What's the point of that? I'm going to look into this.

Shite

404

Nani to fune ga ayashii to ya. Kore wa hosu fune zo to yo.

Why do you suspect something about this boat? This boat is being dried.

Omo

Hosu fune naritomo gatten ga yukanu. Soko nokashime, fune sagasō.

Maybe it's just being dried, but I have to make sure. Get out of the way. I'm going to search it.

SHITE

Nani to fune o sagasō to ya. Ryōshi no mi nite wa fune o sagasaretaru mo ie o sagasaretaru mo onaji koto zo kashi. Mi koso iyashiku omou tomo kono tokoro nite wa okina mo nikkuki mono zo kashi. Mago mo ari hiko mo ari, yamayama tanidani no monodomo, ideaite ano rōzekibito o uchitome sōrae, uchitome sōrae.	What are you going to search it for? For a fisherman to have his boat searched is the same as having his home searched. Maybe you think I'm a lowly fellow [*the shite rises*] and that I don't count for much, but around here I can use my muscles. I have grandsons. I have great-grandsons. [*The shite looks across stage front.*] Come out, come out, from those mountains and valleys over here and there, ho, all of you. Shoot down these intruders. Shoot them down. [*Claps his hands.*]

OMO

Kore kore rōjin. Ryōji o ossharuna. Oite no mono wa haya modoru zo.	Wait a minute. Wait a minute, old man. Don't talk so hastily. We're turning back right away.

ADO

Kono yō na tokoro ni nagai wa muyō. Kochi e watarashime kochi e watarashime.	It's useless to stay long in a place like this. Come on, let's go; come on, let's go.

OMO

Kokoroeta kokoroeta.	Certainly, certainly. [*Exit.*]

[*As the kyōgen make their exit behind the Nō curtain and across the bridge, the tsure rises and stands at center stage and faces the shite.*]

TSURE

(*Kakaru: awazu, yowagin*)

Nō kikoshimese, oite no bushi wa kaeritari.	Listen! Did you hear all that? Those pursuing warriors have all gone away.

SHITE

Ima wa kō yo to ōji muba wa	Now all's well; the ancient man rejoicing with his wife

405

TSURE

ureshi ya chikara o	together pull the boat,

Kuzu

Shite

ei ya   Ho! Heave-ho!

Shite and Tsure

ei ya to.   And ho! Heave-ho!

[*Both the* shite *and the* tsure *go to the boat and pull it right side up as the chorus sings the following high-pitched* ageuta, *during which the* kokata *returns to the* waki *seat and sits on a stool, and the* waki *and his followers resume their former positions.*]

Chorus

(*Ageuta: au, yowagin*)

Fune hikiokoshi	Pull it, turn it right side up
sontai no,	for the noble one,
fune hikiokoshi	pull it, turn it right side up
sontai no	for the noble one
on-tsutsuga naku	who survived this peril well
kawabune no	in the river boat;
kai aru[35] onninochi	truly guided by the worthy oars,
tasukaritamō zo	His Highness's life has been rescued;
arigataki.	we all feel thankful.

[*The chorus sings the following passage, called* kuri, *while the* shite *and the* tsure *take the boat to the* shite *pillar. The* shite *then sits at stage center, and the* tsure *by the flute player's seat. Stage attendants remove the boat. The chorus continues to sing the* kuri.]

Chorus

[6] (*Kuri: awazu, yowagin*)

Sore kimi wa fune[36]	Our lord is a mighty ship;
shin wa mizu.	he is supported
Mizu yoku fune o	by his subjects, as the seas
ukamu to wa	keep the ship afloat.
kono chūkin no	This old metaphor refers
tatoe nari.	to a deed like this.

[*The* waki *sings the following passage, called* sashi.]

Waki

406

(*Sashi: awazu, yowagin*)

Arigata ya	How gratifying!
sashimo sugata wa	Though outwardly they appear
yamagatsu no	just like mountain folks,

Chorus

kokoro wa takaki	true and lofty are their hearts
hakarigoto.	like their great design;

Masterworks of the Nō Theater

Geni kisen ni wa yorazarikeri.	in such things, rank plays no part, whether high or low.

WAKI

Shakuzen no yokei kagiri naku	How immeasurable are virtues heaped up from the past

CHORUS

nagaretaesenu[37] Mimosusogawa nigoreru[38] yo ni wa sumigatashi.	flowing ever ceaselessly down the Gown Rinse River through the world so muddy now where it's hard to live.

KOKATA

Sareba kimi to shite koso tami o hago-kumu narai naru ni kaette tasukuru ko-korozashi	As your sovereign lord, though I should have rescued those who are my subjects according to age-old ways, in reality I have been saved by them instead.

[*The* kokata *and the* shite *face each other. The chorus comes in and sings the following high-pitched* ageuta *passage.*]

CHORUS

(*Ageuta: au, yowagin*)

mi wa shukuzen no kai zo naki,	Blessed by virtues though he can use them now no more;
mi wa shukuzen no kai zo naki	blessed by virtues yet he floats on an oarless boat,
ichiyō no fune no yuku sue	like a leaf, but he will harbor in the future,
hanryō[39] no kumoi tsui ni nado	just as dragons hid in caverns finally ascend
itarazarame ya	to the palace of the clouds
miyakoji ni	by the rightful way
tachikaeritsutsu	to Miyako we will go;
Akitsusu[40] no	then when all is well
yoshi ya yo no naka osamaraba	in the Land of Dragonflies and abundant reeds,
inochi no on o hōzen to	he will pay his debt, he says, for they saved his life;
ringen kimo ni meijitsutsu	touched by these exalted words deep within their hearts,
fūfu no rōjin wa	this old man and the ancient woman
katajikenasa ni	are awe-struck with reverence
nakiitari.	and begin to weep.

407

[*The* shite *and the* tsure *make a* shioru *gesture. Then the chorus sings the following passage.*]

Kuzu

(Sageuta: au, yowagin)

Saru hodo ni
fukeshizumarite
monosugoshi.

As the hours slip by,
night deepens into silence
full of fearfulness.

(Uta: au, yowagin)

Ikani to shite ka
kono hodo no
mi-kokoro nagusame-
mōsubeki.
Shikamo tokoro wa
tsuki yuki no
Miyoshino nare ya

So for now what can we do
to console the heart
of His Highness and comfort him
in his present plight?
For all that, this is the place
where we view the moon
and the snows on Yoshino,

[*The* shite *and the* tsure *rise.*]

hana tori no
iro ne ni yorite
ongaku no
ryoritsu no shirame

and seek the blossoms and birds—
colored bright and sweetly aired
like the melody
playing high and low in tune

[*At the* shite *seat, the* shite *feels as if he were listening to the tune.*]

koto no ne ni⁴¹
mine no matsukaze
kayoikuru⁴²
amatsu otome no
kaesu sode
gosechi⁴³ no hajime
kore nare ya.

with the koto notes;
pine winds from the summit come
mingling back and forth
descend the heavenly maidens,
fluttering their sleeves
in the dance called *gosechi*,
first performed like this.

[*As the chorus finishes singing, the* shite *slowly exits over the bridge, followed by the* tsure*, behind the curtain.*]

Nakairi (Interlude)

PART II

[*Then the* tsure *(Part II), an angel, appears. She wears a* tsuremen *mask, a long black wig (kuro tare), a wig band (kazuraobi), a heavenly crown (tenkan), a collar in red (eri aka), an under kimono with painted gold or silver patterns (surihaku), a "long silk" loose unlined broad-sleeved robe (chōken), a red broad divided skirt (iro ōguchi), a waistband (koshiobi), and a fan (ōgi). She performs the* gaku *dance.*]

Gaku

[*After the* gaku, *the* tsure *continues to dance to the singing of the chorus.*]

[7]

Otomeko ga,[44]	Oh, heavenly maidens,
otomeko ga	oh, heavenly maidens,
sono karatama no	upon the strings of koto
koto no ito	decked with precious stones
hikarekanazuru	from old China you perform
ongaku ni	celestial music;
kamigami mo	so the deities
rairin shi	come and all attend:
Katte[45] Hassho[46]	god Katte with eight more,
kono yama ni	out from this mountain,
Komori no Gozen[47]	Komori, who guards the woods,
Zaō[48] to wa	and then Zaō,

[*The* tsure *moves to the* shite *pillar and looks at the curtain across the bridge as if to welcome the* nochi-jite, *and as the* nochi-jite *begins to sing, the* tsure *goes in front of the flute player and sits down. The* nochi-jite, *Zaō Gongen, wears an* ōtobide *mask, a flowing red wig (*aka gashira*), a headband (*hachimaki*), a flower-pink collar (*eri hanairo*), a "thick board" heavy silk kimono (*atsuita*), a lined hunting robe (*awase kariginu*), a brocade broad divided skirt (*hangiri*), a waistband (*koshiobi*), and a fan (*ōgi*). He appears on the bridge, and at the first pine (*ichi no matsu*), he stands and sings.*]

SHITE

[8] (*Issei: awazu, tsuyogin*)

ō o kakusu ya	who keeps our sovereign hidden
Yoshinoyama	in Mt. Yoshino.

CHORUS

(*Noriji: ōnori, tsuyogin*)

sunawachi sugata o	Hereupon, his sacred presence
arawashite,	manifests itself,
sunawachi sugata o	hereupon his sacred presence
arawashitamaite	augustly manifests itself:

[*The* shite *comes out to center stage.*]

ten o sasu te wa	the hand that points at Heaven

[*With the folded fan, he points upward.*]

409

SHITE

Taizō[49]   shows the Womb World;

CHORUS

chi o mata sasu wa   the hand that points at Earth

Kuzu

[*With the folded fan held* gyakute (*in reversed-hand position), he points downward.*]

Kongō hōseki no[50]	shows the Diamond World, upon whose stone
ue ni tatte	of precious gem he stands,

[*The* shite *stamps the floor.*]

CHORUS

issoku o hissage	and lifts one foot heroically;

[*Lifting up his left foot.*]

tōzai nanboku	eastward, westward, southward, northward,
jippō sekai[51] no	throughout the void which covers
kokū ni higyō shite	the world of ten directions, he flies

[*He circles the stage once and jumps back.*]

futen no shita	underneath the Heaven
sotto no uchi ni	to the farthest ends of Earth.
ōi o ikade ka	How can the great imperial power
karonzen to	be seen contemptible?

[*The* shite *faces the* kokata.]

daiseiriki no	With his vast unbounded strength,
chikara o idashi	he displays his might,
kokudo o aratame	reforming all throughout the land
osamuru mi-yo no	so tranquility may rule
Tenmu[52] no seitai	the days of mighty Tenmu's reign;
kashikoki megumi	blessed by his benevolence
arata narikeru	deeply sacred and divine
tameshi kana.	is his example!

[*The* shite *stamps his feet by the* shite *pillar and makes a stately exit over the bridge, followed by the* tsure, *behind the curtain.*]

410

Nue

Introduction

Nue, a chimera, is the terrifying creator of the nocturnal world, begotten by the abysmal darkness of night. It has the head of an ape, the body of a badger, the tail of a serpent, and the limbs of a tiger. Such subject matter puts this piece into Group V of Nō plays. In its two-part structure, however, the play resembles the warrior piece. This resemblance is significant in that the play does not impart a strange feeling to the audience. The reason for its effect is perhaps that the source of this play is the *Tale of the Heike*, which depicts Minamoto no Yorimasa (1104–80), the noted warrior-poet and great archer of the Genji clan, who slew the dreadful and mysterious Nue. In this play, however, Zeami presents Nue from the viewpoint of the slain prey, instead of from that of Yorimasa, who is glorified in the *Tale of the Heike* for his heroism.

In the first part of the play, the *shite* comes out with the *issei* music, costumed entirely in black from head to foot. "In this piece the *mae-jite* [*shite* in the first part] is already dressed like the *nochi-jite* [*shite* in the second part]," in Setchō's words. The *shite* is a monstrous creature disguised as a boatman. In the *kuri-sashi-kuse* passages, he tells of how he met his fateful death. This section is followed by the *rongi* passage, before the *nakairi* (Interlude). The important section of the play is, indeed, the *kuse*, which, according to Sanari's Kanze text, is marked *iguse*, or the *kuse* that is not accompanied by the *shite*'s dance while the chorus sings the passage. The *shite* is in a sitting position, however, and he makes some gestures that correspond to the meaning of the lines. For instance, he looks up high when the chorus sings the following lines: "As Yorimasa looked up / sternly far above." Or, when the chorus sings the following, on behalf of the *shite*,

411

> Fully drawn and with a twang
> released, the arrow
> responded unto his hand,

the *shite* gestures as if Yorimasa were drawing his bow and shooting an arrow at the phantom. As the prey tumbles down, the *shite* rises from his sitting position and makes a gesture with his folded fan, as if his assistant, I no Hayata, were stabbing the fallen prey many times. Later he raises his folded fan as though it were a torch, and looks at the prey, as in the *maiguse*, or *kuse* accompanied by dance. When Setchō saw Kita Minoru's performance of Nue, he commented on the *kuse*:

> It should be called *hatarakiguse* [in which the *shite* gestures] rather than *maiguse*. In a scene such as this it is very difficult to perform the *shite* role as the *mae-jite* rather than as the *nochi-jite*. A round-table discussion was held the same night after the performance, and the criticism was that the *mae-jite* did not have enough ferocity. Judging from this, I think that it should have more. However, that they have such a feeling is due to the fact that the critics are taken in by the *shite*'s appearance, and while they have come to expect that the *nochi-jite* demands . . . [that] the way the *shite* executes the *kata*, vividly with tenseness, be exhilarating . . . in the *rongi* it is completely altered and gives a somber feeling. After the active part of the performance, which is practically like that of the *Shura* Nō, it required, I thought, this somber stillness.[1]

Following the Interlude and the waiting song, the *nochi-jite* appears in the true form of Nue himself and boasts of how he tormented the emperor: "near the capital I raged / in fury all around. . . ." He continues singing:

> night upon dark night,
> above the royal palace
> I dashed and dived headlong,
> whereupon a pain became
> acutely frequent;
> his noble person
> was plagued with torture
> and terror
> that made him tremble:
> and all these things, he said,
> were of my evil doing too.

But suddenly Yorimasa slays Nue, and Zeami changes the focus to the triumphant warrior, allocating thirty-five lines to a description of the glory bestowed upon him. After this passage, continuing the pattern of contrasts, the spotlight shifts again, back to Nue. In a unique depiction of the viewpoint of the defeated monster, the fallen prey relates the event. Toward the end of the play, the chorus sings the following lines for the *shite*:

> and my dugout boat
> remains to rot away;
> so no moon nor sun is seen
> from raven darkness
> into the path of darkness
> I have gone astray;
> let the light shine bright far out
> from the mountain ridge,
> O, moon, with you the moon . . .
> upon the ocean,
> too, is going down . . .

Masterworks of the Nō Theater

As the chorus sings the final line, the *shite* makes the concluding stamps (*tome byōshi*) on the floor and exits across the bridge beneath the waves of the abysmal darkness of night, leaving behind a melancholy note, with a rich poetic trailing tone.

Here it must be remembered that when the source for a Nō play is the *Tale of the Heike*, the passage chosen should be adapted for the Nō text, as Zeami said: "The image of the warrior. If, for instance, your source is about a famous captain of the Genji or the Heike, take special care to write as it is told in the *Tale of the Heike*."[2] In *Nue*, Zeami has eloquently demonstrated this principle. The twelfth episode of chapter four of the *Tale of the Heike*, entitled "On Nue," which Zeami used for this play, is quoted at the end of this introduction, where it can be seen that much of it has been arranged musically and metrically. The excerpt occupies mostly the *kuri, sashi*, and *kuse* sections of the play, totaling 103 lines! This is very significant because the *kuse* is one of the two most important parts in Nō structure. Zeami called it "the ear-opening section" of the play, while he called the dance segment "the eye-opening section" of the play.

By comparing my translation of the passage from the latest Iwanami edition of the *Tale of the Heike* with the play that follows, one can see that Zeami adapted his Nō play almost word for word from the *Tale of the Heike*. The comparison reveals how he skillfully incorporated the passages into the Nō text.[3] He did so by allocating them to the *shite* and the chorus. The allocated portions are further divided into lines, which normally consist of five and seven syllables for the musical measure of eight beats but range from two to ten syllables. It is also interesting to note that the lyric passages flow seamlessly and may sound too smooth and even flat when read. The reason for the smoothness or flatness of the lines is that when the passages are sung, each line is punctuated, in a way that is uniquely characteristic of Nō, by the appropriate set pattern of the percussion instruments. Therefore, the lyric passage must be smooth and flowing enough to withstand such attacks, so that the total effect will produce the desired poetic cadence as we hear it in performance. In order to achieve the smoothness of the lines in the English translation, I tried on the whole to use the simplest iambic and trochaic meters. If these passages were rich in metrical variation, like lines from great English poetry, for example, and then were cut and punctuated with accentuation by Nō instruments (rather than accompanied by the other instruments, as in opera), the total result would be disastrous. Furthermore, the singing in strict- or free-rhythm *tsuyogin* or *yowagin* style, or in *hiranori, chūnori*, or *ōnori* style, along with the movements of the gorgeously costumed Nō actors, serves to add color and dignity to the entire expression in both lyric and music.

In the second part of the play, the verses of the chorus are in strict-rhythm *tsuyogin* and *chūnori* style, where the shortest line for eight beats is two syllables. For instance:

> Crescent
> like the moon that sets
> low I bend
> my bow so humbly.
> Answering in song,
> he then receives the treasured sword.

Nue

All the above-mentioned points are necessary for the composition and arrangement of the Nō lyric and music into a dramatic whole, in order to create the "flower" Zeami loves. The "flower" so achieved in this play is, indeed, singularly remarkable.

The italicized segments of the following *Heike* excerpt are the portions that Zeami used in his play.[4]

> Especially *in the Ninpei Period, when the former Emperor Konoe was still the reigning monarch, His Majesty* had a fear *night after night. Though priests of wondrous powers and those of highest rank were called to hold* the grand rites and *the rites of intercession, there appeared no signs. The pain would come upon him only when the deepened Hour of the Ox drew near, but from the wooded quarter of the Third Ward in the east, the deep black clouds, in one huge mass, arose, and, hovering above the royal palace, they covered all; without fail, His Majesty would be gripped by fear.* Because of this, *the noble lords held council together. . . .* According to the precedent, *let the warriors be summoned, let them then protect our lord,* they said. *So from the two great houses of the Genpei, the chosen of the bravest of the brave, Yorimasa, was selected and summoned before them. Yorimasa, when all this happened, was still serving as a bureau chief of the armory. . . .* In compliance with His Majesty's command, he went to the court. Yorimasa made *the one retainer, I no Hayata,* from the land of Tōtōmi and whom *he trusted truly* carry on his back the arrows with feathers fastened near the butt. *Only this one gallant he chose to go with him. As for himself, the hunting robe, richly lined, he wore. Fledged with a copper pheasant's tail, with pointed metal heads were his arrows; two he readied for his bow, entwined so tightly close with fine rattan. He attended ever graciously the southern palace hallway.* The reason why he carried two arrows was that Lord Masayori, though he was still no more than a Minor Controller of the Left, selected him, saying, "Yorimasa is the one to shoot the phantom down"; should he fail to do so with the first arrow, he would shoot Masayori's jawbone with the second arrow, we heard. *As expected,* and without fail, as the men said in those days, from the wooded quarter of the Third Ward in the east, *the deep black clouds in one huge mass, arose, and, hovering above the royal palace, they covered it all. As Yorimasa looked up sternly, far above, deep within the clouds, mysterious and malign, lurked a phantom form.* Should he fail to shoot it with his arrow, he would not live in this world, he felt. However, *to the bowstring he fit the arrow. "Glory to Hachiman! O Great Bodhisattva!" he prayed mightily, deep within his heart. Fully drawn and with a twang released, the arrow responded unto his hand and squarely hit the mark. "There I hit it, oh," he shouted a warrior's arrow-cry. As the prey came tumbling down, I no Hayata went near it suddenly,* grasped and held it down, *and in swift succession nine times straight, he thrust his sword close to the hilt and to his fist, deeply through and through it. Then the men,* high and low, *lit up the torches in their hands* to see it closely. The head was like an ape's; the trunk, like a badger's; *the tail, like a snake's; and his hands and feet appeared like a tiger's limbs; then they heard its howling cries like that of Nue.* Terrible is an inadequate word.
>
> *His Majesty was more than gratified, and the treasured sword renowned as Lion King was then presented* to him. *The minister from Uji received it graciously and descended the staircase* halfway-down. *Just then,* as it was about the tenth of April, above the cloud-girt palace *a cuckoo passed by,* singing two or three notes. *The minister responded:*
>
>> *As the cuckoo sings*
>> *above the cloud-girt palace,*
>> *extolling, too, your name,*
>
> so the poem went; *thereupon Yorimasa humbly put his right knee on the ground; then, spreading out his long left sleeve, he looked from the corner of his eye at the moon and said:*

414

Crescent
like the moon that sets
low I bend
my bow so humbly.

Answering in song, he then received the treasured sword and retired from the royal audience.

415

Nue

NUE

By Zeami

Persons: WAKI: *A traveling Buddhist priest*
SHITE (PART I): *A strange boatman*
NOCHI-JITE (PART II): *The spirit of the chimera*
KYŌGEN: *A village man*

Classification: *Primary, Group V; Variant, Group II or IV*
Place: *At Ashiya in the land of Settsu*
Time: *April*
Kogaki: *1*

PART I

[*Following the introductory music, called* shidai, *the* waki, *wearing a pointed hood* (kakubōshi), *a plain, less-formal heavy silk kimono* (muji noshime), *a brown "inferior silk" broad-sleeved robe* (cha shike mizugoromo), *a waistband* (koshiobi), *a fan* (ōgi), *and a rosary* (juzu), *appears at the name-saying seat* (nanoriza), *facing the chorus seat, and sings the following verse, also called* shidai.]

WAKI

[1] *(Shidai: au, yowagin)*

Yo o sutebito[5] no	I renounce this world beneath
tabi no sora,	the sky I travel,
yo o sutebito no	I renounce this world beneath
tabi no sora,	the sky I travel.
koshikata izuku	From which regions to this place
naruran.	do I really come?

[*The chorus sings the* jidori, *a repetition of the above verse, except the third and fourth lines, in a lower key. While the chorus sings, the* waki *faces stage front.*]

CHORUS

(Jidori: au, yowagin)

Yo o sutebito no	I renounce this world beneath
tabi no sora,	the sky I travel.
koshikata izuku	From which regions to this place
naruran.	do I really come?

[*After the* jidori, *the* waki *intones the following prose passage, called* nanori, *which informs the audience of who he is and his purpose.*]

Masterworks of the Nō Theater

(Nanori: awazu, kotoba)

Kore wa shokoku ikken no sō nite sōrō. Ware kono hodo wa Mikumano[6] ni mairite sōrō. Mata kore yori Miyako ni noborabaya to omoi sōrō.

I am a Buddhist priest, going from province to province. Recently I went to Mikumano and now from this place, I think I will go up toward the capital.

[*The* waki *sings the following high-pitched* ageuta *passage, called* michiyuki *(travel song).*]

(Michiyuki: au, yowagin)

Hodo mo naku	In no time we come
kaeri Ki no ji[7]	on our homeward way through Ki,
seki koete,	past its barrier
kaeri Ki no ji no	on our homeward way through Ki,
seki[8] koete	past its barrier,
nao yukusue wa	and to my destination,
Izumi naru	Izumi, where lies
Shinoda no mori[9] o	Shinoda's sacred forest
uchisugite	through which I travel
matsubara mieshi	toward the grove of pines I see
tōzato[10] no	there a far-off town,

[*Facing his right, the* waki *takes two or three steps forward toward stage front and then returns to his former position, indicating that he has traveled long.*]

koko Suminoe[11] ya	here at Suminoe shore
Naniwagata,[12]	by Naniwa's bay
Ashiya no sato[13] ni	the village called Reed Cottage
tsukinikeri,	I have reached at last,
Ashiya no sato ni	the village called Reed Cottage
tsukinikeri.	I have reached at last.

[*After the* michiyuki, *the* waki *faces stage front and intones the following prose passage, called* tsukizerifu, *"arrival speech," in free-rhythm style.*]

(Tsukizerifu: awazu, kotoba)

Isogi sōrō hodo ni kore wa haya Tsu[14] no kuni Ashiya no sato ni tsukite sōrō. Hi no kurete sōrō hodo ni, yado o karabaya to omoi sōrō.

As I journeyed in haste, I have already reached the village called Reed Cottage in the land of Tsu. As day comes to an end, I think I will look for lodgings.

[*The* waki *goes toward the bridge by the* shite *seat.*]

(Mondai: awazu, kotoba)

Tokoro no hito no watari sōrō ka.

Is there anyone about who is a native of this place?

[*The* kyōgen, *wearing a striped, less-formal heavy silk kimono* (shima noshime), *the* kyōgen *two-piece* (kyōgen kamishimo), *a waistband* (koshiobi), *and a fan* (ōgi), *rises from the* kyōgen *seat and stands at the first pine* (ichi no matsu) *along the bridge.*]

Nue

Tokoro no mono to otazune wa, ikayō naru go-yō nite sōrō zo.

You called, asking for some native of this place. Is there something I can do for you?

WAKI

Kore wa shokoku ikken no sō nite sōrō. Ichiya no yado on-kashi sōrae.

I am a Buddhist priest, going from province to province. Please put me up for a night.

KYŌGEN

Sono koto nite sōrō. Kono tokoro no taihō nite ōrai no mono ni yado kasu koto wa kinzei nite sōrō aida, narimō-sumajiku sōrō.

About that question, there is an immutable law here that prohibits giving any lodgings to travelers. We cannot accommodate you.

WAKI

Go-taihō wa saru koto nite sōraedomo, hira ni ichiya o akasasete tamawari sōrae.

Though the immutable law should be observed, still I ask that you give me some lodgings for just a single night.

KYŌGEN

Iya iya, taihō o yaburu koto wa narimō-sazu sōrō. Tōtō o-tōri sōrae.

No, certainly not. We cannot break the immutable law. Quickly, please, go on your way.

WAKI

Sate wa ryōken naku sōrō ka.

Then you have no thoughts of your own, do you? [Going away.]

KYŌGEN

Ara o-yado o mairasetaku sōrō. Nō, nō o-yado o mairashō.

Oh, well, I would like to; yes, I will get some lodgings for you.

[*The* waki *returns to his former position.*]

WAKI

Shūchaku mōshite sōrō.

Thank you for arranging it.

KYŌGEN

Ano susaki no mi-dō e o-tomari sōrae.

Please, stay for the night at that shrine on the sandy point out there.

WAKI

Sono mi-dō wa katagata no tateraretaru
mi-dō nite sōrō ka.

Did you people build that shrine?

KYŌGEN

Warera no tatetaru mi-dō nite wa nashi.
Yoriaite tatetaru dō nite sōrō.

No, no, we did not build it all alone. Ev-
erybody met together and did it.

WAKI

Sono mi-dō ni tomari sōraeba, katagata
ni karu made mo naku sōrō.

If I should stay at that shrine, would I
need their permission?

KYŌGEN

Sarinagara ano dō e wa yona yona hika-
rimono ga agari sōrō aida, kokoroete o-
tomari sōrae.

That may not be necessary, but night after night, a luminous body rises from
the shrine, so please be careful if you
stay there tonight.

WAKI

Hōriki o motte tomari sōrōbeshi.

With the grace of Dharma, I shall stay
for a night.

[*The* waki *goes to the* waki *seat and sits down.*]

KYŌGEN

Ara sunei o-sō ni wa aru.

Oh, what a determined priest he is!

[*Following the introductory music called* issei, *the* shite, *wearing the* mikazuki *mask, a flowing black wig* (kuro gashira), *a headband* (hachimaki), *a collar in navy blue* (eri kon), *a plain, less-formal heavy silk kimono* (muji noshime), *an "inferior silk" broad-sleeved robe* (shike mizugo-romo), *a waistband* (koshiobi), *and a fan* (ōgi), *and carrying a pole* (sao), *appears and stands at the* shite *seat* (jōza); *then facing stage front* (shōmen), *he sings the following* sashi *passage.*]

SHITE

[2] (*Sashi: awazu, tsuyogin*)

Kanashiki kana ya
mi wa rōchō,[15]
kokoro o shireba
mōki no fuboku,[17]
tada anchū ni
mumoregi[18] no
saraba mumore mo
hatezu shite
bōshin nani ni
nokoruran.

How saddened is my body,
trapped like a caged bird!
Like the turtle, blind[16] my soul
seeks out here the drifting wood,
but deep in sightless darkness
the log is buried
could I be too deep to rise,
for I cannot rest;
what draws my straying spirit
still to linger on?

419

Nue

[The shite *continues to sing the following verse, called* issei.]

(Issei: awazu, tsuyogin)

Ukishizumu	Ah, rising, sinking,
namida no nami no	midst the waves of tears I shed
utsuobune[19]	goes my dugout boat,

[The shite *faces to his right.]*

CHORUS

kogarete[20] taenu	paddled by my thoughts that yearn
inishie o	always for the past

[The shite *faces stage front once more.]*

SHITE

shinobihatsubeki	so that there is no moment
hima zo naki.	for my heart to rest.

[The shite *slightly clouds his mask (*shioru*). The following passages, called* kakeai, *are exchanged between the* waki *and the* shite. *The* waki, *facing the* shite, *sings.]*

WAKI

[3] *(Kakeai: awazu, tsuyogin)*

Fushigi ya na,	How mysterious!
yo mo fukegata no	Night thickens with the darkness
uranami ni	deep between the waves
kasuka ni ukami	faintly floating in, it seems
yoru mono o	a form approaches;
mireba kikishi ni	I see it does not differ
kawarazu shite	much from what they told me.
fune no katachi wa	Though it seems to be a boat
arinagara	in form and outline,
tada mumoregi no	only a log, long buried,
gotoku naru ni	appears before me now,
noru hitokage mo	and the rider's figure, too,
sadaka narazu,	is not defined clearly.
ara fushigi no	How strange, how truly strange
mono ya na.	a thing this is!

420

SHITE

Fushigi no mono to uketamawaru. So-nata wa ika naru hito yaran.	What sort of man are you to say that I am very strange?
Moto yori ukimi wa	Foam from the fleeting wretched past,
mumoregi no	"like this flotsam log
hitoshirenu[21] mi to	buried and unknown to man,"
oboshimesaba,	I am, as you must guess.

[*The* shite *makes a* tsumeashi *gesture toward the* waki.]

fushinna nasase- tamai so to yo.	So there can be no reason for you to find me strange.

WAKI

Iya kore wa tada kono satobito no samo fushigi naru funabito no yoru[22] yoru kitaru to iitsuru ni mireba sukoshi mo tagawaneba ware mo fushin o mōsu nari.	No, indeed, I only meant that the villager who spoke of a mysterious, strange boatman who appears about this place night after night was speaking truly, since his tale is quite the same as what I've witnessed; so I was surprised and spoke inadvertently.

SHITE

Kono satobito to wa Ashi no Ya no nada no shio yaku amabito no tagui o nani to utagaitamō.	This villager you speak of is most likely one of the fisher folk of Reed Cottage, who boils brine by the seashore. Why do you doubt him?

WAKI

Shio yaku ama no tagui naraba waza oba nasade itoma arige ni yoru yoru kitaru wa fushin nari.	If this fisherman is one who lives by boiling brine, he seems to neglect his work, as if he had time to spare to come here nightly to this place, which seems suspicious.

SHITE

Geni geni itoma no aru koto o utagai- tamō mo iware ari. Furuki uta ni mo "Ashi no Ya no[23]	Indeed, I understand the reason you are troubled by the fact that he has time to spare. Even in an old song, it is said that "along Reed Cottage,

WAKI

nada no shioyaki itoma nami tsuge no ogushi wa sasazu kinikeri."	by the sea, salt-making girls have no time to spare; without dressing up their hair with their boxwood combs they come."

[*The* shite *sings the following lines in* yowagin *style.*]

❀

Nue

(Yowagin)

Ware mo uki ni wa	In this wretched, floating world
itoma nami no[24]	I have no time to spare

WAKI

shio ni sasarete	as a boatman driven on

SHITE

funabito wa	by the ocean waves,

[*The* shite *makes a* tsumeashi *gesture toward the* waki. *He then faces stage front once more, as the chorus sings the following* ageuta.]

CHORUS

(Ageuta: au, yowagin)

sasade kinikeri	driven, in my dugout boat
utsuobune,	without oars, I come,
sasade kinikeri	driven, in my dugout boat
utsuobune,	without oars, I come;
utsutsu ka yume ka	whether real or just a dream,
akete koso	when it dawns you may
mirume[25] mo	see weeds uncut,
karanu[26]	abandoned,
Ashi no Ya ni	like this Reed Cottage

[*The* shite *goes out slightly toward stage front.*]

hitoyo nete	where you pass this night;
amabito no	for this fisherman

[*The* shite *faces the* waki.]

kokoro no yami o	and for the dark attachment
toitamae.	in his heart, please pray.

[*Changing his mood, the* shite *goes out to the eye-fixing pillar, and, making a turn to his left, he goes to the* shite *seat, while the chorus continues singing for the* shite.]

Arigata ya,	Oh, how blessed you are.
tabibito wa	Oh, good traveler!
yo o nogaretaru	Though you are freed completely
on-mi nari.	from this fleeting world,
Ware wa na nomi zo	I exist in name alone
sute obune,	like a cast-off boat.
nori no chikara o	I call upon the power
tanomu nari,	of the Holy Law,
nori no chikara o	I call upon the power
tanomu nari.	of the Holy Law.

[The following dialogues exchanged between the shite and the waki are called mondai. They intone them from their respective positions, the waki at the waki seat, and the shite at the shite seat.]

WAKI

[4] *(Mondai: awazu, kotoba)*

Nani to mimōsedomo sarani ningen to wa miezu sōrō. Ika naru mono zo, na o nanori sōrae.

No matter how I look at you, somehow, I cannot consider you quite human. Whatever you are, please tell me your name.

SHITE

Kore wa Konne no In[27] no gyo-o ni, Yorimasa[28] ga yasaki ni kakari mei o ushinaishi Nue[29] to mōshishi mono no bōshin nite sōrō. Sono toki no arisama kuwashiku katatte kikasemōshi sōrō-beshi. Ato o tōte tamawari sōrae.

I am the one who in the reign of the ex-Emperor Konne was struck by Yorimasa's arrow and died and then became the specter of the chimera that I once was. Let me tell you in full what happened at that time. Listen to me well, and then please pray for my memory.

WAKI

Sate wa Nue no bōshin nite sōrō ka. Sono toki no arisama kuwashiku katari sōrae. Ato oba nengoro ni tomurai sōrōbeshi.

So then, are you the unsettled specter of a chimera? Tell me all about what happened then so that I can reverently pray for your memory.

[The shite goes to stage center from the front of the musicians and sits down, as the chorus sings the following high-pitched passage, called kuri.]

CHORUS

(Kuri: awazu, tsuyogin)

Sate mo Konne no In no
go-zaii no toki,
Ninpei[30] no korooi
shushō yona yona
go-nō ari.

When the former Emperor Konne
was still the reigning monarch,
in the Ninpei Period,
to His Majesty a pain
came night after night.

[The shite sings the sashi passage in free-rhythm tsuyogin style.]

SHITE

(Sashi: awazu, tsuyogin)

423

Uken no kōsō
kisō ni ōsete
daihō o
shuserarekeredomo
sono shirushi
sara ni nakarikeri.

Though priests of wondrous powers
and those of highest rank were called
to hold the service
and the rites of intercession,
there appeared no signs;
all of them were to no avail.

Nue

CHORUS

Go-nō wa ushi no	The pain would come upon him
koku[31] bakari nite	only when the deepened Hour
arikeru ga	of the Ox drew near;
Tō Sanjō[32] no	but from the wooded quarter
mori no kata yori	of the Third Ward in the east
kokuun hito-mura	the deep black clouds in one huge mass
tachikitatte	arose, and hovering
go-ten no ue ni	above the royal palace,
ōeba	they covered all;
kanarazu obie-	without fail, His Majesty
tamaikeri.	would be gripped by fear.

SHITE

Sunawachi kugyō	Whereupon the noble lords
sengi atte,	held council together:

CHORUS

sadamete henge no	presumably the cause, they thought,
mono narubeshi,	was a demon specter.
bushi ni ōsete	Let the warriors be summoned,
keigo arubeshi tote	let them then protect our lord, they said;
Genpei ryōka no	so from the two great houses
tsuwamono o	of the Genpei,
senzerarekeru hodo ni,	the chosen of the bravest of the brave,
Yorimasa o erami-	Yorimasa, was selected
idasaretari.	and summoned before them.

[*The chorus sings the* kuse *passage, and the* shite *sits still. Hence it is called* iguse.]

CHORUS

(Iguse: au, tsuyogin)

Yorimasa	Yorimasa,
sono toki wa	when all this happened,
Hyōgo no Kami[33] to zo	was serving as a bureau chief
mōshikeru.	of the armory.
Tanomitaru	The one retainer
rōdō ni wa	he trusted truly was
I no Hayata[34]	I no Hayata;
tada ichinin	only this one gallant
meshigushitari.	he chose to go with him.
Waga mi wa	As for himself,
futae no	the hunting robe,
kariginu ni	richly lined, he wore.
yamadori no o[35] nite	Fledged with a copper pheasant's tail,
haidarikeru	with pointed metal heads

424

Masterworks of the Nō Theater

togariya	were his arrows;
futasuji	two he readied
shigedō no yumi[36] ni	for his bow, entwined so tightly
torisoete	close with fine rattan.
go-ten no	As he attended
ōyuka ni	ever graciously
shikō shite	the palace hallway
go-nō no	and for the hour
kokugen o	of unbearable pain,
imaya imaya to	moment after moment now,
machiitari.	he humbly waited;
Saru hodo ni	surely in due course,
an no gotoku	as he had expected,
kurokumo	the deep black clouds
hitomura	in one huge mass
tachikitari	arose, and hovering
go-ten no ue ni	above the royal palace,
ōitari.	they covered it all.

[*The* shite *looks up high above stage front.*]

Yorimasa kitto	As Yorimasa looked up
miagureba	sternly far above,

[*The* shite *looks across to his right.*]

unchū ni	deep within the clouds
ayashiki mono no	mysterious and malign
sugata ari.	lurked a phantom form.

[*The* shite *holds the fan in his right hand and sings the following lines, called* ageha.]

SHITE

(*Ageha*)

Ya totte	To the bowstring
uchitsugai	he fit the arrow.

[*The* shite *lowers his head as if to pray, as the chorus continues to sing the following.*]

CHORUS

Namu	Glory
Hachiman	to Hachiman!
Daibosatsu[37] to	O Great Bodhisattva!
shinjū ni	He prayed mightily
kinen shite	deep within his heart.

425

[*The* shite *gestures as though he were shooting an arrow.*]

yoppiki hyō to	Fully drawn and with a twang
hanatsu ya ni	released, the arrow
tegotae shite	responded unto his hand

Nue

[*The* shite *gazes deeply into space.*]

hata to ataru   and squarely hit the mark.

[*The* shite *holds the fan in reverse (*gyakute ni*), and looks toward the eye-fixing pillar.*]

                    etari ya   "There I hit it,

[*The* shite *rises.*]

          ō to   "oh," he made
          yasakebi shite a warrior's arrow-cry,

[*He goes toward the eye-fixing pillar.*]

          otsuru tokoro o   as the prey came tumbling down,

[*As the chorus continues to sing the following passage, the* shite *rises, goes to the eye-fixing pillar, and kneels down; he holds down the catch with his hands and gestures, as though he were stabbing it with his sword.*]

          I no Hayata   I no Hayata
          tsutsu to yorite   went near it suddenly,
          tsuzukesama ni   and in swift succession,
          kokono   nine times straight,
          katana zo   he thrust his sword
          saitarikeru.   deeply through and through it.

[*The* shite, *regrasping the fan in a normal way, rises and holds it like a torch and looks at the catch.*]

          Sate hi o tomoshi   Then the men lit the torches
          yoku mireba   to see it closely;
          kashira wa saru,[38] the head was like an ape's;
          o wa kuchinawa,   the tail was like a snake's;
          ashi te wa tora no and his hands and feet appeared
          gotoku nite,   like a tiger's limbs;
          naku koe nue ni   then they heard its howling cries,

[*Changing his mood, the* shite *makes a turn to his right and goes to the* shite *seat.*]

          nitarikeri.   like that of *Nue*,
          Osoroshi   more hideous
          nandomo   than one can say;

[*At the* shite *seat, the* shite *faces the* waki, *goes out toward stage center, and sits down.*]

          oroka naru katachi   beyond all words, a horrid sight
          narikeri.   is this dread form!

[*The* shite *faces stage front once more, as the chorus sings the following passage, called* rongi.]

CHORUS

[5] (*Rongi: au, yowagin*)

          Geni kakurenaki   How well known this story is
          yogatari no   all throughout the world!

sono ichinen o	Now you must reverse and change
hirugaeshi	that one attachment
ukamu chikara to	for power to uplift you
naritamae.	from the sunken depths.

SHITE

Ukamubeki	There are no tidings
tayori nagisa[39] no	that help me to float ashore
asamidori	with the light-green waves[40]
mizunokashiwa[41] ni	like the lucky three-leafed spray
araba koso	of the sacred oak

[*The* shite *faces the* waki.]

| shizumu wa ukamu | and change my fate from sinking |
| en narame. | to emerge again. |

[*The* shite *faces stage front once more.*]

CHORUS

| Geni ya tashō no | Waving sleeves at each other |
| en zo tote | is a karmic sign; |

SHITE

| toki mo koso are | as such it is the moment |
| koyoi shi mo | of the eve to meet |

CHORUS

| naki yo no hito ni | such a one not from this world; |
| aitake[42] no | it's not out of joint |

[*The* shite *holds a bamboo pole in his hand.*]

SHITE

| sao torinaoshi | like the bamboo pole he grasps |
| utsuobune | once again as though |

[*The* shite *rises.*]

CHORUS

| noru to mieshi ga | he seems to board the dugout |

427

SHITE

| yoru[43] no nami ni | but midst the surging waves |

[*The* shite *goes to the* shite *seat and then, without stopping, goes to the bridge.*]

Nue

CHORUS

ukinu	of the night,
shizuminu	he floats, he sinks,
mietsu kakure	hiding and appearing,
taedae⁴⁴ ni	faintly, dimly, there,
ikue ni kiku wa	now and then at times we hear
Nue no koe,	Chimera's screeching.
osoroshi ya	How horrifying
susamashi ya	with dreadful terror!
ara osoroshi ya	O, how horrifyingly awful
susamashi ya.	with dreadful terror!

[*At the* shite *pillar, the* shite *throws the pole and makes his exit.*]

Nakairi (Interlude)

[*The* kyōgen *appears near the* shite *pillar (shitebashira).*]

KYŌGEN

(*Mondai: katari, kotoba*)

Saizen ōrai no o-sō no ichiya no yado to ōse sōraedomo taihō no yoshi mōshi, susaki no mi-dō o kashite sōrō. Imada are ni goza aru ka. Mairite mi-mōsabaya to zonzuru. O-sō wa imada kore ni goza sōrō ka.

A while ago, a passing Buddhist priest asked for some lodgings for the night and I told him about our immutable law. But I let him have that shrine on the sandy point. I wonder if he is still out there. I think I'd better go see him. [*Sees the priest.*] Oh, Your Holiness, are you still here?

WAKI

Imada tōryū mōshite sōrō. On-mi wa yazen yado o kasazaru hito nite watari sōrō ka.

I am still here. Are you the one who would not give me a room last night?

KYŌGEN

Nakanaka o-yado mairasetaku sōrae-domo, kono tokoro no taihō nite zehi ni oyobazu sōrō.

Yes, but not really. I wanted to, but because of the immutable law of this place, I could not help it.

428

WAKI

Iya iya kurushikarazu sōrō. Sore ni tsuki tazunetaki koto no sōrō. Mazu chikō on-niri sōrae.

I don't mind it at all. About that law, I have something I would like to ask you. Please come closer.

KYŌGEN

Kashikomatte sōrō. Sate nanigoto o-tazune nasare sōrō zo.

Yes. [*Goes out to stage center and sits down.*] What do you want to know?

Omoi mo yoranu mōshigoto nite sōraedomo inishie Konne no In no gyo-o ni
nue to yū keshō no mono no hatetaru
shisai, go-zonji ni oite wa katatte on-
kikase sōrae.

Indeed, this is something you may
not expect from me, but I hear that in
the reign of the ex-Emperor Konne,
the specter called Nue lost his life here.
Please tell me the story if you know
about it.

Kore wa omoi mo yoranu koto o uketamawari sōrō mono kana. Warera mo
kono atari ni sumai tsukamatsuri sōraedomo sayō no koto kuwashiku wa zonzezu sōraedomo, oyoso uketamawarioyobitaru tōri on-monogatari mōsōzuru
nite sōrō.

How strange that you should ask me
about such things. Though we live in
this neighborhood, I don't know too
much about the details. I will, however,
let you hear the story the way I have
heard it.

Chikagoro nite sōrō.

I would be most grateful.

Saru hodo ni nue no shisai to mōsu wa.
Konne no In no gyo-o ni Tō Sanjō no
mori no kata yori kokuun hitomura
tachikitari, go-ten no ue o ōeba Mikado
go-nō to nasaretamō. Kisō kōsō o shōji
go-kitō aredomo sono shirushi sara
ni nashi. Hakushi o meshite uranawase
goran areba kore wa henge no mono no
waza nari. Bushi ni ōsete ite otosasera-
rubeki tote kugyō sengi ari. Genpei ryō-
ka no tsuwamono o erabi, Yorimasa ni
ōsetsukeraruru. Yorimasa o-ukemōshi I
no Hayata ichinin meshitsure, go-ten no
ōyuka ni maitte go-nō no kokugen o
machi-mōsu ni, an no gotoku kokuun
tachikitari go-ten no ue o ōimōsu. Yorimasa kitto miagureba kanpaku-denka,
sayū no daijin daichūnagon hachiza
nanaben goi rokui shoka no samurai
dōjō dōge ni sode o tsurane, bunbu no
hyakkan kore o mite, katazu o nonde
kenbutsu su. Yorimasa sukoshi mo sa-
wagazu togariya tsugatte yoppiki hyō
to hanatsu ya ayamatazu tegotae shite
ōyuka ni ochiru tokoro o I no Hayata
sutto yotte. Fujishirō no muneatsuita

Well. This is the story about Nue, the
chimera. In the reign of the ex-Emperor
Konne, from the grove of trees at the
East Third Ward, there appeared a cluster of black clouds. As it hovered over
the palace, His Majesty suffered great
pain. Though noble priests and high-
ranking priests were called to perform
rites, there was no effect in the least.
Doctors were called in to tell fortunes,
and they declared the cause was a
demon specter. Let warriors shoot it
down, they said, and the noble lords
held council. Braves were chosen from
the two houses of the Genpei, and Yorimasa was selected. He accepted it,
and allowing only one, I no Hayata, to
accompany him, he went to the wide-
eaved floor of the palace and waited for
the hour of the terrible pain. As he had
expected, a cluster of dark black clouds
came and hovered above the palace. As
he looked up, he saw the chief adviser
to the emperor, the ministers of the
Left and the Right, the chief and middle
counselors of eight ranks and seven

429

Nue

naru katana nite sashitometaru to mōsu. Sate hi o tomoshi goran aru ni, kashira wa saru, o wa kuchinawa, ashi te wa tora no gotoku, naku koe nue ni nitaru tote, sono na o nue to nazuke, utsuobune ni tsukurikomi, Yodogawa sashite nagasareshi ga kono tokoro ni nagare kitari, shibaraku ano nada ni to-matte aritaru to mōsu. Warera no uke-tamawari oyobitaru wa kaku no gotoku nite goza sōrō ga, nanto oboshimeshi o-tazune nasare sōrō zo. Chikagoro fu-shin ni zonji sōrō.

posts, warriors of the fifth and sixth ranks, the court nobles, the high and the low who were lined up sleeve to sleeve. As the officials, both military and civilian, looked at the scene, they held their breath. Yorimasa, undis-mayed, notched his bow with an arrow with a pointed metal head. He released it with a twang and it answered true to his hand. As the prey tumbled to the great floor, I no Hayata went near it and stabbed it with his thick-backed sword made by Fujishiro, I hear. As the men lit their torches to examine it, the head ap-peared like that of an ape, the tail like a snake's, both its hands and feet like tig-er's claws, and its cry like that of a chi-mera. So it was named Nue. Sealed in-side the dugout boat, it was set adrift down the Yodo. Before it reached here, it remained for a while in this open sea, I hear. Well, this is what we have heard. Please tell me why you ask me about this. Lately I have felt something strange around here.

WAKI

Nengoro ni on-monogatari sōrō mono kana. Tazunemōsu mo yo no gi ni ara-zu. Saizen kono mi-dō ni tomari sōrō mae ni, keshitaru hito no utsuobune ni norite kitari sōrō hodo ni fushin o na-shite sōraeba, makoto wa nue no bōkon nari. Utsuobune ni irerare kono tokoro ni nagare tomari sōrō ni yori, ima ni shūshin nokotte kayō ni mie sōrō tote, sono toki no arisama nengoro ni katari utsuobune ni noru to mite sugata o miu-shinōte sōrō yo.

How detailed a story you have told me. The reason I asked you is not too spe-cial. A while ago, before I spent the night at this shrine, a ghost, disguised as a man, came in a dugout boat. As I thought it strange, I asked him what he was. He said that, in fact, he was the spirit of a chimera. Sealed inside the dugout boat, he came adrift to this place, and ever since his attachment re-mained behind, he appeared like this. He told me at length about the time he met his end. He seemed as if he were about to board the boat, when I lost sight of him.

430

KYŌGEN

Kore wa kidoku naru koto o ōse sōrō mono kana. Sate wa nue no shūshin a-raware idetaru to zonji sōrō aida, tomu-rōte o-tōri arekashi to zonji sōrō.

This is most surprising, what you have just said. That must have been the chi-mera's attached spirit that made an ap-pearance. You should, I think, pray for him and go along your way.

WAKI

Chikagoro fushigi naru koto nite sōrō hodo ni, arigataki o-kyō o dokuju shi, kano ato o nengoro ni tomuraimōsō-zuru nite sōrō.	Lately, this has been so strange. So I think I will chant the holy Buddhist sutra and reverently recite prayers for his memory.

KYŌGEN

Go-yō no koto mo sōrawaba kasanete ōse sōrae.	If you should have something for me to do, please call me again.

WAKI

Tanomi sōrōbeshi.	I will. Thank you.

KYŌGEN

Kokoroe mōshite sōrō.	Yes, good priest.

[*The* kyōgen *goes back to the* kyōgen *seat.*]

PART II

[*The* waki, *in a sitting position, sings the following passage, called* machiutai *(waiting song).*]

WAKI

[6] *(Machiutai: au, yowagin)*

Mi-nori no koe mo	The voice that chants the prayer
uranami mo,	and the inlet waves,
mi-nori no koe mo	the voice that chants the prayer
uranami mo	and the inlet waves,
mina jissō no	tell us that the Way of Truth
michi hiroki	opens wide for all;
nori o ukeyo to	so that Nue too receives
yo to tomo ni	its holy blessing
kono on-kyō o	all night long I chant for him
dokuju suru,	the Buddhist sutra,
kono on-kyō o	all night long I chant for him
dokuju suru.	the Buddhist sutra.

[*Following the* deha *music, the* nochi-jite, *the ghost of Chimera, appears on the bridge. He wears a kotobide mask, a flowing red wig (aka gashira), a headband (hachimaki), a collar in indigo (eri kon), a striped heavy-silk kimono (dan atsuita), a gold brocade robe (happi), a brocade broad divided skirt (hangiri), a waistband (koshiobi), and a fan (ōgi). He also wears a staff with a T-shaped head at his waist. As the* nochi-jite *approaches the first pine (ichi no matsu), the* waki *clasps his hands together in prayer with his rosary and sings the following lines.*]

❀

431

Nue

WAKI

(Awazu, tsuyogin)

Ichibutsu jōdō	One Buddha who has won the Way
kanken hōkai	surveys the world of Laws and sees
sōmoku kokudo	that grass, trees, the land itself:
shitsukai jōbutsu.	these all attain enlightenment.

[*While the* waki *is chanting the above lines, the* shite *enters the stage and stands by the* shite *seat. Holding both hands together in prayer, he chants the following.*]

SHITE

Ujō hijō	Sentient and nonsentient
kaigu jōbutsudō.	shall find the Way together.

WAKI

Tanomubeshi.	Depend upon him.

SHITE

Tanomubeshi ya.	Oh, depend upon him.

[*Both the* waki *and the* shite *unfold their hands. The* waki, *rubbing the rosary between the palms of his hands, goes out to the eye-fixing pillar, and, making a turn to his left, he goes to the* shite *seat as the chorus sings.*]

CHORUS

(Noriji: ōnori, tsuyogin)

Gojūnirui[45] mo	Since I'm one among the two
ware dōshō no	and fifty kinds of beings,
nehan ni hikarete	guided by Nirvana Sutra

[*The* waki *sits down at the* waki *seat.*]

shinnyo no tsuki[46] no	underneath the moon of truth,
yojio ni ukamitsutsu	floating in upon the tide of night,
kore made kitareri,	up to this very point I come;
arigata ya.	I feel most grateful.

[*At the* shite *seat, the* shite, *facing the* waki, *folds his hands in prayer.*]

WAKI

(Kakeai: awazu, tsuyogin)

Fushigi ya na,	How mysterious!
mokuzen ni kitaru	When I look upon this one
mono o mireba,	who appears before me,
omote wa saru,	his face is like an ape's,
ashi te wa tora,	and his limbs, a tiger's;
kikishi ni kawaranu	this demon-specter's form is just
henge no sugata,	as was told to me before.

Masterworks of the Nō Theater

ara osoroshi no	How fearsome and how dreadful
arisama ya na.	this thing appears to me!

[*The* shite, *facing the* waki, *sings the following high-pitched passage, called* kuri, *in free-rhythm* tsuyogin *style.*]

SHITE

(Kuri: awazu, tsuyogin)

Sate mo ware	Truly I became
akushin gedō no	a demon with a hate-filled heart,
henge to natte,	prowling through the hellish pathway,
buppō ōbō no	hoping that I might corrupt the laws
sawari to naran to	of the kings and holy Buddhas.
ōjō chikaku	Near the capital I raged

[*The* shite *goes to the bridge.*]

henman shite	in fury all around;

[*The* shite, *facing stage front at the first pine, sings the* sashi *passage.*]

(Sashi: awazu, tsuyogin)

Tō Sanjō no	at the Third Ward in the east,
rintō ni	above the treetops
shibaraku higyō shi	I flew and circled for a while

[*Striding onto the stage, the* shite *dashes to stage front (*norikomi hyoshi*).*]

ushimitsu[47] bakari no	and three-fourths past the Oxen Hour,
yona yona ni	night upon dark night,
go-ten no ue ni	above the royal palace
tobisagareba	I dashed and dived headlong,

[*The chorus sings the following passage in* chūnori *and strict-rhythm* tsuyogin *style. As the chorus starts to sing, the* shite *stamps the floor a few times.*]

CHORUS

(Chūnoriji: au, tsuyogin)

Sunawachi go-nō	whereupon a pain became
shikiri nite	acutely frequent,

[*The* shite *goes out to the eye-fixing pillar and, making a big turn to his left, goes to the front of the flute player.*]

433

gyokutai o	his noble person
nayamashite	was plagued with torture
obie-	and terror
tama irase-	that made him tremble;
tamō koto mo	and all these things, he said,
waga nasu waza yo to	were of my evil doing too.

[*The* shite *goes out slightly and, lifting up the fan, stamps the floor a few times.*]

ikari o nashishi ni	As I boasted all in fury,
omoi mo	so suddenly,
yorazarishi	when least expected,

[The shite *goes to the eye-fixing pillar and, with both hands, puts the end of the fan to his chest; bending backward as he is, he strides back toward the* shite *seat, kneels, and turns himself around on his knee. Facing stage front, he sits cross-legged and lowers his face, while the chorus sings.]*

Yorimasa ga	I was deeply hit
yasaki ni atareba	by Yorimasa's arrow point;
henshin usete,	all disguising powers gone,
rakuraku	crashing downward,
rairai to	smashing downward
chi ni taorete	upon the earth I fell down,[48]
tachimachi ni	and in an instant
messeshi koto,	I was destroyed and died.
omoeba	It seems I think,
Yorimasa ga	Yorimasa shot
yasaki yori wa	more than an arrowhead
kimi no	for his lord;
tenbatto	Heaven's punishment

[The shite *hits the floor hard with his fan.]*

atarikeru yo to	struck me hard and brought me down.

[The shite *gazes at the* waki.*]*

ima koso omoi-	Now at last, I understand
shiraretare.	and accept my fate.

[The shite *changes his mood and, holding the staff in his hands, goes out to stage center from in front of the musicians.]*

Sono toki	At this juncture
shushō	His Majesty
gyo-kan atte	is more than gratified
Shishiō[49] to	and the treasured sword
iu gyo-ken o	renowned as Lion King

[The shite *holds his staff out and looks at it, thinking of the sword.]*

Yorimasa ni	is then presented
kudasarekeru o	to honor Yorimasa.

[The shite *makes a* hiraki *gesture toward stage front.]*

434

Uji no	Thereupon
Daijin[50]	the minister
tamawarite	from Uji receives

[The shite *stamps the floor a few times.]*

kizahashi o	graciously the prize
oritamō ni	and descends the staircase.
orifushi kakkō	Just then a cuckoo passes by
otozurekereba	as it pays a humble call.

[*The* shite *looks above to his right.*]

Daijin   The minister
toriaezu   hastily responds:

[*The* shite, *remaining seated, sings the following lines.*]

SHITE

(*Age no Uta: awazu, tsuyogin*)

Hototogisu   "As the cuckoo sings
na o mo kumoi ni   above the cloud-girt palace,
aguru kana to   extolling, too, your name,"

[*The rest of the passages below are sung in* chūnori *and strict-rhythm* tsuyogin *style. First, the* shite, *facing stage front once more, sings.*]

SHITE

(*Chūnoriji: au, tsuyogin*)

ōserare-   so the poem went;
kereba   thereupon

[*The* shite *goes out to stage front and kneels, as the chorus sings the following.*]

CHORUS

Yorimasa   Yorimasa
migi no   humbly puts
hiza o tsuite   his right knee on the ground,

[*Spreading out his left sleeve, the* shite *looks above to his right.*]

hidari no   then spreading out
sode o hiroge   his long left sleeve he looks
tsuki o sukoshi   from the corner of his eye
me ni kakete   at the moon and says:

[*Keeping his posture as is.*]

yumi-   "Crescent
harizuki[51] no   like the moon that sets
iru[52] ni   low I bend
makasete to,   my bow so humbly."

[*The* shite *moves one knee forward and holds the staff reverently with both hands as if receiving the sword from His Majesty.*]

435

tsukamatsuri,   Answering in song,
gyo-ken o tamawari   he then receives the treasured sword

[*The* shite *rises and steps back to stage center; holding a sword in his right hand, he kneels and bows his head.*]

gozen o   and retires
makarikaereba   from the royal audience.

Yorimasa wa	So Yorimasa
na o agete,	won for himself fame
ware wa	while mine went

[*The* shite *rises, goes in front of the flute player, and comes out to the eye-fixing pillar. Putting the staff behind his neck, he leans backward; he scurries on his toes to the front of the chorus, then back again to the* shite *seat, as if he were being washed away.*]

na o nagasu	downward drifting
utsuobune ni	inside the dugout boat
oshiirerarete	I was deeply thrust down
Yodogawa no	the Yodo River,
yodomitsu	now standing still,
nagaretsu	then floating on
yukusue no	to my destined end
Udono[53] mo onaji	over Udono renowned
Ashi no Ya no	for rushes, as Reed Cottage,
urawa no	by the inlet's

[*The* shite *kneels at the* shite *seat.*]

ukisu ni	emerged sandbar,
nagare tomatte	my downward drift is halted,
kuchinagara	and my dugout boat

[*Throwing the staff away, the* shite, *opening the fan, goes out to the eye-fixing pillar and, making a turn to his left, goes to the* waki *seat.*]

utsuobune no	remains to rot away;
tsuki hi mo miezu	so no moon nor sun is seen
kuraki yori[54]	from raven darkness
kuraki michi ni zo	into the path of darkness

[*Toward the curtain the* shite *makes a* kumo no ōgi *gesture and, beckoning with his fan, goes to the bridge.*]

irinikeru,	I have gone astray;
haruka ni terase	let the light shine bright far out
yama no ha no,	from the mountain ridge,
haruka ni terase	let the light shine bright far out
yama no ha no	from the mountain ridge,
tsuki to tomo ni	O, moon, with you the moon

[*Toward the third pine* (san no matsu) *the* shite *dashes out and suddenly jumps, sits down cross-legged, and hides his face with the fan in his left hand; then he rises and makes a final stamp on the floor, as the chorus finishes singing the last line.*]

436

kaigetsu[55] mo	upon the ocean,
irinikeri,	too, is going down,
kaigetsu to tomo ni	with the moon upon the ocean,
irinikeri.	now I, too, go down.

[*The* shite *exits after he stamps the floor.*]

Taema

Introduction

Taema belongs to Group V of Nō plays, but with its variant versions, called *kogaki*, it can be categorized in the first, third, or fourth group. When a variation is used, it is indicated in the small characters on the lower left of the title of the play to be performed. According to Miyake Noboru, there are five variant *kogaki* versions for *Taema*, among which two specifically indicate a change in categorization, namely, *Waki Nō no shiki* (Group I play) and *Sanbanme no shiki* (Group III play). The other three are *Nidangaeshi* (Second-movement repeat), *Kutsurogi* (Rest), and *Bosa no ka-keri* (Bodhisattva stride). Miyake explains each of them as follows:

(1) *Waki Nō no shiki*: When *Taema* is used for a Group I play, the *hayamai* (quick dance) changes to the *ojikicho* mode. Following the *shin no issei*, instead of the ordinary *issei* music, the *shite* appears from behind the curtain. (2) *Sanbanme no shiki*: The musical accompaniment of both the large and small *tsuzumi* and the flute music called *uchikake* are added to the *kuri*, and a special *tsuzumi* piece called *uchikiri* to the *kuse*; however, now this has become a usual practice. (3) *Nidangaeshi*: After the end of the second movement (*dan*) of the *deha* music, one more *dan* of a different musical set is added. The *shite*'s entrance style changes, too. In the mirror room the *shite* stands in front of the curtain; when the stage attendant calls "Curtain," and as he sweeps the curtain up, the *shite* makes a *migiuke* gesture and then comes out onto the bridge. This is called *maku hanare* (stand off curtain), which adds dignity to the grade (*kurai*) of the play. (4) *Kutsurogi*: After the third movement (*dan*) of the *hayamai*, the *shite* goes to the bridge and rests a little, which is called *kutsurogi*. Then the *shite* comes back to the stage. (5) *Bosa no kakeri*: The *Jo no mai* is replaced by the short *iroe* dance movement. The *shite* goes out toward stage front and folds her hands in prayer. After the music of the small and large *tsuzumi*, the *shite* turns to her right, and at the *shite* seat, with a small turn, she makes a *hiraki* gesture and starts singing. In this case, it is customary to omit the *kuse* passage altogether.[1]

All of the first four *kogaki* versions show how flexible in rhythm the play can be, while the Nō text remains unchanged, except for the *kuse*, which is omitted in the fifth *kogaki* variant. Some of the changes called for in these variations have to do with the tempo; others, with the style of entry, *kata* (gestures), or singing, all of which are contributing factors in the performance, bringing out the best of whichever category of Nō plays *Taema* can assume in relation to other plays in a Nō program. Because the text has such a great capacity, it can actually dictate the form of music, dance, or *kata*, as these variant *kogaki* versions demonstrate.

The play is based on the famous legend pertaining to the temple of Taema, a temple that my family and I visited late one afternoon, before the spring twilight, and that remains fresh in my memory. I can still recall my thoughts, asking myself questions much as the *waki* does in this play. The *shite* and the *tsure*, who appear before the *waki* and through whom the *kuri-sashi-kuse* passages tell the *waki* the story of the temple's treasured Mandala, are the manifestations of Lord Amida and Kannon, in disguise as an old nun and a girl.

The first part of the play is quiet and serene, with hardly any posturing or acting of importance. The mood is refreshing and uplifting, especially in the *iguse* section, without its accompanying dance movement, sung in *tsuyogin* style, which adds an awe-inspiring air of dignity to the passage and deepens its tone. "In the *rongi* section," says Miyake, "there is also no marked acting."[2] Then, at the end of the first part of the play, the *shite* exits while the chorus sings the following concluding passage:

> up the slope, though aged,
> she climbs, and on the cloud
> that rises high she rides
> to ascend above,
> on the purple clouds she rides
> and ascends above.

Miyake states of this scene that "the way the aged old nun carries her feet, and handles the cane, requires deep feeling in the actor's heart, because this passage in the play is the point most worthy of note."[3] Sakamoto Setchō remarked of the 1918 performance of *Taema* by the famous Umewaka Manzaburō (1868–1946), "though I was only looking at his feet, . . . this, too, was most splendid."[4] As the *shite* exited across the bridge, we felt, I recall, the uplifted note vibrating everywhere. "The awe-inspiring refreshed air that fills the quiet first part of the play," Masuda Shōzō comments, "is greatly due to the singing of the *kuse* in *tsuyogin* style. It may well speak of the strength of the spirit's power."[5]

The Interlude that connects the first and second parts of the play comes as welcome relief. Afterwards, the *waki*'s prose opening of Part II is appropriate to usher in the formal wonder-filled *ageuta* called the *machiutai*:

WAKI

Thus how holy this event appears, so I hope to see another miracle.

WAKI AND WAKI-TSURE

. . . as these words are barely said,
wonder fills us all;

Masterworks of the Nō Theater

matchless melodies are heard,
lights begin to glow,
bodhisattvas dance and sing
all before our eyes,
how august these forms appear . . .

As the *nochi-jite* makes her entrance and moves across the stage, the empty space suddenly becomes animated with the charm of Princess Chūjō. The *sashi* passage she chants in *tsuyogin* creates a lofty world of its own in pure and simple form where the lyric swells to a great rendering of prayers. The soul of Princess Chūjō behind the superbly crafted Nō mask is clearly revealed through the "flowers" Zeami created in this play. When *Taema* was performed by Umewaka Manzaburō, Setchō noted the following concerning the *nochi-jite*'s entrance: "I always thought it almost impossible that the *nochi-jite*'s spirit could appear through the singing in *tsuyogin* style, for, indeed, I only get a feeling of majesty and nobility by singing this way. I did not feel it was too strong and I was deeply impressed by it."[6]

The *hayamai* dance that the *shite* performs in *banshō* mode is, indeed, an eloquent realization, symbolizing the deepest sense of holiness in the highest form of musical expression. Moreover, together with the *shite*'s gorgeous costuming, superb carriage, gesture, posturing, and movement, all in harmonious unison, it makes a significantly clear statement that the purpose and meaning of the whole play is much more than can be stated by the short lines from the sutras that appear on the surface several times throughout the text.

Taema, it seems to me, is the kind of Nō play Zeami described in the *Kadensho* with the following words: "In lofty and simple plays, beautiful language and taste are not quite as necessary because this kind of Nō contains noble and classic materials. Such a Nō may sometimes seem to be lacking in delicate charm. Even a talented *shite* may not seem suitable in this kind of play. And even if a mature master should do it, he will not be appreciated if he does not have keen-eyed critics in the audience, and if it is not a dignified performance given on some ceremonial occasion."[7] Indeed, for a great Nō such as this, the well-seasoned Nō master requires a great audience as well as a great occasion.

TAEMA

ATTRIBUTED TO ZEAMI

Persons: WAKI: *A priest of the Jōdo Sect*
WAKI-TSURE: *Attendant priests (two)*
SHITE (PART I): *A nun, the manifestation of Amida*
NOCHI-JITE (PART II): *The Princess Chūjō*
TSURE: *A young girl, the manifestation of the Goddess of Mercy*
KYŌGEN: *A man from the neighborhood*

Classification: *Primary, Group V; Variant, Group I, III, or IV*
Place: *At the Taemaji Temple in the land of Yamato*
Time: *February (at the spring equinox)*
Kogaki: *5*

PART I

[*Following the* shidai *music, the* waki, *accompanied by two assistant priests, appears. The* waki *wears a pointed hood* (kakubōshi), *a small-checked kimono* (kogōshi), *an "inferior silk" broad-sleeved robe* (shike mizugoromo), *a white broad divided skirt* (shiro ōguchi), *a waistband* (ko-shiobi), *a fan* (ōgi), *and a rosary* (juzu). *Accompanying priests wear a pointed hood* (kakubōshi), *a plain, less-formal heavy silk kimono* (muji noshime), *a "shrunk silk" broad-sleeved robe* (yore mizugoromo), *a white broad divided skirt* (shiro ōguchi), *a waistband* (koshiobi), *a fan* (ōgi), *and a rosary* (juzu). *As they enter the stage, they face one another and sing together the following verse, called* shidai.]

WAKI AND WAKI-TSURE

[1] *(Shidai: au, yowagin)*

Oshie ureshiki[8]	How joyous is the teaching
nori no kado,	at the holy gate,
oshie ureshiki	how joyous is the teaching
nori no kado	at the holy gate
hirakuru michi ni	opened wide upon the Way
ijō yo.	man must follow.

[*The chorus sings the* jidori, *repeating the above verse, except the third and fourth lines, in a lower key.*]

440

(Jidori: au, yowagin)

Oshie ureshiki	How joyous is the teaching
nori no kado	at the holy gate
hirakuru michi ni	opened wide upon the Way
ijō yo.	man must follow.

[*After the* jidori, *the* waki, *facing stage front, intones the following passage, called* nanori, *introducing himself to the audience.*]

WAKI

(Nanori: awazu, kotoba)

Kore wa nenbutsu no gyōja nite sōrō. Ware kono tabi Mikumano⁹ ni mairi ge-kōdō ni omomukite sōrō. Mata kore yori Yamatoji ni kakari Taema¹⁰ no on-tera ni mairabaya to omoi sōrō.	I am a priest of the Pure Land Sect, engaged in performing religious austerities. On this occasion it was to Mikumano that I went, and now I am going back home. From this point, I will take the road to Yamato, and on my way I plan to visit the holy temple of Taema.

[*As the* waki *finishes the* nanori, *he faces the companions again and they sing together the following passage, called* michiyuki, *"travel song."*]

WAKI AND WAKI-TSURE

(Michiyuki: au, yowagin)

Hodo mo naku	In no time we come
kaeri Ki no ji no	on our homeward way through Ki
seki koete,	past the barrier,
kaeri Ki no ji¹¹ no	on our homeward way through Ki
seki¹² koete	past the barrier
koya¹³ Mikumano¹⁴ no	toward Mikumano I see
Iwadagawa¹⁵	the waves rush brightly
nami no chiru nari	down the River Iwada
asahikage	in the morning sun;
yoru¹⁶ hiru wakanu	neither day nor night we feel
kokochi shite	different as we
kumo mo sonata ni	journey like the clouds that drift

[*The* waki, *facing stage front, goes forward three or four steps and returns to his former position, indicating that they have traveled and now have come to their destination; the* waki *and the* waki-tsure, *facing one another again, sing the rest.*]

441

tōkarishi	far and far away
Futagamiyama¹⁷ no	Two-Peak Mountain rises high;
fumoto naru	at its base below,
Taema no Tera ni	the temple of Taema
tsukinikeri,	we have reached at last,

Taema

| Taema no Tera ni | the temple of Taema |
| tsukinikeri. | we have reached at last. |

[*After the* michiyuki, *the* waki, *facing stage front, intones the following passage, called* tsuki-zerifu.]

WAKI

(Tsukizerifu: awazu, kotoba)

Isogi sōrō hodo ni kore wa haya Taema	We have traveled so fast that we have
no Tera ni tsukite sōrō. Kokoro shizuka	already arrived at the temple of Taema.
ni sankei mōsōzuru nite sōrō.	Reverently and with tranquil heart, let
	us pay homage.

WAKI-TSURE

| Shikarubyō sōrō. | Yes, let us do that. |

[*The* waki, *accompanied by the* waki-tsure, *goes to the* waki *seat and sits down. Following the* issei *music, the* shite, *preceded by the* tsure, *appears. The* shite *wears an* uba *mask, a wig* (kazura), *a flowered hood* (hana bōshi), *a collar in white* (eri shiro), *an under kimono with painted gold or silver patterns* (surihaku), *a "Cathay fabric" brocade outer kimono without red in "loose" style* (ironashi karaori kinagashi), *and a rosary* (juzu). *The* tsure *wears a* tsuremen *mask, a wig* (kazura), *a wig band* (kazuraobi), *a collar in red* (eri aka), *a "Cathay fabric" brocade outer kimono with red in "loose" style* (iroiri karaori kinagashi), *an under kimono with painted gold or silver patterns* (suri-haku), *and a rosary* (juzu). *The* tsure *stands at the first pine and the* shite, *at the third pine. The* shite, *facing stage front, sings the following* sashi *verse.*]

SHITE

[2] *(Sashi: awazu, yowagin)*

Ichinen Midabutsu[18]	Once we call upon Amida,
sokumetsu muryōzai	countless though our sins may be,
to mo tokaretari.	we're forgiven, as he taught.

TSURE

Hachiman shoshōgyō[19]	Eighty thousand creeds and practices,
kai ze Amida to mo	in the end, they all come down
ari geni sōrō.	to Amida, so he tells us.

SHITE

| Shaka wa yari[20] | Shaka sends for us, |

442

TSURE

| Mida wa michibiku | and Amida guides us all |
| hitosuji ni | straight along the way; |

[*The* shite *and the* tsure *face each other and sing the following verse together.*]

Kokoro yurusuna	follow with unflagging hearts.
Namu Amidabu to	"Lord Amida," we repeat,

[*They face stage front. Then the* shite *sings the following verse, called* issei.]

(*Issei: awazu, yowagin*)

tonōreba[21]	calling out his name
hotoke mo ware mo	till myself and Buddha too
nakarikeri.	vanish all away;

Namu Amidabu no	"Lord Amida," we repeat;
koe bakari	there is just our voice

suzushiki michi[22] wa	on the way, so cool and clear,

SHITE AND TSURE [*Facing each other.*]

tanomoshi ya.	and full of promise.

[*The* shite *and the* tsure *enter the stage. The* tsure *stands at stage center and the* shite, *by the* shite *seat; facing each other, they sing the following* shidai *verse.*]

(*Shidai: au, yowagin*)

Nigori ni shimanu[23]	Unstained by muddied waters
hasu no ito,	are the lotus threads,
nigori ni shimanu	unstained by muddied waters
hasu no ito no	are the threads of lotus;
goshiki ni ikade	how is it they can be dyed
sominuran.	all the five pure hues?

[*The chorus sings the* jidori, *repeating the above verse, except the third and fourth lines, in a lower key.*]

(*Jidori: au, yowagin*)

Nigori ni shimanu	Unstained by muddied waters
hasu no ito	are the lotus threads,
goshiki ni ikade	how is it they can be dyed
sominuran.	all the five pure hues?

[*After the* jidori, *the* shite *faces stage front and sings the following* sashi *passage.*]

Taema

(Sashi: awazu, yowagin)

Arigata ya,	We are most grateful!
shobutsu no chikai	Many Buddhas' promises
samazama naredomo	are indeed all kinds and varied,
wakite chōse no	but the Vow Amida took
higan tote [24]	has transcended all,
mayoi no naka ni mo	even midst our deep delusions,
koto ni nao	and especially

SHITE AND TSURE [*Facing each other.*]

itsutsu no kumo wa [25]	those of carnal fivefold clouds
hare yaranu,	still remain unclear,
amayo no tsuki [26] no	as on rainy nights the light
kage o dani	of the moon is hid
shiranu kokoro no	from our heart, so where to go
yukue o ya	we can hardly know,
nishi e to bakari	but here everyone still longs
tanomuran.	for the holy West.
Geni ya tanomeba	If we ask our Lord for help,
chikaki michi o	the way is short and near.
nani harubaru to	Why does man think of it
omouran.	long and far away?

[*The* shite *and the* tsure *continue to sing the following* sageuta *passage.*]

(Sageuta: au, yowagin)

Sue no yo ni	And in latter days,
mayou warera ga	as we wander all astray,
tame nare ya,	it is for our sake,

[*Now they sing in higher pitch the following* ageuta *passage.*]

(Ageuta: au, yowagin)

444

tokinokosu	the Law Amida
mi-nori wa kore zo,	has taught and left behind,
hitokoe no,	the Law Amida
mi-nori wa kore zo	has taught and left behind
hitokoe no	for us all: one call
Mida no oshie o	he has taught us to repeat.
tanomazu wa	Should we not trust him,
sue no nori [27]	while the ages pass,
yorozu toshidoshi	year by year, through wickedness,
furu made ni	for ten thousand years,
yokyō no nori wa	what other sutra's teaching
yomo araji.	stays to save us all?
Tamatama kono shō ni	Given this rare life, if now we fail

ukamazu wa	to receive his grace,
mata itsu no yo o	in what world can we again
matsu no to[28] no	wait for doors all pine

[*The* shite *and the* tsure *exchange their positions; the* shite *goes to stage center, and the* tsure, *to* waki *stage front* (waki shōmen); *they stand and finish the verse.*]

akureba idete	to open in the morning,
kururu made	till the sun goes down
nori no niwa ni	in this garden mingled
majiru nari,	one and all we pray,
mi-nori no niwa ni	in this garden mingled here
majiru nari.	one and all we pray.

[*The* waki *rises and, facing the* shite, *intones the following prose passage.*]

WAKI

[3] *(Mondai: awazu, mixed)*

Ika ni kore naru katagata ni tazunemō-subeki koto no sōrō.	Ho, there. I have something I would like to ask of you people over there.

SHITE

Nanigoto nite sōrō zo.	What can I do for you?

WAKI [*Facing stage front.*]

Kore wa Taema no on-tera nite sōrō ka.	Is this the holy temple of Taema?

SHITE

San zōrō. Taema no on-tera to mo mō-shi, mata Tōmaji to mo mōshi sōrō.	Yes, this is called the holy temple of Taema, and it is also called the Tōma Temple.

TSURE [*Facing the* waki.]

(Kakaru: awazu, yowagin)

Mata kore naru ike wa	There is also over here the pond
hasu no ito o	where once the lotus threads
susugite kiyomeshi	were truly rinsed and purified,
sono yue ni	and consequently
Somedono no I[29] to mo	then the Well of Somedono
mōsu to ka ya.	too, it is called, I hear.

445

SHITE

Are wa Tōmaji.	That is the Tōma Temple there.

TSURE

Kore wa Somedera.[30]	This is the Some Temple here.

Taema

SHITE

Mata kono ike wa	What is more, this very pond
Somedono no	is Somedono's,

[*The* shite *and the* tsure, *facing each other, sing the following passage together.*]

SHITE AND TSURE

iroiro[31] samazama	well known for multicolored dyes,
tokorodokoro no	as the multitudes who go
nori no kenbutsu	here and there to offer prayers.
monpō aritomo,	So there are ten thousand teachings
sore o mo isa ya	which we do not know but pray
shiraito no[32]	with our single faith

[*Facing toward the* waki.]

tada hitosuji zo	like a pure white thread that makes
isshin furan ni	me say so single-heartedly,
Namu Amidabu.	"Holy Lord Amida!"

WAKI

(*Kakeai: awazu, yowagin*)

Geni arigataki	Indeed, we are all grateful
hito no kotoba,	for the words of people
sunawachi kore koso	as it is the one and only
Mida ikkyō nare.	Lord Amida's holy teaching.

[*The* waki *intones the rest of the following prose passage.*]

Sate mata kore naru hanazakura, tsune no iro ni wa kawaritsutsu kore mo yue aru hōju[33] to mietari.	And over here, the cherry tree, blooming at its best, appears to have a different hue from all the others. This, too, must have a story of its own as the Treasured Tree.

TSURE

(*Kakaru: awazu, yowagin*)

Geni yoku goranji	Well, how thoroughly you notice
wakeraretari.	things with differences;
Are koso hasu no	that is where the lotus threads,
ito o somete	dyed in many colors,

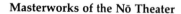

446

SHITE

kakete hosareshi sakuragi no hana mo kokoro no aru yue ni	were hung and left to dry upon that cherry tree, and as its very blossoms also have a soul,

Masterworks of the Nō Theater

hachisu no iro ni	they take on the lotus hues
saku to mo ieri.	as they blossom, it is said.

WAKI

Nakanaka narubeshi	There's great truth in what you stated:
moto yori mo,	grasses, trees and lands,
sōmoku kokudo[34]	all attain enlightenment
jōbutsu no	of their own accord:
iroka ni someru	dyed in these pure fragrant hues
hanagokoro no	these are souls that blossom

SHITE

nori no uruoi	with the dews of holiness
tane soete	nurturing their seeds.

WAKI

nigori ni shimanu	Unstained by muddied waters,
hasu no ito o	grow the threads of lotus,

SHITE

susugite kiyomeshi	which we rinse and purify
hito no kokoro no	and dry men's heart-delusions

WAKI

mayoi o hosu wa	over those ablazing red

SHITE

hizakura[35] no	blooming cherry trees,

[The chorus takes over and sings the following ageuta *passage.]*

CHORUS

(Ageuta: au, yowagin)

iro haete	brightly hued in bloom,
kakeshi hachisu no	draped with lotus threads they are
itozakura[36]	weeping cherry trees;

[As the chorus continues to sing the rest of the passage, the tsure *goes to the front of the chorus and sits down; the* waki *also sits down.]*

447

kakeshi hachisu no	draped with lotus threads they are
itozakura	weeping cherry trees,
hana no nishiki no	weaving blossomed rich brocades
tatenuki ni	in a warp and weft,

Taema

kumo no Taema[37] ni	as from cloud-rift Taima
hare kumoru	light and shadow weave,
yuki mo midori mo	snow the petals, green the leaves,
kurenai mo	red the buds in bloom.

[*The* shite *looks across* waki *stage front (*waki shōmen*).*]

tada hitokoe no	Will one voice alone entice
sasowan ya	all of them along?
nishi fuku[38] aki no	Is it the wind

[*The* shite *looks toward the rich brocade Nō curtain.*]

kaze naran,	blowing to the west?
nishi fuku aki no	Is it the wind of autumn
kaze naran.	blowing to the west?

[*The* waki *intones the following prose passage.*]

WAKI

[4] (*Awazu, yowagin*)

| Nao nao Taema no Mandara no iware | Still more, still more, please tell me in |
| kuwashiku on-monogatari sōrae. | detail the story of the Mandala at Taema. |

[*The* shite *goes out toward stage center and sits on the stool, while the chorus sings the following passage, called* kuri.]

CHORUS

(*Kuri: awazu, yowagin*)

Somosomo	Well, this story
kono Taema no	of the Mandala
Mandara[39] to mōsu wa	at Taema, they say, had started
ninnō	when our sovereign
shijūshichidai no	the Emperor Haitai,
Mikado	was the great
Haitai Tennō[40] no	forty-seventh monarch in his reign;
gyo-o ka to yo.	as I understand
Yokohagi no	then the minister
Udaijin	of the Right, who hailed
Toyonari[41] to	from Yokohagi,
mōshishi hito,	was called Toyonari.

448

[*The* shite *sings the following passage, called* sashi.]

SHITE

(*Sashi: awazu, mixed*)

sono on-sokujo	And his graceful daughter, called
Chūjō-hime	Princess Chūjō,
kono yama ni komori-	is secluded in these mountains
tamaitsutsu	ever graciously

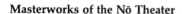

Masterworks of the Nō Theater

Shōsan Jōdo kyō[42]	to chant the Sukhavati Sutra
mainichi dokuju shi-	every day with deep devotion
tamaishi ga	graciously and still
shinjū ni chikai-	deeply in her heart she pledges
tamō yō	ever solemnly,
negawaku wa	pleading with her prayer:
shōjin no Mida	"May Amida Buddha come
raikō atte	in a holy living form
ware ni ogamare-	graciously to welcome me
owashimase to	that I might worship him
isshin furan ni	from my heart in one devotion";
kannen shitamō.	so she determines graciously.

SHITE

Shikarazu wa	"Should Lord Amida
hitsumyō o	not appear at all
go to shite	I would perish,

CHORUS

kono sōan o	never will I leave this hut
ideji to chikatte	thatched with grassy leaves," she pledges,
ikkō ni	as she finds herself
nenbutsu sanmai no	graciously repeating Mida's name
jō ni iritamō.	in the state of meditation.

[*The chorus continues to sing the following passage, called* kuse.]

(*Kuse: au, tsuyogin*)

Tokoro wa yamakage no	Here's the shaded mountainside
matsu fuku kaze mo	where the pine wind blows
suzushikute	so refreshingly,
sanagara natsu o	making anyone forget
wasuremizu no	summer heat, as water
oto mo taedae ni	sounds so faint and intermittent,
shinni o sumasu	sharpening her mind's keen ears
yo mo sugara	all throughout the night
shōmyō kannen no	as she chants his name and meditates
yuka no ue	on the floor, cross-legged,
zazen engetsu no	where the moon shines through the window
mado no uchi	in a perfect sphere,
ryōryō to aru	and, at this very juncture,
orifushi ni	so hushed in silence,
ichinin no	all of a sudden
rōni no	an ancient nun

449

Taema

kotsuzen to kitari-	comes over unexpectedly
tatazumeri.	and before her eyes
Kore wa ika naru	she lingers still. "What sort
hito yaran to	of a person are you?"
tazunesase-	inquires the Princess
tamaishi ni	ever graciously.
rōni kotaete	In reply the ancient nun
notamawaku,	responds by saying:
tare to wa nado ya	"What a foolish thing that you
oroka nari.	ask me who I am.
Yobeba koso	Since you called for me,
kitaritare to	here I come before you."
ōserarekeru	When the ancient nun returns
hodo ni	her answer,
Chūjō-hime wa	Princess Chūjō seems
akiretsutsu	even more amazed!

[*The* shite *sings the following couplet, called* ageha.]

SHITE

(Ageha)

ware wa tare o ka[43]	Whom shall I call and summon,
yobukodori	oh, common cuckoo?

[*The chorus sings the rest of the* kuse *passage.*]

CHORUS

(Kuse: au, tsuyogin)

tazuki mo shiranu	Helplessly I know not where
yamanaka ni	this mountain depth is.
koe tatsuru	What is here that makes
koto tote wa	any sound aloud?
Namu Amidabu no	It is Mida's holy name
tonae narade	I repeat as ever;
mata taji mo	there isn't anything
naki mono o to	other than my prayer.
kotaesase	When she answers back
tamaishi ni	ever graciously,
sore koso	"That is truly
waga na nare	what my name would be;
koe o shirube ni	guided by your calling voice
kitareri to	I have come this way,"
notamaeba	says the ancient nun.
himegimi mo	Then the Princess thought
sate wa kono gan	that her very prayer is now
jōju shite	truly all fulfilled,
shōjin no	for Lord Amida
Amida nyorai	Buddha in his holy

450

geni raikō no	living form comes down for her
jisetsu yo to	on this occasion!
kanrui kimo ni	Deeply touched within her heart,
meijitsutsu	she is moved to tears,
kirae no on-sode mo	and the sleeves of her magnificent robes
shioru bakari ni	seem as if, all soaked with tears,
mietamō.	they are weeping too.

[*The chorus continues to sing the following passage, called* rongi.]

[5] *(Rongi: au, yowagin)*

Geni ya tattoki	How inspiring and august
monogatari,	is the tale we hear!
sunawachi Mida no	That's the lesson Mida taught
oshie zo to	for us all indeed;
omō ni tsukete	so when we think about it,
arigata ya.	we feel most grateful.

SHITE AND TSURE

Koyoi shimo	Now this eve will be
Kisaragi naka[44] no	on the middle of the month
itsuka nite,	of February,
shikamo jishō no	falling even on the time
jisetsu nari.	of the Equinox,
Hōji o nasan tame	for the service we would like to hold
ima kono tera ni	presently at this temple,
kitaritari.	we have come this way.

CHORUS

Hōji no tame ni	You have come this way to hold
kitaru to wa	the Buddhist service,
somo ika naru	you have said, so tell me,
on-koto zo.	what is the reason?

SHITE AND TSURE

Ima wa nani o ka	For by now why should we keep
tsutsumubeki,	all so secret still?
sono inishie no	We are beings from the past,
keni kejo[45] no	a nun and a girl,

451

CHORUS

muchū ni genji	we transformed ourselves and came
kitareri to	in the dream you dream,

SHITE AND TSURE

ii mo aeneba	but no sooner than these words

Taema

CHORUS

hikari sashite	are said, the light shines bright,
hana furi	flowers scatter,
ikyō kunji	rare incense perfumes
ongaku no	sweetly and the voice
koe su nari.	of music rises.
Hazukashi ya	"How ashamed I am,
tabibito yo	holy traveler,
itoma mōshite	now farewell," she says and goes
kaeru yama no	back into the mountain

[*The* shite *rises.*]

nijō no dake to wa	that soars with those too lofty peaks
Futakami no	none has climbed, which is,
Yama to koso	men say, the mountain
hito wa iedo	of those two lofty peaks
makoto wa kono ama ga	but we know the very truth
noborishi yama	that this holy sister
naru yue ni	has ascended high
Nijō no Dake[46] to wa	upon the mountain once, therefore
mōsu nari.	it is called "Nun's Peak."
Oi no saka	Up the slope, though aged,

[*The* shite *goes near the* shite *pillar and, facing stage front, she stretches her body and throws the cane away; then, followed by the* waki, *she makes her exit quietly behind the curtain as the chorus finishes singing.*]

nobori noboru	she climbs, and on the cloud
kumo ni norite	that rises high she rides
agarikeri,	to ascend above,
shiun ni norite	on the purple cloud she rides
agarikeri.	and ascends above.

Nakairi (Interlude)

[*The* kyōgen, *wearing a striped, less-formal heavy silk kimono* (dan noshime), *the* kyōgen *two-piece* (naga kamishimo), *a waistband* (koshiobi), *a fan* (ōgi), *and a small sword* (chiisa gatana), *comes out to the name-saying seat* (nanoriza).]

KYŌGEN

(*Mondai: awazu, kotoba*)

452

Kayō ni sōrō mono wa kono atari ni su-mai suru mono nite sōrō. Kono aida wa hisashiku Taemaji e mairazu sōrō aida kyō wa sankei mōsabaya to zonzuru. Iya kore ni minare mōsanu o-sō no goza sōrō ga izuku yori izukata e o-tōri na-sare sōraeba kore ni wa yasurōte goza sōrō zo.

I am one who lives in this neighbor-hood. I have not visited the Taema Temple recently. So today, I think, I will go there and pay homage. [*Noticing the* waki.] Well, here is a Buddhist priest I am not familiar with. As he is traveling somewhere, he may be just resting here.

Kore wa kaikoku no hijiri[47] nite sōrō. On-mi wa kono atari no hito nite watari sōrō ka.

I am a Buddhist sage, making a pilgrimage around the country. Do you live in this vicinity?

KYŌGEN

Nakanaka kono atari no mono nite sōrō.

Yes, I live in this neighborhood.

WAKI

Sayō sōrawaba mazu chikō onniri sōrae. Tazunetaki koto no sōrō.

If you do, first of all, please come closer. I have something to ask you.

KYŌGEN

Kashikomatte sōrō. Sate o-tazune-nasaretaki to wa ikayō naru go-yō nite sōrō zo.

Yes, Your Holiness. [*Comes out to stage center and sits down.*] What is it you would like to ask me?

WAKI

Omoi mo yoramu mōshigoto nite sōrae-domo tōji no on-iware Chūjō-hime no on-koto ni tsuki samazama shisai aru-beshi. Go-zonji ni oite wa katatte on-kikase sōrae.

This may seem surprising to you, but there must be many stories about this temple and the Princess Chūjō. If you know them, please tell me and let me hear about them.

KYŌGEN

Kore wa omoi no yoranu koto o uketa-mawari sōrō mono kana. Warera mo kono atari ni sumaitsukamatsuri sōrae-domo sayō no koto kuwashiku wa zon-zezu sōrō, sarinagara hajimete o-me ni kakari o-tazune nasare sōrō koto o nani to mo zonzenu to mōsu mo ikaga nite sōraeba oyoso uketamawarioyobitaru tōri on-monogatari mōsōzuru nite sōrō.

This is certainly an unexpected question. Even folks like me who live in this neighborhood don't know much about such things; but since this is the first time we've met and you have asked me a question, it is not nice to say I know nothing at all. I will tell you the story the way I've heard it.

WAKI

Chikagoro nite sōrō.

I would be most grateful.

❋

453

KYŌGEN

Mazu Chūjō-hime to mōshitaru on-kata wa ninnō shijūshichidai Haitai Tennō no gyo-o ni Yokohagi no Udaijin Toyo-nari-kō to mōshitaru on-kata no on-sokujo nite goza aritaru to mōsu. Saru shidai arite Hibariyama ni suterare-

First of all, the gracious one, who was called Princess Chūjō, was the daughter of Lord Toyonari, the minister of the Right from Yokohagi, in the reign of the forty-seventh sovereign, Emperor Hai-tai. For certain reasons, she was aban-

Taema

tamō ga sanchū no koto nareba tsune no mono sate sumaigataku sōrō ni Chūjō-hime wa gonja no on-mi nareba sayō no koto mo itoitamawazu nenbutsu sanmai nite tsukihi o okuritamō ni aru toki chichi no Toyonari-kō on-kari no on-sata sōraite, Hibariyama e wakeiretamō ga aru taniai ni shiba no an o musubite utsukushiki hime no owashimasu. Toyonari-kō fushigi ni oboshimeshi kono sanchū ni ningen nite wa yomo araji. Ika naru mono zo to tazunetamaeba sono toki ni ware wa Yokohagi no Udaijin Toyonari to mōsu mono no musume naru ga keibo no hakarai ni yori kono yamaoku ni suterareshi to on-mōshi sōraeba Toyonari kikoshimeshi gongo dōdan sayō no koto yume ni mo shirazu. Ware koso chichi no Toyonari yo, nanigoto mo ware ni menjite tamaware to Nara no Miyako ni tomonai-tamai, sude ni kisaki ni sonaen to shi-tamō tokoro ni Chūjō-hime wa sayō no koto wa mi-kokoro ni irazu, kōse bodai no koto o nomi oboshimeshi Nara no Miyako o shinobiide kono tera e kitari kore nite on-kami o oroshi ware shōjin no Amida nyorai o ogamitaku to go-ryūgan no okoshitamō ni aru toki Mida nyorai o ogamitamai, masse no shujō saido no tame kidoku o nokoshi-tamae to notamaeba, saraba tote hasu no ito nite gokuraku no myōzō o Mandara ni oriarawashi Chūjō-hime ni ataetamō. Sono toki kono tera no niwa ni i o hori hasu no ito o susugase tamaeba, sunawachi goshiki ni somaritaru to mōsu. Saru ni yotte kono tera o Somedono to mōsu. Mata i o Somedono no I to mōshi sōrō. Toriwake kono sakura no ki e ito o kawakashi tamō aida hana mo goshiki ni saki mōshi sōrō. Mazu warera no uketamawarioyobitaru wa kaku no gotoku nite goza sōrō ga, nani to oboshimeshi o-tazune nasare sōrō zo. Chikagoro fushin ni zonji sōrō.

454

doned on Mt. Skylark. Since it was up in the mountain, even most men find it hard to live there, but as she was one who had temporarily appeared on earth, she did not mind it at all. She passed her days in meditation, repeating Mida's holy name. Then one time Lord Toyonari, her father, ordered a hunting expedition and went into Mt. Skylark. In a certain ravine, a brushwood hut was standing, and a lovely princess was living there. Lord Toyonari thought this so strange. In a mountain such as this, she could not be human. When he asked who she was, "I am the daughter of Lord Toyonari, the minister of the Right from Yokohagi, but due to my stepmother's scheme I was abandoned in this deep mountain," she replied. When Lord Toyonari heard this, he said that this was beyond all words; not even in a dream had such an outrage taken place. "I am your father; for my sake, please forgive everything." So saying, he escorted her back to the capital at Nara. Although the plan to have her installed as empress was ready, a matter such as this never entered the heart of Princess Chūjō. She thought only about enlightenment in the future world. Secretly she slipped away from the capital at Nara, and came to this temple. Here she cut off her hair and prayed that she might worship Lord Amida in his living form. Once when she was worshiping him, she was blessed as she prayed: "For the sake of the multitude in this latter age, bestow upon me some miracle that will lead them to enlightenment." Then, with the lotus threads the wonderful figures of Paradise were woven in the Mandala and this was so bestowed upon her. At that time, it is said, when a well was dug in the temple garden, and the lotus threads were cleansed, they were dyed in five colors. Therefore this temple is called the Somedono; and the well, too, is called the Somedono Well. While upon this cherry tree, in particular, the lotus threads were hung to dry, the flowers bloomed in five colors too. At any rate, this is about all I've heard. I wonder what you were thinking when you asked me that question. Lately I have felt something strange around here.

WAKI

Nengoro ni on-monogatari sōrō mono kana. Tazunemōsu mo yo no gi ni arazu. On-mi izen ni rō ni to wakaki nyoshō no kitaritamaite sōrō hodo ni sunawachi kotoba o kawashite sōraeba tokoro no meisho nado o oshie Taema no Mandara no iware tadaima on-monogatari no gotoku nengoro ni katari inishie no ken kejo no muchū ni genji kitareri to ii mo aezu shiun ni noritamō to mite sugata o miushinōte sōrō yo.

How kindly you have told me this story in such detail. I had no special reason for asking you about it. An aged nun and a young girl came here before me. As we exchanged words, they explained the sights so famous at this place, and kindly told me about the Mandala of Taema in detail, as you have just done. "In a dream we appeared and came, phantom nun and maid of long ago . . ." These words were hardly spoken, when on purple clouds they rose, it seemed, and I lost sight of them.

KYŌGEN

Kore wa kidoku naru koto o uketamawari sōrō mono kana. Sate wa utagai mo naku Chūjō-hime araware-tamaitaru to zonji sōrō aida iyoiyo go-shinjin arite kasanete kidoku o goran arekashi to zonji sōrō.

You have truly told me a miracle. Undoubtedly, Princess Chūjō has appeared. With the greater faith that you have, surely a greater miracle will be shown to you.

WAKI

Chikagoro fushigi naru koto nite sōrō hodo ni, iyoiyo shinjin o itashi kasanete kidoku o miuzuru nite sōrō.

Lately how extraordinary this is! I shall have greater faith than ever, and witness, perhaps, another miracle.

KYŌGEN

Go-yō no koto sōrawaba kasanete ōse sōrae.

If there is something further I can do for you, please do not hesitate to ask.

WAKI

Tanomi sōrōbeshi.

That is kind of you, thank you.

KYŌGEN

Kokoroe mōshite sōrō.

At your service, Your Holiness.

[*The* kyōgen *goes back to the* kyōgen *seat.*]

Taema

PART II

WAKI

[6] *(Au, kotoba)*

Kaku arigataki on-koto nareba kasanete
kidoku o ogaman to

Thus how holy this event appears, so I
hope to see another miracle.

[The waki *and the* waki-tsure *sing the following* ageuta *passage, called* machiutai, *a waiting song.]*

WAKI AND WAKI-TSURE

(Machiutai: awazu, tsuyogin)

ii mo aeneba	As these words are barely said,
fushigi ya na,	we are wonder filled;
ii mo aeneba	as these words are barely said,
fushigi ya na	wonder fills us all;
myōon kikoe	matchless melodies are heard,
hikari sashi	lights begin to glow,
kabu no bosatsu no	bodhisattvas dance and sing
ma no atari,	all before our eyes,
arawaretamō	how august these forms appear
fushigisa yo,	in this miracle!
arawaretamō	How august these forms appear
fushigisa yo.	in this miracle!

[Following the deha *music, the* nochi-jite *appears. She wears a* zō *mask, a heavenly crown decked with a white lotus flower (*tenkan byakuren o itadaku*), a wig (*kazura*), a wig band (*kazuraobi*), a collar in white (*eri shiro*), an under kimono with painted gold or silver patterns (*surihaku*), a dancing robe (*maiginu*), a scarlet broad divided skirt (*hi ōguchi*), a waistband (*koshiobi*), and a fan (*ōgi*). Holding a scroll of sutra in her hand, she enters the stage and stands at the* shite *seat; she then sings the following passage.]*

SHITE

[7] *(Sashi: awazu, tsuyogin)*

Tadaima muchū ni	Now what is revealed before you
arawaretaru wa	in a dream so graciously
Chūjō-hime no	through a vision is the soul
seikon nari.	of Princess Chūjō.
Ware shaba ni	When I spent my days
arishi toki	in the mortal world,
Shōsan Jōdokyō	I read the holy Pure Land Sutra
chōchō jiji ni	every morn and every eve,
okotarazu,	never falling short
shinjin makoto	in the practice of my faith
narishi yue ni	sincerely, so for this,
mimyō anraku no	in the world of joy exquisite
kekkai no	and peace eternal,
shū to nari	with the throng I join
hongaku shinnyo no[48]	on the dais of the perfect

456

engetsu ni zaseri,	shining moon, enlightened truly,
shikaredomo	I am seated now,
koko o saru koto	but whose distance is not far
tōkarazu shite	from this place, among you all
hosshin kyakurai no	in this holy guise, I have returned
hōmi o naseri.	to this world once more.

CHORUS

(Issei: awazu, yowagin)

Arigata ya	We are most grateful,
jinko kūkai[49] no	for magnificent and boundless
shōgon wa	is the shining realm!
manako wa unro ni	On the road of clouds how dazzled
kagayaki	is our vision.

SHITE

tenmyōhōrin no	Here Amida's voice that speaks
onjō wa	of the Turning Wheel
chōbōsetsu[50] no	in the holy Treasure Land
mimi ni miteri.	fills its every corner.

[*The* shite *faces to her right.*]

CHORUS

| Shōzen to aru | Solitude reigns peacefully |
| akatsuki no kokoro. | in the still deep heart of daybreak. |

SHITE

Makoto ni suzushiki	Truly lively and refreshing
michi ni hikaruru	lies Amida's holy Way,
kōin no kokoro.[51]	which leads us to the heart of time!

CHORUS

(Noriji: ōnori, tsuyogin)

| Oshimubeshi ya na, | Guard these precious moments well, |
| oshimubeshi ya na | guard these precious moments well. |

[*The* shite *goes out toward stage center.*]

457

| toki wa hito o mo[52] | Rare occasions do not wait |
| matazaru mono o | on man's leave or pleasure. |

[*The* shite *kneels down and opens the sutra.*]

sunawachi koko zo	This is indeed precisely
yuishin no	the Pure Land Sutra
Jōdokyō,	of holy Mida!
itadakimatsure ya,	Receive it ever graciously!
itadakimatsure ya	Receive it ever graciously!

Taema

[*The* shite *bows her head toward the sutra.*]

sesshu fusha [53]　　All shall rise, none fall.

SHITE [*Giving the feeling that she chants the lines.*]

(*Ei: awazu, tsuyogin*)

i issai seken [54]　　"For the sake of all the world,
sesshi nanshin　　well expounded are these laws

CHORUS

shihō zei jinnan.　　otherwise too recondite for man."

SHITE

(*Noriji: ōnori, tsuyogin*)

Geni mo kono hō　　As these teachings seem, indeed,
hanahadashikereba,　　too profound for comprehension,

CHORUS

shinzuru koto mo　　so believing them is too
katakarubeshi to ya　　difficult for us, we hear.

[*The* shite *rolls the sutra and rises.*]

SHITE

tada tanome　　Just depend on him,

[*The* shite, *chanting, goes to the front of the* waki *and hands the sutra to him.*]

CHORUS

tanome ya tanome.　　oh, depend, depend on him!

[*The* waki *receives the sutra from the* shite.]

SHITE

(*Noriji: ōnori, tsuyogin*)

Jihi kayū [55]　　Mercy saves us all,

[*The* shite, *singing, goes to the* shite *pillar.*]

458

CHORUS

ryōshin furan.　　frees us from our troubled hearts.

SHITE

Midaru na yo.　　Do not be disturbed!

[*The* shite *faces the* waki.]

Masterworks of the Nō Theater

Chorus

Midaru na yo.   Do not be disturbed!

Shite

Tokoe mo   For ten callings,

Chorus

hitokoe zo,   one suffices too.
arigata ya.   We are most grateful.

[*The* waki *bows in reverence to the sutra and puts it in his bosom. The* shite *performs the* hayamai.]

Hayamai

[*After the "Quick Dance," the* shite *sings the following line.*]

Shite

Goya no kane no ne,   Echoes from the temple bell,

[*The* shite *dances to the singing of the chorus as they sing the following concluding passage.*]

Chorus

(Noriji: ōnori, tsuyogin)

goya no kane no ne	echoes from the temple bell,
fushō no hibiki	tolling now at third night-watch
shōmyō no	trail and sound superb,
myōon no	with her voice that chants
kenbutsu monpō no	holy sutras and Amida's name
iroiro no hōji	while many rites she too performs,
geni mo amaneki	everywhere the light of Laws
kōmyō henjō	shines so bright from ten directions
jippō no shujō o	all the thronging multitudes are led
tada saihō ni	only to Amida's West
mukaeyuku	by his greeting boat
mi-nori no fune no	with the familiar pole
minarezao	across the water;
mi-nori no fune no	board his boat for just a while[56]
sao naguru	we shoot the shuttle
ma no yume no	as we dream this night
yo wa honobono to zo	that starts to turn to purple,
narinikeru.	whitening at dawn.

459

Taema

Tōru

Introduction

Tōru belongs to Group V of Nō plays. Historical works about the great minister Tōru portray the events of his splendid life. Zeami shows what the historical record tells, and reveals Tōru's soul eloquently in this Nō play.

The *waki* is a traveling Buddhist priest, who, in Nogami's words, represents the audience.[1] Zeami further informs us that the *waki* is from the eastern provinces, the locality of the original garden that Tōru reproduced. This fact provides the important reason for the priest's journey, as well as why he wants to see Tōru's River Beach Mansion.

Following the *issei* music, the *shite* appears as an old man carrying wooden pails to draw saltwater. Facing stage front at the *shite*'s seat, he sings the following verse:

> The moon is rising
> high already too the tide
> across the inlet
> of Salt Kiln growing lonely
> with its scenic view.

But according to the stage directions in the Kita *utai-bon* text,[2] before the *shite* starts singing the above lines in free-rhythm *tsuyogin* style, he looks toward the Nō curtain across the bridge as though he has caught a glimpse of the moon. This detail is remarkable in that it reveals not only how significant a stage direction can be, but also how subtly it can express insight into this Nō. Equally meaningful is the rising moon, with which Zeami begins the *issei* verse at the *shite*'s entrance, and the setting moon, with which he concludes the play. The moon serves as the important binding image that unifies the entire play into a whole, as does the cherry-blossom image in *Tadanori*. At the same time, it provides the necessary splendor to grace the mid-autumn scenes, especially at the magnificent mansion in its ruined state, and it functions as a magic filter to create the "flower" Zeami called *yūgen*.

Moreover, the *tsuyogin* style of singing adds dignity and depth, which sets the poetic tone of this play.

After the *issei*, the *shite* expresses his deepest feelings, alone, beneath the brilliant harvest moon, through the *sashi*, *ageuta*, and *sageuta* passages. As the *waki* encounters the *shite*, the subject of Tōru is introduced during the dialogue that ensues. The story the *shite* tells to the *waki* moves him to tears. Then, in the question-and-answer form called *mondai*, exchanged between the *waki* and the *shite*, various subjects and many famous spots associated with the moon unfold one after another, through famous lines quoted from Chinese and Japanese poetry in an uplifted tone, as the *shite* seems carried away under the spell of the brilliant moon. This segment depicts the cultural awareness enjoyed by the audience, whom Tōru represents. Consequently, by subtle inference, it shows the poetic side of this noble statesman through the *shite*, the old man, although the *waki* does not know that he is Tōru, the minister, in disguise.

Toward the end of the first part of the play, the chorus sings the following passage in behalf of the *shite*:

> the ocean water
> I must draw
> from the Bay of Pails
> up he holds his salt-stained hem
> tucked in eastern style,
> scooping, too,
> the moon he holds
> in his sleeves
> higher rolls the tide
> ashore he goes . . .
> but mixing with the mists
> of shrouding salt-sea sprays
> and leaving not a trace,
> he vanishes away . . .

In Part II, after the Interlude, the scene begins with the waiting song, and the *shite*, dressed in his elegant, gorgeous attire, appears as the minister, with an air most courtly and magnificently noble. He recollects his splendid life and enjoys himself by giving way to his fantasies of the days of long ago, on a boat under the brilliant full moon or at the wine-party along the crescent stream. His reveries culminate in the *hayamai* dance that symbolizes his glorious life. Thus he entertains his traveling guest and never makes him weary throughout the autumn night. He continues to sing of the moon, with one metaphor after another, in a duet-like heightened exchange with the chorus, till the moon "grows dim." The chorus chants:

> already slanted
> to the west at dawn,
> with the clouds that rise
> as the rain begins,
> lured by the paling glimmer
> of the lunar rays,
> back to the Moon Blessed Palace
> graciously he goes
> with courtly air . . .

The chorus concludes the final line, singing,

> sweetly touched by parting sorrow
> appears his visage,
> touched by parting sorrow
> seems his visage.

Here one more point worthy of note is that throughout the play the *shite* never asks the *waki* to pray for his memory. The reason for this departure from convention is that he is already enlightened and dwells among the heavenly hosts, as the *kiri* passage shows.

The old name for this work is *Shiogama*.[3] The relation between this piece and the play known as *Tōru, the Minister,* the one Zeami's father performed, is not clear. Zeami praised his father's role of the Demon very highly, and it is speculated that Zeami might have rewritten this old *Shura*-piece into the present play. If this is true, then the manner in which he took out the Demon and reworked it is indeed bold and masterly. Whatever the circumstances under which Zeami composed this play, critics all agree that this piece is truly his greatest play. The Nō passages, particularly the lyric parts, are melodious and rich in poetic imagery as well as seamless in rhythmic flow. Even the number of syllables in the lines is harmonious, for the ratio of 5 to 7 is most pleasing to our ears. As Masuda Shōzō states, "This flawless piece of perfect composition and the image of the moon are unified into one whole as Zeami's foremost masterpiece."[4]

462

TŌRU

By Zeami

Persons: SHITE (PART I): *An old man*
NOCHI-JITE (PART II): *The ghost of Tōru*
WAKI: *A traveling Buddhist priest*
KYŌGEN: *A man of the place*

Classification: *Primary, Group V; Variant, Group I or IV*
Place: *At the River Mansion in the Sixth Ward, Kyoto*
Time: *Autumn*
Kogaki: *16*

PART I

Jo no Dan

[*As the musicians, a flute player, two hand-drum players, and a stick drummer, take their respective seats, following the* shidai *music, the* waki, *wearing a pointed hood* (kakubōshi), *a plain, less-formal heavy silk kimono* (muji noshime), *a broad-sleeved robe* (mizugoromo), *a waistband* (koshiobi), *a fan* (ōgi), *and a rosary* (juzu), *enters the stage and, at the name-saying seat* (nanoriza), *facing stage front, intones the following prose passage, called* nanori.]

WAKI

[1] *(Nanori: awazu, kotoba)*

Kore wa Tōgokugata⁵ yori idetaru sō nite sōrō. Ware imada Miyako o mizu sōrō hodo ni kono tabi omoitachi Miyako ni nobori sōrō.	I am a Buddhist priest who comes from the eastern provinces. Since I have not yet seen the capital, on this occasion I have decided that I will go there.

[*The* waki *sings the following passage, called* sageuta.]

WAKI [*Still facing stage front.*]

463

(Sageuta: au, yowagin)

Omoitatsu⁶	Guided by my heart
kokoro zo shirube	that makes me think of going
kumo⁷ o wake	through the clouds I part,
funaji o watari	over distant seas I cross
yama o koe	and climb the mountains;
chisato mo onaji⁸	a thousand miles I journey
hitoashi ni,	starting with a step,

Tōru

chisato mo onaji	a thousand miles I journey
hitoashi ni	starting with a step,

[*The* waki *changes to a high-pitched singing style and sings the following passage, called* ageuta.]

(Ageuta: au, yowagin)

yūbe o kasane	one by one the nights give way
asagoto no,	to the dawning light,
yūbe o kasane	one by one the nights give way

[*The* waki *faces to his right, takes two or three forward steps, and goes back to his former position, indicating that he has traveled.*]

asogato no	to the dawning light,
yado no nagori mo	saddened deeply by farewell
kasanarite	to the inn once more,
Miyako ni hayaku	I arrive ahead of time
tsukinikeri,	at the capital;
Miyako ni hayaku	I arrive ahead of time
tsukinikeri.	at the capital.

[*After the* ageuta, *the* waki, *facing stage front, intones the following prose passage, called* tsukizerifu, *"arrival statement."*]

WAKI

(Tsukizerifu: awazu, kotoba)

Isogi sōrō hodo ni kore wa haya Miyako ni tsukite sōrō. Kono atari oba Rokujō Kawara no In[9] to yaran mōshi sōrō. Shibaraku yasurai ikken sebaya to omoi sōrō.	Since I traveled so fast, I have already reached the capital. This place around here is called the River Beach Mansion of the Sixth Ward. I think I will rest awhile and do some sight-seeing.

[*The* waki *goes to the* waki *seat and sits down.*]

Ha First Dan

[*Following the entrance music called* issei, *the* shite, *an aged man, appears, balancing on his shoulder a pole with wooden pails hanging down from both ends. He wears a* warai jō *mask, an "old-man" wig (*jō gami*), a collar in light yellow (*eri asagi*), a plain, less-formal kimono (*muji noshime*), an "inferior silk" broad-sleeved robe (*shike mizugoromo*), a straw waist skirt (*koshimino*), a waistband (*koshiobi*), and a fan (*ōgi*). The* shite *turns toward the curtain, looks at the moon, and, facing stage front again, sings the following verse, called* issei.]

464

SHITE

[2] (Issei: awazu, tsuyogin)

Tsuki mo haya	The moon is rising
dejio[10] ni narite	high already too the tide
Shiogama[11] no	across the inlet
ura sabi wataru	of Salt Kiln, growing lonely
keshiki kana.	with its scenic view.

[*The* shite *continues to sing the following passage, called* sashi.]

Masterworks of the Nō Theater

Michinoku wa [12]	In Michinoku
izuku wa aredo	there are other lovely spots,
Shiogama no	but here in Salt Kiln,
uramite [13] wataru	where I view its bay, I grow
oi ga mi no	old with deep regrets
yorube mo isa ya	as I have no trusty friends
sadame naki	in this transient life,
kokoro mo sumeru	yet my heart is clear and bright
mizu no omo ni [14]	on the water surface
teru tsukinami o [15]	shines the moon in full each month
kazōreba	when I make the count.
koyoi zo aki no	This night indeed is truly
monaka naru	to be mid-autumn,
geni ya utsuseba	and since this is a copy
Shiogama no	of the old Salt Kiln
tsuki mo Miyako no	transferred here, its moon is too
monaka kana.	midst the capital!

[*The* shite *sings the following* sageuta *verse.*]

(Sageuta: au, tsuyogin)

Aki wa nakaba	At the halfway point the fall
mi wa sude ni	arrives already
oi kasanarite	this old age heaped upon me
moroshiraga,	with my hair all white,

[*The* shite *changes the singing style and sings the following* ageuta *verse.*]

(Ageuta: au, tsuyogin)

yuki to nomi	like the very snows
tsumori zo kinuru	drifting deeper as they pile
toshitsuki no,	through long months and years,
tsumori zo kinuru	drifting deeper as they pile
toshitsuki no [16]	through long months and years
haru o mukae	I welcome spring and autumn
aki o soe	I add upon it
shigururu matsu [17] no	with each rain, awaiting death
kaze made mo	as the pine winds pass
waga mi no ue to	mourning over such life's end
kumite [18] shiru	I know I feel it
shionaregoromo [19]	with the salt sprays soaking cold
sode samuki	through my tear-stained sleeves
urawa no aki no	across the bay in autumn

465

[*Putting down the wooden pails at* waki *stage front, the* shite *stands again by the* shite *seat.*]

yūbe kana,	on this evening,
urawa [20] no aki no	across the bay in autumn
yūbe kana.	on this evening.

Tōru

[Toward the end of the above passage, the waki *rises. Then the* waki *and the* shite *exchange a dialogue, which is called* mondai. *The* waki *stands at the* waki *seat, and the* shite, *at the* shite *seat.]*

Ha Second Dan

WAKI

[3] *(Mondai: awazu, tsuyogin)*

Ika ni kore naru jō-dono on-mi wa kono atari no hito ka.

Ho, there, old man! I wonder if you live about these parts.

SHITE

San zōrō. Kono tokoro no shiokumi nite sōrō.

Yes, I do. I am one of those who draws the saltwater at this place.

WAKI

Fushigi ya. Koko wa kaihen nite mo naki ni, shiokumi to wa ayamaritaru ka jō-dono.

How strange! This place is not by the seashore. So how can you draw saltwater? Did I hear you rightly, old man?

SHITE

Ara nani tomo naya. Sate koko oba izuku to shiroshimesarete sōrō zo.

Well, I am so surprised, but since you ask me . . . Do you know what this place is?

WAKI

Kono tokoro oba Rokujō Kawara no In to koso uketamawarite sōrae.

I have been told that this is the very place where the River Beach Mansion in the Sixth Ward is located.

SHITE

Kawara no In koso Shiogama no Ura zōro yo. Tōru[21] no Otodo Michinoku no Chika[22] no Shiogama o Miyako no uchi ni utsusaretaru kaihen nareba

The River Beach Mansion stands by the Bay of Shiogama, for the beach scene of the Salt Kiln at Chika in Michinoku was reproduced by Lord Tōru in the heart of the capital.

[The shite *faces stage front and sings the following.]*

na ni nagaretaru[23]
Kawara no In no
kasui o mo kume
chisui o mo kume
koko Shiogama no
urabito nareba
shiokumu to nado
obosanu zo ya.

At the River Beach Mansion,
whose fame flows throughout the land,
whether I draw the water
from its stream or from its pond,
since I live upon the shore
before the Bay of Salt Kiln,
why should you not think of me
as one who draws seawater?

Masterworks of the Nō Theater

[*The* shite *makes a* tsumeashi *gesture toward the* waki *and stamps the floor.*]

WAKI

Geni geni Michinoku no Chika no Shio-gama o Miyako no uchi ni utsusaretaru koto uketamawarioyobite sōrō.

Indeed, indeed. I have heard that the Salt Kiln at Chika in Michinoku was reproduced here in the capital.

[*The* waki *looks toward stage front.*]

Sate wa are naru wa Magaki ga Shima[24] sōrō ka.

So then, is that the famous Isle of Hedges over there?

SHITE

San zōrō. Are koso Magaki ga Shima zōrō yo. Tōru no Otodo tsune wa mi-fune o yoserare go-shuen no yūbu sa-mazama narishi tokoro zo kashi. Ya, tsuki koso idete sōrae.

Yes, indeed, that is the Isle of Hedges. [*The* shite *looks toward his right.*] Lord Tōru always rowed over to it in a boat. It is here where he held his banquets, enjoying wines and the various dances. [*The* shite *looks down over the water.*] Oh, indeed, now the moon is rising.

WAKI [*Looking at stage front.*]

Geni geni tsuki no idete sōrō zo ya. Ano Magaki ga Shima no mori no kozue ni tori no shuku shi saezurite, shimon ni utsuru tsukikage made mo koshū ni ka-eru mi no ue ka to omoiiderarete sōrō.

Yes, there the moon is rising, on that Isle of Hedges, in the branches of the stand of trees, the birds take shelter as they chirp and twitter; and even the moonlight shining on the brush-thatched gate reminds me of the old song that somehow makes me feel as though I were the one of whom it was written.

SHITE

Nani to tadaima no menzen no keshiki ga o-sō no on-mi ni shiraruru to wa moshi mo Katō[25] ga kotoba yaran

When you said just now that this scene before you reminds you of your life, oh, holy priest, I wonder if you were thinking of the lines from Chia Tao:

tori wa shuku su[26]
chichū no ki

among the lakeside trees
the birds take shelter;

WAKI

sō wa tataku
gekka no mon,

a priest knocks on the gate
beneath the shining moon;

SHITE

osu mo   whether "push"

Tōru

tataku mo   or "knock" depends

SHITE

kojin no kokoro   on the ancient poet's heart

SHITE AND WAKI

ima mokuzen no   this scene now before my eyes
shūbo ni ari.   across this autumn eve!

[*The chorus sings the following* ageuta; *the* shite *faces stage front as the chorus begins singing.*]

CHORUS

(*Ageuta: au, yowagin*)

Geni ya   How truly
inishie mo   near the past appears
tsuki ni wa Chika [27] no   beneath the moon at Salt Kiln
Shiogama no   that lies in Chika,

[*The* waki *takes a seat at the* waki *seat.*]

tsuki ni wa Chika no   beneath the moon at Salt Kiln
Shiogama no   that lies in Chika,
urawa no aki mo   when autumn is at midpoint

[*The* shite *goes out slightly toward stage front and looks ahead.*]

nakaba nite   about the inlet
matsukaze mo   where the winds begin
tatsu [28] nari ya   rising through the pines

[*The* shite *looks as though he were seeing the island on his right.*]

kiri no   in the mist,
Magaki no   half-hidden, lies
Shimagakure   the Isle of Hedges.

[*Changing his mood, the* shite *faces the* waki.]

iza ware mo   Let me rise and go
tachiwatari   and wander closer

[*Making a turn to his right, the* shite *goes to the* shite *seat.*]

mukashi no ato o   to the place of long ago
Michinoku [29] no   in the Eastern Lands,
Chika no urawa o   to view again the beauty
nagamen ya,   of Chika's inlet,

[*At the* shite *seat, the* shite *faces stage front.*]

Chika no urawa o   to view the inlet beauty
nagamen.   over Chika.

[During the above singing, the ai *(kyōgen) appears inconspicuously through the half-lifted Nō curtain and silently takes the* ai *seat.]*

Ha Third Dan

WAKI

[4] *(Awazu, kotoba)*

Shiogama no ura o Miyako no uchi ni utsusaretaru iware on-monogatari sōrae.

Now, please tell me what you know about this re-creation of the salt kiln at Shiogama inlet here in the capital.

[The shite *goes out to stage center and sits down. He then tells the story, which is called* katari.]*

SHITE

(Katari: awazu, tsuyogin)

Saga no Tennō no Gyo-o ni Tōru no Otodo Michinoku no Chika no Shiogama no chōbō o kikoshimeshi-oyobase tamai kono tokoro ni Shiogama o utsushi, ano Naniwa no Mitsu[30] no Ura yori mo hi-goto ni ushio o kumase koko nite shio o yakasetsutsu isshō gyo-yū no tayori to shitamō; shikaredomo sono nochi wa sōzoku shite moteasobu hito mo nakereba, ura wa sono mama hishio to natte

In the reign of the Emperor Saga, a man known as Tōru had heard of the scenic view of Shiogama at Michinoku. Therefore, he reproduced the salt kiln here at this place. And from Mitsu Bay at Naniwa he had men haul saltwater every day *[looks to his right]* and had them boil it here, taking pleasure in such joy throughout his life. But afterwards, there was no one to inherit it or to enjoy such pleasure. So now the bay lies dry.

chihen ni yodomu
tamarimizu wa
ame no nokori no
furuki[31] e ni
ochiba chiriuku
matsukage no
tsuki dani sumade[32]
akikaze no
oto nomi nokoru
bakari nari.
Sareba uta ni mo
kimi masade[33]
kemuri taenishi
Shiogama no
ura samishiku[34] mo
mie wataru kana to

Scattered here about the pond,
some stagnant pools collect,
left behind by passing rains
on the age-old bay,
where fallen leaves are floating;
even through the pines
the moon doesn't shine so brightly,
and the lonely sounds
of the whirring autumn winds
only now remain.
So even in a poem,
"Without you, my lord,
the smoke no longer rises
from the old Salt Kiln
at the inlet, too forlorn
and desolate the scene appears,"

469

[The shite *faces the* waki.]*

Tsurayuki mo
nagamete sōrō.

Tsurayuki wrote
as he viewed the scenery.

[The chorus takes up the rest of the passage and sings. The shite *faces stage front again.]*

Tōru

(Uta: au, yowagin)

Geni ya'	As I look
nagamureba	all around, indeed,
tsuki nomi miteru[35]	only now the moon alone
Shiogama no	rises here in full

[*The* shite *looks far into the distance on the right.*]

ura samishiku mo	across the Bay of Salt Kiln
are hatsuru	lying desolate

[*Thinking deeply, the* shite *faces stage front.*]

ato no yo made mo	in the world to come all stained
shiojimite	by the salty sprays;

[*Holding his right knee with both hands, he thinks about the past.*]

oi no nami mo	the wave of old age, too,
kaeru yaran.	comes surging over me.
Ara mukashi	Oh, how dear those days
koishi ya.	of the past appear!

[*The chorus continues to sing the following* ageuta. *Lifting up his face, the* shite *holds back his feeling.*]

(Ageuta: au, yowagin)

Koishi ya	How dear those days!
koishi ya to,	Oh, how dear those days!
shitaedomo	Though I yearn for them,
nagekedomo	though I moan for them
kai mo nagisa[36] no	all in vain I have no oars

[*The* shite *cannot bear his feelings any longer, and his knee gives in.*]

urachidori	along the seashore
ne o nomi naku	where the inlet plover
bakari nari	alone is crying,

[*The* shite *covers his face with both hands and weeps. As the chorus sings the last line, the* waki *rises.*]

ne o nomi naku	where the inlet plover
bakari nari	alone is crying.

[*The following dialogues are exchanged between the* shite *and the* waki. *Facing the* shite, *the* waki *intones in free-rhythm style.*]

WAKI

[5] *(Mondai: awazu, tsuyogin)*

Ika ni jō-dono. Miewataritaru yama-yama wa mina meisho nite zo sōrōran. On-oshie sōrae.	Now then, old man. Are those mountain ranges clearly visible over there all famous? Please tell me.

San zōrō. Mina meisho nite sōrō. On-
tazune sōrae, oshie-mōshi sōrōbeshi.

Yes, sir, all of them are famous. Please
ask me whatever you wish and I will
answer.

[*The* shite *rises and goes near the* shite *pillar. The* waki, *facing toward the* waki *pillar, asks the* shite *the following.*]

Mazu are ni mietaru wa Otohayama[37]
zōrō ka.

First of all, is that Mt. Otoha I see over
there?

[*The* shite *faces the same direction as the* waki.]

San zōrō. Are koso Otohayama zōrō yo.

Yes, sir. That is indeed Mt. Otoha.

Otohayama oto ni kikitsutsu Ōsaka[38] no
Seki no konata ni[39] to yomitareba, Ōsakayama[40] mo hodo chikō koso sōrōrame.

Mt. Otoha, according to what we hear,
rises on this side of Ōsaka Barrier, as the
poet sang. Then Mt. Ōsaka must be
close by.

Ōse no gotoku seki no konata ni to wa
yomitaredomo anata ni atareba Ōsaka
no yama wa Otoha no mine ni kakurete

As you said, according to the poet, it is
"on this side of the barrier." But actually, Mt. Ōsaka is on the opposite side
and is hidden by Mt. Otoha's peak.

kono hen yori wa
mienu nari.

We cannot see the mountain
from this neighborhood.

[*The* waki *turns slightly to his right.*]

Sate sate Otoha no mine tsuzuki, shidai
shidai no yamanami no meisho meisho
o kataritamae.

Indeed, well then, please tell me now
about those famous places lying, one after another, along the mountain ranges
from Mt. Otoha's peak.

471

Katari mo tsukusaji koto no ha no[41] uta
no Nakayama[42] Seiganji[43] Imagumano[44]
to wa are zo kashi.

Though I may begin, I can never finish.
Well known in poetry are Nakayama
and Seiganji Temple; that one there is
Imagumano, indeed.

[*The* shite *faces toward the same direction as the* waki. *As they change places with each other, both of them shift their eyes to the right.*]

WAKI

Sate sono sue ni	After you have passed it then,
tsuzukitaru	continuing onward,
sato hitomura[45] no	a village-town is clustered
mori no kodachi.	about a stand of trees.

SHITE

Sore o shirube ni goranze yo madaki	Using the village as your guide, you can
shigure no[46] aki nareba momiji mo aoki	see that it is still too early for the au-
Inariyama.[47]	tumn drizzling rain; the maple leaves
	are green on Mt. Inari.

WAKI

Kaze mo kureyuku	Here the wind is growing dark
kumo no ha no[48]	where clouds are trailing,
kozue mo aoki	there the treetops too are green
aki no iro.	midst the autumn hues.

SHITE

Ima koso aki yo, na ni shiou haru wa	Now, indeed, it's autumn, but well
hana mishi Fuji no Mori.[49]	known and worthy of the flower I saw
	in spring is the Wisteria Grove.

WAKI

Midori no sora mo	Underneath the high blue sky
kage aoki	the light glows greener
noyama ni tsuzuku	beyond the fields and mountains,
sato wa ika ni.	what is that village there?

SHITE

Are koso Yū sareba	That is where "As evening closes

WAKI

nobe no[50] akikaze	winds from the autumn meadows

SHITE

mi ni shimite	pierce me with the chill,

472

WAKI

uzura naku naru	as the quails are crying low

SHITE

Fukakusayama[51] yo.	among the Deep Grass" Mountain.

[*The* shite *goes to the* waki *and takes hold of his sleeve. He lures the* waki *out toward stage front, where they view the scenery, while the chorus sings the following lines, taken from famous place-names, in* yowagin *style.*]

CHORUS

(*Uta: au, yowagin*)

Kowatayama[52]	Next, Kowata Hill,
Fushimino Takeda	Bamboo Lea, Fushimi Field,
Yodo Toba mo	Pool, and Bird Wing, too,
mietari ya.	can be clearly seen.

[*The chorus next sings the passage called* rongi.]

[6] (*Rongi: au, yowagin*)

Nagame yaru[53]	Off in the distance,

[*The* shite *returns to the* shite *seat, and the* waki, *to the* waki *seat; they stand at their respective positions.*]

sonata no sora wa	deep I look across the sky
shirakumo no	with the soft white clouds
haya kuresomuru	as the dusk begins to fall
tōyama no	on distant mountains
mine mo kobukaku	whose peaks seem thickly wooded;
mietaru wa	I gaze upon them,
ikanaru tokoro	wondering what sort of place
naruran.	lies over there.

SHITE

Are koso	That is, indeed,
Ōhara ya.[54]	Ōhara field,

[*The* shite *faces toward* waki *stage front.*]

Oshio no yama mo	then, the hill of Oshio;
kyō koso wa	on this day, indeed,
goranji	for the first time
sometsurame	do you see this scene?
nao nao towase-	And do you have more questions
tamae ya.	to put to me?

CHORUS

473

Kiku ni tsuketemo	Even as I'm asking you,
aki no kaze	here the autumn wind
fuku kata nare ya	comes blowing from the quarter
mine tsuzuki	of those peaks in view
nishi ni miyuru wa	ranging onward to the west.
izuku zo.	What is that place?

Tōru

SHITE

Aki mo haya	Too soon this autumn,
aki mo haya	too soon this autumn

[*Facing the bridge.*]

nakaba fukeyuku	is deepened and half over
Matsu no O[55] no	across Pine Ridge
Arashiyama[56] mo	and Storm Mountain, too, appears
mietari.	before our eyes.

CHORUS

Arashi fukeyuku[57]	The stormy wind blows deeply
aki no yo no	through the autumn night,
sora suminoboru	across the sky how brightly
tsukikage ni	the moon comes rising

SHITE

sasu[58] shiotoki mo	high the tide but now its hour
haya sugite	is past already

CHORUS

hima mo oshiteru[59]	yet all the while too lovely
tsuki ni mede	is the moon he loves!

SHITE

kyō ni jōjite	Enraptured by its splendor,

[*The* shite *goes out slightly forward.*]

CHORUS

mi oba geni	he neglects his work

[*Suddenly he comes to himself and clasps both hands together.*]

wasuretari	and forgets himself
aki no yo no	in the autumn night

[*The* shite *faces the* waki.]

nagamonogatari[60]	long the narrative he tells
yoshi na ya,	ever foolishly.

474

[*Goes near the pails, puts them on his shoulder with a pole, and goes out toward stage front.*]

mazu izaya shio o	But first of all, well now, he says,
kuman tote	the ocean water
motsu ya	I must draw
Tago no Ura[61]	from the Bay of Pails

[*The* shite *looks at the pails on his right and on his left.*]

Masterworks of the Nō Theater

azumakarage no	up he holds his salt-stained hem,
shiogoromo	tucked in eastern style,

[*The* shite *pushes both pails out to the waves as though he were trying to draw some seawater.*]

kumeba	scooping, too,
tsuki o mo	the moon he holds
sode ni	in his sleeves
mochishio[62] no	higher rolls the tide

[*Looks at both pails on his right and left.*]

migiwa ni	ashore he goes
kaeru nami no	back with the ebbing waves
yoru[63] no	in the night

[*Going to the* shite *seat from the front of the* waki *seat.*]

rōjin to	he appears to be
mietsuru ga	an ancient person,

[*Suddenly the* shite *throws the pails away and stops at the* shite *seat as though he has faded away.*]

shiogumori ni	but mixing with the mist
kakimagirete	of shrouding salt-sea sprays
ato mo misezu	and leaving not a trace,
narinikeri,	he vanishes away,
ato o mo miezu	leaving not a trace behind,
narinikeri.	he vanishes away.

[*Quietly the* shite *makes his exit along the bridge and behind the curtain.*]

Nakairi (Interlude)

[*The* kyōgen, *a man of the place, wearing a horizontally striped kimono* (dan noshime), *a long* kyōgen *robe in two pieces* (naga kamishimo), *a waistband* (koshiobi), *a fan* (ōgi), *and a short sword* (chiisa gatana), *comes out to the name-saying seat* (nanoriza) *and intones the following prose dialogue with the* waki.]

(Mondai: katari)

Kayō ni sōrō mono wa kono atari ni sumai suru mono nite sōrō. Kyō wa makariide kokoro o nagusamebaya to zonji sōrō. Iya kore ni minaremōsanu o-sō no onnide nasare sōrō ga izukata yori sankei nasare sōrō zo.

I am a person living in this neighborhood. Today I will go out to amuse myself. [*Sees the* waki.] Well, I see a Buddhist priest unfamiliar to me who comes out here. Where did you come from to make a pilgrimage to this place?

475

Waki

Kore wa shokoku ikken no sō nite sōrō. On-mi wa kono atari no hito nite watari sōrō ka.

I am a wandering Buddhist priest, visiting various provinces. Do you live in this vicinity?

Tōru

Nakanaka kono atari no mono nite sōrō.

Yes, I am from this neighborhood.

Sayō nite sōrawaba mazu chikō onniri sōrae. Tazunetaki koto no sōrō.

If that is so, please come closer. I have something to ask you.

Kashikomatte sōrō. Sate o-tazune nasaretaki to wa ikayō naru go-yō nite sōrō zo.

Yes, holy priest. [*Goes to stage center and sits down.*] What do you want to ask me?

Omoi mo yoranu mōshigoto nite sōraedomo inishie Tōru no Otodo Michinoku no Chika no Shiogama o kono tokoro ni utsusaretaru yōtai go-zonji ni oite wa katatte o-kisase sōrae.

Indeed, this is something you may not expect from me, but I heard that long, long ago, Minister Tōru built a reproduction of Shiogama of Chika in Michinoku at this place. Tell me the story if you know it.

Kore wa omoi mo yoranu koto o uketamawari sōrō mono kana. Warera mo kono atari ni sumaitsukamatsuri sōraedomo sayō no koto kuwashiku wa zonzezu sōrō. Sarinagara hajimete o-me ni kakari o-tazune nasare sōrō koto o nan to mo zonzenu to mōsu mo ikaga nite sōraeba oyoso uketamawarioyobitaru tōri on-monogatari mōsōzuru nite sōrō.

How strange that you should ask about such things. Though we live in this neighborhood, I don't know too much about the details. But since I am asked by a person that I meet for the first time, it would not be right to say that I know nothing about it at all; so I shall tell the story the way I've heard it.

Chikagoro nite sōrō.

I would be most grateful.

Saru hodo ni Tōru no Otodo to mōshitaru on-kata wa jinnō gojūnidai Saga Tennō no sue no on-ko nite goza aritaru to mōsu. Jinnō gojūrokudai Seiwa Tennō no gyo-o Jōgkan jūyonen hachigatsu ni sadaijin ni ninzerare Ninwa san-nen ni wa ju-ichii ni nobori Kanpyō gannen ni wa on-toshi rokujūshichi nite rensha no senji o kōmuritamai makoto ni kan'i hōroku made mo tagui sukunaku, yū ni yasashiki on-kata nite goza aru to mōsu. Mata Otodo wa yo ni masaretaru on-monokonomi nite iroiro no

Well, a person called Minister Tōru was the youngest son of the fifty-second emperor, Saga, I hear. In the reign of the fifty-sixth emperor, Seiwa, he was graciously appointed minister of the Left, in August of the fourth year of the Jōgkan. In the third year of the Ninwa he was promoted to the junior grade of the first court rank. In the first year of the Kanpyō, at the age of sixty-seven, he was bestowed the privilege of the carriage. There were so few who were like him in rank and wealth. He was

on-asobi kazu o tsukushitamau ga, on-mae nite aru hito no mōshi sōro wa Michinoku no Chika no Shiogama no chōbō omoshiroki yoshi, on-monogatari kikoshimeshi, go-gekō atte go-ran aritaku oboshimesedomo, amari engoku no koto nareba, Miyako no uchi e utsushi goran arubeki tote, ezu o motte kono tokoro e Shiogama o utsushi, Kamogawa no mizu o hikikudashi, yarimizu sensui tsukiyama no yōtai o obitadashiku nasare, shio wa Naniwazu Shikitsu Takatsu kono mitsu no ura yori shio o kumase, sanzennin no ninsoku o motte itonamu yue, shioya no kemuri nado no keshiki on-uta ni yomitamō ni sukoshi mo tagawazu. Kore hodo omoshiroki koto wa arumajiki tote, isshō no go-yū no tayori to nasare. Are ni mietaru o Magaki ga Shima to mōshite, ano shima e onnide atte, go-yū samazama arishi orifushi, Otoha no Yama no mine yori mo idetaru tsuki no Magaki ga Shima no mori no kozue ni utsurikagayaku arisama migoto naru yōtai, kisen gunshū o nashi kenbutsu tsukamatsuri sōro. Koro wa Kannazuki otsugomogata ni, kiku momiji no irozuki, chikusa ni miete omoshiroki orifushi wa, kono tokoro e miko kandachime nado owashimashi, kokorobae no onuta nado amata asobashi sōro. Naka ni mo Ariwara no Narihira wa mina hitobito ni yomasehatete, Shiogama ni[64] itsuka kiniken asanagi ni tsuri suru fune wa koko ni yoranan to, kayō ni eizeraretaru onuta makoto ni shushō naru yoshi uketamawari sōro. Sareba toshitsuki no suguru wa hodo mo naku, Otodo hōjitamaite ato wa, onnato o sōzoku shite moteasobu hito mo nakereba, ura wa sono mama hishio to nari, na nomi bakari nite goza sōro. Mata kayō ni arehatetaru tokoro o, Tsurayuki no onuta eizeraretaru to uketamawari sōro. Mazu warera no uketamawarioyobitaru wa kaku no gotoku nite goza sōro ga, nan to oboshimeshi o-tazune nasare sōro zo. Chikagoro fushin ni zonji sōro.

graceful and kind, I hear. The minister had a very highly cultivated sense of beauty. A certain official who served him told the minister the story of how inspiring was the scenic view of Shiogama at Chika in Michinoku; so he wished to take a journey to view the scenery. But since it was too far away, he said he should reproduce it in the capital. Therefore, by working from drawings, they reproduced it at this place. The water was canalled from the Kamo River. Streams, ponds, and artificial hills were constructed extensively. The saltwater was hauled from the three bays, namely Naniwazu, Shikizu, and Takatsu. Since 3000 men were used, the scene of smoke from the salt-making hut was no different from that described in the poems he composed. Since there was nothing as interesting as this, he took pleasure in such joy throughout his life. What you see over there is called the Isle of Hedges. He went out there at times and held many banquets. The moon that rose from Mt. Otoha's peak and shone on the treetops of those groved trees in the Isle of Hedges was so splendid that the people, high and low, came in throngs for sight-seeing. It was about the thirty-first of December, when the chrysanthemums and the maple leaves were in colors, and a countless variety of the plants appeared interesting, that the princes, princesses, and high officials paid their visits and wrote many poems from their hearts. Among them, Ariwara no Narihira composed a poem after the others had all finished their verses:

477

> To Shiogama
> when do they come I wonder
> but at morning calm
> those boats of fishers fishing
> will be stopping at this place.

They said it was truly an admirable poem, I hear. Then time went by so quickly, and after the minister had passed away, there was no one to inherit it or enjoy such pleasure. The bay became dry and remained only in name. Tsurayuki, I hear, wrote a poem about it[65] when this place was lying in wasted ruins. This is what I have heard. I wonder what you had in mind when you asked me the question. Lately I have felt something strange about this place.

WAKI

Nengoro ni on-monogatari sōrō mono kana. Tazunemōsu mo yo no gi ni arazu. On-mi izen ni rōjin hitori shiokumi no tei nite korare sōrō hodo ni, sunawachi kotoba o kawashite sōraeba, Shiogama no shisai nengoro ni katari, tokoro no meisho nado o oshie, nan to yaran yoshi arige nite, shiokumori nite sugata o miushinōte sōrō yo.

How kind of you to tell me all about the story. The reason I asked you about this place is nothing special. A while ago an old man appeared, like those who draw saltwater, and he exchanged words with me and told me about Shiogama in detail. He also explained the famous places here with a meaningful air, it seemed, and through the cloudy salt-sprays, I have lost sight of him.

KYŌGEN

Kore wa kidoku naru koto o ōse sōrō mono kana. Sate wa Tōru-kō no arawa-reidetamaitaru to zonji sōrō. Sore o ika ni to mōsu ni, ima ni mo tsuki no mei-mei taru orifushi wa inishie shio o yakaseraretaru yōtai, on-sata aru yoshi mōshi sōrō ga, o-sō tōtoku mashimasu ni yori, shio o kumu yōtai nite araware-tamai, o-kotoba o kawasaretaru to zonji sōrō aida, shibaraku go-tōryū arite, ka-sanete kidoku o goran arekashi to zonji sōrō.

How strange a story this is that you have told me. Well, Lord Tōru must have appeared to you. You said how he appeared when the moon was about to come up brightly, as he made the salt-water boil long ago. Since you are a holy priest, he appeared in disguise as an old man who draws saltwater and exchanged, I think, words with you. You should stay here a while. Somehow I think you will see that strange thing again.

WAKI

478

Chikagoro fushin naru koto nite sōrō hodo ni, shibaraku tōryū mōshi, kasa-nete kidoku o miuzuru nite sōrō.

This is indeed a strange thing that has happened to me of late. I will stay here for a while, for I would like to see it once more.

KYŌGEN

Go-yō no koto mo sōrawaba kasanete ōse sōrae.

If you have something for me to do, please ask me.

Tanomi sōrōbeshi.   That is kind of you. Thank you.

Kokoroe mōshite sōrō.   Not at all, good priest.

[*The* kyōgen *goes back to his seat.*]

Kyū no Dan

[*Sitting at the* waki *seat, the* waki *sings the following* ageuta, *called "waiting song"* (machiutai).]

[7] (*Machiutai: au, tsuyogin*)

Isomakura[66]	Pillowing on a stone
koke no koromo o	at the beach, half-spread the sleeve
katashikite,	of my moss-hued robe,
koke no koromo o	at the beach, half-spread the sleeve
katashikite	of my moss-hued robe,
iwane no toko ni	bedded midst the rooted rocks,
yo mo sugara	this long night I spend
nao mo kidoku o	so that I'll see the marvel
miru ya tote	further as I sleep
yumemachigao no	with a dream-awaiting look
tabine kana,	upon this journey,
yumemachigao no	with a dream-awaiting look
tabine kana.	upon this journey.

[*Following the* deha *music, the* nochi-jite *appears and stops at the first pine* (ichi no matsu) *and enters the stage. He wears a* chūjō *mask, a headdress* (shokan ei), *a gold brocade headband* (kindan hachimaki), *a collar in white* (eri shiro), *an under kimono with painted gold or silver patterns and an embroidered design on a red ground* (akaji nuihaku), *an unlined hunting robe* (hitoe kariginu), *a broad divided underskirt* (komi ōguchi), *a waistband* (koshiobi), *and a fan* (ōgi). *Facing stage front, he sings the following* sashi.]

[8] (*Sashi: awazu, tsuyogin*)

Wasurete toshi o[67]	I who had forgot this world
heshi mono o	over these long years,
mata inishie ni	come again to see the waves
kaeru nami no[68]	that ebb away and rise
mitsu[69] Shiogama no	high with the tide at Salt Kiln,
urabito no	like a fisherman
koyoi no tsuki o	looking at the moon tonight
Michinoku[70] no	across the inlet
Chika no urawa mo	of Chika in the East Land
tōki yo ni	as in ages past,
sono na o nokosu	when the name was left behind

479

Tōru

mōchikimi	by the noblest one
Tōru no Otodo to wa	known as the Minister Tōru,

[*The* shite *faces the* waki.]

waga koto nari.	who was no less than I.

[*The* shite *faces stage front again.*]

Ware shiogama no	I am he who gave his heart
ura ni kokoro o yose	away all for the Bay of Salt Kiln
ano Magaki ga Shima no	and to that lovely Isle of Hedges
matsukage ni	with its shadowed pines

[*The* shite *looks toward his right.*]

meigetsu ni	and the harvest moon,
fune o ukame	I set my boat afloat
gekkyūden[71] no	for the Palace of the Moon,
hakue no sode mo	where the heavenly maidens' sleeves
sango yachū no	on each three-fives night are white

[*Stamps the floor and makes a* hiraki *gesture.*]

shingetsu no iro	with the newly rising moon,

(*Issei: awazu, tsuyogin*)

chie furu ya[72]	a thousand twirlings,
yuki o megurasu	whirling bright like flakes of snow
kumo no sode	seem the clouds of sleeves,

[*The* shite *makes appropriate dancelike movements to the lines the chorus sings. Turning to his right, the* shite *goes out to stage center.*]

CHORUS

sasu ya[73] katsura no	shining brightly twig on twig
edaeda ni	of the laurel crown,

[*At the center of the stage, the* shite *makes a* hiraki *gesture.*]

SHITE

hikari o hana to[74]	the moonbeams shine and scatter
chirasu yosooi.	like the fluttering flowers!

[*The* shite *points the fan at the water and goes out to the eye-fixing pillar.*]

480

CHORUS

Koko ni mo na ni tatsu	Here is also this White River
Shirakawa no nami no	well known to all, the ripples rise

[*Making a turn to his left, the* shite *goes out, scooping water with his fan.*]

| ara omoshiro ya[75] | so delightfully, there float |
| kyokusui no sakazuki | round the crescent bend the rice-wine cups |

[*Holding a fan with both hands as if it were a wine cup, the* shite *stamps the floor.*]

| uketari uketari | receive, receive them all with joy |
| yūbu no sode | of gaily dancing sleeves. |

Hayamai

Kyū Second Dan

[*The chorus sings the following passage, called* rongi.]

CHORUS

[9] (*Rongi: au, tsuyogin*)

Ara omoshiro no	How delightful indeed are
yūgaku ya.	the dance and music!
Somo meigetsu no	Though the harvest moon comes up
sono naka ni	brightly as a rule,
mada hatsuzuki no	in the third day of the month,
yoiyoi ni	at each evening
kage mo sugata mo	why is it that both its glow
sukunaki wa	and form are meager?

[*Facing stage front, the* shite *stands at the* shite *seat.*]

| ika naru iware | What is the reason for this, |
| naruran. | I wonder why. |

SHITE

| Sore wa | Whenever |
| saishū ni | down the sun descends |

[*The* shite *goes out slightly toward stage front.*]

| irihi no imada | behind the western mountains, |
| chikakereba | near the crests it hangs; |

[*The* shite *stamps the floor a few times.*]

sono kage ni	so the moon is dimmed
kakusaruru.	in its stronger light.
Tatoeba tsuki no	Further, when the moon is out
aru yo wa	at pitch-dark night,

[*The* shite *makes a* hiraki *gesture to his right and stamps the floor once.*]

| hoshi no usuki ga | all the scattered stars appear |
| gotoku nari. | pale across the sky. |

481

[*The* shite *goes out to the eye-fixing pillar.*]

CHORUS

Seiyō no haru no   In the first and faint appearance
hajime ni wa   of the spring's beginning,

[*The* shite *looks off into the distance to his right.*]

SHITE

kasumu yūbe no   as the hazy twilight veils
tōyama   the far-off hills,

[*Making a turn to his right, the* shite *goes to the front of the* waki *seat.*]

CHORUS

mayuzumi no iro ni   outlined in black like eyebrows curved
mikazuki no   is the crescent moon,

[*In front of the* waki *seat, the* shite *points to stage front below with his fan.*]

SHITE

kage o fune ni mo   which looks like a silver boat
tatoetari,   sailing far above,

CHORUS

[*The* shite *stamps the floor a few times.*]

mata suichū no   or mirrored in the water,
yūgyo wa   the fish at play

SHITE

[*The* shite *points above with his fan.*]

tsuribari to   question it as though
utagō   it were a hook,

[*The* shite *looks at the sky.*]

CHORUS

unshō no   and above the clouds,
hichō wa   the birds in flight

482   [*Looking at the water, the* shite *stamps the floor once.*]

SHITE

yumi no kage to mo   take it for a shadowed bow
odoroku: that startles them.

[*Making a turn to his left, the* shite *goes to the front of the musicians.*]

CHORUS

ichirin mo But never has it
kudarazu,   fallen earthward,

[*Pointing stage front ahead with his fan, the* shite *goes forward.*]

SHITE

bansui mo   never has the water
noborazu   run heavenward;

CHORUS

tori wa   here the birds
chihen no   about the pond
ki ni shukushi shelter in the trees;

SHITE

uo wa   and upon

[*Kneeling on the floor on one leg, he makes a pillow of his fan.*]

gekka no   the waves, the fish
nami ni fusu.   sleep beneath the moon.

[*Rising up, the* shite *goes to the eye-fixing pillar.*]

CHORUS

Kiku to mo akaji   What we hear doesn't weary us
aki no yo no   through this autumn night,

[*Listening, the* shite *goes to the* waki *seat.*]

SHITE

tori mo naki   but the rooster calls

CHORUS

kane mo kikoete   as the temple bell is heard;

[*Making a* kumo no ōgi *gesture, the* shite *looks at the western sky.*]

SHITE

tsuki mo haya   the moon is also

[*The* shite *looks at the eastern sky.*]

483

CHORUS

kage   paling,
katamukite   already slanted
akegata no   to the west at dawn,

Tōru

| kumo to nari[76] | with the clouds that rise |
| ame to naru | as the rain begins, |

[*Pointing his fan, the* shite *goes to stage front, and, flipping his sleeve upward and making a turn to his right, he goes to the* shite *seat.*]

kono kōin ni	lured by the paling glimmer
sasowarete	of the lunar rays,
tsuki no miyako ni	back to the Moon Blessed Palace
iritamō	graciously he goes
yosooi	with courtly air
ara nagorioshi no	sweetly touched by parting sorrow

[*At the* shite *seat, the* shite *makes a* hiraki *gesture toward stage front and, facing the* waki *seat, he stamps the floor.*]

omokage ya,	appears his visage,
nagorioshi no	touched by parting sorrow
omokage.	seems his visage.

484

Martin Luther King, Jr.:
A Nō Play

Introduction

When I heard that the birthday of Martin Luther King, Jr., had been designated a national holiday, I was so moved that I felt a sudden urge to compose a Nō play in his honor. I traveled to Memphis, Tennessee, where he was martyred by an assassin's bullet, and to Washington, D.C., where his "I Have a Dream . . ." speech galvanized his followers in the March on Washington and rippled with tidal force through the consciousness of a heretofore complacent nation. Traveling to these now-historic sites gave me necessary information but, more than this, helped me establish a "feel" for those places and events. The emotions and insights thus arising formed rhythms in my head and in my heart, and I began to hear the beginnings of the music and to see the rudiments of the dances out of which the play itself would emerge.

From studying all of King's writings and speeches, I was able to produce many pages of quotations and notes on themes. But more important, I began to form a vision of his soul. This vision was close enough to the reality of King to continue promoting insights into his life and honor to his memory. At the same time, that vision was just distant enough, just abstract enough, that I felt it might serve the *shite* role, pointing to the common yearnings of all humankind.

With this intense, but nebulous, foundation, I looked to the formal structures of Nō for the frameworks into which my untamed thoughts and feelings could flow. Following Zeami, I tried to see how my ideas could be placed into the three sections that form the basic structure of the Nō—the Jo, with one *dan*, the Ha, with three *dan*, and the Kyū, one *dan*. I then had to find how the music would be composed and how it would fit within the five *dan*.

Many of these decisions (or discoveries) would depend on the category of the play and its overall length. So, I had to decide which category the play would represent. I liked the phrase of Ralph David Abernathy, King's successor in the Southern Christian Leadership Council, which labeled King as "the peaceful warrior." King led his people in nonviolent battle against the Confederate flag of the segregated southern cities and the racism it symbolized for many, just as Lincoln's soldiers had fought against the same flag fivescore years before. I felt, therefore, that the structure of this play would be that of the "warrior" play, outlined by Nogami as follows:

> First *dan* (Part I): The *waki* entry (*shidai, michiyuki,* etc.). Jo 1 *dan.*
> Second *dan* (Part I): The *shite* entry (*issei, sashi, sageuta, ageuta,* etc.). Ha 1 *dan.*
> Third *dan* (Part I): *Mondai* and others. Ha 2 *dan. Nakairi.*
> Fourth *dan* (Part II): *Machiutai, nochi-jite* entry (*issei*), *kuri, sashi, kuse.* Ha 3 *dan.*
> Fifth *dan* (Part II): *Kiri.* Kyū 1 *dan.*

Later, as you will see, I would discover that my categorization was in error. But until that moment, I worked in the format just described.

I chose to make the *waki* a recent graduate of Howard University Divinity School in Washington, D.C. He would be traveling to take a post in a small church in the South. He has faith in God, justice, freedom, and peace. He is also about the same age as King was when he took his first post and started to lead the life of a modern warrior with his dream. That dream is echoed in the *shidai,* sung by the *waki* and his companion as the play opens:

> From this dream-filled world of man
> we wake with a start,
> from this dream-filled world of man
> we wake with a start
> on the Way that all must take
> let us hurry.

The *waki* begins his life's new journey from Washington, the city from which King's dream resonated to mark a new journey for America. The *waki* is destined to meet King and to be invited to join in leading the people back to the capital, where they are awaited by Abraham Lincoln, "who had issued forth the Emancipation Proclamation fivescore years ago." The *waki* meets King in Memphis, scene of the assassination but also site of the rebirth and continuation of the ideals the bullet was meant to end.

The time is also important and should have multiple allusions. Thus, I placed the Nō play in April, the month of King's death, the month of Lincoln's death, and the traditional month of Jesus' death. This is revealed in the *kakeai* between the *shite* and the *waki:*

486

SHITE:	April is the cruellest month,
WAKI:	April is the cruellest month,
SHITE:	April is the cruellest month,
	for nineteen hundred
	eighty and some years ago
	our Lord died for the world
	on Good Friday.
WAKI:	On Good Friday
	sixscore years ago
	Lincoln was assassinated

SHITE: and for his country died
from a bullet wound, as I
for my fellow men when lilacs last
in the dooryard bloom'd.

These events are foreshadowed by the beginning of the *sashi* immediately after
the *shidai*. Included is the famous first line from the Prelude to the *Canterbury Tales*
by Geoffrey Chaucer, fused with the title line from Walt Whitman's great poem
"When Lilacs Last in the Dooryard Bloom'd." The lilac, which blooms in April, is
used as the theme flower of the play, binding it into a whole. This *sashi* also serves
as the prelude to the *michiyuki* passage.

Generally, the *michiyuki* has only an *ageuta*, but here I use the *sageuta* and the
ageuta. The music of the two songs differs appropriately, adding color to the passages, but the two together are meant to be recognizably linked by the content
flowing through and connecting them. The general function of the *michiyuki* is to
describe the way by which the *waki* reaches his destination. It is a high-pitched
song with vivid descriptions of the beauty of the fruitful landscapes, usually performed immediately after the *nanori*. It is sung in *hiranori* style. I added lines from
"America, the Beautiful" to intensify the *waki*'s emotional experience and to represent the voice of the American people. The whole structure of the sequence is
dedicated to showing the *waki*'s first journey as memorable and lovely.

Next comes the *shite* entry in the second *dan*. The full-scaled *shite* entry pattern
is usually used for the god-plays, but plays in other categories (such as *Matsukaze*
and *Tōru*) can also use the pattern. The typical structure is *issei* followed by *sashi*,
then *sageuta* followed by *ageuta*. The *sashi* I use here is sung with the same feeling
as the *issei*. Both *sashi* and *issei* depict scenery that will make the *shite* appear in his
best light. The scenic view of the *issei* and *sashi* contains human elements particu-
larized in the *sageuta* and to which the *ageuta* responds. Though the content of the
songs is tightly linked through the sequence, the music must remain appropriately
distinct.

Martin Luther King, Jr.'s message was a call to all Americans for the benefit of
all, but was directed particularly to black people. This focus is reflected in the
sageuta, where I introduce the voice of the black people, in contrast to the voice of
all Americans in the first *dan*. This song is chanted in *chū* and *ge-on*, as the name
implies. The *ageuta* responds to it, uplifting the tone of both the content and the
music.

The *shite* is revealed during the *mondai* and *kakeai* that follow. Through the juxtaposition of the poetically expressed events, the soul of the *shite* is gradually un-
folded, phase by phase, until full realization occurs in the *kuse* segment of the play.
This is the climax called "Opening the Ears," when the lyrics and the music blend
and flow into a harmonious whole and the entire audience should be moved
strongly.

The formal musical structure of the *kuse* comprises the *kuri-sashi-kuse* sequence,
with the *kuri* and the *sashi* serving as prelude pieces to the *kuse*. This relationship
has been described by Japanese masters as the waterfall (*kuri*), the rapids (*sashi*),
and the pool (*kuse*).

Following Zeami's injunctions about the placement of songs for "warrior"
plays, I put the *kuse* at the end of Part II. But something was wrong with this. The
subject of this *kuse* is, naturally, the great March on Washington—the pivotal moment of King's heroic fight against human injustice, where, before the statue of
Lincoln, he delivered the most famous speech of his career. The music and lyrics

487

Martin Luther King, Jr.: A Nō Play

for this speech should need no dance by the *shite*—the audience need not see anything, but only listen. Such a song should be *iguse*, and I found myself pushing the *kuse* back into Part I and changing the category of the play from Category II (warriors) to Category V ("demons," which, paradoxically, can include the lives of saints). I had been wrong about the play and the play was telling me this: that the thrust of King's life, for the masses who followed him, was like that of a bodhisattva or a saint sent down from the Lord. "Freedom" thus becomes bigger than political and economic rights and approaches salvation.

With this revelation, I realized that the climax, the "Opening of the Eyes," should be a *hayamai* dance in the Kyū section. This is a stately and refreshing dance, as opposed to the *kakeri* I had originally chosen for this point to show the suffering of the warrior. This five-movement *hayamai*, which the *shite* performs in the Ōshiki mode (A) and then changes into the Banshiki mode (B), should balance well with the full-structured double *kuse* that "opens the ears" back in Part I. The play closes as the chorus sings,

> welcomed by a band of angels
> singing clear rejoicingly,
> midst the purple-colored clouds,

and the *shite* exits across the Nō bridge. His knee is slightly bent. He straightens up as he disappears behind the brocade curtain. He has ascended into heaven.

488

MARTIN LUTHER KING, JR.
A NŌ PLAY

By Kenneth Yasuda

Persons: WAKI: *A young pastor*
WAKI-TSURE: *His companion*
SHITE (PART I): *The ghost of Martin Luther King, Jr.*
TSURE: *His companion*
NOCHI-JITE (PART II): *Martin Luther King, Jr.*
KYŌGEN: *An old man of the place*

Time: *April*
Place: *Memphis*
Classification: *Group V*

PART I
Jo Dan

[*The* waki, *a young pastor, and the* waki-tsure, *a fellow pastor, enter and proceed quietly down the Nō bridge and onto the stage. Facing the audience, they sing the* shidai, *or prelude song.*]

WAKI AND WAKI-TSURE

[1] *(Shidai)*

From this dream-filled world of man
we wake with a start,
from this dream-filled world of man
we wake with a start
on the Way that all must take,
let us hurry.

[*The chorus then sings the following verse, called the* jidori.]

CHORUS

(Jidori)

From this dream-filled world of man
we wake with a start
on the Way that all must take,
let us hurry.

[*The* waki *then delivers the following prose passage, called the* nanori *(name-saying speech).*]

Martin Luther King, Jr.: A Nō Play

WAKI

(Nanori)

I am a recent graduate of the Divinity School of Howard University in Washington, D.C. I am taking a post offered me by a small church in the South. With my companion, I have decided to visit some noted places on the way. Spring comes early this year.

[*The* waki *and the* waki-tsure *next sing a verse called* sashi.]

WAKI AND WAKI-TSURE

(Sashi)

When April with its showers,[1]
when April with its showers
sweet with fruit has pierced
the drought of March and lilacs[2]
in the dooryard bloom'd,
we taxi through the city,
and in the distance
fade the White House and the Hill,
but remaining bright
loftly still its mighty dome
looms in its splendor
above the waving treetops,
for we drive away,

(Sageuta)

past the Lincoln Memorial,
off in the distant vista
the flower-mist is trailing
around the Tidal Basin.

(Ageuta)

As the scenes have turned
to April for air travelers
this mid-afternoon,
oh, it must be beautiful!
America! America![3]
God shed his grace on thee
and crown thy good with brotherhood,
from sea to shining sea,
bright beneath the deep blue sky
flying, past the clouds that drift
far and far away[4]
landing lights below
mark our descent to Memphis
we have come at last

490

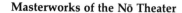

to the airport at Memphis
we have come at last.

[*The* waki *delivers the following passage, called* tsukizerifu *(arrival speech).*]

WAKI

(Tsukizerifu)

Since we have flown so fast, we have arrived at Memphis at sunset. Let us quickly take the bus downtown to the riverfront, while the light is still above the city skyline. There we will look around and ask about a place for the night.

Ha First Dan

[*The* shite, *an old man, and the* tsure, *his companion, enter and proceed slowly down the Nō bridge onto the stage. The* shite *faces the audience and sings the following passage, called* sashi.]

SHITE

[2] *(Sashi)*

How delightful all appears
in this spring season
for the aged oak shelters birds
warbling joyously
and their morning songs will ring
from its leafy folds.

(Issei)

Along the river
to the sloping field in flower
opening in the breeze
the landscapes are enchanting
in the setting sun.

(Sashi)

There behind the shadowed hill
now a voice begins
singing old spirituals
in the echo of the bell
tolling on this eve.

[*The* shite *and* tsure *sing the following passage, called* sageuta, *low-pitched song.*]

SHITE AND TSURE

(Sageuta)

Steal away, steal away,[5]
steal away to Jesus.
Steal away, steal away home,
I hain't got long to stay here.

Martin Luther King, Jr.: A Nō Play

SHITE

My Lord He calls me,
He calls me by the thunder,

TSURE

the trumpet sounds within-a my soul,
I hain't got long to stay here,

SHITE **AND** **T**SURE [*Switch to low-pitched* ageuta.]

(*Ageuta*)

but life should not be weary,
since at Independence Hall,
still at Independence Hall
we can hear the trailing sound
of the Liberty Bell!
How it tolled!
How it told
of the future clear and loud
proclaimed this nation's freedom
and independence
to the four corners of the earth,
telling still the truth that all
men are created equal,

TSURE

created equal,

SHITE

telling still the truth that all
men are created equal,
in this trouble-ridden world
as night approaches,
in this trouble-ridden world
as night approaches
from the darkening trees in bloom
trailing through the dusk.

492

Ha Second Dan

[*The* waki *rises and faces the* shite. *The following exchange between them is called the* mondai.]

WAKI

[3] (*Mondai*)

Ho there, old man. I have something I would like to ask you.

Masterworks of the Nō Theater

SHITE

Are you speaking to me? What can I do for you?

WAKI

Do you live in this vicinity?

SHITE

Yes, sir. I live in this neighborhood.

WAKI

Well then, as the day draws near to a close, would you kindly suggest some motel in this vicinity? Since I have traveled a long way, from Washington to this place, I would like to retire early for sight-seeing tomorrow.

SHITE

Indeed, indeed. First of all, I would suggest the Lorraine Motel[6] nearby. You should keep going west toward the riverfront. You will find the signboard and you won't miss it. As for sight-seeing, on your left, there is an old historical site where you can get all sorts of literature, postcards, and even souvenirs.

There are many noted sites in and around this city. Here close by there is Mason Temple,[7] where a famous speech was delivered at that evening meeting a good many years ago. The speaker was slated to address a meeting of local people, but a storm passed through this city on that day, well into the night.

WAKI

I would like to know about it in detail.

TSURE

That late afternoon I still remember.

SHITE

All heard the tornado warning,
the jagged lightning
rent the leaden skies asunder
with cracks of thunder,
and by nightfall there ensued
the gusty downpour
that lashed aslant the city,
yet at the temple
with so large a press,
television cameras
were waiting for the speaker.

TSURE

As the phone rang,[8]

493

Martin Luther King, Jr.: A Nō Play

SHITE

he went to Mason Temple,,
welcoming the crowd,
and as he spoke, the thunder
rumbled still while lightning flashed
across the window
and against the temple roof.

WAKI

Please continue and tell me about the speaker.

TSURE

Reverend King was his name. Just as his father and his father's father were well-respected ministers, so this speaker was too. He led the march wherever he was helpful—from Montgomery, Birmingham, Washington, Selma, to Memphis. He does not want you to mention that he received a Nobel Peace Prize and a few hundred other awards.

SHITE

That isn't important.[9] It does not matter.[10] It really doesn't matter. I don't know what will happen now. We've got some difficult days ahead. But it doesn't matter with me now. Because I've been to the mountaintop. Like anybody, I would like to live a long life. Longevity has its place. But I'm not concerned about that now. I just want to do God's will. And He's allowed me to go up the mountain.

CHORUS

GO AHEAD.[11]

SHITE

And I've looked over.

CHORUS

YES, DOCTOR.

SHITE

And I've seen the promised land.
I may not get there with you.

CHORUS

YES SIR, GO AHEAD.

SHITE

But I want you to know
that we, as a people, will get
to the promised land.

494

GO AHEAD, GO AHEAD.

SHITE

Mine eyes have seen the glory
of the coming of the Lord.
I have a dream this afternoon.

WAKI

This is the "Mountaintop Speech" I have learned. Please continue.

SHITE

By next mid-morning[12]
in spite of April weather,
the sky grew cloudless,
cloudless like my heart,

CHORUS

for the court approved
the demonstration,[13]

SHITE

as the staff reports to us,[14]

CHORUS

It's time to go to dinner,[15]
all[16] descend the stairs,
but at the iron railing
of the balcony
he stands, and facing

SHITE

a row of poor old buildings,
in some blooming trees

CHORUS

beyond Mulberry Street,[17]
he sees a vision

495

SHITE

of the shining dome
of the Capitol.

Ha Third Dan

[*The chorus sings the* ji shidai, *choral prelude song.*]

Martin Luther King, Jr.: A Nō Play

(Ji shidai)

I am happy now tonight[18]
with no fear of man;
I am happy now tonight
with no fear of man;
mine eyes have seen the glory
of the Lord's coming.

(Jidori)

I am happy now tonight
with no fear of man;
mine eyes have seen the glory
of the Lord's coming.

SHITE

(Issei)

Oh, glory, glory,
for the March on Washington[19]
makes me visualize
another one I'm planning
to lead my people.[20]

CHORUS

(Kuri)

He envisions this
before the iron railing
of the balcony; it is

SHITE

(Sashi)

around the Presidential Mall
people are already thronged,
by morning 25,000
by mid-morning 90,000
and by noon at least
250,000

496

CHORUS

a thousand more are streaming in;
a thousand still are surging in,

SHITE

shoulder to shoulder all singing,

Masterworks of the Nō Theater

CHORUS

keep on singing freedom songs.

[*The* shite *comes out to stage center and sits down while the chorus sings the following passage, which is called* nidanguse *(double* kuse*).*]

(Nidanguse)

They are all pressed together,
thronged on the grassy
tree-skied Ellipse
behind the White House
and below the gentle rise
of the Washington Monument
where those march marshals
are directing them
to the bright reflecting pool,
all marching forward
to the Lincoln Memorial.
They are no soldiers,
but people, people, folks back home
from the southern color belt:
ditchdiggers, black sharecroppers,
cleaning women, janitors,
and among those thronged together
from all directions
there are labor leaders, clerics,
teachers, students, counselors,
gospel singers, movie stars,[21]
black and white, all pressed together,
side by side, all singing.

SHITE

(Ageha)

WE SHALL OVERCOME,
WE SHALL OVERCOME.

CHORUS

Hear old Negro spirituals
bursting loud and clear
into the great refrain
of the Battle Hymn
of the Republic.
Words are the bullets they fire,
hats are the helmets they wear,
and shields they hold are the placards
waving, tossing, swaying,
above the rippling multitudes

497

Martin Luther King, Jr.: A Nō Play

before the statue of Lincoln,
who had issued forth
the Emancipation Proclamation
fivescore years ago.
Now this is the people's park,
and over in the distance,
straight ahead, their Capitol
stately with the shining dome,
and their White House, too,
waiting, waiting eagerly
waiting for them all [22]
awaiting and awaiting
awaiting and awaiting
the major speaker [23]
who addresses them
with his rising voice
in sonorous baritone:

SHITE

(Ageha)

I HAVE A DREAM, [24]
I HAVE A DREAM TODAY

CHORUS

that one day
on the red hills of Georgia
both the sons of former slaves
and slave-owners' sons
will be able to sit down
together at the table
of true brotherhood.
I have a dream today
that one day
a desert state [25]
sweltering with the heat
of injustice and oppression
will turn into an oasis
of freedom and of justice.
I have a dream today
that one day
freedom will ring
from every village
and every town and city,
from every mountaintop,
for I've seen the promised land.
I am happy now tonight
with no fear of man;
mine eyes have seen the glory

498

of the Lord's coming;
no sooner than he finishes
saying the last word
suddenly there is a shot—
hardly can he dodge the bullet
that throws him backward,
down, he crumples to the floor
of the balcony.

SHITE

Men are terror-struck below;
dark horror fills them all
darkness of the dark
shrouds the courtyard instantly
through the sudden rift divine
shines the shaft of golden light

CHORUS

from the mountaintop

SHITE

rare exquisite fragrance fills the air,

CHORUS

and a band of angels comin' after him,
comin' for to carry him home.

SHITE

Swing low, sweet chariot,[26]

CHORUS

comin' for to carry me home.

[*The* shite *performs the* iroe *dance, going gracefully around the stage once.*]

Iroe

SHITE

Mine eyes can see the splendor
of the promised land
where all are free and equal.
I'm really not a dreamer,
but I have a dream.

CHORUS

So he wishes you a dream,
"In your dream you have

Martin Luther King, Jr.: A Nō Play

I will appear before you,"
he whispers softly,
"The Lord is King for ever[27]
and ever King is with you,"
and before he can finish
the final word, he vanishes
in the gathering dusk,
with the coming of the night
he has vanished away.

[*The* shite *and the* tsure *exit down the bridge and behind the curtain.*]

Nakairi (Interlude)

[*The* kyōgen,[28] *a man of the place, comes out to the name-saying seat (*nanoriza*) and recites the following prose passage.*]

KYŌGEN

I live in this neighborhood. It's a fine evening. I will go to the church and attend the service. I haven't been there since I don't know when. So, this evening I think I will go there. [*Noticing the* waki.] Well, there is a young preacher I am not familiar with. As he is going somewhere from someplace, he may be just resting here.

WAKI

I am a young pastor who has come from Washington, since I was offered a post in a little church in a southern town. Do you live in this vicinity?

KYŌGEN

Yes, I am from this neighborhood.

WAKI

If that is so, first of all, please come closer. I have something to ask you.

KYŌGEN

Yes, reverend, what is it you want to ask me?

WAKI

This is something you may not expect from me, but I heard among other things that Reverend King was asked to lead the demonstration in this city. If you know the stories about him, please tell me and let me hear about him.

500

KYŌGEN

How strange that you should ask about such things. Though I live in this neighborhood, to tell you the truth I don't know too much about the stories in detail. But, since we are meeting for the first time, and you have asked me a question, it is not very nice to say I know nothing about it. So I will tell you the story the way I heard it.

I would be most grateful.

KYŌGEN

Well, Reverend King was from Atlanta, they tell me. Just as his father and his father's father were well-respected preachers, so this preacher was too. As a man of peace, he received the Nobel Peace Prize. To churchgoers he appeared a saint, sent down by the Lord.

I think December[29] at Montgomery the Negro leaders met him in the evening and all agreed to boycott the city buses. Early Monday morning the first bus was all empty, and the second bus was too. So it was throughout the day across the city. The students was biking and hitchhiking, old men and women was walking miles and miles to their downtown jobs, and most of the black maids and kitchen help was stepping to the workplaces with only battered umbrellas for protection. For a long time black folks had suffered abuses and humiliations, and now police harassment, threats of every kind, and finally a court order against the black car-pool fell upon them. But the boycott and court battles still kept on until the Supreme Court decision was made in their favor. "It was the miracle of the century at Montgomery." Reverend King's people all shouted in joy.

I still remember the Freedom Rides[30] I've heard about. Black and white boarded the buses together in Washington, D.C., and set out on a journey across the South. As they came through Atlanta, Reverend King had dinner with them and he said that he would help them in Birmingham and Montgomery. Nothing unusual happened until they reached just outside of Anniston, Alabama. There, an armed mob surrounded the first bus and set it on fire. They boarded another bus and when they arrived in Birmingham, they were attacked and beaten by different mobs. A second bus was also later attacked by a thousand armed whites in Montgomery. Several hundred U.S. marshals were ordered out to the city as the violence got out of hand. The I.C.C. (Interstate Commerce Commission) banned all segregated transportation between the states.

WAKI

That indeed gave a death blow to Jim Crow's bus facilities.

KYŌGEN

Yes, sir. Oh, yes, Lord.

WAKI

Please tell me some more.

501

KYŌGEN

Though I forget the name of the Negro organization,[31] it won a court suit to open the town parks to black folks, but Birmingham ordered the parks closed. So Reverend King led the direct-action campaign in the city, which is called Project "C" (Confrontation Birmingham). The first march was not no mass demonstration. As the marchers made their way, they weren't bothered by the police. Then suddenly a group of police blocked the street near City Hall and gave orders to halt. When the marchers kept moving forward, the police was ready for resistance, but the marchers burst out singing and kept on singing freedom songs instead of resisting arrest, while they was herded into police vans. Many mass arrests followed a few days later. Then the Negro community started to unite and demonstrations increased day by day. So the city officials got a court order, stopping demonstrations altogether.

Reverend King and Abernathy protested the court order and led the march the next day and they was arrested. In a dark jail cell, Reverend King wrote his "Letter from the Birmingham Jail." When Reverend King was released after several days, that was the time, he thought, for the big push, but he realized that there wasn't many left outside of jail that could march. That's when Reverend King agreed with his aids to use a Children's Crusade. More than a thousand children gathered around Reverend King and marched on downtown Birmingham, where most of them was arrested. By the next morning over twice that number showed up to march again. The firemen stood pointing high-powered firehoses at the marchers and there was several cops, with German police dogs. When the marchers refused to turn back, the firemen turned on their hoses. Big streams of water hit into children and adults alike, knocking them down and rolling them into the street. Then the dogs was let go and charged into the marchers, jumping at them and biting small children. The next day major newspapers carried front-page reports and tragic photographs of the police brutality. The TV news flashed the same pictures into millions of American living rooms, which brought the anger of Americans down on Birmingham politicians.

Each day the demonstrations grew larger. When Birmingham ministers led more than a few thousand people on the prayer pilgrimage to the city jail and they approached the police barricade, they was told to turn back. When they started forward, the police ordered the firemen to turn on the hoses. The firemen just stood there. They and the cops fell back as the Negroes marched through their ranks. By the next day a few thousand marchers was in jail, but still several thousands was parading and picketing. The police intercepted a few hundred youngsters and dispersed them without arrest. There was no room for them in jail. Birmingham seemed on the edge of disaster. The city's powerful business leaders met downtown to discuss peace. The Project "C" victory indeed made history.

I can still recall clearly the TV picture and news about the March on Washington[32] that summer. It was the greatest crowd that had ever thronged together, as a quarter million Americans, black and white, made a march. Led by Reverend King and other leaders, it turned out to be the largest and most peaceful civil rights demonstration. The gathering was moving and significant. Reverend King's speech was sent straight from heaven.

502

Before Reverend King came to this city in early April a good many years ago, he campaigned to register Negroes to vote in Selma, but I didn't know too much about it. When Reverend King and his party got here in Memphis, several Negroes greeted them at the airport gate and quickly escorted them to the Lorraine Motel. There they had a busy afternoon with meetings and conferences about demonstrations. A day after his famous speech he was shot and killed at the motel's balcony.[33] He died for his people. He was indeed a true peace-loving man.

WAKI

How kind you have been to tell me the story in such detail. An old man came here before you. As we exchanged words, he told me about the places and sites so famous in this city, and he went on to say that here, close by, is the church called Mason Temple, where the famous speech was delivered on that evening a good many years ago, before the demonstration in Memphis. He told me the same thing that you did about the reverend. When I asked him who he was, he said that if I wanted to know his name, I should follow him to the temple of our Lord. And he disappeared into the church at dusk.

KYŌGEN

How strange a story this is that you have told me. Well, Reverend King must have appeared to you and exchanged words with you since you are a young preacher like he once was. You should go to the evening service and offer him a lighted candle.

WAKI

This is indeed a strange thing that has happened to me. I will stay here for this night, so I can offer him a lighted candle at the evening service.

KYŌGEN

If there is anything further I can do for you, please ask me.

WAKI

That is kind of you. Thank you.

KYŌGEN

Not at all, good young preacher.

[*The* kyōgen *goes back to his seat.*]

PART II

Kyū Dan

WAKI

503

[5] *(Sashi)*

Sunset and evening star,[34]
once a poet sang,
twilight and evening bell,
and after that the dark;
the birds retire to rest[35]
in the pond-side trees;

Martin Luther King, Jr.: A Nō Play

beneath the moon the priest
knocks upon the door,

[*The* waki *sings the following* ageuta *passage, called* machiutai, *or waiting song.*]

(*Machiutai*)

as I await the dream
for this night upon the Way;
as I await the dream
for this night upon the Way
we must take and seek
for the holy temple door,
I await the dream.

[*The* shite *enters and moves to the* shite *seat, where he faces the audience.*]

SHITE

(*Sashi*)

As this world is full of dreams,
what you see you dream,
what you dream is my vision
in a form like this
I now return when lilacs
in the dooryard bloom
once again that April night.
April is the cruellest month,[36]

WAKI

April is the cruellest month,

SHITE

April is the cruellest month,
for nineteen hundred
fifty and some years ago
our Lord died for the world
on Good Friday.

WAKI

On Good Friday
sixscore years ago[37]
Lincoln was assassinated

SHITE

and for his country died

504

CHORUS

from a bullet wound, as I
for my fellow men when lilacs last
in the dooryard bloom'd;
April is the cruellest month
with the hermit thrush
singing all alone at eve.

WAKI

Now I find out who you are.
Oh, Lord, your name is King;
you're the Nobel Laureate.

SHITE

That isn't important. It does not matter. It really doesn't matter what will happen
to me now. Because I've been to the mountaintop.

Mine eyes have seen the glory [38]
of the coming of the Lord.

CHORUS

He is trampling out

[*The* shite *performs the* hayamai [39] *dance.*]

Hayamai

SHITE

(Waka)

He is trampling out
the vintage from the harvest
where the grapes of wrath

CHORUS

where the grapes of wrath are stored.

SHITE

(Rongi)

He has loosed the fateful lightning

CHORUS

of his terrible swift sword.

SHITE

His truth is marching on.

505

Martin Luther King, Jr.: A Nō Play

He has sounded forth the trumpets
that shall never call retreat.

SHITE

He is lifting up the spirits

CHORUS

of all of those who suffered
great oppression and injustice
in the trouble-ridden world
the throngs of people
are rising up in protest.

SHITE

Only when it is dark enough,[40]
only when it is dark enough,
can you see the stars.

CHORUS

We see that He is working
everywhere across the land
our God is marching on.

SHITE

Mine eyes have seen the glory
of the coming of the Lord,

CHORUS

and too the bright and morning star[41]
guiding us onto the Way

SHITE

beneath its shining splendor

CHORUS

for the temple of the Lord

SHITE

all pine from every corner,

506

as we chant and march ahead,
marching, shouting joyously,
all together, side by side,
he's let us see the promised land,
he's let us lie down in green pastures,[42]
beside the still waters,
and we go up the mountaintop
as he ascends into heaven
graciously with saintly air
at April daybreak,
welcomed by a band of angels
singing clear rejoicingly,
midst the purple-colored clouds,
FREE AT LAST, FREE AT LAST.

[*The* shite *exits, with slightly bended knees, across the Nō bridge. As he disappears behind the five-colored brocade curtain, he straightens up, as if he is ascending into heaven upon the five rainbow-colored clouds.*]

507

Martin Luther King, Jr.: A Nō Play

NOTES

Frequently cited works have been abbreviated as follows:

KT. Matsushita Daizaburō and Watanabe Fumio, eds., *Kokka Taikan* (The Great Canon of Japanese Poetry), 2 vols. (Tokyo: Kyōbunsha, 1903).

NGS. Nippon Gakujutsu Shinkōkai, *Japanese Noh Drama,* 3 vols. (Tokyo: Nippon Gakujutsu Shinkōkai, 1959–60).

NKBT. *Nihon Koten Bungaku Taikei* series.

Taishō. Takakusu Junjirō and Watanabe Kaikyoku, eds., *Taishō Shinshū Daizōkyō,* 100 vols. (Tokyo: Society for the Promotion of the Taishō Edition of the Tripitaka, 1924–34). *Taishō* citations will give volume number, sutra number, and page and column number.

Preface

1. Sanari Kentarō, ed., *Yōkyoku Taikan,* 5 vols. (Tokyo: Meiji Shoin, 1964).
2. See the glossary for definitions of all Japanese terms.

Himuro

1. Zeami (1363–1443) was a great actor, the head of a distinguished theater troupe, and the author of a large number of the plays still in the current repertoire as well as of a series of critical works on Nō. The citation is from his *Kadensho, Seami Jūroku Bushū,* trans. Shidehara Michitarō and Wilfred Whitehouse, *Monumenta Nipponica* 4, 2 (July 1941): 555.

2. Ibid., p. 553.
3. Ibid.
4. While Zeami makes this remark especially of the opening pieces for night performances, I do not think it violates his thinking to apply it generally to the order of presenting programs. *Kadensho,* p. 554.

509

5. Ibid.
6. *Monumenta Nipponica* 5, 2 (Dec. 1942): 481.
7. For example, *Takasago* deals with the Sumiyoshi Shrine, *Chikubushima* deals with the Chikubushima Shrine, and *Oimatsu* is about the Kitano Tenjin Shrine.
8. Only the shrine of Himuro-jinja, now located in the town of Yaki in Funai-gun in Kyoto Prefecture, might possibly be connected with this Nō. According to Nakamura Yasuo, the shrine is in the mountains, somewhat isolated from the rural houses of the surrounding countryside, and is a rather lonely place, where only children come to play. However, an-

nually on 21 October a festival is held there to honor the enshrined gods, of whom the shrine records give a somewhat garbled history. At any rate, it is a modest rural *jinja* (shrine), not at all well known. *Zoku Nō to Nōmen no Sekai* (Tokyo: Tankōsha, 1963), p. 95.

9. Sanari Kentarō, ed., *Yōkyoku Taikan*, 5 vols. (Tokyo: Meiji Shoin, 1964), vol. 4, p. 2653.

10. Hisamatsu Sen'ichi, ed., *Chūseihen, Nihon Bungaku Hyōronshi*, vol. 3 (Tokyo: Shibundō, 1955), p. 476. One possible translation for *yūgen*, a complex term central to Zeami's thought, is "transcendent beauty." For a translated excerpt from Zeami's discussions, see Donald Keene, *Anthology of Japanese Literature* (Tokyo: Tuttle, 1956), pp. 260–62.

11. Hisamatsu, *Chūseihen*, p. 437.

12. Keene, *Anthology*, p. 26.

13. For illustrations, see Nakamura, *Zoku Nō to Nōmen no Sekai*, p. 86.

14. *Sakamoto Setchō Nōhyō Zenshū*, 2 vols. (Tokyo: Unebi Shobō, 1943), vol. 2, p. 478.

15. *Kadensho*, p. 550.

16. Ibid., pp. 550–51. The bracketed words in quotations indicate the only instances where I have attempted to make Zeami's general terms more specific to the context. Shidehara and Whitehouse most correctly resist the temptation throughout their translation, although well aware of the need: ". . . many technical terms—Hana, Yūgen, Mono-mane—need long interpretation [and] each problem and its solution needs a commentary and interpretation." Ibid., p. 532. For the myriad problems for the translator in handling material of this sort, their procedure of first establishing as literal a text as possible seems to me the optimum method.

17. Mr. Kita indicated in a conversation that because *Himuro* was felt to be a weaker play, the drummer held back, slowing the tempo. In another connection he remarked that the drum at his back was fearsome (*osoroshi*) to him. I took this to mean that it watches him, and he is not free. The counterpoint between the *shite* and drum reaches its zenith in a play such as *Dōjōji*, where the moments of suspended action arising from the patterning between dancer and drum become palpable. In a zenlike paradox, at those moments when the actor is held motionless, he is being the most active.

18. *Hiraki* indicates a conclusion. Three small, almost unnoticeable, backward steps are taken and the arms are held half-extended from the sides, the position in which the *shite* begins the play. It is a difficult moment, as the effectiveness of the exit depends on it. Kita Minoru, *Ennō Shuki* (Tokyo: Yōkyoku Kai, 1939), p. 312.

19. In a conversation.

20. Yamada Chisaburō and James Laughlin, "Contemporary Japanese Art," in *Perspective of Japan: An Atlantic Monthly Supplement* (New York: Intercultural Publications, n.d.), p. 34.

21. The word "Yashima" refers to the eight islands of the Japanese kingdom, meaning Japan.

22. Kameyama no In: Ex-Emperor Kameyama (1249–1305), the ninetieth sovereign (r. 1259–74), third son of the Emperor Godaigo.

23. Kuse no To: Kuseto, located south of Ama no Hashidate, noted for its famous statues of Monju, the Bodhisattva of wisdom and intellect, in the province of Tango in northern Japan.

24. Tsuda: Not yet identified, but probably present-day Murojima, Obama, in the province of Wakasa in northern Japan.

25. Aoba: In the Obama district of Wakasa, marking the boundary between Wakasa and Tango provinces.

26. Nochise: South of Obama in Wakasa Province.

510

27. *Shiratama tsubaki:* "Pearly white camellia," an allusion to a congratulatory poem by Fujiwara no Sukenari (an eleventh-century poet) in the *Goshūishū* (1075–86), an imperial anthology of Japanese poetry. Matsushita Daizaburō and Watanabe Fumio, eds., *Kokka Taikan* (The Great Canon of Japanese Poetry), 2 vols. (Tokyo: Kyōbunsha, 1903), p. 92. Hereafter cited as *KT*.

Kimi ga yo wa	When I take account
shiratama tsubaki	of our Sovereign's glorious rule
yachiyo to mo	the white camellia
nan ni kazoen	comes out forever blooming
kagiri nakereba.	because his reign is endless.

According to Tsuchihashi Yutaka, the term "pearly white" is an epithet indicating "camellia." The flower itself is the main subject used in this poem.

28. *Yachiyo:* "Eight thousand years," or "endless." This modifies the camellia, which had been considered to be a symbol of the strong life-force of the sovereign since the *kiki* period. See Tsuchihashi Yutaka, *Kodai Kayōron* (Tokyo: San'ichi Shobō, 1960), pp. 191–92.

29. *Midori:* "blue." Along with white (*shiro*) and green (*ao*), this is one of the three color words scattered throughout the passage, enriching the texture of the lines.

30. *Midori ni kaeru:* "The blue returns," an allusion to a poem by Minamoto no Michimitsu (1186–1248) in the *Sengohyakuban Utaawase*, #35 743. Matsushita Daizaburō, ed., *Zoku Kokka Taikan* (The Great Canon of Japanese Poetry, Continued), 2 vols. (Tokyo: Kigensha, 1925–26), p. 1055.

Kesa yori wa	The clouds that threatened
yukige no kumo no	with snow-packed shrouds this morning
ato harete	have all cleared away,
midori ni kaeru	graciously, the blue returns
haru no hatsuzora.	to the first sky of the spring.

31. *Haru no Nochise:* The component *nochi* (after) is used here as a pivot device, so the expression can mean either "after the spring" or "spring in Nochise."

32. Himuroyama: Mt. Himuro, or "Icehouse Mountain." In general, this term is used for any mountain that has an icehouse on it. Here, it refers to a mountain in the Kuwada district of Tamba Province, near the capital.

33. *Sore ikke:* "Now, when once the buds." These lines are from the Buddhist work *Kegon Engishō*. Sanari, *Yōkyoku Taikan*, vol. 4, p. 2654.

34. *Geni hōnen:* "A fruitful year," referring to a line from the *Classic of Songs*. Sanari, *Yōkyoku Taikan*, vol. 4, p. 2654.

35. *Chitose no yama:* Literally, *chitose* means a thousand years. This word acts as a *kakeshi* (pun) on the proper name "Chitoseyama" (Millennia Mountain), located in the Kitakuwada district in Tamba Province.

36. *Mifuyu:* "Three winters" (Kita text); "deep winter" (Kanze text).

37. *Mitsuki:* "Native product"; refers to the ice provided for the imperial table. According to the *Engishiki* of 913, the tribute begins on April 1 and ends on September 31. Ice is sent from various provinces such as Yamato, Tamba, Yamashiro, Koshi, and Ōmi. Sanari, *Yōkyoku Taikan*, vol. 4, p. 2655.

38. *Mukashi:* "Long ago," here referring to the reign of the Emperor Nintoku (313–99). See particularly the entry dated 375 in the *Nihonshoki*, which runs as follows:

In this year [375] Prince Onakahiko Mukada went hunting in Tsuge. As he looked down the valley from the top of a hill, there was something shaped like a hut. Therefore he ordered his men to go and investigate. On their return they reported that it was a dug-out house. So the prince called the chief of Tsuge and asked him, "What is that dug-out house in the middle of the field?" The chief replied in awe, "That is the icehouse." The Prince asked, "What does the hut look like? What is it used for?" "The earth is dug out over ten feet," replied the chief, "and it is thatched with grass leaves; pampas grass is spread on the floor. Then ice is gathered and placed there. Through the summer months it does not melt. It is our custom to serve sake with ice in it during the summer heat." Thereupon the Prince carried ice back to the country and presented it to His Majesty, who was pleased. Since then, as each winter season begins, ice is always stored, and at the beginning of June, it is used.

39. *Shisetsu*, etc.: "Purple snow." According to the *Ruijū Zatuyo* (Classification of miscellaneous items), "All ailments will be cured. Depending on the illness take with water or sake. . . . Their names describe their appearance . . . they're like powdered sugar or snow" (Sanari, *Yōkyoku Taikan*, vol. 4, p. 2656).

40. Daiwakoku: The Land of Great Peace. Refers to Yamato Province.

41. Tsuge: Ancient place name in Yamato, which is the present Nara Prefecture.

42. Matsugasaki: "Pine Point" (in English translation), located in the Otagi district of Yamashiro Prefecture, where there was an ancient icehouse.

43. Kitayama: "North Hill" (in English translation); refers to the mountain range to the

north of present Kyoto, where an ancient icehouse was located at a place called Ono, to which Fujiwara no Teika refers in the headnote to his poem (see Sanari, *Yōkyoku Taikan*, vol. 4, p. 2656):

On the day I started from Ono's Himuro Mountain in search of the remaining cherry flowers:

Shita sayuru	Cold and chill it grows
Himuro no yama no	below Himuro Mountain
osozakura	with the cherry trees
kienokorikeru	blossoming so late which seem
yuki ka to zo miru.	like remaining snows unthawed.

44. *Toshi koyureba:* "The year is over." Refers to the lunar calendar.

45. *Tsurayuki:* Ki no Tsurayuki (868?–945?), famous poet who edited the *Kokinshū*, the first imperial anthology of Japanese poetry, about 905.

46. Tsurayuki's poem is found in the *Kokinshū*; see *KT*, p. 2. This poem contains a *kakeshi* (pun) in the original on the words *musubu* (meaning both "to draw up" and "to tie"), and *toku* ("to melt" or to "untie"). The words "tightly" and "loosen" attempt to approximate this pun. Sahaku Umemoto, ed., *Kokinshū, Nihon Koten Bungaku Taikei* (NKBT), vol. 8 (Tokyo: Iwanami, 1967), p. 100.

47. *Sansai:* Heaven, Earth, and Man, according to Chinese tradition.

48. *Kōdo:* "Imperial land" (Kita text). The Kanze text's *kōto*, "imperial design," is a closer citation of a Buddhist prefatory verse. See Sanari, *Yōkyoku Taikan*, vol. 4, p. 2648.

49. *Natsu no hi ni:* "Until the coming . . ." A poem by Minamoto no Yorizane (an eleventh-century poet), found in the *Goshūishū*, an imperial anthology of Japanese poetry compiled in 1086 by Fujiwara no Michitoshi. See *KT*, p. 86.

50. *Tsuchi:* "The earth." An allusion to a poem by Asao, found in chapter 16 in the *Taiheiki* (Record of the great peace), a fourteenth-century historical work that covers the period 1318–67. (See Sanari, *Yōkyoku Taikan*, vol. 4, p. 2659.)

Kusa mo ki mo	Even grass and trees
waga ōgimi no	flourish in this royal land
kuni nareba	of His Majesty:
izuku ka oni no	is there any place, I ask,
sumika narubeki.	where fiends and demons can live?

51. *Ukiyo:* The world of illusion, or the fleeting world, which unenlightened mankind mistakes for the real.

52. *Hi no mono:* "Ice" (*hi*) is used as a *kakeshi* (pun); it also means "sun."

53. *Hatsuharu no:* "In this first new spring." A poem by Ōtomo no Yakamochi (716–85), one of the outstanding poets of the Nara period. The jeweled rake refers to the rakes decorated with good-luck symbols that are distributed at Shintō shrines on New Year's Day, to be used to gather good luck during the coming year. The custom still prevails today. The song conveys an expectation of the auspicious. This poem is numbered 4493 in the *Man-yōshū*, the first and greatest of the many anthologies, the work of numerous editors, of whom Yakamochi was probably the last and the one responsible for the bulk of the work.

54. *Okina:* The *O* in *okina* (old man) serves as a *kakeshi* that also means "word."

55. *Natsukage:* *Na* in *natsukage* is a *kakeshi*, meaning both "summer" and "not at all."

56. *Sumeru:* Used as a *kakeshi*, meaning "to live" and also "clear."

512

57. "Sit" (*shita ni iru*) in Nō refers to the sitting position with the left knee up, according to the Kanze and Hōshō schools, and with the right knee up, according to the Komparu, Kongō, and Kita schools. The left knee is up for the *waki* and the *tsure*, however, regardless of the school. Hereafter "sit" is used in this sense.

58. *Keikō Tennō:* The Emperor Keikō. Perhaps this error (see n. 38) has been purposely inserted to show the *kyōgen*'s lack of historical knowledge and, by implication, his status as a comic figure.

59. *Itsumo no tōri:* "As usual." After their surprise at their actual success, the priest attempts to pretend that it is not unusual.

60. *Kotoriso:* The "Old Bird Measure," which is the name of a musical piece from "Kō-kuri" (the Japanese name for the ancient Korean kingdom Koguryŏ). The music played during the dance is, however, typical Nō music. According to the Kanze text, the dance is to be performed in the spirit of the "Kōkuri" mode, although the dance is in the Nō style.

61. *Isago chōjite wa:* An allusion to what is now the Japanese national anthem, first found in the *Kokinshū* (*KT*, p. 8) with a different first line. The reference to it here seems to be an attempt to enhance the solemnity and importance of the following climactic scene. Cf. n. 194 to *Hagoromo.*

62. *Guren daiguren no kōri:* "Ice from Crimson Lotus Hell, Great Crimson Lotus Hell." Originally these terms referred to the names of the seventh and eighth stages in the Hell of Coldness. They are used here to indicate extreme cold.

63. *Kōri no omote: Kōri* is used as a pivot word in the line, for it means both "ice" and "county" or "country."

64. *Kagami:* "Mirror." Refers to a magic mirror installed at the court of Yama, reflecting everything the dead have done during their lifetimes in this world.

65. *Himuro no kamikaze:* "Himuro's god. . ." Serves as a pivot word.

66. *Yuki:* Used as a *kakeshi* meaning both "to go" and "snow."

67. Kitayama: "North Hill." The element *ki* in Kitayama is a *kakeshi,* meaning "to come."

68. Suwa: A place name in Shinano; it is also used here as an interjection meaning "great heavens" or "good God."

69. Otagi: A place name. The *O* in "Otagi" is used as a *kakeshi* meaning "many," which modifies "places."

70. *Kōri:* Ice. Here it is also used as a *kakeshi* meaning "country" or "county."

Nonomiya

1. Lady Murasaki, *Genji monogatari* (*Tale of Genji*), trans. Arthur Waley (London: George Allen & Unwin, 1935), p. 39. All quotations from the *Tale,* unless otherwise noted, are taken from this translation. The masterly effect of this introduction deepens the sense of the many currents around Genji's life and is a device Murasaki also uses in the case of Princess Asagao. Waley compares it appropriately to Proust's introductions.

2. *Tale,* p. 59.

3. Ibid., p. 154.

4. Ibid., p. 158.

5. Ibid., p. 159.

6. Ibid., p. 163.

7. Ibid.

8. A marriage of convenience for political reasons, but not without its private content.

9. *Tale,* p. 161.

10. Ibid., p. 162.

11. Ibid., pp. 163–65.

12. He is later to remember the expression of Rokujō's spirit as full of "rage and misery." *Tale,* p. 663.

13. Ibid., pp. 166–71.

14. Ibid., pp. 191–93.

15. For a translation, see Nippon Gakujutsu Shinkōkai, *Japanese Noh Drama,* 3 vols. (Tokyo: Nippon Gakujutsu Shinkōkai, 1959), vol. 2, pp. 89–102. Hereafter referred to as "NGS."

16. *Tale,* pp. 191–95.

17. Ibid., p. 192. This close parallel between the two texts has been pointed out by many Japanese critics. Waley's translation is quite free.

18. In his prose works on Nō, Zeami wears many hats: actor, playwright, aesthetician, stage manager, historian, teacher, preserver of secret family traditions, etc. His various pronouncements need to be understood within the context of his role at the moment, as when he seems to equate *yūgen* with the beauty of courtly graces. See especially *Kakyō* in Nose Asaji, ed., *Zeami Jūrokubushū Hyōshaku,* 2 vols. (Tokyo: Iwanami, 1966), vol. 1, p. 358, where Zeami seems to be the master actor, instructing his troupe. For an English translation, see Donald Keene, *Anthology of Japanese Literature* (Tokyo: Tuttle, 1956), pp. 260–62.

19. For pictures of the masks, see Nakamura Yasuo, *Zoku Nō to Nōmen no Sekai* (Tokyo: Tankōsha, 1963), the *deigan,* p. 21; the *hannya,* frontispiece.

20. The *fukai* mask, used by the Kanze school, represents middle-aged women. *Fukai* means "deep," "referring to the deep-set features of a woman who has experienced the vicissitudes of life." NGS, vol. 2, p. xxii. The Kita school uses the *ko-omote* mask, symbolizing the pride, beauty, and confidence of a young girl, according to Mr. Kita, who adds that it "brings out the highest sort of beauty in women." Kita Minoru, Toki Zenmaro, and Kondō Shingo, "*Nonomiya*: Zadankai," *Kita* (December 1965): 11. Obviously the difference in masks used rises from a difference in the tone of the interpretation; the *ko-omote* adds a sensuous beauty to the Kita performance consonant with his total interpretation. For illustrations, see Nakamura Yasuo, *Zoku Nō to Nōmen no Sekai* (Tokyo: Tankōsha, 1963), p. 27 for the *fukai* mask; p. 177 for the *ko-omote* mask.

21. *Kita* (December 1965): 11.

22. Ibid., p. 12.

23. Ibid.

24. While the sound of the Japanese syllable *rin* seems appropriate in an English line, the corresponding *bō* for the wind sound does not carry overtones as it does in Japanese.

25. Nose, *Kakyō*, p. 396.

26. Ibid., p. 376. See also Keene, *Anthology of Japanese Literature*.

27. In the Japanese text, *Rakuyō*. According to the *Teiō Hennenki* (historical documents pertaining to imperial reigns), on "January 15th in the twelfth year of Enryaku (793), the construction of the Heian capital has started. The east city is called Sakyō; the Chinese name is Rakuyō. The west city is called Ukyō; the Chinese name is Chōan." Kuroita Katsumi, ed., *Teiō Hennenki, Shintei Zōho Kokushi Taikei*, vol. 12 (Tokyo: Yoshikawa Kōbunkan, 1962), p. 175.

28. In Saga village, Kadono, Yamashiro Province, northwest of Kyoto.

29. A branch shrine of Ise was built here at Nonomiya. The site is preserved and still visited. The term "Meadow Shrine" is an English translation of "Nonomiya," where an imperial princess stays temporarily for purification rites prior to going to Ise as the priestess. It was once located at Arisugawa, Saga, northwest of present Kyoto. Sakamoto Tarō et al., eds., *Nihongi*, NKBT, vol. 67 (Tokyo: Iwanami, 1967), vol. 1, p. 238.

30. Shintō deities were supposed to be reincarnations of Buddhist gods. Hence the Buddhist priest feels free to worship here.

31. Allusion to her love affair with Genji.

32. Literally, to take possession of the ground. It is always a repetition of the opening verse and states the central matter of the play.

33. The next three lines include a fine example of *engo* or word association, defined by Brower and Miner as the "relation of disparate elements in a poem by the use of a word that has or creates an 'association' with a preceding word or situation, often bringing out an additional dimension of meaning and giving the two expressions a secondary richness" (*Japanese Court Poetry* [Stanford: Stanford University Press, 1961], p. 504). The effect is somewhat like a subtle parallelism. Here the *engo* is "shatter" (*kudakunaru*), which connects "life" and at least five meanings of "dew": the literal dewdrops, which fall no more since the weather is too cold; tears, which wet the sleeves used to wipe them away; the ephemeral, the evanescent; human life, as fragile as dewdrops; beauty, which is frail and fleeting, iridescent with reflected light. These many associations are all perceivable to any ordinarily well-read Japanese. He is given time to seize and enjoy them by the slow tempo of the chanting. As short as the script of this play is, it takes almost two hours to perform.

34. Allusion to Genji's many relationships with women.

35. Extending the meaning from *kusa makura* (pillow of grass), which always connotes travel, I have translated *kusa goromo* as "traveling robes of grass," since the lines contain references to her coming and going between two worlds. However, "robes of grass" does not necessarily connote travel in Japanese. The elaborate verbal play in the text depends on three meanings of *shinobu* (endure or bear, long for, and bracken); "bracken grass" suggests a well-known pattern for printed kimono material. Therefore in the above text, the lover comes clad in a garment printed with a bracken pattern, suggesting unendurable longings. There is a further play on *kite*, meaning both "to wear" and "to come." Cf. the well-known poem in *Hyakunin Isshu* by Minamoto no Tōru (#14), where the added meaning of "tangled" or "confused" emotions (the irregular bracken pattern) also adheres.

36. Rokujō's daughter, Akikonomu. She becomes Genji's ward after her mother's death and through his influence is later elevated to the position of empress.

37. Miyasudokoru refers to Rokujo; it is the official designation for the wife of the crown prince. Sanari Kentarō, *Yōkyoku Taikan*, 5 vols. (Tokyo: Meiji Shoin, 1931), vol. 4, p. 2410.

38. Allusion to the song in the *Kokinshū*, first imperial anthology (*KT*, p. 20):

> As my cottage stands
> at the foot of Mt. Miwa,
> if you long for me,
> call upon me at the gate
> where the cryptomeria grows.

39. See the *Tale*, p. 192.

40. Allusion to a line by Mencius in his *Kaou Tze*, Book VI, Part 2 (Uchimo Kumaichirō, ed., *Mōshi, Shin'yaku Kanbun Taikei*, vol. 4 [1962], p. 423). Zeami uses the same allusion in *Yuya*, where the heroine must conceal her anxiety about her mother.

41. An invention of Murasaki.

42. Probably a well-known Buddhist tag; it occurs also in Book 10 of the widely read *Tale of Heike*. Takagi Ichinosuke, ed., *Heike monogatari*, 2 vols., NKBT, vols. 32, 33 (Tokyo: Iwanami, 1966), vol. 2, p. 282.

43. For events referred to, see introductory note.

44. The following is closely adapted from the *Tale*; see introductory note.

45. A river near Kyoto.

46. *Shirayū*, or in modern Japanese, *gohei*; narrow white strips of paper used in purification rites and here cast adrift.

47. Allusion to a poem by Ono no Komachi in the *Kokinshū* (*KT*, p. 19):

> Desolate and lone,
> I think that I might follow
> like the floating grass
> drifting with its roots cut loose,
> should the water lure me on.

For a masterly analysis of the poem, see Brower and Miner, *Japanese Court Poetry*, p. 222. By the allusion Zeami enhances his own passage; Komachi's renowned beauty and her reputation as a passionate, gifted, ill-fated woman reinforce the image of Rokujō: the echoes of the underlying intensity of Komachi's despair, implicit in the imagery, match the bitterness of Rokujō's poem that follows. According to Tanaka, even in the midst of bitterness, however, there are hints of her coming salvation. *Suzuka*, the river, suggests *suzushi* (cool), while *Take*, a town, suggests *oyako no take*, a congenial filial relationship. In *Chūseihen*, ed. Hisamatsu Sen'ichi, *Nihon Bungakushi*, vol. 3 (Tokyo: Shibundō, 1955), p. 460.

48. A river near Ise. Once they crossed it, the travelers would be considered residents of Ise.

49. Taken directly from the *Tale*, sixth chapter, "The Sacred Tree," *KT*, p. 895.

50. It was not customary for a mother to accompany her daughter, the official Ise priestess, to the shrine itself.

51. Where the palace of *Sainomiya* (head priestess) was located in Ise. *Take* also means "bamboo." See n. 47 above.

52. On being asked, Mr. Kita said of this moment: ". . . I do not move the mask here but move my feeling. To turn to the right in such a way as to seem to vanish is very difficult." *Kita* (December 1965): 13.

53. "Robe of moss" (*kokegoromo*), a standard epithet for a priest; priestly robes were moss colored, symbolizing Buddhistic detachment.

54. Refers to the carriage involved in the famous brawl scene, thus preparing the way for the story; also to the rounds of the seasons, the rounds of fate, etc.

55. Still celebrated in great style in May.

56. Translation of *Aoi no ue*, Genji's official wife.

57. Sins committed in former lives. Salvation can come only through enlightenment or grace of prayer. The Buddhist doctrine of karma, according to which man is condemned to the round of reincarnation, underlies the following lines.

58. See Dr. Toki Zenmaro's deeply perceptive interpretation of this passage; introductory note above. The passages before and after the *Jo no mai* contain some of the most beautiful lyrics in Nō literature.

59. Another example of *engo*: "placed" (*okidokoro*) associates "dew" with "dwelling," thereby attributing to the latter the pathetic, ephemeral quality of dew. There are other subtleties I was not able to render.

60. A pivotal phrase, applying to both the previous clause and the following one. The effect is one of continuity and forward movement. Of the many such phrases in the play, this one is particularly felicitous.

61. The Japanese text renders these two lines in one: *yoso ni zo kawaru*. It can be read either "It was different from others" or "It has changed into something different." In the Japanese text, both meanings are equally and simultaneously operative.

62. I have translated the line according to the implications of the Japanese text since the passage has a limpid, forward flow that would be impeded by a strictly grammatical rendering such as "as the small brush fence . . ."

63. Approximation of the Japanese sounds.

64. An often used figure for the world of flesh and illusion in the Buddhist context. For fuller detail, see NGS, vol. 2, p. 93.

65. This ending is from the Kita text. The Kanze text repeats *gate*. According to Mr. Kita, the omission makes the passage less flat. The same sort of omission occurs in the *kokaki* version of *Hagoromo* and, probably because its effectiveness is generally acknowledged, is given a special name, *kasumi-dome*. A comparable term—*kataku-dome*—is used to designate the above ending. Dr. Toki notes that the continuing process of refinement in the art of the Nō can be seen in a change like this. *Kita* (December 1965): 14.

Funabenkei

1. For a brief summary, see NGS, vol. 1, p. 163.

2. See n. 21, below.

3. Takagi Ichinosuke, ed., *Heike monogatari*, 2 vols., NKBT, vols. 32, 33 (Tokyo: Iwanami, 1966), vol. 2, pp. 389–92.

4. Okami Masao, ed., *Gikeiki*, NKBT, vol. 37 (Tokyo: Iwanami, 1959), pp. 170–81.

5. NGS, vol. 1, p. 165.

6. From his *Kadensho. Seami Jūroku Bushū*, trans. Shidehara Michitarō and Wilfred Whitehouse, *Monumenta Nipponica* 4, 2 (July 1941): 537–38. The term "flower" is central to this work and assumes various shades of meaning as the context shifts; here perhaps it can be understood to imply something of personal charisma. For the curious, I note Professor Furukawa Hisashi's comment that the *kokata* appealed to the homosexual sector of the audience (*Koten Nihon Bungaku Zenshū* [Tokyo: Chikuma Shobō, 1965], vol. 20, p. 346).

7. *Sakamoto Setchō Nōhyō Zenshū* (Tokyo: Unebi Shobō, 1943), vol. 2, p. 449.

8. In this context, a derogatory spectacle or mere theatricalism as show.

9. *Kyō omoitatsu*: *Tatsu* (set out) in *omoitatsu* (plan to journey), serves as an *engo* (related word) with *koromo* (cloth), for it also means "cut out."

10. *Kiraku*: *Ki* (come) in *kiraku* functions as a *kakeshi* (pun) with *koromo* (cloth or robe), for it also means "wear" or "put on."

11. Miyako: The capital, present-day Kyōto.

12. *Jidori*: Literally, to take possession of ground. It is always a repetition of the opening *shidai* verse by the chorus and serves as a refrain that establishes the milieu.

13. Saitō: One of the three complexes of monastic buildings on Mt. Hiei, near Kyōto, the headquarters of the Tendai sect since the ninth century. The other two are known as the East Pagoda and Yokawa. They constitute the Enryakuji Temple. See *Ataka*, n. 108.

14. Musashibō Benkei: One of the trusted followers of Yoshitsune. Yoshitsune is popularly known as Hōgan, his official title. His brother is the Shogun Yoritomo.

15. Mono: Refers to Kajiwara no Kagetoki, an influential captain under Yoshitsune. His deep resentment against Yoshitsune originated during the council of war held on the eve of the battle of Yashima in Shikoku. Kagetoki returned to Kamakura to slander Yoshitsune to his brother, the Shogun Yoritomo.

16. Amagasaki: A port city, located on Ōsaka Bay. Daimotsu Bay lies to the southeast of Amagasaki. Tsu is the abbreviated name of Settsu Province.

516

17. Bunji: The period from 1185 to 1189, under Emperor Gotoba.

18. *Ochikochi: Ochi* (far) in *ochikochi* is a *kakeshi* (pun), for it also means "flee."

19. *Michi sebaku naranu:* "Long before the roads get narrow." Yoritomo, as shogun, had the power to order strict inspections at key barriers along the principal roads to apprehend wanted persons. It was probably in anticipation of this move that Yoshitsune chose to travel by sea.

20. Saikoku: Western Land. It usually refers to districts west of the capital; however, here it means Kyūshū.

21. *Izuru:* Used as a *kakeshi* meaning the moon "comes out," and "leaves" the capital. It implies that Yoshitsune and his ten men, together with Shizuka, leave the capital.

22. *Hitotose:* "A year ago." Refers perhaps to the time when Yoshitsune was preparing to attack the Heike at Yashima on the Inland Sea in 1184.

23. *Tada jūyonin:* "Only ten men or more." This is about the same number of men who follow Yoshitsune in *Ataka.* See p. 396 in *Monumenta Nipponica,* Winter 1972. According to the *Heike monogatari,* they were about 500 strong.

24. *Nobori kudaru ya:* "Drifting up and floating down." Refers to a riverboat used for the trip down the Yodo River. "Ship" in "comradeship" is a related word.

25. *Yo no naka no:* A poem attributed to the god Hachiman. See Kenneth Yasuda, ed., *Funabenkei* (Tokyo: Kōfūsha, 1967), p. 12, n. 10.

26. Iwashimizu: Refers to the Iwashimizu Hachiman Shrine located on Otokoyama in Kyoto. *Iwa* (rock) in Iwashimizu is used as a *kakeshi,* for it also means "to say." "Clear Rock Spring" is the English translation.

27. *Ushio: Ushi* (weary) in *ushio* (tide) is a *kakeshi.*

28. Daimotsu: A beach located to the southwest of Amagasaki City, which has the meaning of "Giant Rock" or "Log."

29. Shizuka: Shizuka-gozen. A famous dancer (*shirabyōshi*) of the late twelfth-century and faithful mistress of Yoshitsune. Beautiful and touching stories are woven around them in the *Heike monogatari, Genpei seisuiki, Gikeiki,* and *Azuma kagami.* See Yasuda, *Funabenkei,* p. 14, n. 13.

30. Shizuka: Here this proper name functions as a *kakeshi* meaning "calm" or "peaceful."

31. *Yūshide:* An older form of the modern *gohei,* a staff with a cluster of white paper strips, which a Shintō priest shakes over worshipers to purify them. Here the strips of hemp cloth are in effect an offering. *Yū* (hemp) in *yūshide* is used as a *kakeshi* (pun), since it also means "to say."

32. *Wakare yori:* A poem by Fujiwara no Kintō (966–1041) in the imperial poetry anthology, *Senzaishū* (circa 1188), edited by Fujiwara no Shunzei (1114–1204), one of the great Japanese poets (*KT,* p. 151).

33. *Kiku no sakazuki:* Allusion to a Chinese legend. Tz'u-t'ung, a young boy unjustly exiled, had been taught a line from a sutra that he was to repeat every day. Afraid that he might forget the words, he wrote them down on the undersides of chrysanthemum leaves. Dew dripping from these leaves gave eternal life and good health to those who drank it. The chrysanthemum festival is based on this legend, which is recounted in the thirteenth book of the *Taiheiki* (Records of the Great Peace). Gotō Tanji and Kamata Kisaburō, eds., *Taiheiki,* 2 vols, NKBT, vols. 34, 35 (Tokyo: Iwanami, 1961), vol. 2, pp. 12–17. See Yasuda, *Funabenkei,* p. 17, n. 17.

34. *Toki no chōshi:* The phrase "to fit" in the English translation means in the original *toki no chōshi,* or a seasonal mode of rhythm. According to the *Ryūchōso* (Book of the dragon's cry), each season had its appropriate musical mode: *soji* for spring, *hyōjo* for autumn, and *banshiki* for winter. In vol. 15 of *Shinko Ruiji* (Tokyo: Naigai Shosei Kabushiki Gaisha), p. 310. See Yokomichi Mario and Omote Akira, eds., *Yōkyokushū,* 2 vols., NKBT, vols. 40, 41 (Tokyo: Iwanami, 1967), vol. 2, p. 431, supplementary n. 50.

517

35. *Toko no yūsen:* From a poem in Chinese by Ono no Takamura (802–52), composed when he was banished to the island of Oki in the Japan Sea. *Wakan Rōeishū,* edited by Fujiwara no Kintō (966–1041).

36. *Tachi mobeku mo:* Allusion to a poem by Genji in chap. 7, "Momijiga" (Celebration of Golden Maple Leaves), in *Genji monogatari,* ed. Yamagichi Tokuhei, 5 vols., NKBT, vols. 14–18 (Tokyo: Iwanami, 1958–63), vol. 1, p. 272. The poem runs as follows: "Longing for

my love, / I can hardly dance a dance / in my present state; / as I motion with my sleeves, / will he understand my heart?" Shizuka is expressing her modesty here as well as her love.

37. *Tsutaekiku:* The story is given in the fifth chapter of *Soga monogatari* (Tale of the Soga Brothers), a highly popular story of revenge undertaken by two brothers. Ichiko Teiji and Ōshima Tatehiko, eds., *Soga monogatari*, NKBT, vol. 88 (Tokyo: Iwanami, 1966), pp. 225–40.

38. *Tsui-ni Go-ō o:* The parallel elements in the Chinese story and Yoshitsune's situation are, of course, clear. Tao Chu-kung is Yoshitsune; King Kuo-chien is his brother, the Shogun Yoritomo; and the defeated King Fu Ch'a of Wu corresponds to the Heike clan. See Yasuda, *Funabenkei*, p. 19, n. 22.

39. *Kō nari:* The passage, taken from the *Soga monogatari,* is based on Lao Tsu.

40. Goko: Another name for T'ai-hu, a lake in Chang-su Province.

41. *Ariyake:* Ari (is) in *ariyake* (daybreak or dawn) functions as a *kakeshi.* In the context of the *shite's* two lines, *ariyake* (*ariake*) means "is," and in the following two lines of the chorus, it means "daybreak" (daywake). The original pun serves deftly in making the transition between the Chinese story and the present situation in the play. In this translation, I have attempted to have the word "awakes" (daywake) convey some sense of the pivotal function of the pun.

42. *Tada tanome:* A poem attributed to the Kannon of Kiyomizu Temple in Kyoto, found in the *Shin Kokinshū,* the eighth imperial poetry anthology completed in 1210, under the aegis of Fujiwara no Teika. *KT,* p. 209.

43. *Idebune:* Ide (comes out) in *idebune* functions as a *kakeshi*: in the original, the passage moves with the characteristic ease and economy of Japanese verse at its best, pivoting on the word *ide,* first meaning that Yoshitsune will rise in the world again or regain his position, and then, combined with boat (*idebune*), meaning that the boat is about to set sail. See Yasuda, *Funabenkei,* p. 22, n. 27. In my English translation, "full sail" is used as a pivot phrase that links the lines that come before and after.

44. *Tokutoku:* Used as a *kakeshi,* meaning both "to loosen" (the hawser) and "to hurry."

45. *Tokutoku to:* Here the phrase is used also as a pivot line, which I imitate in the English translation.

46. *Hitotose:* 1184. Cf. n. 22 above.

47. Watanabe and Fukushima: Both places are now a part of Ōsaka City, from which Yoshitsune attacked Yashima in 1184; cf. note 22 above.

48. *Yūnami no:* Yū (evening) in *yūnami* (evening waves) is a *kakeshi* that also means "say."

49. *Tachisawagitsutsu:* Functions as a pivot or linking phrase between what comes before and after it: in this case, "waves" and "crew." See Yasuda, *Funabenkei,* p. 24, n. 30.

50. *Yūnami ni:* cf. n. 48 above. Here the translated phrase functions as a pivot line, as in linked verse.

51. *Mukoyamaoroshi:* Downblast from Mt. Muko, which is another name for Mt. Rokkō, located in Muko County, outside present Kōbe City.

52. Yuzuriha ga Dake: On Awaji Island in the Inland Sea, facing Mt. Muko.

53. *Kyū-dai:* Ninth generation. Actually, the thirteenth generation. Emperor Kanmu (737–806) was the fiftieth sovereign.

54. Taira no Tomomori: Taira and Heike are synonymous, the first being the Japanese reading, and the second, the Chinese of the same character. Tomomori is the fourth son of Kiyomori, head of the Heike clan, who first established the family fortunes. Tomomori, known for his wisdom and valor, took his own life at the age of thirty-four, after the disastrous battle of Dan no Ura in 1184.

55. *Tomomori:* Tomo in Tomomori functions as a *kakeshi,* for it means "stern."

56. *Yūnami ni:* cf. n. 50 above.

57. *Tōbō Kōzanze:* The five most powerful *myōō,* or protective deities, usually presented in fierce and frightening guises to disperse evil spirits. They are particularly connected with the esoteric schools of Tendai and Shingon Buddhism, more particularly the latter, now centered at Daigoji Temple near Kyoto, where a fine great blue Fudō is enshrined in the upper complex (Kami Daigo). This deity, the best known, is shown with a sword and rope in his hands, while his eyes represent the sun and the moon; he stands in the midst of flames and is regarded as the wrathful form of Dainichi Nyorai, the central figure of the Shingon pantheon.

58. *Ato shiranami:* Shira in *shiranami* is used as a *kakeshi,* meaning both "white" and "not know."

Ataka

1. For a short summary of this cycle, see NGS, vol. 1, p. 163. The NGS translation of *Ataka* appears in vol. 3, pp. 149ff.

2. By the same author, Kanze Kojirō Nobumitsu. Translations appear in NGS, vol. 1, pp. 167ff., and in Part I of this book.

3. A third and new play on this theme is *Hidehira*, by Toki Zenmaro; this play was first performed in 1951.

4. See n. 31, regarding the many felicities of this opening verse, including the justification for my remark about tears.

5. The phrasing here is cumbersome. I wish to express through it the fact that the actors are not intended to be identified with their characters, as they are on the Western stage. This relationship is dealt with in further detail in my introduction to the play *Hagoromo*.

6. For definitions of these terms, see Robert H. Brower and Earl Miner, *Japanese Court Poetry* (Stanford: Stanford University Press, 1961), pp. 503ff.

7. On the *kokata*, see my introduction to *Funabenkei*. Here the assignment of Yoshitsune to a child actor diminishes it as part of the dramatic machinery to exploit the charm of youthfulness and to enhance Benkei's loyalty and faithfulness, which is central to the dramatic "meaning" of the play.

8. In the *utai-bon*, the commonly available Nō texts, no stage directions are given. Actors are expected to learn their art under established masters, through long years of study. Usual scholarly texts give a minimum, generally relating to entrances and exits and to positions taken on the stage. Recently a fuller description has been attempted by Yokomichi Mario and Omote Akira, based on their observations of actual performances. Sakamoto Setchō, that most perceptive of critics, notes them occasionally when he is particularly struck by an exceptional interpretation. In the translation that follows, stage directions are given at certain crucial points; these have been culled from several sources when they seemed to help in establishing the inner line of the play. This particular business is noted by Yokomichi Mario and Omote Akira in *Yōkyokushū*, NKBT, vols. 40, 41 (Tokyo: Iwanami, 1967), vol. 2, p. 175. Hereafter referred to as "Yokomichi."

9. The Japanese text reads, ". . . nani zo to tazunete sōraeba," or "When I asked people what they were." This phrase, puzzling on first consideration since in the previous scene the carrier saw only the heads and no other people, explains how he knows that the monks were running away. It does not appear in the carrier's first description, perhaps because another character would then have to be brought on to give the answer, which would be overly cumbersome. Consideration of why a playwright tolerates minor inconsistencies such as this can provide important clues as to the potential configuration of the play.

10. *Sakamoto Setchō Nōhyō Zenshū*, 2 vols. (Tokyo: Unebi Shobō, 1943), vol. 2, p. 70. Kita Roppeita is one of the greatest masters of recent years.

11. 1121–1206, a monk of the Jōdo sect. He went to China in 1168, and on his return in the following year he was put in charge of the rebuilding of Tōdaiji.

12. *Sakamoto Setchō Nōhyō Zenshū*, pp. 172, 212.

13. Maruoka Akira, *Nōgaku Kanshō Jiten* (Tokyo: Kawade Shobō, 1961), p. 85.

14. In H. D. F. Kitto, *Form and Meaning in Drama* (London: Methuen, 1960), p. 252.

15. Abe Nōsei, "Nō no chikara," in *Nō Kyōgen Meisakushū*, ed. Yokomichi Mario et al., *Koten Nihon Bungaku Zenshu*, vol. 20 (Tokyo: Chikuma Shobō, 1966), p. 364.

16. The late Gotō Ryō, for many years president of the Nō Sculpture Association and creator of many distinguished Nō masks, a number of which are in the imperial collection, said in conversation that there was a sculpture in every line created by the actor on stage, viewed from any angle.

17. These lines, among others, must inevitably bring to mind the fact that the author Kojirō had witnessed the collapse of social order and the chaotic terror during the Ōnin War of 1467–77.

18. The relationship of such terms as *shite* and *waki* to the character represented provides many insights into the nature of characterization in Nō, a subject too lengthy to be discussed here. The issue is dealt with in my introduction to the translation of *Hagoromo*.

19. There are translations in NGS, vol. 2, pp. 33ff., and Kenneth K. Yasuda, *Yuya* (Tokyo: Kōfūsha Shoten, 1967).

20. *Shirabyōshi:* Female professional dancers and singers, usually dressed in white male attire. They first appeared around 1150 and reached their greatest popularity during the

519

Kamakura period, when they enjoyed the favors of influential and highly placed men. See P. G. O'Neill, *Early Nō Drama* (London: Lund Humphries, 1958), pp. 43–46.

21. The qualification on qualification that Zeami piles upon the question of "tear-flavored" Nō is indicative of the austere kind of enjoyable experience he had in mind; in his advice to playwrights, he says, "When it comes to a meeting between parent and child, or brothers and sisters, you may end the Nō with effects to bring out a little the feeling of Nō flavored by tears." Quoted in Nose Asaji, ed., *Zeami Jūrokubushū Hyōshaku*, 2 vols. (Tokyo: Iwanami, 1966), vol. 1, p. 630.

22. In his *Kadensho,* in Nose, *Zeami,* vol. 1, p. 159.

23. Part I: I follow Tanaka's division of the play into three sections: Part I, introduction (*jo*); Part II, development (*ha*); Part III, conclusion (*kyū*). Tanaka Makoto, ed., *Yōkyoku* (Tokyo: Kawade Shobō, 1954), pp. 135ff.

24. *Nanoribue* (name-announcing flute): A set musical flute pattern; it precedes the name-saying prose speech of the *waki* and is so strongly introductory that it often serves as entry music, substituting for the conventional *waki-shidai* entry, as it does here.

25. Kaga no Kuni Togashi: Kaga is the former name for the present Ishikawa Prefecture in which Togashi is located in Ishikawa County.

26. Yoritomo and Yoshitsune: Yoritomo is the head of the Minamoto clan; Yoshitsune is his younger brother.

27. Hōgan: A rank bestowed on Yoshitsune, which came to identify him as if it were his name; for details see NGS, vol. 1, p. 163, nn. 1–3.

28. Oku: Also known as Ōshū, in the northern part of Japan.

29. *Yamabushi:* A mountain monk or priest who belongs to the esoteric Buddhist order and carries a diamond staff (see n. 63) and a trumpet (conch) shell.

30. *Shidai:* A term applicable to both a musical pattern and a lyrical one, it is most often used to introduce the *waki* and/or his followers at the beginning of a play. Its use here to introduce the main actor is unusual. Only in 32 of the 235 plays in the present repertory does the *shite* enter on *shidai* music and verse. (See introduction to *Hagoromo.*) It often expresses in an "enigmatic" way, to use Waley's word, the affective theme of the play.

31. *Tabi no koromo wa . . . . :* This *shidai* verse is a splendid example of the rich texture of Japanese poetry as it exploits the full potential of the language. The second line can also read: hanging (*kake*) from dwarf bamboo (*suzu* read as *shino*). Bamboo is an *engo* (word association) for dew (*tsuyu*) in the next line, connoting tears, sorrow, the ephemeral. (For the many meanings of dew, see n. 33 to *Nonomiya.*) Now the dew is hanging from the bamboo leaves. Their sleeves are soaked by the literal dews and their tears, which they wipe away with their sleeves, connoting sorrow over the ephemeral fortunes of human life. The last line applies not only to their limp sleeves but to their hopes and thus foreshadows their tragic end. Thus, along with the surface, literal meaning flow secondary statements of deep richness; both levels of meaning serve to move the play forward, particularly in the variation in the following verse by the baggage carrier. The above verse occurs also as the opening *shidai* of two other Nō plays: *Settai,* attributed to Miyamasu, and *Kurozuka,* by an unknown author.

32. *Ore ga koromo wa:* Normally this verse would be an exact repetition of the last four lines of the preceding *shidai* verse and would be classed as a *jidori. Jidori* are sung by the chorus in a lower pitch than that of the *shidai* and in a different rhythmic pattern. Through the repeated lines of the *shidai* and *jidori,* which serve as a closure pattern, the basic tonality of the play is set. Here, however, where slightly humorous variations appear as the baggage carrier, a comic character, imitates the monks, the verse cannot technically be called a *jidori* but functions in the same way. The subtlety of the playwright in thus projecting over the enigmatic, fateful sonority of the *shidai* the gayer touch of this verse is most pleasurably adroit. The richly poetic ambiguity of the *shidai* becomes in the *gōriki*'s version appropriately explicit and plain. Bamboo branches no longer drop dew; they tear clothes. In addition, the verse foreshadows the concluding scene of the play, with its lightly rollicking drinking party. This gay, uplifted note is carried over to the reference to Hung-men (see n. 34), but immediately the picture darkens. The shields here at Miyako are broken.

33. *Sashi:* Verse sections so marked are comparable to recitative passages in Western opera. There is a simple melodic movement with some ornamentation. For *sashi* in Western notation, see Tatsuo Minagawa, "Japanese Noh Music," *Journal of the American Musicological Society* 10 (Fall 1956): 190.

520

34. Kōmon: Hung-men. A reference to the thirty-fifth story in the section "Retsuden" of the ancient Chinese history *Shiki*. When Kao-tzu, founder of the dynasty, met Hsiang Yu of Chu at Hung-men in 206 B.C., the latter's retainer tried to kill Kao-tzu during a sword dance. Kao-tzu's follower parried the blow with his shield and saved his master. Noguchi Sadao et al., eds., *Shiki, Chūgoku Koten Bungaku Zenshū*, vol. 5 (Tokyo: Heibonsha, 1959), vol. 2, p. 220.

35. *Tabigoromo: Goromo* (clothes) in *tabigoromo* is an *engo* (related word) with *yabure* (broken), *himo* (cord or strand), and *haru* (stretch).

36. *Hi mo harubaru: Hi* (day or sun) and *mo* (too) function as *kakeshi* (puns), for *himo* as combined *hi* and *mo* means "cord" or "strand." Here *haru* (far) in *harubaru* is a *kakeshi*, for it also means "stretch."

37. Koshiji: Koshi is the old name for the seven provinces to the north of the capital, bordering on the Japan Sea. It also serves as a pun, for it means "to cross" or "crossing." Koshiji refers to the *Hokurikudo*; see n. 65.

38. Ise no Saburō: Ise Saburō Yoshimori, Yoshitsune's vassal.

39. Suruga no Jirō: Suruga Jirō Kiyoshige, Yoshitsune's servant.

40. Kataoka: Kataoka Hachirō Hirotsune from Mutsu.

41. Mashio: Mashio Jūrō Gonnokami (Provincial Chief) Kanefusa, the keeper of Yoshitsune's first and legitimate wife.

42. Hitachibō: Hitachibō Kaison, originally a warrior-priest (*sōhei*) of the Miidera Temple.

43. *Shirayuki no: Shira* (white) in *shirayuki* is a *kakeshi* (pun), for it also means "not know."

44. *Ageuta*: Song in the high-pitch range, of varying length, sung by either the chorus or actors, that deals with lyrics in a moderately heightened manner. It may appear at several points throughout a play. See William P. Malm, *Nagauta* (Tokyo: Tuttle, 1963), pp. 29ff.

45. Kisaragi: Yoshitsune and his followers left the capital in February 1187, according to *Azuma kagami*, or on February 2, 1186, according to *Gikeiki*. Two of his most splendid victories took place in February of other years; the text repeats "the second month" three times, suggesting the tragic contrast in his fall from fortune. This nuance is perhaps brought out by the quality and varying tempo of singing.

46. *Kore ya kono*: A poem by Semimaru found in *Gosenshū*, compiled in 951 by Minamoto no Shitagō (911–83) and others. Poem #170 in *KT*. The last word, *seki*, is omitted from the last line. There is a pun on the proper name Ōsaka, which can also mean "hill of meetings."

47. *Yama kakusu*: Allusion to a poem by Lady Oto in the *Kokinshū* (905), the first imperial anthology of Japanese poetry, compiled by Ki no Tsurayuki. Poem #413 in *KT*.

yama kakusu	In the hills half-hid
haru no kasumi zo	how the trailing mists of spring
urameshiki	linger willfully;
izure Miyako no	which is the one, I wonder,
sakai naruran.	marking off the capital.

48. *Sageuta*: Song in the low-pitch range, usually of shorter length than the *ageuta*, sung by either the chorus or actors, often preceding the *ageuta*. It may appear at several points in a play.

49. Kaizu: A port town located on the north shore of Lake Biwa in Takashima County, Shiga Prefecture.

50. Arachiyama: Allusion to a poem by Kakinomoto no Hitomaro (fl. c. 680–700) in *Shinkokinshū*, edited by Fujiwara no Teika and others. Poem #657 in *KT*.

Yata no sato ni	From Yata Meadows,
asaji irozuku	by morning-colored sedges
Arachiyama	on Mt. Arachi,
mine no awayuki	chilly seems the dappled snow
samuku zo arurashi,	lying light upon the peak.

Mt. Arachi is one of the borders between Shiga and Fukui prefectures.

51. Kei no Umi: Tsuruga Bay in Fukui; the shrine referred to is the Kei Shrine.

52. Kinomeyama: Kinome-tōge (Tree Bud Pass). *Kinome* (tree buds) functions as a pivot word with *matsu* (pine). It is located in Tsuruga County, Fukui Prefecture.

53. Somayamabito: "Forest Hill" is the English translation of *Somayama*, located three miles north of Kinome Pass.

54. Itadori: "Timber Haul" is the English translation of Itadori, a small town located at the foot of Kinome Pass.

55. Asozu: "Ramie Ferry" is the English translation of Asozu, located northeast of Somayama in Ashiha County, Fukui Prefecture.

56. Mikuni no Minato: "Tristate Port" is the English translation. It is located at the mouth of the Kuzu River in Itai County, Fukui Prefecture.

57. Shinowara: "Bamboo Fields" is the English translation; it is now part of Kaga City in Ishikawa Prefecture.

58. *Nabiku arashi no:* There is a foreshadowing of the danger that awaits the band here at Ataka; just as the storms are "fatal to the flowers," so here at "blossoming Ataka" (literally, "house of peace") the peace is threatened.

59. Ataka: Located in Nomi County, Ishikawa Prefecture. It is part of the present Kamatsu City.

60. Abiraunken: Even baggage carriers in Nō have great verbal facility. The last line of the poem is an adaptation of the Sanskrit sounds *A vi ra hum kham.* This is a mandala chant in reference to the five elements of the universe—Earth, Water, Fire, Wind, and Air—all of which are embodied in the Mahavairocana Tathagata.

61. *Nani zo to tazune sōraeba:* (I asked what they were). See n. 9, above.

62. *Geni ya kurenai wa:* A passage from *Gikeiki*, ed. Okami Masao, in NKBT, vol. 37 (Tokyo: Iwanami, 1959), p. 59.

63. Kongōzue: An eight-sided wooden staff used by the *yamabushi:* diamond staff.

64. Nanto Tōdaiji: One of the seven great temples of Nara, built on the order of Emperor Shōmu (r. 724–48); however, it was not completed until 749, in the reign of Empress Kōken. The eye-opening ceremony (dedicatory rites) of the Rushana Buddha in the main hall was held in 752. Fire destroyed most of the building in 1180, when Taira no Shigehira, a Heike general, fought with the warrior priests of Kōfukuji. Nanto is another name for Nara.

65. Hokurikudō: The seven old provinces of Wakasa, Echizen, Kaga, Noto, Etchū, Echigo, and Sado. See n. 37, above.

66. *Notto:* Introductory musical piece for various religious characters, both Shintō and Buddhist. It may be played before a prayer is given by a Buddhist priest or by a mountain monk, as in this case.

67. En no Mubasoku: Another name for En-no Gyōja, who flourished in the latter half of the seventh century and founded the sect of mountain ascetics. This half-legendary figure is said to have established monasteries on Mt. Ōmine in Yamato Province.

68. Fudō Myōō: The god of fire. He is said to be the incarnation of Dainichi Nyorai, the great sun Buddha.

69. *Goji (Gochi):* Skt. *Panca jnanani.* The five wisdoms of esoteric Buddhism, which are said to correspond to the five *tathagatas* (Buddhas): Mahavairocana (Dainichi), Aksobhya (Ashuku), Ratnasansbhava (Hōshō), Amitayus (Muryōju), and Amoghasiddhi (Fukū Jōju).

70. *Jūni innen:* Skt. *Dvadasanga pratityasamutpada.* The twelve-linked chain of cause and effect: (1) ignorance, (2) action produced by the preceding, (3) consciousness, (4) mental functions and matters, (5) the five organs and the mind, (6) contact, (7) perception, (8) desire, (9) attachment, (10) existence, (11) birth, and (12) old age and death.

71. *Kue mandara:* A mandala of nine sections used for meditative visualization in the Shingon sect; more technically, it belongs to the Realm of the Diamond Elements of Nine Divisions. It is also another name for *kongō mandara*, the pictorial representation of the nine sections of the Diamond World (*Kongōkai*), the expression of Dainichi's virtue of Wisdom.

72. Taizō: *Taizōkai*, the Womb World, in contrast to the Diamond World. It expresses Dainichi's virtue of Reason.

73. *Hachiyō no renge:* Eight-petaled lotus blooms. According to Shingon teaching, a symbol of the heart that man originally possessed.

74. *Aun no niji o tonae:* The sounds signify the great beginning (ah) and the great ending (om), associated with the two *niō*, or guardian deities of Buddhist temples. The words "we chant" (*tonae*) are intended as a pivot phrase to introduce the next line, which is a well-known tag.

522

75. Yuya Gongen: Gongen is the title of honor given to a Buddha who appears in another guise. In this case, he manifests himself as a Japanese deity at the Yuya Shrine, an important Shintō shrine in Kii Province to which all the *yamabushi* pay deep homage.

76. *Daion kyoshu:* An honorific title for Shakyamuni.

77. *Aki no tsuki:* "The moon in autumn" is the English translation. Buddhist symbol of pure wisdom.

78. Shōmu: Emperor Shōmu. See n. 64, above.

79. Fujin: Empress Kōmyō, who, in fact, outlived Emperor Shōmu.

80. Rushanabutsu: The shortened form of Birushana-butsu, Vairocana, who is Dainichi Nyorai.

81. Shunjōbō Chōgen: The Jōdo priest, the student of Hōnen. He received an imperial order to rebuild the Tōdaiji Temple, which was destroyed by fire in 1180. See n. 64, above.

82. Hachiman: The spirit of Emperor Ōjin (201–69), enshrined as the guardian deity of the Minamoto clan.

83. *Kuri:* First section of a three-part musical unit marked by the most melodious and heightened musical effects in the play. It is in a higher pitch than the *ageuta* and calls for an ample and splendid attack in the singing of it. The lyrics, sung by the chorus, have no set pattern. The three parts of the unit, the *kuri, sashi,* and *kuse,* are traditionally compared to a waterfall, flowing water, and a deep pool.

84. *Masse:* The later stage of time. A period of corruption, to last from 1,500 to 10,000 years after the passing of Buddha.

85. *Geni ya . . . ka o mite:* This phrase refers to the passage in the Buddhist sutra called *Ingakyō,* which is the shortened title for the *Kako Genzai Ingakyō Sutra.* This work is a life of the Buddha. "Desirous of knowing the basis of the past, examine its outcome in the present. Desirous of knowing the outcome in the future, examine its basis in the present" (*Taishō,* vol. 30, No. 189, 620c–653b).

86. *Kisaragi:* Ki in Kisaragi (the second month) is a *kakeshi* (pun), for it means "come."

87. *Iguse:* The last section of the three-part musical unit, which may also be referred to as *kuse.* The lyrics, often referred to as *kuse,* have no set pattern. It is the most melodious and delicate of the three parts. When the singing of the chorus is accompanied by the dance of the *shite,* it is called *maiguse* (dance *kuse*); without the dance, it is *iguse.*

88. *Kabane o:* A reference to the decisive battle at Dan no Ura, near Shimo no Seki, where Yoshitsune crushed the Heike forces.

89. *Nami: Na* in *nami* (wave) is a *kakeshi* (pun), for it means "not."

90. *Fūha ni / mi o makase:* A reference to Yoshitsune's voyage when he attacked Yashima on February 18, 1185.

91. *Batei mo miezu:* A reference to Yoshitsune when he lost his way in snow over Hiedorigoe Pass before the attack on the Heike rear during the battle at Ichi no Tani on February 2, 1184. See *Atsumori,* n. 13.

92. *Umi sukoshi aru:* A passage from the *Tale of Genji.*

93. Suma: Located west of present-day Kobe on the Inland Sea; *su* in Suma is a *kakeshi* (pun), for it means "does."

94. Akashi: Located west of Suma, on the same stretch of beach.

95. *Tokaku: To* in *tokaku* is a *kakeshi* (pun), for it means "strait." The English word (straight/strait) approximates a pivot word in the Japanese text.

96. *Mitose no:* Refers to Prince Genji, who lived at Suma for three years. Yokomichi, vol. 2, p. 179, n. 39.

97. *Itazura ni:* A pivot phrase.

98. *Sugu naru hito wa:* Refers to Yoshitsune.

99. *Zanshin wa:* Refers to Kajiwara no Kagetoki. See *Funabenkei,* n. 15.

523

100. *Yo ni arite:* A pivot phrase. The "Way" of the next line refers to both the Buddhist way of divine law and an actual geographic distance. With this first meaning, then, it is difficult to make one's way in the fleeting world.

101. *Tōnan no:* "To the East and South" is the English translation. A reference to Yoshitsune's escape to Yoshino after the mishap on the sea on the way back from Daimotsu in November of 1185. See the introduction to *Funabenkei.*

102. *Seihoku no:* "To the West and North" is the English translation. A reference to Yoshitsune's present journey.

103. *Kurehatori:* Rich textiles as well as skilled weavers came from China to Japan during the reign of Emperor Ōjin (201–69), as reported in *Nihonshoki.* The impact of this event

reverberates faintly even to the present day, when dry goods stores are called *gofukuya* (*go* is another reading for Wu). Hence, "goods from Wu" connotes what is rare and precious.

104. *Ayashimeraru na: Aya* in *ayashimeraru na* is a *kakeshi*; it means "figured" or "twilled" fabric.

105. *Kiku no sake:* Chrysanthemum wine. An allusion to a well-known Chinese legend found in the thirteenth book of the *Taiheiki;* see *Funabenkei,* n. 33. Here the allusion serves as a compliment to the lord of Togashi, who brought the rice wine, which the *shite* compares to eternal, life-giving wine.

106. *Ryū ni hikaruru:* An allusion to a poem by Sugawara no Masanori on the "Feast of the Crescent Stream," observed at the court annually on 3 March. The poem is found in *Wakan Roeishū,* ed. Kawaguchi Hisao, NKBT, vol. 73 (Tokyo: Iwanami, 1965), p. 57.

107. *Sode furete:* A pivot phrase that seems particularly graceful.

108. *Santō no:* "Three towers" or "pagodas" is the English translation. Refers to Tōtō (Eastern Tower), Saitō (Western Tower), and Yokawa, the three main divisions of the Enrya-kuji temple complex on Mt. Hiei. Benkei served as a page at Saitō when he was young. See *Funabenkei,* n. 13.

109. *Maiennen no:* Literally, "life-prolonging" dances. These were entertaining pieces set to music after large, public Buddhist ceremonies.

110. A line from an old popular song (*imayō*), used as a lyric for an Ennen Dance. The *imayō* also appears in the play *Okina,* which is still performed at the beginning of a Nō program presented on particularly auspicious occasions, such as New Year's. The song is found in *Ryōjin Hishō,* ed. Shida Nobuyoshi, NKBT, vol. 73 (Tokyo: Iwanami, 1966), pp. 416, 530.

111. *Ageōgi:* A movement of the fan. See Glossary.

112. *Sekimori no hitobito:* A pivot phrase.

113. *Dokuja no kuchi o:* An allusion to a passage describing dangers, in *Hōin Mondō,* the third book of *Heike monogatari.*

Hagoromo

1. For a study of folklore sources, see Howard S. Levy, "Rainbow Skirt and Feather Jacket," *Literature East and West* 13 (1969): 111–40.

2. Arthur Waley, *The Nō Plays of Japan* (London: George Allen and Unwin, 1950), p. 217.

3. Donald Keene gives figures showing the comparative frequency of presentation of several plays, including *Hagoromo,* in his *Nō: The Classical Theatre of Japan* (Tokyo: Kōdansha International, 1966), p. 52.

4. Introduction to the Kanze *utai-bon,* 1966.

5. Sakamoto Setchō, *Sakamoto Setchō Nōhyō Zenshū,* 2 vols. (Tokyo: Unebi Shobō, 1943), vol. 2, p. 291.

6. For *Yamauba,* see NGS, vol. 3, p. xxvii. For *Taema,* see Sanari Kentarō, *Yōkyoku taikan,* 5 vols. (Tokyo: Meiji Shoin, 1965), vol. 3, p. 1839 (hereafter cited as "Sanari"), and Maruoka Akira, ed., *Nōgaku kanshō jiten* (Tokyo: Kawade Shobō, 1961), p. 255.

7. For example, he advises his troupe that the most accomplished actor is not necessar-ily the best troupe manager, and discusses what skills the latter must have. In his *Kadensho,* trans. Shidehara Michitarō and Wilfred Whitehouse, "Seami's Sixteen Treatises," *Monu-menta Nipponica* 5 (1942): 489.

8. P. G. O'Neill, *Early Nō Drama* (London: Lund Humphries, 1958), pp. 71–77.

9. Such remarks are scattered through his writings. See especially *Kakyō,* in *Zeami Jū-rokubushū Hyōshaku,* ed. Nose Asaji, 2 vols. (Tokyo: Iwanami, 1966), vol. 1, pp. 321–22. Hereafter cited as "Nose." See O'Neill, *Early Nō Drama,* pp. 88–89, for an account of the total number of pieces included in a day's program during Zeami's time.

10. Shidehara and Whitehouse, *Monumenta Nipponica* 4 (1941): 553.

11. Japanese texts in Sanari, vols. 4 and 5.

12. For a discussion of the *waki* Nō, see my introduction to *Himuro.*

13. For example, in *Kadensho,* trans. Shidehara and Whitehouse, vol. 4, pp. 552–54 and vol. 5, pp. 478, 486.

14. *Kakyō,* in Nose, vol. 1, p. 321.

15. Ibid., pp. 326–27.

16. Ibid., p. 329.

524

17. O'Neill, *Early Nō Drama*, p. 147.

18. Nose, vol. 2, p. 278. The perhaps reprehensibly expanded translation is based on the interpretations of Nose and Konishi Jin'ichi, *Zeami shū, Nihon no shisō*, vol. 8 (Tokyo: Chikuma Shobō, 1970), p. 357. For an example of the "important details," see Zeami's stage direction in *Sarugaku dangi* for a passage in the play *Obasute* on the handling of a fan, which instantly magnifies the scope of the play. Nose, vol. 2, pp. 350–51.

19. Makoto Ueda, "Implications of the Nō Drama," *Sewanee Review* 69 (1961): 373.

20. These figures are taken from Masuda Shōzō, "Nō genkō kyokumoku," in *Nōgaku Zensho*, ed. Nogami Toyoichirō, 5 vols. (Tokyo: Sōgensha, 1958), vol. 5, pp. 286–96. Hereafter referred to as NZ.

21. Donald Shively, "Buddhahood for the Nonsentient: A Theme in Nō Plays," *HJAS* 20 (1957): 135–61.

22. Sanari, vol. 3, pp. 1550–51. For a description of how the *taiko* functions in a somber play like *Obasute*, see Kakimoto Toyoiji, "Taiko no koto," in *NZ*, vol. 5, p. 221. He describes how its regular and unequivocal rhythm and the control of its tone color can be used as essential elements in underlining the quiet mood of a play.

23. For other types of Buddhist priestly street singers, see William Malm, *Japanese Music and Musical Instruments* (Tokyo: Tuttle, 1959), pp. 73–74.

24. An example is seen in *Kinuta*, where two *issei* occur out of pattern. NGS, vol. 3, pp. 122, 123.

25. Kobayashi Shizuo, "Nō no ongaku," in *NZ*, vol. 3, p. 75.

26. Kazamaki Kejirō, *Yōkyoku, Nihon koten dokuhon*, vol. 8 (Tokyo: Nihon Hyōronsha, 1942), p. 181.

27. Waley, *Nō Plays*, pp. 209–13.

28. For an account of the reasons for Western characterization of Nō as only serious, otherworldly, etc., see Yasuko Stucki's fine article, "Yeats's Drama and the Nō," *Modern Drama* 9 (1966): 107–108.

29. Nose, vol. 1, pp. 614ff.

30. Kazamaki, *Yōkyoku*, pp. 223–24.

31. Poem #1228 in *KT*, p. 733.

32. Poem #362 in *KT*, p. 178, from the *Shinkokinshū*.

33. Akimoto Kichiro, ed., *Fudoki*, NKBT, vol. 2 (Tokyo: Iwanami, 1956), pp. 457–58.

34. According to Sanari, all five schools of Nō have their own texts of the play, which vary slightly from one another (vol. 4, p. 2495). For a description of the oldest known texts, see Omote Akira, *Kuzan bunkobon no kenkyū* (Tokyo: Wan'ya Shoten, 1965), pp. 84, 154. For the Hōshō text, see Yokomichi Mario and Omote Akira, *Yōkyokushū*, 2 vols., NKBT, vols. 40, 41 (Tokyo: Iwanami, 1967), vol. 2, p. 31. Hereafter cited as "Yokomichi."

35. Igarashi Chikara, "Hagoromo ni yorite kokoromi ni yōkyoku ni okeru kakaru no igi yakume oyobi shumi o toku," *Koku bungaku kenkyū* 2.1 (1934): 1–18. (Published by Waseda University.)

36. Miyake Kōichi, *Shidai kara kiri made no utaikata* (Tokyo: Hinoki Shoten, 1953), p. 160.

37. Miyake Noboru, "Nō no tokushu enshutsu," in *NZ*, vol. 3, p. 190. He states that of the 250 plays in the current repertory, 170 have variant forms; altogether, he has identified 600 *kogaki*.

38. William P. Malm, *Nagauta* (Tokyo: Tuttle, 1963), p. 103.

39. Sakamoto, vol. 2, p. 291.

40. Miyake Noboru, "Nō no tokushu enshutsu," pp. 262–63.

41. Introduction to the official Kanze text (*utai-bon*), 1966.

42. Stephen Orgel, *Ben Jonson: The Complete Masques* (New Haven: Yale University Press, 1969), p. 2.

43. *Yūgen* is usually associated with nonjoyous feeling tones. For example, Makoto Ueda says, ". . . *yūgen*, in its broader sense, has the implication of universal sadness." *Literary and Art Theories in Japan* (Cleveland: Case Western Reserve University Press, 1967), p. 61. See also Robert H. Brower and Earl Miner, *Japanese Court Poetry* (Stanford: Stanford University Press, 1961), p. 266: *Yūgen*'s "characteristic tone was one of sadness or wistful melancholy."

44. *Nikyoku santai ezu*, in Nose, vol. 1, p. 500.

45. Sakamoto, vol. 2, pp. 34, 122.

46. Miyake Noboru, "Nō no tokushu enshutsu," pp. 262–63.

525

47. Nose, vol. 2, pp. 639–44, I, 504.

48. Sakamoto, vol. 2, p. 133.

49. Ibid., p. 291.

50. Malm, *Japanese Music*, p. 105.

51. *Shuo-yüan*, attributed to Liu Hsiang (ca. 77–76 B.C.), Ts'ung-shu chi-ch'eng ch'u-pien edition (Shanghai, 1937), p. 92. I am indebted to Dr. Irving Lo for both the citation and translation. Sanari refers to this legend (vol. 4, p. 2486).

52. *Kadensho*, trans. Shidehara and Whitehouse, vol. 5, p. 482. Zeami's authorship of the play is in question at present. The discussion of this particular point in the *Hagoromo* text, whoever its author, in the light of Zeami's critical writings is not an impermissible procedure, however, since Zeami's writings are in part a reflection of the practices current in his day.

53. H. D. F. Kitto, *Form and Meaning in Drama* (London: Methuen, 1960), p. vi.

54. Sanari, among others, seems to believe the error is unintentional, arising from the playwright's mistake. This would be more credible if the misquoted version fit smoothly into the text.

55. The angel's rebuke is found in the *Tango Fudoki* (Akimoto, p. 467).

56. Igarashi, "Hagoromo," p. 13.

57. Malm, *Japanese Music*, p. 111.

58. On the basis of grammar and meaning, Igarashi finds that if the passage is divided among the *waki, shite,* and chorus, the following allocation would be logical (pp. 13–14):

CHORUS: Kono on-kotoba o / kiku yori mo / iyoiyo Hakuryō / chikara o e /
WAKI: moto yori kono mi wa kokoro naki [the following *ama* is a pivot word: fisherman and heaven],
CHORUS: ama no hagoromo torikakushi
WAKI: kanōmaji
CHORUS: tote [i.e., to yutte] / tachinokeba / ima wa sanagara / tennin mo / hane naki tori no / gotoku nite / agaran to sureba / koromo nashi / chi ni mata sumeba / gekai nari /
SHITE: toya aran / kaku ya aran
CHORUS: to [i.e., to yutte] / kanashimedo / Hakuryō koromo o / kaesaneba / chikara oyobazu / senkata mo / namida no tsuyu no / . . .

I am not comfortable with his interpretative suggestions on the dramatic intent of the allocation to the *shite* of the two lines "Hakuryō koromo o / kaesaneba" (p. 15).

59. The play is classified as a one-act dream-play by modern critics, to distinguish it from the "living-person" play. The device of the dream is more common for solving the problem of credibility for nonactual characters, such as the spirit of the cherry tree in *Saigyōzakura* or the ghosts of persons. The play then is understood to have been a vision of the *waki,* who awakes at its close. The dream section corresponds to what is here called the "play within a play."

60. Keene, *Nō,* p. 29.

61. Ibid., p. 71.

62. Kenneth Yasuda, *Yuya* (Tokyo: Kōfūsha Shoten, 1967), p. 25. "CHORUS: If I follow my lord back / to the capital, / once again, I fear, he may / change his gracious mind."

63. Waley renders this speech in the first person.

64. The confusion is compounded in the Hōshō text.

65. Yokomichi, vol. 1, p. 10. The statement is qualified in later discussion.

66. For example, NGS, vol. 3, p. xxv.

67. Donald Richie, "Notes on the Noh," *Hudson Review* 18 (1965): 78.

68. Keene, *Nō,* p. 26. See Tanaka Makoto and Nogami Toyoichirō, eds., *Nōgaku Zenshū,* 3 vols., *Nihon koten zensho* (Tokyo: Asahi Shinbun, 1965), vol. 1, pp. 37–38. The editors state that the first handwritten *utai-bon* were used perhaps only to help the memory of performers. Consequently, there is little marking in them of the melody or rhythm, and even at times of role allocation of the speeches. This edition uses the *Kurumaya-bon,* the first known date for which is 1683, in which generally only the role is named in allocating the speeches; at times, even the role is not named. See, for example, vol. 1, p. 104.

69. Malm, *Japanese Music,* p. 254; Richie, p. 70.

70. Kita Minoru, *Ennō shuki* (Tokyo: Yōkyokukai, 1939), p. 312.

71. Keene, *Nō*, p. 70.

72. Kondō Kanzō, "Jiutai no hanashi," in *NZ*, vol. 5, p. 59.

73. William P. Malm, "The Rhythmic Orientation of Two Drums in the Japanese Nō Drama," *Ethnomusicology* 11 (1958): 89–95.

74. Hōshō Shin, "Waki kata geidan," *NZ*, vol. 5, p. 134.

75. Ibid., p. 141.

76. For example, "The Masque of Beauty," l. 102, p. 65, or "The Golden Age Restored," l. 134, p. 229, in Orgel, *Ben Jonson*.

77. Tatsuo Minagawa gives the number as "approximately 200" in "Japanese Noh Music," *Journal of the American Musicological Society* 10 (1957): 181. Maruoka (p. 74 and pp. 406–19) gives as a total 255 plays, including *Okina*; he includes 4 *shūgen* Nō and 9 non-classified, composed since the Meiji period. Masuda (pp. 281–97) gives a list of only 232 plays; 1 *shūgen* Nō, 15 new Nō plays, and *Okina*. He states that he has eliminated any play acted by only one school when that play is no longer in their active repertory. He compiled his list through contact with each of the five schools of Nō in 1957. NGS gives the total as 240 (vol. 3, pp. xxiii–xxiv). Each school classifies certain plays differently. Consequently, the figures of the above sources vary for the number of plays in each group. Such differences, while they will affect the figures I give, are not large enough to invalidate the general tendencies I attempt to establish. Sanari's list has been compared to the lists given by Masuda and Maruoka, and to the plays edited by Yokomichi and Omote and by Tanaka and Nogami. Four of the plays in Sanari—*Minase, Nakamitsu, Sekihara Yoichi,* and *Urokogata*—are cited by only one other source. All others are cited by two or more other sources. I have changed Sanari's category for 10 plays since I found him in the minority; this has involved 5 plays in Group IV reclassified to Group V; 4 plays in Group III to Group IV; and 1 in Group V to Group IV. These are, respectively: *Sesshuōseki, Taema, Tanikō, Nue,* and *Eboshiori* to Group V; *Unrin'in, Sotoba Komachi, Tatsuta,* and *Ojio* to Group IV; and *Ikkaku Sennin* to Group IV. *Ikarikazuki* was eliminated from Sanari's list as it was variously classified as II (Sanari), V (Masuda), and IV, II, and V (Maruoka). For only 2 of the reclassified plays did Sanari give only one category: *Sotoba Komachi* and *Ikkaku Sennin*. For the 8 remaining titles, reclassification was made to the alternative group he gave for the particular play. The revised classification based on Sanari is given: Group I, 40 plays; Group II, 16; Group III, 40; Group IV, 95; and Group V, 43.

78. In only one play are the music and verse separated when the *shidai* occurs as part of the *waki* entry, according to Sanari; in *Hakurakuten, oki tsuzumi* music is played and the *waki* gives his name in verse, delivers a prose passage, and then sings a *shidai*. This opening pattern is known as a *han-kaiko*. This opening of *Tamanoi* is also in this pattern, with a verse in *sashi* replacing the *shidai*. Both NGS (vol. 2, p. 127) and Yokomichi (vol. 2, p. 418) show *Kagekiyo* opening with a *tsure* entrance with no musical accompaniment, while the first speech is a *shidai* verse. NGS (vol. 3, pp. 59–60) sets the *waki*'s first entrance, together with the *kokata* and others, in *Miidera* to *issei* music, while the first lines are a *shidai*. However, Yokomichi (vol. 2, 387–88) as well as Sanari (vol. 5, pp. 2992–93) shows both music and verse as *shidai*.

79. These plays are: Group I, *Fujisan*; II, *Tomonaga, Atsumori,* and *Ebira*; III, *Minobu, Higaki, Bashō, Nonomiya, Senju, Uneme,* and *Izutsu*; IV, *Ataka, Aizomegawa, Kanawa, Kantan, Genzai Shichimen, Genbuku Soga, Kosode Soga, Shichikiochi, Shun'ei, Sekihara Yoichi, Daibutsu Kuyō, Nishikigi, Fuji taiko, Matsumushi, Miwa, Sotoba Komachi, Dōjōji,* and *Youchi Soga*; V, *Chōbuku Soga, Zegai,* and *Momijigari*. In five of the plays, the *shite-shidai* entry follows a *waki-shidai* entry; in fifteen, the *waki* enters to a *nanori*; in five to an *issei*; two plays have no *waki*. The *waki* entries in the remainder of the plays are fairly unstructured. An analysis of these plays may be particularly revealing for the comparative weights of entry patterns, and their disposition within the dramatic structure of the individual play. The *waki-issei* entries are dealt with in the following text.

80. Waley, *Nō Plays*, p. 52.

81. Translations of all three plays may be found in NGS, vol. 3. These translations will be cited wherever possible, as musical terms are included in them. The *shidai* can be quite specific for its play; *Shunkan* is an example (NGS, vol. 3, p. 138).

82. *Kurozuka* is known as *Adachigahara* in the Kanze school. Other examples of the same *shidai* appearing in more than one play are found in the following pairings: *Iwafune* and

527

Oimatsu, Kinsatsu and *Yōrō,* and *Takasago* and *Makiginu.* In the last pair, the first four lines are the same, while the last *ku* is different. Noël Péri points out that in the Kanze texts, the same *shidai* can be found in *Atsumori* and *Tsuchiguruma;* the Hōshō text has a different *shidai* for *Atsumori,* while the Kongō and Komparu omit the *shidai* (*Le Nô* [Tokyo: Maison Franco-Japonaise, 1944], p. 129). Yokomichi and Omote name only the Kongō school as omitting the *shidai* (vol. 1, p. 234). Although Péri states that *Sotoba Komachi* and *Tomoakira* also have the same *shidai* (p. 38), the Kanze texts for the two plays given in Sanari do not bear this out (vol. 3, p. 1718, and vol. 4, p. 2239). Péri also notes that *Tamura* and *Ōshukubai,* the last no longer played, have the same *shidai* (p. 321).

83. Miyake Kōichi, *Shidai,* p. 82.

84. Minagawa, "Japanese Noh Music," p. 183. Pitch is not so rigidly fixed in Nō as the word connotes in English; see Minagawa, p. 194, and Malm, *Japanese Music,* pp. 127–29.

85. Kobayashi, "Nō no ongaku," p. 68. He gives a good description of the three basic rhythm patterns (p. 63). See also Minagawa, "Japanese Noh Music," pp. 195–96.

86. Masuda Shōzō, "Nō kyōgen yōgo kaisetsu," in *NZ,* vol. 5, p. 363.

87. Kobayashi, "Nō no ongaku," p. 68.

88. Yokomichi, vol. 1, p. 220; Sanari, vol. 3, p. 1859.

89. For the *ji-shidai* in *Kinuta,* see NGS, vol. 3, p. 122; Miyake Kōichi, p. 127.

90. Miyake Kōichi, *Hyōshi seikai* (Tokyo: Hinoki Shoten, 1954), pp. 14–15, and Yokomichi, vol. 2, p. 11.

91. Miyake, *Shidai,* p. 90.

92. NGS, vol. 2.

93. For a detailed description, see Miyake Kōichi, *Fushi no seikai* (Tokyo: Hinoki Shoten, 1952).

94. Miyake, *Shidai,* p. 90.

95. Minagawa, "Japanese Noh Music," p. 195.

96. For *Hakurakuten,* see n. 78. In three plays, the initial *shite* entry is marked by the *issei* verse alone, according to Sanari (Group I, *Iwafune;* Group IV, *Tenko;* Group V, *Tsuchigumo*). Muruoka shows both *Tenko* and *Tsuchigumo* as having *issei* music (pp. 284, 275). In seventeen plays, the entry is marked by *issei* music followed by *sashi* or unidentified verse, according to both sources: I, *Chikubushima, Ukon;* II, *Tadanori, Michimori, Yashima;* IV, *Ashikari, Kamo monogurui, Sumidagawa, Semimaru, Tōsen, Minazukibarai, Kayoi Komachi, Tsuchiguruma, Minase;* V, *Kōu, Taema, Nue.* In nine of these plays, the *sashi* or other verse is followed by an *issei* verse.

97. For a description of the variations possible on the *issei* entry of the *shite,* see Kobayashi, "Nō no ongaku," pp. 76–79. The god-play *Rinzō* has no *mae-jite.*

98. Miyake, *Shidai,* p. 96.

99. "Yōkyoku no kōsei," in *NZ,* vol. 1, pp. 134, 138–39.

100. *Nōsakusho,* in Nose, vol. 1, p. 624.

101. Distribution of the plays lacking a *kuse* is as follows: I, 8; II, 1; III, 4; IV, 35; V, 20. O'Neill gives the figure as 70 (p. 57), as does Nogami. However, Nogami's computation is at fault; based on his own analysis, his total is 71. Nogami's distribution for plays lacking a *kuse* is as follows: I, 8; II, 2; III, 3; IV, 34; V, 24. *Kannami Kiyotsugu* (Tokyo: Kaname Shobō, 1949), pp. 134–35.

102. This confirms the accuracy of Nogami's prototype; "Yōkyoku," pp. 118–19.

103. Ibid., p. 150.

104. Kobayashi, "Nō no ongaku," pp. 77–78. The *shite* in Groups I and V are to a large extent otherworldly beings.

528

105. I have not included *Ikkaku Sennin,* in which the *mae-waki* gives a long *nanori* prior to singing an *issei,* since the *nanori* itself is a strong entry. Sanari shows the *waki* and *waki-tsure* singing the *issei* in *Uchitomōde* (vol. 1, p. 373); this is a misprint as the footnote shows.

106. The *tsure* enter to *shidai* in *Zenji Soga.* Maruoka (*Nōgaku kanshō jiten,* p. 236) marks the *waki*'s first song in *Sekihara Yoichi* an *issei;* Sanari shows it as unmarked verse. In *Momijigari,* a *sashi* precedes the *waki*'s *issei* verse.

107. NGS, vol. 3, p. 143. Although not designated as *ato-waki* in NGS, Sanari has this role designation (vol. 3, p. 1428). Sanari is not consistent in role naming; for example, *ato-waki* is used in *Zegai,* but *waki* in *Daibutsu Kuyō,* although in both plays there is no *mae-waki.*

108. Sanari, vol. 5, p. 2839; for the Komparu text, Tanaka and Nogami, vol. 1, pp. 304–305. The Kanze text is translated in NGS, vol. 3. Yokomichi and Omote (vol. 1,

p. 125) note the *ashirai* entry from the bridge to the stage in *Aoi no Ue*, a translation of which may be found in NGS, vol. 2. A translation of *Ohara gokō* is included in *Twenty Plays of the Nō Theatre*, ed. Donald Keene (New York: Columbia University Press, 1970), pp. 281–97. Musical and lyrical patterns are not indicated.

109. Roy E. Teele, "Translations of Noh Plays," *Bibliography of Comparative Literature* 9 (1957): 353.

110. The translation of *Sagi* by Gaston Renondeau in his *Nô* (Tokyo: Maison Franco-Japonaise, 1953), pp. 251–67, which he states is based on the Kanze text, differs from the Kanze text found in Sanari, particularly in the allocation of speeches to the various roles.

111. *Nikyoku santai ezu*, in Nose, vol. 1, p. 492. *Shikadō*, Nose, vol. 1, p. 439, using an emendation suggested by Konishi (*Zeami*, p. 141).

112. These figures correspond to those given in NGS, vol. 3, p. xxiii: I, 4; II, 0; III, 29; IV, 2; V, 0.

113. O'Neill, *Early Nō Drama*, pp. 141–42. A fuller English translation of the passage may be found in *Anthology of Japanese Literature*, ed. Donald Keene (New York: Grove Press, 1955), p. 260. *Kakyō* may be found in Nose, vol. 1, p. 396.

114. Konishi Jin'ichi, *Nōgakuron kenkyū* (Tokyo: Hanawa Shobō, 1961), pp. 151, 482. The Japanese text of "Kashū ni iu" is found in Nose, vol. 1, pp. 192–93; an English translation in Shidehara and Whitehouse, vol. 5, p. 485. *Yūgen* is consistently translated as "graceful" or "grace."

115. Konishi, *Nōgakuron*, p. 153.

116. Ibid., pp. 154–55 and 134–35. See also Nishio Minoru, "Sabi" in *Nihon bungaku no biteki rinen*, ed. Hisamatsu Sen'ichi et al., *Nippon bungaku kōza*, vol. 7 (Tokyo: Kawade Shobō, 1955), p. 101.

117. *Kyūi*, Nose, vol. 1, p. 547. (English translation in Keene, *Nō*, pp. 29–30.) *Sarugaku dangi*, Nose, vol. 2, p. 308. O'Neill's interpretation of this passage as pejorative criticism of Zōami's acting may need evaluation. He translates *hie ni hietari* as "It was a very thin performance" (p. 143). However, along with Konishi, Kōzai Tsutomu interprets the passage as one of high praise. Kōzai Tsutomu, *Zoku Zeami shinkō* (Tokyo: Wan'ya Shoten, 1970), p. 192.

118. NGS, vol. 1, p. 128.

119. NGS, vol. 3.

120. In *Sōshiarai Komachi*, the Kanze school: (Sanari, vol. 2, p. 1183) uses the *fukai* mask, which Maruoka (p. 58) says is intended to show deep feeling and is suitable for women around thirty-five. Maruoka indicates that the young woman's mask is used (p. 224) but does not specify the schools. Neither Yokomichi and Omote nor Tanaka and Nogami give the masks for the plays in their books. For *Kayoi Komachi*, both Sanari (vol. 2, p. 763) and Maruoka (p. 153) give the *tsure* mask. This last play is a ghost play in which neither Komachi nor her lover (the *shite*) reappears in her or his "true" form. In it, she refers to herself as an old woman (in a chorus passage where the chorus is speaking for her); the *waki* refers to her as a woman (*onna*, *myoshō*). A young girl or young woman is often referred to as *otome*. In the remaining three plays, the old-woman mask (*uba*) is used.

121. While it is known that the source of the reference to Komachi as an old beggar woman is found in *Tamatsukuri no Komachi ga sōsui no sho*, the question here is why this guise is the preferred one for her in Nō.

122. See Nishio Minoru, "Nihon Bungaku no biteki rinen," in *Nihon Bungakushi* (History of Japanese Literature), ed. Hisamatsu Sen'ichi, 6 vols. (Tokyo: Shibundō, 1955–59), p. 101. "*Yūgen* is the womb from which *sabi* was born." He gives historical background and develops the idea.

123. In *Sumizome zakura*, the mask worn by the *shite*, the spirit of the cherry, is the *magojirō*, a lovely young girl. The play appears only in the Kongō repertory.

529

124. See Shively, "Buddhahood," for a discussion of the Buddhistic doctrine in the plays with "nonsentient" *shite*. See also Stucki, "Yeats's Drama," p. 105, for the way in which religious doctrine appears in Nō: ". . . the secular subject matter reflects the Buddhist or Shintoist attitudes emerging spontaneously as a way of looking at human experience."

125. For the effect of *tsuyogin* on melody, see Minagawa, "Japanese Noh Music," pp. 191–92.

126. Ibid., p. 193.

127. For an example of *sashi* in Western notation, see ibid., p. 190.

128. Miyake, *Shidai*, p. 89.

129. It is marked *sashi* by Sanari (vol. 4, p. 2486), NGS (vol. 3, p. 22), and Tanaka Makoto, ed., *Yōkyoku* (Tokyo: Kawade Shobō, 1954), p. 83. Yokomichi and Omote do not mark it.

130. Sanari, vol. 4, p. 2487.

131. Miyake, *Shidai*, p. 97.

132. For a detailed discussion of the divisions and subdivisions of structure, see Yokomichi, vol. 1, pp. 13–25. Tanaka, *Yōkyoku*, pp. 83–95.

133. Miyake, *Shidai*, pp. 99–100.

134. Minagawa, "Japanese Noh Music," p. 199. "Each successive verse begins at a faster tempo than did its predecessor and continues its own cycle of speeds, so that an accelerando gradually builds up through a whole section or play."

135. Miyake characterizes its dual role as a *mondai-ji*, replacing the *ageuta*, and as an introduction to the *kuri* that follows (*Shidai*, pp. 127–28).

136. See Konishi's astute account of the relationship between *renga* and Nō (*Nōgakuron kenkyū*, pp. 96–98). His arguments seem greatly supported by newly discovered documents. See the interesting account of a documented meeting between Zeami and Nijō Yoshimoto, the minister of the Left and great *renga* theorist, in Kozai Tsutomu, *Zoku Nōyō shinkō* (Tokyo: Wan'ya Shoten, 1970), p. 192. For a discussion of the techniques of linking and of Nijō's critical writings, see my introduction to a translation of *Minase sangin hyakuin*, the best known of the classical *renga*. Kenneth K. Yasuda, *Minase Sangin Hyakuin: A Poem of One Hundred Links Composed by Three Poets at Minase* (Tokyo: Kogakusha, 1956).

137. O'Neill considers that the *ji-shidai* is to be considered historically an integral part of this structure in his "The Structure of Kusemai," *BSOAS* 21 (1958): 109–10. Zeami states that the section begins and ends with *shidai* (*Saruguku dangi*, in Nose, vol. 2, p. 400). Zeami's use of the word *shidai* here may apply to the musical pattern rather than to the whole six-line verse pattern, as an examination of the plays cited below indicates, since the *kuse* in them end with the last four lines of the *shidai*; this suggestion is advanced by Toda Matsusaburō, "Kusemai no kenkyū," in *Engekishi kenkyū*, ed. Engekishi Gakkai (Tokyo: Daiichi Shobō, 1932), vol. 2, p. 42. Sanari shows the fourth *dan* beginning with the *ji-shidai*, rather than after it as Tanaka does. See O'Neill's full account of the relationship between the earlier *kusemai* and Nō in his *Early Nō Drama*, pp. 53–58.

138. The pattern can vary considerably. See Miyake, *Shidai*, p. 128; also Toda, "Kusemai," pp. 41–42.

139. Minagawa ("Japanese Noh Music," p. 191) gives a *hon'yuri* in free rhythm in Western notation.

140. Miyake, *Shidai*, pp. 121–22, and Kobayashi, "Nō no ongaku," p. 70.

141. Kobayashi, "Nō no ongaku," p. 70.

142. Miyake, *Shidai*, p. 122.

143. Ibid., p. 123.

144. Yokomichi and Omote state that the *ageha* forms a part of what follows it (vol. 1, p. 17). O'Neill suggests that *ageha* were regarded in the older *kusemai* as part of what precedes them (*Kusemai*, p. 109). Miyake and Kobayashi make no statement on this point.

145. All descriptions of the music are taken from Miyake, *Shidai*, pp. 123–24.

146. Sanari, vol. 4, p. 2494. In this form, the left knee touches the floor and the right foot is placed flat on the floor, according to the Kanze and Hōshō schools. In the other three schools, the right knee and left foot are used. Masuda, "Nō kyōgen," p. 364.

147. NGS, vol. 3.

148. Miyake, *Shidai*, p. 157.

149. Yokomichi, vol. 2, pp. 10–11.

150. For ways in which irregular syllabication is adopted to the eight-beat rhythmic unit, see Minagawa, "Japanese Noh Music," p. 196.

151. Ibid., p. 195.

152. *Shichijū igo kuden*, in Nose, vol. 2, p. 674. In regard to the romanization *sassatsuno*, on a manuscript copy of the score in Western notation, Tanaka Makoto has *sassa(t)'no*; Yokomichi and Omote concur (vol. 2, p. 329). This is an instance of the specialized Nō pronunciation, which perhaps has risen in part from the singing.

153. Nose, vol. 2, p. 676.

154. Masuda, "Nō kyōgen," p. 362.

155. Since Japanese is polysyllabic and its prosody depends on syllabic count as in

classical Greek, Japanese prosody is, I feel, relatively closer to Greek prosody than to English. Here I try to use both to bring out some of the tonal qualities and internal rhythms of the Japanese poetic line.

156. Trans. Shidehara and Whitehouse, vol. 5, p. 484.

157. Miyake Noboru, "Nō no tokushu enshutsu," p. 263.

158. The other five plays are *Yūgao, Yoshino Tennin, Yōkihi, Sumiyoshi mōde,* and *Giō.*

159. Miyake Noboru, "Nō no tokushu enshutsu," p. 263. In the Kanze school, the *shite* stamps at the *shite* seat when the final verse is concluded.

160. In the *Man'yōshū* poem, Mio refers to a place in Hidaka County in Kii Province. In the play, Mio Point is located in Suruga Province. It is a sandbar, about four miles long, which serves as a curving breakwater for Shimizu Harbor, reaching out into Suruga Bay.

161. Poem by an unknown author from the *Man'yōshū,* the oldest and one of the finest anthologies of Japanese verse, compiled during the eighth century by Ōtomo no Yakamochi and others. The last line in the original poem reads "nami tatsurashi mo" (for the waves may start to rise). Poem #1228 in *KT,* p. 733.

162. Quotation from a poem by the Chinese poet Ch'en Wen-hui in the collection entitled *Shijin gyokusetsu.* Yokomichi, vol. 2, p. 438.

163. *Tsuki* serves as a pivot word, functioning in its two meanings, "fade away" and "moon." Literally the line reads: "The mist (fades away—the moon) lingers." "Paling" in the translation is an attempt to provide a word applicable to both the moon and the mist.

164. English translation of a Japanese place name, Kiyomigata, which is part of the Bay of Suruga between Mio Point and Kiyomi Point, near the present town of Okitsu.

165. Allusion to a poem by Lady Nakatsukasa in the *Shokukokinshū,* compiled in 1265 by Fujiwara no Tameie and others. Poem #866 in *KT,* p. 283.

Wasurezu yo	I do not forget
Kiyomi ga seki no	the seashore pines of Mio
namina yori	that come before us
kasumite mieshi	through the mist above the waves
Mio no matsubara	at the Kiyomi Barrier.

With this poem, the playwright has completed a circular view around Kiyomigata Bay.

166. Attributed to Fujiwara no Tamesuke only in the *Yōkyoku shūyōsho,* edited in 1314 by the Buddhist priest Myōkū, according to Tanaka Makoto, ed., *Yōkyoku* (Tokyo: Kawade Shobō, 1954), p. 85. It does not appear in *KT.* The original poem is given:

Kaze muko	Mistaking cloudlets
kumo no ukinami	drifting on before the wind
tatsu tomite	as the rising waves,
tsurisenu saki ni	ere the fishers cast their lines,
kaeru funabito	there they are, returning home.

167. Related words (*engo*) are skillfully used in this passage: pines (*matsu*) and breeze (*kaze*); sound (*oto*) and voice (*koe*). *Ōki* (many) is a pivot word, applying to both the fishers and their boats.

168. *Masse* has two interpretations: "future generations" and "this corrupted age." It probably operates with both meanings in the Japanese prose. The translation here follows Waley (*Nō Plays,* p. 220).

169. The allocation of speeches in this *kakeai* section is made according to the Kanze text. Even this allocation is not free from the incongruity in the Hōshō text discussed previously. The second and fourth speeches of the *waki* here appear inappropriate. The *kakaru* notation is adopted from Tanaka, *Yōkyoku,* p. 86.

170. *Shioshio to* (sorrowfully, too) serves as a pivot line, both in Japanese and in English.

171. The five signs of corruption are variously listed in the sutras and other writings. See, for example, Hanada Ryōun, ed., *Bukkyō daijii,* 6 vols. (Tokyo: Fuzanbō, 1936), vol. 5, p. 3416. In the well-known *Ōjōyōshū,* written by the Buddhist priest Genshin (942–1017), they are listed as follows: (1) the flowers on the coronet wither; (2) the armpits exude sweat; (3) dust gathers on the robes; (4) the eyes lose their vision from time to time; (5) the heavenly

531

being no longer finds joy in his abode. Edited and translated into modern Japanese by Ishida Mizumaro, *Tōyō Bunko*, vol. 8 (Tokyo: Heibonsha, 1963), vol. 1, p. 55.

172. The original poem from the *Tango Fudoki* has the following last line (Akimoto, p. 468): "ieji madoite" (hiding the road to my home).

173. A legendary bird of the Western Paradise, which sings while still in its shell and is unsurpassed as a songbird. The image frequently appeared on the back of metal mirrors imported into Japan from China and Korea, showing the body of a bird with a human head. It is identified with the bulbul of India. Hanada, *Bukkyō daijii*, vol. 1, p. 601.

174. The description of *shioru* (weeping) is taken from Masuda, "No kyōgen," p. 363.

175. The *mondai* notation is made by both Tanaka (*Yōkyoku*, p. 88) and Yokomichi, vol. 2, p. 327.

176. This is my own description. The Kita text has the direction *yuttari*, or "with composure."

177. The rebuke appears in the *Tango Fudoki* (Akimoto, p. 467).

178. The *kakaru* notation is given by Tanaka (*Yōkyoku*, p. 88).

179. The *ashirai* notation is given by Yokomichi, vol. 2, p. 328.

180. The name of a famous musical composition by one Yang Ching-shu, according to Po Chu-i's own note to his poem "Rainbow Skirt and Feather Jacket." *Hakurakuten*, ed. Tanaka Katsumi, *Kanshi taikei*, vol. 12 (Tokyo: Shūeisha, 1964), p. 44, note. Po Chu-i's attribution is noted by Levy, "Rainbow Skirt," p. 111.

181. *Azumaasobi* is a kind of dance-song performed since the Heian period. Originally a folk dance from the eastern province, it was adapted by the court and performed at Shintō festivities. It is presently performed at the shrine of the ancestors of the royal family at court, and at Nikko, Tōshōgū, Kamo, and Hikawa shrines. See Malm, *Japanese Music*, pp. 43–46, for a description of the ancient musical instruments known to have been used. The Suruga dance is one type of *azumaasobi*.

182. The *jidori* is given in Tanaka (*Yōkyoku*, p. 89) and NGS (vol. 3, p. 27); Sanari does not note it. All three state that the Kanze text was used.

183. The direction is given by Yokomichi, vol. 2, p. 328.

184. The two gods are Izanagi and Izanami, who created the Japanese islands.

185. The ten directions are the four quarters, the four corners (southeast, northeast, southwest, and northwest), and the two directions (upward and downward).

186. In the Palace of the Moon, there are fifteen angels dressed in white and fifteen dressed in black. On the thirtieth day of the month, the fifteen angels in black occupy the moon; therefore, the moon is dark. However, on the first day of the month, one angel in white replaces one in black. On the second, another angel in white replaces a second one in black, and so on, until on the fifteenth night, all the angels who occupy the moon are dressed in white. Consequently, the moon is full. From the sixteenth night on, the process is reversed, until on the thirtieth night, the moon is again dark, since all the angels are dressed in black. This description appears as a note in the *Sankaigi*, by the priest Genshin, which repeats material found in his *Ōjōyōshū*. Genshin refers to 160 different sutras and other writings, according to Ishida (p. 342). It is probable, therefore, that the imagery originates from an older religious writing.

187. The legend of the laurel tree in the moon is mentioned in the Chinese collection *Yu-yang tsa-tsu*. For a certain offense, a man who had studied magic (Taoism) was sentenced to chop the tree down, but each cut he made healed as quickly as he made it. *Dai kanwa jiten*, ed. Morohashi Tetsuji, vol. 5, p. 1013.

188. Poem by Ki no Tsurayuki in the *Gosenshū* (951). Poem #18, p. 24, in *KT*. The last line is longer by two syllables (*ran*).

532

189. In contrast to her previous condition.

190. A poem by Abbot Henjō in the *Kokinshū* (905). Poem #872 in *KT*, p. 17.

191. The end of the first section of the three-part *kuse*.

192. Amaterasu Ōmikami, the legendary ancestor of the ruling family, is enshrined in Ise Shrine.

193. An epithet for Japan. This marks the end of the second section of the *kuse*.

194. Refers to a poem that is now the Japanese National Anthem:

Kimi ga yo wa   Oh, thy reign shall stand
chiyo ni yachiyo ni   forever and forever

sazareishi no	until one grain of sand
iwao to narite	grows to be a mighty stone,
koke no musu made.	till the moss be thickly grown.

195. Allusion to a poem in Chinese by Ōe no Sadamoto, which reads as follows (Tanaka, *Yōkyoku*, p. 93):

Seiga haruka ni kikoyu	The panpipe songs are heard afar
koun no ue	on the lonely cloudlets;
seishū raiōsu	the hosts of saints come down to meet
rakujitsu no mae	before the setting sun.

196. Refers to the purple cloud. Yokomichi, vol. 1, p. 269, n. 19.

197. Mt. Sumeru, over three million *li* in height, at the center of the universe, is made of gold, silver, lapis lazuli, and crystal. The sun and moon orbit around it. Its rays color all space in four directions. *Kōjien*, p. 1034.

198. English translation of the place name Ukishima ga hara, which extends along the seashore to the south of Mt. Ashitaka. "Floating" is a pivot word.

199. This marks the end of the *kuse*.

200. The notation is based on Miyake, *Shidai*, p. 157.

201. A bodhisattva (Mahasthamaprapta) named in the sutra *Amitayurdhayana*, well known in Japan through the writings of Zendo (613–81), a Chinese teacher particularly revered by Hōnen, founder of the Jōdo sect. Together with Kannon, he forms a triad with the Amida Buddha as the central figure. He is one who illuminates the world with the light of wisdom and possesses infinite power. When this divinity goes forth, the world shakes in all ten directions. When this bodhisattva seats himself, the world of seven treasures shakes at once. Hanada, *Bukkyō daijii*, vol. 5, p. 3182. See also Charles Eliot, *Japanese Buddhism* (London: Arnold & Co., 1935), p. 122.

202. The direction is given by Yokomichi, vol. 2, p. 329.

203. For *shinnyo*, see Eliot, *Japanese Buddhism*, p. 334; also Shively, "Buddhahood," p. 142.

204. Probably refers to the Buddha's forty-eight vows or prayers for the enlightenment of the people, which can be found in the sutra *Muryōjukyō* (*"Greater" Sukhavati-vyuha*). Mochizuki Nobutaka, ed., *Bukkyō daijiten*, 10 vols. (Tokyo: Sekai Seiten Kankō Kyōkai, 1960), vol. 3, p. 2891.

205. Various precious stones are included in the several lists as they appear in the sutras and commentaries: gold, silver, lapis lazuli, amber, agate, coral, pearl, crystal, and a black stone carved in the shape of a clam.

206. In the Kita school variant, known as the *kasumidome*.

Izutsu

1. *Kakyō*, in *Zeami Jūrokubushū Hyōshaku*, ed. Nose Asaji, 2 vols. (Tokyo: Iwanami, 1966), vol. 1, pp. 402–403. Hereafter cited as "Nose."

2. Uncle of Prince Koretaka, the son of Emperor Montoku (r. 850–58). He was an intimate friend of Narihira's.

3. *Tales of Ise*, trans. Helen Craig McCullough (Stanford: Stanford University Press, 1968), p. 89. In the *Tales*, the man and woman in episode 23 are unnamed. Just when they became identified with Narihira and Aritsune's daughter is not known. See Yokomichi Mario and Omote Akira, *Yōkyokushū*, 2 vols., NKBT, vols. 40–41 (Tokyo: Iwanami, 1967), vol. 1, pp. 446–47. Hereafter cited as "Yokomichi."

4. Robert H. Brower and Earl Miner, *Japanese Court Poetry* (Stanford: Stanford University Press, 1961), p. 161.

5. McCullough, *Tales*, p. 49.

6. Introduction to *Hagoromo*, this volume.

7. Roy E. Teele, "Translations of Noh Plays," *Bibliography of Comparative Literature* 9 (1957): 357.

8. Marvin Rosenberg, "A Metaphor for Dramatic Form," *Journal of Aesthetics and Art Criticism* 17.2 (1958): 176.

533

9. Arthur Waley, *The Nō Plays of Japan* (London: George Allen and Unwin, 1950), p. 52. Aside from Japanese sources, detailed descriptions of lyrical and musical elements are found in Noël Péri, *Le Nô* (Tokyo: Maison Franco-Japonaise, 1944); in Donald Keene, *Nō: The Classical Theatre of Japan* (Tokyo: Kōdansha International, 1966); and in Akira Tamba, *La Structure musicale du Nô* (Paris: Klincksieck, 1974).

10. See the arrow on the diagram of the Nō stage.

11. William P. Malm, *Japanese Music and Musical Instruments* (Tokyo: Tuttle, 1959), pp. 120–21.

12. For definitions, see Brower and Miner, *Japanese Court Poetry*, p. 507.

13. For the characteristics of free rhythm and a diagrammatic representation of the three fixed rhythms, see Tatsuo Minagawa, "Japanese Noh Music," *Journal of the American Musicological Society* 10.3 (1957): 195–96. For a Japanese account, Kobayashi Shizuo, "Nō no ongaku," in *Nōgaku zensho*, ed. Nogami Toyoichirō, 5 vols. (Tokyo: Sōgensha, 1958), vol. 3, pp. 63ff. Hereafter cited as NZ.

14. The division of *Izutsu* into *dan* is taken from Kazamaki Keijirō, *Yōkyoku* (Tokyo: Nihon Hyōronsha, 1942), pp. 126ff.

15. Ibid., pp. 128–29.

16. See introduction to *Hagoromo*.

17. Minagawa, "Japanese Noh Music," p. 183.

18. Sakamoto Setchō, *Sakamoto Setchō nōhyō zenshū*, 2 vols. (Tokyo: Unebi Shobō, 1943), vol. 2, p. 169.

19. Miyake Kōichi, *Shidai kara kiri made no utaikata* (Tokyo: Hinoki Shoten, 1953), pp. 86–87.

20. Introduction to *Hagoromo*. For the number of plays considered and their distribution among the five categories, see *Hagoromo*, n. 77.

21. Miyake, *Shidai*, p. 96.

22. A prime example of this function of *ya* is found in Bashō's haiku beginning *furuike ya*, where the *ya* opens the dimensions of the poem to include not only the grounds about the old pond but the stillness of a hushed, expanding silence made richly audible by the splash of the frog's plunge into the water:

> Furuike ya,   Age-old the pond,
> kawazu tobikomu   a frog plunges into it
> mizu no oto.   with a plashing sound.

23. W. B. Yeats, *Essays and Introductions* (New York: Collier Books, 1968), pp. 234–35.

24. Introduction to *Hagoromo*.

25. A religious rationale for the division of a day's program into five parts is given by Makoto Ueda, "Implications of the Noh Drama," *Sewanee Review* 69 (1961): 371–73; a theatrical rationale in the introduction to *Hagoromo*. Five plays was the normative number; for variations, see P. G. O'Neill, *Early Nō Drama* (London: Lund Humphries, 1958), pp. 88–89.

26. Introduction to *Hagoromo*.

27. They are *Eguchi, Kazuragi, Genji kuyō, Kochō, Sumizome sakura, Teika, Tōboku, Fuji, Hotoke-no-hara, Mutsura, Yugyō yanagi, Yoshino tennin,* and *Obasute*.

28. Miyake, *Shidai*, pp. 99–100.

29. Their distribution is as follows: Group I, *Urokogata*; Group II, *Tomoakira* and *Yorimasa*; Group III, *Hagoromo* in addition to the thirteen named in n. 27 and the three in n. 31; Group IV, *Utō, Tatsuta, Mitsuyama, Ominaeshi*; Group V, *Kumasaka, Kokaji, Shōki, Sesshōseki, Yamauba*.

534

30. *Seiganji, Sekidera Komachi, Yōkihi,* and *Yuki*.

31. These are named according to the *shite* entry: *issei: Ōmu Komachi, Sumiyoshimōde, Matsukaze; shidai: Uneme, Senju, Nonomiya, Bashō, Higaki,* and *Izutsu; yobikake: Ume, Kakitsubata, Futari Shizuka* (in the last, the *tsure* enters first to *issei* music and *issei* verse); *ashirai* music and recitative: *Yoshino Shizuka, Yūgao, Sōshi arai Komachi, Yuya* (in the last, the *tsure* enters first to *shidai*); *ashirai* music and *mondō: Hajitomi*; no music and *mondō: Giō*.

32. These fifteen plays are the following: Group II, *Tomonaga*; Group IV, *Ataka, Aizomegawa, Kanawa, Shunnei, Fuji taiko, Matsumushi, Miwa, Dōjōji*; and the six in Group III previously listed. The two plays without a *waki* in this group are *Youchi Soga* and *Kosode Soga*.

33. NGS, vol. 3, p. xxvi.

34. In his *Go-on sankyokushū*; cited by Sanari Kentarō, ed., *Yōkyoku taikan*, 5 vols. (Tokyo: Meiji Shoin, 1964), vol. 5, p. 3399.

35. For example, Kazamaki, *Yōkyoku*, p. 139. He adds that "there is no sense of anger or hatred at all"; her love "never becomes a pain that tortures her."

36. In emphasizing the sound of these lines I follow the reading of Yokomichi, vol. 1, p. 279. A famous instance of the imagistic technique described here is in the final lines of *Matsukaze*; for a description in English, see *Twenty Plays of the Nō Theatre*, ed. Donald Keene (New York: Columbia University Press, 1970), p. 19.

37. *Sarugaku dangi*, in Nose, vol. 2, p. 458.

38. Sakamoto, vol. 2, p. 169.

39. Ibid., p. 229. These lines are treated in a rhythmically heightened way; see n. 155.

40. *Three Japanese Plays*, ed. Earle Ernst (London: Oxford University Press, 1959), p. 14.

41. Kita Minoru, present head of the Kita school, goes even further, saying that he moved only his "feeling" and not the mask at one moment in *Nonomiya*; Kita Minoru et al., "*Nonomiya: Zadankai*," *Kita* (December 1965): 13. See Kenneth Yasuda, "On the *Nonomiya* of Zeami," in *Asien: Tradition und Fortschritt*, ed. Lydia Brüll and Ulrich Kemper (Wiesbaden: Otto Harrassowitz, 1972), p. 698, n. 26.

42. *Utai kata hyōkō* (Tokyo: Shunjūsha, 1942), p. 122.

43. Keene, *Nō: The Classical Theatre*, p. 29.

44. Introduction to *Hagoromo*.

45. *Sarugaku dangi*, in Nose, vol. 2, p. 474.

46. Miyake, *Shidai*, p. 123.

47. Yokomichi, vol. 1, p. 17.

48. Masuda Shōzō, *Nō no hyōgen* (Tokyo: Chūo Kōron, 1971), p. 67.

49. Although NGS states that *rongi* is intoned rather than sung (vol. 1, p. xiv), both Minagawa ("Japanese Noh Music," p. 184) and Miyake (*Shidai*, p. 132) indicate that it is a song in the high tones.

50. The reluctance usually arises from guilt and shame, since to remain attached to the world because of negative feelings such as hatred or a desire for revenge does not accord with Buddhistic teaching. Here, because of the *shite*'s purity of feeling, her reluctance arises from bashfulness.

51. *Sarugaku dangi*, in Nose, vol. 2, p. 485.

52. Brower and Miner, *Japanese Court Poetry*, p. 503. *Aware* is, among other things, "a deep . . . awareness of the ephemeral beauty of a world in which only change is constant."

53. Minagawa, "Japanese Noh Music," p. 184.

54. Masuda Shōzō, "Nō kyōgen yōgo kaisetsu," in *NZ*, vol. 5, p. 383.

55. The *issei* as a reentry pattern for the *nochi-jite* is discussed in the introduction to *Hagoromo*.

56. Kazamaki, *Yōkyoku*, p. 139. *Shirabyōshi* usually dressed in white male attire. They first appeared around 1150 and in the Kamakura period enjoyed the favor of influential and highly placed men. See O'Neill, *Early Nō Drama*, pp. 43–46.

57. Sakamoto, vol. 2, p. 169.

58. Yokomichi, vol. 1, p. 279.

59. Miyake, *Shidai*, p. 147. It can also be an initial entry pattern; see *Hagoromo*, n. 96.

60. Sanari, vol. 2, p. 1034, for *Genji kuyō*; vol. 4, p. 2730, for *Fuji*.

61. NGS, vol. 2, p. 170; Miyake, *Shidai*, p. 148.

62. Sanari, vol. 4, p. 2442; Yokomichi, vol. 2, p. 404.

63. Sanari, vol. 5, p. 2996; Yokomichi, vol. 2, p. 388; NGS, vol. 3, p. 63.

64. These eight plays are the following: Group II, *Kanehira* and *Tomoakira*; Group IV, *Kōya monogurui*, *Torioi bune*, *Hōkazō*, *Hashi Benkei*, *Hanagatami*, and *Miidera*. Both NGS (vol. 1, pp. 137–38) and Yokomichi (vol. 2, p. 42) show *Bashō* with the same pattern; the latter also so marks *Yorimasa* (vol. 1, p. 261).

65. Introduction to *Hagoromo*.

66. Miyake, *Shidai*, pp. 256–57.

67. Sanari, vol. 1, p. 409. Interestingly, the last line of the *kuse* and the first line of the following *waka* are the same.

68. Miyake, *Shidai*, p. 146.

69. NGS, vol. 3, p. 51, for *Matsukaze* and vol. 1, p. 88, for *Tōboku*.

70. Introduction to *Hagoromo*.

71. Two exceptions I have noted are *Awaji*, where a pair of seven-syllable lines precedes the dance, and *Yūgano*, where the same seven-syllable line is repeated. The 235 plays were checked for only three dance types: *jo no mai*, *chū no mai*, and *kami mai*.

72. Miyake, *Shidai*, p. 148. The passage can be found in Sanari, vol. 5, p. 3307. Yokomichi and Ōmote (vol. 1, p. 261) mark the line as in the high tones followed by *issei*.

73. Helen Julia Bryant, "An Analytical Study of Music in Nō with Special Reference to the Play *Hagoromo*" (Master's thesis, Australian National University, 1972), p. 19. The author studied Nō singing in Japan for some years.

74. *Sarugaku dangi*, in Nose, vol. 2, p. 474.

75. The following are the percentages for two-part plays in all categories with a *machiutai*: I, 37 percent; II, 90 percent; III, 70 percent; IV, 38 percent; V, 24 percent.

76. These fifteen are *Uneme*, *Eguchi*, *Genji kuyō*, *Kochō*, *Sumizome sakura*, *Tōboku*, *Nonomiya*, *Bashō*, *Fuji*, *Hotoke-no-hara*, *Mutsura*, *Yūgao*, *Izutsu*, *Obasute*, and *Higaki*. Sanari does not indicate the entrance music for the *nochi-jite* in *Higaki*; Maruoka Akira shows it as a special *issei* (*Nōgaku kanshō jiten* [Tokyo: Kawade Shobō, 1961], p. 329). The figure for the number of *issei* reentries in Group III was given as eighteen in the introducton to *Hagoromo*, but if we include *Higaki*, it becomes nineteen.

77. These four are *Kazuragi*, *Seiganji*, *Teika*, and *Yugyō yanagi*. For the last, Sanari omits the mention of music; Maruoka (*Nōgaku*, p. 383) and Yokomichi (vol. 2, p. 125) both note the *deha*.

78. Masuda, "Nō kyōgen," p. 371.

79. Malm, *Japanese Music*, p. 125.

80. These four are *Ume*, *Hajitomi*, *Giō*, and *Futari Shizuka*. Sanari omits the music for *Giō*; Maruoka has the *issei* notation (p. 159).

81. A translation of *Ohara gokō* is found in Keene's *Twenty Plays*; some of its musical patterning is given in the introduction to *Hagoromo*.

82. *Higaki* (Yokomichi, vol. 1, pp. 280–86) omits the *ōnori* in the passage preceding the final choral song, while *Bashō* and *Yugyō yanagi* (Yokomichi, vol. 1, pp. 35–45 and pp. 122–28) both conclude in *ōnori*. Some rhythmic notations are given in Sanari, *Yōkyokyu Taikan*, and in Tanaka Makoto, *Yōkyoku* (Tokyo: Kawade Shobō, 1954); they are not as detailed as those in Yokomichi.

83. Yokomichi, vol. 1, p. 437, and Masuda, *Hyōgen*, p. 66.

84. Introduction to *Hagoromo*.

85. Kobayashi, "Nō no ongaku," p. 43.

86. Masuda, *Hyōgen*, p. 66.

87. The texts in Sanari are used.

88. NGS, vol. 1, p. 175. Translation taken from Kenneth Yasuda, *Funabenkei* (Tokyo: Kōfūsha Shoten, 1967), p. 21.

89. NGS, vol. 1, p. 88.

90. Miyake (*Shidai*, pp. 161–62) notes that the *rongi* following the dance in a good number of the god-plays has in performance the same conclusive function for the dance section as does the *waka*, although the former is a succession of 7–5 lines.

91. Ibid., p. 158.

92. Zeami, *Nōsakusho*, in Nose, vol. 1, p. 606.

93. In the basic *hiranori* rhythm of the *sageuta* and *ageuta*, the distribution of the twelve syllables along the eight-beat line shows the propulsive, continuing movement of the regular *ku* of seven and five syllables. As Minagawa's depiction in Western notation shows (p. 196), only in the first seven syllables is there an element of syncopation, while the last five continue regularly, shown as quarter notes on Minagawa's charts. Even for irregular verse lines of fewer than twelve syllables set to *hiranori*, the rhythmic adjustment between the verse line and the eight-beat phrase takes place in the first group of syllables, while the last five continue regularly (Minagawa's example 15). The placement of the first syllable on the final upbeat of the preceding musical phrase also creates "patterns [that] never seem to lose their dynamism but continue to push forward," as Malm says (*Japanese Music*, p. 268).

94. Yokomichi, vol. 1, pp. 8–10.

95. Introduction to *Hagoromo*.

96. Miyake, *Shidai*, pp. 157–58.

97. Minagawa, "Japanese Noh Music," p. 195.

98. All *kata* are described in the text of the play that follows.

536

99. In the line *nagameshi mo* (rendered here "gazing longingly"), the effect of *mo* (too) is to apply the line to the preceding moon poem and to the following well-side poem. The implication then is that Narihira looked as longingly when he wrote the second poem as when he wrote the first. Thus the intensity of feeling around the first poem is transferred to the second. The Japanese nuance is attempted in English by treating the first *tsutsu izutsu* as the place where he sang equally well the poem of the well curb. (The repetitive "well" in the two lines attempts to approximate the alliteration of *itsu* [when] and *tsutsu izutsu* in the two Japanese lines.) The nuance of the Japanese may soften the incongruity noted, but the moon poem is so well known that it might well be overlooked.

100. Miyake Noboru, "Nō no tokushu enshutsu," in *NZ*, vol. 3, p. 227. He describes five variants for *Izutsu*, as does Maruoka (*Nōgaku*, p. 101).

101. Masuda, *Hyōgen*, p. 68.

102. Kita, *Hyōkō*, p. 127.

103. Sakamoto, vol. 2, p. 229.

104. Masuda, *Hyōgen*, p. 68.

105. Miyake, *Shidai*, p. 160.

106. Sakamoto, vol. 2, p. 169.

107. Sahaku Umetomo, ed., *Kokinwakashū*, NKBT, vol. 8 (Tokyo: Iwanami, 1967), p. 100.

108. See McCullough, *Tales*, p. 54.

109. H. D. F. Kitto, *Form and Meaning in Drama* (London: Methuen, 1960), p. vi.

110. Despite the popular ascription of authorship of the anonymous *Ada nari to* poem to Narihira's wife, the context of it in the *Tales*, as created by the poem in reply, which is one of courtly wit and raillery, makes it inappropriate for the play (episode 17; McCullough, *Tales*, p. 82). As for the anonymous *Azusayumi* poem (episode 24; McCullough, *Tales*, p. 90), popularly ascribed to Narihira, in the *Tales* it is sent to a wife rejected for her inconstancy. The most famous of the six poems in the play, *Tsuki ya aranu*, is identified with the story of Narihira's illicit affair with Kōshi, later an imperial consort (episode 4; McCullough, *Tales*, p. 71).

111. See Brower and Miner, *Japanese Court Poetry*, p. 506, for a fuller definition.

112. Introduction to *Hagoromo*; introduction to *Ataka*.

113. Stephen Orgel, *Ben Jonson: The Complete Masques* (New Haven: Yale University Press, 1969), p. 24.

114. Masuda, *Hyōgen*, p. 69.

115. Sakamoto, vol. 2, p. 169.

116. *Lieh-tzu chang-chü hsin-pien*, ed. Yen Ling-feng (Hongkong: Wu-ch'iu-pei Studio, 1950), pp. 21–22. I am indebted to Dr. Irving Lo for the citation.

117. Ernst describes the walk: "His feet, shod in cotton cloth [i.e., *tabi*], are not lifted from the floor, but are slid along it, the toes raised at each step" (*Three Japanese Plays*, p. 7).

118. The southern capital is Nara. The seven temples are Tōdaiji, Kōfukuji, Gangōji, Daianji, Yakushiji, Saidaiji, and Hōryūji.

119. In Yamato Province, where beautiful Hasedera is located.

120. Yokomichi and Omote (vol. 1, p. 446) give three possible locations for Ariwara Temple, all in Nara Prefecture. By the end of the thirteenth century it was in ruins, as shown in the following poem by Fujiwara no Tameko (b. ca. 1250), which appears in the imperial anthology *Gyokuyōshū* (*KT*, p. 417):

Kata bakari	Only these traces
sono nagori tote	serve here as remembrances
Ariwara no	at Ariwara
mukashi no ato o	where the ruins of the past
miru mo natsukashi	I see with tender longings.

121. In free rhythm, *sashi* begins in the high or middle range, with a simple melodic pattern. It ends in the lower tones. Minagawa ("Japanese Noh Music," p. 190) gives an example of one type of *sashi* in Western notation.

122. The old name given to the general area of Furu, Yamanohe-gun in Nara Prefecture. Yoshida Tōgo, ed., *Zōho Dai Nihon chimei jisho*, 8 vols. (Tokyo: Fuzanbō, 1972), vol. 2, p. 396.

123. See n. 160.

124. *Sageuta* begins in the middle or low range of tones, with the melody moving between the low and middle range of tones, ending in the low range. It is in *hiranori*.

125. *Idatsu*: In this position, one foot is flat on the floor, with the knee bent. The other knee touches the floor, with the foot under the body perpendicular to the floor. The body rests on its heel. Masuda, "Nō kyōgen," p. 346.

126. A play on the name Aritsune and *tsune*, meaning "always," combined here with a negative (*tsune naki*). Aritsune, whose name means "to be forever," has belied his name and is no more. *Tsune naki* combined with *yo* (world) then means a world where nothing remains forever, another formulation of the Buddhistic belief in the ephemeral nature of actuality.

127. *Shitai* or *shita ni iru*: In this position, the foot on which the body sits is parallel to the floor. Masuda, "Nō kyōgen," p. 364.

128. The Kanze school uses the *waka-onna* mask; the Kita, the *ko-omote*, which represents a slightly younger girl. Kita, "Zadankai," p. 11.

129. The white indicates her noble character. NGS, vol. 2, p. x.

130. *Aka*, a Japanese approximation of a Sanskrit word meaning clear water to be used as an offering to Buddha.

131. *Samishiki*, here translated as "loneliness," includes a wide spectrum of feeling tones in classical poetry, from unhappiness to pleasantness. Brower and Miner, *Japanese Court Poetry*, pp. 260–62.

132. *Fukesugite* is a pivot line. *Fuke*, meaning to blow and to grow late in time, and *sugite*, meaning to pass on in distance and in time, apply to both the pine winds and the moon.

133. *Katamuku*, a pivot word meaning to sink low and to slant, turns between "moon" and "eaves."

134. *Kusa* (grass) is an *engo*, relating to *wasurete*, suggesting *wasuregusa* (literally, "forgetting grass"), and to *shinobu*, suggesting *shinobugusa* (literally, "yearning grass"), here translated as "bracken." The first is a type of lily; the second, a mosslike fern. McCullough, *Tales*, p. 211, n. 3, and p. 200, n. 2. Her gloss on *shinobu* is particularly full.

135. *Sugishi*, a pivot word meaning to conclude, turns between *wasurete* (to forget) and *inishie* (ancient times).

136. *Shinobu*, as well as being a related word to grass, becomes a pivot word between *inishie* and *kao*; she longs for the past and is filled with longing.

137. *Omoide* pivots between *hito* and *nokoru*; with the first, a person who is longed for, and with the second, memories that remain.

138. *Hitosuji* (straight line) is an *engo* to *ito* (cord), which the Buddha holds.

139. Sanari (vol. 5, p. 3403) cites a passage from the thirtieth chapter, entitled "Tsuru no hayashi" (Grove of Cranes), in the *Eiga monogatari*, attributed to Akazome Emon (ca. 957–64 to ca. 1037–44): "At the time of the passing of the Great Person [Fujiwara no Michinaga], in his hand he held the cord from Holy Buddha's hand." Matsumoto Hiroshi et al., eds., *Eiga monogatari*, NKBT, vol. 76 (Tokyo: Iwanami, 1965), vol. 2, p. 327. In the Jōdo sect, the cord helped the dying man to concentrate on Buddha's grace.

140. Yokomichi and Omote (vol. 1, p. 275) suggest that this line is the prayerful repetition of the Amida Buddha's name, which leads to salvation, according to the Jōdo sect.

141. *Ageuta* begins in the high range of tones, with the melody moving between the high and middle ranges, ending in the low range. It is in *hiranori*.

142. The metaphorical guiding light becomes the imagistic moon, itself a symbol of wisdom in Buddhistic thought.

143. In the Jōdo sect, paradise lies in the west.

144. *Aki*, meaning emptiness and autumn, pivots between *yomo* (literally, "four corners") and *sora* (sky). It is also a homonym for weary, a meaning incorporated in the translation.

145. The division of these five lines follows Yokomichi and Omote, who state that, "In the fixed rhythm sections, the division of lines is to make clear the prosodical and musical matchings" (vol. 1, p. 36). The rules for fitting syllables of verse to the rhythmic line are myriad and explicit; see Miyake Kōichi, *Hyōshi seikai* (Tokyo: Hinoki Shōten, 1954), pp. 45–145. They are a source of expressiveness in Nō singing.

146. *Izuku* (where) pivots between *arashi* (storms) and *sadame naki* (literally, "there is no constancy"). The imagistic storm becomes a metaphor for man's attachment to worldly concerns.

147. Four related words in the preceding lines center on the auditory: *koe* (voice); *kiko-yure* (to hear); *arashi* (storms); *oto* (sounds).

148. *Yume* (dream) is an *engo* to *samete* (to awaken).

149. No Japanese text indicates whether a stage attendant removes the pail and spray. See *Yuya* (Sanari, vol. 5, p. 3244), where an explicit direction is given that a small property is removed.

150. He would not have been surprised to find a priest—i.e., a man—offering prayers.

151. Reference to an opening phrase in many sections of the *Tales of Ise*: "Mukashi otoko arikeri" (In the old days, there was once a man). Since popular tradition held that Narihira was the hero of many of the episodes, the first two words came to denote him.

152. A pivot use of the name, which the repetitive use of "remains" (in the sense of both "traces" and "stays") attempts to echo in English.

153. A pivot use of the name, which the pivot line in English ("of the Man of Ancient Days") attempts to echo.

154. *Oitaru* ("to grow" and "to become aged") pivots between *matsu* (pines) and either *tsuka* (mound) or *kusa* (grass), or possibly both.

155. The division of the following nine lines (Yokomichi, vol. 1, pp. 277ff.) indicates particularly expressive musical treatment. See above, n. 145.

156. *Ho* ("ears," as of grain) pivots between *susuki* (pampas grass) and *izuru* (to become prominent). The site is clearly marked by the earing grain.

157. *Kusa* (grass) and *tsuyu* (dew) are related words. In the translation the pivotal function of "dense" attempts to suggest this.

158. *Furu* ("to fall" and "to become old") pivots between dew and mound. In the translation, the pivotal use of "drops" (as noun and verb) and of the second "deeply still" (adjective and adverb) attempts to suggest the linking.

159. *I* (to remain) pivots between *koko ni* (at this place) and the proper noun.

160. Tatsuta Hill is in the mountain range on the border between Yamato and Kawachi provinces. Since the pass was a notoriously dangerous crossing, the wife expresses her fears for her husband's safety. The pivot word in Japanese (*tatsu*, to rise) connects the introductory first two lines to Tatsutayama. *Shiranami* (white waves) is a metaphor for robbers, adapted from a Chinese term referring to bandits who hid in a ravine named "white waves" (*Kōjien*, ed. Shinmura Izuru [Tokyo: Iwanami, 1955], p. 1092). The editors of *Yamato monogatari*, in which the Tatsutayama poem also appears (149th section) reject this metaphorical meaning without stating the reason: *Taketori monogatari, Ise monogatari, Yamato monogatari*, ed. Sakakura Atsuyoshi, NKBT, vol. 9 (Tokyo: Iwanami, 1967), p. 321. Another name for Kawachi, now a part of Osaka Prefecture, is Kashū, denoting a sandbar or land formed in rivers or lakes. The somewhat free translation of Kawachi in the preceding lines as "River Deltas" is based on this meaning. The area is now solid ground.

161. Miyake, *Shidai*, p. 155.

162. In this and the following six lines, there are two pairs of related words: *kage* (images), *omo* (surface or top) in *omote*, *sokoi* (bottom), *utsuru* (reflect).

163. *Mi* (to see) pivots between *kage* (images) and *mizu-kagami* (water mirror).

164. *Utsuru* ("to reflect" and "to pass on") pivots between *sokoi naku* (bottomless) and *tsukihi* (moon and sun).

165. *Tsuyu* (dew) is an *engo* to *tama* (jeweled); *hana* (flowers) and *iro* (color) are also *engo*.

166. *Tsutsui* denoted a well that has been dug, in contrast to a natural spring, according to Sakakura, p. 126, and Fritz Vos (*Study of the Ise Monogatari* [The Hague: Mouton & Co., 1957], vol. 2, p. 87, n. 3). The meaning of the fourth syllable (*zu*) in the first line is not known and perhaps functions only onomatopoetically. In the *Tales*, the line reads: *tsutsui tsu no*. There is apparently a variant text in which the line appears as in the Nō play, but neither Sakakura nor Vos names it. A well curb in the old days was round; Tokugawa illustrations show it as square, as is the Nō prop now used. *Kakeshi*, given here as "measure," may mean "to begin to speak" (*ii kaketa*) or "to be less than." *Maro* may indicate "you" rather than "little boy." The fourth line in the *Tales* reads: *Suginikerashi na. Imo* is a term of endearment used by a man to a woman.

167. From the twenty-third episode of the *Tales*. *Furiwake-kami* describes a child's hairstyle, parted in the middle and falling only to the shoulders. It was allowed to grow long and was put up as a girl approached a marriageable age (Sakakura, p. 126). The six simple

539

water-references in the kuse, previously mentioned, are found in line 7, *izutsu ni yorite*; line 12, *mizu-kagami*; line 15, *kokoro no mizu mo*; line 26, *kokoro no tsuyu*; the *ageha, izutsu ni kakeshi*; lines 48–49, *tsutsu izutsu no onna*.

168. *Koi* (love) pivots between *ware* (I) and *koromo* (robes).

169. *Ki* (to wear) pivots between *koromo* (robes) and the proper name.

170. *Isa* is an interjection; however, when followed by *shiranu* (see n. 171), it is an intensive. *Nihon kokugo daijiten*, 20 vols. (Tokyo: Shōgakukan, 1976), vol. 2, p. 17.

171. *Na* pivots between *shiranai* (not to know) and *nami* (waves). The division of lines here again allows for expressive treatment.

172. Although not noted by Japanese sources consulted, there may be an *engo* factor here between *tatsu* (to stand) and *izuru* (to emerge); the phrase *tachi izuru* (go out) is common enough. *Tatsu* then is used to echo the mountain's name from the immediately preceding lines, and the name in turn introduces the maples for which Tatsutayama is famous. Such an *engo* function for *tatsu* might reduce the imagistic impact, which seems to me somewhat abrupt here.

173. *Iro* (color) and *momijiba* (maple leaves) are related words.

174. *Ki* (tree) pivots between *momiji* (maple) and the proper name. In the English, "stands" (groves and to appear) is an attempt to approximate the pivotal effect.

175. *Iu* (to say and to tie) pivots between *to* (thus) and *shimenawa* (sacred rope). In the translation, "lines" (words and rope) attempts to approximate it. *Nawa* (rope) is related to *nagaki* (long).

176. *Tsutsu* (nineteen) pivots between *toshi* (age) and *tsutsui* (well), according to Yokomichi, vol. 1, p. 278. The echo of the theme poem is strong in the Japanese.

177. Another name for Yamato.

178. *Kaesu* (to turn back or inside out) pivots between *mukashi* (the past) and *koromo* (robe). The reference is to a poem by Ono no Komachi, where she expresses the common belief that dreams will come if the sleeper's robes are turned inside out. (*Kokinshū*, #554, *KT*, p. 12.)

Ito semete	When my longing thought
koishiki toki wa	overpowers me with love
mubatama no	more than I can bear,
yoru no koromo o	in the blackness of the night
kaeshite zo kiru	inside out I wear my robes.

179. *Koromo* (robe) is related to *koke* (moss); the robes of a Buddhist priest are referred to as *kokegoromo* (robes of moss), perhaps in reference to their color.

180. *Yume* (dream) is related to *makura* (pillow).

181. From the seventeenth episode of the *Tales* (McCullough, p. 82; *KT*, p. 3). Both man and woman in the *Tales* are anonymous, but Narihira is cited as the author of the poem sent in reply in the *Kokinshū* (#63). The witty poem in reply is as follows:

Kyō kozu wa	Had I not come today,
asu wa yuki to zo	snow-like, they would have fallen
furinamashi	upon the morrow,
kiezu wa ari tomo	and even if they stay unthawed,
hana to mimashi ya	will they still seem like these blooms?

540

A paraphrase might be: Had I not come today, tomorrow your affections might have been bestowed elsewhere. And even if they were not, would you still have felt tomorrow as you do today? NGS (vol. 1, p. 103) conserve a lovely subtlety in their translation of the first poem; the errant lover comes "once a year / less for my sake than for theirs [the blossoms]."

182. *Tsutsu* (nineteen) is again used as a pivot between *ware* (I) and *mukashi* (the past), while echoing the well-side poem.

183. Two lines from a poem in the twenty-fourth episode of the *Tales*, sent to an inconstant wife (McCullough, *Tales*, p. 90). The persons are again anonymous.

| Azusayumi | Drawn like crescent bows |
| mayumi tsukiyumi | of birch wood, spindle, and zelkova, |

toshi o hete   many moons have passed;
waga seshi go goto   be as loving now to him [the new husband]
uruwashimi seyo.   as before I was to you.

The first two lines read literally: "birchwood bow / spindle-wood bow, zelkova-wood bow."
They are a *joshi* (introduction) to the poem, with *tsuki* ("zelkova" and "moon") as a pivot to
hete (to pass), and related to *toshi* (years). The enumeration of the three kinds of bows may
be a reference to an old song (*kagura*), which also names the three bows. A bow may also be
a metaphor for a woman, taken with the verb *hikedo* (to pull toward) which is found in the
poem sent as a reply in the *Tales*. Sakakura, p. 193.

    184. *Nari* (to become) pivots between *yo* (world) and Narihira.

    185. *Utsuri* ("to be possessed by a spirit" and "to imitate") pivots between *otoko* (man)
and *mai* (dance).

    186. Masuda, "Nō kyōgen," p. 345.

    187. *Sumeru* ("to dwell" and "clear") pivots between *terai* (temple well) and *tsuki*
(moon).

    188. From the fourth episode of the *Tales* (McCullough, p. 71; *KT*, p. 15). The lady
mourned is supposedly Kōshi, later an imperial consort. This is Narihira's "most famous
poem," according to Brower and Miner, who give a thorough exegesis of it (p. 193), as does
McCullough (pp. 52–53).

Tsuki ya aranu   Is this the moon no more?
haru ya mukashi no   Is this spring no more a spring
haru naranu   as those from before?
waga mi hitotsu wa   Though this self of mine alone
moto no mi ni shite   seems my former self to me.

One paraphrase of the poem might be: The moon and spring, which seemed so beautiful to
me while I had my love, seem different now, though I seem to be the same. But I know I
have been changed through suffering, and thus it is perhaps only I who see nature as
changed. But I suffer so deeply, I am confused and really do not know.

    189. See n. 99 for a justification for the use of this line as part of the Nō text rather than
the poem.

    190. *Oi* is used in its two senses in the repetitive variation: to grow and to grow old.

    191. Kobayashi, "Nō no ongaku," p. 54.

    192. *Bōfu* can mean either a male or female lover who is dead. Yokomichi and Omote
(vol. 1, p. 447) find the reading as a male more appropriate in this context. Masuda (*Hyōgen*,
p. 68) finds both meanings are operative.

    193. *Hana* (flower), *iro* (color), and *nioi* (fragrance) are related words in this quotation
from the *Kokinshū*. The connotation of love in *iro* is also probably present.

    194. *Ari* (to be) pivots between *nioi* and the name.

    195. *Honobono* (faintly) pivots between *kane* (bell) and *akuru* (to dawn).

    196. Stage direction from Yokomichi, vol. 1, p. 279.

    197. *Yume* (dream) and *same* (to awake) are related words.

Atsumori

    1. Nose Asaji, ed., *Zeami Jūrokubushū Hyōshaku* (Tokyo: Iwanami, 1966), vol. 1, p. 57.

    2. Takagi Ichinosuke, ed., *Heike monogatari* (Tale of the Heike), 2 vols., NKBT, vols. 32,
33 (Tokyo: Iwanami, 1966), vol. 2, chap. 9, "Tadanori Saigo" (Tadanori's Last Day), p. 221.

    3. *Atsumori*, in *Nōgaku Techō*, ed. Gondō Yoshikazu (Kyoto: Shinshindō, 1979), p. 23.

    4. *Sakamoto Setchō Nōhyō Zenshū*, 2 vols. (Tokyo: Unebi Shobō, 1943), vol. 2, p. 80.

    5. Tanaka Taishi, "Atsumori ron," *Geinōshi Kenkyū*, no. 77, p. 28.

    6. Kakeri pieces: *Tamura, Yashima, Ebira, Tadanori, Michimori, Tsunemasa, Shunzei Tada-
nori*. Quasi-kakeri pieces: *Yorimasa, Sanemori, Kanehiro Tomoakira, Tomonaga, Kiyotsune,* and
Tomoe. Tanaka Makoto and Nogami Toyoichirō, eds., *Nōgaku Zenshū*, 3 vols. (Tokyo: Asahi
Shinbun, 1965), vol. 1, p. 133.

    7. Gondō, *Nōgaku Techō*, p. 23.

    8. Two Group II Nō plays. See n. 6.

    9. Nogami, *Nōgaku Zensho*, vol. 1, p. 137.

541

10. Ashura (Skt. Asura): Originally, in Hinduism, a titan who fights with the gods headed by Indra. Ashura was introduced into Buddhism and came to be regarded as a demon who is fond of fighting by nature. Ashura World is one of the six worlds among which the souls of living beings transmigrate: hell; the worlds of hungry spirits, animals, ashuras, and men; and heaven.

11. Kumagae no Jirō Naozane: One of the warriors of the Heike and a poet from Kumagae in the land of Musashi. At the battle of Ichi no Tani he slew Atsumori, and, moved by a deep sense of the impermanence of life, he shaved his head under the direction of Priest Hōnen and assumed the Buddhist name Rensei. *Heike monogatari*, chap. 9, pp. 219–22. See *Tōru*, n. 3.

12. Atsumori: The youngest son of Taira no Tsunemori, the brother of Taira no Kiyomori. He was slain at the battle of Ichi no Tani in 1184, when he was seventeen, according to the *Heike monogatari*, chap. 9, pp. 219–22.

13. Ichi no Tani: Located in Muko County in the land of Settsu; the noted battleground where Minamoto no Yoshitsune attacked the Heike in 1184. The English translation used here is "the First Ravine."

14. *Kokonoe no kumoi*: The capital, where the Imperial Court is.

15. *Oguruma*: "Small wheel" is an *engo* (related word) with *meguru* (turn), which, in turn, introduces Yodo (Pool), famous for its waterwheels for mills.

16. Yodo: Located in Yamashiro on the water route that leads to Naniwa from the capital. It is a river port where the four rivers Kamo, Katsura, Uji, and Kitzu, join to form the Yodo River. English translation: "Pool."

17. Yamazaki: Located southwest of Yodo. Here translated as "Mountain Point."

18. Koya no Ike: Famous in Japanese poetry.

19. Ikutagawa: Famous in Japanese poetry; introduced by head rhyme with Ike at the end of the previous line. Located in the east of Kōbe City.

20. *Nami koko moto ya*: Nami (wave) is an *engo* with *kawa* (river) and *mizu* (water); refers to the passage in *Genji monogatari*. See *Matsukaze*, n. 19.

21. Suma no Ura: Located in the county of Muko in Settsu; famous in Japanese poetry and tales, especially the *Genji monogatari*.

22. Ueno: General area on the mountainside of Suma. The English translation used here is "High Meadow."

23. *Kano oka ni*: Refers to a poem by Kakinomoto no Hitomaro in the *Shūishū*, #567, KT, p. 66.

24. *Kotaemashi*: Refers to a poem by Ariwara no Yukihira in the *Kokinshū*, #962; KT, p. 19. See *Matsukaze*, n. 54.

25. *Moshio tare tomo*: Tare is used as a *kakeshi* (pun): "dipping" and "who."

26. *Amari ni nareba*: Ama in *amari* is used as a pun, for it means "fisherman."

27. *Shitashiki dani mo*: Refers to a passage in the preface of the *Kokinshū*, ed. Sahaku Umetomo, NKBT, vol. 8 (Tokyo: Iwanami, 1967), p. 98.

28. *Masaru o mo*: A proverb of the time.

29. *Shōka bokuteki*: Refers to a line by Ki no Saime in *Wakan Rōeishū*, ed. Kawaguchi Hisao, NKBT, vol. 73 (Tokyo: Iwanami, 1965), p. 113.

30. *Fushin na*: Fushi in *fushin na* is used as a *kakeshi*: "joint" and "doubt."

31. *Yoritake*: Yori is used as a *kakeshi*: "drift" and "lean on."

32. Saeda: The name of the bamboo flute Atsumori carried until he died. It was originally conferred to his grandfather, the noted flute player, by Emperor Toba, according to the *Heike monogatari*, chap. 9, p. 222.

33. Semiore: A flute made out of bamboo, presented by the Emperor of T'ang around the time of the reign of the Emperor Toba. The joint of the flute looked like a cicada, but the cicada was broken off from the flute by careless handling, hence it was known as the Broken Cicada, according to the *Heike monogatari*, chap. 15.

34. Komabue: A flute used for music derived from Koguryŏ.

35. Takisashi: Another name perhaps for the famous flute called Kashiradaki (the "Head-Charred Flute," according to *Jikkunshō*). Yokomichi, p. 234, n. 10 to *Atsumori*.

36. *Yūnami no*: Yū in *yūnami* is used as a *kakeshi*: "evening" and "say."

37. Jūnen: Repeating the holy Buddha's name ten times, according to Jōdoshū, the Pure Land sect of Buddhism.

38. *Nyakuga jōbutsu*: Based on a passage in the sutra *Muryōjukyō*; Nakamura Hajime, ed., *Shin Bukkyō jiten* (Tokyo: Seishin Shobo, 1962), p. 101.

39. *Hitokoe:* "One call" refers to a poem by Priest Kūya in the *Shūishū, #1344, KT,* p. 81.

40. *Dohi and Kajiwara:* Dohi refers to Dohi Sanehira, and Kajiwara, to Kajiwara Kagetoki, both of whom are warriors of the Genji.

41. *Awajigata:* Adapted from a poem by Minamoto no Kaneyoshi in the *Kin'yōshū, #288, KT,* p. 119.

42. *Suma no:* Su in *Suma* is used as a *kakeshi:* "do."

43. *Ichinen Midabutsu:* In *Busshin Hōyō* by Genshin, the author of the *Ōjōyōshū, Taishō,* vol. 34 (No. 2682), it was stated that the passage appeared in *Ōjō Hon'enkyō.* See *Taema,* n. 11. Sanari, p. 7842.

44. *Arisoumi: Ari* is used as a *kakeshi:* "is" and "rough."

45. *Fukaki: Fukaki* is used as a *kakeshi:* the sea is "deep," and "deep" sin.

46. *Sore haru no hana:* A like passage appears in *Saigyōzakura;* see n. 16 to that play.

47. *Kinka ichijitsu:* A line from Po Chu-i (772–846). Kawaguchi, *Wakan Rōeishū,* poem #291, p. 121.

48. *Kataki:* Used as a *kakeshi:* "difficult" and "hard."

49. *Hitomukashi:* Generally ten years. According to *Nagato-bon Heike:* "long ago it was considered thirty-three years . . . now it is twenty-one years" (p. 1817, *Kōjien* [Japanese dictionary], ed. Shinmura Izuru [Tokyo: Iwanami, 1955]).

50. *Rōchō no:* Refers to a passage in the *Heike monogatari,* vol. 2, chap. 10, p. 245.

51. *Hi mo:* Used as a *kakeshi:* "strand" or "cord" and "day."

52. *Suma:* Used as a *kakeshi:* "live."

53. *Yoru to naku: Yoru* is used as a *kakeshi:* "night" and "surge."

54. *Sumabito:* Su in *sumabito* is used as a *kakeshi:* "do."

55. *Shiba to yū:* Refers to a passage in Yamagishi Tokuhei, ed., *Genji monogatari,* 5 vols., NKBT, vols. 14–18 (Tokyo: Iwanami, 1958–63), vol. 2, chap. 12, "Suma," p. 45.

56. *Imayō:* A class of songs popular during the later part of the Heian period.

57. *Senkata nami no: Nami* is used as a *kakeshi:* "not" and "wave."

58. *Uchimono:* Used as a *kakeshi:* "hit" and "surge."

59. *Inga wa meguriaitari: Meguri* functions as a pivot word between *inga* and *meguriau.*

60. *Hōji:* Used as a *kakeshi:* "prayers" and "repay."

61. *Rensei hōshi: Hōshi* is used as a *kakeshi:* "repay" and "priest."

Tadanori

1. Takagi Ichinosuke, ed., *Heike monogatari,* 2 vols., NKBT, vols. 32, 33 (Tokyo: Iwanami, 1966), vol. 2, pp. 164–227.

2. Nose Asaji, *Zeami Jūrokubushū Hyōshaku* (Tokyo: Iwanami, 1966), vol. 1, pp. 624–25. See also Shelley Fenno, "Unity and the Three Principles of Composition in a Nō Play" (Ph.D. diss., Indiana University, 1986), p. 89.

3. *Shunzei:* Shunzei is the Sino-Japanese reading of the name Toshinari. Toshinari was the noted poet and critic, known as Fujiwara no Toshinari (1113–1204), who compiled the *Senzaishū* by the order of Retired Emperor Goshirakawa in 1188.

4. *Seinan no rikyū:* Refers to the palace of both Emperor Toba and Emperor Shirakawa, which is located south of the capital, hence this line.

5. *Yamazaki:* Mountain Point is the English translation of the place name Yamazaki, a village situated on the province line between Yamashiro and Settsu. In Japanese, *yama* in *Yamazaki* means *mountain,* which serves as a "buried" pun.

6. *Sekido:* Located west of Yamazaki. In English the name means "Barrier Gate," for it is where the checkpoint was erected during the Heian period.

7. *Akutagawa:* Rubbish River is the English translation of the name of the river, Akutagawa, in Settsu Province, which flows into the Yodo River. The preceding line serves as a *jo,* introduction, as "dust" and "rubbish" are *engo,* related words.

8. *Ina:* The place in Settsu that is famous for bamboo grass, which poets traditionally love to use as a theme; for instance, poem #227 by Hyōe no Naishi in *Shin Goshuishū, KT,* p. 626:

Samidare ni	As I look far out
ozasa ga hara o	at the field of bamboo grass
miwataseba	in the rain of May,
Inano ni tsuzuku	the pool of Koya's water
Koya no ike-mizu.	extends to Ina's meadow.

9. *Koya no Ike:* Located adjacent to Ina's Meadow. *Koya* is used as a pivot word, for it also means "small cottage." See n. 6 to *Atsumori.*

10. *Suminashite:* Used as a pun: *sumi* in *suminashite* means both "clear" and "dwell."

11. *Ashi no hawake no:* Refers to poem #77 in *Shui Gusō,* p. 131 in Matsushita Daizaburō, ed., *Zoku Kokka Taikan* (The Great Canon of Japanese Poetry Continued), 2 vols. (Tokyo: Kigensha, 1925–26). Intended as a supplement to *Kokka Taikan,* this work collects the poems from the personal collections of more than one hundred important court poets as well as poems found in certain unofficial anthologies and records of poetry contests.

Natsumushi no	The summer insects
hikari zo soyogu	flit and flicker with the light
Naniwagata	at Naniwa Bay
ashino hawake ni	as there pass the inlet-winds
suguru ura-kaze.	rustling through the reedy leaves.

12. *Arimayama:* Used as a buried pun, as *ari* in *Arimayama* means "is" or "exists."

13. *Samuru makura ni:* An allusion to poem #1176, by Fujiwara no Munemitsu, in *Shin Chokusenshū, KT,* p. 233:

Akatsuki no	The bell at dawning
kane no aware o	tolls and sounds the knell that adds
uchi-souru	a ring of sadness
ukiyo no yume no	on the pillow where we wake
samuru makura ni.	from the dream of this vain world.

14. *Kane:* The bell refers to that of the Naniwa Temple, i.e., the Tennōji Temple of Ōsaka.

15. *Naruogata:* Used as a buried pun, as *naru* in *Naruo* means "become" and "sound."

16. *Korizuma:* Used as a buried pun, as *kori* in *korizuma* means "learn to one's sorrow," while *korizuma no ura* is another name for Suma no Ura, which is mentioned in the Pillow Book of Sei Shōnagon under the heading of "On Bay."

17. *Naregoromo:* Used as a pun, as *na* in *naregoromo* means "no" or "not."

18. *Ura:* Used as a pun, as *ura* means "the reversed side," while it also means "bay."

19. *Suma:* Used as a pun, as it also means "to live."

20. *Ama no yobikoe:* Refers to poem #238 by Naga no Imiki Okimaro in the *Man'yōshū;* see *KT,* p. 707:

Ōmiya no	We can even hear
uchi made kikoyu	inside the mighty palace
abikisu to	the voices shouting
ago totonouru	for netting by the fishers
ama no yobikoe.	ready for the rope they draw.

21. *Wakurawa ni:* Quoted from poem #962, by Ariwara no Yukihira (818–93), in the *Kokinshū,* edited by Ki no Tsurayuki in 905; *KT,* p. 19.

22. *Michi koso kaware:* One way leads to the mountain for firewood, and the others to the sea.

544

23. *Satobanare:* Refers to the passage from the "Suma" chapter in the *Tale of Genji;* Yamagishi Tokuhei, ed., *Genji monogatari,* 5 vols., NKBT, vols. 14–18 (Tokyo: Iwanami, 1958–63), vol. 2, p. 11. "Mukashi koso hito no sumika nado arikere. Ima wa ito sato-banare kokoro sugokute ama no ie dani mare ni . . ." (In the past there were some houses but now this place lies far from the village and appears terribly lonely to our heart; the fisher's hut can rarely be seen . . .).

24. *Shiba to iu mono no:* Refers to a passage in the same chapter, which runs as follows: "Ama no shio yaku naramu to oboshi wataru wa, owashimasu ushiro no yama ni shita to yū mono fusuburu narikeri" (You think that the fishermen are boiling the brine; it is what all the natives of these parts dismiss as brushwood growing in the mountain which they burn behind the place where you live). *Genji monogatari,* vol. 2, p. 45. See *Atsumori,* n. 54.

25. *Amari:* Used as a buried pun, as *ama* in *amari* means "fisherman."

26. *Suma no wakaki:* Refers to a passage from the "Suma" chapter cited above: "Suma ni

wa toshi kaerite, hi nagaku tsurezure naru ni ueshi waka-gi no sakura honoka ni sakiso-mete . . ." (The year returns to Suma and days grow long and idle; the young cherry trees, newly planted, begin to bloom faintly . . .). *Genji monogatari*, vol. 2, p. 48.

27. *Umi sukoshi danimo hedateneba*: Refers to a passage from the "Suma" chapter cited above: "Suma ni wa itodo kokoro zukushi no akikaze ni, umi wa sukoshi tōkeredo . . ." (At Suma our hearts grow sad and weary with the autumn wind, though the sea is lying at a little distance . . .). *Genji monogatari*, vol. 2, p. 38.

28. *Aruji naramashi*: A poem by Taira no Tadanori (1144–84), which appeared in the ninth chapter of the *Tale of the Heike*, entitled "Tadanori Saigo," vol. 2, chap. 9, pp. 215–17.

29. *Na mo Tadanori no*: Used as a pun, as it also means "only laws."

30. *Yūbe*: Used as a buried pun, as *yū* in *yūbe* means "say."

31. *Yadoriki*: Used as a buried pun, for *yadori* in *yadoriki* means also "to lodge or shelter."

32. Teika: Fujiwara Teika (1162–1241) was the great poet who edited the *Shin Kokinshū* (1205). He was the son of Fujiwara no Shunzei. See n. 3 above.

33. *Yūzuki*: Used as a buried pun, as *yū* in *yūzuki* also means "say." See n. 30, above.

34. *Kagerō*: Used as a buried pun, as *kage* in *kagerō* means "shade" or "shadow," while Kagerō no Ono is a proper name in Yamato.

35. Ono: Used as a pun, as Ono means "Little Field" and also "one's own," another word with the same sound.

36. *Mayō amayo no*: According to Yokomichi, the phrase serves perhaps as a pun that suggests "mayō amari," which means "in the excess of one's delusion," while, based on the conversations among Genji and his friends on the rainy night mentioned in the chapter called "Hōkigi" of the *Tale of Genji*, it serves as a *jo*, or introduction, to the following line. Yokomichi Mario and Omote Akira, eds., *Yōkyokushū*, 2 vols., NKBT, vols. 40, 41 (Tokyo: Iwanami, 1967), vol. 1, p. 246.

37. *Senzaishū*: The seventh imperial anthology of Japanese poetry. See n. 3 above.

38. *Chokkan no mi no*: Refers to the ex-Emperor Goshirakawa's (1159–91) anger toward the Heike clan as the imperial enemy.

39. *Yomibito shirazu*: Refers to the poem by a supposedly unknown author in the *Senzaishū* (#66, *KT*, p. 143), which the editor had selected out of the poems Tadanori entrusted to him when the Taira Clan fled the capital in 1183.

40. *Geni ya waka . . . umare*: Refers to the verse of Tadanori's father, Tadamori (1096–1158), a noted poet whose works appeared in the imperial anthologies of Japanese poetry.

41. Shikishima: Refers to Japan.

42. Goshirakawa: The Emperor Goshirakawa (1127–92) reigned as the seventy-seventh emperor for only three years, but his influence was great even after his abdication in 1158.

43. Gojō no Sanmi: Shunzei is known by this epithet, as he was decorated with the Senior Third Rank and lived at his Fifth Street (Gojō) mansion.

44. *Toki wa Juei*: Refers to the time when the Heike fled from the capital to the west in July of the second year of Juei in 1183, shortly after the imperial order was bestowed on Shunzei to compile the *Senzaishū*.

45. *Kokoro no hana*: A metaphor for the heart that loves poetry.

46. *Rangiku no*: An allusion to the lines of Po Chu-i: "The owls hoot on the branches of the pines and laurels; the foxes hid among chrysanthemums and orchids." Yokomichi, *Yō-kyokushū*, vol. 1, p. 240, n. 21.

47. Kitsunegawa: Refers to the fox (English translation).

48. *Nami no ue*: Refers to the Heike, who fled from Fukuwara to Tsukushi.

49. *Genji no sumidokoro*: Refers to Suma, where Hikaru Genji lived.

50. *Ware mo fune . . . tote*: Hereafter, the description of Tadanori's end follows closely the Heike text; chap. 9, "Tadanori's Last Day." Yokomichi, *Yōkyokushū*, vol. 1, p. 248, n. 28.

51. Okabe no Rokuyata Tadazumi: One of the warriors of Minamoto no Yoshitsune, who commanded the Genji army. *Heike monogatari*, vol. 2, chap. 2, p. 216.

52. *Kōmyō henjō*: Lines from the *Murōjukyō*. *Taishō*, vol. 12, No. 360.

53. *Furimi furazumi*: An allusion to a poem by an unknown author in the *Gosenshū*; #445, *KT*, p. 321:

Kamunazuki	In this October
furimi furazumi	without any settled skies
sadamenaki	the sudden drizzle,

| shigure zo fuyu no | coming on or turning off, |
| hajime narikeri. | will be the start of winter. |

54. *Mireba . . . dai o sue:* Both the *Tale of the Heike* and the *Tale of the Rise and Fall of the Heike* state that the theme was originally entitled "On the Flowers at the Inn."

55. *Arashi:* Used as a buried pun, as *araji* (not) is implied in *arashi* (storm).

56. Hana wa ne ni: An allusion to a poem by Emperor Sutoku (1119–64), in the *Senzai-shū* (#122, *KT*, p. 144):

Hana wa ne ni	To the roots the flowers
tori wa furusu ni	must return themselves, the birds
kaerunari,	to their old dear nests,
haru no tomari o	but there is no one who knows
shiru hito zo naki.	where will be the inn for spring.

Matsukaze

1. Nose Asaji, ed., *Zeami Jūrokubushū Hyōshaku*, 2 vols. (Tokyo: Iwanami, 1966), vol. 2, p. 469.

2. Ibid., vol. 1, p. 657.

3. Ibid., vol. 2, p. 202.

4. Ibid., p. 206.

5. Ibid., p. 491.

6. Ibid., vol. 1, p. 592. See also Shelley Fenno, "Unity and the Three Principles of Composition in a Nō Play" (Ph.D. diss., Indiana University, 1986), p. 84.

7. See notes 19, 20, 24, 31, 32, 33, 34, 36, 53, 57, 60, 79.

8. Sanari Kentarō, ed., *Yōkyoku Taikan*, 5 vols. (Tokyo: Meiji Shoin, 1964), vol. 5, p. 2821.

9. *Sakamoto Setchō Nōhyō Zenshū*, vol. 2, p. 321. See also J. Thomas Rimer and Yamazaki Masakazu, trans., *On the Art of Nō Drama* (Princeton: Princeton University Press, 1984), pp. 217–18.

10. Nose, vol. 2, p. 474.

11. Ibid., p. 478.

12. Tsu: Old name for Settsu Province. Suma is a famous place in Japanese poetry and tales.

13. Matsukaze and Murasame: Names given by Yukihira to the fisher maidens. They are fictitious characters.

14. *Sono mi wa dochū ni:* A line from Po Chu-i in the *Wakan Rōeishū*, originally edited by Fujiwara no Kintō (966–1041); NKBT, vol. 73, ed. Kawaguchi Hisao (Tokyo: Iwanami, 1965), p. 170.

15. *Yamamoto:* The foot of the mountain; refers to the village of Suma.

16. *Wazukanaru:* Used as a buried pun, for *wa* in *wazukanaru* means "wheel."

17. *Ukiyo: Uki* in *ukiyo* is used as a pun: "float" and "wretched."

18. *Meguru* (go round, turn): An *engo* (related word) with *kuruma* (cart), and *wa* (wheel).

19. *Nami koko moto ya:* Refers to a passage in the "Suma" chapter of the *Tale of Genji*. See *Atsumori*, n. 20. Yamagishi Tokuhei, ed., *Genji monogatari*, 5 vols., NKBT, vols. 14–18 (Tokyo: Iwanami, 1958–63), vol. 2, chap. 12, p. 38. See also Tanaka Makoto, ed., *Yōkyoku* (Tokyo: Kawade Shobō, 1954), p. 98. "Hitori me o samashite . . . yomo no arashi o kiki tamō ni, nami tada kokomoto ni tachi-kuru kokochi shite . . ." (As I wake alone and . . . listen to the gales from all directions, I feel that the waves come up only to this place . . .).

20. *Kokorozukushi no:* Refers to a passage (about eleven lines) in the "Suma" chapter of the *Tale of Genji*. *Genji monogatari*, vol. 2, chap. 12, p. 38. Tanaka, *Yōkyoku*, p. 99.

21. Yukihira: A poet and elder brother of Narihira.

22. *Seki fukikoyuru:* A poem by Yukihira in *Shoku Kokinshū*, #871, *KT*, p. 283.

23. *Yoru yoru:* Used as a *kakeshi* (pun): "night" and "surge."

24. *Satobanare naru:* Refers to a passage in the "Suma" chapter of the *Tale of Genji*. *Genji monogatari*, vol. 2., chap. 12, p. 11. Tanaka, *Yōkyoku*, p. 99. The passage runs as follows: "Mukashi koso hito no sumika nado mo arikere, ima wa ito satobanare kokoro sugukute, ama no ie dani mare ni . . ." (In the past, indeed there were houses, but now this place lies far from the village and appears terribly lonely to our eyes; even the fisher's hut can rarely be seen . . .).

25. *Tsuki yori hoka wa:* Refers to the poem by Norihashi Tadayori in the *Kin'yōshū,* #187, *KT,* p. 117.

Kusamakura	Grass for my pillow,
kono tabine koso	I sleep upon my journey
omoishiru	as I come to know,
tsuki yori hoka no	here there is no other friend
tomo nakarikeri.	than the shining moon for me.

26. *Kaku bakari:* Refers to the poem by Fujiwara no Takamitsu (940–94) in the *Shūishū,* #435, *KT,* p. 13.

Kakubakari	The fullest measure
egataku miyuru	of all harshness of our lives
yo no naka ni	in this mortal world,
urayamashiku mo	is our envy of the moon
sumeru tsuki kana.	shining pure and calm and bright.

27. *Sumu:* Used as a *kakeshi:* "live" and "clear."
28. *Dejio:* De in *dejio* is used as a *kakeshi,* meaning "rise" and "come."
29. *Hiku:* Used as a *kakeshi:* "pull" and "ebb."
30. *Kuchimasariyuku:* Kuchi (decay) in *kuchimasariyuku* is used to describe *sutekusa* and *tamato.*
31. *Ama no yobikoe:* Refers to a passage in the "Suma" chapter of the *Tale of Genji. Genji monogatari,* vol. 2, chap. 12, p. 40. Tanaka, *Yōkyoku,* p. 101. "Oki yori fune-domo no utai nonoshirite kogiyuku nado mo kikoyu . . ." (From the offing we can hear the fishermen singing and calling as they row the boats . . .).
32. *Tomochidori:* Refers to a poem in the "Suma" chapter, *Genji monogatari,* vol. 2, chap. 12, p. 40. Tanaka, *Yōkyoku,* p. 101. The poem runs as follows:

Kaki tsurane	Writing line by line
mukashi no koto zo	how I now recall the things
omōuru	of so long ago,
kari wa sono yo no	so ephemeral, though the geese
tomo narane domo.	were no friends at all that night.

(*Monogatari,* #961, *KT,* p. 895.) Also refers to another poem in the same chapter, p. 46:

Tomo chidori	At the break of dawn
morogoe ni naku	when a pair of plovers sing
akatsuki wa	a song together,
hitori nezame no	wakened in my bed alone
toko mo tanomoshi.	I find it full of promises.

33. *Kakaru tokoro no:* Adapted from a passage in the "Suma" chapter, *Genji monogatari,* vol. 2, chap. 12, p. 38. Tanaka, *Yōkyoku,* p. 101.
34. *Aki narikeri:* Refers to a passage from the "Suma" chapter, *Genji monogatari,* vol. 2, chap. 12, p. 38. Tanaka, *Yōkyoku,* p. 103.
35. *Kataonami:* Allusion to the famous poem by Yamabe no Akahito (Nara period) in the *Man'yōshū:* #919, *KT,* p. 726.

Wakanoura ni	As from the Bay of Song
shio michikureba	coming in full tide the waves
kataonami	submerge the beaches,
ashibe o sashite	over to the reedy shore,
tazu naki wataru.	the flocks of cranes fly crying.

36. *Yomo no arashi:* Refers to a passage in the "Suma" chapter, *Genji monogatari,* vol. 2, chap. 12, p. 38. Tanaka, *Yōkyoku,* p. 103.
37. Matsushima: One of the most beautiful spots in Japan, located near Sendai in Mie

Prefecture. The following passages are strewn with famous place-names, known as "Meisho Zukushi," which enrich the lines by association as they move forward.

38. Ojima: The lovely island of Matsushima, famed in Japanese poetry. "Small Island" is the English translation.

39. *Hakobu wa tōki:* Allusion to the story of Tōru.

40. *Michinoku no sono na ya Chika:* Michinoku is an ancient name referring collectively to the remote part of northern Japan, where Matsushima is located. The name contains a buried pun: *michi* means "road." Although the area is actually far away, it sounds "near" because Chika, the old famous name for Shiogama (English translation, "Salt Kiln"), noted for its scenic beauty and salt making, is close to Matsushima; besides, they are inseparably associated whenever either one is mentioned. Chika is used as a *kakeshi:* it means "near."

41. *Shizu ga shioki:* Refers to the poem by Fujiwara no Ieyoshi (1192–1264) in *Shoku Kokinshū,* #1336:

Ise no umi	At the Ise Sea,
ama no mo shioki	learning nothing from driftwood
kori mo sede	and seaweed, fishers
onaji urami ni	look along the hateful bay
toshi zo enikeru.	for these years I passed away.

42. Akogi ga Ura: Refers to the poem by an unknown author in the *Kokin Rokucho,* #3238; Matsushita Daizaburō, ed., *Zoku Kokka Taikan,* 2 vols. (Tokyo: Kigensha, 1925–26), p. 522.

Ōkoto o	Meeting with someone
Akogi ga ura ni	across Akogi Inlet
hiku tsuna mo	up the rope is pulled
tabi kasanareba	over and over again
araware ya sen.	all should appear so clearly.

43. Futami no Ura: "Twice-Seen Bay" is the English translation; a noted place near Ise where twin rocks add a superb touch to the natural beauty of the seascape. Since the scenery is so beautiful, there is a saying that one must have a "second look," hence the name.

44. *Matsu no Muradachi:* Refers to the poem by Unakatomi no Sukehiro (1028–?; banished to Sado Island in 1103) in the *Kin'yōshu,* #580, *KT,* p. 126:

Tamakushige	On this Twice-Seen Beach,
Futami ga Ura no	like the jeweled toilet chest,
kaishigumi	those seashells abound
makie ni miyuru	where the stands of pines
matsu no muradachi	grow as in the painted scroll.

45. Narumigata: Used as a buried pun, as *naru* in *Narumigata* means "become." Narumigata, noted in Japanese poetry, lies in Owari Province.

46. Narumigata: The first two syllables, *naru,* are the same as those in the two place names Naruo and Narumi, which lie far apart. Consequently, near and far are contrasted.

47. *Ashi no ya:* Used as a part of the scenery described, while it serves as a proper name which introduces Nada, noted for salt making and scenic beauty.

48. Nada: Refers to the poem that appeared in the eighty-seventh episode of the *Tale of Ise;* Sakakura Taneyoshi, ed., *Ise monogatari,* NKBT, vol. 9 (Tokyo: Iwanami, 1957), pp. 163–64. *KT,* #889, p. 172.

548

Ashi no ya no	Across Reed Cottage,
Nada no shio yaki	boiling Nada's ocean brine
itoma nami	we've no time to spare,
tsuge no ogushi mo	but to speak with you I come
sasazu kinikeri.	with no little boxwood comb.

49. *Tsuge:* Used as a pun, for it means "to tell" and "boxwood."

50. *Sashikuru:* Sashi in *sashikuru* is used as a pivot word: "wear" and "flow" of the tide.

51. *Tsuki wa hitotsu . . . shio no yoru*: The passages exchanged between the chorus and the *shite* constitute one of the play's most famous scenes, the unity of which is created by the thematic progression. On the one hand, the moon image plays a major part, reflecting the mind of the character, and on the other hand, the number-progression helps the forward movement, binding all the elements mentioned into a poetic whole; for instance, *hitotsu*, *futatsu*, *mitsu*, and *ya* are in English one, two (too), three, and four (for), respectively. *Yo* in *yoru* is a *kakeshi* that means "night" and "approach."

52. *Yokage*: *Yo* in *yokage* is used as the *tōin*, or "head rhyme," which skillfully unifies the lines.

53. *Take no kaki*: Refers to a passage of the "Suma" chapter, *Genji monogatari*, vol. 2, chap. 12, p. 49. Tanaka, *Yōkyoku*, p. 106. The passage reads: "Take ameru kakishi watashite ishi no hashi, matsu no hashira, orosokanaru mono kara, mezuraka ni okashi" (The bamboo-woven fence is put across the stone steps, the pine posts, though they are plain, all look unusually amusing).

54. *Wakurawa ni*: The poem by Arihara no Yukihira (818–93) in the *Kokinshū*, #912, *KT*, p. 19, with the following prefatory note: "Tamura no on-toki, koto ni atatte, Tsu no kuni no Suma to yū tokoro ni komori haberikeru ni, miya no uchi ni haberikeru hito ni tsukawashi-keru" (In the reign of Tamura [Emperor Montoku (849–57)], for some reasons of my own, I secluded myself at a place called Suma in the land of Tsu, and I sent this verse to a person in the palace).

55. *Uchi ni areba*: Refers to the passage in the preface to the *Shin Kokinshū*.

56. *Naki ato*: *Naki* is used as a *kakeshi*: "none" and "dead."

57. *Korizuma no*: Refers to a passage in the "Suma" chapter, *Genji monogatari*, vol. 2, chap. 12, p. 31. Tanaka, *Yōkyoku*, p. 107.

Korizuma no	Still learning nothing
ura no mirume mo	from the thick-haired codium
yukashiki o	lovely in the sea;
shio yaku ama no	I wonder what the fishers,
ika ni omowan.	boiling brine, would think of them.

58. *Tsuki ni mo naruru*: Refers to the poem by Fujiwara no Tameuji (1222–86) in the *Shin Gosenshū*, #361, *KT*, p. 340:

Shiokaze no	Dampened are the garments
nami kake-goromo	splashed by wind-tossed ocean waves,
aki o ete	at passing autumn,
tsuki ni naretaru	with the moon so intimate
Suma no amabito.	grow Suma's fisher maidens.

59. *Matsukaze*: *Matsu* in Matsukaze is used as a pun: "pine" and "wait."

60. *Naregoromo*: Used as a pun, for it also means "body," while the other meaning is "Serpent's Day," which refers to the "Suma" chapter, *Genji monogatari*, vol. 2, chap. 12, p. 52. Tanaka, *Yōkyoku*, p. 110.

61. *Nami*: Used as a buried pun, for *na* in *nami* means "not." In the English translation the pivot line is used instead, as I combine the pun in the preceding line, *kami*.

62. *Aware*: *Awa* in *aware* is a pun: "foam" and "sad" or "pitiful."

63. Suma: Used as a pun: "to live," and the proper name, Suma.

64. *Omoigusa*: Refers to the poem by Minamoto no Toshiyori (1055–1129) in the *Kin'yōshū*, #444, *KT*, p. 123:

549

Omoigusa	The longing flower
hazue ni musubu	forms the drops of dew so white
shiratsuyu no	on its leafy tip
tanatama kite wa	but they come too far apart;
teni mo tamarazu.	hardly can they fill my hand.

65. *Katami koso*: An anonymous poem in the *Kokinshū*, #746, *KT*, p. 15.

66. *Yoi yoi:* The first part of the poem by Ki no Tomonori (mid-Heian period) in the *Kokinshū*, #593, KT, p. 12. The last part of the poem is as follows:

> kakete omowanu   hang it on my very thoughts
> toki no ma mo nashi   that my longing may never cease.

67. *Kakete:* Used as a pun: "hang" and "depend."
68. *Makura yori:* An anonymous poem in the *Kokinshū*, #1023, KT, p. 21. The last two lines run as follows:

> senkatanamizo   Without any help at all I stay
> toko naka ni iru   in the middle of the bed.

69. *Namida: na* in *namida* is used as a pun: "nothing" or "none," and "tear."
70. Mitsusegawa: The Three-Ford Rapids, which run through the netherworld, according to Buddhist tradition.
71. *Matsu to shi kikaba:* Refers to the poem in n. 75, below.
72. Matsukaze: Used as a buried pun, for *matsu* in Matsukaze means "wait," which is described by the preceding word.
73. *Tachikaerikon:* Used as a buried pun, for *tachi* in *tachi-kaeri* means "rise," and acts as a verb for "matsu."
74. *Matsu:* Used as a pun, for it means "pine" and "wait."
75. *Tachi wakare:* The poem by Arihara no Yukihira in the *Kokinshū*, #365, KT, p. 8.
76. *Matsu:* Used as a pun: "pine" and "wait."
77. *Kaeru:* Used as a pivot word, between the phantom and the waves.
78. *Suma:* Used as a pun: "clear" and "live."
79. *Fuku ya ushiro no:* Refers to the mountain that lies behind Suma, mentioned in the "Suma" chapter, *Genji monogatari*, vol. 2, chap. 12, p. 45. Tanaka, *Yōkyoku*, p. 115. The passage runs as follows: ". . . ushiro no yama ni, shiba to yū mono fushuburu narikeri" (at the rear of the mountain, the brushwood, as they call it, is smoldering).
80. *Sekiji:* Refers to Suma Barrier, famed in Japanese poetry.

Higaki

1. Maruoka Akira, ed., *Nōgaku Kanshō Jiten* (Dictionary of Nō Appreciation) (Tokyo: Kawade Shobō, 1961), pp. 329–40.
2. *Sandō,* in *Zeami Jūrokubushū Hyōshaku,* ed. Nose Asaji, 2 vols. (Tokyo: Iwanami, 1966), vol. 1, p. 958.
3. Masuda Shōzō, *Nō no Hyōgen* (Tokyo: Chūō Kōron, 1971), p. 96.
4. *Sakamoto Setchō Nōhyō Zenshū,* 2 vols. (Tokyo: Unebi Shobō, 1943), vol. 2, pp. 101–102.
5. Arthur Waley, *The Nō Plays of Japan* (London: George Allen and Unwin, 1950), p. 52.
6. *Sakamoto Setchō Nōhyō Zenshū,* vol. 2, p. 102.
7. Iwado: "Rock Door" is the English translation; it is a mountain located in the land of Higo (present Kumamoto Prefecture in the central part of Kyūshū).
8. Kanzeon: The Goddess of Mercy is the main figure enshrined at the Unganji Temple on the Iwado Mountain.
9. Shirakawa: A river starting from Mt. Aso that flows into the Bay of Ariake. "White River" is the English translation. *Shira* (white) in *Shirakawa* functions as a *kakeshi* in the original, as in the translation.

10. *Rōchō wa:* Refers to a passage in the tenth chapter, entitled "Yashima Insen," in Takagi Ichinosuke, ed., *Heike monogatari,* 2 vols., NKBT, vols. 32, 33 (Tokyo: Iwanami, 1966), vol. 2, p. 248.
11. *Hinka ni:* Refers to the lines by Tachibana no Aritsura (tenth-century poet), in Kojima Noriyoshi, ed., *Honchō Monzui,* NKBT, vol. 69 (Tokyo: Iwanami, 1964), p. 349.
12. *Aware yo no: Awa* in *aware* is used as a buried pun: "foam."
13. *Kumite: Kumi* in *kumite* is an associated word (*engo*) with water (*mizu*).
14. *Fukaki: Fukaki* is used as a pivot word (*kakekotoba*) with *mizu* (water), and *tsumi* (crime).

15. *Ashibiki no:* A "pillow word" (*makurakotoba*) to *yama* (mountain).

16. *Gosenshū:* The second imperial anthology of Japanese poems, compiled by order of Emperor Murakami in 951.

17. *Toshi fureba:* A poem by the Woman of the Cypress Hedge (*Higaki no Onna*) in the *Gosenshū*, 1220, *KT*, p. 44.

18. *Mitsuwagumu:* Used as a *kakeshi:* "to draw water," and "bent" and "old."

19. Dazaifu: The government office for all of Kyūshū, located in the province of Tsukushi (present Fukuoka Prefecture).

20. *Shirabyōshi:* A professional dancing girl who entertains the audience with songs and dancing.

21. Fujiwara no Okinori: A government official during the reign of Emperor Kōkō (884–87).

22. *Yūmagure: Yū* in *yūmagure* is a *kakeshi:* "to say" and "evening dusk."

23. *Ashita ni:* A couplet from a poem by Fujiwara no Yoshitaka (954–74), in Kawaguchi Hisao, ed., *Wakan Rōeishū*, NKBT, vol. 73 (Tokyo: Iwanami, 1965), #794, p. 255.

24. Shirakawa: *Shira* in Shirakawa is used as a *kakeshi:* "to know" and "white."

25. Mitsusegawa: The river flowing through the netherworld. *Mi* in *Mitsuse* functions as a *kakeshi:* "to see" and "three."

26. *Fukaki: Fukai* (deep) is used as a *kakeshi*, connecting *omoi* (thought) and *sayo*, in which *sa* is "sweet" and *yo* is "night." It is also an *engo* (related or associated word) with *asaku* (shallow).

27. *Tamoto no tsuyu no: Tsuyu* and *tama* are *engo; tamoto* and *tasuki* are also *engo*.

28. *Kage Shirakawa no: Kage* functions as a *kakeshi:* "light" and "put on."

29. *Kōri wa:* A passage from Hsun-tzu (circa 298–238 B.C.). Yokomichi Mario and Omote Akira, *Yōkyokushū*, 2 vols., NKBT, vols. 40, 41 (Tokyo: Iwanami, 1967), vol. 1, p. 284, n. 21.

30. *Kurenai no:* A poem by Fujiwara no Kanesada (1149–1207) in the *Shinchokusenshū*, #668, *KT*, p. 224.

31. *Kazura:* Refers to her tresses.

32. Kefu: A place-name famous for cloth woven with a narrow width. The old poem appeared in *Toshiyori Zuino* (Toshiyori's Poetics), written around 1115 by Minamoto no Toshiyori (1055–1129), a noted poet and critic. Sasaki Nobutsuna, ed., *Nihon Kagaku Taikei* (Great Compendium of Japanese Poetic Writings), 6 vols. (Tokyo: Bunmeisha, 1935), vol. 1.

33. *Aware: Awa* in *aware* is used as a pivot word: "foam" and "pitiful."

34. *Ashitazu: Ashi* in *ashitazu* functions as a pivot word: "foot" and "reed." In the English translation, I use "here" as a *kakeshi*, meaning "hear."

35. *Ne: Ne* is used as a pivot word: "cry" and "root."

Obasute

1. *Sakamoto Setchō Nōhyō Zenshū*, 2 vols. (Tokyo: Unebi Shobō, 1943), vol. 2, p. 10.

2. Nose Asaji, ed., *Zeami Jūrokubushū Hyōshaku*, 2 vols. (Tokyo: Iwanami, 1966), vol. 1, p. 601.

3. Abe Toshiko, ed., *Yamato monogatari*, NKBT, vol. 9 (Tokyo: Iwanami, 1957), episode 156, pp. 327–28.

4. *Konjaku monogatari*, attributed to Minamoto no Takakuni (1003–77), ed. Yamada Yoshio, NKBT, vol. 5 (Tokyo: Iwanami, 1963), episode 50, p. 236.

5. Ichijima Kenkichi, ed., *Toshiyori Kudenshū, Zoku Gunsho Ruijū*, vol. 15 (Tokyo: Kokusho Kankōkai, 1907), #82, p. 220.

6. Sanari Kentarō, ed., *Yōkyoku Taikan*, 5 vols. (Tokyo: Meiji Shoin, 1964), vol. 5, p. 3472.

7. Gondō Yoshikazu, *Nōgaku Techō* (Kyoto: Shinshindō, 1979), p. 64.

8. *Sakamoto Setchō Nōhyō Zenshū*, vol. 2, p. 10.

9. Gondō, *Nōgaku Techō*, p. 64.

10. Sanari, vol. 5, p. 3474.

11. Refers to the most famous moon of the fifteenth day of the eighth month of the lunar calendar. Because it is called "Harvest Moon," Japanese poets refer to it as the "named full moon."

12. Obasuteyama: Located in Sarashina County in the land of Shinano. According to

Konjaku monogatari, "Obasute Mountain was previously called 'Kanmuriyama,' because its shape is like the *kanmuri* (crown) cap."

13. *Sarashina no tsuki*: Generally speaking, refers to the moon on Obasute Mountain

14. *Aki no nakaba*: Fifteenth day of the eighth month, according to the lunar calendar.

15. *Waga kokoro*: A poem by an unknown author in the *Kokinshū*, #878, KT, p. 18.

16. *Katsura no ki*: An *engo*, with moon (*tsuki*).

17. *Mumoregusa*: Mumore in *mumoregusa* is used as a buried pun, meaning "buried."

18. *Kari naru*: Kari is used as a *kakeshi* (pun), meaning "makeshift" and "cut."

19. *Midori mo nokorite*: Refers to the color of the evergreens, *matsu* (pines), and *katsura* (laurel trees) in the previous lines.

20. Hitoeyama: The English translation is "One-Fold Mountain," one of the thirteen scenic spots on Obasute Mountain; it is also called *Jizō Tōge*, "Jizō Pass." *Hitoe* in *Hitoeyama* is used as a pivot word with the light autumnal color of the trees. It also serves to introduce *usugiri*, "thin mist" in the following line.

21. *Sumu tsuki no*: Sumu is used as a pun: "pure" and "clear" moon, and "live" in the mountain.

22. *Yūkage*: Yū in *yūkage* is used as a pun: "evening" shade of the tree, and "say."

23. *Sangoya-chū*: Lines from a poem by Hakurakuten (Po Chu-i, 772–846), in *Wakan Rōeishū*, ed. Kawaguchi Hisao, NKBT, vol. 73 (Tokyo: Iwanami, 1965), p. 108.

24. *Akeba mata*: A poem by Fujiwara no Teika (1162–1241) in *Shinchokusenshū*, #261, KT, p. 18. The fourth line is *katabuku tsuki no*: "with the moon declining low."

25. *Taguinaki*: Refers to the first two lines of the *hokku* by Sōsetsu, a linked-verse poet. The last line is *yūbe kana*: "in the evening." Ijichi Tetsuo, ed., *Rengashū*, NKBT, vol. 39 (Tokyo: Iwanami, 1960), p. 168.

26. *Mochitsuki no*: Mochi in *mochitsuki* is used as a pun, meaning "have" and "view."

27. *Hakue no nyonin*: Refers to the angels dressed in white robes who live in the Moon Palace. See *Hagoromo*, n. 186.

28. *Yūgure*: Yū in *yūgure* is used as a pun: "say" and "evening." See n. 22.

29. *Hana ni oki fusu*: Oki is used as a pun: "waken" and "set" the dew (*tsuyu*) in the line that follows it.

30. *Joroka no*: "Lady flower" is the English translation.

31. *Sarashina no*: Sarashi in *Sarashina* is used as a buried pun: "expose" the face.

32. *Omoigusa*: "Longing grass" is the English translation; another name for *ominaeshi*.

33. *Geni ya kyō ni*: Refers to the Chinese story.

34. *Ichirin miteru*: Refers to the Chinese lines, but the true source is unknown. Yokomichi Mario and Omote Akira, *Yōkyokushū*, 2 vols., NKBT, vols. 40, 41 (Tokyo: Iwanami, 1967), vol. 2, p. 448, supplementary n. 190.

35. *Chōse no higan*: Refers to Amida Buddha's compassionate vow to save all suffering beings; the primal verse: "I establish a vow that transcends this mundane world." This is in the *Muryōjukyō* ("Greater" Sukhavati-vyuha Sutra). *Taishō*, vol. 12, No. 360, 265c–279a.

36. *Sankō*: Refers to the sun, the moon, and the stars.

37. *Tsuki*: Refers to Gattenshi Honchi Daiseishi; see *Hagoromo*, n. 201.

38. *Daiseishi*: See *Hagoromo*, n. 201.

39. *Karyōbinga*: See n. 173 to *Hagoromo*.

40. *Muhenkō*: "Light All Infinite" is the English translation; another name for Daiseishi.

41. *Tsuyu no ma*: Tsuyu is used as a pun. It also means "a very short time."

42. *Kochō no asobi*: Refers to the Komagaku entitled "The Dance of Butterflies." Komagaku is music from the state called Koryŏ (936–1392) in ancient Korea.

43. *Kaese*: Used as a pun: "return" and "flip."

Saigyōzakura

1. Nose Asaji, ed., *Zeami Jūrokubushū Hyōshaku*, 2 vols. (Tokyo: Iwanami, 1966), vol. 2, p. 450.

2. *Sakamoto Setchō Nōhyō Zenshū*, 2 vols. (Tokyo: Unebi Shobō, 1943), vol. 2, pp. 38–39.

3. Masuda Shōzō, *Nō Hyakuban* (Tokyo: Heibonsha, 1979), vol. 1, p. 125.

4. Kanze Kojirō, *Yōgyō-yanagi*, in *Yōkyoku Taikan*, ed. Sanari Kentarō, 5 vols. (Tokyo: Meiji Shoin, 1964), vol. 5, pp. 3191–3206.

5. Nose, vol. 2, pp. 43 and 491.

6. Saigyō (1118–90) was a famous poet and Buddhist priest; his real name was Satō Yoshikiyo. He wrote a collection of poems entitled *Sankashū*.

7. *Nōriki:* One who does miscellaneous work at a temple. Here *nōriki* is simply translated as "an attendant."

8. Miyako: The capital, now known as Kyōto.

9. Shimogyō: Refers to the general area from Third Street to the south of the city.

10. Higashiyama: Translated as "Eastern Hill." A name given to the general mountain area on the east side of the capital, in contrast to that of the north (Kitayama) and the west (Nishiyama, "Western Hill").

11. Jishu: Refers to the famous cherry trees that belonged to Jishu Gongen in the compound of the temple known as Kiyomizudera (Seisuiji) at Higashiyama.

12. Anjitsu: Saigyō's cottage at the foot of Mt. Ogura, which is located in Nishiyama.

13. *Momochidori:* Refers to the poem by an unknown author in the *Kokinshū*, #23, *KT*, p. 2.

Momochidori	Countless are the birds
saezuru haru wa	with their chirping songs in spring
monogoto no	everything's renewed
aratamare domo	yet once again; however,
ware zo furi yuku.	still I go on growing old.

14. *Yayo: Yayo* repeats the same sound in *Yayoi* (March), in the previous line, while it serves as an exclamatory word to call out to the friend.

15. *Shiru mo shiranu mo:* Refers to the poem by Fujiwara no Ietaka (1158–1239) in *Shin Kokinshū*, #113, *KT*, p. 173.

Kono hodo wa	It's around this time
shiru mo shiranu mo	those who know and do not know
tamahoko no	one another cross
yukikō sode wa	upon the road, with their sleeves
hana no ka zo suru.	perfumed with fragrant flowers.

16. *Jōgu honrai no . . . :* Similar lines are used in *Atsumori*. See n. 46 to *Atsumori*. (Yokomichi, n. 17, p. 238).

17. *Sanpuku no:* Refers to the line from the Chinese poem by Minamoto no Fusaakira. Kawaguchi Hisao, ed., *Wakan Rōeishū*, NKBT, vol. 73 (Tokyo: Iwanami, 1965), #940, p. 88.

18. *Hitori:* Refers to a poem by Saigyō in the *Sankashū*, Sanari, *Yōkyoku Taikan*, vol. 2, p. 1172.

Ojika naku	A stag is calling
Ogura no yama no	across Ogura Mountain;
suso chikami	living by myself
tada hitori sumu	closer to its base alone
waga kokoro kana.	are the thoughts within my heart.

19. *Sakurabana:* Refers to the poem by Ki no Tsurayuki (868–945) in the *Kokinshū*, #59, *KT*, p. 3.

20. *Mukashi no . . . :* Refers to a poem by Minamoto no Kaneuji in *Shoku-Senzaishu*, Sanari, *Yōkyoku Taikan*, vol. 2, p. 1173.

553

Hedate yuku	Back to the faces
mukashi no kage no	of the spring of long ago
omokage ni	parting further still,
mata tachi kaeru	once again the snowy clouds
hana no shirakumo.	of the cherry blossoms return.

21. Saga: Located in the northwest of the city, facing opposite Arashiyama, or "Storm Mountain," as in the English translation.

22. *Ukiyo:* Used as a buried pun; *uki* in *ukiyo* means "float" and "miserable" or "wretched."

23. *Saga:* Used as a pun, for it also means "custom"; here in this translation another pun is made from the English word "saga."

24. *Hana min to:* Saigyō's poem appeared in his *Sankashū*, #7068, *KT*, p. 102.

25. *Ieji wasurete:* Refers to a poem by an unknown author in the *Kokinshū*, #72, *KT*, p. 3.

Kono sato ni	Upon our journey
tabine shinubeshi	to this village should we sleep
sakurabana	among the falling petals
chiri no magai ni	of the blooming cherry trees,
ieji wasurete.	we forget our homeward path.

26. *Hito shirenu mi to:* It is still unknown where this poem appeared, though it is stated in *Yōkyokushū* that it is by Saigyō. Yokomichi suggests that the playwright strings these lines together, perhaps, by modeling it on some other *tanka* poem. Yokomichi Mario and Omote Akira, eds., *Yōkyokushū*, 2 vols., NKBT, vols. 40, 41 (Tokyo: Iwanami, 1967), vol. 2, p. 442, supplementary n. 154.

27. *Hana mono iwanu:* A line from a poem in Chinese by Sugawara no Fumitoki (899–981), in Yokomichi, *Yōkyokushū*, vol. 2, p. 292, n. 12.

28. *Yūhana no:* *Yū* is used as a buried pun, for *yū* in *yūhana* means "evening" and "to say."

29. *Mōshihiraku:* *Hiraku* in *mōshihiraku* is used as a pun, for it means "to open," while the other meaning is "to vindicate." Here in English I use "open," which is a related word (*engo*) with flowers.

30. *Hana kanzen ni:* Lines from *Hyakurenshō kai*. Yokomichi, *Yōkyokushū*, vol. 1, p. 447, supplementary n. 155.

31. *Sore ashita ni:* Lines from Po Chu-i. Kawaguchi, *Wakan Rōeishū*, p. 33.

32. *Kasanuran:* *Kasanu* in *kasanuran* is an *engo* (related word) with *kokonoe* and *yaezakura*, meaning "ninefold" and "eightfold" respectively.

33. *Itozakura:* Refers to the famous weeping cherry tree that was at the residence of Konoe Michitsugu and that Ashikaga Yoshimitsu wanted. He transplanted it to his mansion in 1373, according to *Gukanshō*. Yokomichi, *Yōkyokushū*, vol. 1, p. 449, supplementary n. 170.

34. *Miwataseba:* Refers to the poem by Priest Sosei (859–923) in the *Kokinshū*, #56, *KT*, p. 3. The last two lines read: *miyako zo haru no / nishiki narikeri* (and the capital appears / wearing rich brocades of spring).

35. *Chimoto:* Thousand Cherry Lane, which runs north to south in the capital.

36. *Bishamondō:* Famous for cherry flowers; located near Eikandō in Higashiyama.

37. *Shiōden:* Refers to the Four Heavens located half-way up Mt. Sumeru, one of which is the home of Bishamonten. See n. 197 to *Hagoromo*.

38. *Kurodani:* Black Ravine (English translation), located in Higashiyama, where Priest Hōnen founded the Pure Land Sect of Buddhism.

39. *Shimogawara:* Lower River Beach (English translation), located on the west of Eikandō.

40. *Henjō:* A famous poet. Moved with grief by the death of the Emperor Ninmei (r. 833–50), he became a Buddhist priest in 851 and assumed the name Henjō. He died at the age of seventy-five in 890. (*Waka Bungaku Daijiten*, ed. Hisamatsu Sen'ichi et al. [Tokyo: Meiji Shoin, 1962].)

554

41. *Kachōzan:* Mt. Flower Crown (English translation), one of the thirty-six peaks of Higashiyama, which is located southwest of the Nanzenji Temple. Henjō, however, did not live here.

42. *Washi no Mi-yama:* Eagle Mountain (English translation), famous mountain in India where Lord Buddha delivered his sermons.

43. *Tsuru no Hayashi:* The Grove of the Crane (English translation), famous place in India, where the leaves of the trees turned white like the feathers of a crane when Lord Buddha entered into Nirvana. This is mentioned in the *Daihatsu Onhatsu Sutra. Taishō*, vol. 12, No. 374, 365a–603a; 603b.

44. *Seisuiji:* Clear Stream Temple (English translation), located in Higashiyama. See *Taema*.

45. *Matsu fuku kaze no:* Refers to the poem by Fujiwara no Sanekane (1249–1322) in *Shoku-Gosenshū, #237, KT,* p. 46.

Yūsareba	When the eventide comes,
matsu fuku kaze no	the wind blows among the pines
Otohayama	from Mt. Otoha
atari mo suzushi	and how invigorating
yama no shitamichi.	it is down the trail below.

46. Otohayama: The famous mountain in the mountain range located behind the Sei-suiji Temple. *Oto* is used here as a pun, for it means "sound."

47. Arashiyama: Mt. Tempest (English translation), famous in Japanese poetry, located to the northwest of Kyōto.

48. Tonase: The upper reach of the Ōi River that flows below Arashiyama.

49. *Ōigawa: Ōi* in *Ōigawa* functions as a pun, for it means "great" and "increase."

50. *Shunshō ikkoku:* A line from a poem entitled "Spring Night" by Su Shih; *Su Shi Shih-chi,* 48 vols. (Peking: Chung-hua, 1982), vol. 8, p. 2592.

51. *Kane o mo matanu:* Refers to a poem by Fujiwara no Tamesuke (1263–1328), in *Shin-shoku Kokinshū, #1313, KT,* p. 678.

Akuru ma no	Just before it dawns
kane o mo matanu	without waiting for the bell
tsurasa kana	how I feel a pain
yo fukaki tori no	at parting with the crowing
koe ni wakarete.	of the rooster deep at night.

52. Ogura: The place where Saigyō built his cottage in Nishiyama. It is used as a pun, for it also means "slightly dark."

53. *Yozakura: Yo* in *yozakura* is used as a pun, for it means "night" and "world"; *nokoru yo,* "remaining world."

54. *Hana o funde wa . . . :* Refers to the lines from Po Chu-i in Kawaguchi, *Wakan Rō-eishū,* p. 79.

Motomezuka

1. Nose Asaji, ed., *Zeami Jūrokubushū Hyōshaku,* 2 vols. (Tokyo: Iwanami, 1966), vol. 2, p. 211.

2. Muraki Seiichirō, ed., *Yaku Man'yō* (Tokyo: Chikuma Shobō, 1956), vol. 9, pp. 265–66; vol. 19, pp. 586–87.

3. Abe Toshiko, ed., *Yamato monogatari,* NKBT, vol. 9 (Tokyo: Iwanami, 1957), episode 147, pp. 311–16.

4. *Sakamoto Setchō Nōhyō Zenshū,* 2 vols. (Tokyo: Unebi Shobō, 1943), vol. 2, pp. 466–67.

5. Ibid.

6. Gondō Yoshikazu, *Nōhyōshū* (Kyoto: Shinshindō, 1979), p. 241.

7. *Hina:* Means "country," which is used as an antonym with Miyako in a later line. See n. 8.

8. Miyako: Means "capital." *Mi* ("body" or "self") in *Miyako* is an *engo* (related word) with *goromo* ("cloth" or "robe") in *tabigoromo.*

9. *Goromo* (cloth) serves as a related word (*engo*) with *yae* (eightfold), *ura* ("reverse side" or "bay") in *urazutai, kake* ("by way of" or "toward") in *kakete,* and *harubaru* (farther). *Yae* also serves as a pivot word modifying *tabigoromo* and *shioji* (ocean road). These are typical embellishments used in the *michiyuki,* or traveling song.

10. A pivot word.

11. Tsu: Settsu Province.

12. Ikuta: Located in Muko County, Settsu Province, near present San no Miya, Kōbe City.

13. *Wakana:* "Fresh young green," one of the seven spring herbs used on the seventh of January for rice porridge.

14. *Kaeru:* A pun meaning both "stirs" and "turn" or "flip."

555

15. *Ko no me mo haru no:* Refers to a poem by Ki no Tsurayuki (868–945) in the *Kokinshū*, #9, *KT*, p. 2. *Haru*, a pun, means "spring" or "swell."

Kasumi tachi	Though the mists arise
ko no me mo haru no	and the treetops start to swell,
yuki fureba	should spring snow begin
hana naki sato mo	across the flowerless meadow,
hana zo chirikeru.	the petals would seem to scatter.

16. *Miyama ni wa . . . kienaku ni:* A poem by an unknown author in the *Kokinshū*, #18, *KT*, p. 2. The last line reads, "wakana tsumikeri" (they have picked the fresh young greens).

17. *Amazakaru:* A pillow word, *makurakotaba*, for *hina*.

18. *Ikuta:* Iku in *Ikuta* is used as a pivot word (*kakekotoba*) with *inochi* (life) in the preceding line.

19. *Mi: Mi* repeats the sound of *umi no* (of the sea) in the preceding line.

20. *Michi nashi tote mo:* A poem by an unknown author in the *Kokinshū*, #322, *KT*, p. 7.

Waga yado wa	Before my cottage
yuki furi shikite	appear the falling snowflakes,
michi mo nashi	and there is no path
fumi wakete tō	so no one will make his way
hito shi nakereba.	across it for a visit.

21. *Yukima o matsu:* Refers to a poem by Kōgen'in in the *Shin-Senzaishū*, #31, *KT*, p. 600.

Fumi-wakete	On we make our way
nozawa no wakana	by the marshland fields to pick
kyō tsuman	fresh young greens today;
yukima o mataba	for some days would pass if we
hikazu hinubeshi.	wait for time between the snows.

22. *Nanakusa: Na* pivots between *haru toshi mo* and *nanakusa. Na* means "no" or "not," while *nana* in *nanakusa* means "seven."

23. The whole line serves a pivot function.

24. *Ikuta:* Used as a pivot word (*kakekotoba*) with the preceding line; it means numerous, many.

25. Ikuta no Mori: "Ikuta Forest" is a famous site located in the sanctuary of the Ikuta Shrine, in the present city of Kōbe.

26. *Nagaretaru: Nagare* in *nagaretaru* is an *engo* (related word) with Ikuta, the stream or river.

27. Ikutagawa: Ikuta stream starts from Mt. Maya in Settsu Province, flows on the east side of Kōbe, and runs into the Ikuta inlet.

28. Miyoshino: Located in Yoshino County, Yamato; famous for cherry flowers.

29. Shiga: Located in Shiga County, Ōmi; noted for cherry flowers.

30. Tatsuta: Located in Ikoma County, Yamato; renowned for red maple leaves.

31. Hatsuse: Located in Isogi County, Yamato; famous for red maple leaves.

32. *Kajin no ie:* Means "house of the poet." Refers to the passage in chapter 9, "The Old House," in the *Tale of the Heike*; Takagi Ichinosuke, ed., *Heike monogatari*, NKBT, vols. 32, 33 (Tokyo: Iwanami, 1966), vol. 2, p. 197.

33. Motomezuka: Located on Mikage Street, Higashiyama Ward, in the present city of Kōbe; it is also called "Maiden's Mound."

34. *Tabibito no:* A poem by Minamoto no Motoyori (1068–1139), in *Horikawa Hyakushu*. Sasaki Nobutsuna, ed., *Nihon Kagaku Taikei*, 6 vols. (Tokyo: Bunmeisha, 1935), vol. 5, p. 10.

35. *Kasugano no:* A poem by an unknown author in the *Kokinshū*, #18, *KT*, p. 2. The last two lines read: "ima iku-hi arite, / wakana tsumiten" (How many days from now until / we can pick the fresh young greens?).

36. *Kimi ga tame:* A poem by Emperor Kōkō (830–87), in the *Kokinshū*, #21, *KT*, p. 2. The last two lines read: "waga koromode ni / yuki wa furitsutsu" (though upon my garment's sleeves / the flakes of snow are falling).

37. *Haru tachite*: A poem by Taira no Suketaka in the *Shūishū*, #7, *KT*, p. 54.
38. *Ashita no Hara*: "Morning Meadow," famous in *tanka*, located in Yamato.
39. *Furu*: Furu ("fall" and "old") is used as a pivot word with *yuki* (snow).
40. *Haru no no ni*: A poem by Yamabe no Akahito in *Shoku Kokinshū*, #160, *KT*, p. 269. The last two lines read: "no o natsukashimi / hitoyo nenikeru" (and delighted by the field / I have passed the whole night through).
41. *Na ya tsumishi*: Na is used as a pun (*kakeshi*). Na means "greens" and "name," which refers to *wakamurasaki*, or "young purple," suggesting an episode in the *Tale of Genji*.
42. *Imose no hashi*: Refers to the boat bridge (*funahashi*) at Sano in Ueno Province.
43. *Sano no kukutachi*: An *azumauta* in the *Man'yōshū*, #3406, *KT*, p. 772.

Kamitsukenu	In Kamisuke
Sano no kukutachi	at Sano, stalks of rapeweed
orihayashi	I pluck for cooking
are wa wataene	a dish, and I await you
kotoshi kozu to mo.	though you may not come this year.

44. *Chōan*: Chōan was the capital during the T'ang dynasty in China (*kara*), which introduces the next line.
45. *Nazuna*: English translation, shepherd's purse; a variety of watercress.
46. *Karanazuna*: Kara in *karanazuna* is used as a pun (*kakeshi*), meaning "hot" and "China."
47. *Shiromigusa*: Another name for *seri* (watercress); white, green, and purple are all *engo* (related words).
48. *Ariyake*: Ari in *ariyake* is used as a pivot word with *shiromigusa* in the previous line. It means "is."
49. *Shiranami*: Shira in *shiranami* is a pun, meaning "white" and "not to know."
50. Unai Otome: A maiden's name appearing in a long poem by Tanabe no Fukumaro in the *Man'yōshū*, #1801–1803, *KT*, pp. 746–47.
51. *Sumi wabitsu*: A poem by Unai in the *Tale of Yamato*, #687, *KT*, p. 893. "Field of Life" is the English translation of Ikuta, which serves the same function in the English passage as in the original text.
52. *Ikutagawa*: Iku in *Ikutagawa* is used as a pun, meaning "to live."
53. "Tide" here is a buried pun, referring to the river that flows down, and the tide that comes up at evening, and also to the waves that cross each other, as well as the two young men who cross their swords, as in the original text.
54. *Sashichigaete*: Used as a pivot word.
55. The whole line serves a pivot function.
56. *Oshika no tsuno no*: Refers to a poem by Kakinomoto no Hitomaro in the *Shin Kokinshū*, #1373, *KT*, p. 198.
57. *Tsuka no kusa*: A very short time.
58. *Namu yūrei*: A Buddhist prayer.
59. *Hito mare*: Refers to a Chinese line.
60. *Kofun . . .* : A line from the play *Hakurakuten*.
61. *Enbu*: Enbudai (Jambudvipa). In Sanskrit, it refers to one of the four continents located south of Mt. Sumeru, the greatest mountain in the world. Normally it refers to our own world of existence. See *Yuimakyō* (*Vimalakirti Nirdesa Sutra*), *Taishō*, vol. 14, No. 475, 537a–537b, 546b.
62. *Hisakata* ("distant" or "far away"): A *makurakotoba* (pillow word) with any word that begins with *ama* ("heaven" or "heavenly").

63. *Nochi no Horikawa*: Emperor Gohorikawa, who reigned from 1221 to 1232.
64. *Kataku*: A Buddhistic metaphor for this fleeting world; it appears in the *Hokekyō*, *Taishō*, vol. 9, Nos. 262, 263, 264.
65. Daishōnetsu: One of the eight Buddhist hells. See n. 68, below.
66. Sankai: The three Buddhist worlds.
67. Tetchō: A huge bird residing in hell, mentioned in *Ōjōyōshū* by Genshin (942-1017). *Taishō*, vol. 84, No. 2682.
68. *Hachi daijigoku*: Appears in the *Daichidoron* (*Mahaprajnaparamita Spadesa Sutra*), *Taishō*, vol. 25, No. 1509, 57a–756a; 176c. The eight Buddhist hells and their punishments

are: (1) Tōkatsujigoku: beaten to death by iron birds, revived again, and beaten to death; (2) Kuronawajigoku: tied by a rope of red-hot iron; (3) Shugojigoku: suffering caused by the trees of swords on iron mountains; (4) Kyōkajigoku: suffering caused by fierce fires and boiling water; (5) Daikyōkajigoku: suffering caused by most terrible agonies; (6) Ennetsujigoku: suffering caused by high heat; (7) Gokunetsujigoku: suffering caused by extreme high heat; (8) Mugenjigoku: the bottomless hell without end.

69. Motomezuka: *Motome* in *motomezuka* is used as a pun, meaning "search."

70. *Katachi* (figure) is used in the Yokomichi text instead of *kage* (shadow).

Kuzu

1. *Sakamoto Setchō Nōhyō Zenshū*, 2 vols. (Tokyo: Unebi Shobō, 1943), vol. 2, p. 408.

2. Gondō Yoshikazu, *Nōgaku Techō* (Tokyo: Shinshindō, 1979), p. 95.

3. *Tsuki:* "Moon" symbolizes the Emperor Tenmu (624–86), who was unexpectedly forced to flee from the imperial court (*kumoi*). Here *kumoi* is used as a *kakeshi* (pun): "where the clouds stay" and "imperial court."

4. Miyako: The capital.

5. Kuraiyama: Located in the province of Hida; the English translation is "the Crown Mountain." *Noboru* (ascend) implies that the prince will be crowned or regain his throne.

6. *Kamikaze:* "Divine winds" is a *makurakotoba* (pillow word) for Ise, which is implied by the Isuzu Stream.

7. Isuzu: The Isuzu Stream, which flows through the most sacred sanctuary of the Grand Shrine of Ise, where the imperial ancestor, the Goddess of the Sun, is enshrined.

8. *Furuki:* Furu in *furuki* and *suzu* in *Isuzu* are *engo* (related words), and *furu* functions as a *kakeshi* (pun), meaning both "shakes" the bell and "old."

9. Mimosusogawa: Another name for the Isuzu Stream. Here, *mi* in *Mimosusogawa* acts as a *kakeshi* (pun): "self" or "person" who receives (*ukeru*).

10. On-kata: Refers to Ōtomo, the son of Emperor Tenchi. Tenchi's younger brother, Tenmu, became the fortieth emperor after Tenchi's death.

11. On-hakubu: Refers to the son of Emperor Tenchi, actually a nephew of Emperor Tenmu.

12. *Mi-yuki:* Used as a *kakeshi*, as it means "deep snow" and "royal tour." Sanari Kentarō, ed., *Yōkyoku Taikan*, 5 vols. (Tokyo: Meiji Shoin, 1964), vol. 2, p. 894.

13. Akiyama: Name of a mountain in Yamashiro. *Aki* in *Akiyama* is used as a *kakeshi*: "wearied" and "autumn."

14. Uda: Name of a place in Yamato. The famous hunting ground in ancient times. *U* in *Uda* is used as a *kakeshi*: "inconstant," "sad."

15. Ojika: "Stag" is an *engo* (related word) with the Uda hunting ground. It is also closely associated with Kasugayama.

16. Kasugayama: A famous place-name in Japanese poetry. It is also noted for deer; even today numerous deer can be seen roaming freely in the compound of the Kasuga Shrine.

17. Mikasa: "The volume of waters" is an *engo* (related word) with "spring rain." Its sound suggests "Mount Mikasa," another name for Kasugayama.

18. Yoshinogawa: A beautiful river flowing through the region of Yoshino, richly associated with Japanese history.

19. *Kake yo:* Used as a *kakeshi*: "Put trust in" and "carry."

20. *Tsuyu shimo:* "Dew" and "frost" are *engo* (related words) with *sode* (sleeves).

21. *Shiraito:* Shira in *shiraito* is used as a *kakeshi*: "to know" and "white."

22. *Oi ga mi no:* Oi functions as a *kakeshi*: "to live" and "aged."

23. *Wakana:* Waka in *wakana* is used as a pivot word: "young," between *kokoro* (heart) and *na* (green).

24. Rinkan ni taki: Refers to a line of a poem by Po Chu-i (772–846). Kawaguchi Hisao, ed., *Wakan Rōeishū*, NKBT, vol. 73 (Tokyo: Iwanami, 1965), #221, p. 113.

25. *Junsai no atsumono:* Water-shield soup, a famous delicacy; refers to the Chinese story of Chang Han, who took an official post in a remote region but went home when the autumn wind began to blow, recalling the delicacies of hot soup garnished with water shields and lime-flavored bass. Sanari, *Yōkyoku Taikan*, vol. 2, p. 898. Yokomichi Mario and Omote Akira, eds., *Yōkyokushū*, NKBT, vols. 40, 41 (Tokyo: Iwanami, 1967), vol. 2, p. 363, n. 25.

26. *Tameshi ari:* Refers to a legend that appeared in the *Kojiki*, ed. Takeda Yūkichi et al., NKBT, vol. 1 (Tokyo: Iwanami, 1958), p. 233.

27. Tamashimagawa: A river located in the province of Bizen, where the Empress Jingū caught a trout as a sign for her army's victory, according to legend.

28. *Iwa kiru mizu ni*: Refers to a poem by an unknown author in the *Kokinshū*, #492, *KT*, p. 11.

Yoshinogawa	The rushing water
iwa kiritōshi	of the river Yoshino
yuku mizu no	rives through the rocks
oto ni wa tateji	but like them no sound I raise
koi wa shinutomo.	even though my love would die.

29. *Are Miyoshino*: Mi in *Miyoshino* is used as a *kakeshi*: "look."

30. *Namu-sampō*: "Holy Buddha," an equivalent of "holy smoke" in English.

31. Kiyomibara: A place where Emperor Tenmu established his capital.

32. *Kiyomibarae*: A parodic twist of "Kiyomibara": an intentional mishearing.

33. Tosotsu no Naiin: Located in the Buddhist Pure Land, dwelling place of Miroku, one of the bodhisattvas who would appear on judgment day.

34. Godaisan Shōryōsen: Shōryōsen is another name for Godaisan, the famous center of Buddhism in China.

35. *Kai aru*: Kai is used as a *kakeshi*: "be worth (doing)" and "oar."

36. *Sore kimi wa fune*: Refers to a passage from Hsun Tzu (circa 298–38 B.C.). Sanari, *Yōkyoku Taikan*, vol. 2, p. 903.

37. *Nagaretaesenu*: Used as a pivot word, which I try to imitate in the English translation.

38. *Nigoreru*: Refers to or implies the turbulent conditions of the times.

39. *Hanryo*: "Dragon," a symbol of the emperor.

40. Akitsusu: An ancient name for Japan.

41. *Koto no ne ni*: Refers to a poem by Princess Sainomiya in the *Shūishū*, #451, *KT*, p. 63.

Koto no ne ni	With the koto notes
mine ni matsukaze	pine winds from the summit come
kayōrashi	mingling back and forth;
izureno o yori	from whose sweet strings does music
shirabe someken.	swell into a melody?

42. *Kayoikuru*: Functions as a pivot word. Its effect is imitated in the English translation.

43. *Gosechi*: One of the important court functions in which five young maidens perform the dance.

44. *Otomeko ga*: Refers to a song in *Genpei Seisuiki*, vol. 14.

45. Katte: A deity enshrined at the Katte Shrine in Yoshino.

46. Hassho: Refers to the eight deities of Mt. Yoshino.

47. Komori no Gozen: A deity enshrined above the Katte Shrine on Mt. Suibun. *Komori myōjin* in English means "Tree Guardian Deity," and *komori* also means "hide" or "secluded."

48. Zaō: A bodhisattva, Kongōzaō, at the Zaō Hall in Yoshino; one of the sixteen figures in the Kongōkai Mantra (one body with Kongōsatta vajra-sattva). Nakamura Hajime, ed., *Bukkyōgo Daijiten* (Tokyo: Shoseki, 1975), p. 420.

49. Taizō: The World of Reason. See *Ataka*, n. 72.

50. *Kongō hōseki*: Refers to Kongōkai, the World of Wisdom, in contrast to the Womb World, according to the Buddhist concept of the world.

51. *Jippō sekai*: The entire world.

52. Tenmu: Refers to Emperor Tenmu.

Nue

1. *Sakamoto Setchō Nōhyō Zenshū*, 2 vols. (Tokyo: Unebi Shobō, 1943), vol. 2, p. 454.

2. Nose Asaji, ed., *Zeami Jūrokubushū Hyōshaku*, 2 vols. (Tokyo: Iwanami, 1966), vol. 1, pp. 24–26. See also Shelley Fenno, "Unity and the Three Principles of Composition in a Nō Play" (Ph.D. diss., Indiana University, 1986), p. 89.

3. It has not been determined which Heike text was originally used by Zeami.

559

4. Takagi Ichinosuke, ed., *Heike monogatari*, 2 vols., NKBT, vols. 32, 33 (Tokyo: Iwanami, 1966), vol. 1, chap. 4, episode 12, pp. 324–27.

5. *Yo o sutebito:* Refers to one who has renounced the world, meaning a Buddhist priest.

6. *Mikumano:* The Three Shrines at Kumano in the province of Ki.

7. *Ki no ji:* The road to Ki. Ki is the old name of Kii. *Ki* is used here as a *kakeshi* (pun), for it also means "come." The same lines appear in *Taema*.

8. *Seki:* Barrier. Refers to the *Shiratori no seki* (Swan Barrier), located at Yamaguchi Village on the border between Kii and Izumi provinces.

9. *Shinoda no mori:* "Shinoda's sacred forest." The famous forest appeared in Japanese poetry. It is located in the compound of the Katsuha Shrine at Shinoda Village in Izumi (present Ōsaka Prefecture).

10. *Tōzato:* "Far-off town," alluding faintly to Tōzato Ono, located near Suminoe. It serves a pivot function.

11. *Suminoe:* Old name for Sumiyoshi, located in Nishinari County in Settsu Province (a part of Ōsaka).

12. *Naniwagata:* Refers to the body of seawater surrounding Naniwa, the old name for the Ōsaka area.

13. *Ashiya no sato:* Another name for Ashiya ("Reed Cottage" in English translation), located in the Muko County of Settsu Province.

14. Tsu: Another term for Settsu Province.

15. *Rōchō:* Refers to a passage in the *Heike monogatari*, vol. 2, chap. 10, p. 248.

16. Used as a pivot device.

17. *Mōki no fuboku:* Blind turtle. Alludes to a fable that a blind turtle, living in the great ocean, surfaces once every hundred years and sticks his head into a hole in a drifting log. Refers to the passages in *Myōhōrengekyō* (Skt. *Saddharmapundarika Sutra*), *Taishō*, vol. 9, No. 263, 1c–62c; chap. 3 ("On Parables"), 106–66. Yokomichi, *Yōkyokushū*, vol. 1, p. 145, supplementary n. 145.

18. *Mumoregi:* Used as a pivot device. *Mumore* or *umore* (buried) serves a pivot function here.

19. *Utsuobune:* Utsu (hollow) in *utsuobune* is a *kakeshi* (pun), for it also means "lap" or "fold over."

20. *Kogarete:* Paddled or oared. Used as *kakeshi* (pun), for it also means "long" or "yearn" and "burned" or "ablaze."

21. *Hitoshirenu:* "Unknown to man." Refers to a passage in the preface to the *Kokinshū*, ed. Sahaku Umetomo, NKBT, vol. 8 (Tokyo: Iwanami, 1967), p. 197.

22. *Yoru:* Night. Serves as a pun, for it also means "approach."

23. *Ashi no Ya no . . . :* A poem in the seventy-eighth *dan* of the *Tale of Ise*, trans. Helen Craig McCullough (Stanford: Stanford University Press, 1968), p. 130. *Ise monogatari*, #172, KT, p. 88.

24. *Itoma nami no:* Nami (not have or none) is a *kakeshi* (pun), for it also means "wave." In the English translation, "wave" is used similarly.

25. *Mirume:* A kind of seaweed. It is used as a pun, for *miru* means "to see" and *me* means "eye." In the English translation, a similar attempt is made.

26. *Karanu:* Uncut. *Karanu* functions as a *kakeshi* (pun), for it also means "borrow" or "rent."

27. Konne no In: The seventy-sixth emperor, who came to the throne at the age of three in 1141 and died at seventeen in 1155.

28. Yorimasa: Minamoto no Yorimasa (1104–80), a great archer and noted poet, whose fifty-nine poems appeared in the imperial anthologies. In 1180 he raised an army against the Heike, was defeated, and took his own life at Heitōin.

29. Nue: Translated here as "chimera." An imaginary being whose head is like an ape's, its limbs, like a tiger's, and its tail, like a serpent's, as described later in the text. Its voice is like that of a bird called *nue*, hence it is so named.

30. Ninpei: The name given to the period between 1811 and 1813.

31. *Ushi no koku:* Hour of the Ox, which is around 2:00 A.M.

32. Tō Sanjō: Originally Fujiwara no Yoshifusa's huge mansion; at one of the corners there was a grove of trees known as "the God Grove." *Heike monogatari*, p. 324, n. 13.

33. Hyōgo no Kami: The chief of the bureau of the armory.

34. I no Hayata: A native of Tōtōmi. *Heike monogatari*, chap. 4, pp. 32–35.

35. *Yamadori no o*: Copper pheasant's tail feathers are fastened near the butt of the arrow.

36. *Shigetō no yumi*: A fine bow entwined tightly with the choice rattan-cord and lacquered in black. A warrior with the rank of general used such a bow.

37. Hachiman Daibosatsu: A deity of war enshrined at the Hachiman Shrine and honored by the Minamoto warriors.

38. *Kashira wa saru*: "The head was like an ape's": According to the *Heike monogatari*, chap. 4, p. 326, it is described as follows: "The head was like an ape's; the trunk, like a badger's; the tail, like a snake's; and his hands and feet appeared like a tiger's limbs; then they heard its howling cries like that of Nue. Terrible is an inadequate word."

39. *Tayori nagisa*: Tayori has two meanings. First is "news," and another meaning is "help"; *na* in *nagisa* (shore) functions as a *kakeshi* (pun), for it means both "no" and "not." Combining all these, I try to make an English translation where "tiding" is not only a piece of news but also a progressive form of the verb "tide." This, in turn, serves as an associated term with the words "float," "ashore," and "wave" that follow, while the verb "help" also alludes to one of the meanings of *tayori* stated above.

40. The word "waves" is used as a pivot device.

41. *Mizunokashiwa*: The lucky three-leafed spray of the white oak is used to tell fortunes at the Ise Shrine; *mizu* in *mizunokashiwa* functions as a pun, for it also means "water." It is also an associated word (*engo*) with "shore" and "wave."

42. *Aitake*: Ai in *aitake* is a *kakeshi* (pun), for it also means "to meet," while *take* (bamboo) functions similarly and describes the "pole" that follows. *Aitake* is the characteristic way of tuning the shō-flutes together.

43. *Yoru*: Used as a *kakeshi* (pun), meaning "night" and "surging."

44. *Taedae*: Faintly, dimly. Serves as a pivot phrase, describing what comes before and after, namely the form and voice of Chimera.

45. *Gojūnirui*: Fifty-two kinds of beings. Refers to all those who attended at the time of Buddha's great passing. Reference is from *Daihatsu Onhatsukyō, Taishō*, vol. 12, No. 374, 354a–603a, 603b.

46. *Shinnyo no tsuki*: The moon is considered as a symbol of Buddhist Truth.

47. *Ushimitsu*: 2:45 A.M.

48. Down: Used as a pivot device.

49. Shishiō: Name of the famous sword. English translation, "Lion King."

50. Uji no Daijin: Grand Minister Uji. Refers to Fujiwara no Yorinaga, the minister of the Left (1120–56), a prolific writer and a great book collector.

51. *Yumiharizuki*: Crescent moon.

52. *Iru*: Used as a pivot word, for it means "shoot" and "descend" or "set." Here, similarly, I use "low" as a pivot word, for it refers to the moon, which sets "low," and to bowing "low." Also "bend" pivots as a verb, for it means "draw" a bow and "bow in reverence."

53. Udono: Cormorant Hall (English translation); a place famous for rushes, located along the lower reach of the Yodo River flowing through Settsu.

54. *Kuraki yori*: Refers to a poem by Izumi Shikibu in *Shūishū*, #1343, *KT*, p. 81:

Kuraki yori	From raven darkness
kuraki michi ni zo	into the path of darkness
irinubeki,	must I go astray?
haruka ni terase	O moon, let your rays shine bright
yama no ha no tsuki	far out from the mountain ridge.

55. *Kaigetsu . . . :* Ocean moon. Refers to the moon reflected on the ocean.

Taema

1. Miyake Noboru, "Nō no Tokushu Enshutsu," in *Nōgaku Zensho*, ed. Nogami Toyoichirō, 5 vols. (Tokyo: Sōgensha, 1961), vol. 3, p. 253.

2. Ibid., p. 254.

3. Ibid.

4. *Sakamoto Setchō Nōhyō Zenshū*, 2 vols. (Tokyo: Unebi Shobō, 1943), vol. 1, p. 303.

5. Masuda Shōzō, *Nō Hyakuban* (Tokyo: Heibonsha, 1979), vol. 2, p. 30.

6. *Sakamoto Setchō Nōhyō Zenshū*, vol. 1, p. 303.

7. Nose Asaji, ed., *Zeami Jūrokubushū Hyōshaku*, 2 vols. (Tokyo: Iwanami, 1966), vol. 1, p. 204.

8. *Oshie ureshiki*: Refers to a poem by Go-Fushimi-in (1288–1336) in the *Shin Senzaishū*, #824, *KT*, p. 550.

9. Mikumano: Refers to the three shrines at Kumano in the province of Kii. They are Honmiya, Shinmiya, and Nachi.

10. Taema: Located in Taima Village in Kitakusugi County at Yamato. Taema is, perhaps, a corruption of the name Taima. It was first built at the foot of the Futakami Mountain and called Mampō-zōin; later it was moved to its present place at the base of Mt. Maruko, where En no Gyōja is said to have had his hut.

11. *Ki no ji*: Ki is the old name of Kii. It is used here as a *kakeshi* (pun), for it also means "come." The same lines appear in *Nue*.

12. Seki: Refers to the *Shiratori no seki*, Swan Barrier, located at Yamaguchi Village on the border between Kii and Izumi provinces.

13. *Koya*: Ko in *koya* seems to function as a *kakeshi* (pun), for it also means "come."

14. *Mikumano*: Mi (three) in Mikumano is used as a *kakeshi*, for it also means "come."

15. Iwadagawa: A river flowing east of Iwada Village in Kii.

16. *Yoru*: Night. Used as a *kakeshi*, for it also means "to approach" or "come near." *Asa*, *hiru*, and *yoru* are *engo* (related words).

17. Futagamiyama: A mountain with two peaks located in Kitakusugi County in Yamato; Mt. Maruko is below it. See n. 10.

18. *Ichinen Midabutsu*: Literally, "A single thought on the Amida Buddha will immediately dispel an infinite number of evil karmas." The *Ōjōyōshū* by Genshin (942–1017) states, it is said, that this passage is found in the *Ōjōhonryōkukyō*; however, I cannot locate this sutra in the Buddhist Tripitaka.

19. *Hachiman Shoshōgyō*: "The numerous (84,000) teachings of the Buddha are all one with the Amida Buddha." Nakamura Hajime, ed., *Bukkyōgo Daijiten* (Tokyo: Shoseki, 1975), p. 1106.

20. *Shaka wa yari*: A poem by an unidentified author. It is also mentioned in a Nō play entitled *Kashiwazaki*.

21. *Tonōreba*: Refers to a poem that is said to have been written by Priest Ippen (1239–89).

22. *Suzushiki michi*: Buddhist Paradise.

23. *Nigori ni shimanu*: Refers to a poem by Priest Henjō (816–90) in the *Kokinshū*, #165, *KT*, p. 5.

24. *Higan tote*: Refers to Amida Buddha's compassionate vow to save all suffering beings. The primal verse: "I establish a vow that transcends this mundane world." This appears in the *Muryōjukyō* (Skt. "Greater" Sukhavati-vyuha Sutra). *Taishō*, vol. 12, No. 360, 265c–279a.

25. *Itsutsu no kumo wa*: Refers to Saigyō's line. *Saigyō shōnin shū*, #391, *Shikashū Taisei*, ed. Hashimoto Fumio (Tokyo: Meiji Shoin, 1974), vol. 2, p. 59.

26. *Amayo no tsuki*: Refers to a poem by an unknown author in *Gyokuyōshū*, #2607, *KT*, p. 418.

27. *Sue no nori*: A passage by Jion Daishi (631–82), according to Sanari, *Yōkyoku Taikan*, vol. 3, p. 1844. Jion Daishi was a Buddhist scholar of the Hossō school. Nearly one hundred works are attributed to him, but I cannot locate this passage.

28. *Matsu no to*: Matsu (pine) is used as a *kakeshi*, for it also means "wait."

29. Somedono no I: Located opposite the gate of the Sekkōji Temple, about 450 yards from the Taema Temple.

562

30. Somedera: Another name for Sekkōji Temple.

31. *Iroiro: I* in *iroiro* is used as a *kakeshi*, for it also means "well."

32. *Shiraito no*: Shira in *shiraito* functions as a *kakeshi*, for it means "white" and also "not know."

33. *Hōju*: A treasured tree compared to one of the seven holy trees in the Buddhist Paradise.

34. *Sōmoku kokudo . . . :* The complete thought is as follows: Although grass, trees, and realism lack sentiency, they all have the Buddha-nature and are thereby destined to be enlightened (become Buddha). The original idea comes from the Nirvana Sutra, but the quoted line probably comes from the *Daijō-genron* by Chi-tsang, *Taishō*, vol. 45, No. 1853.

35. *Hizakura:* Red flowering cherry tree. *Hi* in *hizakura* is used as a *kakeshi*, for it also means "fire" or "flame."

36. *Itozakura:* Weeping cherry tree. *Ito* in *itozakura* is used as a *kakeshi*, for it also means "strand."

37. *Kumo no Taema:* Rifts among the clouds. Here Taema is echoed.

38. *Nishi fuku:* West implies the direction in which Amida's Paradise is located, according to Buddhist belief.

39. *Mandara:* A picture of the Buddhist world.

40. Haitai ("Deposed") Tennō: Refers to Emperor Junnin (r. 758–64), exiled to Awaji.

41. Toyonari: Refers to Fujiwara no Toyonari (703–65), the minister of the Right during the reign of the forty-seventh sovereign, Emperor Junnin.

42. *Shōsan Jōdo kyō:* Another name for *Amidakyō*, the Sukhavati Sutra.

43. *Tare o ka:* Alludes to a poem by an unknown author in the *Kokinshū*, #29, *KT*, p. 2.

44. *Kisaragi naka:* This seems to refer to the day on which Princess Chūjō passed away; however, she died on 14 March in the sixth year of Hōki (776).

45. *Keni kejo:* Incarnated nun and maid are said to be Amida and Kannon, the Bodhisattva of Mercy, respectively.

46. Nijō no Dake: Nijō is used as a *kakeshi*, which the author coined. It means "two high" peaks, and "nun ascended." In the English translation this effect is imitated by using "two lofty peaks," "too lofty peaks," "none," and "nun."

47. *Hijiri:* A sage. However, here it means a well-learned Buddhist priest.

48. *Hongaku shinnyo no:* The moon symbolizes the state of pure enlightenment.

49. *Jinko kūkai:* Refers to a passage in the *Ōjōyōshū* by Genshin. *Taishō*, vol. 34, No. 2682.

50. *Chōbōsetsu: Bōsetsu* in *chōbōsetsu* means Treasure Land. The world of Buddha.

51. Kōin no kokoro: "A heart of time" refers to Amida's heart. Sanari, *Yōkyoku Taikan*, vol. 3, p. 1853.

52. *Toki wa hito o mo:* A line from T'ao Yuan-ming (365–427). Sanari, ibid.

53. *Sesshu fusha:* Refers to the line in the *Muryōjukyō*. *Taishō*, vol. 12, No. 360.

54. *I issai seken:* Refers to the line in the *Amidakyō*. *Taishō*, vol. 12, No. 362.

55. *Jihi kayū:* Refers to the line in the *Shōsan Jōdokyō*, i.e., *Shōsan Jōdo Bussetsu Shōjukyō*. *Taishō*, vol. 12, No. 367.

56. "While" serves a pivot function. They board his boat for just a while, and also they shoot the shuttle as they "weave" their dreams for just a little while.

Tōru

1. Nogami Toyoichirō, ed. *Nōgaku Zensho*, 5 vols. (Tokyo: Sōgensha, 1965), vol. 1, p. 5.

2. Kita Roppeita, ed., *Tōru* (Tokyo: Kitaryū Kankōkai, 1965), f. 1v.

3. Nose Asaji, ed., *Zeami Jūrokubushū Hyōshaku*, 2 vols. (Tokyo: Iwanami, 1966), vol. 1, p. 660.

4. Masuda Shōzō, *Nō Hyakuban* (Tokyo: Heibonsha, 1979), vol. 2, p. 62.

5. *Tōgokugata: Tōgoku* in *Tōgokugata* means eastern provinces.

6. *Omoitatsu:* An allusion to a poem by Priest Rensei (1172–1259) in the *Shingoshenshū*, #674, *KT*, p. 346. See *Atsumori*, n. 11.

7. *Kumo: Kumo* (cloud) is an *engo* (related word) with *tatsu* (rise) in *omoitatsu*.

8. *Chisato mo onaji:* Refers to a passage of *Tao Te Ching*, chap. 64, by Lao Tzu; trans. D. C. Lau (Harmondsworth: Penguin Books, 1983), p. 125.

9. Rokujō Kawara no In: The Sixth Ward River Beach Mansion refers to Tōru's mansion, located on the Sixth Bridge in the city of Kyoto.

10. *Dejio: De* in *dejio* is used as a *kakeshi* (pun), meaning "rise," "come up," and "flowing" tide. In the English translation this technique is adapted.

11. Shiogama: The old name for the beach of the present city of Shiogama (English translation, "Salt Kiln") in the Miyagi Prefecture. It is a part of the Matsushima inlet, and famous for salt making. Here Tsurayuki's poems, which appear later, are echoed. See n. 33.

12. *Michinoku wa:* Refers to an *Azuma uta* (Eastern song) in the *Kokinshū*, #1088, *KT*, p. 22.

13. *Uramite: Ura* in *uramite* is used as a *kakeshi* (pun), meaning "bay" and "resentment," and *mite* means "see."

14. *Mizu no omo ni:* Refers to a poem by Minamoto no Shitagō (911–83) in the *Shūishū*, #171, *KT*, p. 57.

15. *Tsukinami o: Nami* (wave) in *tsukinami* is an *engo* (related word) with *mizu* (water) in the previous line.

16. *Toshitsuki no:* Used as a pivot phrase or line, which is imitated in the English translation.

17. *Matsu:* Used as a *kakeshi*, meaning both "pine" and "await."

18. *Kumite: Kumi* (draw or scoop) is an *engo* (related word) with *shio* (brine or salt).

19. *Goromo: Goromo* (robe) in *shioaregoromo* is an *engo* (related word) with *sode* (sleeve) in the next line.

20. *Urawa: Ura* (reverse side) in *urawa* is an *engo* (related word) with *sode* and *koromo* above, and it also acts as a *kakeshi*, meaning "inlet."

21. Tōru: The son of the Emperor Saga (r. 809–23). He was given the family name Minamoto. In 873 he became the minister of the Left. He lived in the grand mansion at the Sixth Ward and died at the age of seventy-four in 895.

22. Chika: Old name for Shiogama area.

23. *Nagaretaru*, meaning "flow," is an *engo* (related word) with *kawa* (river) in *kawara* (river or beach).

24. Magaki ga Shima: An island in the offing of Shiogama, famed in Japanese poetry.

25. Katō: Chia Tao (779–849), a noted Chinese poet.

26. *Tori wa shuku su:* Lines from a verse entitled "Inscription on the Hermitage (Wall) of Li Ning" by Chia Tao. *Complete T'ang Poems*, 25 vols. (Shanghai: Shanghai Chunghua Book Company, 1960), vol. 17, p. 6639. This is a reprint from the original edition of the Chin dynasty.

27. Chika: See n. 22, above; here used as a *kakeshi*, for it means "near."

28. *Tatsu*, meaning "rise," serves a pivot function between *matsukaze* (pine wind) and *kiri* (mist).

29. Michinoku: *Mi* in Michinoku is a *kakeshi*, meaning "to see."

30. *Mitsu:* Has the same sound as *mitsu* (to see). It is the ancient port in the Naniwae.

31. *Furuki: Furu* in *furuki* (old) is used as a *kakeshi*, meaning "fall." It also serves as an *engo* (related word) with *ama* (rain) and *ochiba* (falling leaves).

32. *Tsuki dani sumade: Sumade* (not to live) is used as a *kakeshi*, meaning "not to become clear."

33. *Kimi masade:* A poem by Ki no Tsurayuki (868?–945?) in the *Kokinshū*, #852, *KT*, p. 17. The prefatory note runs as follows: "After the minister passed away, I went to the Shiogama Bay, to see the mansion which he reproduced, and I composed the following verse."

34. *Urasamishiku: Ura* (heart-feeling) in *urasamishiku* is a *kakeshi*, which also means "bay," or "inlet."

35. *Miteru: Mi* in *miteru* (becoming full) has the same sound as *mi* (see).

36. *Kai mo nagisa: Na* in *nagisa* (seashore) has the same sound as *na* (not). *Kai* is a *kakeshi*, meaning "fruitful" and "oar."

37. Otohayama: Located southwest of Mt. Minekasa in Uji County in Yamashiro Province; famous in Japanese poetry.

38. Ōsaka: Located on the border between Yamashiro and Ōmi provinces; *Ō* in *Ōsaka* functions as a *kakeshi*, meaning "to meet."

39. *Seki no konata ni:* A poem by Arihara no Motokata in the *Kokinshū*, #473, *KT*, p. 11.

40. Ōsakayama: See n. 38, above. Here it is simply used as a proper name.

41. *Koto no ha no: Engo* (related words) with the previous phrase.

42. Nakayama: A famous mountain path between Seiganji Temple and Imagumano Shrine in Higashiyama in Kyoto.

43. Seiganji: Noted temple.

44. Imagumano: The area located southeast of the noted Sanjū-san-gen-dō, Hall of Thirty-Three Bays, where one thousand and one standing Kannon figures are housed.

45. Hitomura: Used as a *kakeshi*, meaning "a village" and "a stand of trees."

46. *Madaki shigure no:* Refers to a poem by an unknown author in the *Kokinshū*, #763, *KT*, p. 15.

47. Inariyama: Refers to a poem in the *Kokin chomonjū*, #201, *KT*, p. 178. Inariyama is located north of Fukakusayama in Kii County in Yamashiro Province.

48. *Kumo no ha no: Ha* (tip or end) is a *kakeshi*, for it means "leaves"; it is also an *engo* (related word) with *kozue* (treetops).

49. Fuji no Mori: Famous place; it is located south of Inariyama.

50. *Yū sareba nobe no . . . :* A poem by Fujiwara no Shunzei (1113–1204) in the *Senzaishū*, #258, *KT*, p. 147.

51. *Fukakusayama:* Deep Grass Mountain. It extends to the south of Inariyama, and to the east of Fuji no Mori.

52. Kowatayama: Kowatayama is located south of Fukakusa; Fushimino, south of Fukakusa and northwest of Kowata; Takeda, west of Fukakusa; Yodo, southwest of Kowata; Toba, west of Fukakusa and Takeda. All are located in Kii County in Yamashiro Province.

53. *Nagame yaru:* Refers to a poem in the "Ukifune" chapter of the *Tale of Genji*, #1505, *KT*, p. 90.

54. Ōhara ya: A little distance from Fushimi and Fukakusa, to the west, lies Ōhara, and to the south, Oshio, all famed in Japanese poetry. Refers to a poem by Arihara no Narihira in the *Kokinshū*, #258, *KT*, p. 147.

55. Matsu no O: Located to the north of Ōhara.

56. Arashiyama: A place famous in Japanese poetry and located northwest of Matsu no O, both of which serve as *kakeshi*, as *arashi* in *Arashiyama* means "storm," suggesting "pine storm."

57. *Fukeyuku:* Fuke (deepen) in *fukeyuku* is used as a *kakeshi*, for it also means "blow."

58. *Sasu:* Used as an *engo* (related word) with *tsukikage* (moonlight).

59. *Hima mo oshiteru:* Oshi (push) in *oshiteru* is used as a *kakeshi*, for it also means "spare," and "feeling regret."

60. *Naga:* Naga in *nagamonogatari* serves a pivot function: "night long" and "long tale"; I try to achieve this effect in the translation.

61. Tago no Ura: The Bay of Pails. A famous place located in Suruga; *tago* (pails) is used as a pivot word.

62. *Mochishio:* Mochi in *mochishio* (high tide at the harvest moon) functions as a *kakeshi*, meaning "wait."

63. *Yoru:* Used as a *kakeshi*, meaning "night" and "surge" or "come up."

64. *Shiogama ni . . . :* A poem by Narihira in the *Shoku Go-shūishū*, #967, *KT*, p. 483.

65. See n. 33, above.

66. *Isomakura . . . :* The first half of this *machiutai* is the same as that of *Atsumori*. Iso is an *engo* (related word) with *koke* (moss) and *iwa* (rock) in the following lines.

67. *Wasurete toshi o . . . :* Appeared also in *Eguchi, Unrin'in, Umegae, Sekidera Komachi, Sanzan,* and *Matsumushi*, but its source has not been located.

68. *Kaeru nami no:* Kaeru functions as a *kakeshi*, meaning "ebb" and "return."

69. *Mitsu:* Used as a pivot between *nami* (wave) and *shio* (bring).

70. *Michinoku:* Mi in *Michinoku* is used as a *kakeshi*, meaning "see."

71. Gekkyūden: See n. 186 to *Hagoromo*.

72. *Chie furu ya:* Furu is a *kakeshi*, meaning "wave" and "fall."

73. *Sasu ya:* Sasu is a *kakeshi*, meaning "insert" and "shine."

74. *Hikari o hana to . . . :* Alludes to a poem by Minamoto no Hodokosu in the *Kokinshū*, #463, *KT*, p. 11.

75. *Ara omoshiro ya:* Ara is a *kakeshi*, meaning "rough" with waves, and "is" or "exist."

76. *Kumo to nari . . . :* Refers to a poem by Fujiwara no Ariie (1155–1216) in *Shinchokusen wakashū*, #830, *KT*, p. 229.

Martin Luther King, Jr.

1. Refers to the lines from Geoffrey Chaucer, *The Canterbury Tales*, rendered into modern English by J. U. Nicolson (Garden City: Garden City Publishing Co., Inc., 1934), "The Prologue," p. 1.

2. Refers to the lines from Walt Whitman, "When Lilacs Last in the Dooryard Bloom'd," in *The Collected Writings of Walt Whitman*, ed. Harold W. Blodgett and Sculley Bradley (New York: New York University Press, 1965).

3. Refers to the lines from Katharine L. Bates, "America, the Beautiful."

4. A pivot line.

5. Refers to the lines from an old Negro spiritual. The saddened melody of the song and the internal agony of the lyric convey the feeling of the slaves who attended "secret meetings" and found "home" with their personal Lord.

6. Lorraine Motel, located in the waterfront area in Memphis, where King usually stayed while in town.

7. (The Bishop Charles) Mason Temple, the headquarters of the Church of God in Christ, in Memphis, where King delivered "I See the Promised Land" on 3 April 1968.

8. At or about 8:30 P.M., 3 April 1968.

9. Refers to the passage from "The Drum Major Instinct," in *A Testament of Hope*, ed. James Melvin Washington (New York: Harper & Row, 1986), p. 458. See also Stephen Oates, *Let the Trumpet Sound* (New York: Harper & Row, 1982), p. 458.

10. Refers to the passage that follows: "It doesn't matter . . . I've been to the mountaintop," from "I See the Promised Land," which King delivered on the eve of his assassination, at Mason Temple in Memphis, Tennessee, on 3 April 1968; Washington, *Testament*, p. 284; Oates, *Let the Trumpet Sound*, pp. 485–86.

11. A shout used by the audience during King's speech. Oates, *Let the Trumpet Sound*, p. 483.

12. Refers to 4 April 1968.

13. On that afternoon the judge ruled to let the march take place on 8 April 1968.

14. Used as a pivot line; "the staff" refers to Andrew Young and Chauncey Eskridge.

15. A dinner for King and his staff given by the Reverend Samuel Kyles.

16. Ralph Abernathy, Jesse Jackson, Ben Branch, and Samuel Kyles.

17. The street that King faced from the balcony of the Lorraine Motel, when the bullet of a high-powered rifle came from the direction of an old building. Oates, *Let the Trumpet Sound*, pp. 490–91.

18. Refers to the passage from "I See the Promised Land," Washington, *Testament*, p. 286; Oates, *Let the Trumpet Sound*, p. 486.

19. Refers to the March on Washington, 28 August 1963.

20. Refers to the projected march on the nation's capital after the demonstration in Memphis.

21. Refers to Walter Reuther, Mahalia Jackson, Joan Baez, Charlton Heston, Harry Belafonte, Sidney Poitier, and Marlon Brando. Oates, *Let the Trumpet Sound*, p. 259.

22. Used as a pivot word. The Kennedys were waiting for all of them as they were monitoring the march, and distinguished senators like H. Humphrey, J. Javits, and G. Aiken were also waiting for them. Here "all" refers to the people gathered together, too. Oates, *Let the Trumpet Sound*, p. 257.

23. Refers to Martin Luther King, Jr.

24. Refers to the passage from "I Have a Dream," the speech King delivered before the Lincoln Memorial on 28 August 1963. Washington, *Testament*, pp. 219–20; Oates, *Let the Trumpet Sound*, p. 261.

25. Refers to the state of Mississippi.

26. Refers to the lines from the old Negro spiritual "Swing Low, Sweet Chariot."

27. Refers to Psalms 10:16.

28. The *kyōgen* speech was edited and adapted to Afro-American idiom by Professor John McCluskey, Jr.

29. Refers to Friday evening, 2 December 1955, when Mrs. Rosa Park was booked for violating the city bus ordinance.

30. In May 1961 the Freedom Rides began. The first bus was attacked on 4 May just outside Anniston, Alabama, and the second bus was also attacked, in Montgomery on 20 May 1961.

31. Refers to the Alabama Christian Movement for Human Rights. On 3 April 1963 it won the court battle.

32. The march on Washington took place on 28 August 1963.

33. Refers to the evening of 4 April 1968.

34. Refers to the lines from "Crossing the Bar" by Alfred Lord Tennyson.

35. Refers to the lines from a verse entitled "Inscription on the Hermitage (Wall) of Li Ning" by Chia Tao, a later T'ang poet. *Complete T'ang Poems*, 25 vols. (Shanghai: Shanghai Chunghua Book Co., 1960), vol. 17, p. 6639. Thanks to Professor Irving Lo for this information.

36. Refers to the line from "The Waste Land," in T. S. Eliot, *Collected Poems 1909–1933* (New York: Harcourt, Brace & Co., 1936). April is emphasized for its significance as the

following lines refer to Christ's crucifixion, Lincoln's assassination, and King's death from the gunshot wound.

37. Refers to 14 April 1865. "The assassination had occurred on Good Friday, and on the following Sunday, memorable as a 'Black Easter,' hundreds of speakers found a sermon in the event." *Encyclopedia Britannica*, 1965, vol. 14, p. 52.

38. Refers to the lines from "The Battle Hymn of the Republic," by Julia Ward Howe.

39. A Nō dance that is refreshing and refined. The chief instrument used is the flute, with the small and large *tsuzumi* and the *taiko*. The dance is performed in five movements.

40. Refers to the passage from "I See the Promised Land." Washington, *Testament*, p. 280; Oates, *Let the Trumpet Sound*, p. 485.

41. Refers to Revelation 22:16.

42. Refers to Psalms 23:2.

❀

567

GLOSSARY OF NŌ TERMS

Ado. A main comic actor. In the olden days he was also called the *shite* and the *omo*. When there are several of these actors, they are called the first *ado*, the second *ado*, etc.

Ageha. A short verse sung on the high note called *jō-on* by the *shite* (sometimes sung by his companion or the secondary actor). It occurs in about the middle of the important section of the play, the "ear-opening" segment called *kuse* by Zeami. Usually the *ageha* appears once in the *kuse*; however, it may occur twice (in which case the *kuse* is called *nidanguse*, double *kuse*) or not appear at all (which creates a *katakuse*, half *kuse*). The *ageha* is accompanied by a dance pattern called *agehaōgi*, a "raised fan."

Agehaōgi. A dance pattern performed by the *shite* as he sings the *ageha*. This pattern is also used at the beginning of a section of long instrumental dance. The *shite* holds the open fan out horizontally in front of his face as he moves his feet backward, left, right, left; then he raises the fan up and lowers it down on the right. When the *shite* performs this *agehaōgi* as he sings the *waka* after the long instrumental dance, it is called *ageōgi*.

Agemaku. The brocade Nō curtain in five or sometimes three colors hung by a tasseled cord between the "mirror room" (*kagami no ma*) and the bridgeway (*hashigakari*). When the player enters or exits, the curtain is raised from the bottom by two stage attendants sweeping it up with bamboo sticks tied to both sides of the bottom.

Ageōgi. See *agehaōgi*.

Ageuta. A high-pitched song sung in congruent rhythm (*au*). Melodic movement between Jō (d') and Chū (a) is predominant. The song usually comprises five to eight lines, which deal with the description of scenery and the delineation of the actor's feelings.

Ai. An abbreviation of *aikyōgen*. Refers to (a) the role the *kyōgen* actor plays as one of the performers within a Nō piece, and (b) the farce given by the *kyōgen* actors, which is divided into two types. One is called *katari ai*, where the *kyōgen* tells the *waki* the story that connects the first and second parts of the two-part play; the other, the *ashirai ai*, is played by boatmen, sword-bearers, or servants who help the play move forward.

Aikyōgen. See *ai*.

Aka gashira. A flowing red wig. See *kashira*.

Akujō. A fearful old man or a mask portraying such a man. There are varieties of this mask that represent a powerful old god with bulging eyes, thick beard, and wrinkles. It is used in Group I of Nō plays.

Asakura jō. The old man's mask for members of the plebeian class, such as the salt maker in *Tadanori*.

569

Ashirai. (1) A graceful piece of *hayashi* music played for the entrance and exit of the female *shite* and for the *tsure* in general. The former is called *ashirai dashi*, and the latter, *ashirai komi*. (2) To make the whole body face toward the player of an opposite role.

Atoza. The upstage area, eighteen feet by nine feet in dimension, located between the stage proper (eighteen feet by eighteen feet) and the "mirror board," called *kagamiita*, in front of which the musicians sit. Since the floor planks of the *atoza* run at right angles to those used for the flooring of the stage proper, they are also called *yokoita* (horizontal or lateral planks).

Atsuita (thick board). The heavy silk kimono worn by male characters. A garment made of thick, stiff fabric, with the warp of polished silk threads and the woof of unpolished silk threads in various colors, with different inwoven patterns. There are two varieties named after particular designs: *dan-* (striped) and *kōshi-* (checked) *atsuita*.

Atsuita karaori. A heavy silk kimono with *karaori*-like figures woven in relief. See *karaori*.

Au or **hyōshi au** (congruent). The rhythm of the vocal line is called "congruent," or regular, when it keeps the same beat as the drums. It is "fixed" or "strict" to the prescribed patterns of singing, which are called *hiranori*, *chūnori*, and *ōnori*.

Aware. Touching, beautiful, moving to the sensibility.

Awase. Lined robe.

Awase kariginu. A lined *kariginu*. See *kariginu*.

Awazu or **hyōshi awazu** (noncongruent). The rhythm of the vocal line is called "noncongruent," or free, when it does not keep the same beat as the drum. *Sashi*, *issei*, and *kuri* are sung in this style.

Ayakashi (evil spirit). Refers to one of the masks for male wraiths. It is used in Groups IV and V of Nō plays.

Ba (part or act). Refers to the main division of a Nō play, which has either one or two parts. In Nō, in lieu of the curtain falling between Part I and Part II, the *ai* takes place. See also *dan*.

Banshiki. The mode or scale centered on the flute pitch played by closing the top hole only. The quick dance and fast flute entrance music are in this mode. The note B in ancient music. See *yowa*.

Banshikichō. See *ōshikichō*.

Beshimi (tight lip). A group of masks whose outstanding feature is firmly compressed lips. The masks are subdivided into the *ō-* (large) *beshimi* and the *ko-* (small) *beshimi*. The former is painted greenish gray and is used by a long-nosed goblin. The latter is painted reddish brown and is worn by evil deities or devils.

Beshimi akujō. One of the varieties of *akujō* mask used in Group I of Nō plays. See *akujō*.

Bugaku. Dances performed at the imperial court during the Heian period (704–1185).

Chō jōge. Long two-piece garment worn by the *kyōgen* actor.

Chōken (long silk). A loose, unlined, broad-sleeved outer robe, worn chiefly by women. It comes in the colors of white, purple, scarlet, light blue, or green. From the left and right sides of the chest, two long vermilion ornamental cords (*munahimo*) come down. They are tied in a central knot below the breast and end in tassels just above the hem of the garment. A smaller cord is also attached to the bottom of each sleeve. Under this robe, the broad divided Nō skirt called *ōguchi* is worn. The robe is sometimes used over an embroidered gold- or silver-painted under kimono known as *nuihaku*, worn in a style called *koshimaki*.

Chū (middle). The pitch a in the Nō gamut. See *yowa*.

Chūjō (lieutenant general). A mask designed to represent the features of a typical youth of the Heike family.

Chūkei. See *ōgi*.

Chū no mai (medium dance). A Nō dance in moderate tempo. Its chief instrument is the flute, accompanied by the *kotsuzumi* and *ōtsuzumi* or by the stick drum called *taiko*. This dance is performed formally in five movements and informally in three movements. There are two other main Nō dances: *jo no mai* and *ha no mai*.

Chūnori. One of the three basic congruent rhythmic systems of matching the syllables of the text to the beats of the musical measure. The other two are *ōnori* and *hiranori*. In *chūnori* one beat is linked to two syllables. This style is suitable in the last section of certain plays, especially in scenes depicting battles in Group II of Nō plays (*Shuramono*). Hence it is sometimes called *shuranori*.

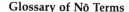

Chū-on. Literally, "middle note," which is the equivalent of the Western note e'.

Chūzayū (medium left-right or zigzag). A dance pattern performed as follows: with the left hand extended straight ahead at shoulder level, a performer takes three forward steps toward the left: left, right, and left; then, with the right hand extended straight ahead at shoulder level, he takes three forward steps toward the right: right, left, and right.

Congruent rhythm. See *au*.

Daijinbashira (minister pillar). The downstage left pillar supporting the roof of the Nō stage. It is also called the *wakibashira* because the *waki*'s seat, the *wakiza*, is located next to it.

Daishō (large and small). Refers to the *ōtsuzumi* (large hand-drum) and *kotsuzumi* (small hand-drum) respectively. The former is held on the left hip and beaten with the right hand. The latter is placed on the left shoulder and beaten with the right hand. *Ōtsuzumi* is also called *ōkawa*.

Daishō jo no mai. A prelude dance accompanied by the large and small *tsuzumi*. See *jo no mai*.

Dan (striped). Used as a prefix to indicate a striped design on a cloth: for example, *dan noshime*.

Dan (man). See *gobandate*.

Dan (section or scene). The basic structure of a Nō play consists of two parts and five *dan*, arranged according to the concept of *Jo-Ha-Kyū*. In dramatic terms, the *Jo-Ha-Kyū* divisions translate as introduction (1 *dan*), development (3 *dan*), and climax (1 *dan*). In musical terms, the divisions are slow (1 *dan*), lively (3 *dan*), and fast (1 *dan*). Between Part I and Part II there is *nakairi*.

Dan atsuita. See *atsuita*.

Dan noshime. See *noshime*.

Deha. Entrance music for the *shite* and the *tsure* in Part II of Nō plays. This music is widely used for deities, demons, spirits, or angels, but not for living persons.

Drummer's calls. See *kakegoe*.

Engo. Related words: for example, oar and boat.

Ennen. Old Buddhist theatricals.

Eri (collars). Beneath the *kitsuke*, the under kimono for women, are worn several unattached collars, one over the other, shaped to run parallel to the neckline of the kimono. They come in white, red, light blue, dark blue-green, and russet. White is considered the noblest, while red is the gayest. Sometimes two or three of the same color are worn; at other times they are all different colors. The combination varies with the nature of the play and the character.

Fukai (deep). Refers to one of the masks for middle-aged women with deep-set features due to the vicissitudes of life. The other is *shakumi* (sunk in middle), which is more haggard than the face of the *fukai* mask.

Gagaku (court music). The music and dance performed in the Nara and Heian courts. At present they are still used in the Imperial Palace and shrines.

Gaku (court dance). This dance, patterned after the court dance called *bugaku*, is performed by the spirit of a deity, a hermit, characters adapted from Chinese stories, etc. The dancer always uses a Chinese fan. Performed in five movements, the dance is very rhythmical and exotic, with many stamps.

Ge (low). The pitch e in the Nō gamut. See *yowa*.

Genzaimono. A Nō play dealing with a living person.

Ge-on. Literally, "low note," which is the equivalent of the Western note b.

Gobandate. A five-play program for a single day, organized according to the order of the five categories of Nō plays. It was officially established in the early Tokugawa period (1600–1868). The following is a chart of a five-play program, designating the characters, subjects, and categories.

CHARACTER	SUBJECT CATEGORY	CATEGORY ACCORDING TO ORDER OF PERFORMANCE
1. *Shin* (god)	*Waki* or *Kami* Nō (god-play)	*Shobanmemono* (Group I of Nō plays)
2. *Dan* (man)	*Shura* Nō (warrior-play)	*Nibanmemono* (Group II of Nō plays)

Glossary of Nō Terms

3. *Jo* (woman)	*Kazura* Nō (wig-play)	*Sanbanmemono* (Group III of Nō plays)
4. *Kyō* (mad person)	*Zatsu* Nō (miscellaneous play)	*Yonbanmemono* (Group IV of Nō plays)
5. *Ki* (demon)	*Kiri* Nō (final or demon-play)	*Gobanmemono* (Group V of Nō plays)

At present it is very rare to have a five-play program for a day. Many programs now consist of two or three Nō plays for a day.

Gobanme (fifth). Group V of Nō plays. See *gobandate*.

Gyaku (reverse). Refers to the way the base of the fan is held in the hand so that the paper lies along the outside of the arm and the fan's tip points toward a person, whereas normally it points away from him. Hence this is called a "reverse hold."

Ha. See *Jo-Ha-Kyū*.

Hakama (divided skirt). Loose pleated pants with slimmer lined black panels without stiffeners. The *hakama* is worn with a kimono with a family crest by the chorus members, musicians, and stage attendants. See also *nagabakama; suō*.

Haku. The kimono made of plain white silk with a satinlike finish, to be used by female characters as a *kitsuke*. A *haku* with a pattern painted in gold or silver is called *surihaku*. There is also another kind of *surihaku* that has an embroidered design. This is called the *nuihaku*, which may be used by a young man as a *kitsuke*, but never by a woman. She, however, may wear it over her kimono as a *koshimaki*.

Hana no bōshi. A silk wimple for a nun. It comes in the colors of white, light yellow, or light tea-brown.

Haneōgi (sweep fan). A dance pattern. The performer takes the open fan in the left hand, lays it on the right arm above the elbow, and then, sweeping it to the left of the body, makes a semicircle.

Hangiri. A broad divided brocade skirt, resembling the *ōguchi* in shape but made of white, red, or light-green brocade, with rich designs in gold. It is worn by an angry god, a devil, or a warrior.

Ha no mai. A short dance in quick tempo performed by the *shite* after the *jo no mai* or *chū no mai*.

Happi. Gold brocade robe with large broad sleeves, resembling the *kariginu* but reaching down only to the hip. Its designs are woven out of gold thread. The robe is either lined or unlined. The lined is for the dragon god, the unlined, for the Heike warrior.

Hashigakari. The bridgeway between the mirror room and the Nō steps, along which the third, second, and first pines are located. See the diagram of the Nō stage.

Hataraki or **maihataraki.** A Nō dance often consisting of vigorous and even wild steps. It contains elements of representation and may embody gestures, called *kata*, which refer to the text. The chief instruments are the large and small *tsuzumi* and the *taiko*, accompanied by the flute. The dance is brief in duration and has a small tonal range. It is suitable for the mad person, the warrior, or the demon.

Hatarakigoto. Refers to *hataraki*.

Hatarakiguse. *Kuse* accompanied by *hataraki*.

Hayabue. (1) Lively entrance music for the *shite* (fierce deity or dragon god) and the *tsure* in Part II of Nō plays. It is performed chiefly by the flute with the large and small *tsuzumi* and the *taiko*. (2) The quick flute music without the *taiko* that expresses the gathering or approach of the armed force.

Hayamai. An elegant, invigorating long dance in five movements.

Hayashi. The Nō ensemble consisting of the flute and the *daishō*. In some plays a *taiko* is also used.

Hayashikata. Musicians who play *daishō*, *taiko*, and flute.

Hie (chill). The highest aesthetic quality, which is not visible but springs from within the Nō actor's heart.

Hi ōguchi. Scarlet broad divided Nō skirt. See *ōguchi*.

Hiraki (open). A performer, taking three steps backward—left, right, and left—spreads his arms out away from the body at about shoulder height. This is perhaps the most common pattern and is used to conclude most series in Nō.

Hiranori. One of the three basic congruent rhythmic structures. Generally speaking, *hiranori*

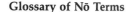

572

is the most common type of Japanese verse. It consists of lines of twelve syllables, divided by a caesura into groups of seven and five. The distribution of twelve syllables among eight beats is accomplished as follows: the seven-syllable line is distributed among 4 1/2 beats, and the five-syllable line among 3 1/2 beats, by giving the first, fourth, and seventh syllables double the duration of the others.

Hitamen. The unmasked *shite*.

Hitatare. A lined hempen robe worn as a rule with a long, trailing divided Nō skirt, called *nagabakama*, of the same color and design. This combination is worn by a warrior.

Hitoe. Unlined robe.

Hitoe kariginu. See *kariginu*.

Ho. Drummer's call. See *kakegoe*.

Hurry door. See *kirido*.

Hyōjō. See *ōshikichō*.

Hyōshi au. See *au*.

Hyōshi awazu. See *awazu*.

Ichi no matsu. The first pine located along the bridgeway near the stage.

Iguse. *Kuse* unaccompanied by a dance, as the *shite* sits while the chorus sings the *kuse* passage. See *kuse*.

Inori (exorcism). A very violent form of action piece, or *hatarakigoto*, showing the combat between the spirit of a demon woman and a Buddhist priest or a mountain monk.

Iro (hue). Refers to red in Nō. See *karaori*.

Iroe (color). (1) Refers to the dance the *shite* performs as the prelude piece to the *kuse*. The *shite* quietly goes around the stage only once to the music played by the *daishō* (rarely with *taiko*) and accompanied by the flute. (2) Refers to this music. (3) In the *kogaki* (variant) called *saishiki* (coloring), the *jo no mai* dance changes to *iroe*, as in *Saigyōzakura*.

Iroiri. See *karaori*.

Ironashi. See *karaori*.

Iro ōguchi. Red *ōguchi*. See *ōguchi*.

Ishō. Costumes.

Issei (first voice). (1) The entry music for the *shite*. It starts from *Jō* d' (High) and ends with *Ge* e (Low). There are coloring ornamental notes ascending to *Kuri* f'. (2) Refers to the entry verse sung in noncongruent rhythm by the *shite*. The prescribed verse form consists of lines of 5, 7–5, and 7–5 syllables. This may be followed by the second verse, called *ni no ku*, consisting of two lines of 7–5 syllables. As a rule, the *tsure* of a *waki* Nō sings the first line, and the *shite* and *tsure*, the second line in unison.

Iya. Drummer's call. See *kakegoe*.

Ji (ground). (1) Abbreviation of *jiutai*, chorus. Designates a passage sung by the *jiutai*. (2) The repeated ground patterns of the flute.

Jibyōshi. The model method of distributing or allocating syllables in the *hiranori* rhythm.

Jidori. See *shidai*.

Jigashira. The chorus leader who sits in the middle of the back row at the *jiutaiza*.

Jishidai. See *shidai*.

Jishō or **jishōmen.** The area, viewed from the *jiutaiza*, extending forward between the center of the stage and the waki stage front (between the *shite* pillar and the eye-fixing pillar).

Jiutai. (1) The chorus, consisting of six to twelve players seated in two rows at the *jiutaiza*. They are from the *shitekata*. (2) Sections of the text sung by the chorus.

Jiutaikata. The members of the chorus.

Jiutaiza. The area where the chorus sits on the Nō stage, at stage left.

Jo (woman). See *gobandate*.

Jo. See *Jo-Ha-Kyū*. See also *kuri*.

Jō (high). Note d' in the Nō scale. See *yowa*.

Jō. Old man.

Jō gami. Old-man wig.

Jo-Ha-Kyū. The term adapted from the *gagaku* and defined philosophically by Zeami as the basic principle governing a day's program, the performance, and the Nō composition. It consists of *jo*, introduction (1 *dan*); *ha*, development (3 *dan*); and *kyū*, climax (1 *dan*). See also *dan*.

Jo no mai (prelude dance). A quiet, graceful, long instrumental dance in slow tempo. The

573

chief instrument is the flute. When it is accompanied by the *daishō*, the dance is called *daishō jo no mai*. When the stick drum is added, it is called *taiko jo no mai*. The latter is somewhat faster in tempo, with a gay air.

Jō-on. Literally, "high note," which is the equivalent of the Western note a'.

Jōza. *Shite* seat located by the *shitebashira*, adjacent to the bridgeway.

Jūroku (sixteen). A young man's mask representing the features of a typical young noble of the Heike clan who was killed in battle at an early age.

Juzu. A Buddhist rosary.

Kadensho. *The Book of the Transmission of the Flower* by Zeami.

Kagamiita (mirror board). The back wall of the Nō stage, decorated with a painting of a huge pine tree, the Yōgō Pine at the Kasuga Shrine in Nara.

Kagami no ma. The "mirror room," in which the actor studies his reflection in the mirror before he makes his entrance.

Kaigen (eye-opening). Zeami's term referring to a scene in a Nō play such as the *jo no mai* or *chū no mai*, a long dance section, which appeals to the eye.

Kaimon (ear-opening). Zeami's term referring to a scene like the *kuse* segment, in which the aural aspect predominates.

Kakae ōgi or **kakeōgi.** These are probably mistaken terms for *kazashi ōgi*, a gesture in which the fan is held high over the forehead with the right hand.

Kakaru. The term indicating the point at which the delivery changes from a passage in prose called *kotoba* to smooth singing in noncongruent rhythm. See *sashi*.

Kakeai (dialogue exchange). After the question-and-answer segment, the *shite* and the *waki* respond to each other in verse. As their exchange grows tense, the lines get shorter and shorter, and finally the chorus takes over.

Kakegoe (drummer's calls). The drummer utters calls before the half-beat in general. There are four drummer's calls: *yo*, delivered before the first and fifth beats; *ho*, before the second, third, sixth, seventh, and sometimes the eighth beats; *iya*, with odd-numbered beats; and *yoi*, at the start of beat two-and-a-half. *Yo* and *ho* are usually written *ha* and *ya* in Japanese syllabary, respectively.

Kakekotoba (pivot word). A word that, by virtue of its position in a line, can be interpreted in two different contexts.

Kakeri or **kakerigoto.** A Nō dance with a dynamic feeling used in warrior-plays and the madwoman piece. The music is played by the *daishō*, accompanied by the flute. A relatively short and simple dance.

Kakeshi. Pun. A play on words.

Kakesuō. See *suō*.

Kakubōshi. A pointed hood for a wandering Buddhist priest.

Kamimai. God dance.

Kami Nō. Refers to a *waki* Nō, or god-play. A *kiri* Nō is never called a *kami* Nō or *shobanme-mono*, even when it features a deity as the *nochi-jite*.

Kamishimo. A two-piece garment for musicians, chorus, and stage attendants.

Kamite. Stage left.

Kanjin Nō. Before the modern period, a subscription Nō performance to which commoners were admitted for a fee.

Karaori (Chinese fabric). A brocade outer kimono with narrow sleeves. It is made of material copied from ancient Cathay brocade in a design and cut that are purely Japanese. Most magnificent is the pattern woven in relief upon unpolished silk, with threads of gold and flossed silk. The kimono is worn loosely over the shoulders, leaving a wide opening between the neck and the collars. The garments are of various colors, but when they contain red they are called *iroiri*; those without red are called *ironashi*. The former is for young female characters and the latter for elderly ones.

574

Kariginu. A hunting robe, an outer garment made of heavy silk with inwoven large patterns for male characters. They are of two kinds: the unlined one is called *hitoe*, and the lined one, *awase*.

Kasezue. See *tsue*.

Kashira (headpiece). A Nō wig, with abundant hair that covers half of the mask in front, hangs down about the shoulders, and flows in tufts to the garment's hem at the back. The wigs come in three colors, red, black, and white, and are called *aka gashira*, *kuro gashira*, and *shiro gashira*, respectively.

Kashira (head). The drummer's call *iya* or a drum pattern incorporating his *kakegoe*.

Kata (pattern). In Nō dance, combinations of arm and leg movements make dance patterns, while in Nō music, patterns known as *te* (hand) are made up of combinations of beats and of drummer's calls.

Kataguse. Half *kuse*. See *kuse*.

Katamaku (half-lifted curtain). When the chorus, stage attendants, etc., appear, one part of the curtain is lifted up for their entry.

Katari. A narrative told by the *waki*, the *shite*, or the *tsure*.

Kazura. Wig.

Kazuramono. "Wig"-piece or Group III of Nō plays. See *gobandate*.

Kazura Nō. See *gobandate*.

Kazuraobi. Wig band or hair band made of an embroidered strip of cloth.

Ki (demon). See *gobandate*.

Kindan hachimaki. A brocade headband.

Kiri. The last part of the Nō play, which is always sung in congruent rhythm.

Kiribyōshi. See *ōnori*.

Kirido. The low door, upstage left, through which the chorus and stage attendants enter and exit. It is also called *okubyōguchi* or *wasureguchi*.

Kiri Nō. Demon-piece or Group V of Nō plays.

Kitsuke (wear). The term for the kimono worn over the underwear in Nō. It refers to the basic garments like *haku* or *atsuita*, over which other garments can be worn.

Kizami. A basic *taiko* pattern.

Kogaki. Literally, "small writing," as they are indicated in a small notation next to a play title on a written program. *Kogaki* are sanctioned variants that can be applied to particular plays. They specify certain allowable changes in performance style.

Kōkenza. The seat for the stage attendant (*kōken*), which is located at the left-hand corner of the rear stage.

Ko-omote. *Ko* means "small," and *omote*, "face." It serves as the prototype of all young-woman masks now in use.

Koshimaki. A style of wearing a brocade silk robe over a kimono. The robe is tied with a waistband and the sleeves come off the shoulders and droop down on the sides.

Koshiobi. Waistband.

Kotoba. A prose passage intoned by a Nō actor.

Kotsuzumi. The smaller of two drums used in Nō. It is held by the left hand near the right shoulder and beaten with the fingers of the right hand. Cf. *ōtsuzumi*.

Kudoki. An emotional passage.

Kudokiguri. A *kuri* passage with emotional content or sentiment.

Kumo no ōgi or **ten no ōgi.** A gesture in which the open fan, held by the right hand, is put on top of the left hand in front of one's face. Then the actor looks up as he raises the fan and lowers the left hand, diagonally opposite each other.

Kuri. An ornate passage in which musical elements predominate. It is also called *jo* (introduction) because it corresponds to the beginning of the popular dance called *kusemai*. It consists chiefly of high notes called *jō-on* and a high-pitched singing that is always accompanied by instruments in noncongruent rhythm style.

Kurogashira. A flowing black wig. See *kashira*.

Kuro tare. A long black wig. See *tare*.

Kuse. The "ear-opening" section of a Nō play. Zeami said that his father, Kannami, adapted it from the *kusemai*, popular at his time. It is sung by the chorus. At the middle of the *kuse* there is generally a short verse sung by the *shite*, which is called *ageha*. If there are two *ageha*, it is called *nidanguse* (double *kuse*). If there is no *ageha* at all, the section is then called *kataguse* (half *kuse*). The *kuse* accompanied by a dance by the *shite* is called *maiguse*, and without the *shite*'s dance, *iguse*, which means that the *shite* sits during the time the chorus sings the *kuse*. The *kuse* accompanied by *hataraki* is called *hatarakiguse*.

575

Kusemai. A dance popular at the time of Zeami's father.

Kutsurogu. (1) The *shite*, turning his back to the audience, pauses for breath at the *jōza* before he starts to dance. (2) The *shite*, turning his back to the audience, kneels and rests at the *kōkenza* during the *monogi*.

Kyō (mad person). See *gobandate*.

Kyōgen. Comic plays used between Nō plays.

Kyōgenkata. Comic actors.

Kyōgenza. Refers to the seat for *kyōgen* players that is located at the near end of the bridge-way and upstage next to the *kōkenza*, the stage attendant's seat.

Kyū. See *Jo-Ha-Kyū.*

Machiutai. Waiting song. A verse sung by the *waki*, who awaits the *nochi-jite*. A kind of *ageuta*.

Mae-jite. The *shite* in Part I of the two-part Nō play. Simply called *shite.*

Magojirō. See *ko-omote.*

Maiginu. A robe for a woman only when she performs a dance. It must be worn in *koshimaki* style or in *tsuboori* style on the *ōguchi.* It resembles somewhat the "long silk," the loose, unlined, broad-sleeved outer robe called *chōken*, but it is not divided in front and back and does not have the chest cords called *munahimo.*

Maiguse. See *kuse.*

Maihataraki. See *hataraki.*

Makurakotoba (pillow word). A rhetorical device consisting of a five-syllable stock phrase that alludes to a specific word or set of words in the seven-syllable line.

Massha raijo. Entry music for the comic actor impersonating a deity of a subordinate shrine.

Matsukaze. Literally, "pine wind."

Metsukebashira (eye-fixing pillar). The downstage-right pillar. The masked *shite* fixes his eyes on it for orientation. The corner area at the *metsukebashira* is called *sumi.*

Michiyuki (travel song). A passage in which the *waki* describes and reacts to the scenery and places passed as he travels on the way to a destination. It is a form of the *ageuta*, sung in congruent *hiranori* style.

Mikazuki (crescent). A mask that belongs to the group of masks for men wraiths. The "crescent" mask is worn, for instance, by the *shite* in Part II of *Funabenkei.*

Mirror board. See *kagamiita.*

Mizugoromo. A broad-sleeved robe, worn by either a man or a woman. An unlined tunic made of one of two types of unpolished silk: "inferior silk," called *shike*, or "shrunk silk," called *yore*, the former being more elegant. The robe comes in the colors of brown, black, light blue, gray, and white. It is striped for the mountain monk. When worn by a woman, the garment hangs loose, but when worn by a man, it is fastened around the waist with a belt.

Mondai or **mondō** (question and answer). Dialogue in prose, called *kotoba*, exchanged between the *waki* and the *shite.*

Monogi (putting things on). The actor changes costumes or puts on some small things during the play. In most cases this activity takes place at the stage attendant's seat in the "rest" position called *kutsurogu*; however, at times it may occur at the center of the stage, as it does in *Matsukaze.*

Monomane (imitation of things). In Nō, imitative gestures are highly stylized and extremely abstracted. See, for example, *shioru.*

Moyō ōguchi. A broad divided Nō skirt with designs. See *ōguchi.*

Muji noshime. See *noshime.*

Munahimo. Chest cord. See *chōken.*

Nagabakama. A long, trailing divided Nō skirt.

Naga kamishimo. A two-piece garment worn by the *kyōgen.*

Nakairi (mid-exit). In the two-part play, the *shite* (at times the *waki* or the companion) exits at the end of Part I. Then, often, the comic actor connects the two parts of the play with the *aikyōgen.*

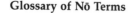

576

Nakairi raijo. See *raijo.*

Nanori (name announcing). A prose speech in which the player identifies himself. It may also relate his intention of making a journey. This speech is delivered only by the male role without a mask.

Nanoribashira. The pillar near which the Nō actor announces his identity. Also called *shitebashira.*

Nanoribue. Entrance music with the Nō flute, played for the actor who makes *nanori* immediately after he appears on the stage.

Nanoriza. Refers to the "name-announcing seat," located near the *shitebashira*, where the "name-announcing" speech is generally delivered. The *nanoriza* is also called the *jōza*, the *shite* seat.

Nashiuchi eboshi. A tall black cap.

Nibanmemono. Refers to the second play to be performed in the five-play program for one day. This is a warrior-play in Group II of Nō plays.

Nidanguse. See *kuse*.

Ni no ku. See *issei*.

Nochi-jite. The *shite* appearing in Part II of the two-part Nō play.

Nōken. The bamboo flute used in Nō.

Noncongruent rhythm. See *awazu*.

Nori (ride). Congruent rhythm in Nō. There are three types: *hiranori*, *ōnori*, and *chūnori*. Its literal meaning refers to the way the verse rides the rhythm.

Noriji. The segment sung in *ōnori*.

Noshime. A heavy silk kimono that is less formal than the "thick board" kimono called *atsuita*. It is woven with unpolished silk for warp and polished silk for woof. There are two kinds: the striped one, called *dan noshime*, and the plain, less heavy one, called *muji noshime*, the latter being more ordinary.

Notto. (1) The Shinto prayer the priest and the priestess offer the the deity. Most of the time they chant it in noncongruent *tsuyogin* style. (2) Music played before the Shinto prayer.

Nuihaku. An embroidered under kimono, painted gold and silver. It is a kind of *surihaku* with embroidered designs. See *haku*.

Omo. See *ado*.

Ōgi (fan). The most commonly used are folding fans, called *chūkei*, carried by an actor in costumed Nō. The spread-tip fan, with the ribs bent outward when folded, is broader at the tip, assuming an elongated triangular shape like a capital "Y." The other type has a slender, closed tip when folded. It is for chorus members, musicians, and stage attendants.

Ōguchi (big mouth). A broad divided Nō skirt. The front part is pleated, while the back is flat, spreading out on both sides, left and right. *Ōguchi* is made of raw silk woven very stiff. It is of various colors and is named by the color used: *shiro ōguchi* for white, *hi ōguchi* for scarlet, *iro ōguchi* for red, and *moyō ōguchi* for one with designs.

Ōkawa. See *ōtsuzumi*.

Okubyōguchi. See *kirido*.

Omo. See *ado*.

Ōnori. One of the three basic structures in congruent rhythm. Each beat is normally linked to a single syllable. This rhythm is ordinarily used in the last section of Nō, creating a calm, majestic effect, while the music that is cast in it is sung with distinct accents. The term *kiribyōshi*, used by Zeami, corresponds to *ōnori*.

Oroshi. In a section of the long instumental dance, the flute plays a special passage and brings the dance to a halt as the dancer remains in place flapping his sleeves or stamping on the stage floor. The tempo becomes slow.

Ōshikichō. Refers to the standard pitch of the Nō flute. The pitch higher than this is called *banshikichō*, and the pitch lower than this, *hyōjō*.

Ōtobide. See *tobide*.

Otokomai. A lively dance performed in quick tempo by an unmasked male player.

Otsuzumi. The larger of the two hand drums, held on the left hip and beaten with the right hand. It is also called *ōkawa*. See also *daishō*.

Ōzayū (large left-right or large zigzag). Refers to a Nō dance pattern, larger than the *sayū*. It covers a large area of the stage. With the left hand extended straight ahead at shoulder level, the dancer takes three or five forward steps and stamps the floor with the left foot, then goes out toward the *wakishōmen*. The number of steps the dancer takes is not fixed; however, seven steps seems to be the standard. See also *sayū*.

577

Raijo. Abbreviation of *nakairi raijo*. Refers to the exit music for the *shite* and the *tsure*.

Rongi (discussion). Ordinarily, the *rongi* comes after the *kuse* and before the *nakairi*. It is a form of *mondai* exchanged between the *shite* and the *waki*. It is written in 5–7 syllable meter and sung in congruent rhythm.

Sabi. Loneliness. The tone of lyric melancholy prized by the Japanese poets during the mid-classical period.

Sageuta. A low-pitched song, a short passage of two or four verses of 7–5 syllable lines sung in congruent rhythm, consisting chiefly of the *chū-on* and *ge-on*.

Saishiki. See *iroe*.

Sakaki. The evergreen called the "sacred tree," whose branches are offered to the gods.

Sanbanmemono. The third play in the five-play Nō program for one day. It is the wig-piece that belongs to Group III of Nō plays.

Sanbengaeshi. See *shidai*.

San yomimono. Three passages from the Nō repertoire in which an actor reads aloud from a document: the petition in *Kiso*, the written pledges in *Shōson*, and the subscription book in *Ataka*.

Sao. Bamboo pole.

Sashi. Recitative style. There are four types of *sashi* passages: (1) the *sashi* between the *kuni* and the *kuse*, (2) the *sashi* the *shite* sings first after his entry, called *sashikoe*, (3) the *sashi* after the *issei*, called *sashikoto*, and (4) the prose segment that changes into verse. *Sashi* starts with the *jō-on* and ends with the *ge-on*. The passage deals with scenery. All four types of *sashi* are sung in noncongruent rhythm.

Sashikoe. See *sashi*.

Sashikoto. See *sashi*.

Sashinuki (strung through). A type of skirt made of ordinary silk dyed in light purple or blue with medallions containing the colors orange, wisteria, etc. This garment is worn over the broad divided inner Nō skirt, called *komiōguchi*, which is tied around the knees like a pair of baggy knickers.

Sayū (left-right or zigzag). A dance pattern. With the left hand extended straight ahead at shoulder level, a dancer takes two forward steps, left, right; then with the right hand extended straight ahead at shoulder level, he takes two forward steps, right, left. See also *ōzayū*.

Shakumi. See *fukai*.

Shidai. Entrance song and music. (1) The lyric verse consists of 7–5, 7–5, and 7–4 syllabic lines, sung by the *waki* or the *shite* in congruent *hiranori* style. The content is "enigmatic," in Waley's words. When the actor is alone, he sings this verse at the *shite* seat, facing the "mirror board." If he is accompanied by the companion, they sing it together, facing each other on the stage. (2) The music used for the player's entrance is also called *shidai*.

After the song is sung by the entering player, the chorus repeats the verse, except the third and fourth lines, in noncongruent-rhythm style in a lower key. This version is called *jidori*. The *shidai* sung by the chorus in the middle of the play is called *ji-shidai*, which is used to alter the scene. The *jidori* is also sung after the *ji-shidai*. When the *shidai* is used for the *waki* entry in a god-play, it is called *shin no shidai*, and the music is in five movements. Following the *shin no shidai* is the only *jidori* that is sung in congruent *hiranori* style. This passage is followed by a repetition of the *shidai*, called *sanbengaeshi*. A shortened form of the *shidai* music is used for the comic actor's entry music.

Shike. See *mizugoromo*.

Shimote. Stage right.

Shin (god). See *gobandate*.

Shin no issei. The music played by the large and small hand-drums, accompanied by the flute, for the entrance of the *shite*, followed by the *tsure* in Part I of the god-play. It is very stately. *Hagoromo* is the only play other than those belonging to the *waki* Nō that has the *shin no issei*.

Shin no raijo. When the *raijo* is used for the *shite* and the *waki* entry, it is called *shin no raijo*, as, for example, in *Tsurukame*.

Shin no shidai. See *shidai*.

Shioru. A *kata* symbolizing "weeping" by stretching out the right-hand fingers together, then bringing the right hand up diagonally before the face so that it "clouds" the mask.

Shirabyōshi. A professional dancer active in the later part of the Heizan period (794–1185).

Shiro aya. A white robe of polished silk with patterns.

Shiro gashira. See *kashira*.

Shiro ōguchi. See *ōguchi*.

Shiro tare. See *tare*.

Shite. The name given to the main role of the Nō play. *Ado*, the chief comic actor, is also called *shite*.

Shitebashira. The pillar located where the bridge and the Nō stage meet. The term is important, as the *shite* stands by this pillar.

Shitekata. Refers to those who belong to the group of actors who play the role of the *shite*.

Shite seat. Called *jōza*, it is located by the *shite* pillar. See also *nanoriza*.

Shiwa jō (wrinkled old man). One of the masks for an old man, used for a dancing role. The *shiwa jō*'s cheeks are suggestively lined. The mask is worn with a *shiro tare*, a *kariginu*, and an *iro ōguchi*.

Shobanmemono. Refers to the god-play. See *gobandate*.

Shōmen or **shō.** Stage front.

Shura. Vengeful spirit of the warrior.

Shuramono. Group II of Nō plays.

Shura Nō. See *gobandate*.

Shuranori. See *chūnori*.

Sumi (corner). Refers to the corner area at the eye-fixing pillar. See *metsukebashira*.

Suō. Unlined hempen over-robe, a simplified form of the lined hempen robe called *hitatare* and worn with a trailing divided skirt, known as *nagabakama*, by the commoner. This two-piece costume is called *suō kamishimo*. When the *suō* is worn over the broad divided Nō skirt (*ōguchi*) as a traveler's costume, it is called *kakesuō*.

Suō kamishimo. See *suō*.

Surihaku. See *haku*.

Tachimawari. A movement in which the actor goes around the Nō stage once, accompanied by the *tsuzumi* and the *fue* (flute).

Tachishū. *Tsure* who enter the stage in a group.

Taiko. The stick drum used in Nō. See also *chū no mai*.

Taiko jo no mai. See *jo no mai*.

Tanka or **waka.** A Japanese verse form consisting of five lines whose syllabication is 5, 7, 5, 7, and 7, respectively. It is also called *uta*.

Tare. The long wig. The hair reaches below the shoulders and is divided into three unequal strands—two thinner ones hanging down on each side of the face, and a third bushy one, falling loosely down the back.

Te. See *kata*.

Tenkan (heavenly crown). A headpiece worn by a heavenly maiden or goddess.

Tennyo no mai. A dance performed by an angel.

Tobide (bulging eye). Refers to the group of masks that have big bulging eyes and a wide-open mouth with a prominent red tongue. The group is divided into two classes: the *ō-* (large) *tobide* and the *ko-* (small) *tobide*. The former is gilded all over and worn with an *akagashira* by the thunder god or some other powerful deity. The latter is painted reddish brown and used with an *akagashira* by a lesser but more lively deity.

Tōin. Literally, "head rhyme." Alliteration.

Tome or **tome byōshi.** (1) Refers to the way the *shite* brings a play to a close by stamping the floor twice. (2) Refers to the concluding stamps at the end of the play.

Tsuboori. The style in which one wears the outer robe for the *kamaori, atsuita, maigoromo*, etc., when it is tucked up at the waist over the *ōguchi*.

Tsue. A staff. The staff with the T-shaped head is called *kasezue*.

Tsukizerifu. Arrival speech delivered by the *waki* at the end of the *jo* section of the play.

Tsukurimono. The props in Nō.

Tsumeashi. The actor takes a step or two toward the opposite player or stage front.

Tsumeru or **tsumeashi.** A dance pattern in which an actor takes one or two steps "closer," toward stage front or toward the player of the opposite role.

Tsure (companion). Refers only to the *shite*'s companion.

Tsuyo or **tsuyogin.** A vocal style based on highly intoned recitation rather than singing. Accent, dynamic stress, tone color, and a specified vocal technique are more important than melodic movements themselves. A scale is as follows:

579

1. *Ken-guri* (Higher *kuri*)
2. *Kuri*
3. *Jō* (High)
4. *Chū* (Middle)
5. *Ge-no-Chū* (Middle of low)
6. *Ge* (low)
7. *Ryo* (Lowest)

In *tsuyo* there are theoretically four main tones: *Jō, Chū, Ge-no-Chū,* and *Ge;* however, in actual performance both *Jō* and *Chū* are the same, as are *Ge-no-Chū* and *Ge.* In general, congratulatory plays are sung in *tsuyo.* In other plays, the descriptive and bright sections are also recited in *tsuyo* style.

Tsuzumi. A hand drum used in Nō. See *kotsuzumi* and *ōtsuzumi.*

Uba (old woman). Refers to the old woman's mask.

Uchiwa. A flat fan.

Uikanmuri. Manhood ceremony crown.

Urokohaku. White under robe with a triangular design representing a serpent's scales, worn by the spirit of a jealous woman.

Uta. Refers to the Japanese poetic form called *waka* or *tanka.*

Utai-bon. Nō chant book.

Waka. Refers to the short musical piece sung by the *shite* in noncongruent rhythm. Its length is thirty-one syllables, like that of the *waka* verse form, according to the general rule.

Waka. See *tanka.*

Wakaonna. The young woman's mask.

Waki. Secondary actor, usually a priest.

Wakibashira. Refers to the *waki* pillar, located downstage left. See *daijinbashira.*

Waki Nō. God-plays or the plays belonging to Group I of Nō plays.

Waki-shōmen. The area, viewed from the *wakiza,* between the *nanoribashira* and the eye-fixing pillar.

Waki-tsure. The *waki*'s companion.

Wakiza. *Waki* seat, located next to the *wakibashira* at stage left.

Warai jō (smiling old man). Refers to a smiling old man's mask.

Warrior play. See *shuramono* or *nibanmemono.*

Wasureguchi. See *kirido.*

Yakuutai. Role song.

Yamabushi. Mountain monk.

Yaseonna. "Lean-woman mask" for a woman who becomes thin because of agony.

Yo. Drummer's call. See *kakegoe.*

Yobikake (calling out). A style of actor's entry used by the *shite* in lieu of the formal standard entry. After the curtain is swept back, the *shite* calls out by saying "nō, nō" from offstage before he appears on the bridgeway.

Yokoita. See *atoza.*

Yōkyoku. Nō singing.

Yomimono. Refers to one of the *san yomimono.* See *san yomimono.*

Yore. See *mizugoromo.*

Yowa or **yowagin.** The vocal melodies of Nō are regulated by *tsuyo* and *yowa.* Literally, *tsuyo* means "strong," and *yowa,* "weak." They are complexes of scales, dynamics, and vocal techniques. A *yowa* scale is as follows:

1. *Kuri*, f′	5. *Chū-Uki*, b	8. *Ge* (Low), e
2. *Jō-Uki*, a′	6. *Chū* (Middle), a	9. *Ge-no-Kuzushi*, d
3. *Jō* (High), d′	7. *Ge-no-Chū*, g	10. *Ryo* (Lowest), B
4. *Sashi-jō*, e′		

Jō, Chū, and *Ge* are the most important notes, functioning as melodic nuclei, while the others are transitional tones, serving as affixes to the important ones. A melody begins with *Jō, Chū, Ge,* and sometimes *Ryo* and most often ends on *Ge.* In general, lyrical and elegant plays, called wig-pieces, are sung in *yowa.* In other plays *yowa* is used for the lyrical and emotional sections.

Yūken. The actor opens the fan, places it against his chest, then lifts it up twice on his right.

Zō or **zō onna.** The Nō mask used to represent young women of a divine nature.

Glossary of Nō Terms

Nō Texts Consulted

Yokomichi Mario and Omote Akira, eds. *Yōkyokushū.* 2 vols. NKBT, vols. 40, 41. Tokyo: Iwanami, 1967. The two volumes contain 133 plays. These are the most reliable and helpful texts.

Sanari Kentarō, ed. *Yōkyoku Taikan.* 5 vols. Tokyo: Meiji Shoin, 1964. The five volumes contain 235 plays. The *ai-kyōgen* are included. Indispensable.

Nippon Gakujutsu Shinkōkai. *Japanese Noh Drama.* 3 vols. Tokyo: Nippon Gakujutsu Shinkōkai, 1959. Thirty plays translated into English. Useful general introductions.

Tanaka Makoto, ed. *Yōkyoku.* Tokyo: Kawade Shobō, 1954. Nineteen plays translated into modern Japanese. Informative.

Ataka: Yōkyokushū, vol. 2; *Yōkyoku Tai kan,* vol. 1; *Yōkyoku;* the Kita *utai-bon*

Atsumori: Yōkyokushū, vol. 1; *Yōkyoku Taikan,* vol. 1; *Japanese Noh Drama,* vol. 1; the Kita text

Funabenkei: Yōkyokushū, vol. 2; *Yōkyoku Taikan,* vol. 4; *Japanese Noh Drama,* vol. 1; the Kita *utai-bon*

Hagoromo: Yōkyokushū, vol. 2; *Yōkyoku Taikan,* vol. 4; *Yōkyoku*

Higaki: Yōkyokushū, vol. 1; *Yōkyoku Taikan,* vol. 4

Himuro: Yōkyoku Taikan, vol. 4; the Kita *utai-bon;* the Kita text

Izutsu: Yōkyokushū, vol. 1; *Yōkyoku Taikan,* vol. 5; *Japanese Noh Drama,* vol. 1

Kuzu: Yōkyokushū, vol. 1; *Yōkyoku Taikan,* vol. 2

Matsukaze: Yōkyokushū, vol. 1; *Yōkyoku Taikan,* vol. 5; *Japanese Noh Drama,* vol. 3; *Yōkyoku*

Motomezuka: Yōkyokushū, vol. 1; *Yōkyoku Taikan,* vol. 5; *Japanese Noh Drama,* vol. 2

Nonomiya: Yōkyokushū, vol. 2; *Yōkyoku Taikan,* vol. 4; *Yōkyoku;* the Kita *utai-bon;* the Kita text

Nue: Yōkyokushū, vol. 1; *Yōkyoku Taikan,* vol. 4

Obasute: Yōkyoku Taikan, vol. 5

Saigyōzakura: Yōkyokushū, vol. 1; *Yōkyoku Taikan,* vol. 2

Tadanori: Yōkyokushū, vol. 1; *Yōkyoku Taikan,* vol. 3; *Japanese Noh Drama,* vol. 2

Taema: Yōkyoku Taikan, vol. 3

Tōru: Yōkyokushū, vol. 1; *Yōkyoku Taikan,* vol. 4; *Yōkyoku*

SELECT BIBLIOGRAPHY

Abe Nosei. "Nō no chikara" (Power of Nō). In *Nō Kyōgen meisaku shū* (Collection of master-works of Nō and kyōgen), edited by Yokomichi Mario et al. Tokyo: Chikuma Shobō, 1966.

Amano Fumio. "*Heike monogatari* to Nō, kyōgen" (The *Tale of the Heike* and its relation to Nō and kyōgen). *Kokubungaku: Kaishaku to kanshō* 47.7 (1982): 125–31.

Bethe, Monica, and Brazell, Karen. *Nō as Performance: An Analysis of the Kuse Scene from Yamaba.* Cornell University East Asia Papers, no. 16 (1978).

Brower, Robert H., and Miner, Earl. *Japanese Court Poetry.* Stanford: Stanford University Press, 1961.

Ernest, Earl. *Three Japanese Plays.* London: Oxford University Press, 1959.

Fenno, Shelley. "Unity and the Three Principles of Composition in a Nō Play." Ph.D. diss., Indiana University, 1986.

Gondō Yoshikazu. *Nōgaku techō* (A Nō handbook). Kyoto: Shinshindō, 1979.

Gōtō Tanji and Okami Maso, eds. *Taiheiki* (Records of the Great Peace). NKBT, vols. 34, 35, 36. Tokyo: Iwanami, 1961.

Hare, Thomas Blenman. *Zeami's Style.* Stanford: Stanford University Press, 1986.

Hisamatsu Sen'ichi, ed. *Chuseihen* (On the classical and medieval periods). *Nihon Bungaku Hyoronsi*, vol. 3. Rev. ed. Tokyo: Shibundō, 1976.

Hisamatsu Sen'ichi and Nishio Minoru, eds. *Karonshū, nōgakuron shū* (Waka theory and Nō theory; two collections). NKBT, vol. 65. Tokyo: Iwanami, 1961.

Honda Yasuji. *Nō oyobi kyōgen kō* (Reflections on Nō and kyōgen). Tokyo: Maruoka Shuppansha, 1943.

Ichiji Tetsuo, ed. *Rengaron shū, nōgakuron shū, hairon shū* (Renga theory, Nō theory, haikai theory; three collections). *Nihon Koten Bungaku Zenshu*, vol. 51. Tokyo: Shōgakukan, 1973.

Itō Masayoshi, ed. *Yōkyokushū* (Collection of Nō texts). *Shinchō Nihon Kotenshū*, vol. 57. Tokyo: Shinchōsha, 1983.

Kawaguchi Hisao and Shida Nobuyoshi, eds. *Wakan Rōeishū, Ryōjin Hishō* (A collection of Chinese poems for recitation and the *Ryōjin Hishō*). NKBT, vol. 73. Tokyo: Iwanami, 1965.

Keene, Donald. *Nō: The Classical Theatre of Japan.* Tokyo: Kodansha International, 1966.

———, ed. *Anthology of Japanese Literature.* Tokyo: Tuttle, 1956.

———. *Twenty Plays of the Nō Theatre.* New York: Columbia University Press, 1970.

Kita Minoru. *Ennō shuki* (Notes on Nō performances). Tokyo: Yōkoku kai, 1939.

Kita Roppeita. *Roppeita geidan* (Kita Roppeita on his art). *Shimin Bunko*, vol. 115. Tokyo: Kawade Shobō, 1952.

Kitagawa Tadahiko. "Zeami to fukushiki mugen nō no tenkai" (Zeami and the evolution of the two-act dream Nō play). *Geinōshi kenkyū* 34 (1971): 1–12.

Kitto, H. D. F. *Form and Meaning in Drama*. London: Methuen, 1960.

Kobayashi Seiki. *Nō: Honsetsu to tenkai* (Nō: Its sources and evolution). Tokyo: Kōfūsha, 1981.

Kojima Hideyuki. "*Yōkoku no ongakuteki tokusei*" (The special musical qualities of Nō). In *Kojima Hideyuki kyoju Taikan Kinen Shuppan*. Tokyo: Ongaku no Tomosha, 1985.

Komparu Kunio. *Nō e no izanai: Jo-ha-kyu to ma no aiensu* (Invitation to Nō: Jo-Ha-kyu and the science of the interval). Kyoto: Tankōsha, 1980.

———. *The Noh Theater: Principles and Perspectives*. Translated by Jane Corddry and Stephen Comee. Tokyo and New York: Weatherhill/Tankōsha, 1983.

———. *Zoku Nō e no izanai* (Sequel to "Invitation to Nō"). Kyoto: Tankōsha, 1984.

Konishi Jin'ichi. *Nōgakuron kenkyū* (A study of Nō theory). 2d ed. *Hanawa Sensho*, vol. 10. Tokyo: Hanawa Shobō, 1964.

Kozai Sei. *Zeami shinkō* (Fresh reflections on Zeami). Tokyo: Wan'ya Shoten, 1962.

———. *Zoku Zeami shinkō* (Fresh reflections on Zeami, continued). Tokyo: Wan'ya Shoten, 1970.

Langer, Susanne K. *Feeling and Form: A Theory of Art*. New York: Charles Scribner's Sons, 1953.

Lau, D. C., trans. *Tao Te Ching*. London: Penguin Books, 1983.

Levy, Howard S. "Rainbow Skirt and Feather Jacket." *Literature East and West* 13 (1969): 111–40.

Malm, William P. "The Rhythmic Orientation of Two Drums in the Japanese Nō Drama." *Ethnomusicology* 2.3 (1958): 89–95.

———. *Japanese Music and Musical Instruments*. Rutland, Vt. and Tokyo: Tuttle, 1963.

———. *Nagauta, the Heart of Kabuki Music*. Rutland, Vt. and Tokyo: Tuttle, 1963.

Maruoka Akira. *Nōgaku kanshō jiten* (Handbook for Nō appreciation). Tokyo: Kawade Shobo, 1961.

———, ed. *Kanze-ryū: Koe no hyakuban shū* (Chant of the Kanze school of Nō: A collection of one hundred plays). Recording, 78 vols. Tokyo: Chikuma Shobō.

Masuda Shōzō. *Nō no Hyōgen* (Nō expression). *Chuko Shinsho*, vol. 260. Tokyo: Chūo Kōronsha, 1971.

———. *Nō no dezain* (The design in Nō). *Kara Shinsho*, vol. 55. Tokyo: Heibonsha, 1978.

Matsushita Daizaburō and Watanabe Fumio, eds. *Kokka Taikan* (The great canon of Japanese poetry). 2 vols. Tokyo: Kyōbunsha, 1903.

Matsushita Daizaburō, ed. *Zoku Kokka Taikan* (The great canon of Japanese poetry, continued). 2 vols. Tokyo: Kigensha, 1925–26.

Minagawa Tatsuo. "Japanese Noh Music." *Journal of the American Musicological Society* 10 (1957).

Miyake Kōichi. *Kanze ryū zōho fushi no seikai* (A detailed analysis of musical modulation in Nō based on the Kanze school). Rev. ed. Tokyo: Hinokishoten, 1960.

———. *Hyoshi no seikai* (A detailed analysis of Nō rhythm). Rev. ed. Tokyo: Hinokishoten, 1979.

Mochizuki Nobutaka, ed. *Mochizuki bukkyō daijiten* (Mochizuki's great Buddhist dictionary). 10 vols. Tokyo: Sekai seiten kankōkyōkai, 1960.

Nagazumi Yasuaki. "Shura-Nō to Heike no monogatari: Zeami no Tadanori o megutte" (Warrior Nō and the *Tales of the Heike*: A study of Zeami's Tadanori). *Kanze* 8 (1970): 3–9.

Nakamura Hajime, ed. *Shin bukkyōjiten* (New Buddhist dictionary). Tokyo: Seinshin Shobō, 1962.

Nakamura Yasuo. *Zoku Noh to Nohmen no Sekai* (Sequel to "The world of Noh and Noh masks"). Tokyo: Tankōsha, 1955.

Nearman, Mark J., trans. "Kakyō: Zeami's Fundamental Principles of Acting." *Monumenta Nipponica* 37.3 (1982): 333–74; 37.4 (1982): 458–96; 38.1 (1983): 49–72.

Nippon Gakujitsu Shinkokai, ed. *Japanese Noh Drama*. 3 vols. Tokyo: Nippon Gakujutsu Shinkokai, 1959–60.

Nogami Toyoichirō. *Nō: Kenkyū to hakken* (Nō: Researches and discoveries). Tokyo: Iwanami, 1930.

Select Bibliography

————, ed. *Kaichū Yōkoku zenshū* (Complete Nō texts with explanatory notes). Rev. ed. 6 vols. Tokyo: Chūō Kōronsha, 1949–51.

————. *Nōgaku Zensho* (Complete writings on Nō). Rev. ed. 5 vols. Tokyo: Sōgensha, 1979–81.

Nose Asaji. *Nōgaku Genryū kō* (Consideration of the origins of Nō). Tokyo: Iwanami, 1938.

————, ed. *Zeami Jūrokubushū Hyōshaku*. (Zeami's *Sixteen Transmissions* with detailed annotations). Enlarged ed. 2 vols. Tokyo: Iwanami, 1966.

Okami Masao, ed. *Gikeiki* (Records of Yoshitsune). NKBT, vol. 37. Tokyo: Iwanami, 1959.

Omote Akira. *Nōgakushi shinkō* (Fresh thoughts on the history of Nō). Tokyo: Wan'ya Shoten, 1979.

O'Neill, P. G. *Early Nō Drama: Its Background, Character, and Development, 1300–1450*. London: Lund Humphries, 1958.

Orgel, Stephen, ed. *Ben Jonson: The Complete Masques*. New Haven: Yale University Press, 1969.

Rimer, J. Thomas, and Yamazaki Masakazu, trans. *On the Art of the Nō Drama: The Major Treatises of Zeami*. Princeton: Princeton University Press, 1984.

Sahaku Umemoto, ed. *Kokinshū* (Anthology of Japanese poems ancient and modern). NKBT, vol. 8. Tokyo: Iwanami, 1959.

Sakakura Shigeyoshi et al., eds. *Taketori monogatari, Ise monogatari, Yamato monogatari* (The Taketori tale, The tales of Ise, and The tales of Yamato). NKBT, vol. 9. Tokyo: Iwanami, 1957.

Sakamoto Setchō. *Sakamoto Setchō Nōhyō Zenshū* (Complete collection of critical writings on Nō by Sakamoto Setchō). 2 vols. Tokyo: Unebi Shobō, 1943.

Samson, G. B. *A Short Cultural History of Japan*. London: The Cresset Press, 1952.

Sanari Kentarō, ed. *Yōkyoku Taikan* (Comprehensive collection of Nō texts). 5 vols. Tokyo: Meiji Shoin, 1964.

Shidehara Michitaro and Wilfred Whitehouse, trans. "Seami Juroku Bushu: Seami's Sixteen Treatises." *Monumenta Nipponica* 4 (July 1941): 204–39; 5 (December 1942): 180–214.

Takagi Ichinosuke, ed. *Heike monogatari* (The tale of the Heike). 2 vols. NKBT, vols. 32, 33. Tokyo: Iwanami, 1966.

Takakusu Junjirō and Watanabe Kaikyoku, eds. *Taishō Shinshū Daizōkyō* (The Taishō edition of the Tripitaka). 100 vols. Tokyo: Society for the Promotion of the Taishō Edition of the Tripitaka, 1924–34.

Takemoto Mikio. "Tennyo mai no kenkyū" (Research on the angel's dance). *Nōgaku Kenkyū* 4 (1973).

Tamba Akira. *La structure musicale du Nô*. Paris: Klincksieck, 1974.

Tanaka Makoto. *Yōkyoku* (Nō plays). Tokyo: Kawade Shobo, 1954.

Tanaka Taishi. "Nōgakuron" (A Nō theory). *Geinōshi kenkyū* 77 (1980).

Tsushihashi Yutaka. *Kodai Kayōron* (A theory on ancient Japanese songs). Tokyo: Sanichi Shobō, 1960.

Ueda Makoto. *Literary and Art Theories in Japan*. Cleveland: Case Western Reserve University Press, 1967.

Umehara Takeshi. *Jigoku no shisō* (Conceptions of hell). *Umehara Takeshi chosaku shu* (Collected writings of Umehara Takeshi), vol. 4. Tokyo: Shueisha, 1981.

Waley, Arthur, trans. *The Nō Plays of Japan*. London: George Allen and Unwin, 1921.

————. *The Tale of Genji*. London: George Allen and Unwin, 1935.

Yamada Chisaburō and James Laughlin, eds. *Contemporary Japanese Art, Perspective of Japan*. New York: Intercultural Publications, n.d.

Yamada Yoshio, ed. *Konjaku monogatari* (The Konjaku tales). 3 vols. NKBT, vols. 22–24. Tokyo: Iwanami, 1960.

Yamagishi Tokuhei, ed. *Genji monogatari* (The tale of Genji). 5 vols. NKBT, vols. 14–18. Tokyo: Iwanami, 1958–63.

Yamazaki Masakazu, ed. and trans. *Zeami*. 2d ed. *Nihon no Meicho*, vol. 10. Tokyo: Chūō Kōronsha, 1969.

Yasuda, Kenneth K. *A Pepper-pod*. New York: Alfred A. Knopf, 1947.

————. *Minase Sangin Hyakuin*. Tokyo: Kōgakusha, 1956.

Yeats, W. B. *Essays and Introduction*. New York: Collier Books, 1968.

Yokomichi Mario. *Nōgei shōyō* (A stroll through Nō dramatics). Tokyo: Chikuma Shobō, 1984.

Yokomichi Mario and Omote Akira, eds. *Yōkyokushū* (Collection of Nō texts). 2 vols. NKBT, vols. 40, 41. Tokyo: Iwanami, 1967.

585

Select Bibliography

KENNETH YASUDA
is an emeritus professor of East Asian Languages and Cultures at Indiana
University. His publications include *The Japanese Haiku* and *A Pepper Pod*,
a collection of original haiku and translations in English. He is a recipient of the
cultural Japanese Imperial Decoration of the Sacred Treasure, Third Order.

EDITOR: *Risë Williamson*
BOOK DESIGNER: *Sharon L. Sklar*
JACKET DESIGNER: *Sharon L. Sklar*
PRODUCTION COORDINATOR: *Harriet Curry*
TYPEFACE: *Palatino*
TYPESETTER: *G & S Typesetters*
PRINTER: *Maple-Vail Book Manufacturing Group*